BRITISH FOOD

ARTS AND TRADITIONS OF THE TABLE

BRITISH FOOD

AN EXTRAORDINARY THOUSAND YEARS OF HISTORY

COLIN SPENCER

Columbia University Press

New York

For my niece, Sandra Winyard, who always asked why

ACKNOWLEDGEMENTS

First and foremost, I am eternally grateful to have been awarded several bursaries; for such a book, which demands years of research, is impossible to write without them. Profound thanks go to my colleagues at the Guild of Food Writers, to the Authors' Foundation and to Fortnum & Mason for their help; this book could not have been written but for them. Many thanks also to the British Library, the Wellcome Library, the London Library and to Mass-Observation at Sussex University Library for their time and patience; all material from the latter has been reproduced with the permission of Curtis Brown Group Ltd., on behalf of the Trustees of the Mass-Observation Archive. I am deeply grateful to have had the enthusiasm and encouragement of my publisher, Anne Dolamore, throughout. I owe a special debt of gratitude to Ron Latham and the labour of love he has performed in picture research and also to his extensive library. I am thankful to Amy Myers for her rigorous editing and that rare ability to perform such a task with humanity and humour. I am also happy to thank friends and colleagues who were eager to help and enlighten, especially Dr Gary Lewis, Catherine Brown, Margaret Shaida, Prue Leith and Darina Allen on areas that were previously obscure to me. Lastly, my thanks to my partner, Claire Clifton, and her own library which has been indispensable.

Columbia University Press
Publishers Since 1893
New York   Chichester, West Sussex
First published by Grub Street, London, England

Library of Congress Cataloging-in-Publication Data
Spencer, Colin, 1933-
  British food : an extraordinary thousand years of history /
Colin Spencer.
    p. cm. -- (Arts and traditions of the table)
Includes bibliographical references and index.
  ISBN 0–231–13110–0 (cloth : alk. paper)
  1. Cookery—Great Britain—History. 2. Food habits—
Great Britain—History. I. Title. II. Series.
  TX717.S754 2003
394.1'0941—dc21

                                        2003048492

Contents

Series Editor's Preface

Sir Winston Churchill, so the apocryphal story goes, proclaimed that the only way to have a decent meal in England was to eat breakfast three times a day. The very title, *British Food*, seems a provocation, and some will view the title as a virtual oxymoron. But that is before they have read this truly revealing book.

Polymath and for many years food columnist of *The Guardian*, Colin Spencer has written wittily and well in a book that will be delightful reading for history buffs, a useful reference tool for secondary reading in British history or in culinary history courses.

With the prominence of food scholarship in cool Britannia (read the prolific and learned Alan Davidson, as well as the ever republished writings of Elizabeth David), the successful Transatlantic implantation of popular UK television shows by Nigella Lawson, *The Naked Chef*, and Gordon Ramsay, *British Food* fills a serious gap in awareness shared by otherwise knowledgeable food historians everywhere.

Few culinary historians outside of the UK know British political, economic, and social history; nor do they realize how rich the culinary arts once were in the land of Falstaff. It is especially important to learn why at certain well-defined historical epochs the quality of British food precipitously declined.

While thoroughly documented, Spencer's chronicle is an easy read, wittily presented, delightfully and usefully illustrated. Above all, he provides convincing historical facts that readily explain the cycle of decline that leads many to grimace in disbelief at the very title *British Food*.

Organized chronologically, each period is treated in the perspective of social history. There were, for example, the well-known "French" invasions: the Norman Conquests (1100–1300 A.D.), which because of the Norman involvement with the Moorish culture of Sicily, brought exotic spices and a new refinement to English cooking.

Later, from the end of the Hundred Years War (1453) to 1558, England lost its "possessions" on the Continent and became an "island" culture, thus leading to rich local production and traditions.

When Henry VIII (with his need for divorce) broke with the Church of Rome, fast days were abolished: the result was that the fishing industry in insular England suffered until foreign laws were passed (and not just by the Catholic-sympathizing Stuarts, but by Elizabeth herself).

British Catholics had treated lean or fasting days (i.e., Lent) as preludes to opulent feasting. The Reformation brought in the Spartan view that food itself was pleasure, hence reprehensible.

When the power of middle classes grew, domestic dishes flourished. As the Royal Navy became the archetypal English "armed force," the need for food preservation led to a quest for "Spice Islands," for foods that would combat scurvy.

One of the many brilliant chapters in this delightful book lays out for the first time the capital influence of *Mrs. Beeton's Book of Household Management* (1859–61), analyzing that key cookbook as a "self-portrait" of a society, seen especially through the optic of its alimentation. Her repeated cautionary notes on sanitation, echoing centuries of English insular phobias about hygiene on the Continent, consecrated the overcooked, parboiled food many think disparagingly of as English "cuisine."

To cover the horrors as if with a sauce, many of the worst dishes were given "French" or bastardized French names. This snobbism only conspired to increase feelings of inferiority on the part of British cooks themselves, confirming their worst inclinations.

But the decline of British Food in the century of British economic, social, and military dominance, the Victorian century, had even more profound roots in social history: the industrial revolution bred a degree of factory urbanization unknown on the Continent until Germany's Ruhr developed. The new capitalist economics in Britain led to the disappearance of the peasant class. There were obviously farmers, but the need to feed masses of urbanized industrial workers destroyed those traditions of quality that landed gentry had cultivated in the eighteenth century. This, when combined with a surface of Victorian prudishness, made quality food virtually taboo.

Among the many insights that this easily read book brings to the reader are topics as various as the careful history of rationing during the two great wars; the depiction of various culinary traditions by diarists like Pepys and Evelyn; food in works of fiction by Fielding and Smollett to the Brontës and on to Dickens; and the importance of foodlovers' guidebooks (Raymond Postgate and *Good Food Guide*) in post–World War II culinary development in the UK.

I have learned something new on virtually every page and that, painlessly, thanks to the elegance with which Colin Spencer carries his learning. *British Food* is an oxymoron no more.

Albert Sonnenfeld

Introduction

How did the mixture of peoples that became the British come to have such definitive culinary tastes? This, of course, is a question we can ask of all nations, but of the British we can also ask: why did their particular style of food decline so direly that it became a world-wide joke, and how is it now climbing back into eminence?

I first became excited by the history of British food when I read some of the earliest known Anglo-Norman recipes[1] that have come to light only in the last 20 years, and realised not only how Lucullan early medieval food was (for that was to be expected with an oppressive, affluent elite intent on ritual and ceremonial), but how extraordinarily stylish, tasteful and contemporary the dishes were. This was food designed to please and satisfy very sophisticated palates, it was food that we would now consider to be the height of gourmet elegance. It was food full of exotic ingredients and Mediterranean influences, with spices and flavourings from all over the then civilised world. As the historian Christopher Hill wrote:

'Each generation asks new questions of the past and finds new areas of sympathy as it re-lives different aspects of the experiences of its predecessors.'[2] This is as true of food studies as anything else and I have noticed that I have found a sympathy and sensual enjoyment of the recipes of the past, where others have expressed dismay and even disgust. A medieval food historian of the 1930s[3] obviously considered the recipes to be thoroughly unpleasant; what is more, not having worked out the amounts of spices per person, he seriously thought that an excessive amount was used and that this must be because they were necessary to mask rotting food. Thus began that particular canard which, though eminent historians since have considered it nonsense, has been difficult to destroy. When there is an amount given for a particular recipe which also states how many people it is meant to feed, the resulting flavour can be worked out; as readers will see on pages 50 and 80, the spices would have bequeathed a subtle sub-text to the finished dish and not overpowered it at all. My own view of this period is that Anglo-Norman cooking reached the heights of gastronomy, which it shared internationally with the courts of Europe, but that its cooking was influenced more by Persia (now Iran), as were the countries of the Mediterranean, than by Paris.

Because we all enjoy food, and there is little debate that it is one of the greatest delights in life, my view about what we ate in the past is a simple one. I think the food of the past was just as delicious as the food of the present. I don't believe people who have any choice in the matter bother to eat gunk. Because of poverty, the majority of people throughout our history were reduced to a very small range of subsistence foods; because all they had to eat was bland and monotonous, they searched for ways to brighten it up into something greatly more appetising. They did that because that's what people are like now and people do not change. Human beings in the past were basically ourselves, driven by the same needs, hopes and desires; though born at a different time and given a different set of cultural influences, notions and beliefs, the palate as a sensual receptor had the same requirements as today, to be satisfied and stimulated.

So I differ from many food historians who have written disparagingly about the food of the past, either considering it gross, such as 'roasting whole carcasses which they ate till the fat ran down their chins and into their beards,'[4] which subscribes to a Hollywood view of the banquet as orgiastic pigswill; or, as I have mentioned above, as rotting meats which only a ton of spices could make palatable. There were hundreds of bye-laws which were used to prosecute cooks and butchers if they were discovered attempting to sell rotting food. Such erroneous impressions also ignore the fact that large carcasses were valued as live creatures which were labouring hard in the fields. You did not slaughter them until they were too old to work. Nor, as meat was so precious, did you cook them without great care and skill. Besides, the wide variety of recipes for sauces to have with different meats would delight any gastronome of whatever era and must surely impress us with the culinary expertise of the medieval cook.

Throughout the period of the first part of this book there were ceaseless struggles between the princes, the church and the nobility for their share and control in the produce of the land. In the course of the twelfth and thirteenth centuries a further group emerges: the privileged town-dwellers, the traders who were to become the bourgeoisie. In England they played a particularly influential role at an early date on our food and cooking. Food was to play a part as a visible celebration of power and affluence in the struggle between the various elites, and food was also the source if not an integral part of the wealth of the new bourgeoisie. When the sumptuary laws began and stopped tells us much about bourgeois affluence and pretension. See, for instance, page 49 on the spicers in the City of London in the twelfth century under Henry II. These traders provide an important clue to how much the new Anglo-Norman nobility treasured the use of spices in their cooking, which meant how much they cared about the flavour and the recipes. Fashion is also a guide: in ages where male courtiers were concerned about the length of hems, shoes and hair, that same aesthetic selectiveness operated at the table. It is unimaginable that such an immaculate and perfumed society sat down to eat coarsely 'while the fat ran down their chins'.

There are close connections between the food we eat and the tumultuous events that made us into the British nation. Meat eating is thought to be central to the British diet, but it is not as simple as that. The history of the vegetable garden in Britain reveals the cultivation of a huge range of vegetables, so though they are not mentioned in the early cookery books we know they were eaten and enjoyed. Tudor meat-eating was stressed at the time and afterwards to draw a clear distinction between what a devout Protestant (and therefore a true Englishman) ate, as opposed to Catholic

Europe and Papist families here, who secretly continued to eat what were basically medieval dishes.

Food reflects everything, it is a microcosm of what is shaping the world at the time. What you eat and how you eat it are the product of what you are doing there and then. We have contemporary examples of this from the Mass-Observation Archive. There can be great ironies, as in the terrifying tragedy of the Black Death, which nevertheless led to improvements in the economy of the peasants. It finally led to them building their own bread ovens and the beginning of rural baking, which became the essence of our own peasant cuisine, just as the series of Enclosures Acts eventually destroyed it. The Reformation radically changed what we ate as did the rise of a rich bourgeoisie in the same century, as did the execution of a monarch, sea voyages of exploration, the legislative oppression of Roman Catholics, the early rise of capitalism on these islands, the vanishing peasant, the solid Hanoverian sensibility, the abundance of country estates, the spread of industry, rails and road, the sado-masochism of the Victorian non-conformists and much, much more.

Throughout these events there is an ever-growing sense of Britishness, but it was at the end of the medieval period that the distinctive characteristics of our food were melded together into one. But how and when did we begin to believe that our food was inferior? At the beginning of the nineteenth century distinguished gastronomes considered our cuisine to be the greatest in Europe. How then did it get a reputation of being so unremittingly disgusting? Why did we think it boring, bland, tasteless and utterly unworthy of the attention of a true gourmet? Basically, good fresh produce was ruined by lack of culinary skill. A dozen or so factors contributed to the decline of our food, not least that it was spurned and thoroughly neglected. Through diffidence, and even at times active dislike, we had allowed our food to become unremittingly mediocre.

Up to the midst of the nineteenth century, our food had had epochs and phases of greatness, which we threw away. Moreover, we not only threw it away, but forgot all about it. This book is an attempt to revive our knowledge of the gastronomic importance of British cuisine, in the belief that we can be genuinely proud of it, and with a passionate hope that we can restore many of its past triumphs so that they will become familiar to us again.

Colin Spencer
East Sussex 2002

CHAPTER 1

Prologue: The Land

Our food begins with the earth. Good food is a successful fusion between the living ingredients that thrive outside dwellings and the human skill and artistry inside, which fashions these disparate elements into harmony.

The land of these islands had been worked for at least four millennia before the Norman Conquest; a land of heath and downland, and of salt marshes, chalk hills and windswept plateaus, of forests filled with oak, elm, lime, ash and birch. Dense pine forests covered the north. The huge diversity of soil types, peat, sandy, lime, chalk and clay, and the mostly temperate climatic conditions dictated how the land would be used. Its main features, the cool hills of the north, the moist, mild variable weather of the west and south-west and the drier, sunnier east and south-east were settled after the last Ice Age receded about 5,500 BC, when Britain finally became an island and was tilled by farmers determined to wrest an existence from this land.

These islands were vulnerable to invasion by other races, for as a land mass it had great advantages over the rest of Europe, many of them due to its smallness; this allowed more efficient communication by water and track, since no part of it was more than 75 miles from the sea coast. Its topsoil was more fertile, it had gold, silver, tin and copper mines, it had coal, salt and wool. Its coastline then was indented with deep and wide river estuaries, providing safe harbours; when rocky it was good for collecting salt, while a strong tidal sea made its flat beaches easy to fish from both line and net. This feature also was always helpful to invasions and possible colonisation. Its forests were not huge or impenetrable, and by the time the Romans had landed there were no areas of woodland left unexplored or unmanaged, as the Celts were great farmers.

Britain's great attraction was its velvet turf, for our climate favours the growth of grass even in winter. Writers and agriculturalists throughout the ages have hymned the green pasture of these islands, where livestock graze and become supple and plump, so that their carcass meat is more appetising than any other. In addition, the soil grew cereals so well that there was often a surplus in livestock and wheat, which could be exported. The Celts, famed as agriculturalists, built underground silos to store their grains so that they could export them to the growing and ever hungry Roman Empire.

After the Romans

As the Roman Empire shrank so invasions from northern Europe began; there were times when harvests were destroyed and people starved. No sooner had the legions left, than the cities and villas with their orchards, fishponds and dovecotes became vulnerable. Three different Germanic tribes began to invade. Under the Romans the land had been well husbanded, and a thriving population reached five million in the first third of the millennium. Much fertile land was drained, cleared and brought under cultivation. The wide spaces of Salisbury Plain, Cranborne Chase and the South Downs became great wheatfields, and in the fourth century Britain became the most important grain-producing country in Europe. At the time of Julian the Apostate, 800 wheat ships left Britain each year to feed the garrisons of Gaul.

What was the inheritance of 400 years of Roman occupation? First was the Roman pattern of farming, a brickwork pattern which fanned out from a farmstead, or large villa; the tilled land formed clusters of irregular shapes, so that the countryside was a patchwork of hedged enclosures, fringed by ditches and wattle fences. This continued for a time because it was simple to go on cultivating the same plants in the same way in the same fields. Yet the demands for cultivating food was much less once the Empire had vanished. The population had declined to barely two million by the time of the Domesday Book, so there was less arable and a great deal more pasture or fields left to grow wild and wooded again. Both farming and communication – for the network of roads fell into disrepair – would suffer for the next 500 years. The people went back to using the old waterways again, if indeed they had ever stopped. The roads were repaired piecemeal, but a skeleton network still existed because we hear of their being used after 1066.

Rabbits had been caged in *leporaria* which were attached to the Roman villas; when they got loose they were devoured by wolves and wild boars. The peacocks, dormice, guinea fowl and pigeons followed suit; the plump dormice, feeding on acorns and chestnuts, ran to cover in the wild and were soon all eaten, while the pigeons flew into the forest and interbred with others. The Romans had also introduced geese and pheasants. The geese became part of the peasant economy, while the pheasant soon naturalised itself in the woods and fields. The first hen that has been recorded in Britain was in 250 BC at Glastonbury, and remains of chickens have been found at Belgic sites, including Colchester. Julius Caesar observed that the Britons did not eat hens, they simply fought with them.

The Romans had introduced the concept of a walled enclosure for fruit trees, the orchard, the vine and a place set aside for pot herbs. Many of these plants now grew wild on river banks, in fields and in forests. Perhaps the most important of these for the future of British cooking was white mustard. The Romans loved mustard, making a sauce in which the seed was crushed and mixed with honey and vinegar. Now the plants grew wild, the seeds gathered only by the perceptive peasant. The landscape of Britain had been enriched by these escapees; from almond, cherry, quince, peach and medlar trees to chervil, dill, coriander and parsley, wild or cultivated, we were to enjoy them for centuries more. The well stocked fishponds and lakes had been fished until they were empty and then they silted up, uncared for and never replenished. Many of the fields that grew barley and wheat were now covered in weeds and thistles.

Four hundred years of occupation must have changed the Britons radically, but all one can pin down from this change are tiny examples of elitist artefacts that were useful to the whole community: lamps became a common form of lighting, with candlesticks made of iron or pottery. The spoon, known before but never accepted as commonplace, and now made from horn, wood or iron in all shapes and sizes, had proved how useful and adept it was, whether on the table or hanging by the cooking pot. The kitchen too might well be far better stocked with bronze or iron pans, even pewter, crockery and cups of glass. British cheese-making was no doubt stimulated by Roman methods and flavours. Palladius (fourth century agriculturalist) made his cheese in May, curdling fresh milk with rennet from a kid, lamb or calf, or with a teasel or sprig of fig. The curd was wrung, pressed, wrapped in salt, pressed again, laid on crates and finally put in a dry place out of draughts. It could also be rolled in crushed pine nuts, thyme or peppercorns.

Under the impact of the new invaders, sporadic battles and the struggle for land, large parts of Britain were neglected; they looked unkempt, tangled and overgrown, yet what riches were hidden there. The marshlands were crammed full of eels, the rivers had plenty of salmon and trout, and other fish such as perch, pike, tench, carp and bream. The forests sheltered such a variety of game birds and red deer that it was a simple matter to trap all the meat you needed. However, forests had to be managed, trees to be coppiced for tools and building, young woodland to be fenced before cutting and replanting. Someone had to organise all this. Natural leaders arose in each community and methods of working grew up to protect the agricultural necessities, the machinery of living, so that a small human group of disparate people might continue to survive. These methods due to custom and practice in time became laws that the community accepted, as a necessity by which they could live together and survive. This changed again when the Angles and Saxons arrived, who, after colonising the eastern coast, moved inexorably into the centre of the whole land. They brought their own laws and customs, and they already had their own leaders and methods of agriculture. Their laws were particularly liberal and just regarding women. (See page 21.)

The Saxon peasants were clothed in wool and leather. Their life expectancy was no more than thirty years, though a few might survive longer and, if still helpful in their advice and guidance, would be revered. From the moment they could walk by themselves, the children would help with all the work. Most of the workers would have been racked with arthritis due to the hard grind of agricultural work; their backs would have been painful, and their hands and feet swollen. They would have suffered throughout their short lives from toothache, due to the grit in the food and most of them would have lost some teeth in their twenties.

Their hearing was acute, able to detect the lie of the land at a distance from the sound of the wind where the pasture changed to bare rock, or where a stream grew shallow or the breathing of a beast in a lair, or which rodent was making that tiny scuffle. Their sense of smell (compared to ours) was selective: unwashed themselves they would be able to distinguish people by their stench as well as the type of beast that even if unseen was nearby; they could smell salt on the wind and describe in walking time, shown by the position of the sun in the sky, how far away the sea was. They slept when it grew dark and awoke at dawn.

In the fifth and sixth centuries the population of Britain declined to about one million, but the soil was cultivated and the beginning of the open field system was created. Barley, oats, rye and wheat were grown, peas, beans and leeks were cultivated, and cattle, sheep and pigs were grazed. Their diet had not changed for hundreds of years back into the past and would not do so for many hundreds more. The peasant survived, and as the bulk of his diet was bread, the harvest was the most important event of the year. However, into this scene of shifting populations the most important cultural change and quite the most long-lasting in its effect on the peasants and their diet was to be the advent of Christianity and the rule of the Church.

The Early Church

Christian missionaries reached Ireland and the west of Scotland following the sea route from the Mediterranean in the fifth century, almost at the time that Rome had relinquished control and the new invasions had begun. These were itinerant pilgrims with staffs of willow who spoke comfortingly to the working people they met. They came obviously in peace and were greeted hospitably as custom decreed; bread and ale were offered and they were given shelter for the night. Their hosts would sing and recite stories and poems that celebrated their heroes. In return the missionaries told stories of Christian relevance, if not of Jesus Himself, and gave advice, counselled on practical matters, and provided consolation for fears of the myriad devils of pagan belief which were everywhere, and which were thought responsible for snagged fishing lines and ruined harvests. The pilgrims went on their way and possibly did not return for a year or two, but within a generation they had been accepted as part of the landscape and their belief in an invisible deity was known.

It was the leaders of the communities, however, that the missionaries needed to speak to and hopefully convert. It took another hundred years before in 565 St Columba founded the settlement on the island of Iona, and it was not until 597 that St Augustine landed in Kent and converted King Ethelbert, whose wife, Bertha, was already a Christian. The first churches to be established were minsters with a body of clergy and these were situated in the manors and estates that seemed to have grown upon the sites of old Roman villas. The minsters were at the heart of local government and also at the centre of the food supply. For the peasant, Church and State were already completely entwined, becoming over the years the one oppressor.

This was a time of economic expansion, and settlements increased by a quarter from the sixth century to 1066; the main growth was in the south, the south-east and the West Midlands. Many hundreds of the villages and towns that we are familiar with now, began then, growing up around the minster. This means that the farming was being well organised and more and more land was under cultivation. The power of the early Church is shown in the account rolls of the minsters and abbeys in the amount of food that they demanded as rent. For example, at the abbey of Bury St Edmund's, one month's food rent amounted to three bushels[1] of malt, a half bushel of wheat, one ox for slaughtering, five sheep, ten flitches of bacon and 1,000 loaves; this was in 1020 in Abbot Ufi's day. A later abbot, Leofstan (1044–65), upped the amounts, adding another bushel of malt, 300 more loaves, another twelve flitches of bacon and ten cheeses.

The type of cheese is unnamed, but abbots in England might have ordered a Casewick made in Lincolnshire, or a Keswick near Norwich, or a Chiswick in Essex or another cheese of the same name from Middlesex or even a Cheswardine from Shropshire. Place names ending in 'wic' meant a place of dairy-making. Hard mature cheeses were eaten by the elite – Church dignitaries and the nobility – while the poor ate fresh cheese or cheese pickled in brine. (The Welsh always used the brine bath method for preserving cheese.) Cheese was made by all households that possessed milch animals, so there was great regional diversity. Even new cheeses could have been hard, however, for in the Leechdoms[2] we read instructions such as the need to shred new cheeses into boiling water. They also very likely had some blue cheese. Dorset Blue is also called Blue Vinney and 'vinney' comes from *vinew/finew* from the Old English *fynig* meaning mouldy.

The most radical manner in which the Church changed the people was in dietary rules, which proliferated over the centuries. It was St Isidore of Seville (c.560–636) who, influenced by Galen's theory, considered that eating meat incited lust. Red meat and gross lechery were twins, therefore the devout Christian must temper his appetite for them. As meat then was only regularly eaten by royalty and nobility this was one method by which the Church could attempt to control the excesses of its worldly rulers. This struggle between Church and State would permeate the whole of the Middle Ages.

Fast days took up two-thirds of the year. Church policy was to erase the pagan by substituting a Christian interpretation, so now fish was to be eaten on a Friday in memory of Good Friday instead of Frigga, the Norse goddess. The pressure against gluttony was immense. Alcuin (732–804), the cleric and foremost scholar of the Carolingian Renaissance, wrote of Adam that 'Through greediness he was overcome, when, by the devil's instruction, he ate the forbidden apple.' He considered gluttony to be the first bodily sin, describing it as an intemperate pleasure in food and drink, from which 'foolish delight, scurrility, frivolity, boastful talk, uncleanness of the body, unsteadiness of mind, drunkenness and lust' all came.[3] Lust was thought to be very close to the stomach for, as Pope Gregory the Great had pointed out, 'The sexual organs appear attached beneath the stomach.' Hence excessive amounts of food were dangerous; food could be made harmless, by eating only small amounts of bland food, which could not stimulate those parts apt to be uncontrolled. (This fear was later taken up by the nonconformist religions and even by the Victorian bourgeoisie.) Alcuin had warned of eating food that was more choice and exquisite than necessary. The theme is referred to in *Metres of Boethius*, possibly composed by King Alfred (849–899): 'I can relate that from excess of each thing, of food and apparel, of the drinking of wine and from sweetmeats, there especially grows a great mad fit of wantonness; this strongly stirs up the conscious mind of each man and from it comes in the greatest degree wicked arrogance, useless strife.'[4]

Eating and drinking became for the Christian church a symbol of worldliness and therefore of the world of sin, yet within the Church itself the libidinous cleric was too common a sight. A poem[5] makes fun of the priests who after mass, when for some hours they should be fasting, instead ran to the tapster and sated themselves with wine and oysters. Patristic tradition saw fasting as a union with the angels, believing that it made the soul clear for reception of divine truth. Meat-eating was seen to reflect Cain's primal crime and was proof of human weakness and cruelty. To abstain from meat was to go some way to recovering primal innocence, for it was observed also that fasting moderated lust. According to Aethelred (c.1009) people were to fast three days on bread, herbs and water on the Monday, Tuesday and Wednesday before Michaelmas, though food might be given to the sick and needy. The 40-weekdays' fast of Lent was of course modelled on Christ's 40-day fast in the wilderness. On fast days one meal was allowed per day; a typical meal might be simply bread washed down with water, but the bread might have a relish of *gitte*, black cumin, described as 'the southern wort good to eat on bread'.[6] Periods of fasting were followed by periods of feasting; even a single day of fasting (children and the infirm were exempt) would be followed by single feast days.

With fast days so numerous the herring industry grew to meet demand and an integral part of the peasant diet was now the salted herring. The arrival of the Vikings, who lived largely from a fish diet, on the east coast of England further developed the fishing industry, including the smoking, salting and drying of fish. By 1066 herrings had become an important part of the economy and Yarmouth became the centre of the trade. Abbeys and manors that owned part of the coastline also installed hedge fishing from their land: a net (which could not be constructed before Roman times) was tied to four stakes, two impaled on the beach above the tide line, and the other two taken out at low tide and stuck into the sand. As the sea came in so did the fish and at high tide the net was pulled in with a catch of mackerel, dabs, young ling, rockling, and grey mullet.[7]

The Church's hold upon society, however, did not stop at making numerous obligatory fast days; to the peasant struggling to survive, fasting changed very little in his daily diet, but the Saxon farmer also had to pay a tithe on all his produce. The tenth foal, calf, lamb and piglet, every tenth sheaf of his harvest, tenth cheese or tenth day's milk, tenth measure of butter, tenth fleece, tenth of the yearly yield of wax and honey, fisheries, brushwood and orchards went to the Church. One-third of these payments went to support the parish priest, one-third to the upkeep of the village church and one-third to the poor. No wonder the Church grew rich and powerful and later was resented for it, fomenting peasant revolt.

Naturally what the Church ate was vastly superior to what the labourers and slaves survived on. In Aelfric's *Colloquy*[8] it is remarked that 'Monks had a good diet for most of the time.' As for everybody else, this was always dependent upon the harvest and clement weather. The novice monk was still allowed to eat flesh meat and also had a daily allowance of vegetables, eggs, fish and cheese: 'Butter and beans and all things that are not taboo I eat very gratefully.' Monastery meals were composed of bread, fish, cheese, vegetables, eggs, butter, beans and milk dishes, with water and ale to drink, and wine for the older, wiser and richer churchmen.

The Countryside

England was criss-crossed with a myriad number of tracks,[9] worn down over the centuries by herdsmen, who travelled with their animals every year towards the summer pasture; here, last year's rough hut would be mended so that the herdsmen were protected from the worst weather. These lands of summer pasture were dotted with grazing herds and small dwellings, and some of these areas have given their names to villages that grew up upon the same land. The syllable 'sell', meaning groups of shelters for animals and herdsmen's huts, turns up in village names such as Breadsell, Bremzells, Boarzell and Drigsell.

In the autumn, the herdsmen travelled back first to the market, where his fattened animals were sold, and then with the few he chose to keep for stud or labour on to the winter homestead. One can imagine him happy to be back with his wife and children after the five summer months, happy to have some fuss and consolation; perhaps his swollen knee was now tended with a green poultice of hot cabbage or leek wrapped around with sheep's wool, or his chesty cough given a hot infusion of hyssop or horehound. Back home the animals were housed inside on the earthen floor while the family slept above. In the winter the plot of land around their dwelling would be cleared and dug for the spring, although some of it would still be growing with winter brassicas. The herdsman and his wife would then return to their craft. Our surnames still reflect much of that work, such as coopering, hammering iron, turnering and tanning, while the wife and daughters would spin, weave and make cloth.

However, the greatest riches the land had for the peasants was the food it contained. When considering the peasant diet, it is vital not to dismiss nature's larder, with which peasants were surrounded, and which they had grown up with, learning from infancy the taste, smell, feel and sound of this thriving edible world; nor the very real and very often intense flavours such ingredients would give to the one-pot cooking or roasting in the embers of the fire which comprised family meals. Terriers were useful in finding small edible mammals such as the hedgehog, curled up beneath hedges, in dry ditches and heather bushes; their cooked white flesh was slightly gamey with a flavour of pork. Red squirrels were caught by throwing 'squails', short sticks loaded with weights; badgers were often smoked over a fire of birchwood, and their fat used for cooking; the brown rat and the dormouse were also eaten. Small birds could be netted, the song thrush, blackbird, wheatear, sparrow, skylark and many others; the eggs of starlings and sparrows, of the mallard, shelduck, wood-pigeon, moorhen, plover and others could be stolen. It was noticed that as long as the eggs were taken before the birds sat on them, the birds flew off and made another nest. In any case (a comforting thought this for children), plenty of larger birds, as well as stoats, rats and weasels, also robbed the nests. The rivers, streams and lakes were stuffed with freshwater fish to be caught: trout, grayling, tench, dace, gudgeon, roach, rudd, eels and pike. There were numerous sea fish that could be caught from the shore: smelt, codling, pollack, whiting, gurnard, as well as all the edible molluscs, whelks, periwinkles, limpets and mussels. Then there were all the wild vegetables, herbs and salad plants (see Appendix I for a fuller list), which were there to be searched out and gathered at different times of the year. The best time for snaring many of the wild mammals was in the autumn when they had built up a layer of fat to keep them throughout the winter months.

However, restrictions limiting the peasants' use of wild land came in early. From bye-laws of 690, we know that some land was privately owned and that timber was highly valued, because fines were exacted if anyone chopped down a tree or set it alight without permission, and fields were fenced or hedged to stop livestock trampling over them. We also know that other land was owned in common. In royal grants of land we see how the natural qualities were valued to describe its boundaries: parts of the grant might be specified as a wood where poles are cut, a stream where watercress grows, or a ford or a heath with heathery pasture. In Saxon charters the most numerous mention is of hedged fields and woods, but rivers, mill streams, ditches, bridges, paths, lanes and roads are also referred to.

Livestock

Whereas the Saxons had brought over with them a stouter, stronger, white ox with large curled horns, the Celts had used a small dark shorthorn ox (*Bos longifrons*). Though this made ploughing easier, these oxen were known to be troublesome and sometimes aggressive. A law of Alfred's states: 'If an ox gore a man or woman so that they die let it be stoned and let not its flesh be eaten.' Even worse, the law went on to add that if the ox had been observed pushing with its horns for several days and the owner had not penned it, then the owner should pay with his life.

Athelstan, King of the West Saxons and Mercians in the tenth century, imported a larger breed of horse from Spain to improve the breed in Britain. The Saxons had begun to use horses for riding in the middle of the seventh century; they were also used for carrying and for pulling laden carts to market. The Celts had always eaten horses and continued to do so throughout the Roman occupation, but Christianity frowned upon the practice as heathen, for horses were sacrificed in rituals that worshipped Thor and Odin. Perhaps it is this that has given the British their traditional repugnance to the thought of horsemeat as edible. The Romans harnessed horses across the throat (which accounts for their heads being held high in relief sculptures) so they could not be used for pulling loads; it was only in the tenth century that iron horseshoes were developed. Soon after, in the eleventh century, the harness was altered so that the horse carried its main load across the shoulders; when the wheeled cart appeared it was then possible to transport grain overland on long journeys.

The most important animal was the pig, which was then a high-backed, long-legged creature akin to the wild boar. Every peasant had at least one pig, but generally more for they cost nothing to keep; they would live off scraps and forage for acorns, beechmast and other riches in the woods. Each sow gave two litters in the year. Laws required pigs to be ringed through the nose to stop them rooting up valuable crops. The rings had two sharp points firmly clinched into the nostrils, so that when the snout was shoved into the earth the points cut into the nose. Men were fined for leaving their pigs unringed, or the pigs could be impounded. The pig was slaughtered at Martinmas (11 November) and salted down for the year, so that on feast days there was generally ham or a scrap of bacon to flavour stock for the pottage (which has developed into modern soup).

As the power of the lords grew, however, they annexed the woods around their properties and the villagers were charged for allowing their pigs to forage. By the tenth century pigs had become more domesticated; swineherds or pig tenants appeared who looked after the herds, surrendering a certain number – generally ten full grown pigs and five piglets – to the lord at Michaelmas (29 September). It was the swineherd's job to singe and scrape the carcasses and to make the bacon and lard, his reward being that he took home the entrails. At his death the pigs under his charge reverted back to the lord.

The Saxons preferred the ancient-horned, long-legged and long-tailed sheep to the hornless variety introduced by the Romans. This could be because the horns were used as drinking vessels and for household implements such as combs and spoons. Apart from the horns, sheep were kept for their wool; their skin was made into vellum for writing upon, their milk was used to make cheese and butter, their dung to fertilise the fields and lastly, their meat was eaten. So sheep were valued for all these products, and only the old sheep who gave no more milk and whose wool was now below standard were slaughtered for meat. The meat might well be salted down for the lean months of winter. Each cottar (a peasant who lived in a tithe cottage) gave his lord a lamb for Easter.

Herds of goats were kept for their milk also but were not as highly valued as the sheep. Each cottar kept a small flock of hens, from which he gave his lord two hens each Martinmas. Geese were also kept but generally always as part of the lord's property. Bees were domesticated under the Saxons, as honey was enormously prized; the sugar cane plantations of North Africa were still undiscovered by northern Europe. Dogs were relied upon to watch the herds of livestock for wolves were a constant danger. Dogs wore collars and were trained; they were expected to work hard and be obedient. Various bye-laws covered their behaviour and fines were exacted from their masters; for example, in the laws of Alfred the fine for a first bite was six shillings, a second twelve and for a third thirty. The heavy cost of these fines shows a certain terror of the dog bite, and there was certainly a knowledge of the existence of rabies.

We have some idea of the work of the peasants from Aelfric's *Colloquy*[11], a work designed to teach Latin to Anglo-Saxon schoolboys. A ploughman is asked to describe his work:

Oh my lord, I labour hard: I go out at daybreak in order to drive the oxen to the field, and I yoke them to a plough. There is not so stark a winter that I dare stay at home for fear of my lord, but having yoked the oxen and fastened the share and coulter to the plough every day I have to plough a full acre or more . . . I have a certain boy driving the oxen with a goad who is also hoarse from cold and shouting . . . I have to fill the stalls of the oxen with hay and water them and carry out their litter . . . Indeed, it is great toil, because I am not free.

Open Field System

Saxons tended to form larger settlements than the tribal hamlets of the Celts. They ignored the Roman remains of villas and cities, but established new villages, apportioned the land and organised it for cultivation. To each family, they shared out land called a 'hide', together with a share of a meadow for hay, pasture and kindling and the common land around the settlement. The hide was probably about 120 acres. The system was basically a response to the demand from villagers for a fair system whereby land is shared out among all, though it carried some obligations to the King such as food rents. Food rents were not just given to the lord and, as we have noted, to the Church but also to the King. In the time of King Ine, King of Wessex in the late seventh and early eighth centuries, the food rent from ten hides was ten vats of honey, 300 loaves, twelve ambers[10] of Welsh ale, thirty ambers of clear ale, two full-grown cows or ten wethers, ten geese, ten hens, ten cheeses, a full amber of butter, five salmon, twenty pounds of fodder and one hundred eels.

It could not last, for social distinctions came into play, and the power of the King's appointed thanes or lords grew. The lords took much of the land, in return for their military service duties for the King, and as time went on the peasant farmers' obligations to the King via his lords increased. Hardship led to loss of freedom for many of the small farmers, bound to serve on the lord's land as well as their own, and they became, in effect, serfs.

Under the lord's protection was the freeman who worked his farm independently. Then there were various classes of unfree men who were tenants on the land; below these were the serfs who were attached to the household of the lord. Then there were the slaves who were captives taken in war, men, women and children; or children of poor families sold into slavery as a preferable option. Each class was delineated by the type and amount of food it ate. However all classes of community had a homestead and land around it where a fenced kitchen garden grew, though both the building and the size of the land became ever more modest.

Arable lands around the villages were divided into three: two were cultivated, one growing cereals and the other peas and beans; the third was left fallow. All the land was fertilised in the winter months by the livestock. Animal dung was treasured as being the source of regeneration in the soil. The whole of this area was divided into long, narrow acre strips a furrow-long – hence furlong, which is forty poles in length and four poles in breadth. These strips were divided from each other by narrow borders of turf called baulks; one can still see the ridges in fields that lie around medieval villages, and where the countryside has not been built on. The strips were scattered across the whole area so that villagers shared the disadvantages of soil and geography and no one person hogged all the land in the best position. These acres under cultivation were carefully fenced around each year to keep out animals. Villagers also retained a share in the hay from meadows and were allowed to pasture their animals on the common land, and had rights of wood-cutting on waste lands.

The system worked well, if the lord and the dignitaries of the Church were all benevolent and behaved with due Christian compassion for those less fortunate than themselves. However, the system was completely open to abuse by these elite, so that the lord could annex the wild land around the village and charge people for the use of it, while the Church could ask in food more than was fair and drive the people into near starvation. When the Normans arrived the system *was* abused and there was greater oppression.

Women and the Law

Anglo-Saxon law stemmed from the German provinces from which the Saxons had come, and it was enlightened. There was clear and sensible legislation as regards women, for example. The prospective husband of a bride had to pay a large sum in land and money called a 'morning gift', which was paid not to the father or her kin but to her, and she then had personal control over this sum; she could give it away, bequeath it, spend it or save and invest it. Sussex field names such as Mayfield, Morgay Farm and Morgay Wood stem from the word for morning gift. In marriage the finances were held in the name of both husband and wife. Furthermore, a woman had the right to walk out of her marriage, and was entitled to take the children and half the property. If the woman had deceived her husband, however, she had to return to her kin and the husband received back the money he gave to her. The wife was not to be held guilty for any criminal activity of the husband. Inheritance laws showed concern for the economic status of the widow, for there was no question of the estate and property passing automatically to the eldest son with the widowed mother left dependent on him. The law also protected women against rape and even seduction: a seducer was fined, although the amount was dependent on the rank of the woman.

The role most consistently linked with women was cloth-making, which involved weaving, spinning and embroidery. Slaves were trained for fine work and specialised in them. There was great demand for wall hangings, seat covers, and tablecloths, as well as for rich Church vestments and the garments of the nobility. Women, of course, also cooked in the home, but men were the cooks in rich households, though it appears that there the role of the lady of the house was to serve drinks. In *Beowulf* it is the Queen herself. The Venerable Bede (c.673-735) mentions the wife of a nobleman who having been cured of an illness 'brought the cup to the bishop and to the rest of us and continued to serve us all with drink until dinner was finished'.[12]

In *Rectitudines*, a text that specifies rights and duties of estate workers, only one woman is named among the male workers who were swineherds, oxherds and foresters, and she was the cheese-maker. 'The cheese-maker is entitled to a hundred cheeses and is to make butter for the lord's table from the whey; and she is to have all the buttermilk except for the herdman's share.'[13] In Aelfric's *Colloquy* the Old English word for cook is *coc* which is a masculine noun, but there are masculine and feminine nouns for the word 'baker'.

All of these laws were swept away under Norman rule (when a woman's role was defined as to marry and serve) and it took a thousand years for some semblance of them to return.

CHAPTER 2

Anglo-Saxon Gastronomy

Though I believe that after the Norman Conquest a peak of English gastronomy was achieved, such cooking used a bedrock of Anglo-Saxon culinary inventiveness which has remained a strong thread within our food. The Normans appropriated for themselves a land that, as we have seen, was rich in produce. The peasants had learned to live using wild foods, and the Anglo-Saxons were learned in herbal lore and adroit in their use of herbal essences. Sadly, this too would later be taken from them by their Norman rulers, for wild game and plants would be sequestered by forestry laws, and herbal knowledge in a vulnerable person would become evidence of witchcraft.

Food and Fasts

One of the great suppositions about our diet is that it was based upon meat-eating. There were certainly great carnivores in our past. Tacitus gives us a clue as to who they are when he talks of the Germanic peoples placing no value on elaborate forms of cookery but preferring simple food: wild fruit, fresh game and curdled milk.[1] Meat-eating took a central role in the Anglo-Saxon and German aristocracy. In the Icelandic sagas a Hollywood vision of the past is given credence by scenes in which drunken warriors throw large animal bones at each other in the hall. The inference is that whole ox or mutton carcasses had been roasted then presented well nigh whole to the table for the warriors to hack and carve themselves. There is an Homeric pride in this kind of consumption; the larger the animal eaten the greater the grandeur and wealth of the provider. We can discern this attitude in Aelfric's *Colloquy* when a cook is confronted with the statement: 'We don't care about your art; it isn't necessary to us, because we can boil things that need boiling and roast things that need roasting.'[2] This exchange tells us that cooking was recognised as being an art even if it was not always pursued – a valuable clue to Anglo-Saxon gastronomy.

However, the Church's teaching (see page 15) confused natural appetites. Both the concept of gastronomy and the idea of asceticism (the control, selection and censoring of foods) come from a basic unease in the early medieval sensibility over the function of eating at all. The anxiety stemmed from how human beings differ from beasts: in the need to consume and defecate there appeared no difference, yet the religious sensibility stated that man was blessed by being created in the image of God and was in control of all the beasts of the field (so could kill and eat them) as well as being in control of the beast within himself. Cooking, spicing and saucing raised food to a level which is beyond that of the beast. Dishes fit for the divine spark within man; fasting and starving the body of nutrients proved that man could become a more rarefied being, more worthy of God's love. In fact, from 960-1216 there was a complete abstinence from meat as a rule throughout the monasteries of England. The rule might be broken in a case of definite illness and poultry was allowed to be eaten.[3]

We obtain glimpses of the monastic diet from the conversations created by the monk Aelfric Bata, and from these lively and colourful exchanges we know the diet was far from monotonous with a large amount of drinking allowed. These conversations are pre-Conquest but the basic life within the monastery would have remained well-nigh unchanged for centuries, except for a gradual erosion of the rules and an accompanying rise in the quality and luxury of the food until the Reformation finally destroyed it all. However, Aelfric Bata at the beginning of the eleventh century gives us a picture that is not in the least austere. They drank good beer or mulled drink, mead or wine, they had hams, poultry and fish, for a monk stole morsels of those from his fellow novices. When the teacher prepared himself for a journey he asked the novice to go to the cellarer and to ask him for a prepared meal, detailing what he wants: 'Wheat bread and a measure of honey and fish, butter and milk, lard and cheese and eggs and toast and whipped cream and beef, pork and mutton, vegetables, peppered dishes, and good beer, and wine and mulled mead and every good thing and a napkin.'[4] This sounds like an ambitious picnic, but the journey by river and road is of several days and the teacher would have been accompanied by two or three others to wait on him. As we will learn from the public cookshops of later years (see page 63), travellers liked to take their own produce with them, such as their own fish from their rivers and lakes, and their own butchered carcasses, for they knew they could trust the quality of these, while on the road they feared being either swindled or poisoned.

The abbey garden is full of medicinal herbs and plants as well as vegetables to eat, which he lists: 'Growing there are the vegetables that can be eaten just about every day: cabbage, celery, mallow, parsley, thyme, garlic, mint, dill and savory.' They divided the vegetables into those that were eaten cooked and those eaten raw; all of these were eaten cooked and the herbs used in cooking. The rest of his list is of herbs eaten raw or used medicinally: 'Also growing there are lovage, woad, sorrel, feverfew, henbane, rubia, rape, mullein, wormwood, hemlock, groundsel, fennel, lupine, violet, ravensfoot, daisy, heliotrope, clary, comfrey, rue, vervain, tansy, milfoil, yarrow, saxifrage, iris, poppy, nettle, angelica, plantain, cinquefoil, periwinkle, horehound, strawberry, cumin, elecampane, watercress, pennyroyal, marjoram, mugwort, sage, thistle, carrot, lily, rose, clover, agrimony, radish, fern and sedge.'[5] A formidable list, any of these would also have been used as flavouring herbs in cooking; they were certainly all used in lotions, potions, ointments and salves as well as warming drinks and in salads.

In a further Colloquy (27), the tools and ironware in the kitchen are listed for the cooking and preparing of the daily meals: 'Practically every day there will be a hearth with coal, flaming logs and brands, hatchets for cutting wood, andiron, a cauldron, frying pan, hook, crocks, bellows for blowing on the fire, spits for roasting, a dish or dishes, a tray, vessel, pitcher, bowl or basin, saw, a vessel of lead, bucket, utensils, wicker basket, barrow, tin vessel, oven, dough, flour, meal, sieve, barrel, vat, bottle, flask, tongs, shears, candlesnuffer and countless other ironware.' Lastly, the teacher asked the novice, 'Oh dear boy, spread my tablecloth, because we don't have a cloth except on feast days. Get my fork, my knife, my spoon, my utensil, my wine jug and my dish. Go quickly and bring some pottage and tasty foods from the kitchen.'[6] Although forks were not widely adopted in northern Europe until the seventeenth century, here is a very early mention of one, as if it is an essential tool with which to eat a meal.

The women and children were kept busy throughout the year, gathering food from the wild, such as innumerable fungi for drying in autumn, as well as sage, rosemary and thyme. Wild celery and alexanders could be picked; greens such as wild spinach or Good King Henry would be tough by then, but with long slow cooking would add a flavour to the stew. Other herbs would be harvested before the frosts destroyed their leaves: dandelion, borage, swinecress, red nettle, orach, scarlet pimpernel, chickweed and plantain. From their plot around the dwelling fenced in by a dead hedge, the women and children would have grown onions, garlic and shallots, which would have been strung earlier. Leeks, kale and cabbages, green onions, hyssop and second-year parsley (which would now seed itself for the next year) could all be left in the ground. Peas and beans had to be podded; they were left on the plants until dried, then stored in earthenware jars and pots.

Peas were slow to become accepted as a field crop, which considering their high nutritive value and the fact that both man and beast can eat them, at first strikes one as puzzling. As late as the thirteenth century there were still some manors not growing them at all. However, dried pulses were basic to the daily pottage (stew-like soup) and I suspect these were grown near the living quarters with the pot herbs. It was the grey pea or field pea (*Pisum arvense*) that was grown, which has an attractive purple flower and grows rapidly to about five feet. It has little taste fresh, but dried it is astonishingly full of a rich, almost meaty flavour, making a purée that is thick and filling. It is then that the colour turns grey and in gastronomic terms it is unappealing, but the flavour and food value are enormous.

Early medieval bye-laws seem eager to protect the harvesting of the peas ('coddling', as it was called), for as they grow to five feet, a person or even a child is hidden when picking them and the open field system was vulnerable to the pods being stolen. One law directs that the poor must not gather the peas on the plough strip but only on the verge. Other laws say that coddling must be done between sunrise and sunset and that people coddling must all enter and leave the field at the same time. The growing peas were being policed, in fact.

Growing the pea just outside the dwellings would solve these problems: two 6 ft x 3 ft beds would give about 12 lb of dried peas; with the dried beans also grown nearby there would have been enough pulses to see a small family through a winter and for seed in early spring. The beans they grew would have been one of ten different varieties of the broad bean (*Vicia cracca*), probably either narbonne vetch (*Vicia narbonensis*) or white vetch (*Vicia sativa*) which was later grown all over northern Europe as a feed for animals.

However, there is abundant evidence in place names that beans were planted in the fields and not only around the dwellings, for example, in Benhall, Benacre and Peasenhall in Suffolk, for that county specialised in the growing of legumes, and Banstead in Surrey was growing them as early as 675. In fact, in the east of England they seemed fond of growing both beans and rye.

So what else, apart from either peas or beans, would have been in this daily family stew? This pottage, with its leaden sound and its association with the Biblical 'mess of pottage', always conjures up a bland and dreary dish. It has been the mainstay of the majority of the people for thousands of years, however, and people then, as now, however poor they were, had a vested interest in the quality of the food they ate. In the first place, however, this food, spooned onto a flat circle of maslin (see below) bread, would have been solid fuel to stifle the growing hunger of their working day. They would also have delighted in flavours that were intense and stimulating, especially on those days and autumn months up to Michaelmas when there were no animal bones, flesh or skin to bequeath a meaty flavour. The main leaf would almost certainly have been a type of kale because it grew abundantly and was very hardy throughout the coldest winter, but every flavouring herb would have been used too. It is unlikely that in the autumn any part of the salted-down pig would be left, but there were the fungi to add richness and the summer's onions and garlic. Any root vegetables were not yet ready, except possibly wild celeriac, skerrit or the roots of flat leaf parsley. Nevertheless, with freshly baked breads (either from the one communal oven if the village was important enough, or more likely homemade cooked flat on an iron placed over the fire) and after the pottage the cheese preserved in brine, there was a meal which kept hunger at bay. Health and vigour must have been preserved by the daily use of wild plant food, a good source of minerals and vitamins. Through the long winter months, when brassicas and land cress are still in leaf, the threat of scurvy must have been erased by gathering from the wild. The pottage was cooked slowly in or over a low fire; to sharpen the flavour there would be wood sorrel, horseradish and mustard, and there might be pickled rock samphire, or relishes of raw onion, leek and garlic.

The peasants fared far better under Anglo-Saxon rule than later under Norman tyranny. According to an ordinance of Athelstan's one destitute Englishman on each of the royal estates was to receive one amber of meal (roughly ground cereals) and a shank of bacon or a wether (a castrated ram) worth fourpence every month. The meal would have been consumed as bread or pottage. Even a male slave was to receive among other things about 3½ lb of corn per day and a female slave 2½ lb, which between them was about 4 lb of bread per day. Slaves were, of course, the basic workforce on the land, so it paid to keep them fed and healthy, especially throughout that sparse time in the bleak winter months. So it was decreed that a male slave received two sheep carcasses and a cow for the winter, while the female slave only got one sheep or threepence for winter food. There was also one sester of beans for Lent and whey in summer or one penny. Both received food at Christmas, Easter and harvest time while both also had a strip of land on which to grow vegetables.[7]

The bread was likely to have been made from maslin flour, which is a mixture of wheat and rye; both cereals were grown together, though the rye ripened at least two weeks before the wheat. The corn would have been milled with a hand quern unless there was a water mill; these first reached Britain in 762 and thereafter proliferated; at the time of Domesday there were 5,624. However, the mill belonged to the landlord, being on the manor's land, so a proportion of peasant grain was taken as a toll. This added expense meant the hand querns continued, even though it was such hard work.

Not only the mill was owned by the manor, but the bread oven too, so if the peasant took his dough to be baked, a proportion of the dough went to the lord or squire. So home baking thrived as well as home-milling. The unleavened hearthcake was called therf-bread; the sour-dough was placed on a round flat iron which had a long handle, the end of which was wood. The iron was supposed to be the width of a man's arm from elbow to wrist, and the bread needed to be thick enough to be held at one side as one would a plate. This could hold a thick pottage heaped up in the centre, while bits of the outside of the rim of the bread could be broken off and dipped into the stew. It was a practical way of eating, for nothing was lost, and the juices of the pottage drained into the centre of the bread to be eaten last.

Bread could be also baked at home if the three-legged cauldron was buried upside down in slow burning peat; the dough went in underneath. That of course required the family not to be using the cauldron for its daily pottage, and few families could afford more than one cooking pot. In what was to become Wales, bread was baked on a griddle set on a tripod covered with an iron lid with the heat produced from furze and clods of earth ranged around it, The yeast was made from barley cleared of beard by being pummelled on a clean floor, sieved three times, then mixed with some boiled grey peas and oats, sieved into a container and left on a warm hearth. Then a handful of hops and flour was added to it and it was left for a day or two. The yeast was so powerful it could not be bottled for the bottles would surely explode.

This way of making yeast continued up to the beginning of this century on the island of Anglesey and in Wales. It was unleavened or barely leavened bread, and would have been eaten daily in round flat cakes. The flour was one hundred per cent rye, barley and oats, with little gluten but nothing removed by sieving. Baking under a pot would have drawn the dough slightly upwards. Even sourdough, which might have used fermented liquor from brewing or the sediment from bottom-fermenting yeasts, was slow acting and would have resulted in a heavy damp bread, perfect as it happens, for its use as a receptacle to a thick soup.

One can understand why wheaten loaves were eaten by the rich and valued so highly as food for feasts and communion food as the Eucharist. The baker was a respected figure. In Aelfric's *Colloquy* he remarks: 'Without my skill every table seems empty and without bread all food is turned to loathing, I gladden the hearts of men, I strengthen folk, and because of this, the little children will not shun me.'

Cooking the Food

When looking at what peasants ate, it is often forgotten that in the summer months much cooking could take place outdoors. Iron tripods made for large cooking pots would stand in the midst of a fire; the pot would take mixed stews of bones, vegetables, herbs and wild game birds with suet puddings stuffed into stomach linings. A boiled suet sausage was a Saxon favourite. This could be tied to the handle and either steamed or boiled. Placing food in earthenware jugs, lighting a fire in a hole, letting it die down, and then burying the jug and leaving it for half a day is an ancient method of cooking and one we still associate with hare. In the winter the fire would have been in the centre of the dwelling with stones used as a fireback, but built onto the earth floor on yesterday's ashes. The fire throughout the winter months would never have gone out; at night the embers would still be warm and porridge could be made overnight. Most meals throughout the year, however, would have been cooked in a cauldron, which hung over the fire and could be lowered when needed.

Modest landowners could afford other cooking equipment: griddle and frying pans, soapstone bowls which were unbreakable on clay floors, other earthenware pots which with a lid could be used for baking, thrust deep into the embers of a fire, and leather vessels which could be used for boiling. Salt meat was simmered with dried peas or beans in the embers for a very long time, salt fish was poached in milk with butter, vegetables were seethed in oil or a mixture of oil and ale, apples, pears and medlars were stewed in wine sweetened with honey. As well as pottage, in Old English the word *brod* is mentioned, meaning broth – in this context a thin broth, though obviously this could be enriched by cream or lots of butter. The Cook in the *Colloquy* mentions a fat, rich broth and also various soups; as well as the obvious bean and pea soup, there is a carrot broth, a mint broth, and a hen and mallow leaf broth; a peppered broth is classed as a delicacy. The art of keeping a fire going all day and allowing it to die down throughout the night meant that cooking was inevitably of the long simmered, one-pot variety; it also necessitated various tools like bellows, fire covers and fire tongs, as well as a steady supply of the right size of logs. It has been estimated that to spit roast a pig of 120 lb in weight you needed 15 cwt of thoroughly seasoned large oak logs a foot long.

A funeral feast receipt costing four ores and seven pence tells us that it was composed of bread, ale, a flitch of bacon and a buck; roast venison would have been a treat. Another grander feast, costing eight ores and twenty-four pence, had a pig, three bucks and a bullock with cheese, fish and milk. All cooking relied on some preserved foods, whether it was only dried fungi on threads. Leechdoms (from the Anglo-Saxon word *laece*, to heal) gave precise instructions on drying foods in the sun and open air, or by the fire or in the oven and kiln. They gave direction as to gathering, drying and powdering of herbs, how to dry seaweed, peas, beans, meat, birds and fish. What foods to salt and smoke and how to pickle.

The salter ranks in importance with the ploughman, fisherman and smith:

> My trade greatly benefits you all. None of you would take any pleasure in
> your meals or food without my hospitable art. How can anyone appreciate
> very sweet foods to the full without the savour of salt? Look, you would
> even lose your butter and cheese and you can't even enjoy your vegetables
> without making use of me.[8]

Food for the Elite

We do have a collection of recipes and observations on digestion. *On the Observance of
Foods*, which dates from the early sixth century (about AD 511), was written by a Greek
physician, Anthimus, ambassador to King Theuderic, King of the Franks (an area of
north-east Gaul around Metz). It is in a form of a letter written to King Theuderic.
To complicate matters, Anthimus had been sent north by his master, King Theodoric,
who was the Ostrogothic king in Italy and whom some historians have confused with
the king of the Franks, owing to the similarity in their names. The letter is highly
informative on the diet at the court: the instructions and observations are imbued with
foods rarely eaten in Italy or Greece: pork, bacon, hams and dairy foods from cattle. I
mention it here, because north-east Gaul's climate was very like Britain's, and as all
worldly monarchs were overseen by the power and jurisdiction of the Papacy, society
was not basically that different. The food of the elite at the court of King Theuderic
would have been similar to that at King Alfred's. The most striking aspect of
Anthimus's letter is not how the shadow of Ancient Rome still looms, but how the
medicinal knowledge is influenced by Arabian thought and its philosophy of
humours, which would come to dominate medieval cooking.

The letter is more concerned with health than with cooking and is a detailed guide
to the foods that are beneficial to the body; thus bread should be white and leavened
otherwise it will weigh heavily upon the stomach. Hares are considered nourishing
foods for one in delicate health. One should not eat pig's kidneys except for the edges
and the kidneys of other animals never.[9] Only the breasts and wings of fowl should be
eaten, never the hinder parts. (Presumably the servants, concerned only with their
hunger and not their health, gladly consumed the rest.) Dark meat, such as cranes',
engendered melancholy humours. Hard egg white should be avoided, only eggs that
are runny should be eaten. Anthimus is suspicious of lampreys because of their dark
blood. He prefers oysters baked instead of raw as it removes the chance of poisoning
from them. He endorses a range of vegetables from mallow, beet, leeks and cabbage
(the latter should only be eaten in the winter), lettuces, turnips, parsnips and carrots.
He approves of both cultivated and wild asparagus: they are boiled with celery and
fennel root and flavoured with coriander and mint, then eaten with salt and oil. Orach,
radishes, garlic, onions and shallots are all good for you.

This list is interesting for historians over the centuries have always bemoaned the
lack of salads and vegetables eaten, as they are rarely mentioned in either kitchen
accounts or recipes. Anthimus also approves of barley, broad beans, chick peas and

lentils; after the latter have been cooked a little vinegar and Syrian sumac are added, then olive oil, coriander and salt. He mentions 'French beans' as being good, even when dried; this is the translator's interpretation of the Latin *fasiolum*, which follows the example of other translators when interpreting the same word in the works of Pliny and Galen, where it is mentioned how short growing the plant is. The bean, in fact, is likely to be the black-eyed pea which came from the East to the Mediterranean countries and would not be a version of *Phaseolus vulgaris* which was waiting to be discovered in the New World.[10]

As to milk being drunk, Anthimus is naturally suspicious, being a Byzantine, so he thinks it should be heated first or have honey, wine or mead mixed with it. He believes that fresh milk will curdle in the stomach (the proof was there in the carcass of calves) and this could be harmful. This belief was to continue up to the nineteenth century, and as milk quickly became contaminated or turned it was perhaps just as well. He likes curdled milk mixed with honey or olive oil, which was either curds or yoghurt; if the latter it is interesting to see it appear as a food so far north. He does not like cheese either, unless it is fresh and sweet. I imagine this to be an Arabic inhibition, as his dislike of cooked cheese was based on a belief that it produced kidney stones.

Anthimus loves quinces, apples, plums, peaches and cherries, but they must all ripen on the tree. Blackberries, mulberries, fresh figs, chestnuts, hazelnuts and almonds are all good, as are pistachios, dried figs, dates and raisins. The Frankish court seems to lack for nothing and from this huge range of ingredients one feels there must have been a lively cuisine. Two recipes have some detail to them, but one gathers that heat from fire could be difficult to control, for roasted meat tends to get burnt, unless it is boiled first. There is, however, much mention of gentle cooking over charcoal, which needs the use of a chafing dish.

First, a recipe for what could be a Beef Daube. The beef, Anthimus says, should be washed in clean water then boiled until almost done. Sharp vinegar and half as much honey, the white part of leeks, pennyroyal, wild celery or fennel, should then be added and the stew simmered for another hour. Then spikenard, pepper, costmary and cloves should be ground, and these spices mixed with wine and added to the stew just before serving. Spices were expensive; spikenard grew high in the Hindu Kush and was exported from the Ganges, so this, even for a royal household, was a recipe for an occasion. The wine added at the end would give aroma and delicacy to the finished sauce. Anthimus also advised that the stew would taste better if cooked in an earthenware pot rather than an iron one. How right he is, for it is an observation other cooks have made and one I can personally agree with. How sophisticated this recipe is; it strikes me as simple but well judged. And though it is sent to a king, something similar with less expensive ingredients would also have been eaten by the Saxon nobility.

Anthimus's next recipe is delicate and again highly sophisticated. It is made from minced chicken and beaten egg white, heaped up upon scallops in a fish sauce, and cooked in a chafing dish; the egg white and chicken cook in the steam from the sauce. When it is served a little wine and honey is poured over it and Anthimus tells us that it is eaten with a spoon. This strikes me as gastronomy – as good as it gets.[11]

As with the peasant household, the implements at a manor kitchen would have been a large cauldron and tripod, but they would have had a much used spit turned by hand and able to hold the occasional large carcass or a string of smaller ones. There were also smaller spits for small birds. Oxen, being labouring beasts, were valued alive, but when past their prime would have been slaughtered; as their meat then was tough they would have been boiled slowly. The most common large carcass to be roasted would have been deer, then wild boar, and occasionally the more elderly sheep and goats; almost certainly they would have been boiled first then spit-roasted.

Further implements in the manor kitchen would have been a gridiron for baking breads, a ladle, iron pots of differing sizes, a mortar and pestle, knives and wooden spoons. The meals would have revolved around boiled and roast wild meats, game and boar. Beyond this basically simple idea of cooking, the concept of a cuisine, where time and skill were expended on food, existed, as we have seen, but if we are to remember the Cook in the *Colloquy* was also somehow resented. Nevertheless, an Anglo-Saxon cuisine of dishes we would consider highly delicious today undoubtedly existed, and many of these have stayed with us and were the basis on which Anglo-Norman cookery was to rise to new heights.

Leechdoms abound with terms like 'work it into a paste', 'beat two eggs in hot water', 'sweeten with honey', 'shred new cheese in front of a gentle fire'. There were sweet omelettes containing flowers and fruit, there were dishes of milk, or cream or curds sometimes mixed with sweet wine and ground cereal – a dish that would come to be known later as flummery.[12] Cows' heels and calves' feet were used to make jellies. Summer puddings used bread to contain fruit, such as blackberries, raspberries and whortleberries.[13] Sweet dishes were called *eft mettas*, literally after meats.

The idea of regional specialities to be sought after had taken root: pigs from Gloucestershire and Buckinghamshire, for example, fed on beech mast, which bequeaths a special nutty flavour, were dearly prized; the hams from Yorkshire and Westmorland, which had been cured with a mixture of common salt, saltpetre, black pepper and honey, were praised. Oven-roasted meat was somehow wrapped in a flour and water paste so that it was steam-baked. Beef was marinaded in vinegar and herbs, and vegetables and apples in wine and honey. Clay was used for wrapping sea birds when roasted in the fire. There is a recipe in a Leechdom for a sage omelette: 'take a handful of sage and grind it very small and twelve peppercorns and grind them up fine, then take six eggs and beat them up with the sage and pepper, take a clean pan and fry the mixture in oil.' There is also another recipe for a vegetable omelette. Perhaps the most impressive recipe is *osterhlfas* (oyster loaf), in which a loaf was hollowed out and the inside filled with a mixture of oysters, minced meat, suet, egg, herbs and seasoning, then baked.

Fruit sauces were traditionally served with meat and fish dishes. The English used a greater number of green herbs for their green sauce than the French did. Some basic cooking procedures were already established: clarifying butter; whipping cream; a prepared mustard referred to as *gerenodne senep*; serving vegetables with butter or oil and vinegar; and a wide range of herbs used to flavour all manner of dishes.

Feast Halls

The high point of Anglo-Saxon cuisine must have been those celebratory meals in the feast halls where the King's throne was also called the gift-seat, for the King rewarded warriors for their triumphs. Beowulf received a golden standard, helmet, mail shirt and eight horses with golden bridles and jewelled saddles. These halls were vast: the foundations of one at Yeavering measure 80 ft by 40 ft with supports for a high roof; another at Cheddar, dating back to the ninth century, is 75 ft in length. Silver gilt mounts for drinking horns and cups of exquisite workmanship have been found and we know that a harp was played as the nobles ate. A horn was blown to summon the guests to the feast. The Great Hall was guarded by doorkeepers, who ensured there were no gatecrashers or anyone entering while the meal was in progress. Hangings, sometimes interwoven with gold used to decorate the walls and tablecloths were in use by the early ninth century, table napkins by the tenth. The diners were seated on cushioned settles.

The function of the royal feast was to emphasise the ruler's power through a lavish display of wealth, and to attract followers and supporters, so that hopefully the feast became a unifying force within society. The King or 'chieftain' provided food and drink that was prestigious in kind and plentiful in quantity; the more rituals attached to the food, the more music and spectacle arranged the greater the ruler appeared. The feast was central to the manner by which the King wielded his power.

Men were in charge of the cooking and the serving of the food; they carried the roasts upon their spits and knelt to serve the diners, carving choice cuts for the King and his favoured guests. They drank beer[14], ale, wine and mead; the bread served was always of wheat, but often made from enriched dough mixtures of flour mixed with eggs and cream, spiced and flavoured, and sprinkled with seeds such as dill, caraway, pepper, fennel and sweet cicely. Meat, fish and game were served. Nor would a feast ignore the dietary knowledge of the time; it would be likely to celebrate it. For example, the inclusion of a sorrel sauce for a fish dish is very likely, because sorrel is mentioned in the Leechdoms, through which we know that the connection between food and health was a strong one. No society before or since placed so much emphasis on the health-giving properties of a huge range of herbs and gave so many recipes for the creation of potions, ointments and dishes to be eaten.

Herbal Knowledge

The Saxons possessed a formidable awareness of the power of herbs upon human and animal metabolism. *The Leech Book of Bald*, which dates from around 900-950, is considered by some to have a much wider knowledge of herbs than the doctors of Salerno. This book, the first medical treatise written in Western Europe after those in the ancient world, is written in the vernacular, so as a work of study it was available to all. One chapter consists of prescriptions sent by Helias, Patriach of Jerusalem, to King Alfred, so it was a work that reflected the thinking upon the subject in the civilised world. It was a manual of a Saxon doctor who refers to two other doctors, Dun and Oxa, who had given him prescriptions. In the *Herbarium* of Apuleius, which included Dioscorides' additions, only 185 plants are mentioned, and in the earliest Herbal, printed in Germany in 1484, 380 plants appear. The Anglo-Saxons had names for at least 500 different plants. Pliny tells us that the Ancient Britons would gather herbs with such striking ceremonies that it would seem as though the Britons had taught them to the Persians. In fact, the *Leech Book* is full of ancient Indo-Germanic beliefs, which shows that trade between the West and the East went far back into prehistory.

As an antidote to many diseases and afflictions some herbs become sacred like watercress, chervil, fennel and camomile and these are but a few. Herb drinks were made by adding pounded mixtures of herbs to ale, milk and honey. There were vapour baths with sweet smelling herbs, sunburn oils and cleansing creams, prescriptions for hair loss, eye mistiness, headaches, snake bites, nose bleeds and wounds. Rooms, people and animals were all fumigated with a mixture of herbs burnt slowly to produce smoke. Plants from the wild were therefore central to the life and vigour of the Anglo-Saxon culture.

Imported spices were enormously valuable. The Venerable Bede on his deathbed in 735 was careful to share his pepper and his incense, while London was already a commercial centre for the sale of expensive and rare spices. Bede describes it as 'an emporium for many nations who come to it by sea and land'. Spices reached northern Europe by way of the Persian Gulf, Red Sea, Egypt and the Levant, and, unlike silver coinage which was frequently debased, peppercorns kept their value. In the 960s Corby Abbey bought from Cambrai sacks of spices which ranged from 120 lb of pepper and cinnamon and 70 lb of ginger to numerous 10 lb parcels of other spices. Although trade was flourishing, the early Church fathers disapproved of it, however. Leo I declared it was difficult for buyers and sellers not to fall into sin. The Anglo-Saxons exported woollen cloaks to the Carolingian Empire, while Cornish tin had been used in Europe's metal industries since Roman times. There was also a brisk business in slaves, generally war captives. At the time of the Domesday Book, twelve per cent of the population were slaves; these were taken in battle and either kept for labouring or sold on.

Export of wool began in the early eleventh century just before the Norman Conquest. By this time the Flemings had a large mercantile fleet. Gold had stemmed from Byzantium and the Muslim Empire and by the tenth century English land purchases had been made with it, pointing to constant trade in the Mediterranean. Peterborough's abbey church had a great cross of solid gold, and English goldsmiths were famous throughout Europe. Pepper doubled in value when it crossed the Mediterranean, and spices, fine silks and taffetas and even wine were all so expensive that only the royal court and the richest of nobility could afford them. Nevertheless, wars, conquests and famine could harm trade and set it back decades. The Danish conquest, for example, with its demands for ransoms in silver, so depleted the English capital and impoverished the English merchants that trade declined. When this occurs, gastronomy is also discouraged, although treacherous weather and the resulting inadequate harvests were the prime enemy and a constant threat.

The Famine Years

The tenth century was full of catastrophes brought on by unseasonable weather of unceasing rain and floods, and months of snow and frost. For a society that relied upon bread as its staple food, a ruined harvest meant famine followed inevitably by plague or pestilence. In the hundred years following the first millennium, England would be conquered yet again by invasion, and further weakened by years of unendurable famine. In 1044 a dreadful famine struck England and the Continent and three years later there was snow and frost and more famine. In 1051 a failed harvest produced extreme dearth where thousands died; again three years later there was a terrible famine, after a comet was seen. In 1068 there was famine and plague after a severe winter and in 1069 the northern counties of England suffered a great dearth after being harried by William I trying to subjugate his northern territory; the mortality was so great that the living could not take care of the sick nor bury the dead. In 1086 there was a murrain[15] of animals and intemperate weather and in the next year pestilence and famine in which many thousands died. In 1093 there was great famine and more mortality.

If we take notice of the number of references to hunger in the early medieval chronicles and legal documents we must recognise that it was a normal, almost everyday, experience. Plagues inevitably followed the famine, exacerbated by the fact that people moved around searching for food. If bad harvests were not enough, eating toxins in the cereals was also a continuing hazard. There was corncockle (*Agrostemma githago*), a weed that grows with the corn and needs to be rooted up before the harvest as the seeds contain *githagen*, which predisposes those that eat it to leprosy. Then there was ergot (*claviceps purpurea*), a fungus disease of cereals especially rye. Ergotism (*ignis sacer*, St Anthony's Fire or erysipelas) was one of the most common complaints dealt with in the Leechdoms, and produced convulsions, gangrene, abortions, often death and certainly hallucinations in both humans and livestock. Ergot flourished in wet conditions for the moulds secreted their dangerous aflatoxins on damp grain, meal or flour, especially where rye was the main crop, which was in the West Midlands.

Another common hazard was that cured pork was a source of botulism; as the curing process did not kill off the parasites. Whipworms (*trichuris trichiura*) leads to severe diarrhoea or Ascarids (*Ascaris lumbricoides*) which are large round worms whose migrating larva can produce hepatitis and damage the lungs. From the coprolite evidence analysed in York, most people carried some worm infestation for most of their lives. Even King Alfred was well aware of this affliction when he wrote to Boethius and commented 'on the small worms that crawl within and without man even sometimes kill him'.[16] There was contamination of milk and dairy products by bacteria, flies and mice lived in food stores, which was why, if milk was not drunk straight from the cow, it could not be kept, but had to be boiled or turned into butter and cheese.

The Anglo-Saxons must have also suffered from vitamin A and C deficiencies in the long winter months, leading to eye, skin and urinary tract diseases and bleeding gums and ulcers. The Leechdoms recommend beet leaves, mallow, brassica, nettle and elder leaves, all of which were good sources for these vitamins. Their teeth show marked wear, a sure sign of a coarse, fibrous diet. They may also have absorbed lead from their food-processing equipment, by salting meat in lead containers; brining creates an acidic medium, which dissolves metal. Lead-lined cider vats and presses might have caused outbreaks of colic and lead poisoning. Many women died from childbirth and attendant complications between twenty and thirty: of those that survived, only a very few lived beyond forty-five, though their stature was greater than in the Iron Age and the later medieval population.

None of these troubles and afflictions was to change after the Norman Conquest. This was the underbelly of a struggling society, clinging onto life and supporting a ruling elite of two per cent with no foreseeable means to improve its wretchedness. All it had, if it was loyal to Christ, free of sin and true to the rituals and regulations of the Church, was the hope of paradise, of an end to pain and suffering and the rewards of heaven. For many that was enough and the rumblings of revolt against an oppressive system would continue for the next few hundred years until the greatest pestilence of all, the Black Death, would scythe down half the population and change the social structure and the food they ate forever.

CHAPTER 3

Norman Gourmets 1100-1300

As we have seen, the roots of British cuisine began, far earlier than has been hitherto supposed, in the sophisticated cooking of the Anglo-Saxon court. This cooking was to reach maturity soon after the Normans colonised these islands, for they brought with them ideas, recipes, spices and ingredients that they had learnt to love from the Mediterranean shores. I believe that the first examples of this new cooking were enjoyed around 1100, and that its character would not have been formed, nor its flavours have been so distinctive (growing independently from any trends in Paris) without the Normans colonising Sicily and travelling in northern Africa on their Holy Wars against the Infidel. British cooking showed independence of spirit and rich ingenuity at this early date.

The Normans
The Normans were acquisitive, greedy and ambitious; they absorbed the culture of others, whether it was France, Sicily, England or North Africa. When they invaded England in 1066, they were also involved in conquering Sicily from the Arabs. That colonisation had begun in 1060 and continued for the next twenty years. Once the Normans ruled Sicily, they were eventually forced to share the island amicably with the Arabs, taking over much of their law, institutions and culture including, of course, their food.

The Crusades began in 1095 and continued until 1270, and during that period there was constant traffic between England and Normandy, Normandy and southern Italy (then a collection of city states), and to the islands of Crete, Cyprus and Rhodes, Turkey, Egypt and the Holy Land. Crusading armies could be there for a decade or more. Bands of knights might split from the main army and travel by themselves, exploring new cultures, new foods and flavours.

So who were the Normans? The name stems from Nortmanii, meaning Northmen. We have met them before as Vikings, the disparate group of Norwegians, Swedish and Danish warriors who colonised the north of England in the eighth and ninth centuries, and who had brought to our shores many new methods of smoking and salting fish, increasing our pleasure in this food. Normandy, the province in France, stems from 911, when their chief, Rollo, led a small fleet up the Seine to Paris and demanded the land. The next year they converted to Christianity and adopted the

French language; within twenty years the old Norse language was forgotten in their capital, Rouen. More significantly, they began to take on the French legal system.

Was it the natural food resources of Normandy that had so attracted them? Its coastal waters teem with fish and shellfish, shad, eel and trout are fished in the rivers, the rich pastures are similar to Britain in that they support herds of dairy cattle and there are expanses of salt meadows where sheep are reared. Froissart described Normandy a few hundred years later as 'a rich and flavoursome country in all its aspects'.[1] Reared upon the Norwegian coast, these tough seafaring men were to be attracted to countries with a rich food heritage before they eventually conquered Britain.

They were pirates, notorious throughout Europe for their lawlessness, able to send mercenary soldiers wherever they were needed. However, they were shrewd enough to see that possessing a legal system was essential to holding onto power, and essential to controlling a society, whether peasants or nobles.

The Normans were thoroughly amoral, yet they were enormously pious, or at least some of them, including Duke William himself, a brilliant tactician, although he led an austere life, totally without the sensuous abandon in which his sons and their court would indulge. However, the old Norse values, built upon a barbaric triumphalism that allowed them to be monstrously cruel to their enemy, were alive and thriving; they would follow a warchief as long as he could inspire and control them, as long as he won victories and distributed the spoils. Duke William fulfilled those demands again and again. Though he was not an attractive person, he had luck on his side and he took advantage of a situation always in an ingenious way. His territorial ambitions were cloaked by concepts of self-righteousness, being a devout fighter for justice. Out of a population in Normandy of about one million he could put over 30,000 soldiers into a campaign. Unlike his sons he was frugal in eating and drinking,[2] and drunkenness was frowned upon at his court. In the Domesday Book forty-five vineyards are mentioned, the most northerly at Ely. There is a note by William of Malmesbury, writing in the twelfth century, of a vineyard that had been planted at the abbey by a Greek monk a hundred years earlier. William enthuses about the wine produced in the Vale of Gloucester:

> In this region the vines are thicker, the grapes more plentiful and their flavour more delightful than any other part of England. Those who drink this wine do not have to purse their lips because of the sharp and unpleasant taste, indeed it is little inferior in French wine in sweetness.[3]

William also noted that the customary heavy drinking of the court at his time could lead great men from cheerfulness, to talkativeness, to quarrels, and to the threat of violence. This was everything that Duke William disapproved of and would not allow, so he was unusual in that he was free of those sins of lechery and gluttony, although, thought St Anselm, full of avarice.

The Normans were efficient and fierce warriors, fostering arduous training for young knights and apprentice trades. By 1060 they had the reputation of being the finest cavalrymen in Europe; their horses were bigger and stronger and they had developed special battle lances that made their mounted charges inevitably disastrous for the enemy. They were explorers and enthusiastic travellers, as well as builders of enormous enterprise and imagination. They were imitative: whatever country they colonised, they took over the culture and institutions and then adapted and improved them. They were energetic and authoritarian, pushy, clever and shrewd.

It is clear then that if these peoples liked a new food, flavourings or ingredient, they would take it over and make it their own. The Normans in Sicily consumed Arab cuisine, Normans from England on their way home from pilgrimages or battle would eat similar highly spiced dishes they had eaten in Aleppo or Jerusalem, and then they would bring those dishes back to England. If when journeying through Greece they found a type of pheasant that they enjoyed, some of the birds would be caged to start a new colony in England.

We have a detailed picture of England after the Conquest from the Domesday Book. Of the population of around two million in Norman England, 10,000 congregated in London, the biggest town; other leading towns were Lincoln, Norwich, Thetford, Winchester and York. It was a land of manors; the lord of the manor ruled (as we have seen in Saxon England) his small kingdom. The manors were worked by peasants to earn income for the lord. But these lords were now Norman, for the English lords had either been killed, imprisoned, or fined and exiled. The Conquest wiped out the whole of the English nobility. By 1086 only a handful of the 180 great landlords were still English and it is thought that the new landowners replaced 4,000-5,000 Saxon thanes. These are terrifyingly large figures, it is amazing that the Norman Conquest has not echoed throughout history as a bloodbath.

William himself owned one-fifth of the land and large amounts of what was left were given to his favourites. This was a small Norman elite, many of them William's family, which controlled half of the country. England was rich and fertile, a prize for any enterprising people; lying at the edge of Europe it had the sea as its natural defence. All its natural riches were pillaged by the Normans. 'Foreigners grew wealthy with the spoils of England,' wrote Orderic Vitalis (1075-1143), 'whilst her own sons were either shamefully slain or driven as exiles to wander hopelessly through foreign kingdoms.'[4]

The Norman Conquest increased the poverty of England. William looted the kingdom of great quantities of gold and silver to pay his mercenary troops, to distribute wealth to Norman monasteries, and to pay for military campaigns in the Welsh marches and northern England. This had a destructive effect on agriculture: lands were laid waste, houses destroyed, populations depleted, and communities could not meet fiscal demands, becoming wanderers and outlaws. William was both bellicose and pious, and his aggression in war was only matched by his devotion to the Church.

Domesday tells us that 81,000 ploughs required a haulage force of 648,000 oxen; with cows and their calves this amounts to about one million cattle and two million sheep, needing about a third of England for grazing. Cows were only milked from May to Michaelmas, each cow giving enough milk for seven stone of cheese. The amounts of stored winter fodder were estimated to work out how many cows it could feed before Martinmas, then the herds were inspected and the weaker were slaughtered, their carcass meat salted down. (There is an eighteenth-century description of cows in the winter months from the Western Isles of Scotland, where they are so weak and skeletal they can hardly rise from the ground. Then: 'They recover as the season becomes more favourable and the grass grows again, and then they acquire new beef which is both sweet and tender; the fat and lean is not so much separated in them as in other cows, but as it were larded, which renders it very agreeable to the taste.'[5])

Ten sheep could give milk which when turned into butter and cheese was equivalent to one cow. Sheep were milked throughout the spring and summer but not after the Nativity of the Blessed Virgin, (8 September) because it was important that they were strong to withstand the rigours of winter. Between Easter and Whitsun the weak and elderly sheep were selected, then shorn early to distinguish them and fattened for sale around St John's Day, 24 June.

Goats declined in popularity under the Normans, but there were still plenty of them. In 1086 they were recorded in 127 farms in Essex. Alexander Neckam (1157-1217), the English scholar, who believed that imparting knowledge lifted the spirit, thought that goats gave more milk than sheep and it was 'efficacious against many diseases'.[6] It is Neckam, too, who tells us that in the manors weasels were often domesticated because they were such skilled hunters of mice and rats, they had a habit of laying their prey at the feet of their mistress. Arsenic was also used to keep down the rat population. But Neckam considers that cats (the old English black variety) for catching mice were indispensable to the peasant.

England did not possess the great impenetrable forests of Europe; in fact, it was not well wooded at all, the woods were small, numerous and well-managed, producing more income than areas of ploughland. Trees were allowed to grow tall as standards for house- and ship-building, while other trees would be coppiced for light timber. Trees could be pollarded (so as to give a crop of poles sprouting from the top) above the reach of browsing animals where the livestock could be grazed.

The Conquest, once the territories were consolidated, was to revolutionise the food that the nobility ate. The Normans built upon the agricultural system that already existed, but exploited it ruthlessly. Their love affair with the French legal system had made them adept at foisting new laws and restrictions upon the peasants, which controlled the amount of land they could till and the amount of forest they could forage in. All the native aristocracy and the gentry had been dispossessed; in matters of family structure, land-tenure and inheritance the Normans observed their own legal and social customs, which were in complete variance with those in pre-Conquest days. To regulate these customs they established a formidable bureaucracy in which the notion of an individual woman hardly appears.

Under the Normans almost half of the peasantry lacked enough land to feed their households. The agricultural serfs had to toil in order to produce the surplus which William's constant wars upon his borders demanded. The Domesday Book itself was the most efficient way of allowing the monarch to know what taxes he should be collecting and what other profits might be being secreted away. The subsistence food of the peasants hardly changed for the next 300 years, and in that time the peasant, struggling under gruelling labours, was to suffer the long famine years where disastrous weather would destroy succeeding harvests. In this time the Norman nobility would be influenced to change the food they ate, turning it into the most sophisticated, fragrant and colourful of cuisines, creating new methods of preparation, new combinations of produce, and new ways of cooking, while importing new foods and ingredients. The changes were radical and achieved astonishing results. Few cultures ever before or since have been so deeply influenced by a tyrannical enemy it longed to defeat.

The Earliest Recipes

The earliest extant recipes were written down sometime before 1280, and are likely to have been court favourites, passed down from master cook to apprentices over decades, if not for almost 200 years, from the time of the Conqueror. There are also a few other recipes that we can date more precisely which occur in Neckam's *De Utensilibus.* These all appear in later medieval sources and are again obvious favourites, such as stewed hen with cumin sauce[7] and fish poached in wine and water with green sauce, so we know that sophisticated cooking at least goes back to the twelfth century. I would argue that its inspiration is likely to have been the Norman invasion of southern Italy and Sicily, and that many of its influences came via the Arabs from Persia.

The year 1280 is in the mid-reign of Edward I, not himself known as a gastronome, for Edward Longshanks (proved to have been 6 ft 2 in tall when his tomb was opened in 1774) was a notorious warmonger, slaughtering Welsh and Scots alike with great ferocity. In the short intervals of peace his expenditure upon spices (a term that included both almonds and sugar) was excessive. These early recipes show a high degree of gastronomic sophistication, and many of them could be eaten today without suspecting their early provenance. Of course, these dishes were made for the nobility and primarily for the royal household, for they all include protein – meat, fish or eggs; so this is food for only two per cent of the population. Animal protein comprised a third to a half of their consumption, for everyone in a magnate household would have had about a pound of meat or fish per day.[8] The fact that these recipes were written down at all shows that they were used for special celebrations.

Here is a description of a selection of them:

Noodles *(Cressee):* pasta dough flavoured with ginger and sugar and coloured with saffron, served with grated cheese.

Ravioli: pasta dough stuffed with parsley, sage, shallots, cheese, butter and cream, served with grated cheese.

Oranges: balls of minced pork and egg yolk poached in stock then placed on spits, roasted, then rolled in raw egg, roasted for a moment to colour, then rolled in egg white and dusted with sugar. (See later.)

White pancakes: batter made from white flour, wine and egg white, fried, sprinkled with sugar and served with the 'oranges'.

Jelly: young pig and chicken cut into chunks, poached in white wine spiced with cloves, galingale and ginger, then left cold to jelly.

Sage sauce: ground ginger, cloves, cinnamon, galingale, sage, hardboiled egg yolk mixed with wine or cider, to be served with suckling pigs' trotters.

Nag's Tail: suckling pigs' trotters and ears cooked in wine, then roasted, cut into chunks mixed with fried onions and moistened with the cooking liquor, so that the pieces of meat are covered in an onion sauce.

White Elder: chickens cut into chunks and cooked in stock, then thickened with egg yolk and almond milk, then flavoured with elder flowers ground with salt. Can be made with fish. Gather elder flowers in full bloom, dry them, then grind them and keep them throughout year.

Veal stew *(Hausgeme)*: a mixture of diced veal and minced veal simmered in almond milk, flavoured with galingale, cinnamon and sugar, thickened with rice flour and coloured with sandragon red.[9]

Poached chicken *(Hauseleamye)*: mutton hock boiled with grapes to make a broth, sharpened with verjuice, strained, then the chicken is cut up and poached in the broth, then flavoured with ground ginger and parsley to colour it green.

Chicken: poached in a broth sharpened with verjuice, parsley, cloves, mace and cubebs (see page 81) coloured with saffron

Mawmenny: minced chicken and pork poached in wine flavoured with spices including cloves and fried almonds, thickened with ground almonds and coloured red. (There are many variations of this recipe in various colours and flavours; it continued to be a firm favourite throughout the Middle Ages, with the recipe changing over time. But the white mawmenny was perhaps the most popular version which came to be the basis of the Victorian 'shape' and our blancmange.)

Nut Tarts: pastry cases, made from chestnut flour coloured with saffron, containing a mixture of pistachio or pine nuts which have been mixed with wine and sugar, honey, ground ginger and cloves and boiled to a syrup.

Rose Pottage: almond milk flavoured with ground rose petals thickened with breadcrumbs and eggs, coloured with saffron and sprinkled with sugar. These could be made with ground hawthorn blossom, with wild strawberries, blackberries or elderflowers.

Food of Cyprus: Almond milk flavoured with a generous amount of ground ginger and ground pistachio nuts, thickened with rice flour.

My first impression when reading these was that English cooking had never since achieved such gastronomic brilliance; these are marvellous dishes, some of which I have cooked. My second impression was of the influence of the eastern Mediterranean; my third was of the amount of ginger and sugar, with hardly ever any mention of salt. As no amounts are ever given, the sugar in many cases could have been as little as a pinch, the kind of added touch that Chinese stir-fry cooking needs today. For example, the ginger noodles need a tiny amount of sugar, not enough to sweeten them, but to bring out the flavour of the ginger. Salt is not mentioned because so many of the foods came out of a brine or had been de-salted first; in fact, there are instructions on how to save a dish when it is too salty. (Into a napkin place oatmeal, tie the napkin, place it into the sauce or soup and take it off the fire, leave to get cool, then take the napkin out. The oatmeal will have absorbed the salt.)

This is highly sophisticated cooking: consider the tarts made from chestnut flour with their nutty fillings, or the almond milk desserts flavoured with rose petals. Consider the use of well-flavoured stocks, or wine to poach food in, the intensity of those flavours, the love of jellied dishes which would have been much decorated, the delicacy of the white pancakes, the richness of the ravioli, the delight in radiant colours. Their creators were artists and skilled craftsmen, full of pride and love for their dishes, and taking painstaking care over all the details.

How early are these recipes? Those written down in, say, 1275, could date back to those early years of the Norman Conquest. If they contained sugar, as many of them do, then they would have been created only after 1205 when sugar first appears in the Royal Rolls. Returning Crusaders were likely to have brought in their own supplies for many years, for they discovered sugar cane growing in North Africa or Sicily. The introduction of sugar to Europe finds its gateway in Sicily: the word for sugar there, *zuccaru*, stems from Arabic *sukkar*, as do those in English, German, Dutch, and most Romance languages.[10]

The recipes hold other clues. They show a dislike of the Turk or the Saracen, for there is one where a mock Turk's head is made out of rice. There are also white, green and yellow Syrian foods (types of mawmenny again); one was made from almonds and minced chicken thickened with rice flour and flavoured with ginger; parsley coloured the green one and saffron the yellow.[11] There is a sense of mischief in the recipes, in making food look like something else: *aloes* were stuffed meat rolls made to look like larks. There is also gilding and vivid colouring, which is a sure sign of great skill in the kitchens. Overall, in their love of spices and ginger they show the influence of the Arab cuisine (stemming from Persian) far more strongly than Parisian recipes of that time.[12]

The use of a flour paste in noodles, ravioli and later in *macerouns*, an early version of macaroni where the pasta is in flat ribbons, not tubes, also evokes Sicily. Macaroni, *pasta secca*, was a food invented by the Arabs in Sicily to take advantage of the discovery and dispersal of hard wheat because its high gluten and low water content allowed for a long shelf life that was ideal in the famine-ridden middle ages and convenient for nomadic and transhumant populations who often had to bring their food with them. Macaroni was but one of the foods associated with the medieval Arab-Sicilian culture which was brought back by the Normans to England. I noted above the Norman love of joke food such as in oranges or *arancina*, deep-fried balls of saffron-coloured rice, stuffed with a meat ragout and mozzarella cheese; these acquired their name from their resemblance to the small oranges from the Arabic *arangio*, meaning bitter orange; it was the Arabs who introduced the bitter orange to Sicily.[13] The bitter orange was first mentioned in Sicily in 1094. This was the time the Normans were colonising both Sicily and southern Italy, and 'oranges' appear in the list of those first recipes, where they have lost the rice, but are made from minced pork.

I showed these recipes to an expert on Persian cookery[14] who saw distinct and numerous borrowings from the repertoire of the Persian cuisine. Flower blossoms, almond milk, wheat starch and eggs are all long-time Persian ingredients and they appear in the Rose Pottage and its variations. The Nut Tarts and the Food of Cyprus are very Persian, except for the pine nuts which are Arabic. All the pasta dishes are Persian, except that, of course, cheese, butter and cream are quite alien. All white dishes are very Persian so the White Elder shows its influence as well. There can be little doubt where the major influence in our cooking stemmed from.

If we take a closer look at the great range of sauces, we can see even more vividly how skilled and sophisticated the cooks were. The Normans placed great emphasis on the art of making a sauce, for separate parts of the kitchens were specially built as a saucery. The first one we read of was early in the thirteenth century. Henry II had his own saucer, Master William, for whom a special sauceboat was purchased in 1265. These sauce-servers had to know that mustard went with brawn, beef or salt mutton and ginger sauce with lamb, suckling pig or fawn as well as dozens of other variations and refinements.

Medieval Sauces

These recipes come from later sources, but from references to the staff and the buildings they were clearly made earlier; the dishes were named after the sauce.

Civey: An onion sauce thickened with bread and flavoured with pepper and mixed spices. This is a sauce for hare or rabbit or even mallard on a meat day. Also a sauce on fast days for tench, sole or oysters.

Gravey: A purée of almonds, ginger and sweetened with sugar. A sauce for rabbit, chicken, eels or oysters. This sauce could be further thickened and enriched with egg yolks (first boiled then pounded) and grated cheese melted into it – then called gravey enforced. The word is thought to be based on Old French *graine* meaning meat.

Charlet: For meat days was ground pork mixed with eggs, milk and saffron. For feast days the sauce might also have ginger, sugar and sweet spices floating on the top. On fish days, almond milk and fish was used, either codling or haddock which would purée well.

Bukkenade: Another meat sauce made from pounded veal or pork and meat broth, with added herbs and spices, thickened with egg yolks, sharpened with either verjuice or vinegar, to be served on kid, veal, chicken or rabbit. Another version adds dried fruits, sugar and spices to the meats, while the broth is thickened with ground almonds and amidon (wheat flour).

Egerdouce: a sweet and sour sauce made from sugar or honey and young red wine or vinegar and dried fruits, cooked with rabbit or chicken.

Other favourite dishes where the main ingredient and the sauce mingled so that they were so thick they could be moulded were: mortrews, Blanc Dessore, mawmenny. These are all different names for much the same dish: pork or chicken ground to a pulp mixed with breadcrumbs and egg yolks, spiced and coloured, then moulded, and served cold, sprinkled with powdered ginger. A white mortrew was combined with almond milk and rice flour.

Blanc Dessore: could be eaten with a sweet, spicy red wine sauce. Mawmenny tended to be made from richer ingredients: pheasant, partridge or capon mixed with pine nuts and spices. A red wine sauce with added currants and chardequince (marmalade) reinforced with *aqua vitae* would be poured over it and set alight, then served flaming.

Blancmange: This is very similar to the dishes above, but was much blander, as all the strong spices were omitted. It was made from grounded capon flesh, almond milk, egg yolks and sugar, then decorated with aniseed comfits or blanched almonds.

All of these could also be made from fish for fast days. They were also referred to as pottages, though they have little affinity with the survival grub of the peasant. All of these dishes are marvellously and imaginatively seasoned. If you think of a slice of chicken breast in a sauce of almond, ginger and lemon you realise how beautifully judged the cooking is. These sauces, mopped up with white bread, would slip down a treat. And that is the point: there would be very little to chew or bite here. Even the roast meats were so well cooked, they must have fallen off the bone and the flesh then disintegrated into its sinews; they would have been chewed for a moment and then swallowed. The cooking shows us, as nothing else does, what a bad state people's teeth must have been in. Tooth decay must have been a continuing and wretched problem, especially when sugar began to be imported after the Crusaders first saw it growing on the plains of Tripoli at the end of the eleventh century. One of the very few advantages that the peasants had was that their teeth stayed healthy, even though they were greatly worn by the fibre within their diet.

Egerdouce: could also be a sauce on its own with chunks of fried fish. Onions, cloves, mace, cubebs were cooked with vinegar and sugar. Another sauce with fried fish was rapeye, made from pounded dried fruit, vinegar, sugar and thickened with rice flour and breadcrumbs. Each meat or bird had its own particular sauce.

Mustard sauce: brawn, beef or salt mutton.

Chawdron: a black sauce made from boiled giblets and offal, mostly the liver, with spices and thickened with brown breadcrumbs: served with swan.

Ginger sauce: served with lamb, kid, suckling pig, fawn, partridge and pheasant. Obviously a favourite sauce.

Camelyn: another dark sauce made from ground currants and walnuts and cinnamon mixed with breadcrumbs and vinegar: for herons, egret, crane, bittern, shoveller, plover and bustard.

Alepevere: a garlic sauce; with roast beef.

Green sauce: made from parsley, mint, garlic, thyme and sage with vinegar thickened with breadcrumbs. Eaten with green fish, that is raw fish pickled in brine.

Gauncil or garlic sauce: made from garlic, saffron seethed in milk and thickened with wheat flour. Served with goose, and thought essential.

English recipes are more specific on the actual spices and the amounts ('great plenty of sugar to abate the strength of the spices') than French recipes of the time. There are also a great number of English recipes that do not appear in French collections, but appear in Italian. It is likely that English cooks were imitated on the Continent. 'There can be little doubt that some of the basic characteristics of aristocratic cookery in Western Europe and England of the time came from the east, either via Spain and/or Italy or as direct importations by returning Crusaders.'[15]

As the royal household was the centre of any culinary innovations it is worthwhile taking a closer look at the Norman and Angevin kings and noting which ones might have encouraged gastronomy. Another clue to discovering when the English cuisine became inspired is to discover how the spicers fared in London, for the trade in spices is fundamental to the question of when English cooking first flowered. If the Normans encouraged the use of spices and therefore created the characteristics of our English cuisine, then this would show in the number of spicers making a living in the City of London; the imports and range of spices would swell in tonnage and number after 1066, while the royal household accounts would show their purchase.

Spice and Splendour

There is a clue to what William the Conqueror's court might have been like in a description of a feast in a Latin poem quoted by William of Malmesbury (1090-1143) and written by a contemporary. The poem purports to be a feast to celebrate the coronation of King Athelstan (895-939) who was buried at Malmesbury Abbey, but scholars believe it is a portrait of a Norman court. The King seems dour and the courtiers are afraid; one feels this could be the Conqueror or at least one of his sons. The courtiers are eager to show their affection and loyalty with a mixture of hope and fear.

> The Palace seethes and overflows with royal splendour. Wine foams everywhere, the great hall resounds with tumult, pages scurry to and fro, servers speed on their tasks; stomachs are filled with delicacies, minds with songs . . . the king drinks in this honour with eager gaze, graciously bestowing due courtesy on all.[16]

The picture of pages and servers feeding the courtiers with delicacies is the first glimpse we have of the beginnings of an English cuisine. But is it the court of one of the Williams, or could it be a picture of the coronation of Henry I, a scene that the anonymous writer might have seen himself? As we know, William was frugal and disliked drunkenness, so this poem is more likely to have conjured up the court of Henry I, although we cannot be sure. There is one other clue to William's palate: the white soup made with dill, called Dillegrout. It was served traditionally at coronation feasts because it was thought that William the Conqueror gave to his cook, Tezelin, the lordship of the Manor of Addington, as a reward for creating the soup. From then on, dill was an important herb in the kitchen garden and used in soups and sauces.

The Conqueror's son, William Rufus, appears to have been both a lecher and a fighter: the church chroniclers were appalled at his lack of piety and the amorality of the court. As he was such a pleasure-lover, he may have fostered a delight in eating, but he was coarse, so there was in his short reign of thirteen years little time for the arts; spices if they were used at all would have been mainly for medicinal purposes. Though by the time of William's reign Barcelona had become a specialist market for spices, there is no record of English merchants buying there until 1130 when they were selling cloth and other goods at Compostela, the centre of pilgrim devotion from all parts of Europe including the south of England. The merchants brought back spices and silks, including Spanish leather, called cordwain as it was from the city of Cordova. By 1120 Peter Alphonsi, a converted Spanish Jew, physician to Henry I, had arrived in London bringing with him a knowledge of Arabic medicine[17] where spices were used as both a tonic and a cure. Henry, the third son of William the Conqueror, ascended the throne in 1100 and was to reign for thirty-five years, a period of stability in a court which delighted in fashion.

After Henry's death we find the appearance of spice rents, which shows a shortage of coinage that is not surprising as civil war raged (1139-1153) between Stephen and Matilda, rival claimants for the throne. Records in Winchester in 1148 show rent as a pound of peppercorns. In 1154 Henry II ascended the throne and there was for the next thirty-five years another period of stability. Gastronomy cannot flower without a secure context. The first hundred years of Norman oppression were unlikely to foster an uninterrupted period of great cooking, except at the beginning of the twelfth century. The chronicler Orderic Vitalis inveighs against the godlessness of court life and the passion that young courtiers had for fashion, including the length of their sleeves, the point of their shoes and the curls and length of their hair. When the elite take so much trouble on their appearance they do not consume meals which are untouched by aesthetics; a culture of a period is all of a piece, and a rich elite fascinated by hem lines, shades of dye, types of fur lining and curling tongs also want the food they eat to have the same skill, time and delicacy spent upon it. My guess is that the first enthusiasm for creating significant dishes in the English cuisine occurred from 1100 to 1135 (this date would also fit in with the poem quoted above), engendered by court life, which was much influenced by ideas, ingredients and recipes coming from the Levant and Sicily where the Normans also ruled.

Around 1110 Alexius I Comnenus sent an embassy to Henry I bearing letters and gifts from Byzantium. The embassy was headed by an Englishman, Wulfric of Lincoln. The gifts included pieces of the True Cross and a scrap of Christ's foreskin or umbilical cord (the monks were unsure which); this relic ended up at Henry's foundation at Reading. We can also be certain that among the gifts were silks, perfumes and spices. Also, we should not underestimate the effect upon the nobility of the first crusade, the discovery of Byzantium and the Holy Land, or of the countries they travelled through. On the first crusade the Conqueror's eldest son,

Robert Duke of Normandy, commanded over 1,000 knights plus infantry. As both southern Italy and Sicily were now ruled by Normans, many of the families would have been related to the Crusaders, and Robert's army passed the winter of 1096-7 with Roger Borsa, now Duke of Apulia and Calabria. In the summer of 1099 knights and footsoldiers stormed Jerusalem, returning it to Christian rule for the first time since the seventh century; soon afterwards it became a new Catholic kingdom, while other crusading states – Tripoli, Antioch and Edessa – covered the Levant coast, extending inland to the other side of the Euphrates.

Here were Christian knights ruling countries in torrid summer heat surrounded by a scorched countryside, consuming everyday fruits and foods almost entirely alien to them, which had strange and singular intense flavours that they must have grown to love. The second crusade was in 1147 with English sailors from London, East Anglia, Kent, Hastings, Southampton and Bristol among the 164 vessels that assembled at Dartmouth. These men in times of peace were fishermen or peasants, intrigued by stories of treasure and the exotic pleasures and adventures that could change their lives. The men that survived voyages and warfare would also have tasted these new foods and returned to tell of them. As I've shown earlier, there can be no doubt that the Crusades and the Christian territories in the Levant and the Mediterranean made England familiar with the flavours and foods of the Middle East. What is remarkable is that these foods and flavours were absorbed by the cuisine of an island on the edge of northern Europe.

Although the English cuisine was born at the beginning of the twelfth century civil war would have interrupted its infancy. Its adolescence was to arrive, however, once Henry II ascended the throne in 1154, for then England stretched from the Pyrenees to Scotland; England's queen was Eleanor of Aquitaine. In 1158 the Winchester Pipe Rolls record the purchase of pepper, cumin, cinnamon and almonds specially for the Queen. In the 1160s, a Spanish Jew, Benjamin de Tudela, travelled from Saragossa to Italy, Egypt and the Middle East and described in detail the communities of merchants he met on his travels. There were Muslim merchants at Montpellier who had come from Egypt, and Christian merchants, including the English, in Palestine and Alexandria, the centre of the spice trade. The English community in Genoa, led by Robert of London, bought pepper at 123 Genovese pounds (about twenty hundredweight) and sold English cloth in return. According to William FitzStephen (d.1190) there was gold from Arabia, palm oil from Babylon, silks from China, gems from Africa, sables from Russia as well as wine and spices arriving at the port of London. In the reign of King John a taste for luxuries became even more pronounced: between 1205 and 1207 pepper, almonds, cumin, rice, cloves, ginger, saffron and nutmeg were listed in the royal accounts, as well as the newly discovered sugar. The Crusaders would have eaten fruits cooked and preserved in syrup. Sugar was to remain expensive, but it became part of English cooking, kept exclusively for the royal kitchens and the nobility, from then on. The English acquired a sweet tooth early.

Eleanor of Aquitaine was highly cultured, influencing both music and poetry, so it is likely that she also took a close interest in food and how the ingredients of southern

Europe were used. She would also have been aware of the Sicilian court, the popularity of its king (her son-in-law, William II), his love of the arts and the esoteric, the Arab dishes eaten at his court and his adoption of many other Arabic customs. William the Good read and wrote Arabic, kept Moslem concubines and black slaves, and paid much attention to Moslem physicians and astrologers. It was said that the whole city of Palermo was imbued with the Islamic spirit. William would also have learnt of the theory of the four humours and seen that the food he ate observed this theory (see pages 51); it is likely that from his reign and awareness of the relationship between food and health, the theory permeated through the whole of medieval Europe.

Sicily was filled with wheatfields, almond orchards, orange, lemon and melon groves. Market gardens surrounded Palermo with machines for irrigation, the Arab love of water, fountains, conduits and waterfalls in the royal gardens would have bewitched these northern knights, as must have the perfumes of orange blossom, the citrus fruits, the flavour of ripe figs, pistachio and pine nuts, pomegranate seeds and syrup, tahina paste and preserved lemons. English cooking shows the impact of all these new flavours and a search, once in colder climes, for an acceptable substitution for some of them.

Throughout the last half of the twelfth century the trade in spices grew enormously; by now the English provinces had also got a taste for them, for provincial spicers began to appear in the records. Walter lived in Bristol in 1194, Ralph the Spicer in Oxford in 1190 and Robert the Spicer in Boston in 1200. The spicers were retailers who also worked as apothecaries and with the growth of medical knowledge from Arabic sources, spices began to be used far more than the indigenous herbs that the Anglo-Saxons had relied on, so the spicer needed to make up cures and tonics from the spices in his stock. By the end of the thirteenth century the spicer becomes the apothecary, and his shop and stall are the beginning of what we know as the pharmacist. The term 'pepperer' was used in the great trading centres like Montpellier, which also dealt in a growing range of spices; by the thirteenth century, however, a distinction between them was apparent, for the pepperer was soon to become the grocer, one who sold his goods by gross. In London the spicers tended to have their stalls and shops on Cheapside while the pepperers were in Sopers Lane.

In the midst of the twelfth century a pound of pepper was fixed at 7d or 8d, but by the 1170s the price had dropped to 5d. Roughly a pound of pepper cost nearly a week's wages for a carpenter. The London Pepperers' Guild was formed at this time to organise disparate traders and to combat greater competition in the trade. There had been a greater demand from Africa and the Levant for English cloth and foreign traders were beginning to bring spices into London themselves. We know from the extant accounts of King John's taxation of merchandise, however, that this was a losing battle. Other ports, Boston, Southampton, Lincoln and Lynn did almost as much trade in foreign merchandise, which included spices, as London[18], and so it is clear that the liking for spices was now shared by all the nobility and not just in the royal household. We can speculate, of course, that the royal table would have set fashions for style and content of dishes, but these figures from ports all over England show it to be so. The sophistication of English cuisine came not only far earlier than hitherto thought but was also far more widespread.

As spicer-apothecary[19] to King Henry III, Robert de Montpellier opened the City of London's first pharmacy in 1245 where he supplied spiced wine, spices, medicines and confections to the court, including electuaries. These were concoctions of various herbs and spices bound by sugar and given to the sick or queasy or just faintly off colour. Once sugar had entered the diet of the rich, electuaries were undoubtedly popular; rose and violet sugar, coloured and flavoured by the spicers, or pyonada made up from ground pine nuts. These early medieval spicers became rich and important; we remember them now because they were rich enough to buy property, to hold office and to leave substantial wills. In 1250 John Adrian was paid over £54 for dates, gingerbread, cinnamon and other spices.

A feast at St Augustine's, Canterbury, to celebrate the installation of Abbot Ralph in 1309 used 1,000 geese, thirty-four swans, 200 sheep, 200 sucking pigs and thirty oxen. The food and drink cost £253 6s of which £1 14s was spent on saffron and pepper, £3 18s on 500lb of almonds and £28 on spices. Spices cost then about thirteen per cent of the whole.[20] In the accounts of Eleanor, Countess of Leicester, sister of King Henry III, we find that in 1265 spices cost her £54. We know that spices were considered to be precious and highly prized, for they were kept with other valuables, away from the kitchen locked up in the Royal Wardrobe. Henry III in 1239 ordered the bailiffs of Winchester to go with Roger, his tailor to fetch raisins, dates and figs from the Wardrobe.

In these first few hundred years of Norman rule the years of peace and stability plainly show in the amount of spices sold. The first rise was from 1100 to 1135 when Henry I ruled, then the trade declined through the civil war, picked up again when Henry II ascended in 1154 and continued into the following century. We know that King John had sybaritic tastes and it shows, as it does a hundred years later in Edward II's reign, when the number of grocers doubled within ten years. At times of civil war in Henry III's reign in the thirteenth century and in the latter years of Edward II's, there was a fall in the trade, pointing to times of uncertainty and fear when eating became a fleeting necessity not a pleasure. Trade declined further still in the terrible famine years of 1315-1318 when torrential rains destroyed crops and rotted the seeds in the ground, and livestock grew sick and died. It was to herald a climatic change when it grew colder (and we could no longer grow vines), as it had in 1310 when the Thames had frozen over from Southwark to Westminster; fires had been lit in the middle of the river, and people, carts and horses used it as the main thoroughfare.

We should not omit another highly influential factor on the cooking of the royal kitchens – the queens. Of the twelve queens up to Queen Philippa, wife of Edward III, only two came from the British Isles; the rest came from Flanders, France, Navarre, Castile, Provence and Aquitaine, bringing with them the flavours and customs of their homes. Eleanor of Provence, wife of Henry III, had a special saucery built in 1264 in the upper bailey of Windsor Castle, a sure sign of her interest in food. Eleanor of Castile, beloved wife of Edward I, sent her clerks to buy fruit from every Spanish ship that came to the ports of southern England from Dartmouth to

Sandwich, for she so loved figs, pomegranates, oranges and lemons. These women, often the most cultured and educated of their time, were no doubt also eager to recapture the flavours of their childhood in the cooking of their new northern home.

Spices were always expensive, so they were used in cooking judiciously; in later recipes the spices are counted as in thirty grains of pepper, or six sage leaves; if not the recipe writer will say, 'Use them with care.' There's no reason to think that spices were used recklessly in the twelfth century if they were so careful in the fourteenth. Both white and black peppercorns were undoubtedly the favourite spice, but ginger came a close second, then grains of paradise which look like grey peppercorns but have a slight gingery taste. Next came an enthusiasm for cinnamon and cloves, followed by mace and nutmeg, long pepper, saffron, spikenard, galingale and cumin. Our own indigenous herbs were not overlooked, for parsley, sage, mint and sorrel were liked for their colour as much as their flavour. Spices and herbs were ground with the pestle and mortar and kept in leather pouches hanging up near where the cook could reach them. The range of spices was immense, 53 varieties were sold at Boston Fair in 1299.[21]

The spice market was dominated by the demand and purchasing power of the royal household. In 1285-86 the Wardrobe spent £1,775 11s 7d on spices out of a total of £9,446 9s spent on luxurious goods. 25,000 lb of almonds were bought at 2d a lb, and 3,000 lb of rice bought in 1303. The royal household grew very fond of sugar: in 1287-8 the Great Wardrobe issued 6,900 lb of sugar, together with 1,434 lb of rose and violet sugar. It is interesting to note that when Edward I returned from his military campaigns the expenditure on luxuries rocketed, while when fighting they were extremely modest. In 1301 the King owed a Genovese nobleman, Antonio Pessagno, just over £1,000 for spices; he was still selling the same amount to the court ten years later. Throughout 1301-4 ginger varied in price from 2s 4d to 3s 4d a lb. Ginger was bought as a powder, dried in its root form, or preserved in sugar or packed in gourds. Sugar was sold by loaf at 2d a lb. Durham Abbey bought 51 lb of sugar from Boston Fair in 1299.

It was once thought that the amount of spices used in medieval cooking was excessive. There is one example of a rich mawmenny cooked for 160 people, which was seasoned with 4 oz minced ginger, 8 oz cinnamon powder, 2 oz cloves and 2 oz ginger powder. The finished dish would have been very faintly flavoured, leaving only a subtle sub-text resonant upon the palate. The same is true of a *Viande Cyprus* (literally, Cyprus Meat, a rich white sweet stew using chicken), also made for 160 people, which used 8 lb pine nuts, 3 lb cooked dates, 4 lb Cyprus sugar, rice flour, sweet wine and 4 oz of powdered cinnamon. Another strange idea that was once commonly held was that the large amount of spices (which I hope I've shown above was nothing of the sort) was used to disguise rotting meat or fish.[22] Apart from the fact that there were various bye-laws that insisted on the freshness for sale of carcass meats, the stink of it is so objectionable that no amount of spices could possibly hide it. Only the very poor and starving might have eaten such wasted foods and they would have eaten them raw where they found them. Households rich enough to have a store of spices under lock and key and to care about the refinements of cooking would also have been particular about the freshness and quality of their ingredients.

Colouring

The love of colouring dishes as well as flavouring them shows us not only the wish to impress and please the royal household and its distinguished visitors, but also an awareness of aesthetics and the visual appeal of such dishes; it also shows skill and knowledge, for it would be easy to colour a dish a stunning hue and make it inedible – even toxic. So colouring requires great care, a scientific knowledge (see *Gozophoria tinctoria* below) and experience.

White was simple enough, achieved with almonds, rice and milk; yellow was always saffron ('the King of all medieval colourants'[23]) or egg yolk or a mixture of both or from the flowers of Dyer's Broom (*Genista tinctoria*). Green came from parsley juice, herb bennet, basil, vine sprouts, sage, onion tops and newly sprouted wheat. There was also a gaudy green colour, a yellowish green, which came from vergay. A shade of peacock blue derived from carrot peel, for all carrots were purple then and the dye is soluble. For a lighter blue, columbine flowers were picked at dawn, before they opened, and crushed and mixed with honey. Black came from cooked blood, cooked liver or burnt toast. Shades of pink came from rose petals. Red Sanders (*Pterocarpus santalina*) gave the colour red, which was similar to sandalwood (*Santalum album*); both came from India. For another shade of red, there was *Alkanet tinctoria*; the name *Alkanet* is a diminutive of the Spanish *alcanna* which comes from the Arabic *al-henna*, the henna plant.[24] It was still used until recently for colouring the liquid in thermometers and tinting the liquid in the large decorative bottles in chemists' shops. Only the root was used: to get a deep red colour it had to be cooked in oil, and the oil was then sieved and bottled.[25] If boiled in water the colour was brown. There was also the potherb bloodwort (*Rumex sanguineus*) which was commonly used and eaten as well as cornel berries. For purple they used the black root of indigo (*Baptisia tinctoria*), or turnsole or heliotrope. An orchis lichen (*Gozophoria tinctoria*) was naturally blue but turned red under the influence of acids and back to blue again if mixed with alkalis. Both gold and silver leaf were also used, the leaf stuck onto the surface by having a wash of egg white painted on first.

Of course, with so much colour the temptation to present multi-coloured dishes was overwhelming. Dishes of blue, red, silver and gold might be made in honour of a special guest or for a wedding feast bearing the heraldic arms of the groom. After the dish was finished it was further decorated with roasted almonds, pine nuts or pistachio, stuck with cloves, or scattered with powdered spices or comfits.

The Four Humours

Today, sophisticated gastronomes have a concept of what a healthy meal is: selecting ingredients and proportions, carefully balancing protein against carbohydrate, and ensuring there's fibre, fresh fruit and vegetables and small amounts of dairy produce. Much of this selection occurs unconsciously, and we hardly have to think about it to get it right. We are in fact eating to a plan, a theory that best suits our bodies, and that is socially acceptable in our contemporary milieu. These theories change as new ideas are accepted and social demands vary. The Middle Ages were no different to any other age in this respect; though we might find their theories odd today, they were believed and pursued with reverence and profound seriousness then.

The Greek physician Galen claimed that all living things were composed of four humours: warm, cold, dry and moist. Human beings were influenced by earth, air, water and fire. Food was created by earth, water and air and to make it palatable it had to undergo fire and be cooked. This theory re-emerged in Arabic thinking and was taken up by medieval physicians who used it to identify and treat disease. So each dish was composed of a combination of these four humours that would be suitable for the person eating it. (We, of course, still do this but use a different set of values to judge the food.) A king's physician would stand behind the monarch and scrutinise each dish offered to him and then advise on its suitability. In fact, physicians would collect recipes they considered to be healthy, as we have seen in Anthimus (see page 29).

Cooking techniques were also considered in the light of the four humours. Roasting dries out a food while boiling warms it but also adds moisture; baking dries and warms in moderation. The cook's choice of cooking method had to adjust the inherent humour of the ingredient, so that beef being a dry meat always had to be boiled (giving the medieval kitchen its endless supply of beef bouillon, an excellent basis for numerous sauces), but pork, being a moist meat, was always roasted. Boiled salted beef became, of course, a national dish, as did the crisp crackling of a roasted leg of pork. Fish, being cold and moist, was always initially fried – another taste that has stayed with us as a nation.[26]

Meats that were only moderately moist like veal, poultry and small game birds could be protected from the drying heat of an oven by a pastry shell, further helped by additions of fat inserted into the pie. Venison was thought very dry so it should first be larded, then boiled before being roasted (a perfect way of treating the rather tough wild venison.) All vegetables were very dry as they came from the earth, so these had to be chopped small and boiled. Onions were fried to remove their moisture. Fruits were extremely moist so had to be roasted or baked, including melons, pumpkins and cucumbers which were thought so cold and moist that they were dangerous, with a tendency to putrefy in the stomach and generate fevers. (Cucumbers continued to be cooked as a vegetable until well into the nineteenth century.)

The anxiety about adjusting the humours of each ingredient had the end effect of mixing opposites as in bitter and sweet. So vinegar was much used in the kitchen, as well as wine that had turned and was too expensive to waste. Vinegar, however, was thought cold and dry, so this had to be adjusted by copious amounts of sugar (thought warm and moist) or honey. The latter was thought to cleanse the stomach and purge the abdomen, heating the blood, and so very suitable for people with cold moist temperaments. Honey was an important component of mead, which was for hundreds of years the staple drink in northern Europe.

Another result of the theory was that as all foods had to be modified in some way by their opposite, foods were chopped, small or ground into powder then sieved and strained, so that they could become united with their opposite. Generally the recipe called for several ingredients to be well mixed into the dish. Sauces were thought to be first invented as the perfect vehicle for this modifying influence, since they often had a dozen or so components in order to harmonise together and adjust the main ingredient.

These ideas must have percolated through from Spain and the Mediterranean soon after the Norman Conquest, but they were only regulated in the royal kitchens once Peter Alphonsi became physician to Henry I in 1120. From then on they gave a firm basis to all the recipes, methods of preparation and cooking; they are another factor in my belief that sophisticated gourmet cooking began in that decade; many of these ideas are with us still, for they were pragmatic solutions to a food's character.

Fasting

The tradition of fasting continued: a conviction that underlined medieval food was that on certain days throughout the year one should eat no food at all, or at least give up eating meat, or as happened in less pious households, substitute other foods that were acceptable, such as fish. Fast days or periods when Christians would please God with their sacrifice and become more worthy to commune with him became ingrained in all classes throughout the age; this idea radically altered what people ate; it gave them a rigid discipline, which clerics and royalty might with great ingenuity bypass, although it could not finally be erased until the Reformation, if then.

Lent was the yearly celebration of Christ's fast in the desert, and the other main fast was Advent, the 30 days before Christmas. It also became obligatory to forgo meat and animal fats on Wednesdays and Fridays. However fast periods were not consistent and were frequently changed by the Church.

There is no doubt that in royal kitchens having to invest the humble herring (such as the dried and salted red herring, the mainstay of the peasant) with gastronomic worth was a spur to invention – and a boned fillet of herring in white garlic sauce sounds inviting. In the same way, being unable to use butter and cream resulted in the invention of almond butter, almond cream and almond milk which became such a staple in fasting, but which also was one of the most delicious of culinary inventions. Another effect of fasting was the high demand for almonds which all had to be imported: the staggering amount of 48,000 lb was consumed by the royal household in the reign of Edward I in the two years of 1286–87.[27]

For the peasant, fast days made little difference; he might have to forgo his tiny amount of butter and cheese, but his pottage remained the same and so did the maslin bread with which he soaked it up. The fact that half of the year was taken up by fasting was a fact of life of which he was hardly aware. The high point of his year was the harvest and the way his diet improved over those weeks. To a lesser extent he would have also looked forward to the festivals of Easter and Christmas, which involved a celebratory meal.

The two main periods of fasting happened to be convenient ones. Lent came at the end of winter when there were few animals left to be slaughtered and when the preserved meats must have become boring. Advent came after Martinmas (11 November) when all the livestock were slaughtered (except for those kept for stud and labour) and which was a busy time preserving the meats for the coming winter.

Whether monasteries kept strictly to the rules of fasting is a moot point; how far such rules were adhered to would have been governed by how conscientious the abbot happened to be. Certainly there was a growing tendency for the Church to become more worldly throughout the medieval period. Both prelates and monks chose more luxurious foods and wines, growing ever more fat and idle, so that they gradually dissipated the reverence that the peasants had once held them in.

Fish

Because there were so many fast days fish was in great demand. Every coastal hamlet had its fishing boats and as the industry expanded larger boats and longer lines baited with many hooks were used so that the larger white fish could be caught – mostly the sluggish cod family with their flaky white flesh – that lived at the sea bottom. Certain ports became famous for a particular fish: we find plaice from Winchelsea, merling (*Merlangius merlangus*), what we now know as whiting, from Rye and cod from Grimsby all appearing in the household accounts. Much of the whitefish caught was salted on board or immediately on return to port and was then sent inland.

There was already a large herring industry before the Conquest, which with renewed demand from the great Norman abbeys now began to prosper. Herrings were caught from off the coast of the Shetland Isles in June, and then all through the summer off the coasts of Scotland, Ireland and the north of England. When the herrings were young and lean they were successfully dried and preserved in the colder climate of the north. The Scottish dried herring industry began in the 1240s. Once the herrings had reached the coast of East Anglia they were fat and oily, difficult to preserve because their fat oxidised in the air and they became rancid, so they were gutted and immediately soaked for a day in brine, before being layered between coarse salt and sold off in barrels. Sprats were also dried and salted, their season conveniently arriving after the herrings. Pilchards were caught by the Devon and Cornish fishermen. Yarmouth was the centre of the English herring industry and its autumn fair was famous for its herring delicacies, pickled, salted and dried. Smoked herrings arrived in the last quarter of the thirteenth century; they were first soaked in a strong brine, then hung in specially built chimneys for a day. They turned a golden yellow and were praised for having their roes safe within them. Yarmouth's Herring Fair was held each year from Michaelmas to Martinmas.

Fish greater than the herring went straight to the manors and abbeys. If whales were grounded upon the beach they were crown property, though the insoluble problem of how to convey this great bulk of meat and blubber to the royal presence made it essential (and several Norman charters spell this out) that the whale remain as the property of the tenant and only the tongue be sent to the monarch. Then the whale was cut up and salted, preserved in barrels and kept for Lent.

The poor could gather whelks, cockles, mussels, clams and oysters and sell them inland, though this was work thought suitable for a woman. On 20 March 1343, the Le Stranges of Hunstanton bought a farthingsworth of cockles from Maud, daughter of

Joan of Burnham.[28] Oysters were available either in their shells or else taken out and pickled in barrels; later we find records of four or five cartloads of oysters being sold to the royal household by an oystermonger, who would also sell lobsters and crabs. In 1298 oysters sold at twopence a gallon, which was cheap compared with other fresh fish. In the Severn estuary there are remains of medieval fishtraps, which would have caught thornback ray, gurnard, sea bream, salmon, grey mullet, plaice and other flat fish.

The range of fish eaten was so large it has the power to amaze us now: bass, brett, cod, conger, cuttlefish, coalfish, dogfish, flounder, garfish, gurnard and red gurnard, haddock, hake, halibut, lamprey, mackerel, grey mullet, plaice, rayfish, salmon, salmon trout, sea shad, seal, skate, sole, smelt, sturgeon, turbot and whiting. Salmon from both Ireland and Scotland were barrelled in brine and sent to London.

In the rivers, lakes and ponds there were barbel, crayfish, chub, eel, dace, lamprill, lampern, perch, pike, pimpernel (small eels) and tench. Many of these ponds were artificial, dug out as part of the moat or park of the castle or monastery, so fresh fish was part of the diet of the nobility. To construct a series of ponds with wooden conduits and pipes and to maintain these as a clean environment for the fish cost money. Westminster Abbey's pools at Knowle in Warwickshire in 1294-5 cost £7 14s 11d to clean, a sum that could have bought 15 cattle or paid a skilled building craftsman for two years.[29] In cooking terms fish were further sub-divided into round (herrings) and flat (sole).

Amazingly, considering transport problems, sea fish were often consumed inland: John Catesby of Ashby St Ledgers bought sea fish at the market at Coventry, including mussels, oysters, haddock and porpoise. We often forget that waterways were used as frequently as we use roads today and barges had seawater tanks, made from canvas slung in barrels, to keep the fish alive until they were sold at market. The live fish were also wrapped in wet moss, interleaved with straw and carried in wicker baskets or panniers and sent by pack-horse. Large households maintained anglers on their staff to catch the fish from the estate's ponds and rivers.

Henry III gave a fish feast on St Edward's Day on 13 October 1257 for which 250 bream, 15,000 eels and 300 pike were collected from all over the country. John Hales, the bishop of Coventry and Lichfield, and his household over a period of four months in the summer of 1461 ate 639 sea fish and 258 freshwater fish, as well as a bulk of salt fish and stockfish; the fresh fish cost more than the seawater fish. The main freshwater fish were eels, followed by bream, pike, roach and tench. Salmon were eaten in all households whether they came from sea or river.[30] Accounts show us, however, that the nobility at the top table ate the freshwater fish in sauces enriched with cream, eggs and spices, while the household servants made do with stockfish, salt fish or herrings.

Sometimes, the English took to fasting rather grudgingly; the first Norman abbot at Winchester found the monks still eating meat, so (a wise and benign abbot this) he ordered particularly tempting fish dishes to be served. The Normans loved food too passionately to be able to make fast days into a spartan exercise; the Benedictines at Westminster Abbey ate fish on 215 days. They ate well, for this was a style of diet comparable to a wealthy merchant's; we can gain some insight into how various foods were considered from their accounts. Small shellfish were not highly thought of; the monks ate molluscs, cockles and mussels but only at supper. Of the 570 dishes of fish served throughout the year fifty per cent consisted of preserved fish; of the other half nearly all were from the sea, only a small proportion were fresh. Cod, either as ling or haburdens (summer-cured dried cod), makes up half of the quantity of fish eaten, though plaice appears frequently between April and October. Herrings hardly appear at all, another clue to the abbot's idea of his place in society.[31]

As fish were thought to be both cool and wet, their method of cooking had to be dry and warm, and sauces to be eaten with the fish should have those qualities. So fish tended to be roasted on a grill. Lampreys had to be killed by being placed live in wine, which possessed both warmth and dryness. Eels would be put in a bath of salt and left for three days, then fried or roasted or made into a pie. Eels were found all over England from the Severn to the Fens, but our love of them was so great that large numbers were also imported from the Netherlands.

Alexander Neckam considered that fish should be boiled in wine and water and eaten with a green sauce; the latter was a green herb sauce; the prime ingredient was parsley which gave a vivid hue, but it also contained sage, mint, onion tops, thyme and pepper. Neckam pointed out that sharp knives were essential in the preparation of fish and finely grated breadcrumbs were necessary to roll the small fish in before frying. Fried parsley was also served with the fish.[32] Some dishes never change in a thousand years.

The Peasant Diet

From the beginning of the fourteenth century, a time of climactic change when a series of bad harvests led to great hardship, we have the accounts of Argentine Manor, at Melbourn in Cambridgeshire. The lord of the manor boarded seven men; two ploughmen, a carter, a shepherd, two plough drivers and a reeve. They began the day with pottage and each of them ate eight quartern loaves a week at dinner and supper. A quartern loaf is simply a quarter of a large loaf, so each of them had two large (estimated at anything between 4 lb and 8 lb) loaves a week. The quality of the bread, because of the harvests, was inferior: usually it was made from wheat and barley with a little rye and pea flour added (half a pint each of rye and pea to half a peck each of wheat and barley). The reeve made the bread out of a mixture of tail-wheat, maslin (a mixture of wheat and rye), pea and mill corn (the lord's perquisite from the tenants' corn); and the labourers were allowed two large loaves each a week, though the woman servant was only allowed 1½ loaves a week. This works out at each adult per year eating 4½ quarters of bread grains, as a quarter is eight bushels and a bushel equals 36.40 litres, roughly two large sackfuls, which is roughly seventy-two sackfuls of bread grain a year. Though this seems an awesome amount it is probably correct because bread was by far the major part of the diet. The oats for the pottage were only two bushels per year, say four large sackfuls.

More details of the farmservants' diet comes from Peterborough Abbey Manor at Kettering in Northamptonshire in 1294, where thirty-two quarters of maslin went in a year's rations to a dairymaid, two carters, a shepherd and a cowherd, which amounts to 512 sackfuls of grain per year for five adults. One boy in return for care of the calves received six bushels or twelve sackfuls. They also ate sixteen bushels of oats and three bushels of peas and beans for the pottage. This farm throughout a year made 160 cheeses, each cheese weighing 6 stones; the manor ate sixteen of these cheeses and sold the rest. The servants ate about ¹/₂ oz of cheese a day. The farm also produced 18¹/₂ stones of butter and the servants ate ¹/₄ oz of butter each day. It was worked out that the servants consumed each day 5¹/₄ lb of rye bread, 2³/₄ oz of oats, less than 1 oz of peas and beans, ¹/₂ oz of cheese and ¹/₄ oz of butter. This comes to 6,035 calories, but the amount of bread takes up the bulk of that at 5,440 calories while the oatmeal is 317. The only animal protein and fat in this diet are the tiny amount of cheese and butter.

Maslin flour for the bread was usually a mixture of wheat and rye, but it could also be rye and barley; in times of hardship it could contain pea or bean flour and perhaps also the seeds of numerous vetches and weeds, which might be hallucinogenic or toxic. For Lent 'drage' was used, a mixture of wheat, barley and oats, which would have made an even heavier loaf than usual. The daily bread then for the workers was very dark and coarse. How many loaves might one get out of a quarter of barley? It is thought 216, at 1 lb 2 oz a loaf, though these would be small, since loaves were generally between 4 lb and 8 lb in weight.

In some accounts the dried peas and beans were always made into flour, in others they were used as part of the pottage; in still others, according to the the accounts from manors or abbeys, the legumes were eaten as a food in themselves. The dried peas by themselves were made into pease pottage which was a favourite staple of the medieval table whether rich or poor. There are numerous recipes for this dish throughout this period, some with white wine, garlic and spices, others with ginger, butter and sorrel. The peasants, however, would have had theirs just with salt and garlic, or with a relish of raw onion, so thick that it could be eaten with the fingers or placed on the bread.

From prehistory food became a symbol of class distinction, and we see this clearly in the Church accounts where the kind of bread is specified for the class of person. Sometimes the richer gentry spent their last years living in the monasteries, where they were called corrodians. In 1256 a corrodian received a white wheaten loaf and a black loaf each day with a gallon of ale plus meat and fish. On a fast day the canon of the abbey was allowed four herrings or five eggs. At the Priory of Dunstable both the canons and the conversi (the better class of corrodian) were given seven loaves a week: there was *albus panis*, *albae michiae*, or *dominicus panis canonicorum*, which were all white bread, a small white loaf or the abbot's special bread, while their servants only received *surae michiae* and *bisae michiae* or *cobbi*, all types of small brown loaves.

There were all kinds of little treats at harvest time, when the workers' diet was augmented by what were known as white meats, that is milk, eggs and cheese. Milk was drunk, both sour and sweet, and whey, the usual thirst quencher, was given out. Also, this was the time of ale drinking as getting a harvest in safely was a huge celebration; records suggest that a gallon of ale was given to each person per day. One wonders if the harvest took a week or more to cut, whether anyone was capable of work after the third day. Herrings, both white and red, and three a day for each man, were a harvest treat, and were given out at all the manors along the east coast. Though the servants received no herrings at other times of the year, they were given to the poor with bread and ale or oatcakes. Eels were part of the harvest food at Feltwell in Norfolk and Wisbech in Cambridgeshire, while greenfish or cod was the harvester's food at Linden End in the same county. At Holme Cultram in Cumberland the lucky harvesters had cod and salmon, while in Marley in Sussex they ate whiting. It is obvious that whenever there was a large catch in August the peasant harvesters shared in it. It was a time in which though equality could never exist between lord and peasant, the bounty was at least shared out for that one month in the year, because the harvest affected them both.

Manors vied with each other in promising good food so as to ensure they had a workforce, and the staff of each manor was joined by itinerant hired help. In 1273 the 34 staff of the manor at Sedgeford in Norfolk hired eleven extra men for thirty-nine days and a cook was employed full time. The main meal of each day was eaten late in the evening by candlelight (so that all the daylight hours could be given over to work) at the lord's table with the supervisors of the workforce seated at a trestle table covered with a canvas tablecloth. The morning meal was eaten out of doors; a servant carried the food and drink to the fields, and the food was eaten from dishes, plates and bowls of wood with wooden spoons. It consisted of barley bread with a large amount of cheese washed down with strong ale. The meat (a rare treat) was mainly bacon though fresh beef was eaten in 1286; fish was mainly salt cod and preserved herring. The quality of these foods improved (bread was made from wheat and more fresh meat, both beef and mutton, was eaten) after the Black Death in the fourteenth and fifteenth centuries. Nevertheless the sparse diet of these early years though meant to be luxurious, shows how very inadequate and poor the daily diet of the agricultural worker was.[33]

There were rare manors that occasionally gave their servants some meat, mostly mutton, but sometimes bacon or pork. There are no accounts of the servants eating beef, poultry or fish. At harvest there were a very few instances of their being given beef to eat, but more often it was mutton. The sheep would have been killed at the end of its working life, for its milk, wool, hide, skin and dung were treasured far more than its meat.

There is only one account of a generous and magnificent feast for ending the harvest: this was given at Grove in Bedfordshire at the end of five weeks of hard work from 15 August to 29 September 1341, just seven years before the Black Death was to decimate the population. It was given for a chaplain, clerk, bailiff, two stackers, two pitchers, a reaper and his lad, two threshers, one winnower, one cook and fifty mowers who consumed throughout that time, including the feast itself: seven quarters and six bushels of wheat, in malting barley ten quarters were brewed; twelve small bacons, two wethers, 5s 5d worth of purchased meat, 4s 8d of herrings and fish, four gallons of butter, cheese worth 10s 6d, sixteen ducklings, six chickens, forty pigeons and pepper worth three halfpence. At the feast they also had a canvas tablecloth and 7 lb of candles, so we know that it must have continued well into the night. At another feast in 1342, the workers ate even more pigeons, eighty instead of forty, had saffron as well as pepper and finished the meal with a Melton cheese.

After the Black Death and after the peasants recovered from the great series of plagues that continued for thirty years, it is interesting to note that the harvest foods also improved in quality and amount, for none of them were by now without meat.

Preservation

In a time before refrigeration, meat, fish and milk had to be consumed on the spot or preserved quickly. Animals were slaughtered outside the kitchens or in the street then butchered, prepared and cooked immediately. (Bye-laws, as we shall see, attempted to control the stench and waste products which ended up in the Thames.) Meat not immediately needed was preserved by salting. Fish could be kept alive in tanks or ponds until needed, but a huge catch would have to be dealt with by salting. Milk was occasionally drunk straight from the beast, but not often for it was regarded as too valuable a product when turned into cream, butter or cheese, so the whey was drunk instead. The further north you lived and the colder it became the more milk was drunk, but contamination with bacteria was also a problem so it was better to boil it or turn it than drink it fresh. Butter in fact was highly salted in order to preserve it, but this was of little use when needed for a dessert recipe. Later medieval recipes abound with directions for de-salting butter, the most common being that to melt it in front of a fire, so that the salt is left as a deposit at the bottom of the dish.

Embedding meat in salt to preserve it was an expensive business, for the amount of salt needed cost forty per cent of the meat itself. It was therefore only good meat that was considered worth preserving, for bad meat was not worth the salt. Also, only good salt guaranteed perfect preservation, as poorer quality salt did not penetrate quickly enough leaving the inner parts of the meat to deteriorate before the salt reached them. A large wooden cask was used and the pieces of meat, cut into portions that fitted the cask, were rubbed all over with salt, then placed upon layers of salt; more salt covered the meat before another piece of meat was placed over it. The top was compressed with a board and a stone so that the juice flowed out and the meat gradually contracted and dried.

Salt then was a valuable product and its collection vital. Bede mentions salt pits, into which the sea flowed at high tide. The Celts first used pottery vessels filled with seawater, and heated to evaporate it. This method was used extensively all around the coast; in the Domesday Book there are 284 salt pans in Sussex alone, and forty-five salt pans are listed in the Maldon area, which is still a source of fine sea salt.

Another source of salt was underground deposits, brought to the peasants' attention by animals which would gravitate towards salt licks, or by their exploring caves and discovering salt springs; those in Worcestershire and Cheshire were much used. Worcestershire salt was considered superior and had fifty *salinae*; there were ten in Cheshire, eight in Herefordshire, seven in Gloucestershire, six in Shropshire, three in Warwickshire and one in Oxford. Salt from geological deposits in Worcestershire was being extracted from salt springs as early as the seventh century. Droitwich in Hereford and Worcester was famous before the Norman conquest for the salt obtained from its brine springs. In 1215 the town obtained its Royal Charter in return for a yearly rental of a £100 from the springs. There were salt pedlars transporting salt from these areas and from the salt pans on the coast to the areas where there was little resource, if any, of salt at all.

It was not enough, however, for by the reign of King John salt was being imported from France; produced from the Bay of Bourgneuf, it was called Bay Salt, a name that became used for salt imported from both Spain and Portugal. In these southern countries the process only needed sun to evaporate the seawater, but the salt was coarse and full of impurities. In its favour, however, was the fact that it only cost half the price. Moreover it was excellent for preserving as its coarseness penetrated flesh more easily.[34]

Game

Medieval cuisine would be unrecognisable if we took the great range of game dishes away. Nor, one speculates, would the peasant population have survived as hardily as they did, without their traps, slings and nets, which ensnared small birds to boil in and liven up the daily pottage, or which, wrapped in wet mud and placed in the embers of the fire, could be baked until the dried casing of the mud was broken taking the feathers and skin with it. The types and numbers of small birds were numerous: finches, tits, sparrows, starlings, wagtail, larks, house martins, swallows, swifts, rooks (only the breast was eaten for the rest was bitter), and wood pigeons. All these could easily be caught on common land and if by chance within the net or snare there was pheasant or partridge then all to the good. If such an incident had been seen, however, then such larger birds would have to be relinquished to the lord as a token tithe; they would be kept in a special poultry enclosure near the kitchens to be killed and prepared on the day they were eaten.

Hunting was the main pursuit of the lord of the manor; falconry and the training of the birds were one of the skills and delights of the age. Deer and wild boar were the chief animals pursued, but there were different methods of hunting the prey. Hares were caught at sunset with the hunters and their greyhounds well hidden in undergrowth until the hares appeared. Bustards – now extinct – which grazed in flocks were also caught by the greyhound, as being heavy they could not take flight with ease. Nets were put over rabbit burrows and a muzzled ferret placed into the burrow, so that the rabbits ran into the nets. Spaniels were used to sniff out game in woods and fields, so that the birds would fly up and be caught by the trained birds of prey.

Swan was the most expensive of all wild birds, although it was also thought tough and indigestible. The neck was cut off, stuffed and served separately. Swan was served with chawdron, the black sauce made from the bird's own guts, diced small, boiled with its own blood, vinegar and spices. A favourite recipe for goose was to stuff it with herbs, quinces, pears, garlic and grapes; after roasting, the bird was sliced in half and a sauce made with the stuffing combined with wine and spices.

Fast Food[35]

William FitzStephen (d.1190), the biographer of Thomas à Becket, wrote a description of London which includes his comments on a cookshop, which was open all day and night, one of several in St Martin Vintry:

> On the river bank in London, amid the wine that is sold from ships, and wine sellers a public cook shop. If friends, weary with travel should suddenly visit and it is not their pleasure to wait for food to be bought, prepared and cooked, they can hasten to the river bank and there all things desirable are ready to hand. There daily according to the season you may find viands, dishes roast, fried and boiled meats, fish great and small, coarse flesh for the poor, the more delicate flesh for the rich such as venison and birds both big and little. There is also sturgeon, guinea fowl and Ionian frankolin.[36]

The latter were pheasants from Greece which shows us that at some time previously some birds had been brought back to these shores and reared successively. What the cookshop is selling is street food, cooked and hot, ready to eat with your fingers as you walked or sat by the river. The cook shop also sold ribs of beef and in the summer peasecods, fresh peas boiled in their pods which you ate like artichoke leaves, dragging the peas away from the pod, but first dipping them into melted butter with added salt, pepper and vinegar. (This was called 'scaldings of peas', still being sold in exactly the same way in the 1850s.) They also sold ready made pottages and spice mixtures and every possible sort of pie, tarts with eggs called crustards, pasties, closed and open pies, mixtures of meat, herbs and egg yolks.

These cookshops must have catered primarily for the river boatmen, dockworkers and travellers. We shall see later that nobles and rich churchmen disdained their product. Cookshops all selling hot food straight from the fire were popular in provincial towns. Norwich in the 1280s had nineteen cookshops, as well as streetsellers of pork sausages, puddings and mustard. York had thirty-five commercial cooks in 1304 and Leicester almost the same number. In London by the late thirteenth century there were several specialist street cooks, flan-makers, cheesemongers, sauce-makers (the favourite being garlic or ginger), waferers making griddle cakes (a flavoured batter poured onto a hot iron), mustard sellers and pie bakers. The list of fast foods stimulates our palates today: well-spiced pasties of chopped pork, chicken or veal, pasties of fish or eel, cooked meats, roasted beef, veal, pork, lamb, kid, pigeon, capon and goose; flan makers sold cheese cakes, tarts and flans made from bread, eggs and soft cheese. Cooks would also wrap the customers' chicken or meat in dough and then bake it. In London regulations in 1350 forbade cooks to take more than a penny for putting a capon or rabbit in a pasty, on pain of imprisonment. To help wash all these delicious snacks down taverners would offer either white wine from Alsace or red wine from Gascony or the Rhine or Rochelle.

Streetsellers would walk through London calling out their food, the street cries in

Piers Plowman evoked by Langland are 'hot pies, hot, good piglets and geese, go dine, go.' There were also cries from the cookshop urging passers-by to sit down and eat bread, ale, wine and fat ribs of beef. In Cheapside peddlers hawked hot peasecods, fresh strawberries and cherries; in Candlewick Street there were hot sheeps' feet and in Eastcheap cooks proclaimed beef ribs and meat pies. The emphasis was on hot food – even in the summer – hot vegetables and breads, pies, ribs and sheep's feet, hot roasted meats and poultry, hot cakes, wafers, pancakes, flans and tarts.

By 1280 the cooks had moved from the docks to cluster in Friday Street near St Paul's remaining there until the early 1300s, but by the 1320s they had shifted again to the east of Bread Street and by the 1350s both Bread Steet and Ironmonger Lane were recognized cookshop districts. This ceaseless moving around must have been stimulated by the fact that one aspect of the trade was a public nuisance, the problem of the waste from the carcasses killed in the street; the guts and blood were flung into the Fleet or the Thames or just left for beggars or the pigs to consume. The stench must have been considerable and the records tell us that cooks had a reputation for uncleanliness and dishonesty, despite the hygiene regulations. In Norwich a cook was punished in 1287 for making sausages and puddings from measled pigs and a few years later the cooks and pastry-makers were accused of reheating pasties and meat two or three days old. A ruling in 1301 forbade cooks to buy fresh meat in summertime more than one day old.

Hence the nobility were not keen to buy the cooked food on offer. The earliest surviving household accounts from the late 1100s list the daily expenses of a lord's household: bread, pottage, eggs, fish, spices (salt, pepper, cumin, saffron and sugar) wine, flour, apples, herbs (garlic, onions, savory), mustard, peas and milk. There is no mention of meat, poultry or fish, for these must have travelled from the lord's estate. Further evidence that the nobility avoided the produce from the commercial cooks is given by an account in 1267 of Sir Roger Leybourn's visit to Canterbury where he stayed for three days from 6-8 March, which was the beginning of Lent. There he purchased shellfish, almonds, rice, oil, dried fruit, spices, wine, bread, ale, mustard and vinegar. He also bought cinnamon and ginger specifically to make sauces. How one wishes to know the details of the dishes which his cook made from these ingredients.

On 1 June he returned from France and stayed for one day to give a banquet for two French counts and 100 knights; this time the only thing he buys ready made are sixty-eight capon pasties. Provisions for the banquet include great carcasses of beef, bacon, mutton, geese, chicken, pigs, various fish, a porpoise, as well as bread, wine, ale, almonds, rice, new beans (in season, of course), cloves and ginger. Six peacocks also arrived as gifts. His kitchen expenses came to £9 15s 7¹/₄d.

The practicalities of cooking a capon or a rabbit in dough are intriguing. To begin with, was it a yeast dough or a sheet of pastry? Was it the whole carcass of the chicken or rabbit? The answer lies in the cookshop's penny charge, which would have been a substantial sum for just borrowing the heat of the oven and the space the bird was cooked in. The cook jointed and boned the bird (or rabbit) for in cooking flesh shrinks and bones jut out and pierce any covering. Each pasty made would have taken about half the meat and been enough for two people. The boned meat would have been sprinkled with fresh herbs, salt and pepper, dabbed with butter and rolled in pastry (not dough) and placed in the hot bread oven for fifteen minutes or so, when the outside would be golden brown and the inside cooked through and bubbling hot. This was a quick supper dish for two people, and when the crust was broken the smell of sage, thyme, butter and chicken would ascend to seduce the palate.

The most expensive dish the cookshop sold in the thirteenth and fourteenth centuries was roast bittern, the marsh bird commonplace in East Anglia, which remained a delicacy of the table for centuries.[37] Bittern cost 1s 8d, followed by heron at 1s 6d and pheasant at 1s 1d, which were game birds for gentlemen. However again we find that both the church nobility and the gentry hardly ever used such ready cooked food. In 1337 the abbot of Ramsey travelled to London; his party rode fifteen to twenty miles each day, taking four days, and when the abbot reached London he stayed in his town house. Along the route they bought bread, ale, oysters, smoked herring, fresh fish and stock fish (salted cod), garlic and mustard, some of these foods they brought with them, but at night they mostly cooked their meals from local ingredients. At Ware they stayed at an inn and purchased mutton, pork, eggs, flour and saffron. Once in London the only hot foods the abbot bought were a pennyworth of pottage each day, fifteen pasties for 4d and 2d worth of baked lampreys.

On the much travelled routes from London to the north and the west there were not only numerous inns as stopping places for the night, but market stalls lining the route with peasants selling their produce. Travellers never had any difficulty in buying all the foods they were used to having at home. When the earl of Ross (an old campaigner in the Scottish wars) travelled from London to Scotland in October 1303 he bought ale, bread, meat, fish, poultry and eggs wherever he stopped. Even in York where he stayed for four days he did not avail himself of the many cookshops, and only bought some pease pottage and bread.

We have to conclude that the main customers of the numerous cookshops were the poor who had no means to cook food,[38] so enjoyed the hot foods on sale. Their diet at home was maslin bread eaten with curds, onions, leeks and garlic washed down with whey. Even in the country Langland tells us that in the winter and spring poor peasants ate bread made of pea or bean flour and the only hot food was pottage and vegetables or baked apples.

The number of cookshops in a town is an indication of how numerous the urban poor were; when a city's population declined the cookshop declined well below the number of bakers. As Martha Carlin sums up: 'Fast food flourished in medieval English towns among those who could least afford it, but whose circumstances made it irresistible.' *Plus ça change.*

The Kitchen

In the kitchen of a merchant or wealthy tradesman the huge hearth with its fire would have dominated the room, for it was hung with equipment, chimney cranes, pot hangers, hook and chain with teeth to lower the cauldron when necessary, the fire dogs and basket spit, the dogs with their iron cups on top to hold a bowl with sauce or soup to be warmed, and other spits in various sizes. Beside the hearth there would have been iron trivets waiting to be used as well as fire tongs, pokers, bellows and a supply of logs and twigs in various sizes, for it was the custom to keep the fire burning all night.[39] A large brass or copper cover or 'curfew' from the French *couvre-feu* covered the embers at night.

The main work surface was a heavy table of oak planks, where bean and peas would be shelled, cabbage, onions and leeks sliced, meat butchered. On it there would be a large pestle and mortar. Around the room there were pots of brass, copper or earthenware of all sizes, a large knife sharpener with a rack for its knifes, tripods and a large cauldron. Hanging from a rack would be an iron flesh hook (a long wooden handled fork with hooked prongs at the side) to pull out large joints of meat from the cauldron, a long slotted spoon for skimming, frying and griddle pans. Elsewhere there would be a pickling vat and a cupboard where the cook kept the aromatic spices, the sugar loaves and the almonds locked away as well as the sieved flour, though many households bought in their loaves from the bakers. In one corner there would have been a cleaning place where the poultry was degutted and dressed, with boiling water ready to scald the birds, and where fish would be scaled and prepared; near there would have been a garde-robe pit through which the filth of the kitchen could have been removed. In a small side room, the pantry, there would have been clean towels, tablecloths and napkins and an ordinary hand towel hung from a pole to avoid the mice. In this room there would also have been stored the tableware, the salt cellars, ewers, spoons and plate as well as a store of wax candles. On the flagstone floor, barrels of verjuice and vinegar, honey, ale and wine.

We catch a glimpse of the kitchen equipment of the wealthy, middle-class urban family from Richard Lyons whose goods were seized in 1376 from his riverside mansion. The house included a pantry, buttery, larder and kitchen. His metal pots, pans and utensils were valued at just under £6 10s and they included 4½ hundredweight of ironware and six hundredweight of brassware: eight spits, three trivets, a gridiron, two andirons, two frying pans, two racks, two grease pans, two dressing knives, another knife, one iron flesh hook, two massive iron pestles (weighing four hundredweight), eight brass pots, a chafing dish and small basin, six brass pails and three brass mortars. No wood or pottery was listed, but he would certainly have had salting and kneading troughs. His staples in the larder were honey, salt, vinegar, verjuice, almonds and the spices kept locked away in the Wardrobe included 6 lb of gingerbread – a chewy, fairly hard candy resembling toffee made from honey and spices. Bread was bought from the bakers because he had no stores of flour or grain.

Fruit and Vegetables

Why, when we know that they were grown, do vegetables appear so rarely in the recipes? We know the peasants grew and ate them, as they had in the Anglo-Saxon period, and that vegetables and herbs were the mainstay of the daily pottage, but their recipes were not recorded, only handed on from generation to generation. We also know that many of the gardens mentioned in the Domesday Book were set outside the walls of London at Fulham and Westminster or on the fringes of towns at Grantham, Oxford and Warwick. There is a mention of a garden in 1110 at Winchester in the western suburb of the city. All of these gardens were fenced to keep animals from doing damage; in fact records tell us that people were often fined large amounts for not keeping control of their animals or allowing fencing to fall into disrepair. From the small plots which every peasant kept around his hovel to the splendour of abbey and castle gardens arable horticulture was flourishing; as we shall see, these gardens were to grow in acreage throughout the medieval period and by the fifteenth century their range of vegetables and herbs are astonishingly impressive, growing many which we have now lost.

In the earlier period, the twelfth and thirteenth centuries, the peasants grew their staples; onions, leeks, garlic, kale, peas and beans. These vegetables appeared in the manor and castle gardens as well and they were amalgamated into the recipes without being much noted, one feels, because they were both cheap and ubiquitous. They certainly do not appear in the household accounts because they came straight from the seigneurial gardens. However, in the manor kitchens there was a suspicion that these vegetables belonged to the poor and should not grace a lord's table. Fresh green vegetables were also thought to be unhealthy. Lettuce was treated as a pot herb, either used medicinally (the seed makes an oil which was thought to soothe headaches and the milky sap in the stem is a soporific) or cooked as part of a sauce.

Apples, at 4d-8d per quarter in the late thirteenth century were cheaper than wheat and onions at 6s. There were cabbage-mongers, garlic-mongers and leek-mongers selling in the streets of London and Oxford. We know that Glastonbury Abbey was supplied with 80,000 bulbs of garlic in a year. It seems a formidable amount but bulbs of garlic were smaller then; it works out as one quarter of a bulb each day for each person. The monks of Westminster had a 27-acre garden, later named Covent Garden; they also had a thriving piggery and their surplus would be sold at market. Fruit and vegetables were sold on the south side of St Paul's Churchyard, as well as apples and pears, cherries and nuts (filberts, walnuts and sweet chestnuts), beans, cabbages and turnips, radishes and skirrets. (The last three were brought to Britain by the Romans and Pliny noted that they grew better here.) Parsnips were valued for their sweetness; they were crushed to a pulp, their juice drawn off, then boiled and used as a substitute for honey. From analysis of fossils from latrines we know that people ate a mass of apples, pears, plums, cherries, grapes, damsons, gooseberries and strawberries as well as wild fruits such as blackberries and sloes.[40]

Consumption of fruit and vegetables then was so commonplace and so cheap in cost it hardly merited a mention in the accounts, nevertheless they were the mainstay of the peasant diet. There were bye-laws that allowed the poor to pick peas and beans in the fields for their own consumption during the 'hungry time' of the early summer before the grain harvest. The daily pottage, sometimes made and given out by the manorial kitchens, had a basis of oats, barley or dried beans or peas and was flavoured with leeks, onions, kale and herbs. This was peasant food until the fourteenth century, when the advent of the Black Death and the Peasants' Revolt changed the class structure forever.

The Anglo-Norman Cuisine

Was there a cuisine formed in the two hundred years of the Anglo-Norman period that was distinct from the international cuisine of the continent? Furthermore, was this cuisine typically English in that it would become the source of future traditional cooking? Though similar dishes occurred in Italian, French and Spanish cooking as in the Anglo-Norman cuisine, they were all different, showing already their individual character. Of the four cuisines it is only the French that absorbed less of the Arabic influences, which, of course, all stemmed from the Persian cuisine.

What is remarkable is not only that southern Italian food and the food of the Iberian pensinsula showed Arabic influence, for they were close neighbours, but that we did, and did so positively and enthusiastically in our offshore islands in the North Sea. Our love of dried fruits and flowers in savoury dishes, of white meat stews with elder flowers, of red meat stews with rose petals, of strawberry sauce with boiled meats, is not reflected in French cuisine (until La Varenne and his roast turkey with raspberries, see page 168). Similar dishes do, however, belong to the Persian cuisine and go back into antiquity. Other influences that we soaked up but which Paris ignored included the use of perfumes in food. Pliny reported that in Persia they were used lavishly in food. We loved the same spices, pepper, ginger, cloves, mace, nutmeg and cardamoms, while colouring dishes was, as we have seen, essential.

What is so fascinating about the Anglo-Norman cuisine that developed after 1100 is that it became firmly grounded upon what had gone before; the northern love of pies and tarts was lightened by the use of dried fruits and spices, roast meats were served with sweet and sour sauces, which were comprised of dried fruits and verjuice. We took from Anglo-Saxon cooking a love of flavoured omelettes, of cream and curd dishes, of custard tarts with dried fruit, of fruits soaked in wine and honey, of fruit jellies and summer puddings.

However, as Constance Hieatt points out, the Anglo-Norman cuisine is more complicated than recipes of that time in the French sources. She quotes a *soutil brouet d'Angleterre* which was chestnuts, hard-boiled egg yolks, ground-up pork liver with spices and saffron mixed up into balls and fried. The idea that there was in the early medieval period an international cuisine influenced by Paris is nonsense. All the cuisines, Italian, Spanish, English and French, were influenced by ancient Persia in some way or other, but the French much less than ours. Nevertheless, it is also true to say that up to the fifteenth century dishes eaten at the royal court at Westminster would be similar to those eaten in Paris or Rome. Most of the recipes would not be identical, however, and the differences point to the stirrings of a national cuisine in each country.

The Significance of the Cuisine

The royal feast was a theatrical display communicating a ritual of undreamt wealth and eminence, the source of myth and fairy tale. Rank and hierarchy were precisely indicated by where each person sat at the table, as were the ornateness of the seat, the tableware and decorations that surrounded him and the delicacy of the dishes that were presented to that part of the table. 'The most expensively spiced dishes were given only to the monarch and those of the blood royal; all food was carefully graded to reflect rank down to the meanest portion for a foot soldier.'

The monarch and his family ate at the high table, raised above all other tables by a dais; the rest of the tables on the lower level ran at right angles and the household and guests would be seated in descending order of importance. Only the high table would be a heavily carved stable piece of furniture, the rest were likely to be trestle tables, which could be set up and removed quickly. Both the court and the baronial families were itinerant, always on the move from one estate to another and much of their furniture was taken with them, even down to portable urinals. Guests would carry their own knives to dinner, sometimes as part of a set with scissors and file. Spoons were used for the pottages (twenty-four silver spoons were made for Henry III's children at Windsor in 1254 at a cost of 27s 8d) and much else, for all those delicate minced poultry and meat dishes could not be eaten with a knife, however thickened they might be with rice flour and curds. Fingers were used as well as knives to collect portions of meat that could be dipped into sauces. Many of the dishes were small tarts, pies or coffyns, easily picked up and transferred to the mouth by fingers. Forks, though used on Byzantine feasts and in European kitchens, were not accepted on the English table until the seventeenth century, though some certainly existed, as we have noted in Anglo-Saxon Britain. After Piers Gaveston was murdered in 1310 a fork was found among his belongings, an example of the singular aesthetic taste that both he and Edward II showed, much to the fury of their more uncouth barons.

The top table would be covered with a white cloth, while the embroidered and decorated overcloth, the *sanap*, would be laid down over it; upon it would be the ornate salt cellar, silver or gold and sometimes jewel encrusted. Other decorations could be table fountains spouting wine or perfumed waters. Goblets or tankards were made from glass or metal, covered pitchers and flagons with decorated finials and hands were used to pour the wine or ale. Before the meal hands were washed with warm perfumed water. The first to wash was the monarch or the host; servants poured the water from a ewer and dried the hands with a fresh towel.

The theatricality of the event is best seen in the food itself, for the dishes had become both sculptures and games. Cooked peacocks were placed back inside their befeathered skins, live birds fluttered out of a cooked pastry shell, acrobats and dwarves leapt out of giant puddings; great pastry castles were surrounded by green sward with pheasants, partridges and doves, all cooked and edible but painted to look as if alive. The cockatrice was half suckling pig and half chicken which had been roasted, bisected, and then sewn together; it was then covered in a thick paste of egg yolk and flour, and roasted again to turn the outside gold. Then there were the jokes: fish roe tinted green with parsley juice, mixed with egg and flour and rolled into tiny balls to represent garden peas; the pork or chicken meatballs, dyed either green or orange and made to seem like apples and oranges; pies that resembled hedgehogs, marmots and porcupines; dried fruits strung on cord, dipped in batter, fried and made to resemble *haslet* (the cooked entrails of the wild boar); and the *appraylere* – a mixture of spices, breadcrumbs, eggs and ground meat – which was cooked in an earthenware pitcher and brought to the table when cool, so that the diners expected wine or water to be poured; the pitcher was then broken and the dish, shaped as a pitcher, could be cut and eaten. Perhaps the most disgusting joke though was the idea of serving a piece of meat that was alive and wriggling with worms; this illusion was achieved by mincing a piece of raw heart and flinging it on top of a sizzling piece of steak, whereupon the pieces of heart began to move about as if alive. There were even joke recipes: 'Finally prepare a tasty little dish of stickleback stomach and flies' feet and larks' tongues, titmouse legs and frogs' throats.'[41] Possibly this recipe was the source of the myth that a dish of larks' tongues was actually prepared and eaten as a special delicacy.

These are jokes, japes, fun and teasing, with a background of music and dancing. In 1300 a saltatrix or acrobatic dancer called Maud Makejoy performed several times at the royal court, while minstrels sang to lutes, harps, dulcimers and pipes. The music would be as carefully planned as the dishes, both melody, instrument and voices would be changed with each course. People were expected to be able to read music, to sing, dance and play. Sometimes on the last course roundels were passed around with sweet comfits resting on the paper, while on the underside were lyrics or poems which could then be sung in unison.

The significance of the feast which bound society together into an oppressive hierarchy and the intricate cuisine that expressed it was to become stronger throughout the fourteenth century, even though the century was full of catastrophe, tragedy and suffering.

CHAPTER 4

Anarchy and Haute Cuisine 1300–1500

'War is probably the single most powerful instrument of dietary change in human experience.'[1] When a nation survives through periods of violence – civil wars and revolutions – that traverse geography and class, one of the results is that the diet dramatically changes. In the 200 years that complete the medieval epoch we can discern the birth of national cuisines all over Europe.

Though there are many diverse factors that contribute to the birth of a national cuisine, a social climate that allows a synthesis to begin, which crosses all classes and regions, succeeds in uniting discordant elements. A social milieu that encouraged the elitist and rarefied cooking for the royal table to filter down to the simplest farmstead began to occur in the fourteenth and fifteenth centuries; while just as importantly the ideas that stimulated rustic cooking at the lowest economic level, with its reliance on wild herbs and intense flavourings, could also rise through differing classes until that inspiration too found its way to the noblest of kitchens. Sumptuary legislation is a graphic illustration of this process, in which lesser classes emulate their superiors, and we shall examine it later. Civil war, also, is an ideal battleground for the mixing of regions, bringing ideas from north to south and west to east, showing populations new ideas and flavours and influencing them.

For the peasant the fourteenth century was a terrifying and tormented one, but ironically at the end of it, peasants were in a stronger social position. Many of them had become small landowners, and their daily diet was much improved. Indeed, from the end of the century one could date the beginnings of a rural cuisine, our own version of French country cooking, a cuisine redolent of the earth, its herbs and produce, which would later be destroyed by a series of Enclosure Acts.

We have seen how the harvest workers would espy, smell and occasionally taste those dishes served to the top table at the three-yearly celebrations of Easter, Harvest and Christmas. We know that the less impoverished would have tried out such dishes at home, experimenting possibly with more economic versions. The food at the manor merely aped the food at the castle, just as the castle aped that of the royal kitchens. This food, as it continued downwards in society, might well have been more and more a shadow of its original self, but in that transformation it also became stronger and heartier. Sometimes the food did not change at all, it was merely lusted after for its pure sensual pleasure and for its symbolism of belonging to the upper classes.

The best white wheaten bread, made from the finest flour, which had been two or three times sieved through woollen and linen bolting cloths, was made for the nobility and the very wealthy, while the poor still ate coarse dark bread made from rye with added pea or bean flour. The white bread stamped with a cross, called wastel or pandemain (from *panis domini*, the sacramental bread) was never intended for the peasant, yet as the beggars and the poor waited outside the doors of manor kitchens for the scraps, some of that bread got thrown out with the trenchers and bones. The poor knew the feel of it upon their tongues; that silky luxuriousness was entirely foreign to their palates, but they loved it. White bread, they discovered, was what they wanted to eat; besides, to be seen to be eating white bread was a clear example of status in society. In 1375 the poet, John Gower (1330-1408) seemed horrified that the peasants were demanding food that was above their station in life. 'Labourers of old were not wont to eat of wheaten bread; their meat was of beans or coarser corn and their drink of water alone . . .'[2] As the peasant class began to be destroyed by famine and plague and then redefine itself as small landowners, some of whom became anarchists and rebels, the rise in consumption of white bread was a potent symbol of how articulate and aware the peasant class had become. In London in 1304 there were thirty-two bakers of brown bread and twenty-one bakers of white; by 1574 there were thirty-six bakers of brown bread and sixty-two of white.

What makes this period crucial is that there was a widespread breakdown of authority which brought to the fore a new class of nobles enriched by war, enclosures (for they began early)[3], and sheep-farming, who kept private armies with which they backed their dubious and illegal claims to other people's land; this feudal gangsterism was to lead to great social upheaval and the Wars of the Roses. Because of the former, society was turned into a stewpot of ideas and influences, a rich, fertile, inventive atmosphere which was to revolutionise art and society; this helped to fuse opposing elements in the food eaten into the beginnings of a cuisine that we recognise as being our own and one that was recognisable internationally.

Famine and Feast

The failed harvests in 1293-95 were followed by more failed harvests in 1310-12, and disastrous weather from 1315-18, when unceasing rain seemed like a biblical deluge with ruinous floods, caused the Great Famine in which ten to fifteen per cent of the people died. There was a sheep plague in 1313 and a cattle plague in 1319, which caused the worst agrarian crisis since the Norman Conquest. At least 600,000 people died in these years, and, adding the toll from the other years, nearly a million people died from starvation. An inevitable outcome was high food prices from 1290 to 1325. If the harvests failed there was no wheat, rye, barley or oats, nothing to make the bread that was the daily staple. Bread had to be made from bean or pea flour augmented with whatever scraps of cereals could be garnered from the fields. Throughout these years there was a rise in crime as people stole to eat. The chronicler of the *Annals of Bermondsey* told of how the poor ate dogs, cats, the dung of doves and their own children. Alms were reduced and the supply of charity dried up. Grain and livestock prices almost doubled between 1305 and 1310.

Nor was there any help given to alleviate the suffering of the peasants at the beginning of these years by an ageing Edward I, obsessed with winning the war with Scotland, nor after his death in 1307 by his son, Edward II. He was equally obsessed, but this time by love for Piers Gaveston and by his quarrels with a belligerent group of barons, and could give no time or thought to a dwindling and starving populace. The country was split between monarch and nobility and civil war broke out several times, adding to the peasants' misery and discontent. By 1327 Edward had been murdered and his son Edward III gave stable government, until he in turn became obsessed[4] with French territories and the beginnings of the Hundred Years War.

Throughout these bleak times the royal feast remained a pre-eminent ritual of significance. It is astonishing to us in a more cohesive society where one class is aware of its obligations to another less fortunate, that the elite of Edward II's court feasted without caring about the poor and the starving. The King, an aesthete born before his time, who designed a string instrument which was the forerunner of the violin – the *crwth* – loved music, theatricals, rowing, swimming, jewels, clothes and food. So it is highly likely that in his troubled reign from 1307 to 1327 his interest and enjoyment of gastronomy would have spurred royal cooks on to produce dishes of ever greater delicacy.

In his childhood Edward, brought up with his five sisters, must have had a sweet tooth, for one of the most common foods appearing in the royal accounts was sugar loaves and sugar candy with fresh fruit, spices, nuts and baskets of dried fruit, figs and raisins imported from Spain. Later, as a youth in his own modest royal palace at Langley, the chronicler of St Peter's Priory, Dunstable, twelve miles away, complains that 200 dishes a day were not enough for the Prince of Wales' kitchen, that his officials took all the supplies of the market, even the cheese and eggs without paying for it. 'They took bread from the bakers and beer from the ale-wives or, if they had none, they forced them to make bread and beer.'[6] As a child Edward was engaged to Margaret, the daughter of the King of Norway, and called the Maid of Norway or the Damsel of Scotland, since she was also the heiress to the throne of Scotland. A great ship was built and provisioned at Great Yarmouth to collect the princess; its supplies included casks of wine, beer, salted beef, dried fish, peas, beans, nuts, dried fruits, sugar and spices. But Margaret, aged seven, died when she reached Orkney and her body was taken back to Bergen for burial.

For Edward's coronation in the spring of 1308, one thousand tons of good wine were ordered from Gascony and Bordeaux (paid for by Frescobaldi, the King's moneylenders). London merchants supplied the ale and large cattle, boars, wood, large and small fish, while lampreys were brought from Gloucester. Great attention was paid to fashion in these years. Piers Gaveston's clothes for Edward's coronation were considered far too sumptuous for his station; he wore purple embroidered with pearls outshining the King. An element of transvestism was even celebrated. Henry Knighton, the chronicler of the abbey at Leicester, says that when tournaments were held women would come to join the sport dressed in the most sumptuous of male costumes. 'They used to wear partly coloured tunics, one colour or pattern on the right side and another on the left, with short hoods and pendants like ropes wound round their necks and belts thickly studded in gold and silver . . . there they wearied their bodies with fooleries and wanton buffoonery.'[7] We can suppose that the same attention was given to the food.

Even in the midst of war when Edward was campaigning against Scotland, the court ate well, for we know that sturgeon were especially sent to the court from Germany. Later, in 1322, we can see how the economic effects of the war were disastrous for the nation: in order to feed the army provisions poured into Newcastle from all parts of the country. The county sheriffs were responsible for supplying the army, and the sheriff of Surrey and Sussex was ordered to organise the collection of large amounts of grain, salted meat and fish which were packed into barrels and sent by sea from Seaford and Shoreham to Newcastle.[8] Few ships reached their destination. Even in war, however, there was no privation at court; during Christmas 1322 Edward resided at York and his clerk of the kitchens ordered supplies of beef, mutton and pork, wild boar, veal, venison, rabbits, bream, salmon, pike, lampreys, eels, porpoise, sturgeon, crabs, swans, peacocks, capons, herons and pigeons. There was so much plenty, in fact, that the King sent presents of twenty pieces of sturgeon to the Queen and thirteen pieces of sturgeon to the wife of his new lover, Henry Despenser. Other close friends received gifts of deer and venison and the Dominicans at his home at Langley were not forgotten, for they were sent eleven pike.

However life was very different out of court. Before the worst ravages of the early famine years in 1314 Stow's *Annals* record: 'No flesh could be had, capons and geese could not be found, eggs were hard to come by, sheep died of rot, swine were out of the way, a quarter of wheat beans and peas were sold for 20 shillings, a quarter of malt for a mark, a quarter of salt for 35 shillings.' For the following year Stow goes on: 'Horseflesh was counted a great delicacy, the poor stole fat dogs to eat, some, it was said, were compelled through famine to eat the flesh of their own children and some stole others which they devoured.'

The King's quarrels with the barons and their efforts to restrain his excesses coupled with famine and Scottish victories led to economic disaster. There was a decline in landlords' revenues, a fall in agricultural income and a shortage of coin due to a falling output of silver itself. However, the pepperers had now become important people in the city of London; the spice trade was lucrative and flourishing, so rich traders liked to apprentice their sons in the business. Pepperers, among fishmongers and wool merchants, were now aldermen, part of the city council and had become mayors of London. So rich and influential were they that at times of civil war each warring side wanted their support. Alien traders were taking much of their profit, however, and they wanted legislation to halt it; both King and barons made promises which they broke, and the pepperers saw that in order to protect their interests they must possess more power as a governing body. The beginnings of mercantile power through spices and the wool trade laid the foundations for the new middle classes, a force that would grow ever greater, but one which throughout the fourteenth century would be constantly threatened by the new powers of the rebellious peasant.

The Black Death

In 1348 the Black Death reached the shores of England and raged for two years. At the end of it almost half the population was dead and it was, of course, the peasants, the lowest class of all in town and country, who suffered the greatest loss. It is estimated that a population of 4 3/4 million before the Black Death fell to 2 million by the end of the century. There is an inscription on the walls of the tower in Ashwell Church in Hertfordshire which reads: 'miserable . . . wild . . . distracted . . . dregs of a people alone survive to witness'. The plague was known as the Great Mortality; it was thought that God had become deaf and could not hear the anguish of His people.

For a population well versed in Old Testament dramas, this was their own Sodom and Gomorrah; they knew how deep in sin they were, how decadent the Church was, how full of avarice, greed, envy, lechery and gluttony they had become and God had no mercy or forgiveness for them. He slew them in the fields, at the hearth, at the very altar where they clung calling out for mercy.

It is Henry Knighton who gives us the most vivid picture of the Black Death. The first English city to be affected was Bristol, which lost 10,000 inhabitants. 'There died suddenly overwhelmed by death almost the whole strength of the town, for few were sick for more than three days, or two days or half a day even.' Knighton also records the effect on the countryside:

> A great number of sheep died throughout the whole country, so much so that in one field alone more than five thousand sheep were slain. Their bodies were so corrupted by the plague that neither beast nor bird would touch them. The price of every commodity fell heavily since, because of their death, men seemed to have lost their interest in wealth or in worldly goods . . . sheep and cattle were left to wander through the fields and among the standing crops, since there was no one to drive them off or collect them; for want of people to look after them they died in untold numbers in the hedgerows and ditches all over the country. So few labourers and servants were left that nobody knew where to turn for help.[9]

There were further outbreaks of plague in 1361, which were called the Pestilence of the Children for they appeared to strike the infants most; there were more in 1368-9, 1371, 1375, 1390 and 1405, but the 1348 outbreak was the most traumatic and it changed society forever, leading to a complete revolution in the occupation of the land. For by far the greatest percentage of fatalities was among the most vulnerable, the poorest, the agricultural labourer. This helped the few that were left, so that the lord's vassal became a free man working for a wage. For the first time it placed the landlord in a weak position. The peasant who worked for wages before now demanded more, and those who worked in return for a hovel and a scrap of land could now demand more wages and their own land. With almost half the population dead and the same amount of land to cultivate, the landlord was forced to pay higher wages, even though, because of reduced demand, he now obtained lower prices for his produce. Government legislation attempted to put the clock back, to check increased wages and the free movement of labour, but on the whole failed. Cases such as the Lincolnshire ploughman who refused to serve except by the day and unless he had fresh meat instead of salt and if he did not get what he wanted would offer his services elsewhere, had become commonplace.[10]

Wages rose rapidly and substantially, in some areas they doubled, in others they rose by a third. At the same time the price of wool, because of lack of demand, fell, while the cost of manufactured products rose, because though everyone knew how to cut hay, few were competent to make a nail or shoe a horse. What emerged from this painful chaos of new changes was that the peasant was possessed of a new awareness of his worth; he now had a say in the terms of his employment and he could seek his fortune elsewhere if such rights were denied him. He also had more land, for land was now plentiful and labour scarce to grow food; he also had silver and copper coins to buy manufactured goods such as kitchen equipment to cook the food with. What is more, because there was a grave shortage of people qualified to teach French, the language of the nobility, the vernacular now became commonplace within bureaucratic society, so that the business of life for the first time, in the law courts and elsewhere, was communicated in the everyday language of the medieval labourer. He was now part of society with the power to rise and better himself.

There is, of course, no quicker way to show to others new social status than in the clothes one wears and the food one eats. Society as well as the economy was deeply disturbed, for the biggest increase in wages went to the humblest citizen, which struck at the very heart of the class system. To the lord and the merchant this state of affairs was unjust, for the poor were expected to keep their place. In time this feeling of grievance grew so that new sumptuary laws were constantly passed which built on and extended statutes such as the one of 1336 which reads: 'No man of what state or condition soever he be, shall cause himself to be served in his house or elsewhere, at dinner, meal or supper, or at any other time, with more than two courses and each mess of two sorts of victuals at the utmost, be it Flesh or Fish, with the common sorts of pottage, without sauce or any sort of victuals . . . except only on the principal feasts of the year . . ., on which days every man may be served with three courses at the utmost, after the manner aforesaid.'[5] A law that attempts to control how many courses a man may have at a meal seems extraordinary to us now. How on earth would such a law be enforced? Why the need for such a law? The preamble to the statute gives us some clues as to the anxieties of government: 'Whereas heretofor, through the excessive and over many sorts of costly meats which the people of this Realm have used more than elsewhere, many mischiefs have happened to the people of this Realm: for the great men by these excesses have been sore grieved, and the lesser people who only endeavour to imitate the greater ones in such sorts of meat are much impoverished; whereby they are not able to air themselves nor their liege Lord, in times of need, as they ought.' So these people who had wealth but no nobility were aping the nobles, and the nobles feared that they would have no financial resources on which to call. It was merely, of course, that the elite could not endure the challenge of new money; Gower spoke for them. Food dearths and famine also haunted this edict: if all the people ate too much then surely there would not be enough food to go around? The sumptuary laws continued throughout the century and concerned themselves with dress, apparel and livery as well as food. They attempted to provide restraints upon the competitive struggle between classes, but were only ineffectual acts in a century of torment and chaos. As we have seen, this disturbed the poet, John Gower: 'It seems to me that lethargy has put the lords to sleep so they do not guard against the folly of the common people, but they allow that nettle to grow which is too violent in its nature.'

Because working men and women on the lord's manor had always eaten celebratory meals in the manor house at Harvest suppers, Christmas and Easter, they were familiar with the cooking of the nobility. They would not have been given delicate dishes of great complexity, or with expensive spices and other ingredients, which were kept for the elite, but they would have caught glimpses of them, smelt the aromas, seen something of their colour and gilding. Nevertheless, they could now begin to replicate at home the pies and roasts they ate at the manor house, even if in a much more modest manner. They were also bound to have added the touches of additional herbs and greens from the wild, with which they had always augmented their diet.

Throughout this time of horror and privation Edward III was waging war in France over his French possessions and for a while the French king was imprisoned in England. For the peasant it must have seemed that not only had the Church deserted them, for no amount of prayer and sacrifice saved them from plague or starvation, but also the monarch with his unending battles across the Channel was unconcerned with their fate. No wonder their feelings of resentment and anger at the injustice of their lives led in the last quarter of the century to what was known as the Peasants' Revolt. It was misnamed, because the leaders of the protest were mostly all small landowners who had acquired their plots after the Black Death.

The government had attempted to prop up the status quo by legislation. An Ordinance of Labourers (1349) and a Statute of Labourers (1351) tried to peg prices down to what they had been before the plague, and attempted to stop labourers from travelling and selling their labour to the highest bidder, but these laws only succeeded in engendering great resentment. A popular slogan asked: 'When Adam delved and Eve span/Who was then the gentleman?' A proposal that gained great popularity was that the lands held by the Church should be confiscated and distributed among the peasants. The government ignored much of this by increasing fines and attempting to levy a poll tax. In 1380 to pay for the war in France a poll tax was set up at one shilling per head with the proviso that the rich should help the poor to pay it. It was hopelessly inequitable and impossible to collect, and in 1381 the whole of south-east England was on the edge of rebellion. The rebels marched on London to attack the King's councillors and to demand redress. The young Richard II (1377-99) rode out to meet the rebels and promised them charters to liberate them from serfdom. On the following day he promised to redress all of their grievances. As their leader, Wat Tyler, had been killed they agreed to return home. Thomas of Walsingham wrote that the 'Serfs went in and out like lords; and swineherds set themselves above soldiers, although not knights but rustics.'

There was great irony in the Black Death and the further plagues of the fourteenth century, however. In decimating the peasant population it had greatly improved the material rewards of those left. Now they could demand, and in the end they received, a small cottage instead of a hovel, and perhaps greatest of all, built into the wall a brick oven shaped like a beehive inside. Now, they no longer had to take their dough to the Manor House and leave a tenth of it behind in payment for the baking. All the bread was baked at home on one day in the week when the oven was hottest; the smaller items followed afterwards. The Black Death, in fact, instigated rural cooking, the beginnings of a peasant cuisine based on baking, and the produce of the small farmhouse had now begun.

The Forme of Cury

Despite turmoil, the royal banquets continued throughout the fourteenth century. The four-course feasts with fifty or so different dishes, full of fantasy, music and gastronomic invention, dedicated to display at its most splendid and grandiose, flourished. Surely no nobility since ancient Rome had lived and eaten with such excessive indulgence? It is from the end of the fourteenth century that the first cookery book exists: *The Forme of Cury* (the proper method of cookery) was compiled by the master cooks to Richard II,[11] that same king who had confronted the peasants' revolt, made them promises and quickly broke them all.

There are around 200 recipes, ranging from simple soups and broad beans served in a sauce made from almond milk and butter, rabbits in onion sauce, meat balls fried in batter and served with a Saracen sauce (almond milk, white wine, spices and egg yolks to thicken) to a choice of sixteen different stews (called *bruets*) to a veal dish which is simply a medieval version of Blanquette de Veau. How interesting that so many dishes bear the names of their North African origin even though the Crusades had long ended, and that in a society renowned for its devotion to Christianity and its erection of the most magnificent cathedrals ever created, its daily diet should recall and celebrate heathen tastes. Of course, the imprint of the Saracen upon its food had long been forgotten; these influences had been absorbed into the celebratory dishes of the feast and were thought of as English, as they still are. They were ablaze with colour, and a table crammed with dishes at a feast would have looked like a stained glass window or the bejewelled robe of a monarch. The cathedrals too were full of colour and decoration, nearly all of it lost to us now, though the restored Sanctuary roof of Tewkesbury Cathedral gives us some idea of their vividness and intensity.

The recipes of *The Forme of Cury* are practical, efficient and craftsmanslike and we shall look more closely at them later. What impresses one on first glance is the sheer range of ingredients cooked in the royal kitchens at this time. There are hens, capons, partridge, curlew, pigeon, cranes, heron, duck, goose, chicken. Of other birds there are quail, lark, bittern, plover, rail, dove, cygnet, peacock, egret, woodcock, snipe, dotterel, gull and teal. These were occasionally boiled first and then always spit-roasted and generally endored (basted with a paste of saffron, egg yolks and flour to give a gilded appearance). Alternatively, they were sometimes stewed in a thick, spicy sweet and sour sauce.

Of the meats there are roasted oxen, mutton, beef, kid, deer and pork, which were all sliced by the carver and served with a pungent vinegar or verjuice-based sauce, or one of the sauces listed on page 43. Boiled pork was often minced or ground and mixed with spices to stuff a pie or encased in pastry shells for *tartlettes*. (These are like won-tons, tiny parcels cooked in a broth.)

Of the fish you could eat porpoise, haddock, codling, hake, salmon, tench, pike, eel, turbot, plaice, roach, rays, mackerel, gurnard, oysters, mussels and lampreys. Other recipe sources mention: bream, flounder, gudgeon, marling, halibut, whelks, perch, sturgeon, trout, crab and carp. The fish was either fried and served with a spicy sauce or if lightly pickled served always with a green parsley sauce (we still serve jellied eels with a similar sauce today) or baked in a pie, boiled in a stew, or prepared and set beneath its jelly.

We know that salads were grown and eaten, as no manor or abbey was without its garden. Herbs and leaves were divided in the garden into those used for soup, just over fifty different kinds are listed, including alexanders (now growing rampant over the coast in my native Sussex), basil, borage, chervil, chives, caraway, fennel, leek, lettuce, nettle, orach, spinach and thyme. These, of course, include those much used herbs, parsley, mint and sage. Other herbs are listed to make sauces: dittander, hartstongue, masterwort, pellitory, sorrel, violet, garlic and mustard. Over twenty other herbs are used for salad, among them are calamint, chickweed, cress, daisies, dandelion, primrose buds, purslane, rampion, ransoms, rocket and violets.[12] These show an enthusiastic love of fresh leaves in the diet, and are selected, one feels, for their aesthetic visual appeal as much as their flavour, texture, impact upon the palate and medicinal qualities. In fact, one of the recipes given shows all of these aspects: a salad made up of finely chopped garlic, shallots, onions and leeks, moistened with oil, vinegar and salt, with parsley, sage, borage, fennel, cress, rue, rosemary, mint and purslane then added.

The order of serving the dishes prevailed from the twelfth to the sixteenth centuries with little change. Meals began with pottages, the standard dish for everyone, soups made of vegetables, or fish for fast days, thickened with dried peas or beans, or made with different meats on other days; cabbage, leeks and onions were the vegetables most used, for they withstand hard winters, while onions could be stored in dry barns. These soups were never coarse: a leek, parsley and mussel soup that became a smooth purée (pounded and sieved) would have looked vibrant and tasted fragrant. Greens were also served as a vegetable side dish; they were boiled then thoroughly drained, any water was squeezed out of them, and then they were tossed in butter and diced white bread. Another side dish of greens would cook them in a meat broth with bacon, and then mince them into a purée. Another serves dried broad beans, well soaked with their skins removed, cooked thoroughly then served in a sauce of almond milk and butter thickened with breadcrumbs. It is delicious for the earthiness of the bean is lightened by the almond milk, enriched by the butter and made velvety by the white bread thickener. These were recipes for highly cultured palates.

After the soups come the substantial dishes: the roast meats, the venison, oxen, mutton, the swans, peacocks and pheasants dressed in their own plumage, but this course was lightened by egg and fish dishes, followed by pies and pasties. These were often small, to be eaten easily with the fingers. Then came fried dishes like the meat balls in batter served with a sharp sauce. Then followed small game birds, counting as part of a dessert (the source of our savoury) with sweet wafers, tarts, fritters, preserved fruits and cakes made of nuts and dried fruits (not unlike panforte) for this dish can be traced back to Cyprus. In the sixteenth century, this last sweet course was to become a separate one altogether and to be called a 'banquet'; special buildings where it would all be eaten were built for it in the gardens or upon the roof of grand houses, as in Longleat (see Chapter 5).

It stemmed from the French ceremony of *voidée* or void, because the spiced wine and sweet comfits were given after the tables had been cleared. *Voidée* is derived from *voider*, to clear the table, but it also means to make empty and so refers to the departure of guests. We are told that Edward IV never 'taketh a voyd of comfittes and other spices but standing.'[13] Standing was perhaps necessary as tables were cleared and moved; the spiced wine and sugar comfits were delicate finger food, which could be taken while moving around, walking in the gardens, dancing or playing games. This also enabled the servants to sit down and eat their dinner, as the sugar course could be laid out enticingly well before the main meal.

In *The Forme of Cury* is the original recipe for Beef Olives, that last mysterious word being a corruption of the Old French *aloues*, meaning larks. Here a piece of beefsteak was hammered thin; over it was strewn beef suet and bone marrow, finely chopped onions, parsley, thyme, marjoram, then salt and pepper; it was rolled up, then tied and grilled or braised in wine and broth. If grilled it was suggested that a batter is poured over; once the top is set the Olives were turned and more batter poured until that too was set.[14] These would have made excellent finger food. Pieces of chicken were stewed in white wine and broth flavoured with cloves, mace and mixed spices, the liquor was thickened with ground almonds and rice flour. Chunks of veal were cooked in chicken broth with ginger thickened with ground almonds. Pieces of kid were stewed in white wine and beef broth with onions, parsley, sage, mint, thyme, marjoram, rosemary, cloves, mace, cinnamon, ginger and a pinch of saffron; it was thickened with breadcrumbs. Turbot was baked in white wine flavoured with ginger and orange juice. Sole was served with a sauce of onions, saffron, honey and salt, plaice with a sauce of ginger, pepper and cinnamon thickened with bread.

Favourite recipes appear in various versions: the source of what later came to be called blancmange or 'shape' went under various names, Blaunche de sorre (see also page 44), Blaw Maungere or Blaunch doucet to name but three. This was a cold chicken pudding which could be flavoured with ginger, almonds, sugar and spices; the chicken flesh was poached and then shredded along the grain; one Italian recipe advises that the shreds should be as fine as hair; then it was mixed with almond milk, sugar and flavourings and thickened with rice flour, poured into a mould and left to cool. When unmoulded it was decorated with candied fruits and violets. On fast days the dish was made with fish instead of chicken.

It was felt to be natural to eat the most substantial foods first, saving the more delicate dishes until later. In households that were more spartan due to excessive religious devotion, delicate cooking was renounced and only the roast was eaten. That first course was all that the more lowly members of the household were entitled to; on fast days one dish of salt fish and one of fresh fish with butter was all that was allowed.

At the court of the young King, Richard II, 10,000 people were fed each day. His person was guarded by 200 men, which included thirteen bishops as well as barons, knights, esquires and others. We hear of the 'Doctoure of Physique' who must counsel the King and his cooks as to what dishes would suit the King best. (See page 46.) Of course, from the concept of humours (what was cold, warm, wet or dry), came much of the stimulus for the imaginative sauces and methods of cooking. A household of 10,000 seems an outrageous number; farms and market gardens around and within medieval London supplied the daily produce. Only the royal nucleus of nobility and advisors would benefit from the expensive dishes; the food was carefully graded as the social eminence of the diner fell[15]. Grooms and blacksmiths would be eating pottage and a chunk of bread and cheese with the chance of gnawing on any meat bones that were thrown out. Nor is it likely that when large roasts of meat or fowl were carved up that the portions would be generous. We know this from the records of Alice de Bryene who was born in Suffolk around 1360, and kept detailed accounts of her estate at Acton. She died in 1435 aged 75.

A Country Household

In the year 1412-1413 Alice de Bryene served more than 16,500 meals in her manor house, roughly forty-five meals a day. Sometimes, as in her New Year's feast she had more than 300 people dining with her, at other times there would be only three guests sitting down with Dame Alice and her household. These could be the bailiffs of one of her manors, or important visitors from London who were powerful at court and protective of the widow's interests, or visiting clerics and quite often her relations. Her household ate per person per day on average a 2 lb loaf of bread, 3½ pints of ale, 1 lb of meat, several varieties of fish and shellfish, dried and smoked fish and a plentiful supply of dairy produce. Guests of Alice's class also drank wine from Gascony or the Rhône instead of home-brewed ale. Alice spent sixty-five per cent of her income upon food and drink, higher than the average fifty to sixty per cent. (Now we only spend ten per cent.) The wealthier the establishment the more money seemed to have been spent; at Battle Abbey, for example, food expenditure reached two-thirds of income. But this is not true of the very poor.

Eating in the hall was a communal affair, and it must have been the high point of the day. Dame Alice, friends and family dined on the high table, raised by a dais which crossed the width of the hall, while other tables ran at right angles down the hall, where the retainers, house servants, grooms and agricultural labourers all ate. The food that was served also observed such social differences, the high table being given the more delicate dishes, or the ones that had had expensive spices used in them, though Dame Alice's expenditure on these items was low – only $1/2$ oz of spice was used per day. That most expensive spice of all, saffron, she used with care, making do with $3/4$ lb throughout the year of 1418-19; that same year she used 5 lb pepper, $2^1/2$ lb ginger, 3 lb cinnamon, $1^1/4$ lb cloves and $1^1/4$ lb mace. If Dame Alice served the same number of meals that year, her amount of spices works out at a tenth of an ounce in each meal for each person, which is no more than a pinch.

The expense of saffron drove people to experiment with its cultivation in England, and gardening manuals suggested growing it among the pot herbs. Growing just a few crocuses, however, yields such a miniscule amount it is not worth doing; the fiddly business of gathering the stigmas seems to indicate cultivating it on large areas, or not at all. Hence the cultivation began in Cambridgeshire and Essex in the middle of the fourteenth century around the town of Walden, which would soon be renamed. This then flourishing industry was not too far from where Alice lived and we can be certain that her saffron was therefore English in origin, but, wily housekeeper as she was, she would have noticed that there was little difference in the price whether it came from Walden or Spain.

Dame Alice was generous in her hospitality, and her doors were open to all and sundry. Two carpenters who were staying in February to mend a plough dined one evening (and this was considered part of their wage) while Dame Alice's sister-in-law, Lady Waldegrave, was also there. On that evening the women and friends may well have eaten an English stew of peeled chestnuts, liver, kidneys and hard-boiled eggs flavoured with pepper and saffron, while they all ate, including the carpenters, the roast venison which had supplied the offal. On nearly every day, there was also stewed pigeon and rabbit, both flavoured with the winter herbs easily plucked from the garden, sage, rosemary and thyme. Dame Alice's tenants from her larger properties would also be asked to dine and one imagines that the richer ones would have been flattered with dishes where time and trouble had been expressed, finishing their meal perhaps with stuffed sweet omelettes flavoured with ginger, or cheese pastries filled with dried fruit and honey. Two friars from Sudbury dined and stayed overnight to commemorate the death of Alice's parents. They, of course, would have been made a great fuss of, their favourite foods known beforehand, planned for and cooked especially. Chaucer's Friar is insistent in eating only a capon's liver and having a roasted pig's head to follow. One imagines that these Sudbury friars might be given roast goose, pike cooked in wine with ginger sauce, or stewed partridge with dried fruits poached in wine and broth.[16]

For the New Year's feast there were two pigs, two swans, twelve geese, two joints of mutton, twenty-four capons, seventeen rabbits, beef, veal, and suckling pig; sweet dishes were made from spices, sugar, twelve gallons of milk and eggs.[17] However, when this amount is divided up into 300 portions it is not such a huge amount: it allows one goose to every twenty-five people, and one capon between ten; one rather doubts whether the lower orders would have tasted anything of the swan, suckling pig or veal – they would have dined instead on rabbit and mutton. We are not told how this feast was cooked, but if the capons and rabbits had been stewed with cabbage, onions, garlic and herbs, with plenty of bread to soak up the juices, then the amounts would have stretched more easily. And what of the excessive amount of milk? One imagines those marvellous sweet and spicy desserts that ended the meals, such as the milk turned to curds and flavoured with ginger and sugar, used in tarts, flavoured with elderflowers or eaten with preserved quinces.

Mixed spices were often specified in recipes. The three most popular ones were, firstly, *blanch* powder, which was pale, made up from white sugar and white ginger, and used to sprinkle over fruit – baked apples, quinces or wardens (a variety of pear that was particularly hard and so excellent for cooking). A white blancmange, for example, would have been sprinkled with blanch powder and fried almonds. Secondly, *Powder fort*, which was a powerful mixture based on pepper, cloves and ginger. Thirdly, *Powder douce*, which was a mild mixture containing sugar. There was also *Powder marchant*, which was a little like *quatre épices* and the mixture we call pickling spices. All of these were ground and ready mixed, bought from the market, and in the store cupboard ready for use in the kitchen. Other popular spices that have fallen into disuse were two cousins of the ginger family, zedoary and galingale, as well as cubebs which the herbalist John Parkinson described as 'small berries somewhat sweete, no bigger than pepper cornes but more rugged and crested not so black nor solid . . . and having each a small short stalke at them like a taile.'[18] Grains of paradise were also enormously popular; they are indigenous to West Africa along the Gulf of Guinea and are related to cardamom. They have a hot peppery taste and show the medieval addiction to really strong hot flavours in their cooking. They would have been an ingredient in many of the sauces used with roasted meats. In the fourteenth and fifteenth centuries their cultivation was of such economic importance that the coastline became renamed as the Grain Coast or Melegueta Coast, the alternative name for the spice. The production of the spice must have been abundant for its price in 1284 was no more than fourpence a pound. That price of course was far too expensive for any peasant whose yearly income would only have been just over £3.

Alice sent her groom to Colchester every Sunday throughout Lent to buy oysters and mussels. The shellfish were then cooked in a little broth or ale with spices, mace and cloves. Mussels could be stewed in wine with pepper and minced onions until 'they beginneth to gape'. They were then served up in their shells.[19] (*Moules Marinières*, of course.) Alice also bought four barrels of white herrings and a quarter of a barrel of salted sturgeon to last through a year; this latter was a luxury. One wonders whether it would be saved for the friars or given to the visiting courtiers. Whoever enjoyed it, the salted sturgeon would have been sliced thinly, soaked to get rid of excess salt, dried and served with a green sauce, made from parsley and other green herbs and mixed with honey, verjuice or vinegar.

On meat days they ate pigeon almost every day; one entry records for May 'a quarter of bacon, one capon, two chickens and twenty pigeons'. They came from the manor's dovecote and pigeons being obligingly fecund, as I know from personal experience, they would need constant culling. On Easter Day they ate boiled eggs with green sauce, for eggs were banned throughout the whole of Lent. Cream was regularly used, turned into egg custards with spices, sugar and breadcrumbs. One of the greatest treats for all manor and farmhouses with cows that were calving was what they did with the beistyn.[20] This was the first milk that the calf received which was thick, yellow and the consistency of egg yolk, necessary to the health of the calf; nature as always is too generous, so that some of this thick milk must be taken away. Desserts would be made whereby the beistyn was thinned down four times with plain milk, sweetened, flavoured with vanilla or cinnamon and allowed to set in a cool place. For special occasions the top was covered in sugar and placed under a hot salamander so that it melted and bubbled, then allowed to cool again.[21] This dish called Burnt Cream must have been a yearly favourite in spring and remained so for hundreds of years; in the late nineteenth century several people believed the recipe derived from Cambridge University.[22] Now it appears on menus as Crème Brûlée, with no clue that it stemmed from the poorest medieval farmyard kitchen.

Dame Alice's household did not consume a great deal of rice, for she only purchased 3 lb in the whole year, at a penny a pound. Dame Alice and her family ate white bread: every week the kitchen baked 220 white loaves and thirty black loaves. As the number of black loaves was so small, most of her servants, one imagines, must have also eaten white bread. The household ate 1 gallon 2½ quarts of honey throughout the year and only a single pound of sugar. This would have been honey from her own bees for the amount of wax used in her house for lighting was considerable and hives were essential to every well run manor house. She also bought 40 lb of almonds. Her most favoured spice was mustard, for in the year 1418-19 the household consumed 84 lb of mustard seed. They ate mustard with almost everything, with fresh and salt meat, with brawn, both fresh fish and stock. The seed was ground up in a mortar with added vinegar and honey. Mustard is another example of a food that originally came from the Anglo-Saxon peasant diet. Dame Alice's household brewed its own ale with equal parts of barley, malt and drage (a mixture of barley and oats) every week except in January and February when barley malt alone was used.

In the year 1418-19 the household consumed forty-six beef cattle, ninety-seven sheep, eighty-seven pigs, 1,584 poultry birds, but only twenty-six game birds and 102 rabbits, although this list does not include the vast numbers of pigeons. Dame Alice seemed to have managed to keep some of her cattle throughout the winter on hay and pasture, so that fresh meat could be eaten throughout the year. Only seventeen cattle were killed between October and November, the rest at other times of the year. Of the sheep, thirty-one were killed before June and fifty after shearing in the summer and late autumn.[23] This reflects the fact that in the fifteenth century more pasture was enclosed and much less livestock was slaughtered at Martinmas. It is apparent from these accounts that a meal at the manor house was a significant part of the social custom of the time; it marked a business meeting, or for the workmen was part of the overall wage for a job, or it could mark religious observance of a festival or a saint's day. Dame Alice was at the centre of a nucleus of people who were nourished and sustained by her farm and the produce grown there. The manor was at the centre of rural life.

The Medieval Housewife

We have the details of another efficient housekeeper, Margaret Paston, for her letters to her husband and her son (both called John) have survived. Margaret married around 1440, when the English were suffering a series of military defeats in the closing years of the Hundred Years War with France, due, among other factors, to the incompetence and later the imbecility of King Henry VI.

We must remember that the marriage contract in the medieval world was a commercial arrangement. When a man chose his wife he chose her for the size of her dowry and the social standing of her family. To marry for love could occur among the poor, one surmises, but because of widespread illiteracy we have, alas, no love letters or poems to cite examples. One also imagines that the struggle simply to survive would be of such grinding exhaustion that though the bonds of sexual desire and parenthood would be strong, affectionate love tokens would hardly have room or time to bloom. Love occurred outside marriage and belonged to concepts of romance and knightly heroism sung by troubadours. Marriage contracts were a method of social climbing, to enlarge one's properties and lands and therefore the income from rent. In the Pastons' story territory plays the most important role: they inherited properties from Sir John Falstaff, which were later fought over; they lost some, sold some and disputed others through the courts. Their story illustrates the reckless lawlessness of the century, but throughout, of course, food was of paramount importance.

Margaret raised eight children; she also supervised the breadmaking, ale-brewing, winemaking, dairy, poultry and pigs, and oversaw the spinning, weaving, sewing and needlework; in preparing for the long winter season she organized the smoking of the ham and bacon, the drying of fruit, the storage of onions, garlic and grain.

A wife was there to manage the estates and from a tender age and was taught by her own mother the range of duties expected of her. The first essential was to plan ahead, to preserve, store and spin. The kitchen and pantry had to be well supplied with produce to keep family and servants well fed. The daily breakfast that Margaret Paston supplied for her family was 'a manchet a quarte of beer a dysch of butter a pece of saltfisch a dysch of sproitts or white herrying'.[24] The beer, butter and bread were, of course, all made on the estate. The sprats would have been salted and bought in a barrel, while the white herring was fresh and plentiful, because the Pastons lived in Norfolk and so were close to Yarmouth, the centre of the herring industry. Richard Calle, the Pastons' bailiff, notified her: 'I have got me a friend in Lowestoft to help to buy me seven or eight barrel of herring and shall not cost me above 6 shillings and eightpence a barrel.' Margaret wrote to her husband: 'As for herring, I have bought a horseload for 4/6. I can get no eels yet.'

The herrings that were not eaten on the day (a portion was four to five fish, according to the monks at Westminster who based their food habits upon the affluent)[25] would have been all preserved in one way or another. There were 215 fast days in the year, so fish had a high priority in the stores; they were preserved by being either salted, dried, smoked or pickled in brine. About half of the fish eaten came from the preserved stores, the rest were sea fish or freshwater fish from the household's rivers, lakes or ponds. The most popular fish by far was the cod family. Conger eel was a delicacy and with pike and salmon was thought suitable for a grand meal. For fifty-two people to dine a cook needed 40-48 lb of fish for a dish of stewed eel and 20-24 lb for a dish of baked eel.[26]

On meat days they had mutton bones and boiled beef, while the bailiff writes to Margaret Paston that he has now bought enough beef to last the household from late autumn until Lent. In a letter to her son, Margaret asks him to enquire about the price of pepper, cloves, ginger, cynamon, almonds, rice, saffron, 'raysons of Corons, and galingal'. Currants were called 'raisons of Corinth' and hence became referred to just as Corinth. We can see that from this list Margaret Paston, unlike Dame Alice some twenty years before, kept up with the very latest trends and fashions dictated by the court and nobility. She frequently asked for loaves of sugar: 'I pray you that you will vouchsafe to send me another sugar loaf for my old one is done.' Treacle, which was a medicinal electuary, was very popular, often mentioned and ordered from town. She writes to her son:

> I have sent my Uncle Berney the pot of treacle that you did buy for him. Also, I pray you heartily that you will send me a pot with treacle in haste for I have been right evil at ease, and your daughter both, since you rode hence . . .

Sir John then sent three pots of treacle from Genoa, explaining to his mother which of the three pots would be the best. Dates and oranges were a favourite food for pregnant women; they were accepted as a recognisable fad at such times and the women should be indulged, so much so that John Paston felt he should apologise when he asked for dates and oranges to be sent to Elizabeth Calthorpe, 'who longed for them even though she be not with child'. Margaret Paston constantly enquired about the price of food in London and compared it to the prices at her local market in Norwich, often finding the London prices cheaper.

In every fifteenth-century manor house there was a brewhouse, a bakehouse, a dairy and other buildings of like nature. Bishop Latimer, in his first sermon to Edward IV, mentioned that his mother milked thirty cows every day. The housewife of this time worked hard from dawn to dusk. We can see from the Paston letters that it is Margaret who negotiates with the farmers, it is she who receives overtures for leases and threats of lawsuits, who manages every detail on their estate, but she also writes to her husband fully explaining the business that has been transacted. Yet it is not all mercenary business. When Margaret of Anjou, Queen to Henry VI, was staying at Norwich, Margaret begs her husband in London to send her some jewels for her neck; in the end she had to borrow jewellery from her cousin, 'for I durst not for shame go with my beads among so many fresh gentlewomen as were here at that time'.

Milk Drinking
It is difficult to find exact figures of milk yields in medieval Britain. In cheese-making country, the yield of two cows or twenty ewes in the fourteenth century was set at one

stone of cheese and half a gallon of whey butter a week.[27] (When full milk was renneted for cheese, the residue was a rich whey, which was then skimmed to make whey butter.) On the one hand we have treatises on husbandry that state what a dairy cow should provide and on the other manor accounts. The anonymous author of *Hosebonderie* (fourteenth century) claimed that a cow should produce between 1 May and Michaelmas enough milk for 98 lb of cheese and 14 lb of butter. In all the manor accounts a cow produced about a third of this. In the manors of Werrington and Hurdwick a cow was expected to yield only 32 lb cheese and about 4 lb butter.[28] It seems very unlikely that any of this milk would have been drunk straight from the cow when the butter and cheese was so prized. In all the manors most of the milk came from the ewes. When the harvest was brought in the peasants were given extra foods to celebrate. These accounts are meticulous and very detailed, so it is interesting to note how rare it is that they were given milk.

Only at five places in Essex was milk drunk at harvest-time and that was not always fresh. In Nettleswell they drank both sour and sweet milk. At Whepstead they drank *lac de matutino* (See Glossary). At Brightwolton in Berkshire the harvesters were given whey in the years 1283 to 1312. At Hadleigh in Sussex and Aldenham in Hertfordshire, they were given *morterel* (bread and milk).[29]

The priority for cows, however, was to bear calves, and the extra milk was a bonus. It was estimated that the ratio between cows and oxen was that every team of eight oxen needed two cows to replenish it, and in some counties this ratio was fewer. This was insufficient for cows to contribute much to the dairy output.[30] It was only after the Reformation when almond milk was no longer drunk that the dairy herds begin to grow.

Settlement names throw light upon what crops and livestock were grown and reared. In the Domesday survey very few milk names appear at all; there are Mulbarton in Norfolk, Melchbourne in Bedfordshire and Melksham in Wiltshire, while there are a large number of cheese and butter names and others that derive from goats and swine.[31]

Once the cows were milked, the cream was skimmed off and sent up to the lord of the manor, his family, friends and guests. Alexander Neckam describes cream and curds brought into the lord's table on round platters. The more affluent peasant with his one cow could also enjoy cream in the summer months if he did not sell it, but Neckam warned of the risk taken: 'Raw cream undecocted eaten with strawberries . . . is a rural man's banquet. I have known such banquets hath put men in jeopardy of their lives.'[32] How interesting it is to note that the lord and his guests were not warned against the cream, only the rural man. Cream and curds were used extensively in the medieval kitchen and hot posset drinks were made with the milk curdled by ale. Andrew Boorde describes one of hot milk and cold ale that is beneficial for a drinker with a hot liver if cold herbs be sodden in it.[33] But this is not drinking the milk fresh.

In medieval towns fresh milk was carried in panniers from a donkey or upon the back of the streetseller. Inevitably in warm summers, with the jostling effect of the movement, the milk curdled. Milk-sellers also too often adulterated the milk by adding water. No wonder almond milk was so popular, not only on fast days (which took up two-thirds of the year) but also for cooking in meat recipes, especially those that used chicken or pork.

The *Menagier de Paris* advised against the drinking of cows' milk for invalids. Cows' milk comes last in the medieval valuation which prizes, as well it might, first of all women's milk, followed by that of asses, ewes and goats. Though it was recognised that: 'A man may live with milk alone, and it will serve instead of meat and drink and medicine.'[34] A comment that describes all milk, for the type is not thought important enough to mention.

It was known that milk was more nutritious in spring and summer than in winter. In fact many farmers did not milk their ewes at all after the summer for fear of weakening them. All dairy products were referred to as 'white meats' and these were considered festive food for the poor. It was meat and spices which distinguished the food of the rich; though dairy foods could be used in its cuisine, they were mixed in with egg yolks, much sugar and spices. The rich were nervous at the thought of drinking milk in its raw state for they had seen slaughtered calves and knew well how milk curdled in the stomach. So physicians constantly warned against it, allowing that milk (and again the type is not specified) might be good for children and the very old, if it is first boiled and then sweetened with sugar.

Of course, the main objection to drinking fresh milk, unless it was straight from the cow, was that it could so easily become dirty and curdle (see Chapter 8). It was noticed that people often got sick, and had stomach upsets with much vomiting; far safer then to avoid the milk in that state and make butter and cheese from it.

Pilgrim Food

In the Prologue of Chaucer's *Canterbury Tales* three characters are expressly linked with food, the Summoner, the Monk, and the Franklin, although there are brief mentions in other tales, including that of the Cook (whose tale is unfinished.) In his Prologue the Host tells us that he has flies in his cookshop, then goes on to complain that many a pasty is stale with no gravy and that people have felt queasy over eating the parsley stuffing with the stubble-fed goose or twice warmed up Jack-of-Dover pie. Note that the flies are linked with stale food which makes people ill. Also, in the Prologue Chaucer laments that the Cook has an ulcer on his shin for he makes chicken pudding with the best of them.

Madame Eglantine, the Prioress, feeds her little dogs with roast meat, milk and white bread, while showing at table her good breeding. Her manners were exemplary, and we learn something of what must have been expected of the courtier when dining. A far cry indeed from the rough, gauche behaviour depicted so often in the cinema when evoking royal feasts in the past. The Prioress never let a crumb fall from her mouth, while only the piece of food was dipped into the sauce, never her fingers; then when she lifted the food to her lips not a crumb ever dropped upon her breast, nor a spot of grease was ever seen in her cup after drinking from it, for she wiped her lips scrupulously. She always reached daintily for her food, for she took pains to imitate courtly behaviour and cultivate a dignified bearing.

All we know of the Summoner's tastes in food (he is an unpleasant-looking character, covered in red pustules and pimples) is that he has a great affection for garlic, onions and leeks and for drinking strong red wine. He also carries a great round cake like a shield. These vegetables were still the main flavourings in the peasant diet and the main additions with kale to the daily pottage. Meat, rabbit and poultry stews, cooked slowly in the embers of a fire, were also flavoured with one or more of them.

The Monk was remarkably fine-looking and loved hunting; he was obviously a stylish fellow with bells on his harness and his favourite dish was roast swan. As chicken cost $2^1/_2$d and swan six or seven shillings, the most expensive bird of all, the Monk was indulging himself. It also shows a certain snobbism for swans were only eaten at feasts given by the rich, even though the flesh was still thought tough and hard to digest; by the sixteenth century only young cygnets were favoured if they were fattened with oats. Swan was always eaten with the sauce chawdron, the black sauce made from the offal and boiled giblets, with added spices thickened with brown breadcrumbs. A recipe for potted swan had the flesh beaten hard then mixed with fat bacon until it was like dough, then well seasoned with salt, pepper and other spices before it was baked. This recipe was only written down in 1727 however, so we cannot tell how far back it goes.[35] Swans were also part of other game bird flesh that was mixed together for raised pies.

The Franklin, part of the landed gentry (franklins presided at Sessions of Justice and were often Members of Parliament for their shires) was a true son of Epicurus, his house a source of plenty that snowed food and drink. The quality of his bread and wine never varied, different dishes were served according to the season of the year, there was every kind of delicacy that you could think of, he had an abundance of fat partridges in his coops, his fishponds were well stocked with bream and pike, his cook found himself in trouble if a sauce was not piquant enough or sharp, and his hall table was kept laid up and ready for guests throughout the day. Here is a picture of a well off and civilised man dispensing hospitality, able to offer a meal at a laid table, where a sauce had to be perfectly seasoned if the cook was not to be chastised.

Sadly, Chaucer does not tell us what the Pilgrims ate on their way to Canterbury. But there were over fifty saints' shrines dotted over England and catering for pilgrimages was a commercial enterprise. Cookshops gathered around shrines while inns and market stalls sprang up along pilgrim routes to feed and care for pilgrims. The poor peasant believed in miracles and such faith was rewarded by them happening. New saints, like Edward II at Gloucester and his arch-enemy Thomas of Lancaster, became centres for fervent adoration. If a king went on a pilgrimage as they frequently did, supplies had to be more adequate and munificent than cookshops and market stalls. On 6 March 1255 six tuns of wine were sent to King Henry III at St Albans for his breakfast as well as all the fish which came from Winchelsea to London without delay. In the following year he had twelve bucks delivered and twenty-five gallons of nut oil together with 2,000 chestnuts. In the spring during Lent, while at Bury St Edmunds, the King ordered a daily supply of mackerel, some of it salted and some packed in bread.[36]

The Aristocratic Diet

Great quantities of meat and fish were consumed by the aristocracy in roughly equal amounts, for fish was eaten on Wednesdays, Fridays and Saturdays and for six weeks over Lent, and on the vigils before important feasts. At least half of the total amount of meat eaten came from cattle, and at least half of that were oxen, cows and bulls slaughtered after a lifetime's labour. So there is little doubt that the consumption of beef became the most important of all the meats early on in the medieval period. Next in preference came pork and mutton and lastly poultry and game birds, though it is difficult to estimate the last as household accounts rarely registered them. Of course, some households showed a marked preference one way or the other. Sir Walter Skipworth of South Ormsby in Lincolnshire ate his way through so much beef it amounted to three-quarters of all the meat consumed, and much of that was young beasts, while at Beaulieu Abbey they ate as little as fifteen per cent. How much venison was eaten corresponded to the amount of hunting enjoyed in a household, and as hunting parties were the principal entertainment for the aristocracy, game, deer, boar and numerous birds were an integral part of their diet. The household of the bishop of Coventry and Lichfield, John Hales, when he was staying in south Staffordshire near Cannock Chase, ate twenty-three deer throughout a four-month summer period as well as eleven cattle. Game birds, swans, herons, pheasants, partridges, plovers, larks and thrushes made their appearance at almost every meal; they represented the food of the elite for they were bred in private parks and protected in forests and chases. At feasts venison was exclusive to the top table.[37]

An enormous amount of the fish eaten was salted and dried and came from trade with Norway and Iceland, while the freshwater species derived from the manor lakes, ponds and rivers. Herrings, referred to as white, were salted while the red kind were smoked; cod was dried and became stockfish (see page 55) and even salmon, sturgeon and eels were salted and preserved. Of the freshwater fish only pike and bream were thought important enough to make their appearance at feasts, though lampreys were considered a huge delicacy[38] (one king – Henry I – died of a surfeit of them); smaller varieties like dace, roach and chub were eaten by the retainers and servants.

The household accounts fail to give us any details of how all this food was cooked and presented; all we can surmise is that recipes eaten at court would have been copied and enjoyed at home, for social emulation was always a driving force and even if the lord arriving home after a hard morning's hunting wanted nothing but roast venison, one can be almost certain that his wife would have requested and fostered the production of other more delicate dishes. Capons in egg sauce for example, where the capons are poached in wine and broth until tender with the sauce thickened with many egg yolks and white breadcrumbs; or rabbits in onion sauce flavoured with ginger, pepper and cinnamon, or oysters in an onion and almond milk sauce.

There are many recipes for *bruets*, the stew that required cooked meat; obviously these were a range of recipes which used up the roasted carcasses that had been carved the day before. Much of this meat would also have been eaten by household servants and some of those gnawed bones thrown to the dogs or the beggars in the yard outside.

But there were enough economically-run households that must have insisted on left-over meat being carved off the bone and used in these dishes. A Bruet of Lombardy was popular, which is cut up chicken in a sauce of almond milk flavoured with mace, nutmeg, ginger and thickened with egg yolks, white bread, then finished with chopped parsley; or a Bruet of Almayn which is made with poultry, rabbit or veal or a Spanish Bruet which is made from venison in a sweet and sour sauce. Other stews tended to have less sauce than *bruets*; a Lombard stew made with cooked pork, red wine and onions is flavoured with ginger, saffron, cloves and mace.

Venison was always hung for a few days or more to tenderise the heavily sinewed flesh; if there was a surplus then it was salted. Roast venison was served with the pepper, bread and vinegar sauce peverade, or cinnamon and powdered ginger. When the venison was boiled it was always served with frumenty (the origin of our bread sauce with fowl); this was made by boiling wheat in water until the grains burst, then once cooled they were mixed with cows' or almond milk, thickened with egg yolks and coloured yellow with saffron. Frumenty was also eaten with porpoise on fish days. Further north it was made from oats and is recognisably the Scots porridge we are familiar with. The use of oats as a cereal is a British characteristic; when oats are mentioned in an Italian cookery book the author qualifies their mention as being 'in the English tradition'.

Left-over venison flesh was minced and made up into pies and pasties; the flesh was seasoned and spiced, then mixed with butter. Sometimes the venison cold cuts would be marinaded overnight in ale, wine or vinegar, before being used in the pie. Both fresh and salt venison were used, the blood was also saved and used in soups or to enrich the pies. Both hares and rabbits were roasted and used in stews and pies. Hares in talbotays (meaning blood) was where the carcass was cut into chunks then stewed with herbs and pepper in ale, the blood was poured into the sauce which was thickened with bread. A simple enough recipe, which we still use, as in jugged hare. Hare was also cooked in onion sauce, a recipe that Hieatt points out is similar to the French recipe for *Civet de Lièvres*. Wild boar was roasted, but the head was often used for brawn: pine nuts, currants, onions and the meat were boiled in wine to make a soup called *boor in brasey*, which would be decorated with slices of brawn.

The pastry cook must have been a favoured person in the household for his skills were called upon daily; apprentice cooks would have followed the master cook's craft with close attention. There were various types of paste. A strong dough was made from wholemeal flour, beef suet and boiling water for the standing crust for great pies or coffins; these shells were baked blind, four of them joined together to make a fifth in the centre, and their tops cut into castellations. Then they could be filled with different coloured mixtures, so that when cut the various colours would show. One of the triumphs of the pastrymaker's art was the numerous small pies that were constantly served at meals and eaten as finger food. There were *chewettes* with a filling of pork, onion, chicken and spices or for fish days, a filling of haddock, cod, cream and herbs, or the *darioles*, filled with egg, cream, chopped dates, figs, prunes and sugar. These pasties were sometimes fried instead of baked. By the later part of the fifteenth century these pasties, filled with minced pork or veal, spices and herbs, were given the name of 'hats'. Then later the shape changed again to one of peasecods. In the reign of Richard II a flour paste was also used for making pasta, both, as we have seen earlier, a form of ravioli and another flat noodle called *macrows* which appears to be the birth of macaroni. Both recipes after boiling the pasta serve it with cheese and butter.

Sausages were also a great favourite; indeed from Greek times they appeared to have been a staple of the kitchen in all countries. Perhaps the reason lies in their economical way of using all the odd bits of the carcass and once well seasoned, moistened with tasty fat, the smoking and drying intensifying the flavour; they become almost an addiction in a country's food, reflecting the tastes of a region in their use of particular flavourings. Some aspects of the Roman Lucanian sausage had remained with the Anglo-Saxons (the word is used in their vocabulary). This was a highly seasoned sausage with pepper, cumin, savory, rue and mixed herbs packed into the cleaned intestine and then smoked. The Normans brought their own varieties of sausage. Neckam names three of them as suitable for provisioning a castle under siege: *aundulyes*, *saucistres*, *pudingis* were all were made when the pig was killed. The latter was made with the animal's blood mixed with minced onions and diced fat, spiced with ginger, cloves and pepper, then stuffed into long lengths of intestine. We have never lost our love of the sausage, and share this liking with nearly all cuisines. However, the manner of serving may be different; though all the smoked sausages could be boiled or grilled and served with mustard, there are recipes where the sausage is sliced and fried then served in a sauce of butter thickened with egg yolks and flavoured with sage. This appears to be where the humble sausage is elevated into gastronomy.[39]

Late autumn was the time to make black puddings, which became a delicacy to be eaten on feast days. There could be puddings of porpoise, mixed with oatmeal, seasoning and blood, or of capon's neck where the stuffing was forced into the neck then roasted with the bird. White puddings were also made from pig's liver mixed with cream, egg and white wheaten bread, flavoured with raisins, dates, cloves, mace, sugar and saffron. Marrow bones were another medieval preference: the marrow was scraped from the bones and used in pies, mixed with dried fruit, eggs and cream; marrow was also used to enrich stuffings for poultry and sausages. The Normans also had a great liking for a dish they called Jelly of Flesh, a speciality that we have come to know as aspic jelly.[40] Pig's feet, snout and ears were boiled with calves' feet, capons and rabbits; wine and vinegar were added, then the whole mixture was boiled for hours and left to cool; the fat was then skimmed off and the liquid strained through a fine cloth, it was seasoned and turned gold with saffron. Varieties of cold cuts were then set out on a platter and the rich stock was poured over. It was left to set, then decorated with herbs and painted leaves. Aspic has an erroneous French derivation, but it is undoubtedly a simplification of this Norman speciality, which became so popular in the English medieval kitchen.

How much spice was used in recipes must have been a personal choice partly dictated by economics. The use of dried fruits in many of the meat dishes was universal, but currants, dates, figs, prunes and raisins were fairly cheap, from 1d to 4d per pound. Modest households always had a few pounds as did Alice de Bryene, while nobler establishments kept many hundreds of pounds, in order to feed the hundreds of people each day. Saffron was the most expensive spice, costing 12s to 15s per pound, while cinnamon, cloves, ginger, mace, pepper and sugar cost 1s to 3s per pound. The Duke of Buckingham in 1452-3 got through 2 lb mixed spices every day, though the Bryene household only used half an ounce. With more modest households, the spices tended to be saved up and then used for a special meal, as when Katherine de Norwich celebrated the anniversary of her husband's death on 20 January 1378.[41] The feasts and meals of the nobility were always completed by a final course of fruits, spices and wafers; baked apples and pears with ginger, mace and cloves was a popular dish. Served with this course was Hippocras, a spiced sweet drink that took its name from the apothecary's bag through which it was strained. Spices such as cinnamon, grain of paradise, nutmeg, mace, galingale, cardamom and cloves were mixed with sugar and added to red wine then simmered for a while, strained and served. More spices were served as comfits, sugared almonds and candied aniseed. Sugar candy and rose- and violet-scented sugars were imported; they were considered to be helpful in curing the common cold. Twisted stems of sugar called penidia, to be renamed later as barley sugar, were popular.

Though sugar was expensive it quickly became immensely popular because it was eaten in large quantities at court. A spiced sugar paste was imported from the Mediterranean, called *paste royale*, flavoured with ginger and mace and made more supple by the addition of honey. There was also a spiced almond paste and a spiced quince jelly (*chardequynce*) and all these pastes became the materials for the making of *sotelties*, those astonishing sugar confections of landscapes with castles, figures and animals, presented at great feasts to mark the interval between courses. By the end of the fifteenth century gum tragacanth was introduced, a resin obtained from a shrub growing in the eastern Mediterranean, which helped to bond and strengthen the paste so that even more astonishing sugar sculptures could be created. Bitter oranges, lemons and pomegranates were shipped to England from Spain from the thirteenth century. Pots containing orange or lemon peel, or the whole fruits preserved in sugar syrup, were imported from southern Europe, and called *succade*, while other fruit and vegetable conserves were called wet sucket or sucket candy; though these started out as medicine they were far too delicious to be reserved for the sick, so they came to be eaten at the end of the meal.[42]

Wafers, which were served with the fruit, were made from batter poured onto a hot iron with another iron covering the top, exactly as we now toast sandwiches. They came over with the Normans, and were called *gaufres*; and as we have seen, they were a popular food at the cookshops. One such batter might be made from flour, white of egg, sugar and ginger, another could have egg yolks, cream, flour, salt and cheese. When cooked these were sprinkled with blanch powder and served with the fruit. Another flour paste recipe was lozenges, made from flour, water, sugar and spices, made into a dough then cut in a lozenge pattern and fried in oil; these were served in a wine syrup with added dried fruit and spices.

The use of eggs and dairy produce was also very much a personal choice; one imagines again that the lady of the household might have a preference for curd dishes, fried curd or sweetened egg custard tarts stuffed with dried fruits – called crustades. Liquid milk is only mentioned in relation to a child's diet or when cooked in the kitchen. Cheese in itself seems not to be a major item and one surmises that it was despised as being part of the peasant diet and not for the high table.

There were four types of cheese: hard, made of skimmed milk and stored for a length of time; soft cheese, made from full cream or semi-skimmed milk matured for a time but still retaining moisture; green cheese, which was newly made curd eaten within a few days and a main ingredient for many desserts; and, lastly, there were the full cream milk cheeses, and only these were sent to the lord's table. Hard cheese was frowned upon by the medical opinion of the time. The yield of two cows or twenty ewes was set at a wey (probably a stone) of cheese and half a gallon of whey butter. Cheese-making was confined to the summer months.

The making of cheese was fraught with problems, however. Hard cheese could be white, dry and too salty, or swollen with its own gas or full of whey, or be tough, spotted and full of hairs. The turning of milk and factors like the temperature and humidity of the air were all improperly understood.[43]

The Peasant Diet

We know something of what peasants ate from the maintenance agreements between sons and their fathers, for when the head of the family retired a legal agreement was signed setting out the amounts of food provided to him annually. These agreements were a type of annuity for sometimes the peasant exchanged or sold them. The grants reflect the amount of land held. In 1330 Beatrice atte Lane, for example, was surrendering 24 acres and she was promised sufficient cereal for an ample diet of bread and ale, while in the same village (Langtoft in Lincolnshire) Sara Bateman who had had 4^1/$_2$ acres only had enough cereals for bread, pottage and water. The average amounts, however, provide for a daily allowance of about 1^1/$_2$ lb of bread per day. These would have been augmented by eggs from their own poultry and sides of bacon and ham from their pig, while they still had their garden plots and grew brassicas, leeks, onions and garlic; if they were not too frail they could also snare rabbits and small birds.[44]

Harvest accounts are also another source of information for the peasant diet. In them we see the dramatic improvement in the quality of the diet from the thirteenth compared to that of the fifteenth century. From 1250 for just over a hundred years the bulk of the diet was bread, with meat playing a very small part, and fish, dairy produce and ale remained fairly constant in that time. After the Black Death there was a sudden rise in the amount of meat and ale consumed and a decline in the bread eaten. After 1400 the amount of meat and ale rose still more, while fish and dairy products shrank a little. Peasant workers were now allowed at harvest time 1 lb meat for every 2 lb bread, compared with an ounce or two of meat to 2 lb bread 150 years earlier. What is more, the bread was of much higher quality, made from wheat rather than barley or rye; the meat tended to be fresh beef and mutton rather than bacon, and the fish was fresh and not salt; they drank strong ale, instead of small ale, cider, milk or water.[45]

We can see that the wheat consumption increased in the maintenance agreements, for the amounts of barley and rye dwindled. Peasants began to bake their own bread, eating cereals in this manner rather than boiling oats in pottages; hence more houses now possessed ovens rather than depending upon a communal one; they also now drank more ale which led to the development of permanent ale houses in villages which were licensed by the lord of the manor and because they now ate more meat, butchery began to be a thriving trade with rural butchers opening up. Here suddenly, at the beginning of the fifteenth century is a recognisable English village, with a peasantry becoming more and more independent.

We have no details of what the peasant ate in the fourteenth century when the diet began to improve, but we know from peasant inventories of household goods that meals were a ceremony. The head of the household sat in a chair at one end of the table, while others in the household had a bench or stools; there would have been a linen or canvas table cloth, hands would have been washed beforehand using a metal basin and ewer then dried with a towel. There were cooking utensils of brass pots and pans with tripods, barrels, vats, tubs; all of which indicate an industrious kitchen, cooking more than just pottage and baking bread.

We know too that the basis of peasant cooking was preservation, necessary to get the peasant family through months of real deprivation which occurred annually after Christmas and through into early summer. Some supplies like corn could be stored in barns and bins; the peas and beans could be dried, the pig could be salted and smoked, much of it made into sausages kept hanging near the hearth, onions and garlic could be stringed and hung, and wild foods like fungi dried. Much of their supplies had to be eaten fresh, however, such as the eggs and green leaf vegetables, poultry and game birds. It would be another hundred or so years before the art of potting meat and fish and sealing with clarified butter was to appear, partly because though the peasant diet had improved there was still no surplus. If a surplus existed, as it did with a slightly more prosperous peasant who cultivated thirty acres instead of four, then the surplus had to be sold to pay rent with only a little over to be saved for years of drought or famine.

The rise in the consumption of wheat and the home oven also tells us that wheat was prized for its gluten content (for barley, rye and oats have little gluten and therefore make a flat dense bread) so dough was worked and yeasty bread baked. The oven also made it possible to make flour pastes, wrap food in them and bake meat and fish in sealed packages, and thus the rural pie was born. It also made possible the packed lunch of meat wrapped in pastry as an edible form of travelling food, fit for pilgrims and field workers. The pie, as we have seen, was a staple of the cookshops, but it was now to become a staple of home cooking in all sizes and shapes.

Another staple would be the sausage; with the sheep's stomach as a casing, the mixture was a handy method of using up the bits and pieces of a carcass, the flesh from the pig's ribs and the chopped entrails with generous bits of fat and ample seasoning of herbs, hung up in the heat and smoke of the fire for five days. When the time came to eat them they were boiled or grilled, or even cut up into slices and fried. When the pig was killed black puddings were also a great mainstay of the peasant kitchen and would remain so for the next 600 years. Out of the annual pig killing came such dishes as brawn, souse[46] – the ears, cheeks, snout and trotters all pickled in brine or ale – as well as the puddings, enjoyed as festive food around Christmastide. At the manor house it was the servants who were given the souse. These pieces were pickled until the fat was so soft that a straw could pierce it through; they were then taken from the brine and placed into another pot into a mixture of verjuice and small ale, there the pieces would be left until eaten cold with mustard.

Nothing of the carcass was ever wasted, even the bones, for marrow was much prized. So the bones were used in soup or they were split and the marrow served separately. In the peasant household such bones were only too quickly used.

The Church

Members of the clergy and the monastic orders ate as well as affluent merchants and the minor nobility. The Rules of St Benedict had laid down that monks were to eat two meals per day, dinner and supper, but the second meal should only be allowed from Easter to September and flesh meats were forbidden to all except the sick. This regime was not adhered to, and by the 1150s every form of meat and fowl was eaten, while the second meal of supper was consumed throughout the year.

The monks ate dinner at 11 or 11.30 in the morning; they had been up by then for four to five hours and they had not eaten cooked food since their supper the night before, though most of them would have breakfasted on ale and bread. Dinner began with pottage based on meat or fish depending on whether it was a fast day or not. At Westminster Abbey by 1500, a daily dish of beef had been substituted for the soup, which preceded several other meat dishes, such as boiled mutton, roast pork or fritters, and the meal ended with cheese. The ordinary monk, however, would not partake of the delicate dishes or those that contained pike or small game birds, which were eaten by the abbot and honoured guests. They appeared not to have eaten from bread trenchers, but used pewter plate.

In the years 1495 to 1525 each monk at Westminster cost 7d per day or 4s a week in food and drink. The convent's outlay represented thirty-seven per cent of its income on food and drink, which is a smaller proportion than many of the nobility, yet they lived well.[47] A peasant at this time would have earned about 4d a day, so his standard of living was about half that of an ordinary monk. A bucket cost 6d, a chair 3d and a mattress 1d.

Fish was eaten on average about 215 days in the year. On Fridays there were only two fish dishes but on other fast days there were always three. About half of the fish cooked came from preserved stores, either salted, smoked or dried, the bulk of the fish came from the sea and only a little from the abbey's pond in the infirmary garden or the River Thames itself. The abbey's kitchener went by boat up the river two or three times a week to shop at the fish market; small fish like dace and roach were served often but pike served with a cinnamon and ginger sauce was kept for feast days. The monks had a tithe on all the fish caught in the River Thames from Staines to Gravesend and salmon might well have been eaten frequently, but it is only recorded when bought. A tenth part of such a catch must have been a considerable amount of fish, which economically greatly benefited the abbey and would have been much resented by the Thames fishermen. On about fifteen days out of the year the kitchener served shrimps at dinner but never molluscs, which were thought to be food for the poor, a slur which they were to bear for several hundred more years, and from which whelks and cockles still suffer.

The bulk of the fish came from the cod family. A considerable amount of it was pickled and eaten with green sauce, as were also plaice and whiting; the more fatty fish were also eaten, the favourite being eel, followed by herring and mackerel. Herring tended to be despised and eaten only at Lent with salted eels; conger eel was a delicacy, which appeared on feast days eaten with a sauce of bread, herbs, spices, garlic and vinegar. At the abbot's table they ate turbot, ray, gurnard and sole; gurnards were filleted, fried then pickled in a sweet spiced vinegar, the dish we now know as Escabeche.[48] The earliest Catalan recipe (fourteenth century) for this dish requires nuts, raisins and onions to be added to the sauce. Salmon and conger eel appeared often at the abbot's table and infrequently at the ordinary monks'. The kitchener required 40 lb to 48 lb fish for a dish of stewed eel and 20 lb to 24 lb for a dish of baked eel; these amounts made fifty-two messes; as this was fish, this meant a small mess for one.

A large mess, containing food for four monks, was typical of meat days; meat was eaten seventy-five days of the year for both dinner and supper. Four dishes were eaten at dinner and one of them inevitably was beef while only one would be served at supper. There would be a dish of boiled meat and two of roast, veal, mutton, pork or goose. Boiled mutton would be served every day, killed after four years, the carcass was boiled with bugloss, borage and parsley roots and eaten with mustard. In the course of a year the kitchener provided 600 dishes of meat at dinner and a further 150 at supper, using 136 hundredweight of meat. Barbara Harvey comments: '. . . only an upper-class household could have afforded the sheer quantity of meat placed before the monks. If any proof is needed that Benedictine monks belonged to upper class society, it is found in these proportions.' A mess of beef for four contained about 3 lb, so monks could eat from three or four dishes at dinner and perhaps another at supper; that has been roughly estimated as one monk eating between 2¹/₄ lb and 3 lb meat per day, which is a considerable amount.

Lamb was eaten in spring and early summer, veal throughout the year, poultry appeared at dinner and supper, while on feast days there was swan or cygnet, teal and snipe. Chicken appears to have always been served with mutton as an accompaniment, but if the hens were boiled they were served with a white sauce made from ground almonds, verjuice and ginger. As there were no slaughtering premises in the abbey the meat was bought from local butchers, who could supply various cuts of meat in quantity, so shoulders of mutton might be served to all. Each of the cuts had its own specific method of cooking: chine of pork was boiled, loin and shoulder of mutton roasted. Goose was eaten twice a year in spring and autumn and always roasted. Geese were plucked regularly five times a year to supply quill pens which were in great demand and goosedown for feather beds. As a rich meat it was thought to be indigestible without garlic sauce. Neckam suggested a strong garlic sauce made with wine or verjuice of grapes or crab apples. The winter goose was stuffed with herbs, quinces and pears, garlic and grapes; after roasting this stuffing was removed and combined with wine and spices to make a *sauce madame*, which was poured over the sliced flesh.

Not only did the abbey consume large amounts of meat, but also of animal fat, though much of this was used for tallow in lighting. On 30 October 1459 when 110 were present for supper at Lambeth Palace, use of tallow candles which was usually around 7 lb per day went up to 16 lb; wax was used for ecclesiastical purposes and feast days always were well lit. The Purification or Candlemas was always marked by the purchase of wax candles and offerings to the Virgin. Sometimes these were specially coloured: Eleanor of Castile had hers coloured green and vermilion.[49] The main cooking medium was lard and butter; puddings were made from beef suet, minced veal and dried fruits and boiled in a sheep's stomach container, thoroughly scalded and washed. Principal Pudding was one such, made as a festal dish for a feast; it used 6 lb of currants, 300 eggs, breadcrumbs and 18 lb of suet. These boiled suet puddings were flavoured with mace, nutmeg, cinnamon, ginger, every kind of dried fruit and ground almonds, and sometimes with rosewater, orangeflower water, musk and ambergris to intensify the perfume.

The monks also consumed every day much bread and ale made by themselves, and every monk received an allowance of a gallon of ale per day. Ale was also used in cooking, sheep's entrails were cooked in it for instance, and the dish flavoured with spices and thickened with breadcrumbs. On solemn vigils and feast days the monks drank wine. Their bread was made from wheaten flour baked at the abbey, though the abbot of Westminster ate the finer wastel bread, which was bought in; the name stems from the Norman French *gastel* or cake. The very finest white bread was manchet, which was made in small loaves weighing about 6 oz. Occasionally the monks also ate enriched bread, made with eggs, cream and dried fruit and spices, to celebrate an anniversary.

Both eggs and cheese were eaten regularly; outside Lent the monks ate about five eggs per day. They were very fond of cheese flans made from cream and eggs; they also ate charlet, a milky dish with boiled shredded pork, ginger, sugar and saffron. On fast days charlet could be made with flaked cod or haddock poached in almond milk. Another dish, gravey was ground almonds mixed with broth with diced rabbit, chicken, oysters or eel, flavoured with sugar and ginger; when this pottage was thickened with egg yolks and diced cheeses it was called 'gravey enforced'. This last dish and others like it, civey, bukkenade and egerdouce, count as pottages or sauces (they could be both) that the abbot was sure to have had made for him, but it is likely that other monks on feast days would have benefited from such rich dishes. As we have seen earlier, they had been favourite soups ever since the Normans had brought them over to England. Civey was the thick onion soup with diced hare or mallard, and on fast days it could be made with tench, sole and oysters; it was thickened with breadcrumbs and flavoured with pepper and mixed spices. Bukkenade was the meat broth with veal, kid, chicken or rabbit, seasoned with herbs and spices, thickened with egg yolks and sharpened with verjuice or vinegar. Egerdouce was a sweet-sour broth made from wine and honey in which kid and rabbit were poached; it was eaten cold with pieces of sliced brawn floating on the surface. There were also soups where the broth was strained and clarified so that a clear stock was poured over pieces of meat or fish and the surface would be garnished with spice powder.

The abbey grew its own fruit and vegetables and these were much prized so went to the abbot's table first. In 1510 Abbot John Islip ate quinces, apples and warden pears at the beginning of the year (obviously beautifully stored). He imported oranges three or four times from January to April (could this have been the first import of sweet oranges, which had arrived in the Mediterranean about thirty years before?) and ate homegrown strawberries in June and July. The monks ate fresh peas and beans throughout the short summer season; the dried version they ate throughout the winter in pottages, and the bulk of them would have been fed to pigs. In their gardens at Covent Garden they grew grapes, cabbages, leeks, garlic, herbs and salad leaves.

What is most striking about the abbey's food consumption is how far away it had moved from the original sixth-century strictures of St Benedict's Rules. Fast days were an absurdity, for the fish dishes became small gastronomical masterpieces, as did everything made using almond milk; there were no culinary sacrifices at all made by the clergy. This became obvious to the layman, who after the Black Death became scornful and critical of the ecclesiastical population. Food inequalities and food hypocrisy were particularly galling; few other issues set up such anger and resentment. The seeds for the Reformation had all been sown.

However, English clergy were feeling more and more resentful of the demands of Rome; between 1450 and 1530 Rome demanded a subsidy from the English clergy on twelve occasions, but they responded only twice. In this time the number of monks fell, although as we have seen above their standard of living rose. The Cistercians at Whalley Abbey in Lancashire were spending two-thirds of their income on food and drink, much more than at Westminster.

John Wycliffe began preaching in 1378, urging that the Bible should be translated into English and be placed in the hands of every clerk and layman; he condemned monasticism, advocated the marriage of the clergy, questioned the doctrines of the mass and demanded a dissolution of the Church's corporate wealth. Lollardy[50] was born, the most organised of fourteenth-century protests. It was stamped out as an academic heresy in its birthplace Oxford in 1411. But Wycliffe's ideas had taken root with the Lollards who attracted disciples not only in London but in country districts, in the Chilterns and in Kent; they demanded the disestablishment of the Church and the redistribution of property. This was the time when the legends about Robin Hood are first mentioned, when heroes were upholders of justice seeking not to destroy society but to redress its wrongs. Wycliffe's translation of the Bible into the vernacular was suppressed, but a hundred copies survived.

The Wars of the Roses[51]

A preamble to a 1378 statute described how armed bands were taking possession of houses and manors 'having no consideration of God, nor to the laws of Holy Church, nor of the land, nor to right, nor to justice'. As we know from the Paston letters, the lords behaved as badly as the outlaws; the lords robbed, raped, kidnapped and murdered, getting away with all these crimes if they fought for the King or the Church. Feuding between great magnates loomed larger than peasant protests.[52] The dynastic wars (1455-85) between the houses of York and Lancaster over who was the rightful heir to the crown were less bloody and less disruptive than the thirteenth-century civil war between Stephen and Matilda. Towns were not sacked, nor churches desecrated, battles stopped for harvests to be brought in, the food supply was respected, and trade continued struggling on through war and piracy.

England was now one of the nodal points in European trade where north met south. The Hundred Years War had dominated the politics of western Europe. Armies absorbed manpower and resources and the development of the national state made it possible for rulers to exploit their subjects to a far greater degree than had previously been possible. Taxation was constant and heavy, war interfered with trade and incited piracy. England was now an integral part of the North Sea-eastern Atlantic economy linked to the Mediterranean by sea routes; our main market for wool and cloth was still Flanders and the Low Countries, in return came gold, silver and food products, especially fish. In the south-west of France we sold cloth and grain in exchange for wine from Spain and Portugal.

Wages for both farm workers and urban craftsmen remained high throughout this century; cereal prices were low and steady until a series of bad harvests in the 1480s forced up the price of wheat. So food was plentiful for most of the century, in fact the lawyer and writer Sir John Fortescue (1394-1476) described the commons in England as 'the best fed and best clas of any Natyon crystn or hethen'.[53] Sheep-farming had now become highly profitable; seven years after the Black Death, 40,000 sacks of wool were exported annually. Exports of cloth rose. However this trend from arable to pasture saw the beginning of the enclosure of land that was to have such devastating effect upon the farm labourer in the eighteenth century. This was a fact not lost on people then, who were dismayed and horrified at the destruction of hamlets where all the land once used commonly had been fenced in for sheep-rearing. 'The root of this evil is greed,' a Warwickshire antiquary rightly claimed.[54] The towns that rose to prominence in the fifteenth century, Coventry, Exeter and Southampton, were all cloth towns. The new towns began to have their own problems of overcrowding, noise (iron shod wheels of carts were banned, and there was an injunction not to drive carts too quickly after they were unloaded), smoke pollution, 'the stink and badness of the air' and animals. A citizen's petition of 1444 complained of 'swannes, gees, herons, and ewes and other pultrie whereof the ordure and standing of them is of grate stenche and so evel savour that it causeth grete and parlous inffecting of the people.'[55]

Everyday life went on throughout the Wars of the Roses. A French chronicler recorded: 'England enjoyed this peculiar mercy above all other kingdoms, that neither the country nor the people, nor the houses were wasted, destroyed or demolished; but the calamities and misfortunes of the war fell only upon the soldiers . . .'[56] There were only thirteen weeks of real fighting during the thirty-two years of the war. At St Albans in 1455 when the Duke of York defeated the forces of Henry VI under the Duke of Somerset, he only had 3,000 men under his command, while Somerset's army comprised 2,000. It was nothing but a brief scuffle in the streets.

When peace came at last under Edward IV, who had secretly married a commoner, Elizabeth Woodville, he turned out to be a *bon viveur* who encouraged trade, investing himself in imports and exports. He was the first King not to die in debt for nearly 300 years. His Queen, from the evidence of her journal, was alive to the nuances of good cooking; in 1451 aged fourteen and newly married to her first husband, she writes:

> Six o'clock, breakfasted, the buttock of beef rather too much boiled and the ale a little the stalest. Memorandum: tell the cook about the first fault, and to mend the second myself by tapping a fresh barrel directly. Seven o'clock. Supper at the table, the goose pie too much baked and the loin of pork almost roasted to rags.[57]

In an age when the Church was heavily criticised and sometimes scorned, Edward (like later Tudor monarchs even after the Reformation, as we shall see) was keen to keep the fast days. Not only was it good for men's spirits, 'but that these days,' he said markedly, 'considered the fishers and men using the trade of living by fishing in the sea, may thereby rather be set on work, and that by eating of fish much flesh shall be saved and increased.'[58]

What is extraordinary in this age of conflict and despair is that its architecture was of almost 'castles in the air', of lightness and delicacy, though castles themselves were becoming transformed into houses, having huge windows to let in light, for comfort and pleasure was much valued, while churches became symbols of the spirit soaring towards God: King's College Chapel, Cambridge and Eton College Chapel, Windsor, for instance. We can only imagine what the subtleties spun from sugar must have been like. Yet also within this warring, quarrelsome agitated society there was for the first time a new sense of being English; not only had the cuisine fused together into something recognisably English, but the language and the people had an identity which separated them from the Continent. All the French possessions except Calais had been lost, Henry VI was the last English King to also term himself King of France. A sense of national identity had occurred all over Europe, however; it was a time when writers began to typify nations with characteristics. Erasmus (1466-1536) made Charon say that he did not mind ferrying Spaniards across the Styx because they were abstemious, but the English were so crammed with food that they nearly sank the boat.

The most momentous event which was about to change the world took place in the last decade of the fifteenth century – the discovery of the New World – but did not add much to the English diet in the new century. Yet within that century our diet was to alter dramatically. What combination of factors wrought such huge change?

CHAPTER 5

Tudor Wealth and Domesticity

A new national identity was born in those years from the end of the Hundred Years War to the loss of Calais, when between 1453 and 1558 England, without realising it, became an island separate from Europe. Before England had acted as a province, or a group of provinces within the Anglo-French unit; it was enmeshed in and absorbed by defeats and triumphs in France. Now disentangled from the continent it began to improve its land, reclaim its forests, drain its marshes and fertilise its heaths. Her territory was reduced to manageable proportions, and now she was cultivating it, she would be preparing to become a force in the world market.

Two other elements also contributed to this new role in the world. When the first Tudor, Henry VII, became King in 1485, he found that after the slaughter of the Wars of the Roses there were only remnants left of the old aristocracy. The great families, which had opposed the Tudors – the de la Poles, the Staffords, the Courtenays – had all died out in the struggle. It was now the minor gentry and the bourgeois purchasers of land who stepped into their places. In itself this was not new, but the scale of it changed the nature of the elite. These were people who were practical, and hard-working, who could farm and cultivate land; by 1540 a new aristocracy had become established and they were further to be enriched. This was another major difference with France, its own aristocracy and its influence upon food, which was to affect the specific nature of each cuisine. Because in England an aristocrat was defined by the amount of land he owned with a permeable boundary between him and what would later be known as the gentry, the aristocracy was far more open than in France. Middle and upper classes could merge under the unifying power of money. How this was to affect food we shall see in Chapter 8.

The other key element that was to distinguish England, and which did not occur in the rest of Europe, was the break with Rome in the years 1529-33. The Reformation spoke the language of nationalism: the King became head of the Anglican Church, and so in his own country was Pope. Church and State were one. The confiscation and sale of Church lands, properties and rare works of art were to give a huge boost to the English economy and enrich the aristocracy and middle classes. Their effect on our diet, not hitherto taken into account by historians, was also radical.

The Reformation was a deep divergence within European society; it set the new Protestants firmly outside Papist unity in an unfathomable way; it occurred because of the deep-set anger and resentment against the Church within the people. The monarch's desire for an heir merely triggered the explosion. The Reformation, however, was only one of the changes that affected the diet in the century of the Tudors. There was a huge rise in population, and with it a rise in literacy, because of the new invention of printing, which enabled books to be published in the vernacular (cookery books were among the first books published). There was a rise in inflation. Food prices generally rose about 120 per cent between 1541 and 1641 – wages did not.

There was also a blurring of social class: in the reign of Henry VIII loyalty to the crown was rewarded with deeds of land, and feudal and monastic rights were given to a rising middle class. This comprised hard-working, commercially-minded people who married their children off to indigents of noble birth; the Heralds' Office made a lucrative business of discovering forgotten pedigrees and armorial bearings in old registers. Nevertheless, this was still a fiercely hierarchical society, for the more mobile a society is the more acutely conscious it becomes of social mores that denote status. Thomas Nashe, poet, pamphleteer and dramatist, wrote: 'In London the rich disdain the poor, the courtier the citizen, the citizen the countryman, the merchant the retailer, the retailer the craftsman . . .' The distinctions, as always, were seen in the diet. William Harrison, the clergyman and topographer whose *Description of England* was published in 1577, pointed out that the gentility ate wheaten bread while 'their household and poor neighbours rye or barley bread, and in time of dearth bread made of beans, peas or oats'. Nothing much had changed here then from the few hundred years before.

As the power of the middle classes grew, a display of wealth could be exhibited in a range of manners, not just in food and clothes where it had been largely kept in the previous 500 years. It was an age of social aspiration where the emulation of foods eaten by the elite could be pursued, but this food was adapted to their own particular needs. This was also an age of exploration where long sea voyages demanded new ways of preserving all manner of foods. As a sense of nationhood began to creep into the awareness of the individual countries of Europe, we first gained an instinctual Englishness which found its expression in our food. Together, these factors caused a swing away from court food to domestic dishes, away from complication, which required a large labour force and much time expended, to a simpler response to the country produce gathered. This was a century when we can clearly recognise our own cooking, our own food, our own traditional dishes, ways and methods in the recipes that have come down to us.

Reformation

What happened to the fast day when England broke from the Catholic Church? If fasting for two-thirds of the year no longer became habitual, as a sign of personal devotion to God instigated and approved by that holy institution, the Roman Church, then fish consumption would surely decline? If nothing else, one would expect those gourmet dishes made with almond milk and fish would now fade away as there was no reason for their continued creation and consumption. So the Reformation should have made a huge difference to our national cuisine; it should have radically altered it, so that we might have lost a whole range of remarkable dishes forever. In fact, many of them were being cooked in France and some would return 150 years later under a French name,[1] while others were secretly kept alive (as if they possessed an element of now being a precious votive offering) within noble Catholic families, to reappear 100 years later in the pages of Robert May's book, *The Accomplisht Cook*, published in 1660.

In 1530 Henry VIII accused all the clergy of *praemunire*; he had charged Cardinal Wolsey with the same crime the year before, meaning that Wolsey had been exerting unlawful jurisdiction over the people. Wolsey died, however, before he could be tried and executed. The clergy, after they had paid a huge fine and recognised the King as the supreme head of the Church of England, were pardoned after two months. The churches and monasteries then endured a period of barbaric destruction: every wall-painting was defaced or painted over, every sculpture broken, walls were white-washed and adorned only with biblical text, the altar, now a wooden table, was moved down into the body of the church, and the priest wore no rich vestments but a plain surplice. Anyone criticising the King's actions was executed, and Carthusian monks were tortured, hanged, drawn and quartered. All this barbaric zeal was based, of course, not upon religious devotions but on human greed. What we lost aesthetically was a great tragedy, for relics and images, which were the centre of pilgrimages, were melted down or transported to the royal palaces in London, and the shrines of the saints were levelled to the ground. The dissolution of the monasteries was carried out in two operations: it began in 1536 with 374 houses with an annual income of less than £200,000, and continued in 1538–40 with the 186 'great and solemn monasteries'. Royal power was now immense for all the riches of the church were being transferred to the crown and it needed a new agency, the Court of Augmentation, to deal with all the new assets.

Ironically enough, the crown did not keep all its new wealth. By the end of Henry's reign two-thirds had been sold off to peerage and gentry; two out of every three peers were either granted or purchased monastic estates. In Yorkshire, for example, over a quarter of the gentry of 1642 owned property that before 1540 had been held by monasteries. Naves speedily became farmhouses, chantries became parlours and towers became kitchens; a Gloucester clothier, Thomas Bell, turned a Dominican priory into a factory, while a furnace and forge were set up on the site of a Sussex monastery at Robertsbridge.[2]

How did all this affect our cuisine? The middle classes were growing, because the enrichment at the top of society (all stolen from the immense riches of the Church) was filtering downwards. Cooking became more domesticated, the woman of the household being the centre of an economic unit that controlled the produce of the farmstead, resulting in a range of food and medicinal products.

These huge changes were noted by everyone; a Venetian observer described it as 'the greatest alteration that could possibly arise in the nation because a revolution in customs, laws, obedience and lastly, in the very nature of the state itself, necessarily follows'. The fact that they were carried out so quickly was because a ground-swell of anti-clericalism had empowered them, a feeling the clergy were well aware of, the fear of which hastened their own willingness to accept the changes.

Saints' days structure the liturgical year, designating when the faithful should feast, fast and toil. In 1534 Parliament lifted the medieval heresy laws and put in place an Act for the Advancement of True Religion, while fasting and holy days were to be specified in the new prayer book. The first English Prayer Book in 1549 dispensed with all the non-scriptural saints, leaving a bare skeleton of holy days, Christmas, Easter, Whitsun, the feast days of the Apostles, the evangelists, John the Baptist, Mary Magdalene and the Virgin Mary. Saints were no longer the intermediaries between the believer and God; instead believers were encouraged to emulate their devotion. It was not until 1563, however, that John Foxe's *Book of Martyrs* appeared, which erased all the old Catholic saints and replaced them with Protestant ones; its intention was to reform the new Church of England and purge the reformed churches of any lingering Roman presence. Foxe's book was based on the twenty or so fixed festivals of the Church year; these ancient festivals were preserved including the feasts of the Apostles and the early martyrs as well as the days connected with the great high points of the year. Protestant martyrs superseded the numerous Catholic saints with their year of death and an account of their suffering, like Bishop's Hooper, Ridley and Latimer, Bishops Farrar of Saint David's and Archbishop Cranmer; Lollards and Wycliffe were given prominence in the beginning of the year. Some 60 new saints' days, including those of Augustine of Canterbury and Saxon saints Etheldreda, Edmund and Edward, were scattered throughout the year. What did all these strange names mean to the people who since childhood had put aside certain days and made certain dishes for other saints who were suddenly banished? What happened to fasting in itself?

The Protestants took over the idea of fasting but made it spartan when it had been sensual. Though Catholicism condemned luxury as a personal sin of pride, we know that both the Church and royalty celebrated it as a means to social self-assertion. But Protestantism was more concerned with the consequences that were attributed to this vice, namely with immorality and dissoluteness. Days of fasting became popular, where people met to pray and listen to sermons 'humbly waiting on grace'; living off bread and water for two or three days was thought to engender the gift of prophesying. The old abbots of Westminster, sitting down on a fast day to dishes of pike poached in wine with a herb and garlic sauce thickened with almonds, would have been most put out at this revolutionary change, yet this is where the connection between Puritanism and bleak and tasteless food began. In 1536 a royal proclamation decreed the reduction of fast days and the observance of feast days in honour of the saints was subjected to official attack. Two Cornish fishermen in the spring of 1537 commissioned a local painter to produce a banner with Henry VIII and his Queen together with Christ, Our Lady and St John, but the painter reported them for this Papist image, and they were both hanged in chains at Helston.

The situation became very muddled, and changed with whoever was on the throne: a Martin Marprelate tract of 1588 states that the new bishops were not to forbid public fasts, for they were popular expressions of faith. The wily and most intelligent of Queens, Elizabeth, obviously did not trust the effect of rigorous fasts, making a pronouncement in 1581 that no public fast could be appointed except by her. She explained that she 'liked well of fasting, prayers and sermons' but she objected to the way they were done, 'tending to innovation . . . intruding upon her Highness's authority ecclesiastical'.[3] Whether this stopped the practice is debatable for Richard Rogers, a minister, wrote in his diary on 22 December 1587: 'We fasted betwixt of selve ministers to the stirringe upp of ourselves to greater godliness . . .' Fasting was of even greater value to the Puritans, though they were very insistent that it was not the superstitious fasting of the Papist.

It was of course the women who determined whether their household fasted or feasted, for it was they who saw the religious significance of food, women who were nursing mothers and had a devotion to the eucharist, women who observed their own bodies lactating or not and the miracle of nurturing the newborn. It was up to the women to observe the new saints or not and there were many accounts of women rebelling in Tudor and Stuart times, even to extremes. Dorothy Hazzard, as a Puritan, refused to acknowledge Christmas as a special day; instead she sat sewing in the door of her grocer's shop in the High Street in Bristol in the late 1630s, keeping her shop open as a witness to God. Lady Elizabeth Brooke refused to keep the fasts or thanksgivings of the usurpers in the 1650s.[4] A rich diet was linked with the stimulation of the flesh, rich food gave one lascivious thoughts, so self-denial was an option for all women who ran a household, since they controlled the purchase, preparation and cooking of the food. For a wealthy woman piety was shown by the choice of a simple and frugal diet. Margaret Clitheroe, wife of a prosperous citizen of York, tried to avoid accompanying her husband to banquets and when she was a carver, she took the worst piece of meat for herself. Katherine Stubbs 'ate sparingly refusing to pamper her bodie with delicate meats, wines or stronge drinke, but refrained from them altogether'.[5] Dorothy Traske ate only vegetables and water. When women were tempted it was by the devil who offered them food.

The opposing view was that all fasts were vain and popish. Philip Gammon in 1535 denounced them as 'nothing in value for the health of man's soul'.[6] Popular confidence in the future of Catholic practices was undermined by the spectacle of gentlemen demolishing crosses or seizing ritual apparatus, as was done at Exeter by Sir Roger Bluett, or encouraging the break of Lenten fasts as did Mr Charles of Tavistock. Poverty goes some way to explain the decline of support in Catholic devotion; it was also a strong motive for theft from churches, which were a rich treasury of all manner of silver, gold, precious stones and ornate plate which could be stolen and melted down. Poverty also led to strong resistance to financial demands from priests. When brought before the Mayor of Exeter for violating Lenten fast in 1556, an inhabitant of the city confessed that his poverty had compelled him to make a soup from forbidden scraps of bacon. The Mayor dismissed the case.[7]

For hundreds of years before the Reformation the monks had kept large herb gardens containing a great variety of herbs and medicinal plants, the inheritance of the huge range that the Anglo–Saxon herbalists had grown. From these plants the monks had made cordials, salves, syrups and medicinal waters, which they sold on. Many of these had been used in cooking; rose water, for instance, once introduced in the early medieval period from the Arabs, began to be made here, becoming one of the most popular and fragrant of essences; it was used to flavour soft cheeses and many different desserts. The monks had also made cough syrups and fruit and herb syrups for every imaginable ailment. Now, with the dissolution of the monasteries, this source of wisdom and healing was wiped out within a few months. Realising the loss to a local community of such specialised knowledge with its cache of prophylactics, the wives of the local squire and landowner now stepped into this role, studying and adding to their knowledge. Stillrooms quickly became part of the architecture in the new houses that were built, for confectionery also used many of the flavourings and the techniques. The wife or housekeeper chose which medicinal water would be made and the housekeeper supervised the distilling of it, though no doubt a manservant looked after the furnace. Citrus peels and angelica stalks, for example, had to be very slowly boiled for wet sucket and sucket candy (see pages 91), and the furnace room became a useful place for drying out sticky sugar confections and a store place for the 'banquetting stuffe' which would become a separate course and feature in this century.

Many changes tend to happen slowly over several decades yet the decline in popular Catholicism was rapid; even in the favourable conditions in Mary's reign from 1553-8 its recovery was no more than partial. It was as if the great resentment towards the Church that began at the beginning of the famine years in the fourteenth century now reached its full expression. Early in Queen Elizabeth's reign laws were passed that none of the Queen's subjects was allowed to eat meat during Lent or on Fridays. The law's expressly stated object was to maintain seafaring and to revive decayed coastal towns – essential for the preservation and expansion of the navy. Even contemporary writers felt the need to encourage fish-eating; Andrew Boorde in his *Compendyous Regyment or a Dyetary of Helth* (1562) claims: 'Of all nacyons and countres, England is best served of Fysshe, not onely of al matter of see-fysshe, but also of fresh water fysshe and of all manner of sortes of salte-fysshe.'

Hence, it was purely the secular demands of possessing a flourishing navy which induced parliament to enforce that fasting in Lent be retained, that meat be given up within this time and fish eaten twice daily. During this change from devotional practice to pragmatic observance the subtleties in the use of almond milk were lost; the dairy cow became supreme, and her butter, cream and cheese were to become an integral part of British cookery from then on.

In reaction against the Papist associations of fancy fast day cooking came a new emphasis on meat, and on mutton, beef and venison in particular. There was a new national pride in their carcass beauty, so that there seemed to be a particular Englishness about eating great haunches of well roasted meat, cooked in the simplest fashion – as if boiled and then well-judged roasting could be wrought without notable kitchen skills. Nevertheless, the distinctions were there, so that made-up dishes, those same dishes eaten for hundreds of years, now began to have French associations – fancy cooking – where sauces could hide inferior ingredients and so deceive the diner.

Meat, cooked separately from its sauce was somehow more truthful, more upright and worthy and undeniably English.

Royal Proclamations

Tudor monarchs governed by proclamation; food and its supply especially to the major urban centres like London were a considerable anxiety, which these laws attempted to control. An early definition of the proclamation was given by John Rastell in 1629, who claimed: 'It was not just a notice publicly given of anything whereof the monarch thinks it good to advertise his subjects.'[8] They were statutes, some stemming from personal royal interference, but others responding to a crisis, and had been passed under the great seal, made by the advice and consent of the Council. Imagine the scene:

> The Sheriffs and other officials of London, mounted on horseback and dazzling in their robes and insignia of office, waited with their retinues just within the City, watching the procession move toward them from the west. When it had arrived, the heralds detached themselves from the entourage with which they had moved throughout Middlesex from the palace at Westminster, and joined the Londoners waiting just within the Temple Bar. The new procession wound its way through the city streets, stopping now at the end of Chancery Lane near Fleet Street, again at the great cross in Cheapside, moving on to Leadenhall and then finally to St Magnus's corner. At each place, after the sounds of the trumpets' blast and the criers' oyez had died away, her heralds with great solemnity proclaimed the words of the Queen's proclamation. Soon the same words would be repeated at market crosses, in front of guildhalls, and at other customary places throughout the realm, solemnized in the traditional way by the officials in the respective areas.[9]

There were in all 437 proclamations issued in the 68-year period during which the three Tudor kings reigned. The first stage in a proclamation was detecting a need, which could come about as a result of information received by the King and council, or from a petition. A significant number of proclamations originated in petitions from the Mayor and aldermen of London, some of them related to the vital question of the food supply to London; other proclamations on placing restraints on food exports were a response to grain shortages and the high price of food in England. On 17 April 1548 the Court of Aldermen agreed that the Mayor, on his next visit to the King's council, would ask 'for the staying of butter, cheese and tallow here within the realm'. It worked immediately, for on 24 April a proclamation imposed a restraint. Food shortages continued, for in the same year on 18 September a messenger from the Court of Aldermen was commissioned to ride to the Lord Chancellor 'desiring his lordship in my lord mayor's name and my masters', the aldermen, to intercede with Thomas Somerset, lord high admiral of England, 'that a restraint may be had with expedition by proclamation'. Eight days later a proclamation forbade unlicensed export of victuals.

Many of the price controls on meat in the 1530s can be traced to the needs of London. A royal proclamation reaffirmed the authority of the mayor and aldermen to set prices on fish and to regulate fishing in the Thames. The hoarding of grain brought forth royal proclamations as it caused shortages and drove up prices. In 1532 there was a grain shortage in East Anglia and justices of the peace were ordered to search for grain and command that it be brought to market. In the following year the treasurer of Berwick, George Lawson, specifically recommended 'a proclamation be made throughout the country to thresh out their corn reasonably and at a reasonable price there would be enough and sufficient'. In 1533 Thomas Cromwell, chancellor of the Exchequer, became aware that high grain prices had caused a dearth and that people with plenty were buying grain; a proclamation ordered that no one was to buy wheat or rye for resale except for the supply of London, or for baking bread and the provision of the fleet. Those with sufficient grain for seed and their household could not buy more. A proclamation two years earlier had made it a crime to export grain without a licence. This was still not effective, for in 1534 punishments were ordered for grain hoarders and a proclamation set fines and penalties.

A proclamation on feast and fast days on 22 July 1541 was directly ordered by the King, and on 8 July 1546 he took a personal interest in the proclamation prohibiting heretical books, for the month before he had written to Mary of Hungary complaining that books written by 'heretical and wicked men both in Latin and English are sent over'. The proclamation prohibited the import of any religious books printed abroad without special licence by the King.

One of the most detailed proclamations on food and the only surviving one that attempts to regulate its consumption was that of 31 May 1517, which set regulations on the number of courses that could be eaten at meals and the type of food they contained. A cardinal may have nine dishes served at one meal; a duke, archbishop, marquis, earl or bishop could have seven; lords 'under the degree of an earl', mayors of the city of London, knights of the garter and abbots could have six; and so on down until those with an income of between £40 and £100 a year could have three dishes. As a dish meant one swan, bustard, peacock or 'fowls of like greatness', or four plovers, partridge, woodcock or similar birds (except in the case of the cardinal, who was allowed six), eight quail, dotterels and twelve very small birds such as larks, they were hardly limited in their choice. Anyone who disobeyed was to be 'taken as a man of even order contemptuously disobeying the direction of the King's highness and his council' and was 'to be sent for to be corrected and punished at the King's pleasure to the example of other'. This statute was made thirteen years before the Reformation and one can see clearly how cardinals are favoured; it is all about status and the display of wealth. It was now becoming possible for individuals to rise in the world, and if you had money you flaunted it. Sumptuary laws attempted to keep control of the social hierarchy, and the wealthy were supposed to limit their spending to about ten per cent of the value of their property.

A statute authorised Henry VIII in 1543 to use royal proclamations to fix retail and wholesale prices, so that price-fixing could be flexible to economic pressures. In the Middle Ages local government set price controls, but Tudor legislation under Cardinal Wolsey began to control first of all poultry prices in London; and by 1529 the price of veal, beef and mutton were set by direct orders of the King's council. This set specific prices per pound and ordered butchers to be bound in recognizances to sell meat by weight. The butchers were furious saying that the graziers charged too much for the livestock and they could not earn enough profit. So the graziers were ordered to sell 'after such reasonable prices as the butchers may reasonably accomplish'. Graziers who did not obey were threatened with the King's 'indignation and displeasure and to suffer punishment for the same at his will'. A circular letter was sent to the justices of the peace instructing them how to enforce such a proclamation. However, the graziers were no more compliant than the butchers had been, so the justices were authorised to seize 'beefs, muttons and veals' and to sell them 'according to the rate of the statute'. In the following year, 1534, another proclamation denounced butchers and graziers and named fines for their offences. Local officials were commanded to see that offenders went to prison. The butchers were not to be controlled, however, for they went on complaining that they could not make a living under the statutory prices until 1542 when Parliament repealed the statutes.

In the summer of 1550 the young King, Edward VI, son of Henry, was beset with the problem of grave food shortages caused by bad harvests. All food exports were banned except to Calais, England's last French possession (soon in the next reign to be lost), all the ships and goods would be forfeited, the buying of grain for resale was to be forbidden, except to bakers, brewers and innkeepers, farmers were compelled to come to market bringing their surplus, and those who refused would be fined. Fines were set at 13s 4d for every bushel of grain retained and 2s for every pound of butter and cheese. Farmers complained that the prices set for the produce were too low: 'The great number of such as have the greatest quantity of grains, butter and cheese in their hands . . . do refuse to bring their corn, butter and cheese to the market in such sort as has been commanded.'

In Mary's reign of five years there were sixty-four proclamations covering seventy-four topics; in Elizabeth's much longer reign there were 382 proclamations covering 395 topics. Half of these dealt with fishing and Lent, wine, and grain; over forty-five years, this makes nearly 200 pronouncements that were attempts at adjustments to the food supply. Elizabeth was keen to bolster the fishing industry by making sure that people consumed fish in Lent and on fast days, because her fleet partly depended on the availability of the fishermen and their craft. She built upon a law of Edward VI that forbade eating flesh during Lent by creating new offences for butchers, innkeepers and other victuallers who made meat available at such times. However, though these new laws must have stimulated fish consumption any Papist connection would have been considered heretical nor, of course, was there any attempt to revive the fish dishes of the past with the use of almond milk or almond butter.

Sumptuary Laws were unenforceable, however, and royal proclamations faded away as Stuart monarchs were vilified and parliament alienated or placed in abeyance. In the sixteenth and seventeenth centuries nothing could stop the gentry from flaunting their riches in food and clothing. Sir Thomas Tresham engaged himself in a series of elaborate building projects which increased his burgeoning debts, but he claimed that his Rothwell Market House was a statement of his concern for the good governance of the country, no doubt his lavish entertaining was too. They, of course, had the common design of emphasising his wealth and social standing. Expenses could also be generated within his establishments by prodigal housekeeping. Tresham maintained a large entourage of 'gentlemen servitors' at Rushton and gloried in the hospitality that he regarded as an essential family tradition. Lavish entertainment was provided for friends and neighbours, and for their followers 'to the number of twenty, forty, yea sometimes an hundred'. Frescheville Holles, though he received only a 'narrow' allowance during his father's lifetime, insisted that he must 'live according to his quality', a determination that resulted in a heavy burden of debt. Hospitality was a major aspect of this expensive concern for an appropriate lifestyle: Holles would 'never set down to meales unless he had some of his friends or neighbours with him, and in case they came not he would send for them.'[10]

Tudor Farming

This was a time of population increase where towns were obliged to seek more food from the countryside, but every village too found itself supporting a larger number of families. Land had to grow more and pasture had to be improved to support more livestock. There was a general move towards cows' milk away from ewe and goats' milk, though these animals in the uplands of the north and especially in Wales and Scotland still thrived and their milk was used to make huge, hard sharp-flavoured cheeses.

Contemporary writings on husbandry are full of exhortations to improve the yield, so with economy and ingenuity everything was used in the battle to wrest food from the land; a new interest in the wild began, in wild foods, flowers, herbs, insects, weeds, all used to improve the health of both human and beast. Animals were cured with mugwort, rue, rosemary, savory, bloodwort among much else. When harvests were inadequate, the hungry mixed beechmast and chestnuts into their bread flour; when they were without ale they distilled liquors from gorse flowers, aniseed, fennel and caraway. Every hedge should be planted with fruit trees, hemp could be grown on scraps of weed infested land, willows could do well on marshy land.

J. Norden in *The Surveyor's Dialogue* claimed that there was no kind of soil, 'be it ever so wild, boggy, clay or sandy, but will not yield one kind of beneficial fruit or another'. Farming has always been a conservative business, however, and farmers did not always want to learn new ways. Norden was obviously peeved: 'We have indeed a kind of plodding course of husbandry hereabouts,' he wrote. The land was still distributed largely in bits and pieces on the medieval system and a neighbour's land covered in molehills and weeds did not encourage the others. There were many complaints about bad farming by people who exhausted their land and skimped ploughing. Village bye-laws were needed to maintain minimum standards of husbandry. It was commonly believed that all land had once been forest and that only by the efforts of the farmer had pasture and corn land been cleared, so the arable farmer was always thought superior to the pasture farmer.[11]

The commonest arable crops were still wheat, rye, barley, oats, beans and peas with the addition of a little buckwheat, vetches and lentils. Two species of wheat were grown, rivet or cone wheat (*Triticum turgidum*) which produces a mealy flour suitable for biscuits and bread wheat (*Triticum vulgare*) which yields a strong flour, suitable for bread-making. The domestic variety of bean was grown in gardens only; the small horse bean sown in February liked stiff clay soils and grew in the north and the midlands; it was used to fatten pigs, to feed pigeons, horses and sheep and in lean years to be added to bread. Lentils were considered the best pulse for feeding calves and pigeons, and were grown in south Lancashire and Oxfordshire. Buckwheat liked sandy soil and was used for fattening poultry and pigs and in years of famine it was mixed with barley to make bread: 'a very hearty and well relished bread'. It helped to promote the poultry business in Norfolk and Suffolk where the largest acreages of buckwheat were grown on the sands and brecks where hundreds of turkeys, geese, chickens and ducks were fattened for the table.

People were on the look-out for new crop varieties: Barnaby Googe, a Lincolnshire squire, saw rape or coleseed growing in the principality of Cleves and recognised it as indigenous to our own seashore; he publicised it in print in *The Four Bookes of Husbandry* in 1577 commending it as a green manure, as sheep fodder and as a source of oil. It took until the 1590s for rape to be grown on a large scale, enough for it to be exported from East Anglia. As rape is more productive of oil than either linseed or hempseed and as at that time we were searching for ways to reduce the imports of foreign oils, Barnaby Googe deserved a knighthood. However, the cultivation of rape may not have been due to him as it is likely that the seed was introduced into East Anglia by refugees fleeing from Spanish oppression.

Other crops urged upon the enterprising farmer were weld or dyer's weed which produced a yellow dye grown on the chalklands of Kent around Canterbury; and woad, which grew wild in various parts of England, was grown in Somerset and Surrey, and used to dye wool; or madder for red dye. That crop took three years to reach perfection, so it became popular in gardens grown for the apothecary. Saffron was used as a dye as well as a condiment; it was planted in midsummer and was ready to crop the following autumn. It was said to prepare the ground for excellent harvests of barley. Tobacco was first cultivated in England in 1571; as it was so profitable it spread from the countries around London to Lincolnshire, Yorkshire and even the Channel Islands.

Hops were introduced around 1530 and grown in Suffolk, Kent, Surrey and Essex. They had been dismissed earlier as a pernicious weed but now they became a staple ingredient of beer. This was criticised by traditionalists: 'Hops, Reformation, Beys[12] and Beer/Came to England in one bad year.' Caraway was grown in Oxfordshire, mustard in the Norfolk fens, onions in the Lincolnshire fens, liquorice at Worksop, carrots in east Suffolk and at Colchester in Essex. The demands of London made

Fulham a centre for market gardening where salad leaves, fruits, peas and beans and root vegetables like carrots, parsnips and turnips were grown. Vegetables from the New World were treated with suspicion; as both the tomato and the potato were relatives of deadly nightshade they were thought to be poisonous. Sweet potatoes were grown in the summer and recipes for them were written down by the end of the century.[13]

In the cattle-breeding areas of the north and west, calves were given a good start by being left to run with the cows all the year. In dairying areas they were weaned at between two and eight weeks and the milk sent to the dairies throughout the summer and autumn for making into butter and cheese. In Essex and Hertfordshire calves were fattened for the butcher as there was a demand for veal in London, but elsewhere it was years before beef was ready for the butcher. They were sent to fattening areas in the Midlands, the counties near to London and East Anglia between August and October and fattened for sale throughout the winter. Barren cows and oxen were used for draught until they were about ten years old, then fattened on hay, vetches, peas, boiled barley or beans and sold to the butcher.

England had a high reputation for great carcass meat and writers of husbandry considered that this was because of its three principal breeds. The long-horned cattle bred in Yorkshire, Derbyshire, Lancashire and Staffordshire, had black square bodies, short legs and large white horns. They were prized for tallow, hide and horn, they gave a good quantity of milk and were strong in labour. Then there were the Lincolnshire cattle of the fens and marshes, which were tall with large pied bodies with small crooked horns, strong for labour-giving good meat. Lastly there were the red Somerset and Gloucestershire cattle with tall, large bodies that made excellent milkers. Also, there were 100,000 Irish cattle imported into England every year, as well as Frisian cattle which came into Cumberland around 1590.

English pride centred upon its mutton, however, and the most prized livestock of all was sheep. 'Sheep in my opinion is the most profitablest cattle that a man can have,' wrote Master Fitzherbert in *The Book of Husbandry* and this belief showed in the care taken of them. In southern England they were regarded as tender animals unable to endure the cold so they were housed in stables in the winter. The lambs were born in April when the pasture was ready for them, and they were weaned from 16-18 weeks, for meat from suckled lambs was regarded as superior to meat from grass lambs. The sheep were shorn about mid-June, then culled at Michaelmas. The regular and wholesale slaughter of all animals at this time had now almost stopped; only the fat animals were killed off, leaving the rest to be overwintered on grass, hay, straw, chaff, peas, mashes of barley, beans and acorn. Great fortunes were made out of sheep-farming: Sir Henry Poole, Elinor Fettiplace's father, owned rich sheep-farming land around Cirencester in the Cotswolds. Both the Spencers of Althorp and the Russells of Woburn built up their estates and wealth on sheep-farming.

Horses were reared in great numbers in all the forests of England, the packhorse was needed for cross country transport and the cart-horse for labour in the fields. But horses were imported also from abroad for saddle and coach; Gervase Markham recommended that for the saddle an English mare be bred with a Turk or Irish

Hobbie. One of the peasant's standbys was pig-keeping; pigs were thought to be 'the husbandmen's best scavenger, the housewife's most wholesome sink'. The brined, butchered carcasses were hung from the rafters and smoked, keeping a family in meat throughout the winter. It was only the better off peasant, however, who had enough kitchen waste to feed a pig and could afford to keep it. Dairymen kept pigs as they could be fed on the whey; in the forests the pigs were fattened on acorns, beechmast, crab apples, medlars and hazelnuts.

Poultry was also kept by peasants; nearly everyone had a few hens and sometimes ducks, while those that had generous common rights also kept geese. They earned something from the sale of feathers and grease as well as the meat. Turkeys were introduced into Europe from Mexico after 1510, and by the end of the century there were considerable numbers in Norfolk; buckwheat was grown in East Anglia for feeding them, and carrots and turnips were also used. Turkeys were also fed on sodden barley and oats; chickens gorged on wheatmeal and milk for 14 days. Capons were crammed with corn and peas, penned in cages so that they could hardly move and fed on barley malt.

Orchards began to increase in number throughout the century; great emphasis was placed on fruit growing as a profitable industry and was given royal encouragement. Cherries became hugely popular: 600 cherry trees at 6d a hundred were ordered for the great orchard at Hampton Court. Henry VIII's gardener, Richard Harris, was one of the first to import French grafts of cherry, pear and apple, 'the sweet cherry, the temperate Pipyn and the golden Renate'; and among apples 'especially pippins, before which time there were no pippins in England'. The anonymous writer added in 1609 that Harris's orchard at Teynham in Kent was 'the chief mother of all other orchards for those kinds of fruit in Kent and divers other places'. Another of the King's gardeners, Wolf, introduced the apricot around 1524 while gooseberries had been planted in the royal gardens in 1509. This is thought to be a reintroduction of the berry earlier introduced in the reign of Edward I, but then lost with other plants in the social unrest of the next few hundred years. (The wild gooseberry grew all over Britain.) Gooseberry growing now became popular, though it was called different names in different parts of the country.[14] Thomas Tusser in his *Five Hundreth Pointes of Good Husbandrie* in 1573 refers to it as the 'Gooseberry'; it is thought it got that name because it quickly became popular to make it into a sauce with goose. As our vines had all disappeared there would have been a lack of verjuice for those favourite sharp sauces, so the sour fruitiness of the gooseberry must have been welcomed.[15] Fruit-growing spread from the Canterbury area of Kent to other districts on the edge of the Weald.

The creation and maintenance of great gardens as part of the estate depleted many a fortune. Throughout Elizabeth's reign ambitious courtiers spent vast amounts on their houses and gardens hoping that the Queen might visit. A foreign traveller, Paul Hentzer, marvelled at the great variety of trees and labyrinths in Lord Burghley's garden who was advised by John Gerard, author of the *Herball* (1597), and employed forty gardeners at a total wage of £10 a week. Burghley had four gardens at Theobalds:

the great garden, the old and new privy gardens, and the cook's garden for produce. Every gentleman's house had not only its kitchen garden, but its formal garden of flowers and shrubs 'for delectation sake unto the eye and their odoriferous savours unto the nose'. Here, exotics from America, the Canaries and other outlandish parts 'do begin to wax so well acquainted without soils', says Harrison, 'that we may almost account them as part of our commodities'.

Among the new varieties introduced to the Elizabethan garden were larkspur and laburnum, Christmas roses, passion flowers and orange blossom. Home-grown melons, cucumbers, radishes, carrots, turnips, pumpkins, parsnips and cabbages appeared; as well as apples, pears and cherries, orchards were producing apricots, peaches, almonds and figs, even oranges, lemons and capers.[16] At Robert Cecil's garden at Hatfield there was a separate rose garden, a vineyard, a knot garden and a maze.

Red beetroot with its sweet root was introduced from Italy in the 1580s. Salsify or tragopogon grew plentifully in the fields about London, Islington and Putney. Artichokes were eaten raw with pepper and salt or boiled, while asparagus was eaten boiled with salt, oil and vinegar. Kidney beans from the New World, so called because of their shape and thought efficacious for that organ, were mentioned in the 1550s but not grown here. They were welcomed in France, however, where they were called haricot beans; we knew them later as French beans when they were still green. Romane or garden peas, lentils and lupin seeds were all eaten and Tusser gives Roncivall or Runcivall peas as a delicacy, which were large marrowfat peas. Chervil, young sow thistle, corn salad, leaves of clary and spotted cowslip were all used in salads with varieties of lettuce, purslane, tarragon, cress, succory, endive, root of rampion which was boiled, flowers of borage, radishes and onions imported from Flanders. Chives were thought to make one thin and to engender 'hot and gross vapours' as well as being 'hurtful to the eyes and brain' and to cause troublesome dreams.

Throughout the century more acreage came under the plough, and heavy manuring of land points to greater numbers of livestock. There was an improved supply of spring grazing through the management and watering of meadows and the reclamation of coastal marshland and fen. The population of England by the end of Elizabeth's reign in 1603 reached around four million. With the rise in population the agricultural worker lost his bargaining power, which he had first enjoyed after the Black Death; while prices rose wages stayed the same. After 1551 the demand for wool lessened (because of the 'new draperies') and there was a fall in sheep population with a shift among farmers to move towards meat and cheese production.

Food of the Star Chamber

Near the old Palace of Westminster there was a large room set apart for the use of the Lords of the Privy Council; it had a painted ceiling of golden stars on a sky-blue background and became known as the Star Chamber. The Lords of the Star Chamber were a law unto themselves; there was no appeal allowed after they had passed sentence. The Lords sat on Wednesdays and Fridays from nine o'clock until dinner time, which they ate in another room called the Inner Star Chamber. Their dinners were carefully recorded in the accounts that have survived from 1519 to 1639. The accounts begin with sums for boat hire, down river towards the City or Southwark where the food markets were; apart from food the accounts list sums spent for candles, coal, salt, wine, vinegar, glass and napkins. Simon selects dinners from 1567 to 1605.[17]

By far the biggest entry was for the meat consumed, beef being the most common; it appears as either plain 'beef' or as 'pottage beef' and 'boiling beef' or as joints to roast, sirloins, ribs, rumps and 'double rump'. The cost over the years remained roughly the same – 20d per stone (14 lb). Veal also appears, though it was never eaten with the same gusto as on the Continent, perhaps because some writers tended to think it unhealthy. As a physician, Thomas Muffet, observed: 'Veal is unwholesome if dry roasted.' He considers mutton to be 'generally commended of all physicians as long as it not be too old.' The best mutton should be about four years, for the 'elder sort is sodden with bugloss, barrage and persly roots'. Lamb met the physician's approval too though it was 'more dainty than wholesome being moist and apt to ingender flegmaticke humours'. Pork was too much a plebeian taste to appear for the Lords of the Privy Council and it only appears once, though brawn made from a pig's head was eaten at the beginning of a meal.

On all the meat days capons, hens and chickens were provided; geese also appear as do pigeons. Gulls were expensive, possibly because they were caught, then kept in cages and fed on salt beef to make them fat and tasty. They cost 5s per bird which was very expensive compared with beef. A huge range of other birds appear, swans, cranes, bustards, curlews, green and grey plovers, lapwings, teals, oxebirds, crocards and oliffs, winders, wild duck and mallards. Capons appear most frequently either roasted or boiled, as did conies or rabbits costing only 6d for each, though by 1590 the price had doubled. The conies were cooked in the medieval manner; one recipe parboiled them, chopped them then added wine, dates raison, mace, pine nuts, sugar, saffron, pepper, ground ginger and vinegar.

In 1563 William Cecil (later Lord Burghley) created a bill for 'the increase of fish and navy days' by making every Wednesday a fish day. Fish eating was already compulsory on Fridays, Saturdays, Ember Days, all vigils and the whole of Lent. In that same year the importation of cod and ling from other countries was prohibited on the pretext that the fish was badly packed in barrels.

In some of the Star Chamber accounts signed by Cecil himself we see that on fish days they consumed poultry and game as well as the fish, showing that their consumption was for political reasons and nothing to do with the old Papist ideas of discipline and penance.

Cod, both fresh and salt, was the staple fish appearing on all the fish days. In 1567 one great cod cost 3s 4d. They also ate whiting, haddock, turbot, sole, herring and mullet, plaice and flounders. 'White herring' was fresh herring immediately gutted, washed and left in a strong brine for twenty-four hours, then drained dry and barrelled; in this state it was transported inland, then cooked in pies, grilled or fried. Gurnards were also eaten on almost every fish day, and oysters, crabs and shrimps appear frequently. Rarer fish were grey mullet, only eaten once, John Dory, eaten three times, and the expensive conger eel. Lobsters, prawns and porpoise also appear infrequently, the last only on two occasions and with no record of how much it cost.

Freshwater fish was cheaper and appears frequently, not only salmon from the Thames, both fresh and salted (in 1602 one whole salmon cost 40s) but trout also, though salmon trout is only mentioned once. Eels were also in great demand to be roasted or placed in pies or even salted. Lampreys were eaten frequently at the beginning of Elizabeth's reign on all the fish days from 1567 to 1590, then only once in 1605, which might show that the fashion for them had almost passed, or that they had begun to disappear from our rivers. The latter is unlikely as the last mention of them in great quantity was by Frederick Furnivall in 1866, in *Early English Meals and Manners*, where he noticed that the 'lamperns had been taken in extraordinary quantities from the Thames at Teddington'. Crayfish, pike, carp, perch, tench and bream are also all eaten. Conger was scalded and cleaned, then lightly poached, cooled then a sauce was made from parsley, mint, pellitory, rosemary, sage, breadcrumbs, garlic, salt, vinegar and wine, poured over and served.

Vegetables appear in the accounts under the heading of herbs and onions; these might have been cabbage, leeks, sorrel, spinach, lettuce and endive, all grown at the time. The vegetables that appear under their specific name were artichokes, beans, carrots, cauliflower and peas. A compound salad was made up of 'young buds and knots of all manner of wholesome herbs at their first springing; as red sage, mint, lettuce, violets, marigolds, spinach mixed together then served up with vinegar, salad oil and sugar.'[18]

A glance at the daily purchases gives some idea of the cooking practices. For an October fish day in 1567, there are ling, salt salmon, great pikes, whitings, codmops, flounders, great eels, soles, roaches, tenches and green fish. It seems a great quantity, not to say variety of fish for 30 lords. One imagines them having appetisers of salted salmon and green fish strips on sops of bread in green sauce. One imagines perhaps some of the other fish, the pike, flounders, soles, the side of porpoise, lampreys and eels being baked. There were salads of spinach and carrot. There were red wardens to be baked with rosewater, medlars and barberries. There was a gallon of cream and a 100 eggs to make custards.

A couple of weeks later, on Monday, 3 November, the meal begins with brawn, then there was beef and mutton boiled with pork chines. (This cut of meat appears frequently; it is unknown now, but was used up to the twentieth century. It is part of the backbone of the pig with a hefty bit of spinal marrow, necessary for the stockpot.) To roast, there are three geese, one turkey cock (possibly guinea fowl as there was some confusion between the two for a time), three joints of veal, four capons, rabbits, pheasants, curlew, partridges, plovers, snipes and thirty-six larks. There are prunes and cream to make tarts as well as more red wardens, barberries and medlars, also beef suet, rosewater, oranges, spices and 100 eggs. A huge steamed fruit pudding seems to be one of the dishes on offer.

In 1590 the most expensive ingredient over the year is the bill for spices at £29; the next most expensive is the coals for cooking at £15; coming third are the wages for the master cook, Mr Stephen Treagle, for cooking fifteen dinners at 6s a day, which came to £4 10s. The Cheshire cheeses over the year come to 15s.

On Wednesday, 9 June 1602, there is a record of 44 stone of beef bought (about 279 kilos), over 20 lb per lord. There must have been much over which the retainers and other servants were to enjoy. In addition there were also five joints of veal, eight joints of mutton, a lamb and nine geese, eighteen ducklings, seven capons as well as twelve rabbits and fifteen pigeons. There were also artichokes and peas, both in season, as well as strawberries, gooseberries, cherries, oranges and lemons.

You could not find food of higher quality than that which is reflected in these accounts. The Lords of the Privy Council were the monarch's closest advisors, the most important group governing the country. Apart from the sheer magnitude of the amounts ordered, the food appears to reflect a simplicity of cooking; meat was boiled and roasted, and all sorts of pies and tarts were made, which was not true of the medieval period. Robert May (see Chapter 6) was apprenticed to the Star Chamber cook for a few years after he returned from France, yet the food in his book strikes a still grander note than the recipes suggested by the above ingredients. A Tudor recipe for sole, for example, was poached, then served with an onion, saffron and bread sauce, which is a lot simpler than May's rich recipes for his Papist masters. The Lords of the Privy Council were definitely not Papists (in fact there is new evidence that some of them may have been secret atheists). The ideological influence upon food and particular recipes is explored in the next chapter.

Tudor Cooking

Because of the growth and wealth of the middle classes, food throughout the century gradually moved steadily away from complication and grandeur, from food designed to impress and fill the spectator and diner with awe, towards food that was born out of a domestic kitchen from a small workforce. Surely food at court and at functions aimed at impressing guests, who were often foreign, with a sense of power and affluence was still a necessary part of government? This is true, but the first Henry Tudor to reign was of a parsimonious nature; the royal court was one of scrupulous economy and notorious for penny-pinching.

We also have to take into account the fact that the nobility had radically changed after the old elite had, for the most part, been swept away in the ravages of the Wars of the Roses. In the 1530s John Leland noticed the great number of ruined castles on his tour of England. This elite, which still ruled in the rest of Europe, was divorced from the realities of medieval life; it is doubtful whether it would know the difference between a hoe and a rake, or have any knowledge of the income from dairy herds dotted over perhaps 5,000 acres from three different estates. The cooking of the medieval era for this elite had been thoroughly denatured: meats had been pummelled and ground into pastes which were spiced, egged and creamed, then reshaped into moulds which looked and tasted quite different from the original product. This was food from which the provenance and source had been totally erased, its humble beginnings of farmyard and millpond had vanished in the preparation and cooking.

There had also been medieval food that was presented back in its full glory, like wild boar with its glistening tusked head, roasted pheasant back in its skin and tail feathers or gilded and crowned swans. This had all been food that represented the elite's power and wealth, food that informed the guests that their hosts were monarchs of the wild forests, rivers and seas, and food that reflected the image they had of themselves.

The men ennobled by the new Tudor King were small farmers and tradesmen with a quite different image of themselves, men who had worked all their lives and would continue to work, who were fully aware of the difference between a duck and a hen's egg, who relished the flavour of the new pippin apple because they had planted orchards, who knew that the season for Seville oranges was a short one and expected their wives to oversee the making of 'marmelada', a term that covered a thick preserve from all fruits, not just oranges, and made to last the whole year. When they sat down to dine they wanted their food to reflect everything they worked for. They wanted their Colchester oysters raw, not cooked with spices, cream and eggs; they valued their mutton from Romney, to be plainly roasted without stuffing, a cheese from Swaledale to be eaten as it was, not used in sauces and stuffings.

A medieval recipe for stuffed fresh figs (expensive because imported from the Mediterranean) sums up its age: make an indentation in the fresh fig and fill it with chopped hard boiled egg, cinnamon and salt, then dredge it all in flour and deep-fry. This was designed to be finger food and once bitten into might have surprised the palate with its different textures and flavours. Such recipes vanish in the following century; figs are only mentioned as an ingredient in syrups or medicinal waters. Gerard thought that figs were a remedy for stomach pains and coughs. This practical approach is what colours Tudor cooking, though the medieval urge to turn everything into hash took time to die out.

Because books were now printed in the vernacular, literacy rose throughout the century, which spread among the English people an independence of thought and a certain wilfulness to authority. Reading became a grass roots force for justice and free thinking, even though the people's reading skills were chiefly based upon Biblical text. Wycliffe's aim to have an open English Bible in every home was beginning to be fulfilled, though it would take another two or three hundred years to complete.

Printed cookery books also grew in popularity. The very first one to be published, *This is the Boke of Cokery*, bears a date of 1500 but was more widely seen after 1533; it is described as 'a noble booke of feastes royall, and of Cookerie for Princes householde', and is typical of many others throughout the century. These books and those in the following century were aspirational. They were often collections of recipes from royal households or noble estates, and a mixture of medicinal recipes – cordials and physics – with preparation techniques for carcasses, fish and fowl and their cooking, techniques of cheese-making and preserving. They often contained practical advice on these techniques, though this was frequently sketchy and might be difficult to follow precisely, perhaps because the writer had only observed the slaughter and butchering of a pig and not actually wielded the knife. The recipes for cosmetics and beauty treatment all swear effectiveness and many a woman must have followed these instructions with the same slavish attention as they do now, believing that if it works for a royal household it would inevitably be just as effective in their more humble abode.

A fuller version of this first printed book has recently (June 2002) been discovered in the archives at Longleat. It is divided into three parts: the first gives details of the coronation feast of Henry V and a feast for George Nevill who became Archbishop of York in 1465; the second a calendar of seasonal foods; and the third a list of ingredients. It is a perfect example of the huge social change that printed books heralded, for it was designed for the aspiring gentry newly affluent through trade, so that they might replicate the dishes eaten at court.

This aspirational stimulus is inherent in the popularity of the cooking recipes. Many of them are highly complicated; one can imagine the servants cutting corners, since they would be following the instructions read out (or learnt by heart) by the housekeeper; or one can imagine the housekeeper doing her own more sensible adaptations of the recipes on the excuse that the master and mistress prefer it done this way. What is certain is that books of recipes then and now do not tell us necessarily what people eat, only what they aspire to eat, or what they imagine they should be eating so that their wealth and position will be envied by their neighbours.

The same is true of books that cover the whole range of a housewife's activities. *The Boke of Husbandrie* of 1523 shows how intensive the work of the middle-class housewife could and should be: she had to winnow all corn, to make malt, wash and wring, to make hay, shear corn, and in time of need help her husband to fill the wain or dung cart, drive the plough, load hay and corn, ride to the market to sell butter, cheese, milk, eggs, chickens, capons, hens, pigs and geese as well as looking after the dairy and doing the household accounts, 'to make a true reckoning and accompt to her husband what she hath received and what she hath paid'. She also had to cook and preserve the produce that was harvested.[19] This book is valuable information on what was considered to be the proper role of the housewife which had changed very little since the medieval period. It was to begin to change at the end of the seventeenth century.

One of the earliest printed cookery books in England is *A Proper Newe Booke of Cookerye*, 1545.[20] It was the first of a series of short cookery books which often contained the same recipes or very similar ones, for they were part of the publishers' routine production. It gave information on seasonal meats and how they should be dressed and served at the table. Some of the recipes seem esoteric to us now and perhaps they did then to the general reader – a tart of borage flowers, or marigolds, primroses and cowslips?

The consumption of spices by the nobility was still high in the first third of the sixteenth century. In May 1535 Lord Lisle's London agent sent him a box which contained 91 lb sugar, 10 lb pepper, 2 lb each of cinnamon and ginger, 1 lb each of cloves and mace. The dishes in the recipe books tend to be simplified versions of medieval ones where the meat is minced or grounded then flavoured and spiced. William Harris (1546-1602) describes what the nobility ate: 'Tthere is no daie in manner that passeth over their heads, wherein they have not onelie beefe, mutton, veale, lambe, porke, conie, capon, pig, or so many of these as the season yeeldeth; but also some portion of the red or fallow deere, beside great varietie of fish and wild foule and thereto sundrie other delicates . . .'[21] Much food was sent as presents or just necessary supplies. The letters to Lord Lisle are full of references: in 1534 he was sent sturgeon and baked crane; in the following year it is venison and several dishes for a banquet (the separate course after the meal), which were cheeses, crystallised fruits, sweetmeats and wine.[22]

Shakespeare's Master Shallow's idea of a modest repast was 'a couple of short-legged hens, a joint of mutton, and any pretty little tiny kickshaws'. The last was a rendering of *quelque choses*, meaning a dish of no great consequence; kickshaws then were small fancy dishes either sweet or savoury. The term faded by the eighteenth century. Robert May (see page 142), using the French term, gives a few egg recipes.

During three months of 1589, William Darrell, a Wiltshire squire of frugal tastes, when detained in London lodgings with a skeleton staff of servants over a tangle of lawsuits, ate beef and mutton for both dinner and supper, with side dishes of game – a brace or more of pullets, rabbits, or occasionally pheasants and pigeons – and sometimes veal and once lamb. Bread and beer were always there and often butter and cheese, but soup or broth and 'sallets' were rare and peas seem to have been the only vegetable. Friday is a fish day with ling, plaice, whiting and conger; he ignored the law enjoining two fish days a week. In 1563 the fine for non-observance of a secular fish day was £3 or three months' imprisonment, unless one obtained a special licence to eat meat on these days. 'Lords of Parliament and their wives shall pay for a licence 26s 8d yearly to the poor men's box in their parish, Knights and their wives shall pay 13s 4d and lesser persons 6s 8d.' Darrell dismisses pastries and jellies for dessert but has a quart of strawberries with cream in season. The cost of each meal ranged between five and ten shillings. Darrell's household wages bill only came to £50 per annum.

Harrison, the topographer, claims a merchant does as well as a gentleman; the multitude of dishes enables each guest to choose his particular fancy and no one consumes more than half a dozen of them on guest days or two or three en famille. What is left over supplements the basic diets of the household staff and a gentleman must at all costs be openhanded. Harrison says that gentlemen do not habitually over-eat or over-drink; it is the meaner sort of husbandman who guzzles and becomes drunk at public feasts to compensate for long weeks of broth and porridge, dairy produce, the inevitable bacon and rye or barley bread, with beer, cider or mead according to district. In a modest merchant's household with two or three maids, including the children's nurse, the highest wage per year would be £4 and the food bill might be no more than 30s a week.[23]

Foreigners seemed to be impressed by our food. 'Very sumptuous and love good fare,' was the comment of a Dutch physician, Levinus Lemnius, who visited England in 1560. Perhaps he had tasted Sir Hugh Plat's Polonian sawsedge: 'Take the fillers of a hog, chop them very small with a handfull of red sage, season it hot with ginger and pepper, then put it into a sheeps gut, then let it lie three nights in brine, then boil it and hang it upp in a chimney where fire is usually kept and these sawsedges will last one whole year. They are good for sallades: or to garnish boyled meats or to make one relish a cup of wine.'[24]

The Ancaster family laid in white herrings at 23s 4d a barrel and Bess of Hardwick had a passion for shrimps. Smoked and pressed pilchards were exported from Cornwall to Spain. Sir Hugh Plat's fish paste is white fish boned then mixed with white breadcrumbs, four spices and isinglass and made into the shapes and forms of little fishes. Quail were imported live from the Lowlands. The crane, the bittern, the wild and tame swan, the brant, the lark and two kinds of plover, teal, widgeon, mallard, shelldrake and shoveller, the peewit, scamen knot, olicet, dun bird, partridge and pheasant, were all hunted or snared, eaten and enjoyed. Sir Hugh Plat gives a recipe for cooking sparrows. Larks cost from 1d to 10d a dozen, pigeons were thought to be 'a hurtful fowl by reason of their multitude'. There were also, 'peacocks of the Ind', hens, geese, ducks and turkeys. Harrison says: 'We do not, thanks be to God and the liberty of our princes, dine or sup with a quarter of a hen, or make repast with a cock's comb as they do in some countries[25]; but if occasion serve the whole carcases of many capons, hens, pigeons and suchlike do oft go to wrack besides beef, mutton, veal and lamb, all of which at every feast are taken as necessary dishes among the Communality of England.' Big country feast days were Plough Monday, Shrove Tuesday, sheep shearing and Harvest Home.

Sir William Petre (1505–1572), who was a secretary of state to Elizabeth and lived at Ingatestone Hall in Essex, observed the fish days fairly regularly because of the Royal Proclamations which declared them necessary to the fishing industry; if he had held them on religious grounds he would have been prosecuted for heresy. At a wedding celebration Petre hired a master cook from London to take charge with four other cooks beneath him. His own resident cook travelled with him wherever he went. There were some perquisites in the position; cooks were allowed to keep the dripping and rabbit skins as well as candle ends (which could be melted down) and all the leavings from the table. Sir William had only twenty indoor and outdoor servants, but his ovens turned out 20,000 loaves of bread in a year and the dovecote had to provide over a thousand birds. The estate provided the household with nearly all their food as well as the Petres' London house, except for wine, dried fruit, sugar and spices. Gifts of food were very popular; when Petre's son, John, was christened a friend sent them a guinea fowl, a mallard, a woodcock, two teals, a basket of wafers and various cakes for the christening feast.[26]

On the table there would be pewter and silverware, also such pieces as ceremonial salts (the Earl of Leicester's was made of mother-of-pearl and shaped like a galleon). When not upon the table they would be arranged upon the sideboard with ornate spice boxes, pepper-casters, pomanders, candlesticks and clocks. Spoons were made of silver and laid on the table with knives, forks had been introduced from Italy but did not catch on, for they are not mentioned in any inventory until 1660. Goblets were made in silver, gold and glass and horn tankards were ornamented with silver bands. So much silver was a product of the mines in the New World, which boosted the currency as well as ending up in warming pans and chandeliers.

Mutton was the meat eaten most frequently at Ingatestone Hall, followed by beef, venison and pork. Eggs and cheese were much enjoyed; the household used about one pound of cheese to every egg. Fish came from the east coast, oysters, flatfish and mackerel with the occasional bass and salmon, the estate pond was full of carp. Several dozen larks are referred to as presents in the kitchen books of the Hall; a neighbour also sent a present of a crane. A 'birder' was paid for catching wildfowl, sparrows, blackbirds, starlings and thrushes. The kitchen book also shows that they ate mallard, widgeons, teals, shovelards, woodcocks, curlews, redshanks and plovers. Between Easter and Michaelmas in 1552 the household ate over 1,000 pigeons from the dove-house.

On a Lenten Thursday, Ingatestone Hall prepared for dinner 'a jowl of ling, half a hakerdin [halibut], 2 mudfishes [plaice], 40 white herrings, 50 red herrings, 2 cakes of butter'. And for supper: 'A tail of ling, 3 mudfishes, 30 white herrings, 2 cakes of butter, 6 eggs'. A cake of butter weighed generally about 4½ lb.

The cellar contained barrels of verjuice for cooking as well as ale and beer. The stocktaking in 1551 reveals that they also had a butt of sack, two puncheons of French wine, a hogshead of French wine, Gascon wine and Rhenish wine as well as 4 gallons of malmsey. They made their own perry from their apples, mead and various flower and fruit wines, as did Elinor Fettiplace later (see page 198) who gives many a recipe. In a sheltered south-west corner of his orchard, Sir William had built a banqueting house, the small pavilion in which the last sweet and fruit course was served to guests in the summer; next to this building was the cook's garden, with chives, sweet marjoram, purslane, cauliflower, leeks and mustard. Next to that were the brick dove-house, which contained thousands of birds, and ponds well stocked with fresh water fish. This is food that still reflects the medieval traditions, but simplified, one feels, because the labour in the kitchen, with only twenty servants, is so much more limited. There is little doubt that Petre, though living in a grand house, lived modestly and within his means.

William Harrison, in his *Description of England* in 1577, speaks of gentlemen taking pride in their kitchens but not overeating; meat and bread remained the principal foods, though salads were very popular, dishes of cucumber, peas, olives and artichokes were more common than in the past. The Petres' servants ate very well; just before Christmas in 1551 when Sir William and family were still in London, the servants had twelve local people for guests at dinner and between them they ate three joints of boiled beef and one roasted, a neat's tongue[27], a baked leg of mutton, two rabbits and a partridge; for Christmas they ate much the same but finished with eight baked pear pies.

The food has a much more familiar ring to it now than the recipes cooked for Richard II; it has lost the esoteric glamour, the touch of strangeness that in the medieval world both entices and alienates. Because these people are not estranged from the source of food as was the medieval elite, they are hard at work producing the food they cook and eat. The new nobility appeared to work unremittingly. Lady Hoby records mornings spent dyeing wool, winding yarn, making oil and spinning; she dried fruits, made quince jelly and damson jam, dried rose leaves for pot pourris, prepared candies and syrups and distilled cordials. She was the wife of Sir Thomas Posthumus Hoby, the ambassador to France, and knew as much if not more of their estates than her husband did. 'I walked with Mr Hoby about the town to spy out the best places where cottages might be builded, after supper I talked a good deal with Mr Hoby of husbandry and household matters.'[28]

The food of the Tudors seems to be the same food that we eat now. In *The French Garden*,[29] a dialogue written by two Huguenot refugees who taught French in London, we recognise the hostess of a dinner party and sympathise with her anxieties. Her guests were offered oysters with brown bread, salt, pepper and vinegar, which, however, were declined by all on the grounds that shellfish should not be eaten in the dog days. (The hottest time of the year; the dog days begin on 3 July and end on 11 August, so called from the rising of the great dog star, Sirius, and the lesser dog star, Procyon.) They dined from a table covered with a damask table cloth, used damask napkins and a silver chafing dish; they had wine from a silver jug, and drank from glass, the glasses being rinsed before being refilled. They ate roast beef and salt beef, veal and a leg of mutton with a galantine sauce (red wine and cinnamon thickened with breadcrumbs); there was also turkey, boiled capon served with oranges, a hen boiled with leeks, partridge, pheasant, larks, quails, snipe and woodcock. They also had wild boar as well as domestic pig; the boar was thought the better as it had more flavour. Salmon, sole, turbot and whiting with lobster, crayfish and shrimps were eaten, but an eel and a pike were sent away from the table untasted. Young rabbits and marrow on toasts tempted those who did not care for the gross meats; then there were artichokes, turnips, green peas, capers, cucumbers and olives. The turnips were from Normandy where grew the best; they were small and had a much better flavour than our large English ones. (How right they were then and now.) There were salads of lettuce, spinach, endive, and of sage, rosemary and violet buds. There was quince pie (the quinces must have been bottled from the previous autumn), almond tart, cherries, gooseberries and prunes. There was also Dutch cheese, Angelot[30], Auvergne and Parmesan[31]; grated cheese was mixed with sage and sugar, and there was also a mild cheese from Banbury.[32] There were strawberries, raspberries, peaches and apricots, served with cream and green walnuts but no chestnuts. What a delicious feast this all sounds. We must not think, however, that this was typical as one of the guests remarked: 'In truth I have not seen of a long time all at once so much poultry, nor fowl nor so good fish.'

The chafing dish mentioned above was a dish with burning coals in it to keep food hot, but this method was also used for cooking and became much more common within the century. It was usually a round dish with hot charcoal in it covered with another dish used for the cooking; this sat on a movable tripod, and allowed for cooking over a gentle heat. Meat could be stewed, fish could be poached, delicate liaison with egg yolk and broth could be wrought without accidents and burnings. The chafing dish had a long history, for both Cicero and Seneca refer to them and they were certainly used in the medieval kitchen; in the sixteenth century, however, the dish is often specified for particular recipes.

In a far less grand noonday meal there were sausages and cabbage with porridge for the children, though hospitality induced the host to offer a pike with a high Dutch sauce and also black birds, larks, woodcock and partridge. This elicited from one of the diners the remark: 'Here is too much meat, me thinketh that we be at a wedding.'[33] Three or four hours were spent over this meal: 'The nobility, gentlemen and merchant men sit till three o'clock of the afternoon so that it is a hard matter to rise from the table to go to evening prayers.' Supper was supposed to be a lighter meal taken between five and six. A roast shoulder of mutton, three fried rabbits, bread, beer and a pint of claret seems, however, to have been the typical meal for a solitary gentleman living in lodgings in London in 1589.[34]

Almond milk is now conspicuously absent from most of the recipes, and some popular dishes now have cows' milk substituted. Flummery was a favourite dish of Tudor and Stuart banquets. It began as a lechemeat based on calves' foot broth and almond milk with added spices; it was left to cool and set and then was cut into leches or slices. Now it was made with a spiced cream set with calves' foot, isinglass or hartshorn,[35] It was eaten with cream or a wine sauce poured over it, but elaborate dishes could be made where the flummery was poured into egg-shaped moulds then set into a nest of shredded lemon peel jelly, or moulded into fish and presented in a jelly pond. (It originated in a far simpler Welsh dish, *llymru*, made from soaked oats, see page 199.)

Dishes made with cream became a new passion: there were trifles, fools and white pots. An Elizabethan trifle was a thick cream flavoured with sugar, ginger, and rosewater. A fool was a flavoured cream mixed with eggs and heated gently until it thickened; the whitepot had dried fruit added to this mixture and it was baked like an egg custard. Sage cream was made with red sage, rosewater and sugar. Clotted cream was made by leaving new milk for several hours in shallow bowls over a slight heat, for it must not boil.

A book published in 1573, *The Treasurie of Commodious Conceits and Hidden Secrets* by John Partridge, reflects the social changes that have occurred in the century. The title page indicates that this is a book for all men and women of whatever quality; the receipts have been gathered from men of great knowledge, which have made the book a treasury for profit. This is a book that contains hidden secrets and sundry experiments, and it is intended for a housewife's closet. It was a book that became highly influential, and was reprinted until 1637. It claims to disseminate to the general populace secrets that once belonged to Guilds; the receipts are for marchpane, marzipans, tarts, blaunch powder, conserves of roots, flowers, fruits, syrups, lozenges, medicines and perfumes. Many of these at the beginning of the century would have been made by monks or imported from Spain. Some of them, the sugar work and sugar pastes, encroach upon the apothecaries, who had attempted to place a form of protectionism over their sugar-work. In the twelfth century, as we have seen, these were the medicinal comfits. Partridge is aware of what he is doing and exults in it, claiming that he might suffer from a backlash of jealousy from the rich (for it is also their secrets of the still-room that he divulges) or the physicians and surgeons might well blacklist him or simply refuse to buy his book. This was the first people's cookbook, making arcane knowledge available to all.

Another form of cookery book was, of course, the collection of receipts kept within a family and passed down from generation to generation. Some of these waited hundreds of years to be published, so that a wider public might enjoy and learn from them. *The Receipt Book*[36] written by Lady Fettiplace (fl.1604) is one such, and it is here that we can see most clearly the changes that had occurred in English cooking throughout the Tudor century. If it began still within the medieval traditions, by Elizabeth's death it was well into a new age. This collection of recipes is without the mainstay of medieval cooking that hung on into the recipe books to the middle of the century, such as the generously spiced meat hash or that great favourite, the sweet and sour sauce. Many of the medieval influences are still clearly to be seen, however, although they are all modified. There's a recipe for saffron buns, but that is the only time the ingredient is used. Her colouring was achieved by more natural means than in medieval recipes. She gives several almond recipes, for buns, a custard and a pudding which she calls a 'blanchmane' which is a flavoured almond custard, and obviously the heir to the medieval *mawmenny*; by now, however, it is totally without the minced chicken and colouring and is close to what the Victorians knew as blancmange. She also gives a recipe for almond butter, to be eaten as a dessert for it becomes a thick cream, which is flavoured with rosewater and which later Nicholas Culpeper suggested should be eaten with violets. She does use fruit sauces in savoury dishes, and this is still one of the great characteristics of our cooking. She uses egg yolk for thickening sauces instead of breadcrumbs, but she retains some Arab influence by a generous use of rosewater (there are rosewater pancakes) and a liking for currants. In her cooking flavours are clear and separate: two or three spices might be used but not seven or eight; there are rich vegetable dishes such as spinach with cream, egg yolks and butter, or charming ideas like stewed oysters flavoured with the juice of Seville oranges. Fettiplace provides a rich storehouse of ideas that we might well explore, such as a white wine sauce thickened with egg yolks for boiled mutton, mutton flavoured with the peel of Seville oranges, or rabbit pie well flavoured with nutmeg. She pots crayfish (Mrs Beeton's recipe, 300 years later, is similar); she preserves apricots, peaches and green walnuts in syrup, makes rose-petal jam and uses both a lettuce and a spinach sauce with boiled chicken. She gives one recipe that stems from the Anglo-Saxons and which was to remain a favourite for another 200 years – sops in wine. These are slices of bread placed in a wine sauce and then baked, so that the top is toasted while the underside of the bread soaks up the sauce; the sops are then buttered and served. These were presented as an appetiser or as a snack after a hard day's travelling.[37]

Elinor Fettiplace is circumspect in her use of spices keeping them for her mince pies, plum puddings and fruit cakes, as we tend to do today. Pies of all sorts are a staple for they were a way of preserving meat and could be taken and eaten as travelling food. They were expected to keep for a quarter of a year sealed with clarified butter. Pies were sent as presents by country people to friends and relations in town. They could be made from venison, wild boar, swan, elk or porpoise. They were often of vast size made with rye-flour paste (which was not eaten) and baked in a bread oven for six to eight hours; then the juices were poured off and they were sealed with clarified butter. Smaller pies were also made with wheat flour crust, which was expected to be eaten; the meat inside was possibly chicken, rabbit and ham, or mixtures of small game birds, or turkey. These too were filled with clarified butter and were often kept upon the sideboard, a slice to be offered to guests.

Lady Fettiplace uses vegetable rennet made from thistles, artichokes, ginger or the green rind of fig trees, to turn her cheese that was to be eaten throughout Lent. She makes simple cream and curd cheeses throughout the summer, but also in a vat she makes Angelot cheese which is obviously her own Brie-like cheese. Owners of dairy cattle now found it more profitable to turn their milk into butter and cheese, for milk could not be sold at the market for fear of its separating; the whey and buttermilk were sold, but the rest of it was used as pig food. The big estates of the nobility now had quantities of milk to be used daily, and this was turned into curds of various kinds for fear of milk fermenting in the stomach.

From then on, therefore, every cookery book devoted a large section to recipes that used curds in their different forms. They were mixed with butter, cream and spices to make fresh cheeses. They were mixed with fruit, lemon juice and sugar to make puddings. They made syllabubs, custards and cheese-cakes. Naturally, cream was also now being added to more and more dishes and sauces. Syllabubs became a favourite dessert made from wine or cider, sweetened with sugar, nutmeg and lemon to which cream was forcefully added, sometimes from a great height, to make it froth up. The milk was even squirted into the wine straight from the cow. French cheese was the fresh creamy curd flavoured with cinnamon, rosewater and sugar, and it was eaten with fresh cream poured over.[38] Alternatively, whites of egg were beaten, then stirred into the cream cheese with nutmeg, rosewater and lemon juice. Various fruit creams were made by heating cream with white of egg flavoured with mace and lemon; then when well boiled they were sweetened and fruit such as raspberries stirred in. (These were, of course, egg custard without yolks and could be baked in a low oven.) Spiced cheese tarts were made and in the following century were known as cheese-cakes. Curd fritters also continued to be made and enjoyed; they were spiced and eaten with added sugar. Cabbage cream was a form of clotted cream: a dish of thick cream was allowed to form a skin; this was then carefully lifted from the dish and arranged on a platter, where it was folded to resemble a cabbage leaf; rosewater was sprinkled over it, then more creamskins were lifted and arranged – the rosewater stopped them from sticking together. Then it was placed in the stillroom for two days and before being served it was sprinkled with sugar, ginger and a light dusting of nutmeg. Dishes made from cows' milk were now a central part of our diet.

The traveller Fynes Morrison who wrote an itinerary over 10 years covering his journeys in 1617, thought that the English ate fallow deer more often than any other nation. It was baked into pasties which were dainty and not found in any other kingdom; nor was brawn. No kingdom had as many dove-houses or roasted their meat as well as the English; they also ate more hens and geese and plenty of rabbits, which were both fat and tender and more delicate than any elsewhere. The geese they ate twice a year, when they were young around Whitsun and after the harvest, when they had eaten off the stubble; they are then both roast and boiled.

Preserving

Before the Age of Discovery the sailor's diet had been just about adequate, preserved meat, ale, ship's biscuits and dried peas, but then voyages were short, no longer than a few weeks. There was no shortage of sailors because the meat allowance of 8lb of salt beef per man per week was generous, but there was much corruption and the men were often short-changed on supplies which led to anger, resentment and mutiny. The mutineers on the *Golden Lion* sailing on Drake's Cadiz voyage in 1587 wrote: 'for what is a piece of beef of half a pound among four men to dinner, or half a dried stockfish for four days in the week . . . you make no men of us but beasts.'[39] Once long voyages began, a new disease struck the sailors down – scurvy. It had not affected the Vikings on their long voyages of discovery for they took with them cranberries and cloudberries. The Dutch treated land scurvy with brooklime, cress, scurvy grass and strawberry leaves. Sir Richard Hawkins had been a prisoner of the Spanish in the Netherlands and learnt that sour oranges and lemons were a cure. This was not generally accepted, however. Scurvy was thought to be engendered by fog, damp, and sea salt and other remedies were tried like vinegar and oil of vitriol.

As always the officers and gentlemen ate well, for they had fresh meat, and sheep and goats for milk at the beginning of the voyage; then, with the pigs, they were butchered and eaten; they also kept hens for fresh eggs and supplies of fresh vegetables and fruits whenever they landed for provisions. They were also well supplied with preserved foods from home. Pastes of potted meat and fish were kept under a seal of clarified butter, or the meat was chopped up small and baked in a low oven for six to eight hours; then the juices were poured away, the meat was crushed and pressed hard down in a large stone jar, and clarified butter was poured over. Hare pie was made by first boning the meat, then the flesh was hashed and beaten to a pulp with a mortar; it was seasoned, larded and baked, then the juices were poured off and claret wine poured in. Once cool, it was sealed with clarified butter and a double layer of brown paper. Hams and bacon were smoked and dried using honey, salt, juniper, pine tar and much else to contrive a meat that would survive the heat of tropical climes. Fresh garden peas were potted in clarified butter, watercress grew in glass jars, broom buds were pickled. Many types of fish like herrings, mackerel, char, salmon, lobster and crab were smoked, salted, dried and potted. Potted shrimps, a standby and a delicacy still for the British, were created at this time for the officers' table. Provisions included dried beans, nuts – walnuts and almonds – clotted cream (boiled with sugar till it was quite stiff); waxed eggs (they were greased in hot lard and packed in sawdust); pickled eggs flavoured with allspice, ginger and garlic, and pickled vegetables in brine or vinegar; there were also many different pastes of smoked fish, cheese and mushrooms. There were barrels of figs and sacks of dried fruit, raisins and prunes, dried pears and apples, and marmalade that was boiled for longer than usual so that it became a stiff jelly and could be sliced. There was bottled spring water and cinnamon water to aid the digestion. Of course, there was also wine and sugar to add to it. These provisions were all for the 'banketting on shipboard of persons of credite'.

Sir Hugh Plat, worried about how to keep meat fresh at sea, suggested that it be placed in a perforated cask and dragged astern. The cold salt seawater would keep it fresh and sweet. A ship in 1576, setting off to catch the 'Whale Fish' in Russia, was provisioned with bread, cedar oil, hog's-heads of beef, salt beans, peas, salt fish, wine and mustard seed.

This urge to provision husbands, fathers and brothers obviously inspired households to create new recipes and flavourings, many of which became an integral part of the British repertoire. Voyages to the New World and to the Orient turned the west of England ports like Bristol, Plymouth and Liverpool into flourishing market centres.

Each harvested product was stored differently in the home: apples were cored, dried and threaded in rings; mushrooms the same; lemons, oranges, pumpkins and onions were hung in nets; dried roots were wrapped in linen; and husked walnuts stored in wet salt. Dried stockfish and herrings were hung in a dry attic, bacon and bath chaps (the cheek of a pig boned, brined and cooked) stored in a keg of sawdust, dried beef hung near the smoke hole, and cheeses were wrapped in cloth to preserve their moisture and aroma.[40]

Wealth and Commerce

Throughout the century the middle classes were growing more prosperous and literate. They were the new consumers, eager to absorb fashionable trends in clothes, architecture and food. We were the first modern commercial nation, and there is evidence that well over half or even two-thirds of all households received some part at least of their income in wages.[41] New industries were adding to the wealth of the nation and the population was expanding (of the four million population 200,000 of them lived in London) and these new industries were assisted by foreign immigrants. 'What country in the world is there,' a Member of Parliament asked in 1596, 'that nourisheth so many aliens from all parts of the world as England doth?' A clergyman, William Lee, invented a knitting frame, which the hosiery industry in the east Midlands used with alacrity, making a fortune, but leaving the clergyman penniless. Other new industries were papermaking, printing, gun-founding and the manufacture of gunpowder; there was substantial growth in the lead, copper and iron industries and steel was first produced in 1565. The new gentry and nobility, being a practical lot, often invested in iron mines, blast furnaces and ironworks located on their own land; if not, they were shrewd enough to purchase a neighbour's land and then borrow the money to invest in fuel, raw materials and wages.

Enclosures of land, as we have noted, had already begun and contemporaries were anxious to distinguish between a farmer's enclosure of his land for improvement (Thomas Tusser's *A Hundreth Good Pointes of Husbandrie* had appeared in 1557[42]) and a rich man's enclosure of 'other men's commons'. Writers also pointed out the difference between enclosure by force and enclosure by consent. Rioting against enclosures had already occurred in 1548. The old medieval horror of usury had entirely vanished; it was legalised in 1571 and loans of money at high interest levels were now commonplace. The now affluent middle classes had bonded with the nobility in their love of money and both resented government if it interfered in matters of enclosure or usury. Land was necessary for the new industries and textiles were the biggest export of all for there was a growing demand for English cloth abroad, which boomed from 1559 to 1603. Cloth-making was a cottage industry, clothiers collected orders, hired out looms and put out work. The huge looms would take up nearly all of the space in the one single room that a family inhabited. London bought cloth in its unfinished form from these provincial markets where prices were low and then saw to the finishing and dyeing, which counted for a great deal more in the value of the fabric. The cloth market in London, Blackwell Hall, was built as early as 1397, but rebuilt in 1558; after it was again burnt down, in the Fire of London in 1666, it was rebuilt to huge dimensions in 1672.

Household interiors were full of fabrics with curtains, hangings, tapestries and the linen cupboards piled with sheets, fine linens, napkins and tablecloths. Social vanity grew to its height in the 16th century and would remain a driving factor in matters of fashion and food until the present day. Nicholas Barbon wrote in 1690: 'Fashion or the alteration of Dress is a great promoter of trade because it urges people to spend money on clothes before the old ones are worn out: it is the life and soul of commerce . . . it is an invention which makes man live in perpetual springtime, without ever seeing the autumn of his clothes.'[43] One of the new palaces to be built upon the river Thames was Craven House, home of the Craven family founded by Sir William Craven who was a Lord Mayor of London and had made his fortune out of tailoring.

Basinghall Street, where Blackwell Hall stood, became the centre of commerce in London. Throughout the century covered markets and market stalls grew up in provincial cities and towns as never before. Between 1500 and 1640 there were 800 market towns in England and Wales; 300 of these confined themselves to single trades, some specialising in grain, others in malt; ninety-two were cattle markets, thirty fish, twenty-one wildfowl and poultry and a few specialised in the odd and idiosyncratic, such as Wymondham which dealt exclusively in wooden spoons, taps and handles. It has been worked out that each market town catered for between 6,000 and 7,000 people, while the average population of the locality was around 1,000.

London, with its growing population, absorbed food from almost the whole of Britain: herrings came from Scotland and cattle from Wales, but most of its produce stemmed from the Thames valley. Uxbridge, Brentford, Kingston, Hampstead, Watford, St Albans, Hertford, Croydon, and Dartford busied themselves in the city's service, grinding grain and sending in flour, preparing malt, harvesting fruits and vegetables and dispatching game birds, mutton carcasses, butter, cream and cheese. The orchards and hops of Kent flourished near London, its forests were also rich in game: pheasant, partridge, quail, teal, wild duck and the wheatear or English ortolan which Daniel Defoe thought 'the most delicious taste for a creature of one mouthful,

Medieval Cooking and Dining

Top: This drawing from the tenth century shows a small Anglo-Saxon dinner party, where the diners are being served an early example of kebab perhaps, though the pieces of meat look large enough for the diners to slice off what they want. There are also fish and bread rolls on the table. (1)

Bottom left: A ninth century manuscript shows an Anglo-Saxon cook stirring a kettle with a vigorous fire beneath. His double-hooked implement allows him to keep the pieces apart as he stirs and to select and take out any already cooked. (1)

Bottom right: A tenth century illustration of a heavenly meal where the most notable substance seems to be the nectar. (1)

Top left: A fourteenth century drawing of an outdoor meal being prepared. Geese are being spit-roasted while the pot they have just been blanched in is still simmering for broth upon the fire. The sign on the building on the right shows it to be an inn. (1)

Top right: A fourteenth century depiction of a cook taking a boar's head from the pot and placing it upon a serving dish. (1)

Middle: Servants were often preceded by musicians; here they play for a monarch at dinner with his companions in an early fourteenth-century illustration. They appear to be eating decorative pastries and chicken. (1)

Bottom right: This fifteenth century drawing shows a steward leading the servants who are carrying the main dishes into the hall. Note the dishes are covered which allows two to be stacked. (1)

Royal Dining Down the Centuries

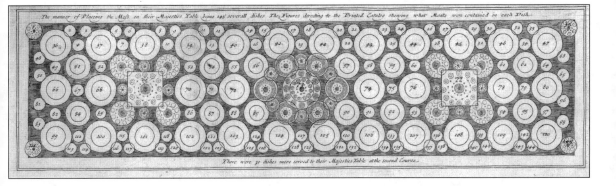

The manner of Placing the Mess on their Majesties Table being 145 severall dishes. The Figures directing to the Printed Catalog shewing what Meats were contained in each Dish.

There were 30 dishes more served to their Majesties Table at the second Course.

A *CATALOGUE* of the several *MEATS* contained in the MESS ferved up to Their MAJESTIES Table at the Upper End of *Weftminfter-Hall*, for Their *Coronation-Dinner*, 23 April 1685. The Figures following referring to the Numbers marked on the feveral Difhes in the Sculpture reprefenting the faid Table.

1. Piftachio Cream in Glaffes.
2. Anchoviz,
3. Cuftards, } cold.
4. Collar'd Veal,
5. Lamb-Stones, } hot.
6. Cocks-Combs,
7. Marrow Patie,
8. Jelly,
9. Sallet, } cold.
10. Stags Tongues,
11. Sweet-Breads,
12. Patty Pidgeon, } hot.
13. Petty-Toes,
14. Cray Fifh,
15. Blumange, } cold.
16. Bolonia Saufages,
17. Collops and Eggs,
18. Frigafe Chick, } hot.
19. Rabbets Ragou,
20. Oyfters Pickled,
21. Portugal Eggs, } cold.
22. Dutch Beef,
23. Andolioes,
24. Mufhroomes, } hot.
25. Veal,
26. Hogs Tongues,
27. Cheefe-Cakes, } cold.
28. Ciprus Birds,
29. Tanfie,
30. Afparagus, } hot.
31. A Pudding,
32. Ragou of Oyfters,
33. Scallops, } cold.
34. Salamagundy,
35. Three Dozen Glaffes of Lemon Jelly.
36. Five Neats Tongues, cold.
37. Four Dozen of wild Pidgeons, Twelve Larded, cold.
38. A whole Salmon, cold.
39. Eight Pheafants, three Larded, cold.
40. Nine fmall Pidgeon Pyes, cold.
41. Twenty four Fat Chickens, fix Larded, hot.
42. Twelve Crabs, cold.
43. Twenty four Partridges, fix Larded, hot.
44. A Difh of Tarts.
45. Soles Marinated, cold.
46. Twenty four Tame Pidgeons, fix Larded, hot.
47. Four Pullets la Dobe, hot.
48. Four Fawns, two Larded, hot.
49. Twelve Quails, } hot.
50. Four Partridges haffet,
51. Ten Oyfter Pyes, hot.
52. Sallet.
53. Peafe.
54. Four Dozen of Puddings, hot.
55. Artichokes.
56. Beef a la Royal, hot.
57. An Oglio, hot.
58. Peafe.
59. A Betalia Pye.
60. Artichokes.
61. Sallet.
62. Three Turkeys a la Royal, hot.
63. Four Chicks,
64. Bacon Gammon, } hot.
65. Spinage.
66. Three Pigs, hot.
67. Almond Puff.
68. Twelve Stump Pyes, cold.
69. A fquare Pyramide, rifing from Four large Difhes on the Angles, and Four leffer Difhes on the Sides, containing the feveral Fruits in feafon, and all manner of Sweet-Meats.
70. A whole Lamb Larded, hot.
71. Twelve Ruffs.
72. Four Dozen of Egg-Pyes, cold.
73. A very large Circular Pyramide in the middle of the Table, rifing from twelve Difhes in the Circumference, fix of which were large, and

and the other fix lefs, containing the feveral Fruits in feafon, and all manner of Sweet-Meats.
74. Six Mullets large Souc'd.
75. Eight Godwits.
76. Eight Neats Tongues and Udders roafted, hot.
77. A fquare Pyramide, rifing from four large Difhes on the Angles, and four leffer on the Sides, containing the feveral Fruits in feafon, and all manner of Sweet-Meats.
78. Eighteen Minc'd Pyes, cold.
79. Matrow Tofts.
80. Eight Wild Ducks Marinated, hot.
81. Goofeberry Tarts,
82. Lampreys, } cold.
83. Shrimps,
84. Twenty four Puffins, cold.
85. Smelts.
86. Truffles.
87. Four Dozen of Petit-Paties, hot.
88. Morels.
89. Five Carps, cold.
90. Blumange in Shells, cold.
91. Mufhrooms.
92. Four Doz. of Almond Puddings, hot.
93. Afparagus.
94. Eight Ortelans.
95. Lamb Sallet, cold.
96. Five Partridge Pyes,
97. Smelts Marinated, } cold.
98. Turt. de Moil,
99. Eighteen Turky Chicks, fix Larded, hot.
100. Twelve Lobfters, cold.
101. Nine Pullets, four Larded, hot.
102. Bacon, two Gammons, cold.
103. Twelve Leverets, four Larded, hot.
104. Sturgeon, cold.
105. Twenty four Ducklings, fix Larded, hot.
106. Collar'd Beef, cold.
107. Eight Capons, three Larded, hot.
108. Five Puller Pyes, cold.
109. Eight Geefe, three Larded, hot.
110. Three Souc'd Pigs, cold.
111. Three Dozen Glaffes of Jelly.
112. Botargo,
113. Gerkins, } cold.
114. Souc'd Trout,
115. Sheeps Tongues,
116. Skirrets, } hot.
117. Cabbage Pudding,
118. Eight Teals Marin.
119. French Beans, } cold.
120. Leveret Pye,
121. Lemon Sallet,
122. Smelts Pickl'd, } cold.
123. Periwinkles,
124. Chicks, Marb'd,
125. Cavear, } cold.
126. Olives,
127. Prawns,
128. Samphire, } cold.
129. Trotter Pye,
130. Taffata Tarts,
131. Razar Fifh, } cold.
132. Broom Buds,
133. Collar'd Pigs,
134. Parmazan, } cold.
135. Capers,
136. Spinage Tart,
137. Whitings Marinated, } cold.
138. Cockles,
139. Pickl'd Mufhrooms,
140. Prawns, } cold.
141. Mangoes,
142. Bacon Pye,
143. Cardoons, } cold.
144. Souc'd Tench,
145. Three Dozen Glaffes of Blumange, cold.

Befides thefe 145 Difhes, there were Thirty more ferved up to Their MAJESTIES Table, at the Second Courfe. In all, 175 Difhes.

The Coronation Feast of James II held in Westminster Hall in 1684. The feast was a masterpiece of culinary art by the royal cook, Patrick Lamb.

Top: The table plan for the King's Table. Similar tables were provided for the two other estates present – the Peers and Peeresses and the Senior Clergy and Barons. (2)

Bottom left and *bottom right:* The dishes for the King's table; note the mixture of cold and hot, of sweet and savoury, reminiscent of a medieval banquet. The puffins are served cold while the larded turkey chicks are hot. There are plenty of

vegetable dishes – skirrets, peas, cardoons, artichokes and spinach. A 'Betalia Pye' is a pie of choice titbits such as cockscombs and sweetbreads – from the French *beatilles* and the Latin *beatillae*. Note too, dessert dishes like 69, 73 and 77 which would have looked spectacular, the descendant of the medieval 'subtlety' and the obvious ancestor of the Victorian epergne. There is little French influence, if any, in this array of dishes. (2)

Next page: The Feast in Westminster Hall. (2)

BALMORAL.

Her Majesty's Dinner.
Potages.
La purée de Taupinambours.
Hochepot de Gibier.
Poissons.
Les Aigrefins à la maitre d'hotel.
Les Truites frites.
Entrées.
Les Croquettes de Ris de Veau.
La Blanquette de Volaille.
Relevés.
La Poularde aux Choux fleurs.
Le Boeuf rôti.
Rots.
Les Faisans. Le Poulet.
Entremêts.
Les Epinards.
Reisz Kuchen mit Ananas.
Les Pains de la Mecque.

The Royal Luncheon
Sunday January 1st 1893
Indian Dish
Chicken Curry
Scotch Broth
Deutsche Venison Steaks
Les Poulets au Macaroni
Les Cailles rôties
Les Epinards

Hot & Cold Fowls. Tongue
Baron of Beef Boars Head
Game Pie Brawn
Rt Loin Mutton

La Bouilli gratinée
Le Gateau Moltais
Les Pommes cuites

BUCKINGHAM PALACE
THURSDAY, 20TH NOVEMBER, 1947
WEDDING BREAKFAST

Filet de Sole Mountbatten

Perdreau en Casserole
Haricots Verts   Pommes Noisette
Salade Royale

Bombe Glacée Princesse Elizabeth
Friandises

Déssert

Café

MENU
Mousse de Saumon Ecossaise

Escalope de Porc Sautée
Sauce Diable
Choux de Printemps
Pommes Normande

Salade

Summer Pudding

LES VINS

Mülheimer Sonnenlay Auslese 1976
Château Fourcas Dupré 1970
Croft 1963

MERCREDI, LE 16 JUIN, 1982   WINDSOR CASTLE

Top left and *top right:* On a simpler level the menus for Queen Victoria dining privately at Balmoral in about 1870 and 1893. At this time royal eating habits are solidly conservative and lacking innovation. (3)

Middle right: The Wedding Breakfast for Princess Elizabeth and Prince Philip in 1947 in the midst of post-war rationing could well have been a table d'hôte menu from an expensive London restaurant of the time. (3)

Bottom right: In 1982 the dinner menu for Queen Elizabeth strikes an interesting note with a sweet white wine being drunk with the salmon mousse. (3)

The Rich Middle Classes – Private Dining in the 1840s

DINNER PARTY AT HOME.

BILL OF FARE
FOR EIGHT PERSONS.

1 SOUP.
French Pot au Feu.

1 FISH.
3 Slices of Salmon en matelote.

2 REMOVES.
Braised Fowls with spring vegetables.
Leg of Mutton basted with devil's tears.

2 ENTREES.
Lamb Cutlets with asparagus, peas.
Salmi of Plovers with mushrooms.

2 ROASTS.
2 Ducklings.
4 Pigeons barded with vine leaves.

4 ENTREMETS.
Orange Jelly.   Omelette, with fine herbs.
Green peas.   Gooseberry Tart, with cream.

1 REMOVE.
Iced Cake with fruits.

Asparagus.   *New Potatoes.*

Nothing but light wine is drunk at the first course, but at the second r
guests are at liberty to drink wines of any other description, intercepting the
with several hors d'œuvres, which are small dishes of French pickled olives a
sardines, thin slices of Bologna sausage, fillets of anchovies, cibonlettes, or ve
small green onions, radishes, etc.; also a plain dressed salade à la Francais
(for which see end of the entrées, Kitchen at Home), fromage de brie Neufchat
or even Windsor cheese, when it can be procured. The coffee and dessert
usually leave to the good taste and economy of my menagere.

Top: How the wealthy dined in the 1840s. (4)

Bottom left: A kitchen from a middle-class home in the 1840s. Note that it is in the basement lit only from above. A piece of meat hangs in front of a roaring fire with a mechanism that allows it to turn slowly, a kettle and a saucepan sit on the hobs simmering. A large dresser occupies one wall with platters, jelly moulds, tankards and bottles upon it. Carcasses of a duck and a fish wait to be prepared for cooking. On the opposite wall there is a hand mincer in use in almost every home until the electric food mixer arrived in the 1960s. A black cat slumbers on a chair ready for a busy night ahead catching mice. (5)

Above: A typical menu for a dinner at home in 1846. The sheer amount of food and win on display is astonishing; conspicuous was was an essential part of living well. (4)

Public Dining in the 1840s

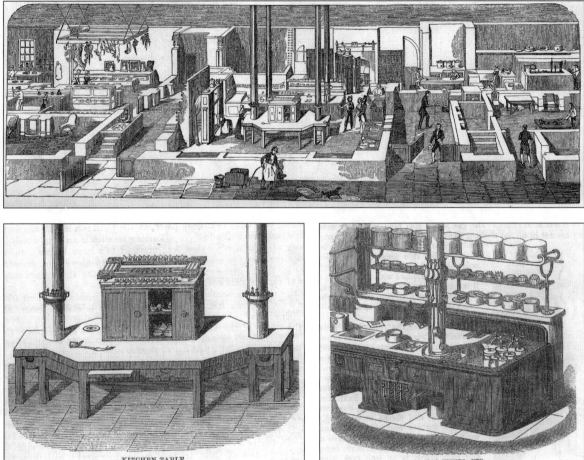

KITCHEN TABLE.

GAS STOVES, ETC.

Top: An unusual diagram of the kitchen at the Reform Club in London in 1846. The chef at the time was Alexis Soyer, an innovative chef and caterer. The kitchen is modern in concept, the meat and game larder is in the top left hand corner with the pastry and confectionery room just below it. The main kitchen is the large room in the centre. The scullery is in the top right hand corner. Soyer's office, looking like a comfortable drawing room, is in the bottom left hand corner. (4)

Middle left: The carefully designed main kitchen table in the Reform Club kitchen. (4)

Middle right: Soyer was an early user of gas in the kitchen. This gas stove was in use in the Reform Club kitchen in 1846. (4)

Bottom right: A typical dinner menu at the Reform Club in 1846. Note that there are eight courses for ten people and that it is all in French – the language of gastronomy. This leads to some absurdities like the capon stuffed in the Nelson style, about the last person the French would want to honour, and the French hors-d'oeuvres containing tunny in the Italian style. However, the range of ingredients is large and Soyer's style is adventurous – a cucumber purée with sweetbreads sounds fascinating. (4)

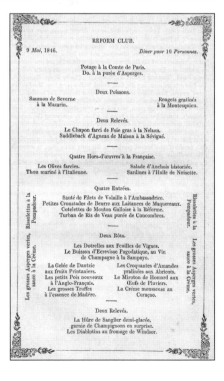

REFORM CLUB.

9 *Mai*, 1846.   *Diner pour* 10 *Personnes.*

Potage à la Comte de Paris.
Do. à la purée d'Asperges.

Deux Poissons.

Saumon de Severne   Rougets gratinés
à la Mazarin.   à la Montesquieu.

Deux Relevés.

Le Chapon farci de Foie gras à la Nelson.
Saddleback d'Agneau de Maison à la Sévigné.

Quatre Hors-d'œuvres à la Française.

Les Olives farcies.   Salade d'Anchois historiée.
Thon mariné à l'Italienne.   Sardines à l'Huile de Noisette.

Quatre Entrées.

Sauté de Filets de Volaille à l'Ambassadrice.
Petites Croustades de Beurre aux Laitances de Maquereaux.
Cotelettes de Mouton Galloise à la Réforme.
Turban de Ris de Veau purée de Concombres.

Deux Rôts.

Les Dotrelles aux Feuilles de Vignes.
Le Buisson d'Ecrevisse Pagodatique, au Vin
de Champagne à la Sampayo.

La Gelée de Dantzic   Les Croquantes d'Amandes
aux fruits Printaniers.   pralinées aux Abricots.
Les petits Pois nouveaux   Le Miroton de Homard aux
à l'Anglo-Français.   Œufs de Pluviers.
Les grosses Truffes   La Crème mousseuse au
à l'essence de Madère.   Curaçao.

Deux Relevés.

La Hûre de Sanglier demi-glacée,
garnie de Champignons en surprise.
Les Diablotins au fromage de Windsor.

Middle and Upper Class Dining in the Late Eighteenth Century

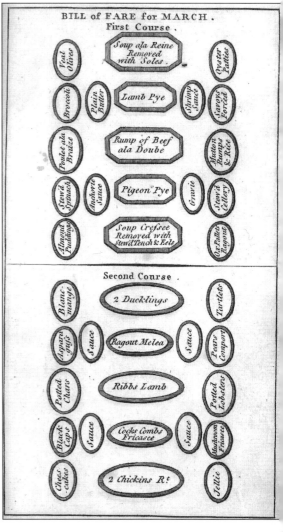

Lamb Pie.

TAKE a loin of lamb, cut off the fkin and fome of the kidney-fat, cut it into thin chops, and feafon them with pepper and falt; lay a thin fheet of pafte round the edge of the difh, put in the meat, with half a pint of water; put puff-pafte over it, clofe it, ornament the top, bake it well, and fend it to table hot.

Top left: A typical kitchen scene from 1790, note that the lady of the house is handing the housekeeper a cookery book. Meats are being roasted at the fire, while a pot is simmering and the butler is carving. (6)

Top right: A Bill of Fare from 1788. (7)

Above and *right:* Richard Brigg's recipes for two of the dishes on the Bill of Fare from 1788 – Lamb Pie and Potted Chars. (7)

Chars.

THESE fifh are peculiar to the lakes in Weftmoreland, and much admired, and are potted thus: fkin, gut, and wafh them clean, cut off the heads, fins, and tails, fcour them well with falt, and wipe them dry with a cloth; turn them round in round potting-pots, or lay them lengthways in a long potting-pot; firft feafon them with beaten cloves, mace, pepper, and falt, cover them with butter, and bake them half an hour in a quick oven; then take them out, and lay them on a coarfe cloth to drain; when they are cold feafon them afrefh, and lay them in your pots; then take the butter they were baked in clean from the gravy of the fifh, put it in a difh before the fire to melt, and when it is melted pour the clear butter over the fifh, and when they are cold put a little more clarified butter half an inch thick over them, and tie them over with paper.

for t'is little more, that can ever be imagined'. The appetite of the Court, the Navy and the Army, all centred within the city of London, was prodigious. The increasing prosperity of its surrounding countryside made an impact upon all travellers. Servant girls at the Inns were mistaken for ladies of gentility so very neatly were they dressed. The peasants appeared well-clothed and ate white bread; they did not wear clogs like the French and were even seen to ride on horseback.

Because the distance between the producer of the food and the buyer had now become too great, food consumption required secondary go-betweens, the merchant who bought from the producer, the carrier who took the produce and the retailer who sold to the market stall. This is why food prices rose throughout the century; the demands of population growth created new jobs for people who took their percentage. Traditional customs of buying and selling food began to vanish forever. We shall see in the next chapter how this is explained trenchantly by Daniel Defoe in *The Complete English Tradesman*, published in 1726.

At the beginning of the sixteenth century chickens had cost 1½d each, eggs were ¾d a dozen, rabbits 1s 4d for nine and a gallon of gooseberries 2d. By 1558 gooseberries and rabbits had doubled in price and chickens trebled. Seven geese cost 9s 4d, two breasts of veal 2s 4d, two necks of mutton 1s and 36 gallons of beer 4s 8d.

Class

People, in this new economic climate, adapted and changed, for human nature insists that new wealth has to be displayed to show everyone else how prosperous a family has become. There was no better way than to buy land and to build a family house in the new style using the latest materials, which were brick and glass. Country estates grew up outside market towns, modest medieval farmhouses were torn down or greatly enlarged, so that they were buried beneath grand facades and long galleries. A new style, Tudor-Gothic, came into being, built from bricks, which by the turn of the century had become very fashionable (both Hampton Court and St James's Palace had been built with them). Cupolas sprang up on top of towers, chimneystacks were ornately finished, gables had painted beasts and entrance porches sprouted finials. There was a passion for windows, so much so that Hardwick Hall, built in the 1590s, gave rise to a jingle: 'Hardwick Hall, more glass than wall'. Though it was a master mason who drew up plans for the house to his client's requirements, it is interesting to note that a new word came into the language by 1563: that of architect.[44] There was little use in living in new large houses with many windows if no one visited, however, so entertaining was important and the food and wine chosen for such entertainment reflected, as always, the court.

Queen Elizabeth was an intellectual and highly civilised, and greatly disdained soporific indulgence in huge banquets and orgies of drinking (which was to happen in the next reign). Her show of restraint and circumspection was obviously something that was absorbed by the rest of society, if the evidence of Elinor Fettiplace is to be accepted. The Queen was an early riser; when she gave audience to Mary, Queen of Scots' ambassador, Sir James Melvil, she bade him arrive at Whitehall at eight a.m.

where he found her walking in the garden, having attended to her devotions, various civil affairs and had had her breakfast; this consisted of manchet, ale, beer, wine and a good pottage, like a farmer's, made of mutton or beef with 'real bones'.

The menu for her dinner on 17 November 1576, a date that marked the eighteenth anniversary of her succession, was not a special one. Her menus varied little over the years. A first course of choice of beef, mutton, veal, swan or goose, capon, conies, fruit, custard and fritters, manchet (the best white bread made up in small loaves), ale and wine. Second course provided lamb or kid, herons or pheasants, cocks or godwits, chickens, pigeons, larks, tart, butter and fritters. Supper was also a two-course meal with a first course of boiled mutton, roast mutton, capon, herons, 'chicken bake', congers, beer, ale and manchet. Authorities tell us the Queen ate very little (she never became fat or gross like her father), and she rarely drank wine, preferring beer or ale and these only in moderation.

Raleigh in his instructions to his son is especially detailed about the horrors of drunkenness. 'Take especial care that thou delight not in wine, for there never was any man that came to honour or preferment that loved it; for it transformeth a man into a beast, decayeth health, poisoneth the breath, destroyeth natural heat, brings man's stomach to an artificial heat, deformeth the face, rotteth the teeth, and, to conclude, maketh a man contemptible . . .' A German traveller in 1598 reported: 'The Queen dines and sups alone, with very few Attendants, and it is very seldom that any Body, Foreigner or Native, is admitted at that Time, and then only at the Intercession of somebody in Power.'[45]

Hentzner describes an account of the ritual attendant upon the Queen's dining. First, two gentlemen, one bearing a rod, the other wearing a cloak, entered the hall, knelt three times, spread a cloth upon the table and then left. Second, two more gentlemen appeared carrying the salt, a plate, and bread. They too knelt three times, placed these things upon the table and disappeared. Third, came an unmarried lady (a countess, he says) and a married one who bore a tasting knife. They curtsied three times, went to the table, and rubbed the plate with bread and salt 'with as much devotion as if the Queen was present'. They stayed in the room. Finally, the Yeomen of the Guard, bareheaded and in scarlet livery with a golden rose embroidered on the back, came in bringing a course of twenty-four dishes served in plate, mostly gold. As each was brought in, it was received by a gentleman yeoman and placed on the table. The married lady who wielded the tasting knife then gave each yeoman a morsel from the dish he had brought in to try it for poison, for there had been attempts – foreign of course – to poison the Queen. All the time while this was going on twelve trumpeters and two kettledrums 'made the hall ring'. Then the dishes were taken to the Queen by the women; she selected what she wanted to eat and the ladies got the rest.

Though the Queen always dined alone or with a few friends, when the day's work was done she often enjoyed supper with friends and attendants 'whom she would cheer up with mirth, discourse and civility'. After or during supper she would often admit Tarleton, the great comedian and talker, or other entertainers to amuse her with 'stories of the town, common jests and accidents'.

By the time of Elizabeth the old dining hall where masters, servants, guests and travellers all dined together had been jettisoned and a new small, intimate room at one end of the big hall became the new dining room, where the master and his family ate alone. The old dining hall became the great chamber now used for games, dancing, plays and household prayers. This, the largest and grandest room in the house was also built as an entrance hall to stun the visitor with its size and beauty.

Etiquette ruled the nobility as well as the wealthy middle classes who were aspiring to join them. *The Boke of Kervynge* by Wynkyn de Worde, though only a short book of twenty-four pages, was first published in 1508 and was reprinted throughout the century. It is highly detailed on the manner of carving, giving precise instructions on how to carve fish, flesh, beast or fowl. It gives instructions to the butler and the panter, knives must be polished and spoons kept clean, cloths, towels and napkins folded in a closet. In all seasons butter, cheese, apples, pears, nuts, plums, grapes, dates, figs, raisins, green ginger and quince jam must be kept in the larder. For feasting there must be butter, plums, damsons, cherries and grapes; after a meal, pears, nuts, wild strawberries, whortleberries, hard cheese, apples and caraway comfits.

This produce was all part of the banquet, the course of sweetmeats taken after the main meal, for which separate rooms were now provided, built in the gardens, and referred to as the banqueting house. In 1533 an arbour was built on top of a mount at Hampton Court; the South or Great Round Arbour was three storeys high, nearly all windows, and topped with an onion dome with a gilded crown. Sir William Petre had one built at Ingatestone Hall. Queen Elizabeth's favourite palace at Nonsuch had a banqueting house three storeys high built on the highest hill in the park; guests would have wandered through the rooms, up into the turrets and out onto the balconies to survey the countryside below. Banqueting was a movable feast: laid out like a buffet you picked out what you wanted, took a glass and conversed as you moved around the company. It all sounds very familiar to us now, though we tend to keep this activity to functions and parties, where we eat, drink and talk while we admire the setting.

The foods served were preserved citrus peels, quince marmalades, conserves of soft fruit, sugar candies, spiced sweet dry cakes, spiced fruit breads and to drink there was spiced hippocras (considered to be a digestive), Rhenish claret wine and beer. These were drunk from Venetian glass, another fashionable necessity. (The New World had made gold and silver relatively cheap so now the gentility spurned them.) Venetian law decreed death for any Venetian glassmaker who took his secrets abroad; nevertheless Giacomo Verzellini arrived in England in 1574 and obtained a patent for making Murano drinking glasses. He eventually became glassmaker to the Queen and retired a rich man in 1592. By that time there were glassworks in Sussex, Surrey and Kent.

During Elizabeth's reign sugar refining began in England and grocers stocked sugar loaves, bits of which were broken off by a sugar chopper. Barbary sugar was known and used, ordinary sugar was imported in loaves of 100 lb and broken up for selling. At the beginning of the century sugar cost from 4d to 10d a pound, but by 1600 the price had risen to 1s or 1s 6d.

The best sugar is made from the tears or liquor of sugar canes, replenished so with juice that they crack againe. The best sugar is hard, solid, light, exceeding white and sweet, glistring like snow, close and not spungy, melting very speedily in any liquor. Such cometh from Madeira in little loaves of three or four pound apiece . . . Barbary and Canary sugar is next to that. Your Common or Coarse sugar (called commonly St. Omers sugar) is white without and brown within, of a most gluish substance, altogether unfit for candying or preserving, but serving well enough for common syrups and seasoning of meat.[46]

By the end of the century the list of banquet delicacies was huge: apart from locally grown fruit and imported dried fruit, there were fruit flavoured stiff jellies and sugar pastes, biscuit breads, cream jellies, sugar candies, marzipan and gingerbread. As the dairy herds grew so did the consumption of cream throughout the whole meal, and syllabubs and flavoured cream cheeses began to appear as part of this last movable feast.[47]

Succade, the sugar preserve of orange and lemon peel, had been imported into England from Spain ever since the thirteenth century, and, as we have seen, the banqueting course itself stemmed from the last course of the medieval feast where all manner of sweet dishes, sugared fruits, spices and nuts and sugary comfits were served. Sugar was seen as partly medicine, partly a preserving agent and as a form of decoration. By the 1530s the name of 'banquet' came to stand for both the sweetmeats themselves, the course where they were eaten and the place in which they were enjoyed. It was due in the main to the large amount of sugar produced in Madeira (where sugar cane replaced wheat by 1460); lesser amounts came from the Canaries, the Azores, North Africa and the Mediterranean. Increased production meant far more imports to northern Europe. However, the Portuguese who owned Madeira had also moved sugar production to Brazil which throughout the century became the biggest supplier of sugar to northern Europe. By 1610 Brazil had 400 mills producing 57,000 tons of sugar annually. This was the beginning of the triangular slave trade in the Caribbean, which increased profits to almost unbelievable heights.

Sugar started as a luxury, presented as gifts from one prince to another.[48] By 1500, however, sugar had taken the place of honey and it was big business; in Antwerp in 1550 there were nineteen sugar refineries, but the real money was made at the wholesale end where in London barrels of various kinds of sugar were sold to grocers. Sugar, in itself, but also as the prime ingredient of the banqueting course, was a symbol of untold luxury and pleasure, but people also clung to the old medieval idea that it was medicinal, so the course also became a *digestif*. The appurtenances to the course, the house, the gardens, the views, and the musicians playing in a glade, underlined the excessive wealth that had contributed to this moment. Indeed, to build a banqueting house was a symbol in the sixteenth century that you had reached the very highest social position possible.

In contrast a very small object – if made from silver – was to become another symbol of class. It was first observed by Thomas Coryat on his travels in Italy and he wrote about it in his *Crudities* in some detail:

> The Italians do always at their meals use a little fork when they cut their meat. For a while with their knife, which they hold in one hand, they cut the meat out of the dish, they fasten their fork, which they hold in their other hand . . . this form of feeding I understand is generally used in all places of Italy, their forks being for the most part made of iron and steel, and some of silver, but those are used only by gentlemen.[49]

Coryat was laughed at for using his fork back home, and it remained unacceptable for another fifty years, then quickly became a status symbol.

Within society there existed an angry stratum of class hostility, the elite feared the poor while they felt a passionate virulence against their masters. A Scottish observer commented in 1614 on the 'bitter and distrustful attitude of English common people towards the gentry and nobility'.[50] Only the landed ruling class were allowed to carry weapons; there was a deliberate policy not to allow the 'meaner sort of people and servants' to serve in the militia. In 1588 when the whole population was called to arms to fight the Spanish Armada there was a general fear that servants trained as soldiers would become unruly and unwilling to continue to serve their masters. These feelings of profound discontent within the lower classes, who had to cope with rising prices and to exist on scraps from their masters, and whose diet otherwise was bread, beans, whey, ale and cheese, would be tapped in the following century by the Parliamentarians in their revolt against the monarchy.

CHAPTER 6

A Divided Century

A civil war, the execution of a monarch, a short-lived republic which thrived for only eleven years, the return of the Stuart monarchy, a bloodless coup and an exiled King: all these dramatic events affected the food the British ate and were to sharpen the differences between ourselves and the continent. Under the Stuarts before 1640 the English ruling class aped Spanish, French and Italian fashions and ideas, for it was sympathetic in every way, including its cooking, to Catholic Europe. 'By the 1620s and 1630s, England seemed to be moving steadily nearer to a system of government modelled on that of Richelieu, with absolute authority and aristocratic privilege centred on a glittering court.'[1]

After 1688, the year of the Bloodless Revolution when William of Orange became King, we led Europe, though not necessarily in our cooking, despite its admirers. In all else, however, much of our strength in politics, culture, literature, military and naval expansion had been laid down in policies brought about by the Civil War and the Interregnum. It was because of this that we were to become the first industrial power of Europe. It was because of this that our diet, our recipes, and the daily food we ate became firmly recognisable as our own for better or worse.

Civil War
Essentially, the English revolution was a bourgeois revolution: it increased the power, wealth and importance of the bourgeoisie; and it created a particularly rich and varied diet for a people not concerned with weight gain, and who saw fatness and physical size as a sign of a profitable existence. Except for Holland, whose commercial prowess was always in competition with our own throughout these years, the substantial influence of the bourgeoisie in the other European countries was to occur 200 years later. How did a war, which is generally considered destructive to almost the whole of society, benefit the middle classes, who had not necessarily fought for the Parliamentarians anyway?

The explanations for the Civil War have been grossly simplified and given religious labels, when in fact at the heart of the dispute were money, commercial trading and land. Under the first two Stuart Kings the issues of land and the monopoly system were at the centre of social unrest and discontent, for land meant food and your family's survival, while the monopoly system, which touched every aspect of life, kept power, patronage and commercial wealth within the monarchy and the immediate court circle. The social mobility that the commercial age of the Tudors had started made government uneasy and suspicious; the rapid enrichment of capitalists and the fluctuations of the market, which led to unemployment and social unrest, caused great unease among the nobility, who sought to control it by granting privileges and placing hindrances in the way of mobility and freedom of movement and contract.[2] So at the beginning of the Stuart period governments thought it their duty to regulate industry, wages and working conditions. They tended to slow down industrial development by controlling it through guilds and monopolies. The industries that held these court-granted monopolies, like the drapers of Shrewsbury and Oswestry, the shoemakers and glovers of Chester, and the metallurgical industry around Birmingham, were unsurprisingly Royalist in the Civil War. The nobility who had been refused under the monopoly system became Parliamentarians. The monopoly system made the market inflexible, unable to react to the demands of a free market. Monopolies were only available to those with influence at court; the producers of rock salt, for example, had to bribe courtiers to get a charter of incorporation, and thus the courtiers acquired control of a new company.[3]

Butter, currants, red herrings, salmon, lobsters, salt, pepper, vinegar, wine and spirits, and every other foodstuff imaginable, were owned by different monopolies which blocked anyone else attempting to trade or produce the goods. Not only the food, but the clothes, the soap, starch, feathers, lace, linen, leather, and gold thread were monopoly-owned; so were the lute strings which played the music, the Bibles and Latin grammars, the coaches and sedan chairs, and even the mousetraps and lighthouses. In 1621 there were 700 different monopolies. They affected the life of hundreds of thousands of Englishmen and by the end of the 1630s they were bringing nearly £100,000 a year into the Exchequer. Business could not endure to be bled in this way; increases in the price of the produce only caused a decline in sales and added resentment and rage when it was known that not only the monarch was enjoying a percentage but so were, as happened in the soap monopoly, foreign Papists. In 1664, when a Bill before Parliament proposed to revive a pin monopoly, a member declared that the late King had lost his head for granting such patents and the Bill was allowed to drop. The Civil War was about trade and commerce. Religion gives convenient labels to a ragbag of resentments; it is commercial injustice that makes men fly to arms.

The struggle succeeded in wresting control of capital from the crown and allowed the entrepreneur to have a free hand. Of the salt industry, Professor Hughes said: 'The first condition of healthy industrial growth was the exclusion of the parasitic entourage of the court.'[4] Abolition of feudal tenures and the Court of Wards turned lordship into absolute ownership, so that lands could now be bought, sold and mortgaged, making long term investment in agriculture possible for the first time. This was the decisive change in English history that made it different from that of the continent. 'A capitalist agricultural economy sprang ready-armed from the great manorial aristocratic system, opening a new chapter in the history of the rural world.'[5] New farming techniques had been popularised by agricultural reformers in the

Interregnum, so most of the obstacles to enclosure were removed. Parliament encouraged enclosure and cultivation of wastelands, it protected farmers against imports and authorised corn hoarding.[6]

Gentlewomen's Secrets

How did the economic repression and the sudden social inflexibility before the Civil War affect what people ate? They heightened social aspiration. Of the twenty cookery books published in the first fifty years of the century, almost all are collections from titled ladies telling of their secrets, both in the kitchen and in the boudoir. Recipes, whether for food or for beauty, were medicinally geared towards health and vigour, as if the secrets of the nobility and how they retained their power were all due to potions and herbal remedies. The literate classes, finding their social mobility blocked or hindered in other ways, could at least dream in these pages of being rich and powerful. The cookery book almost immediately became a stimulus to fantasy.

When the Civil War broke out and the Interregnum began, the collection of recipes of a gentlewoman must have been even more treasured, possibly guiltily, as a memoir of a past age, which might not recur; hence the value placed upon these books was high. How far these recipes were slavishly followed is another question, for often they were too complicated for domestic use. Their advice must have filtered down in some form or other, however; many a housekeeper in an aspiring middle-class home must have instructed an illiterate kitchen staff of two or three young women on how to preserve and pickle the market produce, reading the sentences out slowly, repeating them, then going on to explain how to bone a fish or make a cake the way of a royal princess.

At the end of the century in 1698, Charles Davenant wrote: 'There is no country in the world where the inferior rank of men are better clothed, and fed, and more at ease than in this Kingdom.'[7] Davenant was not considering vagabonds and beggars, he was talking of clerks and servants. Perhaps he was noticing that a large social change had occurred. We had beheaded a king and created a republic, if only for a brief interval. But Davenant's observation was a superficial one. Two years earlier, the engraver and statesman Gregory King (1648-1712) had estimated in his *Natural and Political Observations and Conclusions upon the State and Condition of England* the number of cottagers and paupers to be one quarter of the population, and labouring people and outservants to be another quarter; both groups, he estimated, had to spend more to survive than they ever earned. Half the population then were in permanent debt and poverty. They had barely enough to eat and were certainly almost illiterate and not likely to be reading any books, much less a cookery book.

The bourgeoisie, once they became people of property, inherited a horror of the ignorant, irrational populace. The poor were non-persons, they made no wills and left no inventories, their daughters had no dowries, they did not serve in the militia, but they could be conscripted into army or navy for service overseas. A Yorkshire MP, Captain Adam Baynes, speaking in Parliament in 1659, remarked: 'All government is built on property, else the poor must rule it.'[8]

Some food writers in the past have indicted the Puritan movement as being the cause for the decline in quality of English cooking.[9] This is a conclusion I cannot endorse. But the Puritan movement did affect our diet in a profound manner, for it was to abolish feudal tenures and arbitrary taxation, both of which hugely benefited the common man and therefore improved his ability to grow his own crops. Furthermore it established the sacred rights of property and gave political power to the propertied class. This was, of course, a huge boost to the middle classes and inflated their prestige and power. The Civil War thus eased the plight of the working class for a brief while, before the leviathan of industrial power was again to deplete it; but more particularly it strengthened the bourgeoisie and from that class were born throughout the next few hundred years women cookery writers – a phenomenon totally unknown in France, because of the dominance of the royal male cooks. Women see the providing of a hot meal quite differently from men being paid for their artistry; women see food in a far more pragmatic manner and would be liable to provide nutrition in all its appetising subtlety in a more direct manner. This gender difference was to be apparent in Britain in the centuries to follow.

The Puritan movement also improved the lot of working class women. In all the radical sects considered to be Free Spirits, which vied with each other for authority, there were many women preachers, equal in God's eyes with the menfolk, for, it was said, does not Christ's mercy affect women as much as men? Mrs Chidley in 1641 argued that a husband had no more right to control his wife's conscience than the magistrate had to control his.[10] Also, within these sects there was greater sexual freedom: divorce was approved of, changing partners and even sleeping with two women at once were not considered great sins. In this period there was a breakdown in the Church courts and so freedom was enjoyed from moral supervision; men and women freely met together and publicly denied the existence of heaven and hell, of the devil, of a historical Christ, and of the after life. They rejected a state church, its clergy and its tithes. Hence the sensual aspects of food and drink were as much enjoyed as other pleasures. In fact the Free Spirits sometimes gave a religious and metaphysical significance to food: 'One of them took a piece of beef in his hand tearing it asunder and said to his companion: "This is the flesh of Christ, take and eat."'[11] This could also have been a blasphemous joke, of course, many of which were enjoyed at the time. For a short while ordinary people were freer from the authority of Church and social superiors than they had ever been before or would ever be again until recent times.

The most important manifestation of new thinking, however, was by the Levellers. Their name was given to them by their enemies to suggest that their aim was to 'level men's estates'. They originated around 1645 in the midst of the Civil War when they demanded that sovereignty and real power should be transferred from the crown to the House of Commons. They put forward a plan of economic reform to benefit small property holders: the abolition of all trading monopolies; the reopening of all enclosed land; the security of land tenure; the abolition of tithes; and the complete freedom of religious worship. Sadly, such radical energy and imaginative exploration were suppressed in the 1650s by Cromwell who feared their anarchy. Some of the Levellers' ideas were taken up by the Quakers.

Surely within this ferment of ideas there should be a person who would represent new thoughts upon food itself. Thomas Tryon was born in 1634, a few years after Charles I dissolved Parliament. He rose from the rural working class and educated himself to become an author of fifteen books.[12] He propounded the goodness to health of a vegetable diet and his work and ideas were to influence both Benjamin Franklin and the poet Shelley. What is interesting is that established ideas about food were being questioned, and new answers were being discovered. They had little influence at the time, but they were far from being suppressed, for Tryon was published and read. Within a new and changing social order people were intrigued.

The Bedford Kitchen

Throughout the Interregnum, the old aristocracy kept a low profile, clinging to what was left of the old established values. The Earl of Bedford at Woburn House concentrated on his estates and led a modest life (we have his household accounts) with his expenditure on food being carefully controlled. His estates brought in an income of £8,500; £1,000 came from the sale of wood, malt, tallow, sheepskins, hay and other produce and the rest from rents and fines. In April 1653 he spent 4d on scurvy grass for putting into the children's ale (a common practice in the spring when signs of scurvy were liable to show) and two years later for Lady Anne, aged five, he spent 1s 4d on six sweet oranges and some cherries.

During the Interregnum economies were a necessity; the kitchen fed forty staff as well as the family, the Earl and Countess and their nine children. In 1653, 1654 and 1655 the food cost £280, £260 and £310 respectively. They ate venison from the deer park, rabbits and an occasional hog, while fish came from the Woburn ponds. Cattle were driven from markets at Luton and Leighton Buzzard and meat cost £45-£50 per year. From the Earl's other estates small game birds would be sent, including knots and dotterels (two wading birds still in existence but now uncommon), which were tame enough to be easily snared, and snipe and larks were bought from the markets. They got through a prodigious amount of butter, 30 lb a week, which was bought from six different tenants at 6d a pound. Though in 1654 butter was bought from Hackney, which cost 10d a pound. Farmers' wives supplied cream and eggs; in 1653 cream cost 3d a pint. Fruit and vegetables came from the Woburn gardens but artichokes (costing 3d each), spinach, turnips, beans and peas, salads, herbs and potherbs were bought from the markets. In the summer they bought strawberries and cherries, apricots, quinces (seven for a penny) and apples.

The fish they ate was usually pike and perch from the ponds, but sides of salt fish were eaten by the staff, and flounders, herrings and whiting were bought in. Occasionally a barrel of oysters would be sent from London, and in March 1655 three lobsters, costing 8d each were eaten.

After the Restoration in 1660 all economic caution waned; by 1668 kitchen expenditure had risen to £870, four times the amount of the decade before. By 1671 it had zoomed up to £1,465, but this expense now included the household at Bedford House in the Strand. Keeping a servant was estimated at a cost of 10s a week. A prodigious amount of beef was now eaten; six or seven bullocks arrived almost every month, driven over from the Thorney estate in the fens. Following the Dutch example, this estate had been drained, a process begun thirty years earlier. Thorney supplied all the corn needed at Woburn, as well as oats and hempseed. The Flemings also introduced coleseed (*Brassica arvensis* which we now know as rape), which when crushed was made into a cake for feeding cattle, while the oil, colza, was used for lighting. The rich natural resources of the Fens also ensured a supply of fish and birds: fat swans, quails, knots, dotterels, ruffs and reeves were sent to Woburn for the table. Nevertheless, the breeding of cattle was now seen as important as the growing of corn.

At Woburn improvements to the gardens and orchards began in the 1660s, producing cherries, mascelline[13], apricots, violet musk peaches and Roman nectarines. Many different vegetables were also grown from seeds taken from the gardens of other more enterprising gentry or from the seedsmen in the Strand.

Their groceries came from Nathaniel Child. The largest expenditure in October 1671 was upon sugar, on which they spent £5 12s for 2 cwt at 6d per pound. In November they bought more sugar, both refined and powdered. From 1670 the accounts show the occasional purchase of small quantities of coffee for the personal use of the Earl and the Countess; for the same year there is a mention of the purchase of a coffee pot, a china dish and nine shillingsworth of coffee. In the following year a coffee set was bought for the Countess so that she could entertain her friends. Dried fruit, currants, raisins and prunes were ordered from Nathaniel Child, but the range of spices was small. A medieval noble would have considered the Earl's kitchen to be impoverished, having only mace, cloves, nutmegs and ginger. But this is an example of what was happening within the English kitchen; the Earl, whether he knew it or not, was in fact reflecting the staples of a bourgeois home. These few spices would remain constant within English cooking for the next few hundred years, except for the influence of the Anglo-Indian dishes and ketchups, which would start to infiltrate English society the following century.

The Rise of the Market Garden

In the 1590s immigrants from the Low Countries showed how market gardening could be a profitable venture and the Gardeners' Company received its first charter in 1605. In addition to Kent, other areas around London became centres of fruit and vegetable growing: Westminster, Lambeth, Battersea, Fulham, Putney and Brentford and towards the Thames estuary, Whitechapel, Stepney, Hackney and Greenwich. The districts were chosen for their easy access to the river, for night soil (sewage) was used to fertilise the gardens; barges would unload the dung, then take on board the produce. There were also market garden centres in Surrey and at Colchester and Sandwich, both busy ports with daily goods being sent by sea to London. It became a profitable venture because the London middle classes were aware that the gentry were eating fruits and vegetables cultivated on their country estates, which were not available to them.

Vegetable gardening was now fashionable with the upper classes; a walled garden that grew fruit and vegetables was essential on the country estate. When the nobility moved to London in the winter much of their country produce was sent to them weekly, and market gardens around London could also supply them daily. The fashionable vegetables were artichokes, asparagus, cauliflowers, cucumbers, French beans (the haricot beans from the New World which were first eaten in any quantity in France), green peas (as opposed to the dried pea still eaten by the poor), lettuce, mushrooms and spinach. In the country house garden with glasshouses and hotbeds, the gentry could grow oranges, peaches, apricots, grapes, melons and figs. Market gardens did not try to compete; in the summer they could provide soft fruit, such as strawberries (which were still small), gooseberries, and red, black and white currants. In 1629 John Parkinson, the King's herbalist, first mentions the black currant, suggesting that both the fruit and the leaves should be used in sauces eaten with 'meates'. Francis Bacon wrote: 'The standards to be roses, juniper, holly, berberries (but here and there, because of the smell of their blossom), red currants, gooseberries, rosemary, bays, sweet briar, and such like'.[14]

Root vegetables were a staple food of the poor, but in the winter, when other vegetables were scarce, they were also eaten by the middle classes. They were very cheap, roots, cabbages and beans came to London by the cartload costing 2d to 6d. Roots were also being fed to cattle, however, so they were a despised vegetable and the cookery books tended to dismiss them altogether. An aldermanic report of 1635 speaks of 24,000 loads of roots (carrots, parsnips and turnips) being sold annually in London and Westminster.

By the middle of the century the market gardens around London needed a labour force of 1,500 people to supply the green vegetables. Satisfying the tastes of the gentry proved to be hard work. In 1675 John Worlidge was delighted to discover that if you took up the old roots of the asparagus at the beginning of January and planted them on a hotbed you could have asparagus as early as February.[15] However, in these gardens it was the staple vegetables like cauliflowers and cabbages that took up the most space, though there were some under glass, so that they were ready early in the year. Other favourite crops were radishes and carrots. Fast-growing crops, such as lettuces and radishes, were planted in rows between slow-growing ones like cauliflowers and celery. Thames water was used for irrigation, although sometimes this could be a health hazard. An outbreak of contagious spotted fever in 1623 was put down to the plentiful supply of cucumbers, which to bring them on were over-watered from Thames ditches which were low because of lack of rain. Human excrement as well as animal dung was used as a general fertiliser and to build up the hotbeds. These too, were copied from the walled gardens of the gentry; essentially a hotbed was a pile of dung covered in a thin layer of soil, and the whole covered in glass. One gardener bought 600 loads of dung annually from town for his nine acres of land.[16] It worked miraculously; tender salad plants could be raised in the winter and sent to market. Market gardens boosted the production of glass and London became the centre of its manufacture until the nineteenth century. At Michaelmas gardens could still produce onions, corn salad, spinach, artichokes, celery and asparagus. Melons too needed hotbeds; the Neat House gardens became famous for their melons as early as 1632 and they remained their speciality for the next hundred years. The market gardens made extra money by opening to the public and serving beer, and those next to the Thames became popular ones to stroll in. In August 1666 Pepys took a party on the Thames and visited the Neat House: 'I landed and bought a million melon.'

All this garden produce went by barge on the Thames to Covent Garden; in the early morning the Thames upstream would be full of gardeners' boats going to the various street markets of London. Produce for the markets further from the river went by cart into London; in the evening the same cart would return with dung. It was usual for women to be selling at the stall, while the men acted as porters moving the produce in their huge round baskets, often balanced upon their heads, a familiar sight at Covent Garden until recently.

Of course, London retailers also bought produce from much further afield than the market gardens: cheese came from Suffolk, apples and cherries from Kent. 'The corn growers of Cambridgeshire, the dairy farmers of Suffolk, the graziers of the south Midlands, all looked to the London market as the hub of their economic universe.'[17]

The Accomplisht Cook

Robert May was born in the year of the Armada, his father was a cook and the family known Catholics. Robert rose to be a cook to Royalist nobility – they all fought on the King's side in the Civil War – and worked for them throughout his whole life. In his preface to *The Accomplisht Cook* May says that 'God and my own Conscience would not permit me to bury these experiences in the Grave.' So his life's work, the food and recipes the book contains, is given a religious significance, which, I believe, has been overlooked. Aged fourteen he was sent to France to be a kitchen apprentice and stayed there for five years. When he returned he joined the Worshipful Company of Cooks, which had been incorporated in the fifteenth century and was apprenticed to the cook at the Star Chamber, the food of which we have already examined.

May's collection of over 1,300 recipes[18] was published in 1660, the year that Charles II returned to the throne, and for May such an event must have been a celebration of immense jubilance. For though the King had to pretend to pursue Protestant policy, all knew that he and his family had strong Papist sympathies and a love of France and French cooking. The food they ate was imbued with it. In May's recipes we see a world where the Reformation had never happened, for it recalls medieval food with clarity. May's five years in France must have helped immeasurably, for there, without the traumatic experience of a Reformation, the same recipes were being prepared and cooked as the nobility had eaten for hundreds of years. The French influence may also be seen in his nine recipes for snails and the one for baking frogs. Indeed, May does not hide it, but says in his preface: 'As I live in France and had the language and have been an eye witness of their cookeries as well, as a peruser of their manuscripts and printed authors whatever I found good in them I have inserted in this volume.' It was expected of Stuart noblemen that they should keep open house in the country and be lavish in their hospitality; also the French influence upon the aristocrat demanded conspicuous consumption as part of his role. May's book reflects what must have been uncomfortable demands upon him; it sometimes veers from the occasional simple rustic dish to the lavish spectacle feasting of a medieval monarch.

The medieval influence is most clearly seen at the beginning of May's book, entitled 'Triumphs and Trophies in Cookery to be used at Festival Times': here a ship is made from paste with flags, streamers and guns, or a castle with battlements, portcullis, gates and drawbridges. The perfect spectacle, May suggests, was a pie containing live frogs and another full of live birds; a galleon and a castle, complete with guns, and a stag with an arrow in its side, all made of confectioner's paste. The guns have trains of real gunpowder and the stag is full of claret:

> Being all placed in order upon the Table, before you fire the trains of powder, order it so that some of the Ladies may be persuaded to pluck the Arrow out of the Stag, then will the Claret wine follow as blood running out of a wound. This being done with admiration to the beholders, after some short pause, fire the train of the Castle, that the pieces (guns) all of one side may go off; then fire the trains of one side of the Ship as in a battle . . . to sweeten the stink of the powder, let the ladies take the (blown) egg shells full of sweet waters, and throw them at each other. All dangers being seemingly over, by this time you may suppose they will desire to see what is in the pies; where lifting first the lid of one pie, out skips some Frogs, which makes the Ladies to skip and shriek; next after the other pie, whence comes out the birds; who by a natural instinct flying at the light, will put out the candles: so that what with the flying birds, and skipping frogs, the one above, the other beneath, will cause much delight and pleasure to the whole company.[19]

This extraordinary mixture of spectacle, magic and theatre remained unchanged in court circles for two to three hundred years – May is at the very end of it. One wonders at the hardiness of the women content for their silk, satin and lace to be besmirched with coloured sugared water and slimy frogs, and defecating birds flying in their panic into intricate coiffures. The rough and tumble of this entertainment is not to present taste, but there can be little doubt that in May's time it was still popular as otherwise he would not have made reference to it. This medieval spirit permeates the book in its instructions on how to bake lampreys or the number of almond recipes, or make marrow pies and medlar tarts. This is firmly from an era of pre-Reformation cooking, recalling an age in which the world was secure beneath the yoke of Rome. May even looks back on his youth before the Civil War with nostalgia: 'Then was hospitality esteemed, neighbourhood preserved, the poor cherished and God honoured; then was Religion less talked on, and more practiced; then was atheism and schism less in fashion: then did men strive to be good, rather than to seem to.'

May's recipes for turbot and halibut, which since Roman times had been eaten only by the elite, illustrate this courtly and complicated manner of cooking. The fish is poached in half white wine and water, with added sliced onion and ginger, mace, cloves, thyme, rosemary, bay leaf, lemon or orange peel, and finished off with butter, more spices and barberries. Compare this method with Patrick Lamb's recipe (see page 165), who was the official court cook to five different English monarchs.

May is not alone, however, for all the recipe books published in his lifetime are influenced by the early Stuart court of James I and his son, Charles I; though published after the Civil War and the Interregnum, in the midst of the Restoration period they still recall a golden age that is inherently medieval. Hannah Woolley wrote several cookery books which went into many editions and sold well into the next century; she was clever and cultured and worked hard to improve herself. Speaking French fluently, she read aloud French plays to her master, Sir Henry Wroth, and became stewardess to his wife after first being their cook. They were Royalists and Hannah boasts of having cooked a banquet for King Charles I. In 1661 she wrote her first book, *The Ladies Directory*; it begins, as so many of the collections do, with a section on preserving and candying: apricots in jelly, white quinces (to keep them white they were boiled fast and quickly in pippin water, which is of jellying quality), a conserve of red roses, a paste of plums, almond gingerbread, gooseberry custard, cherry water and naturally, almond butter. There are marmalades of damsons, warden pears and quinces. There are syrups for colds, coughs and an *aqua mirabilis*, which was sack and aqua vitae mixed with many spices – altogether nearly 200 recipes.

The next section, called 'The Exact Cook or The Art of Dressing all sorts of Flesh, fowl and fish', begins with recipes for pickling both cucumbers and purslane. Then follow recipes to stretch and clean sheep's guts, soaking them in water for nine days, but one must be sure to move them about to make them easy to fill. There is no logic in the order of recipes (as there was in May): we go from orange pudding to making French Bread (a brioche, in fact, made with eggs and milk). A chicken pie is seasoned with nutmeg, sugar, pepper, salt and raisins. A herb pie is made with lettuce, spinach and flavoured with butter, nutmeg, sugar and salt; when cold clotted cream, sack and more sugar are added – almost an exact medieval recipe. Plaice and flounders are poached in white wine flavoured with lemon, salt, cloves, mace and small onions. There is a pie of eels and oysters, one for hare, pumpkin and lamb, others for steak, neat's tongue, venison, calves' foot and pig. There is even a recipe for a potato pie (but this would have been the sweet potato); Hannah adds marrow, cinnamon, sugar, mace, white wine, butter and yolks of eggs. Chickens and pigeons are boiled with a sauce of gooseberries or grapes. She tells us how to pickle oysters, to make a trifle, a lemon syllabub and cabbage cream. This is stunning cooking but almost unchanged since 1400. A modern version of the recipes, including all the beef stews, in which Hannah specialises, was published in 1988.[20] Its author and his friends delighted in the flavours of fruit and savoury mixed, which in some cases are similar, if not identical, to the series of *bruets* in *An Ordinance of Pottage* discussed on page 88. Later in her life Hannah went on to cook for another Royalist family, that of Sir Henry Cary.

Another greatly successful book was *The Queen's Closet Opened*, which has a portrait of Henrietta Maria, the wife of Charles I, as frontispiece. This was printed by

Nathaniel Brook in 1655, and purports to be transcribed from Her Majesty's own receipt books by W.M., one of her servants. The sub-title is 'Incomparable secrets in physick, preserving and candying and cookery'. The volume consists of three books: 'The Pearle of Practice', 'A Queen's Delight' and 'The Compleat Cook'; the last was sometimes published by itself. The title page boasts that the recipes stem from Italy, Spain or France (the Queen was French and spent most of her life there in exile). Indeed on page 5 we are told how to dress a pig in the French manner: it is chopped up and boiled in white wine, and flavoured with nutmeg, anchovies, elderflower vinegar and butter. A capon larded with lemons is flavoured in a medieval manner, and cooked with verjuice, white wine and a bundle of herbs; but beef marrow, mace and dates are added and the broth is thickened with almonds. This clearly informs us that the rather complicated cooking of an early period continues in a royal household, unlike the simplicity of Lady Fettiplace. A recipe for boiled pigeons is fairly simple: they are stuffed with parsley and butter, placed in an earthenware dish with more butter and baked; then parsley, thyme and spinach are chopped small and added to the dish; the sauce is thickened with egg yolks and verjuice and the pigeons are served in the sauce on slices of bread. You may learn here how to prepare and dress snails, a long and complicated recipe as the snails are boiled for hours, then minced and turned into a soup; there is mention of one clove of garlic with onions as flavouring with lemon and herbs.

The French influence (or, as I hope I am making clear, the medieval and Roman Catholic) continues in the anonymous *The Accomplished Lady's Delight* (1675). The third section is 'The Compleat Cook's Guide, or, directions for dressing all sorts of Flesh, fowl and Fish, both in the English and the French mode, with all sauces and sallets and the making Pyes, Pasties, Tarts, and custards, with the Forms and Shapes of many of them'. A sauce for a shoulder of mutton is made from oysters, herbs, white wine, nutmeg, mace and lemon. If you have no oysters use capers instead. A leg of mutton is stuffed with herbs and egg. A boiled chicken is cooked with a small piece of mutton, and lettuce, marigold leaves, spinach and endive. Flounders are cooked in the French fashion, it tells us, in white wine, verjuice, mace and rosemary. Yet this recipe is again a medieval English one.

The Closet of Sir Kenelm Digby (1669) is the work that Robert May most admired. One feels that the title and religious faith of the author influenced May's opinion. Digby (1603-1665) even fought a duel in Paris in defence of Charles I; he was chancellor to Henrietta Maria and pleaded Charles's cause with Pope Innocent X; he also discovered the necessity of oxygen to the life of plants. The most striking aspect of Digby's book is the huge number of recipes for making drinks, as if this were his first priority, which it may well have been: there are fifty recipes for making meath, another fifty for metheglin (fermented herbal drinks with honey), in addition to recipes for hydromel, stepony, bragot, strawberry wine and cock-ale.

Queen Henrietta Maria began her day with a light broth and Kenelm Digby gives us a recipe. It was made with lean veal, beef and mutton boiled with a hen; then an onion, perhaps even a clove of garlic, parsley, thyme, mint, coriander, saffron, pepper, salt and a clove were added. This is boiled together then poured on toast and stewed again until the toast has amalgamated with the broth; this is repeated until you have a good potage. However it is not yet finished, for then you can add parsley roots, leeks, cabbages or endive and in the summer you put in lettuce, purslane, borage and bugloss. A *Bouillon de Santé*, the good Digby suggests. Then Sir Kenelm recommends finishing the breakfast with two poached eggs with a few collops of bacon. Little did he know that this simple postscript to the broth with its involved cooking and many ingredients would in a further 300 years become the only British meal worth praising throughout the world.

Digby's recipe for an 'Ordinary Potage' is also worth glancing at, for there is little ordinary about it. First, a leg of beef and scrag end of necks of veal and mutton are boiled in a ten-quart pot filled with water. (This was begun at six in the morning to have the soup ready by noon.) It is skimmed, and two or three onions in quarters, half a loaf of light French bread and the bottom crust of a Venison Pasty are added. (See below.) This will all dissolve in the broth. Season with salt, pepper and a few cloves, then add borage, bugloss, purslane, sorrel, lettuce, endive and whatever else you like! After three hours boil a hen or a capon in it. Then slice some French bread and toast it in front of the fire; lay the slices in a chafing dish and pour some of the broth over; then lay the hen over them with the herbs and roots about it; let it cook a little longer, then squeeze some orange or lemon juice over (or put some verjuice in it) and finish with perhaps adding two or three egg yolks to the broth.

No ordinary person, of course, would ever be able to sup from such a dish; but perhaps within the ranks of the nobility such a soup would strike them as ordinary. To make a barley pottage, according to Digby, barley is added to this broth and then poured over the capon, hen, mutton or veal. There are several recipes for *potage de santé*, which are all based on a broth of boiled chicken and meats with herbs.

The old end of a venison pasty, too dried out to enjoy by itself, would give the broth a much desired spicy tang. Both the bread and the pasty thickened the broth slightly; obviously the liquid was reduced, for Digby mentions that the Queen's light broth 'was boiled to less than a pint'. A nourishing broth had more meat bones in it, with bones broken so that the marrow spilt out; it was allowed to jelly, the fat skimmed from the top, and the dregs removed from the bottom; then the melted jelly was served with a yolk of egg beaten with orange juice added. This sounds something akin to nectar. This food is not for mere mortals; it was eaten at court and at the homes of the great Catholic families if they were still in funds. The food of the rising middle classes, the people who crowded the streets of London and other growing towns, was plainer, quickly and easily cooked, or supplied by the cookshops which they could eat there or take home.

It is interesting to see that a peasant staple dish – pease pottage – appears under the name of Lord Lumley, who was one of Robert May's employers and patrons. His recipe, made with the inevitable dried peas, has as flavouring coriander seed, onion, mint, parsley, winter savory and marjoram. It is strained, then a great deal of butter is added and finally it is seasoned with pepper and salt. Pea soup appears by this time to be a quite classless dish: Pepys enjoys it and Mrs Pepys makes a point of ordering it at a particular eating house; and Evelyn gives two different recipes. The dish that had kept the peasants from starving has now become a favourite throughout society, and henceforward no cookery book was ever without a recipe for it.

New Beverages

In 1637 at Oxford John Evelyn wrote in his diary:

> There came in my tyme to the College one Nathanial Conopios, out of Greece, from Cyrill the Patriarch of Constantinople, who returning many years after was made (as I understand) Bishop of Smyrna. He was the first I ever saw drink coffee, which custom came not to England till 30 years after.

Paris had tasted its first cups of coffee in 1644 but it was not until 1650 that the first coffee house in England (and only the second in Europe) was opened at Oxford, advertised as 'a simple Innocent thing, incomparable good for those that are troubled with melancholy'. But from the very beginning coffee houses proved to be centres of intellectual debate, visited by writers, scholars, wits and politicians. At Oxford the coffee house was run by Jacob the Jew, who benefited from Cromwell's toleration of religion. This was the Interregnum when England was enjoying its first open society and there was much for intellectuals to debate. Oxford was somehow politically tainted, however, for it had been the centre of the Royalist faction and London, the Parliamentary base, needed its own coffee house.

Daniel Edwards, a merchant from Turkey who married the daughter of a London alderman, one Hodges, drank two or three cups of coffee a day and it was he who set up his Turkish servant, Pasqua, to provide coffee in a shed in the churchyard in St Michael's Cornhill. Pasqua recommended coffee as a digestif, which should be taken at three or four in the afternoon after dinner as well as in the morning. He claimed it would prevent drowsiness and so make one fit for business. As this was one claim that customers found was astonishingly true, coffee drinking became an almost overnight success. Seeing this, Alderman Hodges turned the shed into a house and with his coachman, Bowman, became partners of Pasqua and Edwards. Coffee houses quickly became centres of radical discussion to discuss the merits and flaws of the Republic.

An advertisement of 1662 extols the virtues of a coffee powder costing from 4s to 6s 8d a pound; various types are praised, such as a Turkish berry and an East Indian berry. They also sell 'chocolatta' at 2s 6d a pound, sherbet flavoured with lemons, roses or violets and 'Tea according to its goodness'. By 1675 London was thought to have 3,000 coffee houses, but this was an absurd exaggeration; an early London Directory for 1739 listed 551 houses, 144 of them within the City. However, it seemed that more coffee was drunk in London than any other city in the world, and coffee houses had now spread into the provinces as far north as York. Women, brewers and innkeepers disliked them, complaining bitterly of the ills the beverage caused. In 1674

The Women's Petition Against Coffee Houses alleged that 'Coffee makes a man barren as the desert out of which this unlucky berry has been imported.'[21]

Each coffee house had its own distinct character and different type of customer, whether they were lawyers, writers or politicians. After the Restoration, however, their radical character disturbed the monarch; in 1675 Charles II attempted to suppress them, because of 'the multitude of Coffee Houses lately set up and kept within this Kingdom, and the great resort of the idle and dissipated persons in them, having produced very evil, and dangerous effects'. When it was passed, the law caused such fury that it was never enforced. Coffee houses were far too important: they were the first men's clubs, 'penny universities' that disseminated the latest news and gossip, discussion groups and reading libraries. On the corner of Bow Street in Covent Garden stood Will's Coffee House, which was termed Wits' Coffee House and patronised by both Pepys and Dryden. Defoe thought that the best company generally went to Tom's or Will's Coffee Houses. Addison and Steele, Pope and Swift went to Buttons. Coffee houses also became centres of commerce; both Jonathan's and Garraway's served for three-quarters of a century as England's main stock exchanges; Virginia and the Baltic doubled as the mercantile shipping exchange and Lloyd's Cafe became the world's largest insurance company.

Coffee cost 1d or 2d a cup; you could stay as long as you wished, read papers, chat to friends or do business. At first the coffee was served straight without additions, though one could add honey, cloves, ginger, cinnamon and spearmint if inclined. Within two decades milk, cream and sugar were also offered to soften the bitterness. House rules forbade swearing, gambling, quarrelling and profane language and all clients were considered to be equal. These limitations, so readily accepted by the clients, proved to be the beginning of a civilising process within society. By the 1690s alcoholic drinks were also on sale in the coffee houses as well as tea and chocolate, though these already had a feminine image. By the turn of the century coffee had begun to appear not only in the most aristocratic of households but also in the wealthiest. We have seen that the Bedfords had some as early as 1670; now the affluent urban households drank coffee at breakfast and after dinner. At breakfast it took over from ale or wine and the meal of meats, game and fish that was served with them; now a variety of breads and preserves were on offer. In 1685 powdered coffee for domestic use was being sold at 3s a pound and Thomas Garwar, the proprieter of the Sultanese Head, was warning his customers that the powder 'if kept two days looseth much of its first goodness', so he advised buying beans and to grind them in a mill whenever needed.[22]

Tea's feminine image was partly because it was introduced to England by Catherine of Braganza, the Portuguese Queen to Charles II; it was also associated with a panoply of china and porcelain, teapots and tea dishes, gilded mahogany tea-tables and silver teapots, tea-kettles and tongs, cream jugs and tea-spoons which all involved a tea ceremony from the lady of the house at the centre of a circle of friends. Tea drinking was not the instant hit that coffee had been, it took a much longer time to become the staple beverage of the nation (See Chapter 8). From the beginning, however, it was helped upon its way by medicinal claims on its health-giving properties.

Chocolate was introduced to France in 1615 and from there it moved slowly across the Channel until by the 1650s it was served as an alternative in the coffee houses. Two of them, The Cocoa Tree and Whites, specialised in the drink, but it never caught on with any enthusiasm, possibly because it was too thick to drink easily; the butterfat content made it particularly viscous so that it needed constant stirring.

Samuel Pepys

We can gather a vivid impression of what people ate in the seventeenth century from the diaries of Pepys, and a glance at the two food books of Evelyn. We have already said that the recipe books that stemmed from the court and the nobility are aspirational. We have seen, too, that the recipes are complicated and owe much to medieval traditions; they also undoubtedly have a symbolic reference to what was still considered by many to be the one true religion. With the Restoration, French dishes had become fashionable, but they had the associations of Stuart royalty and Roman Catholicism to which courtiers were sympathetic, if not secretly devoted. Samuel Pepys was not a Catholic, but because he was ambitious and mixed constantly with the gentry, he had to be diplomatic. The bourgeoisie was largely Protestant and mercantile, however, and the food they wanted to eat throughout the day had to be convenient, so that it fitted into a busy commercial life. What is perhaps not too surprising is how commerce reacted to the demand, for London was now crammed with eating places.

Tavern food was hugely popular. Pepys visited over 100 in Westminster and London alone. Of the inns, strong-water houses and varied eating places, the most popular were taverns, where you could get a private room and have a pot-boy bring in the food and drink; the room would have a fireplace, table and chairs. The food would be brought in from a cookshop or a market stall, and you could entertain friends, write letters and do business with tradesmen. Naturally Pepys used the coffee houses too. In 1664 he met Sir William Petty at one, where they conversed about waking and dreaming and how one could possibly tell the difference.

Pepys mentions eating game most frequently, followed by poultry, then beef; he appears to eat less of pork and mutton and veal, and marrowbones, tongue and tripe only occasionally.[23] The game was largely comprised of venison and Pepys at times got sick of it. When Lord Sandwich gave him 'half a buck' Pepys passed it on to his mother 'to dispose of as she pleased'. Poached venison and game birds were sold openly in the London market and they were often on the tavern menus; Pepys ate the venison there in a pasty.

Dinner at the King's Head at Charing Cross, one of the most fashionable of taverns, cost 2s 6d; here the food was roasts and pies, vegetables were boiled and then served with butter. There were more modest eating houses called ordinaries, where a meal of two courses would cost 1s. Pepys used the Cocke at the end of Suffolk Street where on 15 March 1669 he began with soup and went on to roasted pullets. A month later he and his wife were dining there again when his wife had a strange desire to partake of their green pea soup. This favourite soup had many different versions: in 1694 Ann Blencowe adds spinach, sorrel, cabbage, lettuce, chervil and endive to hers, as well as mint, butter and strong broth.[24] Thickened with the dried green peas, this would have been a marvellously tasty and nutritious dish of a fetching green hue. The soups made at the cookshops would have been almost a meal in themselves, based as they were on meat, poultry bones and ham hocks, with vegetables and herbs added.

This is not convenience food as we know it today, synthetic and chemically flavoured pre-cooked in a million portions; the dishes were individually cooked from a wealth of fresh foods, bought in the market that morning. They were certainly reasonably priced meals based on meat, soups, vegetables, puddings and bread, washed down with ale, beer or wine. They owe nothing to court medieval tradition and everything to a busy, small Tudor kitchen. These meals were more than adequate, more reminiscent today perhaps of an unpretentious restaurant sited near a cattle market. The meat was nearly always beef, cut in thick slices with a sauce made from the drippings and the stock from boiled mutton, beef or chicken. The most common vegetable would have been cabbage boiled in the mutton stock, drained and served with butter. 'Five or six heaps of cabbage, carrots, turnips, or some other herbs or roots, well peppered and salted and swimming in butter', the French refugee author Henri Misson wrote in 1690. The bread would have been wheaten; loaves cost depending on the size anything between a halfpenny and twopence.

Boiled suet puddings had been a staple of the rustic kitchen. As a flavoured suet with dried fruits, mixed with eggs, curds or cream, tied into a sheep's stomach and hung in a slow boiling cauldron with the rest of the meal, it could be left for the day. These too were made at some of the eating houses; the pudding cloth came into use at the beginning of the century and boiled puddings of various kinds became commonplace. May gives recipes for puddings made from bread, rice and oatmeal, flavoured with cinnamon, nutmeg, cloves and currants, all of which are baked. Then there are the savoury and blood puddings, which are made in animal guts and boiled. He uses a cloth for making various other sweet puddings made from bread, flour, cream and eggs, which are all boiled. Pepys does not mention eating these, but generally he ends his meal with a fruit tart and sometimes a syllabub or tansy.

Cheese came in many varieties; great quantities of it were brought to London by barge down the Thames from Gloucestershire and Wiltshire with bacon and malt. There was Stilton carried down from Huntingdonshire, called the English Parmesan, which according to Defoe was brought to the table 'with the mites and maggots round it, so thick, that they bring the spoon with them for you to eat the mites with as you do the cheese'. Pepys never mentions this experience so perhaps it was not so common fifty years earlier, but he would have eaten Cheddar, which Defoe describes on a visit to the village, which had a large green or common on which the whole herd of cows belonging to everyone fed.

The milk of all the town cows is brought together every day into a common room, where the persons appointed, or trusted for the

management, measure every man's quantity, and set it down in a book;
when the quantities are adjusted, the milk is all put together, and every
meal's milk makes one cheese, and no more; so that the cheese is bigger,
or less, as the cows yield more, or less milk. By this method, the goodness
of the cheese is preserved, and, without all dispute, it is the best cheese
that England affords, if not, that the whole world affords.[25]

Defoe goes on to explain that the people who have only one cow and less milk have to
wait longer to be paid, for they wait until their share amounts to one whole cheese.
Cheddar was sold for 6d to 8d a pound. Pepys might also have eaten a cows' milk
cheese from Cheshire, mentioned in the Domesday book, or Eppynt from north
Wales, which was kept for two to six months before being eaten, and which came to
be called Caerphilly; then there were the great cheeses that stemmed from the
medieval monasteries of Yorkshire: Swaledale, Wensleydale and Coverdale. Dutch and
Italian cheeses were popular too, Parmesan was perhaps the favourite: so precious was
it that Pepys buried his with the wine in the garden when the Fire of London
appeared to be getting near his home.

Dairying and keeping pigs went together because the pigs were fed on the
skimmed milk and whey, so dairy farmers also produced much pork, ham and bacon.
All farmers, however small they were, kept a few pigs, as they were obliging animals
that ate all the scraps and could forage on the common and in the woods. It was these
modest farmsteads that suffered so brutally when the enclosure acts, which had begun
in Tudor times, began to bite, for once the woodland was cultivated and the common
land was hedged by the local landowner there was nowhere for the pigs to forage. Pigs
were also fed on the waste products from distilleries and piggeries were now found
near breweries around the outskirts of London and other towns.

Of the butcher's meat, Pepys' favourite was roast beef, but it was a dish too good
to be eaten alone at home. The meat Pepys ate came from animals that might well have
started their journey to London from as far afield as Scotland, or Wales. They were
driven near to London where they rested and grew fat. St Faiths was a little village
north of Norwich where the Scottish cattle were fattened. Defoe describes it: 'These
Scottish runts coming out of the cold and barren mountains of the Highlands feed so
eagerly on the rich pastures in these marshes that they thrive in an unusual manner,
and grow monstrously fat; and the beef is so delicious for taste, that the inhabitants
prefer them to the English cattle, which are much larger and fairer to look at.'[26] Defoe
estimated that there were 40,000 of these cattle fed in England every year, most of
them in the marshes in the triangle of Norwich, Beccles and Yarmouth. Large
quantities of Lincolnshire and Leicestershire sheep were kept in the Essex marshes
near Tilbury, and fattened in the autumn for the Christmas market. The greatest
sheep fair was held annually at Weyhill near Andover where the downs appeared
covered in the animals; Defoe was told by a grazier that there were around 5,000 sheep
sold at the fair.

Beginning in the autumn turkeys and geese were driven down from Norfolk and

Suffolk, feeding on the harvest stubbles as they walked. 'They have counted 300 droves of turkeys pass in one season over Stratford Bridge on the River Stour,' Defoe noted. The bridge forms the boundary between Suffolk and Essex. He went on to say that the droves generally contained 300 to 1,000 birds and to mention that lately the farmers had invented a carriage (Defoe is writing in the 1720s) with four storeys of cages on each cart to carry the birds in. The carts were driven by two horses and by changing the horses they travelled by day and night, so that they bring the fowls as much as 100 miles in two days and a night. Pepys was given a turkey as a gift five times, four of these at Christmas, for turkey was already a Christmas dish; in all, seventeen turkeys are recorded as being eaten by him. Rabbits were purchased from farmers' wives at Stocks and Leadenhall, or simply from the poulterers in Newgate Market. Pullets, which were served roasted, are mentioned frequently. Roasting is obviously the preferred method of cooking, followed by making pies, tarts and pasties. He enjoyed a sauce invented by the Duke of York (the future James II) who had got it from the Spanish ambassador, 'made from parsley and dry toast beat in a mortar together with vinegar, salt and a little pepper'.

We gain some idea of what a celebratory dinner might be for a comfortably off middle-class family if we look at the menu that Pepys provided in 1663 for his annual anniversary of his operation of cutting the stone, which had taken place on 26 March. (The removal of a kidney stone was a common one, but dangerous and exceedingly painful.) There were eight guests and the ten of them ate a 'Fricasse of rabbets and chicken – a leg of mutton boiled – three carps in a dish – a great dish of a side of lamb – a dish of roasted pigeons – a dish of four lobsters – three tarts – a Lampry pie, a most rare pie – a dish of anchovies – good wine of several sorts; and all things mighty noble and to my great content.'[27] At first glance this seems a great deal of food: there are two roasts, mutton and lamb and perhaps five roasted pigeons, but between ten people, over conversation and wine, it would go quickly. It was customary to serve boiled meats first, then the roasted, then the baked and finally the pies, tarts and dishes of fruit and sweetmeats. As to the rest, such as the fricassée, this would probably have been the simplest form of made-up dish, as they had only the one cook who must have been worked off her feet that evening; she had to serve at the table as well, for she had no temporary cook to help her, as had happened on other anniversaries.

For the fricassée the rabbit and chicken would have been jointed, floured, then fried in butter and when tender, wine, nutmeg and cream added. For our tastes the fact that the courses seem so similar (both courses have fish, pies and meat) seems odd. However, they would have arrived as they were cooked; the roasts would have been put on the table to pick at while another dish was still being finished in the kitchen. The lamprey pies were made in Wales and sent to London, the lobsters were bought already boiled and served cold. The pies also could have been bought ready made, for there were pork pies from the north, veal and ham pies from the midlands, steak and kidney pies, chicken pies, eel pies from the Lake District and venison and pigeon pies. Pie moulds made out of sycamore were made in all sizes, the pastry was wrapped around them, decorated, then the mould was lifted out and the centre filled. Flat pies were made in earthenware, slipglazed shallow dishes.

The year before Pepys had given his guests a brace of stewed carps, six roasted chickens, hot salmon and for a first course a spinach tansy and two ox tongues. The tansy was eggs and cream, with the juice of the spinach (to colour it) thickened with a little breadcrumb and flavoured with nutmeg. (Tansy leaves, a very bitter herb *Tanacetum vulgare*, once flavoured this dish. It was eaten for medicinal reasons and it was finished by being strewn with sugar.) In 1660 Pepys' wife had had a new oven and he found her making 'pyes and tarts' but 'not knowing the nature of it did heat it too hot and so did a little overbake her things, but knows how to do better another time'. A great deal of guesswork and experiment must have gone on when a wood-fired oven was new; only experience would inform the cook how the oven would work.

Over those few years after the Restoration Pepys records visits to taverns and cookshops where he ate various foods like gammon and cheesecakes; sausages washed down with raspberry sack; roasted pork, or ox tongue; he breakfasted on cold turkey-pie and a goose then later ate a venison pasty which he detected had been made from beef – Pepys was not pleased. Yet this was a common practice, and indeed Robert May gives instructions 'to bake beef, red-Deer fashion in Pies or Pasties either Surloin, Brisket, Buttock, or Fillet, larded or not'. Seasoning it correctly might have been part of the secret; May tells you to add ginger, nutmegs, cloves and bay leaves.

At the Mulberry Garden in April 1663 Pepys is treated by a Mr Sheres to a Spanish Oleo which he finds a very noble dish; he is given one by the Spanish Ambassador a month later, but he did not think highly of it. The oleo (or olio) was a highly fashionable dish of the century; essentially, it was a spiced stew of various meats and vegetables, though this description makes it seem mundane, the very last epithet it should attract. It was immensely popular in Paris and had been brought over to England by Charles II; the dish stayed in favour until the end of the seventeenth century, and then seems to have passed away with the decline of the Stuart monarchy, although some of the cookery writers of the next century, with their eye on the nobility such as Charles Carter, include it in their books. The name derived from *olio podrida*, the Latin word *olla* meaning a cooking pot. The dish was a movable feast, as almost anything could be added: in May's Olio Royal there is mutton, veal, twelve baby pigeons, eight baby chickens, a piece of larded bacon, a minced roast capon, oranges, mace, cloves, anchovies, nutmeg, beef marrow, sage and butter, together with artichokes, asparagus, skirrets, pistachios, sheep's tongues, wine, carved lemons, spinach and parsley. He continues with a list of various garnishes, which include cocks' combs. This indeed, is a recipe for royalty and it was unlikely to be anything like the one Pepys enjoyed. But May's everyday recipe for the dish, which includes Bologna sausages, as well as root vegetables and cabbage, is also highly complicated. What was certain was that an oleo included different game birds, poultry and mutton or beef, with root vegetables, spinach and sorrel and depending on the grandeur of the company artichokes, asparagus, saffron and almonds could also be added.

How interesting that Pepys refers to it as 'a noble dish', for that is what it had become, a dish that in using all the most expensive ingredients was a luxury. Yet in essence this was a dish of the Spanish peasant, where anything available was put into a large cauldron and simmered for hours. John Evelyn gives two recipes for oleo: one, which he refers to as the French version, is merely an excellent pease pottage, flavoured with garlic, coriander, butter, parsley and onion. His 'Spanish Olio' is more recognisable, having beef, bacon, pork, a neck of mutton, a knuckle of veal, a pullet or three pigeons boiled with cabbage, ginger, nutmeg, cloves and turnips. These are modest recipes, eschewing the grandeur of May's. Another earlier recipe is from Sir Kenelm Digby, and entitled 'A Plain but Good Spanish Oglia'; it is the only one to mention *Garavanzas* (chick peas), which would have been essential to the original Spanish recipe. Digby also likes to add a venison piecrust to the stew; otherwise it is similar to Evelyn's and must have been very like the one that Pepys ate.

Since Cromwell had banished them, Friday and Lenten fasts were no longer observed (except by the Roman Catholic families who were discreet in such habits) but Pepys and his milieu ate fish often. There were fishmongers like Pepys' Uncle Wight who were often very wealthy men and their livery company was an important city company. The English and Scottish fishing fleets supplied London with herring, cod, ling and haddock, a portion of it always dried and salted. Shellfish was plentiful and cheap and Pepys frequently mentions eating oysters and lobsters. The most expensive fish were the freshwater varieties such as salmon, pike and perch, which had to be kept fresh in tanks and watercarts. Lobsters, crayfish and prawns were made into patties, mixed with egg, butter, minced anchovy (which were sent in barrels from Italy) and lemon, wrapped in pastry and baked. On a visit to Hungerford, Pepys eats eels, trout and crayfish straight from the river. On a dinner with Sir W. Batten he eats a ling and herring pie and remarks how very good it is; at Deptford he has some cod and prawns in Fishstreet. Were the prawns potted like shrimps? May has a recipe which uses wine, nutmeg, orange juice and butter. Possibly not, for Pepys would have been certain to have mentioned it. It was customary to treat unexpected guests with anchovies and wine at all times of the day; anchovies were always served at dinner parties among the dishes in the second course. Pepys often returned home with a barrel of oysters; oysters were eaten as snacks in the street and were often served as a preliminary appetiser to the main meal.

The main meal of the day was dinner, which was eaten at midday – Pepys notes: 'At noon home to dinner'. If there were guests and some of them arrived late, as did happen, they sat down in the afternoon. Sometimes his own work kept him late and he did not dine until four when it would be at a tavern. Breakfast was a 'morning draught' of beer, ale or wine; solid food might be taken any time before eleven and would be cold meats, bread and butter. On several occasions he takes chocolate instead of ale, showing that he is in the midst of the transition between the medieval start to the day and what would be customary in the eighteenth century. Supper, taken almost any time in the evening, would also be a cold meal; meats cut from the carcasses of dinner, cheese, bread and butter. Entertaining at home is something that Pepys obviously enjoys, but it is quite informal; friends quite often just turn up and cards are generally played after dinner.

He entirely ignores fast days: in 1661 he records his intention of keeping Lent, but within a month he weakens, finding others who continue to keep it rather ridiculous. The Restoration court, in its fierce anti-Cromwellian stance and sympathy with France and Roman Catholicism, would want to observe Lent and other fast days, but it is too hedonist in spirit to care; Pepys who is Protestant is indifferent, so as we have seen, though fish is eaten and enjoyed, it is no longer eaten as food for fasting.

How very familiar this food is becoming: the medieval influences have waned, and are only discernible now in dishes such as the Tansy. The flavourings of spices are less, except for the Oleo, but spices are still expensive. This is cooking for an expanding class of bourgeoisie, a thriving commercial class eager for success and social position and not hidebound by too strict rules governing the way they dined. Yet certain dishes like venison are designed more for entertaining than are others, and there is an emphasis on a display of plate, folded napkins and what was to be worn when they visited the theatre or Hyde Park. It is a world we recognise very easily.

John Evelyn

John Evelyn (1620-1706) was an intellectual: his architectural and environmental treatises were prophetic; in matters of aesthetics he was a purist, so one would expect his tastes in food to be refined; he is the first writer on food to communicate ideals and to treat food as another cultural pursuit. His garden at Sayes Court was organised to give a mixed green salad every day of the year; he had a calendar drawn up to help the gardener, which was published in 1664 and went into ten editions. When Denis Papin, a refugee from Huguenot persecution and a member of the Royal Society, demonstrated his pressure cooker, the Digester, Evelyn gave an account of the meal they all ate: 'This philosophical supper raised much mirth amongst us, and exceedingly pleased all the company.'

In 1685 he wrote to his sister warning her against 'trash and sweetmeats which have chiefly been the cause of [his wife] Mary's death. She eat those filthy things so constantly at My lady Falkland's that it was impossible to overcome the tough phlegm that had bred in her.' Nowhere in his writings are there the expressions of delight and greed that so humanise the diary of Pepys. Evelyn sees food much more as a scientist might, noting its characteristics, what affects it and how it flourishes. This is highly civilised food; he also sees very clearly the relationship between food and health, and his *Acetaria* is a prose hymn to salad growing and eating.

Evelyn was travelling in Europe through much of the time of the Civil War: he eats his first truffles in Vienne in France, and notes that in Bologna, apart from the famous sausages and great quantities of Parmesan cheese, they also sell botargo[28] and caviare and how agreeable the smell in the streets was. In Venice he loves the small oysters similar to the ones at Colchester; in Paris for dinner at Lord Stanhops, while complaining at the amount drunk he also takes down a recipe for seasoning cherries (stewed in butter and sugar on white bread). Back home in Bristol he notes down the method of refining sugar and casting it into loaves, where the workers also fried eggs in the sugar furnace and drank them with Spanish wine. In Wiltshire he dined with friends at Hungerford and was fascinated by the way they speared the trout at night;

the fish were drawn to a light at the stern of the boat. He had an excellent dinner there of pigeons, rabbits and fowl in abundance. In Colchester he observes the eringo industry where the giant roots were dug up on the seashore, then taken away to be peeled, cut and candied. *Eryngium maritum* (eringo) grows on the seashore and its phallic-like roots, when boiled, taste like chestnuts and was thought to be an aphrodisiac. The industry at Colchester was thriving until the nineteenth century when the inhibitions of that age made it unpopular.

In August 1668 at a reception given by Charles II for the French Ambassador, Colbert, he sees his first King-Pine: 'His Majestie having cut it up, was pleased to give me a piece off his owne plate to tast of, but in my opinion it falls short of those ravishing varieties of deliciousnesse . . . but possibly it might be (& certainly was) much impaired on coming so farr: it has yet a gratefull acidity, but tasts more of the Quince and Melon.' Ten years later he dines with the Portuguese Ambassador and finds the food disappointing: 'Besids a good Olio the dishes were trifling, hashed and Condited[29] after their way, not at all fit for an English stomac, which is for solid meate; there was yet good fowle but roaste to Coale; nor were the sweetmeates good.' It is not the lack of meat that Evelyn complains of, but the way it is cooked in a sauce; one sees here clearly how he is associating a simple roast with an English style.

How much happier Evelyn is in 1681 when he stays at the estate of Mr Denzil Onslow at Purford where there was much company and an extraordinary feast. What made it so remarkable, he notes, is that everything came from the Estate: venison, rabbits, hares, pheasants, partridge, pigeons, quail, poultry and fresh fish. It was this relationship between the cultivation of a well-managed estate and the produce harvested from it that so fascinated Evelyn. In 1685 he stays with Lord Clarendon at Swallowfield in Berkshire where 'the gardens and waters' as elegant as 'tis possible to make . . . with art and industry and no means expenses, my Lady being so extraordinary skill'd in the flowry part & the diligence of my Lord in the planting'. He enthuses over the orchards, the fishponds and the kitchen gardens and one can almost see him creating recipes from the produce he sees growing.

The relationship between the animal and the food was, of course, so much more intimate then, than now. In a letter from his wife, Mary instructs him:

> When the next hog is killed, the butcher should cut a little more flesh to the chine, and not chop off the hog's snout from the head. I shall be glad Margaret should send some part of the sauce when she sends hog puddings, spare rib and chine. Let the gardener know the apples were very well packed and kept from bruising, but he laid too much hay between the rows, so that we have fewer apples than he might have sent.

Was there no pleasing Mary, one wonders? There is evidence that Mary was a very good cook; what is more she believed in the efficacy of food in itself. She had commented to her husband when travelling down to Bath: 'I find discreet hospitality assists very much towards governing the nation, for common people are led by the mouth with moderate management, and without a little popularity they are perfect mules and ungovernable.'[30]

Evelyn's very personal manuscript recipe book was a collection he began shortly after his travels in France and Italy, which he added to at intervals throughout his life. He collected them from members of his family, and from friends: there is a gooseberry wine recipe from Sir Christopher Wren; from the English Ambassador in Madrid we learn how to make an air-dried sausage; from Lady Harrington, a cake; and from Lady Fitzharding, a recipe for puffs. This is a sweet pastry made with wine, milk and many eggs, cut into small pieces then fried in butter, and served strewn with more sugar (like a flavoured *pâté* a *choux*, fried instead of baked). A recipe titled *Manjar Blanc*, given to Evelyn by the Duke of Arcoat's cook in Madrid, is our old friend mawmenny. This recipe owes much to the original one: the hen's flesh is pulled into pieces like thread, then washed, then milk and rice flour are added with sugar, salt and orange flower water; it is boiled until it is thick, left to get cold, then sliced. In an earlier recipe for the same dish, Evelyn notes that it will keep for four to six days and is excellent food for a journey. What has been omitted from both recipes is all the extra spicing, and especially the ginger, which the original Arabic recipe once had. It is interesting, however, that it is still served to the nobility some 200 years after the Moors have left Spain. Other remnants of medieval cookery that Evelyn includes are almond cakes, puddings, custards and creams.

There are tips on how to spit-roast a turkey, and on how to bake venison or beef to keep all the year. They are cooked in spices and sugar and when tender placed in a pot with a weight on top, then covered and sealed with clarified butter. There are two recipes for neat's tongue pies: in one the cooked meat is minced, mixed with beef suet. dried fruit, apple, rosewater and verjuice, aniseed and orange peel; in the second recipe the cooked meat is sliced, then marinaded in verjuice with nutmeg, mace and cinnamon, then placed in the pie with butter. There are recipes for stewing oysters, for making cheesecakes, syllabubs and cream tarts, for pickling capers, walnuts and mushrooms, and to make rice, oatmeal and bread puddings. All in all, it is an exciting collection, which could still be used today with very small adjustments.

That this collection includes medieval recipes owes more to Evelyn's friends and colleagues, who all came from the nobility or foreign diplomacy, than to his own chosen style of living. For in his *Acetaria*, perhaps one of the finest books ever written on vegetables, he shows he is a sensitive cook, concerned never to ruin a vegetable, and critical of French methods of cutting vegetables into contrived shapes merely to adorn a salad. However, he still reviews plants and their effect on our health through the structure of the medieval four humours. Lettuce is cold and moist for example while fennel is aromatic, hot and dry. Small, young artichokes are fried in butter and served with fried crisp parsley. Cabbage must be moderately boiled, clary should be added to omelettes with cream, only young nettle tops should be used in soups, cucumbers should be dressed with orange or lemon juice and oil, salt and pepper, and boiled cucumber should be eaten with vinegar and honey. Sadly, he does not allow garlic into his salads, for it offends not only the ladies: it has by now become associated with the poor; garlic should be kept for northern rustics 'especially living in uliginous and moist places'. He describes many different varieties of lettuce, a 'dwarf kind, the oak leaf, Roman, shell, and Silesian, hard and crimp (esteemed of the best and rarest) with divers more'. He notes that three or four of these, with unblanched endive, succory and purslane, were the only salad ever served at the best tables.

Evelyn praises the Emperor Tacitus who was satisfied with a salad and a small chicken; frugality for Evelyn is equated with a natural appetite and an honest meal is defined as without so much as a grain of exotic spice. He wanted a salad to be composed harmoniously like music, counterbalancing natural flavours with judicious seasoning from a restricted range of condiments. He is, in fact, taking another step forward in defining an English temperament in food, though not necessarily British.

The Rise of Capitalism

In 1673 the French Ambassador had to leave his house because it was being knocked down to make way for new buildings. He looked in vain for new lodgings and found it difficult as most of the large houses had been torn down to make way for shops, or small lodgings for merchants; he complained there were very few to let and those that were charged exorbitant prices. In 1663 the mercers numbered only about fifty or sixty in the whole city, by the end of the century there were 300 or 400.

Becoming a shopkeeper, generally moving one rung up the ladder from a stallholder, was the quickest way to become wealthy. Shops of all categories came to dominate and devour the town. Luxury shops had walls covered in mirrors and gilded columns, bronze ornaments and candelabra and glass windows, which much impressed the French; they displayed the goods to the passers-by, but also kept the dust off. Defoe mocked fashion in the *Weekly Review* in 1708: 'Such is the power of a mode as we saw our persons of quality dressed in Indian carpets.' He was also amused by the fact that maidservants took to the cheap Indian carpets with great enthusiasm, which were then taken up by their mistresses, so that there was a general blurring of status.

London expanded rapidly, as it became the potentially attractive goal for labourers who were out of work, vagabonds and itinerants, uprooted from the countryside because of enclosures committed by avaricious landowners. The government's policy on how to get rid of the malcontents was wishful thinking; an argument for colonising Ireland in 1594 was that the poor and seditious could be exiled there from the City of London, and exactly the same reasons were given a little later for colonising Virginia.

By the second half of the seventeenth century London was at the centre of world trade: the navy had been built up in the years of the Interregnum to become a strong trading force; and Britain, as the hub of a growing empire, like ancient Rome before it, began to think of the world as its larder – an attitude that would grow considerably throughout the next few hundred years. London had also become the nucleus for all the trading goods for the British Isles, as it held a virtual monopoly on all exports and imports controlling the production and redistribution over the island. There were over 1,000 miles of navigable rivers, and few people now lived more than fifteen miles from a road, which began to improve with the toll system. Defoe points out that once a manufactured product had been finished in some county outside London, it was then sent to London to a warehouse keeper who sold it either to a London shopkeeper who retailed it, or to an export merchant, or to a wholesaler who distributed it for retailing elsewhere in the various regions of England. As each middleman took his cut so the final price of the product rose. Defoe in *The Complete English Tradesman*, who saw only benefit and good come from such a system, explained: 'The sheepmaster who shears and sells the fleece, and the shopkeeper who sells the cloth or clothes ready made, by retail, are the first and last tradesmen concerned in the whole trade; and the more hands this manufacture . . . passes through either in the workmanship or carriage, or sale of the goods . . . so much the greater benefit is that manufacture to the public stock of the nation, because the employment of the people is the great and main benefit of the Kingdom.'

Because of this affluence a new being stepped onto the stage – the parvenu. For the first time a poor man born of humble parentage could live very comfortably and occasionally amass a huge fortune. Great wealth could accrue through trade in the East India Company and the New World colonies. These new affluent middle classes brought a certain structure into the daily life of society, and the arrangement of our meals; breakfast, lunch and dinner became set within this century.

This was the century that saw the beginnings of consumerism: another familiar figure entered the world stage, the Joneses, the couple that everyone had to keep up with. Servants mimicking their masters is an age old phenomenon; one rank in society eager to join a higher one is just as old. This was the first time in history, however, that such a desire could be crowned with success. Social mobility could be achieved and to do so social imitation and emulative spending began on a scale never imagined before. The Joneses play a significant part in any history of food. At the end of the seventeenth century there was an explosion of industrialised objects.

> Who bought the cottons, woollens, linens and silks of the burgeoning textile industries? Who consumed the massive increases in beer production? Who bought the crockery which poured from the Staffordshire potteries? Who bought the buckles, the buttons, the pins and the minor metal products on which Birmingham fortunes were built? Who bought the Sheffield cutlery, the books from the booming publishers, the women's journals, the children's toys, the products of the nurseryman? Which families purchased the products of the early consumer industries?[31]

All these goods were bought by the emerging middle classes, people neither very poor nor very rich, people who were benefiting from jobs in trade and merchandise, the more substantial farmers, the new engineers, clerks and accountants who were all part of the Industrial Revolution that had only just begun. In these last few years of the seventeenth century industry was creating thousands of non-essential goods, frivolities like pins, buttons, lace, brooches and toothpicks, flowering plants, novels, games and table ornaments. Food is the perfect commodity to show who you are, your social position, your wealth, taste and sophistication. The route which food was now to take was firmly in the hands of this new powerful class, unlike France where the development of what happened to food was limited to the royal kitchens and the ingenuity of the 1,000 chefs kept by Louis XIV: 'The development of an absolutist court-society in England was nipped in the bud in the mid-seventeenth century, while that in France continued to develop for another century and a half.'[32]

Capitalism redefined gender. Our ideas of what is male and female were created in the seventeenth century: the female bimbo was born and the male chauvinist gained respectability. To be an entrepreneur you were bellicose and competitive, while your wife was a status symbol wearing the silks and satins that your commercial labours had won for her, living within a stylish house filled with elegant furniture which reflected on how astute and shrewd your business sense was. Before, as we have seen, the wives of country landowners were hard-working people running large estates and equal in business acumen with their husbands. Now the wives' terrain was limited to clothes, food and entertainment, the genteel arts of embroidery and needlework. The accounts were the duty of a clerk, while farmworkers worked the scythes and winnowed the corn, jobs that a century before she had controlled and helped at. The sight of a slaughtered beast now made her faint; the art of stilling and making aqua vitaes was yet another duty that went to the housekeeper, as did drying fruits and making quince jelly and damson preserve, though she would express her delight when the finished products were displayed to her. She was no longer a skilled nurse who knew how to apply poultices and tie bandages, nor did she know a thing about the medicinal qualities of herbs that grew profusely around her in the woods and fields of her estate. She was a status symbol for her husband of leisure and wealth.

New Thoughts on Farming[33]

The spread of new crops and new systems of farming was led by a few gentleman farmers at the end of the sixteenth century, the grandsons and great-grandsons of the new minor nobility who swept in after the Wars of the Roses, and were intrigued by exploring ways to improve their estates and seeing them efficiently administered. They wrote books on husbandry, and this new literature opened men's eyes to greater possibilities. English landlords and large farmers had seen that when food rose in price there was an obvious demand which would continue to grow, bringing with it new problems and benefits. These new writers finished up as farmers, eager to work the plough themselves and not just watch their servants doing so. Thomas Tusser farmed at Braham Hall in Suffolk. Gervase Markham was both scholar and soldier, yet valued being a husbandman most of all. He translated works from the French and German, he wrote carefully and clearly, and seemed always aware that the readers for whom he was writing were not accustomed to receiving instructions from books but by word of mouth. By 1637 this viewpoint and missionary purpose had become commonplace among writers in all branches of agriculture.[34] In 1620 the ship *Supply*, taking stores to Virginia, included Markham's works and others on husbandry and there was advise to guard the books well.

In 1616 Markham underlined the financial rewards to be earned by those who attended to the refined tastes of the well-to-do in foodstuffs. He wrote: 'Such cooks as can contrive and make of some one stuff, either by adding of some few things (and those not costly), or else by their labour or manner of preparing many both pleasant and wholesome dishes, are had in high account and estimation.'

By 1660 farmers were exploiting many more ways of making a living than at the turn of the century. They had discovered that efficiently reared swine, pigeons, turkeys, ducks and bees could all make money; that there were more profitable crops than corn, liquorice could earn £200 an acre, saffron £40, mustard £30, carrots on sand made many small fortunes. Coleseed when crushed for oil left a residue for making rape cake to be fed to milking cows. There was a passion for farming rabbits. It was reckoned that one could keep 200 couples worth £20 per annum at a cost of only £2.

After the Restoration, however, this spirit of exploration was tempered. The new edition of Ralph Austen's *Treatise of Fruit Trees* was censored; no longer did it say that there was an urgent need to employ the poor and that this was a major justification in planting new orchards; now the prime consideration was the financial profit to the grower. The Royal Society was founded in 1659 and in 1662 John Beale proposed the growing of cider fruit all over England. In March 1663 Mr Buckland, a Somerset gentleman, proposed that potatoes be planted throughout England. Mr Boyle described how potatoes had saved thousands of poor from starving in Ireland. They were then being recommended as vegetables to make flour with; the flour could be mixed with wheat and be used in bread, cakes and pastry, while any over would probably do as a feed for poultry and other livestock. The committee agreed to urge all members of the Society who owned land to begin planting potatoes and persuade their friends to do the same. John Evelyn agreed to insert some instructions on growing them in a treatise he was writing on trees. When Evelyn's *Sylva* was published it passed through many editions. He went on, encouraged by the Society, to write *Acetaria: A Discourse of Sallets*, which drew on information given by Charles II's principal gardener, Mr London. The Royal Society's activities were limited in their impact, however; it only had around 200 members and most of them lived in London; they were aristocrats, courtiers, gentlemen, doctors, scholars and clerics, and when there was a lecture on agricultural matters the audience was tiny.

By the end of the century the range of topics covered in new books was impressive. Gentlemen now favoured orchards, vineyards, vegetable gardens, woodland plantations, deer parks, fishponds, rabbit warrens and dovecotes. The middle ranks of yeomen and husbandmen favoured orchards and hops, coleseed and dye crops, while smallholders turned to vegetable gardening, growing onions, artichokes, asparagus, saffron and liquorice, and some even that new vegetable – the potato.

After 1640 a growth in cattle droves with Scotland had begun, and briefly Ireland joined Wales as a source of supply for English markets. In the 1630s grain production hardly ever reached a surplus, but by 1750, the peak year, grain exports were one-tenth of the domestic output. There was a startling growth in imports of sugar, coffee and chocolate throughout the seventeenth century, and in the following century in tea and rum. Gregory King analysed the average household food expenditure of 1695 in percentages: the greatest amount, twenty-seven, was spent on ale and beer; twenty was spent on bread and cereals; meat took fifteen and dairy produce eleven; fish, fowls and eggs took eight and wine and spirits six; fruit, roots and garden produce accounted for five per cent, and the same was spent on salt, oils and other groceries.

Much of the new money and the variety of produce were due to new agricultural techniques and, with the increasing enclosures, the acreage in which to employ them. New plants also played their part. Many of the new ideas had been suggested in Cromwell's time.[35] In 1645 Sir Richard Weston described the field cultivation of artificial grasses and turnips in Brabant and Flanders in a circulated manuscript, which was then printed in 1650; its ideas were so warmly received that another printing happened the following year. The most influential change was to the fodder crops; two legumes, sainfoin and clover, and the turnip were introduced. Sainfoin, a perennial herb (*Onobrychis sativa*) was established in Worcestershire in 1650; clover was grown all over the south, and floated water meadows also began to be used. Dutch immigrants brought the turnip to Norwich soon after 1565, but by the end of the seventeenth century it was grown all over south-eastern England; in the following century it moved down towards Cornwall. The Norfolk four-course shift of wheat, turnips, barley and clover was used on new land enclosed by Acts of Parliament, which were at their zenith in the eighteenth century. Now all stock could be fed over winter; there was the forced grass from the water meadows, with the irrigation of streamside pasture; the harvest of sainfoin, clover and turnips increased the supply of feed and also gave more dung to the land. Both livestock, where there were advances in breeding, and cereal production rose steadily.

Farming was not without its snobbery; it was considered that many of the new farmers had risen from 'servants of the lowest class and never had the opportunity to look beyond the limits of their immediate birth and servitude. Their knowledge is of course confined and the spirit of improvement deeply buried under an accumulation of custom and prejudice.'[36]

Cows' Milk

In the seventeenth and eighteenth centuries, towns began to grow enormously, and the milking of a dairy herd was done in their centres. Often the cows were driven around the streets and milked at the door, a practice that was popular as the housewife could clearly see that no water was added. The best milk in London was from the cows seen grazing in St James's Park, where the milk could be bought and drunk on the spot. Asses' milk was still considered the most efficacious, especially for invalids and young children. Whey and buttermilk were also popular drinks sold in the streets.

Women's milk was still the most highly prized and wet nurses were employed for invalids and old people. Pepys tells of hearing a story from Dr Whistler on 21 November 1667: '. . . of Dr Cayus that built Key's College: that being very old and lived only at that time on women's milk, he, while he fed upon the milk of an angry fretful woman, was so himself; and then being advised to take of a good-natured patient woman, he did become so, beyond the temper of his age.'[37] This story is told by Dr Thomas Moffett in *Healths Improvement* (1655) where he makes it clear that Dr Cayus sucked the woman's breast. Moffett adds, 'Similarly, what made Jupiter and Aegystus so lecherous, but that they were chiefly fed with goats milk?' Obviously, the concept of 'we are what we eat' goes back centuries.

Cows' milk was now used in puddings and desserts, ousting the use of almond milk almost completely, so there was a steady rise in milk consumption. Milk puddings, mixed then heated and baked with bread, sago, rice and oatmeal, sugar and spices, became almost a daily staple. The rich continued to use cream: cabbage cream was still a favourite, for it appeared in so many recipe books in much the same form as earlier (see page 125). White leach, that medieval favourite, also remained popular: cream flavoured with musk, rose water mixed with isinglass or hartshorn to set it firm, poured into a mould and then sliced and decorated when served.

Other fruit creams appeared this century, which remain popular today, such as raspberry cream, where the juice of raspberries was mixed with beaten egg whites, sugar, cream and lemon. This simple recipe was made with gooseberries and currants, even sorrel; the recipe was akin to the 'foole' made with cream, egg yolks and flavouring. One recipe suggest sippets dipped in cream should be put at the bottom of the dish before the cream, egg yolks, rosewater, sugar and lemon are added, which makes the 'foole' into what would soon be called a trifle.

Other popular cream and milk drinks were possets, which could be taken hot or warm. They were sweetened and spiced, then curdled with hot ale or wine. There were rich ones made with cream and egg yolks with added sherry. Others, once fast-day drinks, were made with almond milk, and obviously so well liked that they were retained after the Reformation.

A Coronation and Patrick Lamb, Court Cook

An account of the feast at the coronation of James II appears in a book[38] which is the history of the coronation itself; it has details of Their Majesties' most splendid processions and their royal and magnificent feast in Westminster Hall. There were 145 dishes, but Their Majesties also had served to them thirty more, a mixture of hot and cold. The list begins with pistachio creams served in glasses, cold of course, as were the pickled oysters, salad, jelly, Portugal eggs, egg pies, a whole salmon, cold pheasants, pigeon pies, crabs, Dutch beef, scollops, salamagundy, botargo, sturgeon, cucumbers, periwinkels, gherkins, caviar, olives, prawns, samphire and Trotter pie. Of the hot dishes there were oyster pies, rabbit ragout, roasted capons, turkey chicks, ducklings, leverets, geese, beef à *la royale*, quails, three fawns, one larded, Bolonia sausages, mushrooms, veal, asparagus (the month is April so the asparagus was forced especially for the occasion), spinach tart and bacon pie. Of the sweet dishes there was cold blancmange in shells, gooseberry and taffata tarts, gooseberry and apricot tart, sweetmeats, mangoes, glasses of lemon jelly and cheese cakes. This impressive spread is reminiscent of Robert May and his uneasy combination of medieval splendour and rustic simplicity, for on the same table foods like caviare and black pudding nestle together.

Each ritual is painstakingly detailed:

> Then 32 dishes of Hot Meat, brought up by Gentlemen Pensioners Bareheaded; which service should have been performed by Knights of the Bath, had any been created at this Coronation: After which there were brought up a Supply of 14 dishes more of hot meat by Private Gentlemen. Then followed the mess of pottage, or Gruel, called Dillegrout, prepared by Patrick Lamb Esqu; the King's Master Cook, and brought up to the table by John Leigh Esqu; in pursuance of his claim as Lord of the Manor of Addington in Surrey.

Dillegrout was a white soup made from dill leaves; it was traditionally served because it was thought that William the Conqueror gave to his cook, Tezelin, the lordship of the Manor of Addington, as a reward for creating the soup. From then on dill was an important herb in the kitchen garden and used in soups and sauces.

Patrick Lamb was, as his frontispiece to his *Royal Cookery or, The Compleat Court-Cook*, states: 'for near fifty years Master-Cook to their late Majesties, King Charles II, King James II, King William and Queen Mary and Queen Anne'. His book, published in 1710, contains: 'the choicest recipes in all the several branches of cookery, viz. for making Soops, Biques, Olio's, Terrines, Surtouts, Puptons, Ragoos, Forc'd Meats, Sauces, Pattys, Pies, Tarts, Tansies, Cakes, Puddings, Jellies, etc.'

In the preface there are certain explanations such as 'Bisque is a soop with a Ragoo in it. Blanc-manger signifies white food, a sort of Jelly so called.' (So this is what mawmenny has come to.)

> Braise is a certain way of stewing most sorts of fish as well as flesh, which extremely heightens the tastes of them and is very much in vogue. The several ways of seeing it may be seen in the receipts. Court-Bouillon is a certain way of boiling any large fish. Entremets are the lesser sort of dishes that compose the courses. Hors-d'Oeuvres are the choice little dishes or plates that are served in between the courses at banquets and Entertainments.

A Surtout was a French dish; the word means overcoat, or a centrepiece on a dinner table, such as pigeons (though it could be any game bird) stuffed then larded with veal, wrapped up in paper (hence the overcoat), roasted then served with a ragout or coulis. On anchovies, he tells us that they are commonly eaten as a salad with sliced lemon, capers and olives, but he adds he also makes a 'ramoulade' from a coulis of anchovies which can be added to ragouts. A dictionary of 1725 gives a more detailed description of a 'ramoulade' as being chopped anchovies mixed with chopped parsley, capers, pepper, salt, oil, vinegar, lemon juice and nutmeg, to be sprinkled on fish.

Puptons (the word comes from the French *pupe*, meaning chrysalis or case) were a dish long gone out of favour, but they sound deliciously intriguing; you could make them from game birds, fish or even fruit. A forcemeat stuffing is made, which is used like pastry – hence it is wrapped like a chrysalis. It is bound with eggs, the pigeons are laid on it and then more forcemeat stuffing is laid over like a pastry covering and it is baked. Often puptons were made from various fish; a salmon and carp stuffing was placed at the bottom of a dish; this was layered with mushrooms and slices of salmon, crayfish tails and asparagus tips, then more stuffing covered it all; then it was protected with paper and baked. Before serving, the paper was peeled off, a hole was made in the centre and a crayfish coulis poured in. The fruit puptons seem to be less complicated; they could be merely an apple purée mixed with egg yolks, breadcrumbs, flavoured with sugar and cinnamon, baked slowly in a mould and then turned out.

Lamb gives seven recipes for artichokes: the bottoms could be fried in egg and breadcrumbs, then served with butter and lemon; or dipped in egg and flour, fried in butter and served with fried parsley; or boiled and eaten with nutmeg-flavoured butter. Very young artichokes could be cut in quarters, then blanched and served with pepper and salt; or boiled, then cooked in cream with chives and parsley, and the sauce thickened with egg yolks. A purée could be made from them, and they could also be pickled. There are four recipes for asparagus: cooked in cream and herbs, in broth with a mutton gravy flavoured with lemon, eaten with a butter sauce thickened with egg yolk or pickled.

Bain-marie was then a beef consommé, made from beef, veal and mutton, and a partridge and capon stuffed with rice; it was boiled slowly for five hours, then the broth was skimmed, sieved and served with crusts of bread. Beef could be braised, the fat cut away, larded with bacon, flavoured with spices, herbs, onions and mushrooms, then stewed in a tightly fitting pan and served with a ragout of cardoons, succory[39] or celery, or of roasted onions or cucumber.

Beef is also stuffed before being roasted, stuffed with a salpicon, which is referred to as a sort of ragout. It is an amazing mixture of ingredients: ham, breast of chickens, livers, sweetbreads, mushrooms, truffles, cucumbers, chives, onions, and parsley, all minced and cooked with herbs, pepper and salt, bound and moistened with a coulis of veal or ham. The beef is stuffed between the skin and the bone and then sewn together. At serving the skin is taken away and the stuffing is eaten with a spoon.

A 'cullis', from the French *coulis*, was an incredibly strong broth, used, as it is today, as a finishing sauce, but also added to soups for extra flavour and as a thickener. Lamb gives many recipes for different kinds of cullis. Though they are all sieved they would have thickened very slightly as bread crusts were used in their making. His cullis for adding to flesh-soops was made from sirloin of beef roasted very brown then ground into a paste with a mortar with carcasses of partridges and other fowl, bread crusts cooked in a pan with added gravy and strong broth, seasoned with salt, pepper, cloves, thyme, lemon slices and basil, which is all boiled again for another two or three minutes, then sieved and added to soup with more lemon juice. Lamb places no reliance on verjuice, though it was added to eggs in one recipe before they were scrambled. Lemons are added for a huge range of dishes, however, either their juice or in slices; obviously enough lemons were now being imported from Spain and elsewhere to make verjuice almost redundant, although John Evelyn notes it as an ingredient quite frequently. There were cullis for partridge, ducks, capon and pigeons. A white cullis was made from a roast pullet, sweet almonds, veal, ham, onion, carrot and parsnip and the yolks of four hard boiled eggs mixed with good broth seasoned with truffles, mushrooms, leek, parsley and basil, all cooked and pounded together, and then sieved. There was another white cullis made from fish, and one made from vegetable roots to add to vegetable soups. The intensity of flavour, though there are no instructions for reducing the broth, must still have been astonishing, adding much greater depth to the dishes.

Lamb stuffs cabbage in a manner familiar to us with a stuffing made from bacon, veal, breadcrumbs and cheese. Cauliflowers were cooked quickly, then served with a butter, lemon and nutmeg sauce. A capon was braised with a cullis of crayfish, or a cullis of ham with a ragout of oysters. There is a 'fricassy' of chicken cooked in butter with mushrooms, truffles and cock-combs poached in strong broth, then finished with two glasses of champagne and thickened with egg yolks. Cocks-combs were much used in ragouts and bisques; they were also sometimes split, then stuffed and fried. They remained prominent in French cooking until the last century, when their use died out after the First World War. (Larousse comments: 'Fleshy excrescence often voluminous, found on the heads of cocks. It is used chiefly as a garnish for entrées.') They had to be prepared by washing the blood from out of them, blanched, skinned, then poached in a court bouillon for 35 minutes; then they were finally prepared and cooked in whichever manner selected.

Ducks are cooked with oranges, with succory, celery, oysters, cucumbers and olives and served with green peas. A daube is made with beef, green goose or veal, to be eaten cold. There are poached eggs on a bed of cooked lettuce with a cullis of crayfish. Egg yolks are beaten into a strong veal and ham broth, cooked in cream thickened with pounded almonds, poached over cucumbers and crayfish or celery. Crayfish is much used but nearly always as a cullis, in which the shells are broken and cooked with parsnip, onion, carrot and almonds. The crayfish themselves are also made into a ragout and are always an essential part of bisques.

If you compare Lamb's recipe for turbot, which is poached in milk with a parsley sauce, with Robert May's (see page 142) there is a remarkable difference: Lamb's is simplicity itself, while May's, with his addition of ginger, mace and nutmeg, is still clinging to medieval flavourings. The astonishing fact is that both were cooking for nobility, but Lamb cooked for succeeding monarchs; yet May's dish is pretentious, while Lamb's is simply plain good fare. True, Lamb does give a more complicated recipe where the turbot is stewed in a veal gravy with champagne, herbs, truffles, mushrooms, and a ragout of crayfish, but this owes nothing to medieval sources.

Truffle sauce is made from sliced peeled truffles poached in a light cullis of veal and ham then seasoned. An anchovy sauce is made from mincing the anchovies then heating them in a cullis of veal and ham. A poivrade sauce is made from veal stock, vinegar, leek, onion and slices of lemon boiled and strained, (a poivrade sauce, as defined by Larousse, now has many more vegetable ingredients, and this is the only instance where Lamb appears to have less).

As Lamb presides over fifty years of court cooking at the end of the seventeenth century and at the beginning of the eighteenth, his influence was huge. An examination of his collection impresses one with the vigour of his range and the delicate flavours and fine taste that his craftsmanship must have created; these are remarkable recipes which influenced the future of English cooking. A cursory glance at Hannah Glasse (see Chapter 8), writing only thirty years later, shows what a debt she must have owed to Lamb.

England is now less vulnerable than it was in the time of the early Stuarts; at the beginning of the eighteenth century its remarkable military successes under the Duke of Marlborough against the army of Louis XIV placed it in the forefront of Europe. Yet it was anxious about its religious role, after James II had attempted his Catholic coup, failed and had to flee the land; this new Protestant nation was paranoid about secret Catholics attempting to reconvert it. That these feelings touched and influenced cookery might seem to some readers to be extraordinary, but it did, as we shall see in Chapter 8. Already within the seventeenth century some of the gentry, who were either Catholic or sympathetic both to France and Papism, employed French chefs who naturally used French titles for their dishes, all of which were derived from medieval ideas common to both countries. Already, the idea that French food (still celebrating Papist traditions) was better than English food (imbued with Reformation independence) had taken root. The time has come to have a closer look at the issue.

La Varenne

The French Cook by La Varenne was translated and published in English in 1653, only two years after it had appeared in France. The dedication begins: 'Of all the Cookes in the World, the French are esteem'd the best.' The book was an immediate success in France, and no wonder with that chauvinist trumpet call; it went into thirteen editions in the next decade and was also translated into German. Food historians consider the book innovative and paramount in the French influence upon English cooking. The book's appearance was all the more dramatic because it was published in France after a long gap of half a century when no cookery books appeared at all. However a number of English cookery books such as Sir Kenelm Digby's, which detailed Court cookery and was much influenced by the French, were published, so we know something of what was happening at that time.

Varenne is misleadingly thought to have been the first cook to have made fricassées, hashes and braises popular, and more particularly to have created the made-up dish, as opposed to a plain roast, as the essentially stylish centre of a meal. He is also credited with introducing fungi and the bouquet garni into dishes. He was indeed the first to use flour as a thickening for a sauce, to have a recipe for an omelette and to have created caramel, and in his work culinary terms that have now become familiar were used for the first time: for instance, *au naturel*, *au bleu* and *à la mode*. He eschews most spices except for pepper which he uses a lot, and he never uses sugar in savoury dishes.

Innovative wizards do not suddenly appear, however; they develop ideas to which apprenticeship in their chosen trade has exposed them. We find Fynes Moryson, the observant Scots traveller, commenting, when in France in 1605-17:

> Their Feasts are more sumptuous than ours, and consist for the most part of made fantasticall meates and sallets, and sumptuous compositions, rather than flesh or birds. And the cooks are most esteemed, who have best invention in new made and compounded meats.

So from the beginning of the seventeenth century court feasts had been served with made-up dishes and not roasts, and there had been stimuli for apprentices to invent more dishes.

We also know from English cookery books of the early part of the century, that fricassées, hashes and braises were well known, and that they were part of the repertoire of any skilled cook. Indeed, they were all well known methods which go back to at least the fourteenth century. Surely both French and English cookery must have continued with this tradition, even though in England after the Reformation the made-up dish had had Papist associations. Cooks had therefore turned to roasting and boiling, as a statement of belief throughout the Tudor period. In the seventeenth century under the Stuarts, however, this distinction had become blurred; cookery recipes from the court might have had Papist associations, but they were also touched with the royal aura, and so had enormous elitist attraction for a socially mobile society.

Varenne used flour in many ways throughout his cooking: he sprinkled flour on boiling liquid, he floured meat and vegetables before braising, and he used the *fleur frite*, which was to become the 'roux'; he used lard instead of butter, mixed with flour to a paste, then thinned it down with stock and vinegar. Varenne also uses other thickeners, such as almonds and breadcrumbs.[40] The English cookery books used everything except flour. Most particularly they seemed fondest of adding butter to the sauce and beating until an emulsion occurred; a wholly lighter sauce would then have been created, preferable for our own contemporary taste to a sauce made heavy with lard and flour. All the most courtly and French-influenced of the English cookery books ignore the flour-based liaison, which seems odd as they were basing their knowledge and recipes on French chefs and kitchens. It is not odd, however, if we accept that they tried the sauces and felt no enthusiasm for them. One practical reason for Varenne to have used them was that the made-up dishes displayed upon the table had to remain appetising for some length of time; a butter emulsion would have lost its liaison, while the flour sauces would have gelled and got thicker.

As for spices, Varenne never uses ginger and nor do the English, having fallen out of love with this spice at this time. Both Varenne and the English use pepper, however, but the latter use it more. Varenne used fungi in his cooking at a time when the English had never stopped using them. The innovations for which Varenne is praised had surely been common in French cookery practice for some decades before the book was published. Varenne obviously practised them, and then wrote them down.

The French/English controversy over who influenced what is an emotive one, because British gourmets have been placed in an invidious position for purely historical reasons (which will be explored later in this book); if they are devoted admirers of French cooking then inevitably they are placed in the position of disparaging British culinary art. Yet there were plenty of Frenchmen critical of their own cuisine; often the French cook started to speak like an Englishman. Take Nicholas de Bonnefon in his introduction to *Les Délices de la Campagne* (1654) who attacked the cooking of La Varenne: '. . . let the cabbage soup taste entirely of cabbage, a leek soup of leeks, a turnip soup of turnips, and so on, leaving elaborate mixtures of chopped meat, diced vegetables, breadcrumbs and other deceptions for the kind of dishes which are for simply tasting rather than filling oneself up on . . .' Or there is L.S.R. who wrote *L'Art de bien Traiter* (1674), another attack on La Varenne: 'Look at his shin of veal fried in breadcrumbs, his stuffed turkey with raspberries, his shoulder of mutton with olives, his ragout of tripe, his roe deer's liver omelette, his ragout of chicken in a bottle . . . and any number of other villainies . . .'[41] Less than a quarter of a century after La Varenne's publication, Mennell writes, other writers are 'pinpointing and deriding the medieval survivals and peasant like elements in La Varenne's recipes'. Certainly that recipe for roasted turkey with raspberries is an absurd one, for the turkey is roasted in the normal way, then just before being served a few raspberries are thrown over it.

French cooking in the seventeenth and eighteenth centuries had the reputation of being fussy and fancy, drowned in sauces and over-spiced, but it is obvious that only some dishes fell into this category. In the seventeenth century certainly there were more similarities in both nations' cooking than there were differences. As to La Varenne's influence, it has been much exaggerated, for most of the innovations he is praised for already existed on both sides of the Channel, and as to one innovation that was to feature so largely in nineteenth-century British cooking, the flour-based sauce – well, we had the good sense not to use it at all for the next few decades.

CHAPTER 7

Other Island Appetites

In 1707 the Act of Union made Scotland an integral part of English legislation. From then on England, Scotland and Wales became known as Great Britain; the term the United Kingdom was created in 1801 when Ireland joined Great Britain. This chapter covers Wales and Scotland as well as Ireland, because although they were part of Britain, they remained isolated culturally. All three in their geography, climate and habitat and because of their history and traditions have socially an entirely distinct character, which owes nothing to the English. They share a defiance, a strong individualism and a resolute need to celebrate themselves. Hence, the diets of these different Celtic peoples are patently different from the English, although they share some characteristics among themselves, largely because the extremes of their climate made it impossible to grow wheat and they all relied more on oats, barley and rye. They also had a richness of dairy produce which they used to the full, and easy access to sea foods. For the majority in rural districts, living conditions were basic and often, throughout history, their survival was a desperate struggle. This was not helped by their richer neighbour, who exploited and ravaged their countries. In order to survive at all, they were forced to sell their quality produce to England for well nigh most of their history.

Early Medieval Ireland
The Irish poem *The Vision of MacConglinne*, though first written down around 1250 as a *fabliau* to be sung or narrated, must have been performed some many hundreds of years earlier. In it one gets a picture of a starving people, living in miserable poverty, undeniably pagan. Indeed, the whole poem is a celebration of pagan folklore and ridicules the early Church. It tells of King Cathal who has a malevolent spirit within him, which has turned him into a great glutton. For breakfast he would eat a pig, cow, a bull calf, three score cakes of pure wheat, a vat of new ale and thirty hen's eggs. MacConglinne is a clerical student, poet and minstrel, a *goliardi*, the Latin term for 'riotous and unthrifty scholars who attended on the table of the richer ecclesiastics and gained their living and clothing by practising the profession of buffoons and jesters.'[1] MacConglinne has not eaten for several days, but all he is offered to eat by the abbot is a half cup of whey water (this is the whey from the curds mixed with water, the usual thirst-quencher), which MacConglinne refuses, reviling the Church.

He is found guilty of slandering the abbot and sentenced to be crucified the following day. Minstrels and jongleurs, it should be pointed out, were a despised lot, not allowed to take communion or be admitted to monastic life. The anonymous author includes many lines of invective against the monks. 'Ye curs and ye robbers and dunghounds and unlettered brutes, ye shifting, blundering, hang-head monks of Cork,' MacConglinne calls them while he is cutting down the tree on which he is to be crucified.

In the night he has a vision of a land where everything is composed of food. Parts of this vision are written as verse and seem older than the prose. It is also a parody of the beatific vision that the saints experience, describing an edible world where the whole landscape can be consumed and which sometimes swallows the humans themselves.

The food described in the *Vision* by the phantom Wheatlet from the Fairy Knoll of Eating, the son of Milklet, son of Juicy Bacon, is the plain survival food of a peasant economy. 'Only among a cattle breeding population at a primitive stage of culture could this legend arise.'[2] (I would quarrel with his use of the word 'primitive', which he employed, I imagine, because of the poem's anti-Christian message.) The food in the poem is pottage, curds, kale, oatmeal gruel, nuts, mead and tripe, where fat is the supreme luxury. MacConglinne gets into a coracle made of beef-fat, with a coating of tallow, its thwarts of curds, its prow of lard, its stern of butter, its thole pins of marrow, its oars flitches of old boar. It rows across a lake of milk, through seas of broth, rivermouths of mead, waves of butter-milk, past springs of savoury lard and islands of cheeses.[3]

In much of the poem food is used to parody sacred ritual; they swear 'in the name of cheese'. A church is made up solely of food with an altar of fat, a knocker of butter and a door of curds. The doorkeeper wears food: a girdle of salmon skin, sandals of old bacon, leggings of potmeat, a seven-filleted crown of butter on his head, in each fillet seven ridges of pure leeks, and seven badges of tripe about his neck. His steed has legs of custard with four hoofs of coarse oaten bread, ears of curds and eyes of honey. MacConglinne reaches the Hermitage where the Wizard Doctor, father of Wheatlet, is in control.

It is the Wizard Doctor who diagnoses MacConglinne's illness:

> Three hags have attacked thee, even scarcity and death and famine, with sharp beaks of hunger . . . for thine is not the look of a full-suckled milk-fed calf, tended by the hands of a good cook. Thou hast not the corslet look of a well-nourished blood, but that of a youth badly reared under the vapours of bad feeding.[4]

He also asks MacConglinne what he thinks ails him. MacConglinne describes in great detail all the foods he longs to eat but cannot for he is too poor. 'My wish would be, that the various numerous wonderful viands of the world were before my gorge, that I might gratify my desires, and satisfy my greed.'

The Wizard Doctor gives him directions, which includes love-making with a beautiful woman, in order to achieve a banquet throughout his life: fresh pork, loins of fat, boiled mutton, salted beef, mead, old bacon, stale curds, new milk, carrots, ale, butter, bread, cheese, juicy kale, white porridge, broth, sheep's tripe, salt, sweet apples, hen's eggs and kernels. On the morning of his crucifixion MacConglinne begs to be allowed to relate his vision to the gluttonous king and when he reaches the end of this list of foods, the demon is so entranced by the appetising description that it leaves the king's throat to listen and is destroyed by a steaming cauldron. Both the king and MacConglinne are saved, while the abbot is in disgrace.

This poem shows how vigorous the pagan culture was as it co-existed with Christianity, the new religion. No wonder the abbot wants to crucify this poet, who has a vision of fairies, wizards and phantoms, and a place where food is all that is sacred and where salvation is a night of romantic love-making in front of a fire.

The poem is astonishingly clear on what ails people: starvation. We also get a vivid picture of the diet of fifth- or sixth-century Ireland, which must have remained the same for hundreds of years and was a diet that would have been shared by all the countries of northern Europe.

For peasants the diet was meagre with very little to eat on most days except garnered scraps. For the landowners, churchmen and ruling elite there were oats for bread and porridge, mead, ale and milk to drink, hard cheese and soft curds, butter, lard, pork, boar, tripe, mutton, bacon and salted beef; while the vegetables were onions, leeks, carrots and kale. Furthermore, we learn that salt was imported from England, milk with honey was a drink for children, pigs' intestines were stuffed and boiled, eggs were made into fritters, salmon was dressed with honey, wheaten cakes were dipped in salt and honey, while dulse was dried and also called Salt Leaf.

Old Irish texts make it clear that around any prosperous farm there was an enclosed garden. In Old Irish there is no distinction between the word for vegetable and herb; the one word *lub* includes vegetables that are eaten and plants taken for medicinal purposes. Plant cultivation, however, is associated with the monasteries; the gardener is listed among the seven officers of the church; there is no mention of a gardener in the servants around a king. The most commonly mentioned vegetable is the onion, and from the evidence it would seem to be a bunching onion, pulled green out of the earth and able to be broken up into cloves. One law text deals with an invalid's entitlement to a supply of onions, unless the physician forbids it on medical grounds. Another text specifies the food that a client must provide for the annual visit of his lord. The amount depends on the rank of the lord: the lowest-ranking lord is entitled to four loaves of bread for each member of his visiting party of four men; the bread must be served with a relish which may consist of honey, fish, cheese or salt meat; the text continues that there must be sixteen cloves of onion for each loaf, or four onion plants for each loaf.[5]

In conjunction with the onion a vegetable referred to as *imus* is mentioned, which is thought to be either celery or alexanders. Then there was *borlus*, which is included in the annual food rent due to a lord, which is thought to be leek, as it is referred to as 16 inches in length. Wild cabbage featured in monastic diets and it is likely that was cultivated by them; a ninth-century monastic rule forbids monks to eat cabbage that has been cooked on a Sunday. Only one root vegetable appears to have been mentioned, *cerrbachan*, which could be the skirret (*Sisum sisarum*).

The main meal was normally eaten in the afternoon or evening, supposedly once the sun went down, while light meals and snacks were mentioned at other times of the day. A man was expected to eat a loaf of bread in the day and another at night. The texts appreciate the difference between winter and summer food; winter food rent, for example, consisted of a bullock, a flitch of bacon, three bushels of malt and a half bushel of dried grain; while summer food was mainly dairy products, curds, butter and milk. The summer food rent includes a wether and vegetables.

It is clear that a person of higher rank enjoyed a greater variety of food than one of lower rank, that a lord was given a supply of meat in greater quantity than anyone else and with his bread was entitled to the three condiments, honey, onions and celery. The lord was given in food rent a substantial amount of produce, in fact most of the food eaten within his household. He received live animals, meat, milk products, grain, malt, bread and vegetables, and the law texts specify that these must be of adequate size and quality. The rules of hospitality are binding, as they were in all early societies, but Irish law specifies precisely the amounts of food offered according to social status; for example, a master-builder was entitled to salted meat as a relish with his loaf and a generous ration of beer or fresh milk, while his assistant is only allowed salt and a vegetable and a lot less to drink.

Milk and its products are central to the diet. A tenth-century tale, *Tochmarc Ailbe*, thinks milk is the best food because it is 'good when fresh, good when old, good when thick, good when thin'. The comic tale *Aislinge Meic Con Glinne* speaks of 'very thick milk, milk which is not very thick, milk which is thick but flowing, milk of medium thickness, yellow bubbling milk the swallowing of which requires chewing'. Milk was drunk sometimes with the addition of water, rennet was added to give a thick milk, fresh milk was used in the making of porridge and made into a herbal broth, and cream kept in a cool place was palatable for all of a week, although it was thought the gradual souring improved the flavour.

Butter was made from the cream using a churn dash and a wooden churn, and was considered a luxury food to which lords were entitled, and it appears in the food rent; low ranking people at table were not given butter at all. The language shows that there was a rich diversity of names for cheese, which was eaten at various stages; even the type of curd is delineated. Cheeses were pressed, salted and dried; the harder the cheese the more useful it was to take on journeys. The name of one cheese indicates that it was so hard it could have been dangerous if thrown; in fact the story *Aided Meidbe* tells of the death of Queen Medb from a piece of cheese hurled from a sling.[6]

Inevitably it is Ireland's climate and its heavy rainfall that dictate this diet. In 1185 Gerald of Wales tells us that there is rich pasture, good fishing and hunting but poorly developed agriculture and 'little use for the money making of towns'. Cattle and sheep had excellent pasture but livestock were owned only by the rich, so dairy foods were out of reach of the peasantry. As we have seen, butter was valuable and was buried in the peat bogs (see below), as if it were gold. Swine were easily raised and could fatten on the forest floor, but they were the meat preferred for feasting; the haunch or loin was kept for the lord or king. Oddly enough, though eggs were eaten, there is no mention of poultry as food. Perhaps they were merely kept for cock-fighting, as in England.

Pagan rituals continued well into the medieval period, and there was a definite connection between the idea of a good king and a fertile land. The king was married to the land and his union with her should bring about a rich progeny. At the inauguration rite of a king, he was wedded to the goddess Eriu or to some other local goddess. Many foods possessed magical powers and there was a certain prescription that gave life to the king: 'fish from the Boyne, the deer of Luibnech, the mast of Mana, the bilberries of Bri Leith, the cress of Brossnach, water from the well of Tlachtga, the hares of Naas'. If all these were brought to the king of Tara on the feast of Lugnasad (1 August) and the king consumed them, that year did not count as life spent and he would be victorious in battle.[7]

There is plenty of evidence of the cultivation of oats, barley, rye and even wheat in ancient Ireland; there are references to bread, ploughing and mills in early literature and a large number of querns for home grinding of corn have survived. Oats were the chief grain crop followed by barley, and bread was made from both of them. There are references to porridge or stirabout in the early literature. The law tract *Senchas Mor* is precise in the most chilling manner about the kinds of porridge to be fed to the children from different classes.

> The children of the inferior grades are fed to a bare sufficiency on stirabout made from oatmeal on buttermilk or water, and it is taken with stale butter. The sons of the chieftain grades are fed to satiety on stirabout made of barley meal upon new milk, taken with fresh butter. The sons of the kings are fed on stirabout made of wheaten meal upon new milk, taken with honey.[8]

Wheaten bread was regarded, as in England, to be far superior to any other, and therefore the only bread fit for kings and chieftains; it was also made especially for feast days and other important social occasions. So the small wheat harvest was kept separate for the nobility.

Of all societies Ireland must have been notable for its reliance in the diet of milk; the great expanses of lush green pasture which flourished under the amount of rain gave added nutritional value, flavour and fat, to the milk from livestock. Early references in literature, both profane and hagiographical, place milk at the centre of the diet, and this continued well into the eighteenth century. Then it was referred to as 'whitemeats'. A traveller in Ireland in the seventeenth century commented:

> They are the greatest lovers of milk I ever saw, which they eat and drink in about twenty different ways and love it best when sourest. They drink milk sweet, sour, thick, thin and in summertime eat sour curds . . .[9]

Milk was thought highly precious. A law text of the eighth century lays down the punishment when someone has given food which contains a dead mouse and weasel; the food is thrown away, but it adds that if the food is porridge thickened with milk then only the part around the dead rodent should be thrown out.

Hospitality was a duty in Irish society and butter was thought so necessary for bread that if there was none to offer, it was an insult to the guest. With copious amounts of milk, butter was churned in great quantities; it was eaten fresh or salted, and flavoured with herbs, leeks or garlic. Butter was also enclosed in wooden tubs and buried in bogs. No one quite knows why, apart from the fact that it was highly valued, but there are two theories: one that butter was regarded as a winter food and this saved it for the lean days before the supply of milk resumed with the fresh pasture of the late spring; secondly, that peat bogs provide an antiseptic storage condition whatever the time of year. All kinds of cheese were made: cow, sheep and goat, pressed cream and dry cheese. Its consumption declined in the eighteenth century, as there was a rise in rents, civil war and redistribution of people and the export trade expired. (See below.)

Later Medieval Period

The Norman invasion of England with its sophisticated cooking and the influences brought from Persia and the Mediterranean hardly affected Ireland, though the Normans were quick to notice the habitat of their new near neighbours. They saw the preponderance of pastoral farming and the relative absence of urban and commercial life. They thought the Irish despised agriculture and lived a pastoral life. William of Malmesbury contrasted the half-starved rural Irish with 'the English and French, who have a more civilised style of life and inhabit trading towns'. The Normans were too greedy and ambitious (The Earl of Pembroke, William Marshall, had an estate which included lands in Normandy, England, Wales and Ireland) to ignore the green island to the west; it was only a 122 nautical miles from the mouth of the Liffey to the mouth of the Mersey. The Anglo-Saxons had exploited Ireland as a market for buying slaves and selling furs, but in the twelfth century the Normans saw it as a field of conquest and colonisation.

In 1169 Anglo-Norman forces under Henry II landed in Ireland and brought the Anglo-Norman lords already established there to submission. They formed a Lordship of Ireland, which took its legislative structure from a system of counties with sheriffs and coroners that was modelled on those of England. Parts of Ireland were then divided up into knight's fees and granted out to an immigrant aristocracy, men of English, French, Welsh or even Flemish descent who created new lordships secured by castles with feudal tenures.

Did these Anglo-Irish lords bring with them the grandeur and pomp that we glimpse in the awestruck words of Henry of Huntingdon, who entered the household of the bishop of Lincoln, Robert Bloet (1093–1123), as a young boy? 'When I saw the glory of our bishop Robert, the handsome knights, noble youths, valuable horses, golden and gilded vessels, the number of dishes, the splendour of those who served them, the purple and satin garments, then I thought nothing could be more blessed.'[10]

The size of a great lord's household was about thirty-five, while a knight had a mere dozen or so. Pomp and grandeur need a large staff to augment and maintain them. Sophisticated cooking needs not only a skilled, intelligent and experienced master cook, but a trained staff of at least a dozen even to begin to create some of the dishes we know were eaten at the English court. Such cooking also demands a steady supply of produce, not only spices and sugar, but dried fruits from Mediterranean countries. Such supplies may have come once a year, and so one imagines the cooking within the Irish castles to have been plain, revolving around boiling and spit-roasting, but to have been richly supplied by local country produce.

The Anglo-Normans brought to Ireland the cultivation of peas and beans, especially in the south-east, so that for the first time there was a supply of pulses for the pottage, that staple dish within the diet for poor and rich alike. They also controlled the estates with more commercial acumen, exporting cattle, bacon, butter and cheese to England. The rich pasture gave high quality meat and dairy products, so the Anglo-Normans lived well off roasted pork, beef and mutton, and off poultry, eggs and cream. The earliest visitors were impressed by the huge lakes, mighty rivers and wide estuaries which abounded in fish, 'surpassing in size those of other countries I have visited,' said Gerald of Wales in the twelfth century. He especially noticed the salmon, trout and oily shad.

The people that lived near the coast made use of the rich store of seafood; they gathered up the shellfish, cockles, clams, mussels, oysters, limpets and periwinkles and made use of the seaweeds. Dulse is mentioned in the ancient laws, but sloke and carrageen moss were also eaten; some seaweeds were dried until brittle, then broken up and added to soup; others were boiled and turned into a slush, then mixed with cereal and fried. Herrings were caught, dried and salted and were sold from markets all over Ireland. Inland fish were caught with nets, traps, lines and spears; pike and herring were the fish of the poor, but cod, mackerel, pollock, whiting, trout, eel, plaice, sole, lobster, crab and oysters were all eaten. Seals were thought to be humans who had suffered some form of magical enchantment, so these were not caught and eaten; on the contrary they were treated with awe.

In a cauldron over a peat fire, the poor cooked soups enriched with wild leaves, nettles, wild garlic, sorrel, watercress and fungi; the soups would be thickened with oats or barley and eaten with flat bread cooked on a griddle. Baking bread was vital to Ireland, for as with the medieval peasant in England, bread was the staple food that kept the poor alive. A seventh- to eighth-century lawtext, *Cain Iarraith* (Law of the Fosterage Fee), which outlines the rules of fosterage, stipulates that foster-parents are legally obliged to teach the skills of flour-sieving, kneading and baking to young girls.[11] The poor seldom ate meat at all, as it was a rich man's food; what sheep the poor kept they reared for their wool, milk, horn and hide, so when a sheep was slaughtered mutton would be eaten. There are very few references to the eating of meat in early literature, but we know that pigs were reared, for there are mentions of swineherds and oak mast as fattening food. Pieces of bacon hung from the rafters of the poorest cottage, often far too precious to be eaten but saved and used in small scraps as flavouring for the soups. (See Potato and Point, page 177.)

The Potato and Famine

When did that other great staple, the potato, first become part of the Irish diet? There are differing theories. One is that it was introduced when they were planted in 1586 at Sir Walter Raleigh's property in Youghal, near Cork, but as the evidence points to the fact that it was the sweet potato which Raleigh brought from the New World it is doubtful that it would have grown at all. Another idea is that the potato was introduced early in the seventeenth century through trade with Flanders. The theory I prefer is that the potato formed part of the store of foods in the Spanish Armada of 1588. We know that Spain grew them in Galicia and used them as staple foods for its army, navy and prisons. When the ships from the Armada were wrecked on the west coast of Ireland, the potatoes could easily have survived. They float and sprout easily; a woman finding them while gathering seaweed and molluscs might very well have planted them in her garden plot. Or if they were plentiful on a particular beach a group of women might very well have boiled some of them and seen what they tasted like. Whatever the truth, potatoes were being grown in Ireland in the decade immediately after the Armada and quickly became a popular crop.

It was appreciated by the Irish that one of their huge advantages (only discovered on the Continent throughout the Napoleonic wars) was that fierce battles could occur over potato fields and the crop remain unharmed below. The raising of cows (the main commercial product up to then) demanded a considerable amount of grazing land, but this had been made scarce by the Anglo-Irish landlords confiscating land and redistributing the population in the sixteenth and seventeenth centuries. The ravages of war had destroyed many of the herds, for the Crown forces as a wartime tactic either slaughtered or drove the cattle off. It was also customary to destroy the cereal crops before the harvest; if not burnt, they were trampled over. In September 1567 the English Lord Deputy, Sir Henry Sidney, wrote that his army stayed in South Tyrone, 'to destroy the corn, we burned the country for 24 miles compass and we found by experience that now was the time of year to do the rebel most hurt.' So in the late sixteenth century there was a scarcity in cereals to make bread and in cattle to provide milk, the two staples the Irish had for centuries relied on.

Besides, potatoes were an accommodating crop; they could be fitted into scraps of land allowing a family to exist on a very little land; they could be stored easily throughout the winter, allowing the family to economise on the consumption of oats and milk. They needed little time or skill to cook them; they needn't even be boiled but could be put into the embers of a fire. And if it was necessary to flee to the hills and mountains to avoid the English soldiers, potatoes could even be planted up there.

Agricultural writers were quick to see the advantages of the potato as a food crop: 'Potatoes are a very profitable root for husbandmen or others that have numerous families.'[12] 'I advise you only to sow potatoes and turnips,' Lord Bellhaven wrote in 1699, 'but rather potatoes because being once planted they will never fail, they require little more labour than to keep the ground where they grow free from grass.'[13] He goes on: 'The Flandrian Bovvers make so much use of this root and had such plenty thereof, that both the Confederate and French Army found great support thereby by feeding the common soldiers most plentiously, it is both delicious and wholesome.' He continues by explaining how the poor people cook them: 'Boyl them, dry them, mix them with a little meal, knead them and make them up in Bread, which is a most useful and wholesome Food, especially in times of scarcity . . . or stilled, they make most excellent Aquavitae.'

Ireland exported to England cattle, sheep, pork and bacon, butter and cheese. Charles II and William III prohibited these imports as they were depressing English sales of the same goods; this prohibition continued until the third quarter of the eighteenth century when the increasing pressure of population on food resources, created concern and discontent, and led to the relaxation of the laws on Irish imports.

For the farm labourer food was scarce long before the famine of the nineteenth century. The cause was clear: the agricultural worker toiled in the fields, the crop was flourishing, but the harvest was carried to the nearest port and sent to England, while he returned home to a meal of potatoes. The worst time of year was the month of July; all the old potatoes had been eaten and the new crop was not yet ready. It was called Hungry July or July of the cabbage, for the new crop was not dug until the first day of August.

However, a few farmers who owned land were still fortunate: 'The food of the farmers is plain, wholesome and substantial, consisting of fried bacon or hung beef, boiled beef (chiefly in broth). Excellent broth made of beef, groats and oatmeal, leeks and cabbage is a favourite and comfortable dish.' So recorded James Boyle in his *Ordnance Survey Memoirs* in 1838.[14] The beef was salted and so was some of the butter to preserve it and these farmers were small landowners, so their diet was substantial, as Boyle says. The poorer families made do with sheep's head broths and plenty of cabbage, kale and leek, and by the time Boyle was writing there was real impoverishment. There had been an astonishing rise in the Irish population of four million between 1780 and 1841, because farm labourers married very young compared with the farming class of small landowners who were bound by the conventions of matchmaker and dowry. Once married, labourers produced large families of ten or more children. So from the beginning of the nineteenth century the standard of living for the farm labourer gradually declined to a subsistence level.

By the middle of the century seven families out of ten were barely surviving; they had no surplus money or goods, so nothing that could now be sold in exchange for food. On the eve of the famine (named afterwards as The Great Hunger) Irish people needed seven million tons of potatoes; the very poor, the cottiers, smallholders and landless labourers required at least five million tons just to survive, for the average male adult consumed upwards of 10 lb pounds of potatoes per day; the rest of the population needed another two million for food, another five million were needed for animal consumption and two million for seed, making a total requirement of fourteen million tons.[15]

There were potato failures due to blight in 1845, 1846 and 1847; the population of Ireland in 1841 was just over 8 million, in 1851 it had dropped to just over 6½ million, although by the normal rate of population increase it should have reached over 9 million; so at least 2¹/₂ million people were lost through the famine; a million people had emigrated, many of them dying before they reached the promised land. Between 1848 and 1864 £13,000,000 were sent home to Ireland by emigrants in America to bring relatives out, so there was a steady drain of the best and most enterprising to enrich other countries.[16]

It was the west coast of Ireland that had suffered most in the famine, yet the Atlantic broke upon these shores and the sea was full of shoals of herring and mackerel in immense quantities which swam near the shore, and further out there were cod, ling, sole, turbot and haddock. But sea fishing was a neglected industry; one of the problems was that there were no trees, hence no wood to make seaworthy craft for deep-sea fishing. There was the curragh, a frail craft, made of wickerwork covered in stretched hides or tarred canvas, but it was not suitable for nets for deep-sea fishing; a vessel of 50 tons was needed, laden with nets, in order to combat the heavy swell. The coast nearer the shore was perilous, full of great rocks, cliffs, treacherous currents and sudden squalls. The fishermen were heroic but the odds were impossible. When the potato harvest failed, many of the fishermen stripped their boats and sold all their gear, in order to buy food for their families. In such circumstances one might expect the British Government to have provided a fishing fleet, or at least the wood to build one, but it was not to be. Soup kitchens were set up and emergency rations distributed to three million people, and with that the British Government considered that its responsibility towards starving Ireland was almost at an end.

It is astonishing that throughout this terrible tragedy, and in the years before and after, the potato was still one of the few staple foods, however poor and hungry a family was. They could not, as they might have done centuries before, search the fields for wild greens, herbs and fungi, for the soil belonged to a landowner who fiercely protected his rights. Such knowledge of wild foods had gone. The potatoes were boiled in their skins over an open fire and were drained in a shallow basket called *sciathoga*; the family gathered around the kitchen table, or huddled in the middle of the floor. If they were fortunate they also were able to drink milk and eat the potatoes with butter. It is here that the dish 'Potatoes and Point' was born: to pick up your potato and point it at the scrap of dried bacon hanging from the rafters, somehow endowed the potato with a touch of salty bacon flavour.

It is even more astonishing that from this Irish experience a now equivocal attitude to the potato was born. Great potato dishes emerged, central to Irish cuisine, and at least two of them have emigrated happily to other countries. Firstly, there is Colcannon, for which the potatoes are mashed, then mixed with cabbage and cooked leeks or spring onion, with masses of butter. Secondly, there is Boxty, a potato cake, made so that it could be carried as travelling food; it is also known as 'tatties' or 'parleys'. The mashed potato and butter are mixed with flour, made into a dough, then cut into rounds and cooked over a griddle. There are potato puddings, potato pies and potato bread. The Irish cuisine revolves around butter and milk as much as the potato, as well as oats and mutton stew. It is food to warm the body, to keep out the damp; it is hearty, rich and basic.

Modern Period

Irish food changed very slowly. American bacon, jam, tea and sugar all became established at the end of the nineteenth century. The fish and chip shop arrived in 1900. However, it was the corner store that changed what the Irish ate; the goods from abroad, such as tinned fruits, salmon and ham, were considered better than home-produced ones and were designated as treats, designed for high tea with soda bread. Nevertheless, right through to the 1950s the staples still remained potatoes, butter and cabbage, which for the majority of people comprised the main meal of each day. Throughout the 1960s French, Italian and Chinese foods were introduced and quickly accepted in urban areas, followed in the 1970s by the American hamburger. It is only recently, in the last two decades, that a renaissance of traditional Irish foods has occurred, in which a real pride and skill in the making of farmhouse cheeses have created remarkable products equal to any great continental cheeses. Irish salmon, smoked or fresh, is renowned. Foods such as the seaweeds have become chic and valued for their health-giving properties.

Many of the traditional dishes are rightly famous: the broths and soups made with wild foods, then thickened with oatmeal, were often made from shellfish, the free harvest of the shores; Irish Stew made with mutton, onions and potatoes could not be more basic, yet if made with care with all the fat skimmed off it is a fine dish. The original recipe needed the fat and the potatoes obligingly soaked up much of it. Some Irish cooks flavoured it with thyme or rosemary and many added carrots and dumplings. Cabbage and bacon is another hearty dish, with the cabbage boiled in the bacon water for the last eight minutes. Many of the dishes now prized stem from the Anglo-Irish kitchens of great estates whose old recipe books have come to light; all the game pies, for example, and fish dishes like scallops with cream and hot buttered lobster have their origin here. The Irish poor had a way with offal, and Drisheen, from stuffed lamb's intestines, is still made in Cork, while both black and white puddings as well as a goose pudding are still eaten with great enjoyment. There are also a host of cakes and bread mixtures such as Barm Brack, which is usually a yeast dough with dried fruit, candied peel and lemon peel and carraway seed added, or Irish plum cake made with sour milk, an enormous amount of butter as well as currants, raisins and mixed peel. Irish Soda Bread is one of the great breads of the world – and there are very few of those left.[17]

Scotland

In the fifth century when the Roman legions left Britain and the invasions from the north and east began, the sixth-century British writer Gildas tells us that it was a British king who invited these tribes to defend his kingdom against the Picts and Scots. If they were invited, they certainly outstayed their welcome. The Jutes from the Rhineland, the Angles from the Cimbric Peninsula and the Saxons from the north-western coast of Germany, saw the rich abundance of the country and stayed to fight the British themselves, until the British fell back into Devon, Cornwall, lowland Scotland and the Welsh Marches. Within the next hundred years all distinctions between these German tribes had vanished and they regarded themselves as one nation, though it was divided into several kingdoms.

The British, thrust back to the edge of these islands, were the last inheritors of the Roman culture and in the sixth century a literature of verses and ballad poetry, often intensely lyrical, but which also celebrated sacrifice in battle and the heroism of warriors, was written. These works mention food in passing: reflecting Homer, it is the food of warriors, roasting meats and drinking mead and wine:

> Men went to Catraeth at dawn:
> Their high spirits lessened their life spans.
> They drank mead, gold and sweet, ensnaring.[18]

We learn that the soldiers sat around a large vessel which held the mead or wine, and with their pann – a scoop or drinking bowl – dipped into the communal bowl. Mead and ale were drunk from vessels made from horn, while for wine they used glass, gold or silver. They grew oats which made a flat round bread baked on an iron, they hunted deer, boar and grouse, they kept cattle, while the soldiers had a fondness for apples and for tending kitchen gardens.

There had always been huge difficulties in wresting an adequate food supply from the landscape of Scotland; more than three-fifths of the land consists of mountain, moor and hill. In the south is the plateau of the southern uplands, a slaty rock, which runs across from south-west to north-east for 120 miles. The Highlands are granite rock with a thin topsoil where the frequent rains from the south-west wash away the soluble minerals. Much of the valley ground is marsh or bog, where the acidity of the peaty soil and the poorness of natural drainage add almost insuperable difficulties to cultivating anything. So great stretches of Scotland were regions where very little would grow. Dr Johnson, as always, summed it all up, by saying that in Scotland a tree elicited some of the curiosity bestowed on rarities, and went on to remark that at Tobermory he saw 'what they called a wood, which I unluckily took for heath'.[19]

Much of the farming technique in the early years was basic, devoted to growing oats, barley and kale and forcing the soil to give a return until it was exhausted then moving onto another virgin patch. This worked while there was still plenty of land to move around on, but once settlements began, the land never had any opportunity to rest and recuperate which resulted in a decline in its quality.

Over the extent of this small country there were huge differences in the quality and amount of food, as there was between what the majority had to survive on and what the nobility clustered around the monarch enjoyed; for example, the nobility relied on a substantial amount of imported goods. What the poor ate in Edinburgh was vastly different from what the poor ate in the coastal regions and islands.

Early Agriculture

The struggle against the elements had always been a harrowing one. The actual growing season for the crops was short, so there were never enough cereals to extend through the year. The summer, often up to the late nineteenth century, was a breadless period and cereal products might only be available for four to five months of the year. The oats or barley prior to grinding was dried in a kiln, or put into a pot to parch over the fire or even placed in the ash; if the grain was placed in the fire the process avoided threshing and parched the grain simultaneously, thus preparing it for the hand mill or quern. Once ground, the grains were boiled to make porridge, which was the staple daily dish and eaten with milk and salt. Meat was eaten very occasionally and very early methods of cooking meat still remained in the Hebrides and Highlands; animal skins were sewn into a pouch and the meat was boiled in this bag over a fire or the animal's stomach was used as a container. This practice was still in use in the Hebrides in the late eighteenth century; it was common in the Highlands until after 1759, when a range of mass-produced cast-iron domestic cooking utensils became available through the development of the Scottish iron industry.

A late eighteenth-century traveller met a man on the island of Rum, who did not taste bread until he was fifty and for the rest of his life (he lived to 103) never ate it from March till October, but only took fish and milk, like everyone else in Rum. It was even considered unmanly to toil with spades for such an unnecessary luxury. Fish in fresh or preserved form might have to be a substitute for bread or other cereal products for fifty per cent or more of the year.[20]

In these coastal areas wild foods that could be gathered were paramount in the diet: eggs from sea birds, small shellfish, clams, limpets (but see below) and mussels, seaweeds like dulse and *alaria esculenta*, edible algae called slake or slawk, and vegetables that grew on the beaches like sea kale and wild skirret (when boiled the last was a substitute for bread). The staple fish was coley which could be caught in small boats close to the shore, or with a rod and line from the cliffs and rocks; it was eaten fresh, rolled in breadcrumbs and fried, or dried and salted; its livers were also eaten and sometimes stuffed into the heads of cod or haddock, a dish that came to be called Crappit Heid (Stuffed Head). Walter Scott mentions 'crappit heads' in his novel *Guy Mannering*. An oil was made from the livers on the Isle of Skye, described as dark like port wine, thin but effective.

Wind Blown Fish was made by cleaning the fish, taking out the eyes and passing a string through, then covering the fish with salt and hanging the fish in a draught for the night; the next morning the fish was cooked slowly over a low fire. As in Ireland, seaweeds were used in soups and a jelly made from carrageen; a seaweed referred to as tangle was thought very good for the eyesight, and was both eaten raw and boiled with butter. Limpet shells have been discovered from the earliest times; they were used as fish bait as well as food, but whether eaten cooked or raw they were tough and tasteless, and people who ate them were looked down upon, for limpets were eaten in times of famine and extreme poverty. Yet a soup, stew or 'skink' was made from them, boiled in milk, because it was thought to increase the milk in nursing mothers. Whelks and periwinkles were also eaten, and in Barra the cockle was collected from April to August; horseloads were gathered at a single tide. They were boiled and eaten from the shell, or sometimes boiled in milk and made into a soup. On the east coast fishergirls from Ardersier gathered cockles and sold them in Inverness.

On the Highlands and the Islands dairy products were a central part of the diet; in fact, as in Ireland, newly made butter was often buried in the peat bogs. Butter was made in the summer months when the livestock were on the hills grazing; this was called the 'shieling' system of transhumance necessary with subsistence farming on poor terrain, a term that referred to both the summer pasture and the hut in which the shepherds, who in this case were the women, lived. In the summer period, these women made the butter in clay pots, called crogans, which they also made by hand and left to dry by the hearth. Crogans were used as milking pails, to carry water and ale and to store oil. Crogans made especially to churn butter had holes perforated in one side to allow the gases to escape, otherwise the crogan would have exploded. The method was partially to fill the crogan with milk, to tie a piece of cloth or skin tightly over the circular mouth and to rock the vessel backwards and forwards until the butter was made; this process could take up to nine or ten hours.[21] It is odd that the churning tool and wooden churn common in early Ireland did not find their way north across the water.

Before the Act of Union roads were very few and what existed were well-nigh impassable; wheeled traffic was completely impossible, and travel on foot was often the quickest way as stepping stones could be utilised while horses simply slipped, fell or got stuck in the mud. Winter feeding of livestock was unknown; the milch cows and sheep that were housed had to starve on straw, boiled chaff, mashed wins, dry benty grass and coarse rushes, which had been cut in autumn from the marsh lands with an occasional sheaf of oats. The animals that survived staggered outside dizzy with weakness, sometimes so feeble they had to be carried to the pasture; for the first few days they had to be dragged out of the bogs and marshes into which they had been tempted by the sprouting vegetation on the surface but were then too weak to extricate their clogged feet.[22] That these animals could slowly recover, grow stronger on the new grass and then be sold on, going on long journeys over these rough tracks seems astonishing.

The chief industry of the south-west and the Highlands of Scotland was the trade in cattle with England. From Galloway came the black, polled, shaggy cattle which were good grazing stock and were readily sold in England. Large herds were driven from the north to the cattle trysts at Crieff and Falkirk where they were sold to English drovers. The Highland cattle, which had been well nigh starved in the winters, were small, hardy, lean and active; they were, not unexpectedly, poor milkers (they calved only every second year), giving in the height of summer only $1\frac{1}{2}$ gallons per day. In the Lowlands double that amount was given.

A few swine were kept in the Lowlands, but none at all in the Highlands as they refused to eat pork. An old Cavalier song ridicules them as 'the Jewish Scots that scorn to eat the flesh of swine'. (James VI of Scotland and I of England also disliked pork.)

They kept small flocks of sheep to provide wool for domestic purposes; these fed on the hill slopes, but often had to be driven through snow to distant sheltered valleys, a journey on which many died. They had to be housed at night, as they could be attacked by eagles, wild cats and foxes. The ewes were milked for a few weeks after weaning, the milk being made into cheese or butter; they were a small, narrow-framed, unshapely breed, slow in growth, varying between 28 lb and 36 lb in the carcass, producing mutton and wool of poor quality.

The Food

Jean de Froissart (1333-1400), European medieval poet and court historian who travelled to Italy, France, and the Iberian peninsula as well as Scotland, wrote an impressive account of the Scots army campaigning. He was astonished at its mobility, advancing seventy miles in a day, sweeping into the north of England on horseback, its knights and squires on fine strong horses, the commoners on small ponies. Its secret was that it dispensed with the baggage carts; each soldier took with him a bag of oats and a flat stone kept between the saddle and the saddle cloth. The army lived on water, underdone meat and thin oat cake. It drank river water without wine, slaughtered cattle from the surrounding countryside and cooked the meat in the hides over a fire; the water was then mixed with the oats, the stone laid over the fire and the thin cake spread over the stone. Froissart ends his account with the remark, 'It is not surprising that they can travel faster than other armies.' He goes on to describe the discomfort of living in Scottish burghs, the lack of refinement among the nobles and gentry and the violent Byzantine barbarity of the court. This was at the beginning of the Auld Alliance when French soldiers came to Scotland to help fight the English. From Froissart one gets the impression that the Scottish court remained uninfluenced by French manners, certainly at the table. However, Froissart was impressed by the fact that the farmers were not downtrodden by the nobility as they were in France.

In the medieval period, from the few scattered accounts of consumption, one gathers that meat-eating was prominent, at least in the military, the navy and the towns and cities. Visiting Denmark in 1564, a Scottish recruiting officer declared that the men he offered to bring over from Scotland to fight the Swedes would need but few provisions – water and milk for drink, fresh flesh and a little bread. In 1513 the *James*, one of James IV's great ships, had forty men on board and was provisioned daily. Each man's ration was 15 oz bread, 3 oz mutton, 12 oz herring and a good deal of ale, which would have supplied 3,500 calories. In the 1380s John Fordoun thought that 'the Scots were a people rarely indulging in food before sunset and contenting themselves, moreover with meat, and food prepared from milk.' Aeneas Sylvius Piccolomini, envoy to the Pope and the future Pope Pius II, visited Scotland to report on life there a few decades later, thought the country bleak and wild with few trees and very little corn.

> Sulphurous stone dug out of the ground (coal) was used as fuel. The
> towns were without walls, the houses built without mortar, with doors of

ox-hide, the common people are poor, and destitute of all refinement. They eat flesh and fish, and bread was a luxury. Trading with Flanders the people exported hides, wool, salt fish, and pearls.

Perhaps, understandably as all nations do, the Scots put on a show for these foreign visitors, for in 1498 Don Pedro de Ayala noted that 'they have more meat in great and small animals than they want' and in 1545 Nicander Nucius wrote that 'the Scots have so many oxen and so many flocks of sheep that wonder arises in the beholders on account of the multitude of them,' adding, 'they abound in butter, cheese and milk.' Estienne Perlin, writing in 1551-2, found plentiful and cheap provisions, not least meat: 'They have plenty of cows and calves, on which account their flesh is cheap; and in my time bread was tolerably cheap.'[23]

There is other evidence which points to meat being plentiful up to the beginning of the seventeenth century which is that at times of famine and dearth the Privy Council took measures to halt all exports of fish, flesh, cheese and butter. The eating of meat in 1565 and 1567 was banned by the Privy Council in Lent, not for religious reasons, but to conserve supplies, 'for the common weill', as there had been bad harvests; these regulations continued in the 1570s and 1580s. In the famine of 1598, when Dumfries was short of food, the local magistrates purchased cattle from the surrounding countryside and had them brought into the burgh.[24] Unless the townpeople regularly ate meat this, of course, would not have happened. At these times of food shortages Parliament rationed the food according to rank: in 1551 a Parliamentary order maintained 'that having respect to the great and exorbitant dearth risen in this realm of victuals and other stuff for the sustenation of mankind . . . it is decided and ordained that no archbishop, bishop, nor earl shall have at his mess but eight dishes of meat, nor baron nor freeholder have but four dishes of meat, nor no burgess or other substantious man, spiritual or temporal, shall have at his mess but three dishes, and but one kind of meat in every dish.' This, in fact, is a temporary sumptuary law employed at a time of famine. There were penalties if any of the grandees exceeded their limits, though one doubts that the higher orders were ever fined a £100 for an infringement. In 1572 in the midst of these meat bans Lord Lovat's accounts show that he consumed seventy fat oxen a year as well as venison, fish, poultry, lamb, veal and huge quantities of game birds, as well as imported wines, sugars and spices from France.

Very early in the following century the authorities ceased to concern themselves with meat supplies at times of food shortages. In the famine years of 1622-4, the Privy Council never attempted to control meat supplies. Exports of hides also declined in this century, but the export of live cattle increased; up to 48,000 beasts crossed the border to England in the 1660s, rising to 60,000 by the 1690s. What had occurred was that the English were now eating the Scottish beef, while the Scots had to eat something else. Even throughout the medieval period, there must have been regions of Scotland that rarely ate meat at all.

Bishop Leslie in 1568 said of the Highlanders that they were accustomed to a mixed diet of rye, pease, beans, wheat and especially oats, but their 'greatest delyte' was beef. Of the Borderers he comments that they lived mainly on flesh, milk, cheese and 'sodden' beir (barley supposedly in broths), adding that they made little use of bread. Not so long afterwards in 1598, Fynes Morison described the Lowland population as eating 'little fresh meate'; he added: 'They vulgarly eate harth Cakes of Oates, but in Cities have also wheaten bread.' In 1605 Sir Thomas Craig, investigating the possibilities of a union between the two countries, for now they shared the same monarch, saw a striking difference between the Lowlands and the Highlands. 'Nowadays,' he pointed out, 'national plenty is a question of food and clothing; and in the matter of food we are as well off as any other people.' He claimed that fewer Scots died of starvation than the English, that nowhere else was fish so plentiful, and that there was meat of every kind and barley bread as pure and white as that of England and France. He was impressed by the servants 'who are content with oatmeal, which makes them hardy and long lived. The greater number of our farmhands eat bread made of peas and beans.' Craig described the Highlanders as robust, long-lived active people, in spite of their entire dependence on cheese, flesh and milk like the Scythians.[25]

The first known reference to porridge is from Richard James (1592-1638), an English traveller, who spoke of a 'pottage' made of oatmeal flour boiled in water which was eaten with butter, milk or ale; he speaks of it as being 'eaten by the common people and school children at breakfast and by Ladies also'. He also speaks of the 'meaner' sort in Berwickshire eating pease bread, while he enthuses over the food he has eaten in the gentlemen's houses he stayed at – the boiled meat dishes, broths and stews. All references to the Lowland diet now emphasise the staple food, oatmeal, and hardly mention meat at all. Even the seventeenth-century army diet is now without meat, allowing for two soldiers 2 lb oatbread and 28 oz wheatbread with a pint of ale per day. In 1689 the provisions for 100 men for a month provided two-thirds of the nutrition from oatmeal, with a quarter from butter and cheese and the rest from ale and brandy. In 1649 an orphan's diet from Hutcheson's Hospital in Glasgow shows that eight-two per cent of the nutrition came from oatbread, eight from meat and three from fish. An analysis of other institutional diets shows roughly the same ratio.[26]

Highland food was described by Bishop Pococke in 1760 as milk, curds, whey and oatmeal. Pennant, in his *Tour of Scotland* (1769), described the food on Arran as 'chiefly potatoes and meal, and during the winter some dried mutton or goat is added to their hard fare'. He describes three groups that drank milk: the Highland shepherds who drank 'milk, whey and sometimes by way of indulgence, whisky'; the married servants on Skye who as their common food had Brochan, a thick meal-pudding with milk, butter or treacle; and the inhabitants of Lismore who were forced to live off boiled sheep's milk throughout the spring in the absence of anything else. Marshall, in his survey of the Highlands in 1794, told of a peasantry that lived predominantly on oatmeal and milk; if butter and cheese was made from it, they could not give any to their children, for it all had to be sold at the market.

The food the tenant farmers ate was both monotonous and inadequate. The families gathered around one wooden dish and helped themselves with a horn spoon which each carried about them. Table knives and forks were not even provided at inns, so travellers learnt to carry their own. Oatmeal of the poorest quality was the staple food; it was boiled with water to make a porridge and eaten with thin milk or ale; bread was thin oatcakes cooked over a griddle. The food was further rendered insipid by the absence of salt, since the salt tax made that commodity a luxury. Oatmeal and pease-meal mixed together provided a dish called 'brose', made by pouring over water which had had greens boiled in it, or kail, which was a broth made from cabbage leaves thickened with coarse barley or groats of oats. These dishes were sometimes flavoured with a piece of salt meat, but meat was a luxury eaten only at a wedding or a christening, or when an animal died of starvation or disease. The slightly better off farmer at the end of autumn killed and salted one or two animals to be kept throughout the winter. In 1795 a traveller commented that 'among the ordinary tenants not five pounds of meat were consumed in the family in a year; that an egg, and still more a fowl was a luxury seldom enjoyed; and that an occasional haddock was regarded as a wonderful regalement.'[27] Elizabeth Hamilton complained of the slovenly methods adopted by the people in making cheese and butter and the filthy state of these articles when ready for use.[28] 'The butter was of twenty different colours and stuck with hairs like mortar.' A black pudding was sometimes made by bleeding the cows and mixing the blood with oatmeal and boiling it together. Tenants who lived above a Highland stream could supplement this meagre diet by catching salmon and other fish. Further north in the Orkneys, the diet was little better, the daily fare consisted of 'morning piece', which was half a bannock of bread made from bere (a form of barley which had its grains in four rows and sometimes contained almost twice as many grains as ordinary barley) mixed with seeds from wild plants. Breakfast was porridge made from the native black oats and more wild seeds, and fish with nettle broth formed the main meal. The water in which the fish was boiled was kept to cook the cabbage reserved for supper, and the scourings from the pots and platters were mixed with the following morning's porridge. Salt water supplied the only seasoning. Reuthie bread, made from the seeds of wild mustard, filled the gap between the exhaustion of the old crop and the harvest of new grain.

The French Influence

The Auld Alliance goes back certainly as far as 1239 when Alexander II of Scotland married Mary de Courcy of Picardy, who survived him to act as Regent for her son. (Norman influences could have entered Scotland earlier after Alexander I married the daughter of Henry I of England.) From then on there must have been cultural influences from across the Channel entering the Scottish court and inevitably moulding some of the food eaten. James I (1406-1437) is said to have had a French cook and James II (1437-1460) married a French wife. Did they bring French cookery books with them, contemporary versions of *Le Viandier* and the *Grand Cuisinier*?[29] If so, the influences were only detected later in the midst of the sixteenth century. The court of James IV was considered the most romantic and brilliant in Europe; its praises were sung by the Italian poet Ariosto, and it is the subject of a finely painted frieze in Siena. The poet Dunbar wrote of the swans, cranes, partridges and plovers and every fish that swam in the rivers adorning the tables with wines from the Rhine, so one must conclude that gastronomy was of a high order. But whether this was specifically French is another matter. Court dishes, as we have seen, were almost international in their character.

Historians think it was Mary of Guise, Queen to James V, who brought French food and recipes to the court of Scotland. Throughout her 18-year regency, while her daughter, the future Mary Queen of Scots, was growing up, that French influence in Scotland reached its zenith. Her family, Cardinal de Guise and the Duke of Lorraine, did all they could to tighten the bonds between France and Scotland, and also to stem the advance of Protestant Reformers. The Duke of Lorraine sent French miners to help the Scots develop their coal-mining and engineers, masons and master builders, carvers, glaziers and decorators, clothmakers and cooks followed. The Scots began to drink their wine from silver 'tassies' and cut their meat with a 'jockteleg' after Jacques de Liège, the inventor of the table knife; they ate thin triangles of shortbread called 'Petticoatails' from *petites Gatelles*, and liked cod in a horseradish and egg sauce, or 'cabbieclaw'[30] from *cabillaud*. French cookery terms have passed into Scots: others include ashet from the French *assiette*, meaning meat dish, battry (*batterie de cuisine*) for kitchen utensils, pottisea for *patissier* and mange for meal.[31] F. Marian McNeill lists over 150 Franco-Scottish domestic terms in her book *The Scots Kitchen*; she quotes a Colonsay woman who was cook to a great Highland chief in the Jacobite period as saying that she thought French and Scottish methods of cooking were similar:

> The way we cook up meat and vegetables together, and go in so much for braising and stewing. I often think their charcoal stoves are very like our peat embers that keep the broth boiling so gently and bake the potatoes on the top.

Once Mary Stuart came to the throne she continued to improve the court manners and table. Feather Fowlie appears to be a rendition of *Velouté de Volaille*, while Lorraine Soup, with almonds, eggs, chicken, breadcrumbs, lemon, nutmeg and cream was possibly a tribute to the Queen Regent, as was *Soupe à la Reine*, a white soup, made from veal, chicken and herbs. Veal Flory, a veal stew with herbs and mushrooms, is supposed to have arrived via Paris and Florence.

There are also two puddings that bear the same word Flory, Almond Flory and Prune Flory. Meg Dods (see page 196) thinks the nuns of Florence and France were the source of much confectionery and many Scottish puddings: 'caramelled and candied fruits, fruits en chemise, chantilly and caramel baskets'. *Archangelica officinalis*, green angelica which is candied, has been grown in Scotland since 1568, the only place in the British Isles where it is cultivated. A 'crokain' is a pudding made from sugar, water and lemon and derives from *croque en bouche*; another pudding, Nun's Beads, is a kind of *beignet soufflé*, while Haggis is a corruption of *hachis*, French for mince.[32]

George Buchanan was delighted with the feasting at the Duke of Atholl's table, where he was regaled 'with all sich deliciosus and sumptuous meattis as was to be had in Scotland for fleschis, fischis, and all kinds of fyne wyne, and spyces requisite for ane prince'.[33]

At the end of the sixteenth century Fynes Morrison travelled around the country and gives a picture of the diet of the people:

> They eat much colewort and cabbage but little fresh meat, using to salt their mutton and geese . . . The gentlemen reckon their revenues not by rents of money, but by cauldrons of victuals . . .

He explains he was at a knight's house, attended by many servants wearing blue caps, who when they had finished eating sat down at the end of the table and were given great platters of porridge with a small piece of boiled meat, but the more senior servants had a pullet and some prunes in a broth instead of porridge. There was a difference, he explained, between the food of the country and the food of the city: in the former they vulgarly ate hearth cakes of oats, while in the latter they have wheaten bread bought by courtiers, gentlemen and the best sort of citizen. 'They drink pure wines not with sugar as the English, yet at feasts they put Comfits in the wine after the French manner.'

The Eighteenth Century

Travellers to Scotland found getting around a hazardous business while the food at the inns outraged them. 'A couple of roasted hens, very poor, new killed, the skins much broke with plucking, black with smoke and greased with bad butter,' remarked one traveller in 1801.[34] At breakfast in the inn at Inveroran Dorothy Wordsworth found the butter 'not eatable, the barley cakes fusty, the oatbread so hard that I could not chew it and there were only four eggs in the house which they had boiled as hard as stones'. At an Edinburgh inn Dr Spier ate a dinner of 'salt haddock, cold chicken in a periwig of feathers, tarts covered in black dirt instead of white sugar which seemed to have been first tasted by the mice'.[35]

As always the nobility did very well. Not only did they take valuable food from their tenants, but they could afford to buy the best imported food if they wished. In addition to money rent, the Earl of Dunnottar had corn, fodder butter, eggs, capons, hens and swine. Stewart of Appin is said to have received as part of his rent an ox or cow for every week and a goat or wether for every day of the year. In the *Arniston Memoirs*, a bill of fare for a week in December 1748 for Lord Arniston mentions cocky-leekie, boiled beef and greens, roast goose, shoulder of mutton, eggs, rice and milk, pea soup, boiled turkey, roast beef, apple pie, sheep's head broth, rabbits, boiled hens with oyster sauce, mince pie, calves' head, moorfowl, roast pig, hare soup, jugged hare, roast ducks, tongue, tarts and jellies, claret wine, white wine and ale. Dr Johnson was astonished at the high standard of living in the Hebrides. 'I forgot to enquire how they were supplied with so much exotic luxury.' The luxury could have been explained by the merchants of Inverness, who exported quantities of cured fish to France, Spain, Italy, Holland and Sweden, and in return imported glass, silk, muslin, tea, coffee, raisins, spices, oranges and lemons, wine and brandy. Dr Johnson continued to be amazed at the scale and magnificence of Scottish hospitality that he enjoyed: 'veal in Edinburgh, roasted kid in Inverness, admirable venison and generous wine in the castle of Dunvegan'.

In 1784, the French traveller Faujas de St Fond tells us:

> At the Duke of Argyll's table, the different courses and the aftermeats were all done as in France, and with the same variety and abundance. We had delicate water-fowl, excellent fish and the vegetables which did honour to the Scotch gardeners. At the dessert, the cloth and napkins disappeared and the mahogany table was covered with brilliant decanters filled with the most exquisite wines, vases of porcelain and crystal glass containing comfits, and beautiful baskets, replete with choice fruits, which could scarely have been expected in this cold climate, even with every assistance from art . . .[36]

When John Knox dined at Brahan Castle near Dingwall in the 1780s there was beef, mutton, veal, lamb, pork, venison, hare, pigeons, fowls, tame and wild ducks, tame and wild geese, partridges and a great variety of moorfowl. From Lord Seaforth's own boat came cod, haddock, whiting, mackerel, skate, sole, flounders, lythe, salmon and trout; the fish caught in the bay before the house were thrown in a heap on the kitchen floor, the cook chose what she wanted for his Lordship's table and the rest went to the poor. Knox claimed that all these items, as well as the garden produce, was what a Highland laird or chieftain had at his dinner. For breakfast there were French rolls, oat and barley bread, tea and coffee, honey in the comb, red and blackcurrant jellies, marmalades, conserves, cream, a plateful of fresh eggs, fresh and salted herrings boiled, fresh and salted haddocks, a cold round of venison, beef and mutton hams. While to begin the meal there were drams of whisky, gin, rum or brandy, plain or infused with berries that grow among the heath.[37]

There is a Highland breakfast described in Tobias Smollett's *Humphry Clinker* where laid out upon the table are piles of boiled eggs, butter and cream, 'an entire cheese made of goat's milk; a large earthenware pot, full of honey; the best part of a ham; a cold venison pasty; a bushel of oatmeal, made into thin cakes and bannocks; with a small wheaten loaf in the middle, for the strangers; a stone bottle full of whisky; another of brandy, and a kilderkin of ale.' A rather more sophisticated breakfast was found by the French visitor, Faujas de St Fond in 1784: 'Plates of smoked beef, cheese of the country and English cheese, fresh eggs, salted herrings, butter, milk, and cream; a sort of boullie of oatmeal and water, in eating which each spoonful is plunged into a basin of cream; milk worked up with yolks of eggs, sugar, and rum; currant jelly, conserve of myrtle, a wild fruit that grows among the heath; tea, coffee, three kinds of bread (sea biscuits, oatmeal cakes, and very thin and fine barley cakes); and Jamaica rum.' This breakfast is interesting for its medieval dishes; the *boullie* is flummery or the Welsh llymru (see page 199) and the flavoured milk is eggnog or syllabub. One wonders whether the beef was smoked or wind dried. Meg Dods, the one authority to inform us on this matter, does not mention beef in her chapter on curing (see page 193).

Scottish breakfasts were understandably praised, but another meal in which the Scots would excel was about to appear, when Mary of Modena, the wife of James II of England, introduced tea in 1681 when her husband as Duke of York was Lord High Commissioner of Scotland. By 1750 tea had become a meal that gave great impetus to the national flair for baking. Henry Mackenzie, born in 1745, wrote of his childhood:

> Tea was the meal of ceremony and we had fifty odd kinds of teabread.
> One Scott made a little fortune by his milk-bakes. His shop in Forrester's
> Wynd was surrounded at five o'clock by a great concourse of servant
> maids . . .[38]

One Scottish lady living in London despised the meal there, writing back to a friend that they only have flimsy bread and butter and 'no such thing as short-bread, seed cake, bun, marmlet or jeely to be seen . . .'[39]

There is a yawning gap between the food of the poor and that of the rich; the injustice of these social conditions strikes one as unbearable, especially as no one seemed moved to redress the situation. The irony was that oatmeal provides the basis for an extremely healthy diet and though the food of the Scottish poor was limited and bland it was highly nutritious. Francis Douglas, writing in 1782 of the food of small farmers in the north-east, remarked that they lived on 'oatmeal, milk and vegetables, chiefly red cabbage in the winter seasons and coleworts for the summer and spring', while flesh was never seen in their houses except at Christmas and Shrove Tuesday and at baptisms and weddings: 'Nevertheless they are strong and active and live to a good old age.'

A very dismal view of Scottish cattle and their poor milk yield because of the scarcity of pasture is given in 1813 by a Mr Robertson in a book called *A General View of Inverness*. 'The best cows in the Island afford only a Scots Quart (about 3 English pints) of milk a day; of which the calf gets a Choppin (one and a half pints) in the morning and the same quantity in the evening; but many of them yield not daily above a pint (one and a half quarts) of milk.'[40]

Very soon afterwards the potato was added to this diet. The first mention of it is in 1683 in Sutherland's *Hortus Medicus Edinburghensis* and it found its way into the gardens of a few landowners as an occasional vegetable dish. In 1701 in the household book of the Duchess of Buccleuch there is an item of one peck of potatoes brought from Edinburgh for 2s 6d; in 1731 potatoes are mentioned several times as a supper dish in another household book of the Eglinton family.[41] On the Marchmont estate field cultivation was practised at an early date for that part of Scotland. Among the directions for farm work in 1757 are the following: 'The little valley below full of thistles to be planted with potatoes', and 'Potatoes to be planted in the ground next to the pond below the Old Parterre to supply the family'. A letter written in 1726 by John Cockburn to his favourite tenant, Alexander Wight, reads: 'As your potato ground was well dunged and in order I doubt nothing of your having a good crop of barley upon it . . . the profit from the one fourth acre potatoes upon the bad land opposite the church is so great that I hope you will go on with them, especially as you find good crops after them.' It was quickly realised that potatoes planted on 'bad land' broke up the soil, aerated it and were excellent as the first cultivating crop. Yet the Scottish people initially were suspicious about eating these tubers, and there were stories of the workers compelled to grow them laying the crop at the laird's gate, as if to say they were not going to be made to eat them.

This was quickly to change, however:

> Potatoes are used chiefly in lieu of bread by the great mass of Hebrideans plain boiled and without anything else but a little milk or salt; and in winter some salted meat or herrings. One fourth of the quantity raised is given to cattle, horses and pigs between the beginnings of February and the middle of March.[42]

The traveller who wrote thus was obviously suspicious of the potato, and his dislike of it is communicated in the best civil servant manner, on whether it can really be good for these people. He wrote: 'It has been questioned whether potatoes are in fact advantageous to the Highlands or ought to be encouraged, as they tend to discountenance industry by affording so great a quantity of sustenance with so little labour.'[43] Yet by the end he thinks they should be cultivated as long as they are confined to waste land. He tells us that a Hebridean would consume 8 lb potatoes per day.

However, as in Ireland, allowing the potato to become a staple food of the poor was to lead to disaster. There is little doubt that it was a major contributory factor to over population in the Hebrides and Highlands, so that by the second half of the eighteenth century population was overrunning resources. A combination of smallholdings, inefficient farming systems and the lack of integrated national markets in basic foodstuffs put the population at risk. From the 1690s the Highlands continued to suffer periodic famine periods, the worst one being in 1782. People, having nothing to eat at home, took to the road and begged; one commentator estimated that the numbers of begging poor had doubled to 200,000 during the later 1690s.

The crucial factor that changed Highland policy and the temperament of the chieftains themselves was the collapse of the 1745 Jacobite rebellion. The Highlands had always remained apart from the rest of Scotland; dominated by a feudal regime, clan chieftains enjoyed medieval judicial and military privileges, achieving devoted loyalty from their tenants. Now the British Government abolished the chieftains' authority and extended the royal system of shires and judges as they had done in the sixteenth century in Wales. Though the chieftains' status was destroyed they did not suffer economically, for they became landlords on estates that before they had held in trust for their clans. Loyalty in the feudal system had been a one-way process, but now the new policies were all to the detriment of the crofter who had to pay rent for his land, a rent which the chieftain kept on raising.

Emigration overseas now increased greatly. It was the small farmers who left in their thousands, for the sub-tenants were too poor to emigrate. The Highland farmer could raise the money for himself and his family by selling his livestock. Dr Johnson discovered the plight from his host at Anach in Glenmoriston:

> From him we first heard of the general dissatisfaction which is now driving the Highlanders into the other hemisphere; and when I asked him whether they could stay at home if they were well treated, he answered with indignation that no man willingly left his native country. Of the farm, which he himself had occupied, the rent had in twenty five years, been advanced from five to twenty pounds which he found himself so little able to pay that he would be glad to try his fortune in some other place.[44]

Consolidation of farms accompanied the rise in rents and emigration, and from this time too there was a changeover to sheep-farming. *The Scots Magazine* of July 1772 thought the emigration of hundreds of people to America from the north of Scotland was caused by the coming of opulent farmers from the Lowlands who turned the Highlands into sheep runs. In 1784 the export of wool from Inverness was only 1 ton 3 hundredweight, but in 1804 it had increased to 131 tons 10 hundredweight. The growing wealth of the country was all part of the industrial revolution, which had created the iron and steel trade, the expansion of the linen industry, woollen manufactures and the cotton industry in the west. This in turn made new and increasing demands on agricultural produce which could now reach the market towns by travelling efficiently on the new highways.

At the end of the century an artificial stimulus was given to the economy by the war with France. The price of wheat continued to rise throughout the Napoleonic Wars, and the result of the new prosperity was the erection of new farms and threshing mills, new agricultural implements and the making of enclosures. There was also a substantial increase in the wages of agricultural labourers. A ploughman's wage in 1720 was £2 per year, in 1809 it was £24; a servant maid earned 16 shillings a year which went up to £10. There was general improvement in the social conditions of the people. One writer pointed out that in 1760 no wheat was sown in the parish, except one half acre by the minister and no kail or potatoes were planted in the open field; in 1790 above 100 acres of wheat were cultivated and three-fifths of the ground was under grasses, turnips, kail and potatoes; the whole parish was completely enclosed. In 1760 there was only one eight-day clock in the parish and one tea kettle; in 1790 there were thirty clocks, above 100 watches and at least 160 tea kettles, 'there being scarce a family that have one and many that have two'. Wheaten bread, sweet milk, butter, cheese, eggs, tea and sometimes roast meat were added to the general diet.[45] Good roads for carts and horses had replaced the mud tracks of 1750, so that some hundred pounds value annually of wheaten bread was brought from

Kirkintilloch and Glasgow. 'The houses of every decent inhabitant of this parish consist at least of a kitchen and one room, generally two rooms ceiled above, and often laid with deal floors, with elegant glass windows and, I believe, few of the tradesmen sit down to dinner without flesh meat on the table and malt liquor to drink.'[46] Another writer remarked that 'as ministers to our luxury we have in the same street an oilman, who advertises the sale of Quin sauce, Genoa capers, Gorgona anchovies etc.'[47]

Public roadhouses now also improved: one traveller commented on the cheapness of the tariff, a dinner of 'fine fresh trout, a shoulder of mutton, two fowls and bacon, hung beef and salmon salted, vegetables, cheese and an excellent bottle of port, cost only four shillings and twopence'.[48] Oatmeal still remained the staple food for breakfast and supper in many parts of Scotland. Among the poorer tenants, potatoes, milk and salted herrings came as a welcome change from the eternal brose and sowens, but if they kept a pig it provided them with pickled pork for part of the year, the lard dressed the potatoes and vegetables and the bones gave relish to the broth, if they kept poultry they had eggs which they could sell to buy tea and sugar.

In 1826 Meg Dods was impressed by the advances made in the last few years 'to improve the quality, hasten the seasons and to spread the cultivation of vegetables'. She remarked in her *The Cook and Housewife's Manual* that now upon a gentleman's table when there had just been peas, broccoli, cauliflower, there was now asparagus, seakale, endive and artichoke. She spoke of the vegetable market improving 'so that a healthful luxury is now within reach of all classes'. However, it was another story if you lived in the Highlands. In 1812 Elizabeth Grant of Rothiemurchus wrote:

> We were so remote from markets that we had to depend on our own produce . . . we brewed our own beer, made our bread, made our candles, nothing was brought from afar but, wine, groceries and flour for wheat did not ripen so high above the sea. Yet we lived in luxury; game was plentiful, red deer, roes, hare, grouse, ptarmigan and partridge; the rivers provided trout and salmon, the different lochs, pike and char; the garden abounded in common fruits and common vegetables; cranberries and raspberries ran over the country and the poultry yard was ever well furnished.[49]

The diet became less frugal in the cottage too. Mrs Katherine Grant from Appin in Argyll, recalled the ordinary diet as being porridge or potatoes with milk, cheese, eggs, scones, oatcakes and an occasional potful of cock-a-leekie, but a night's fishing could bring in a harvest of shellfish and they would dry ling and codfish with herring and saithe and preserve them in barrels. A slaughtered sheep would be salted down and packed into a barrel, tripe had to be cleaned, suet transformed into candles and any left went into white puddings. Nothing was ever wasted: sheep's head, barley broth, haggis, hash and fine mince patties. Meg Dods sums up this pragmatic and imaginative cooking when she writes: 'We are convinced that the art of preparing cheap dishes is much better understood by the intelligent poor than by those who assume the task of instructing them.'

The industrial revolution brought the making of new roads, bridges and canals, giving work to thousands of agricultural labourers; these men left home and experienced new places and different foods. Moralists saw great benefits: 'They have returned to their native districts with the advantages of using the most perfect sort of tools and utensils or they have been usefully distributed through other parts of the country . . . wheelwrights and cartwrights have been established, the plough has been introduced . . . the moral habits of the great masses of working classes are changed . . .'[50]

The Role of Women

From the earliest days, as in England, until greater urbanisation and the industrial revolution, women laboured in the fields besides their husbands and sons. It was not only the milking and feeding of livestock, but they spread the manure, carried the sheaves for threshing, cleaned out the byres and stables and helped winnow the corn, as an account from the Lothians in 1656 makes clear.[51] A fit and able wife was essential to any adult male agricultural worker. It was also expected that not only were they the cooks for the main daily meal, but that bread would have been baked and at times of glut for any fruit and vegetable, it would be preserved, bottled, pickled or dried.

Women's work was not confined to farming. In the seventeenth and eighteenth centuries, coal-mining women were part of the workforce; colliers in the east Lothian had to provide bearers to carry the coal to the surface, and generally they chose their wives and daughters. In pits such as Loanhead in Midlothian in the 1680s or Bo'ness in West Lothian during the 1760s women outnumbered men by two to one. This phenomenon was almost unknown in England. Women who lived around large towns could market vegetables, fruit and dairy products; fishwives from Fishmerrow and Prestonpans walked to Edinburgh to sell the fish caught by their husbands and fathers. Rural domestic industry was important, especially in the textile industry, and in the mid-eighteenth century roughly eighty per cent of adult women were involved in spinning. Women's participation in trade was generally limited to shop-keeping. In the late seventeenth century, a Fife woman, Isobel Anderson, dealt in pepper, sugar, candy, soap, starch and hemp, in addition to a ton of tea from Bruges. These women also cooked, cleaned and mended in their homes; they looked after the children and made clothes for the family. The concept of a 'housewife' (a married woman who simply looked after her house and family) did not exist until the eighteenth century, until with greater urbanisation the burgeoning of the middle classes occurred and female leisure became an indication of the husband's social status.

Scottish Cookery

Cookery books began to appear for this new woman, books which she would read and then give to the housekeeper to pass to the cook. One of the later ones, Mrs Frazer's *The Practice of Cookery*, appeared in 1800: she writes in her preface: 'These recipes were originally intended for the Author's own private life, but at the request and solicitation of her scholars, and several respectable friends, she was induced to publish them.' The cloak of respectability is thick upon this volume; it is much concerned with the appearances of food, giving great detail on how to dress and garnish it. There are four pages on how to dress a turtle, then three more on how to dress it the West Indian way; making an ornamental salmagundy entailed making a pound of butter into the shape of a pineapple – no instructions are given for this effect. It is obvious that how the food looks is the first priority; its appearance must impress and strike the onlooker with awe, but whether they found this appetising is not recorded.

These are books about social aspiration: indeed there are long homilies in *Cookery and Domestic Economy* by Mrs Somerville (Practical Teacher of the Art), which she published herself in 1862, and which is respectfully dedicated to the Ladies of Scotland. The book begins with a piece on the young housekeeper and her duties, which starts with the many difficulties that will meet her on her initiation into the duties of her new sphere of life. She must avoid all wasteful expenditure, in personal attire she will be neat and tasteful without extravagance: 'rich adornments and gaudy jewellery are not the standard by which the real lady is judged'. It goes on to point out that 'Many good husbands have been sadly changed by ill cooked and ill-timed dinners.' This is followed by sections on cleanliness; 'to dispel odours from the kitchen heat a coal shovel and pour a little coarse vinegar upon it and carry it about for a few moments in the lower hall and kitchen.' Punctuality: 'Without this qualification it is impossible to get on well, if indeed at all.' 'The kitchen time piece should be regularly attended to, to prevent the possibility of a mistake.' We catch a glimpse of how the dinner dishes had to be made, all of them prepared some time before (soup should be made the day before), so that everything could be served at once. Fish, for example, should be prepared a few hours previously, vegetables laid in salt and water until boiled, then drained and kept warm.

Among the recipes for soup there are two, one called Summer Hotch-potch and the other Winter Hotch-potch (from the French *hochepot*) that do not inspire confidence. (However, see Chapter 10 on the art of left-overs, a Victorian practice, which began earlier if Mrs Somerville's book is to be trusted as reflecting a social trend. Mrs Glasse's [see page 219] recipe for Hodge-podge is made from fresh ingredients and so is Meg Dods'.) The recipe for turtle soup begins by taking the turtle out of the water, laying it on its back, tying its feet and cutting off its head. It ends with the remark that turtle fins make a nice corner dish. She is woefully inadequate, however, on instructions for nettles and dandelions, which, she says, 'are esteemed by some and are said to be very wholesome; they are dressed in small bundles and served on toast with melted butter on them.' The Victorian tendency to provide cheaper substitutes as in Mock Turtle soup made from a calf's head here appears in Mrs Somerville's recipe for mock ginger made from sliced apple soaked in salt water and flavoured with ginger. An extract of calves' feet is used to make jelly for setting various puddings, such as white vanilla cream, strawberry or ginger cream. Fritters of left-over pudding, were made by dipping slices into pancake batter, frying them, then dusting them with sugar. Cold left-over rice is mixed with flour and fried.

A recipe for cow-heel, a mould of jellied beef with hard boiled eggs, ends with the remark 'This is an economical dish.'

The one cookery book of great authority is *The Cook and Housewife's Manual* (1826), written under the authorship of 'Mrs Margaret [Meg] Dods', who is a character in Sir Walter Scott's *St Ronan's Well*, the termagant landlady of the Cleikum Inn. The writer was really a Mrs Johnston, the wife of an Edinburgh publisher; she was the author *The Edinburgh Tales* and other works, and was later editor of *Tait's Magazine*. She considers Anglo-Gallican cookery to be the best the world has ever known, but regards both the conceit of French cooks and the affectation of juvenile gastronomers as detrimental. She thinks that the French took the lead of all European peoples in soups and broths, while the Scots ranked second and the Welsh next; the English were at the very bottom of the scale. (Miss Acton complains only a little later that the English appeared to have forgotten how to make soup, see page 246.) Dods gives thirty pages on making stock and various game soups as well as five more pages on fish soups. Her Oyster Soup is made from a quart of oysters, pounded and simmered for half an hour, then strained and another dozen added, poached for eight minutes, seasoned with mace and cayenne, then thickened with three egg yolks. She adds a note: 'Any other flavour that is relished may be given to this luscious soup. We like lemon: mustard and vinegar are used, and tarragon or garlic, for those who relish foreign cookery.' Note, she does not say French cookery but foreign, yet these are two flavourings we would now associate with French cuisine. Apart from the chicken and leek, her Cock-a-Leekie also has prunes and like the Oyster Soup has two lots of leeks, the first cooked to a purée, the second cut into chunks and added later.

She advises the Rumford Steamer for vegetables and deplores them boiled and watery. She cooks peas with lettuce, parsley and young onions. She advises potatoes cut into rounds and fried in goose fat, cutting endive into slices and stewing it in veal gravy; she wants white turnips to be the size of marbles before frying them in butter, she stews red cabbage, in only the water still clinging to it after being washed, with cayenne and a glass of vinegar, and cooks sorrel with butter. In short her ideas and methods are sound, her cooking brief; everything in her fresh vegetables is designed to retain the maximum flavour.

She likes her fish to be 'ripened' for two days or more, for she considers fresh fish harsh, while ripened fish is more delicate and sapid. (This liking is hardly shared by us today.) The Scots had a predilection for slightly high fish: on the Island of Lewis they hung up skate unsalted for a few days to be eaten 'high'. Another method with skate was to earth-dry it: the skate were placed on damp grass and covered with sods (grass side down) for a day or two, because they were too tough if eaten fresh. On the Islands salmon was poached in sea water; for overripe salmon, as Dods puts it, horse-radish is added to the water.

Much of Meg Dods could still be used today and certainly her book is well worth reading. McNeill believes it is a work 'not unworthy to be placed alongside its French contemporary, Brillat Savarin's *Physiologie du Gout*'. How far, however, did the aspirations of these cookery books, both the good ones like Dods and the execrable like

Somerville, influence staple fare in middle-class homes? It is impossible to say, one suspects that the central basis of traditional Scottish food was retained, plain fare cooked simply, but using the very best of fresh ingredients, butter and cream, beef and mutton, potatoes, oats. In the hands of inspired cooks such ingredients were to become the best food imaginable. There is a description of a nineteenth-century larder at Conan House in Ross-shire that makes the mouth water: of jam pots by the hundred, shelves of preserved candied apricots and Magnum Bonum plums, smoked sheep and deer tongues, strings of threaded artichoke bottoms for adding to soups, gooseberry and currant wines, raspberry vinegar and ginger beer.[52]

McNeill's book is a collection of traditional Scottish recipes from many reliable sources; she correctly claims that you can only make nettle soup in the early spring because it must be made from the young shoots. (As does Mrs Somerville, a later Scottish writer, Elizabeth Craig, entirely omits this point, making one suspect she had never made this soup, for if you make it with anything else but the young shoots you'll end up with a fibrous skein which is entirely inedible. After all, old nettles are as good as flax for making cloth; better, some say, than any species of linen.) McNeill's collection also includes Scots Hare Soup (Bawd Bree), Mussel Brose which is made with oatmeal, milk and water, Cullen Skink, that great soup of smoked haddock and potatoes, and Partan Bree, a crab soup. Her traditional dishes continue through game, meat, fish, puddings, bannock, shortbreads and much else.

This is a cuisine that is a far cry from the English one. It has its own very distinctive tone and flavour, described as 'pastoral cooking, brightly influenced by old ties with France'. It is heard clearly today in the work of Scottish food writers.

Wales

A land that juts out into the Irish Sea, half of it mountainous where the Britons, once part of Rome, were beaten back by the Angles, Jutes and Saxons made invasion a slow process. Once the Roman Empire had retracted in the early fifth century, the invasions began in 476 and were not complete for another 200 years. In the uplands they grew oats which made a flat round bread baked on an iron, they hunted deer, boar and grouse, they kept cattle and sheep, milking both and making both butter and cheese.

British cheese making was no doubt stimulated by Roman methods and flavours. Palladius made his cheese in May, curdling fresh milk with rennet from a kid, lamb or calf, or with a teasel or sprig of fig. As elsewhere transhumance was practised, taking the livestock up from the valleys at sowing time into the hills as the pasture there began to come to life. It was at the *hafod*, or smaller hill farm, that the butter and cheese were made; the butter churns were the right size to take oatcakes made in the winter in the valley farms for summer eating. The curd was wrung, pressed, wrapped in salt, pressed again, laid on slats and finally stored in a dry place out of draughts. Welsh cheese was stored for some time in barrels of brine.

Early Riches

Material from the middens at Dinas Powys suggests that soldiers in the fifth-seventh centuries ate well on pork and beef, with poultry, shellfish, salmon or sea trout, bread and vegetables.[53] The soldiers also had a fondness for apples and for tending kitchen gardens. Apples would have grown well in the eastern part of the country, in what would become the counties of Breconshire, Radnorshire and Monmouthshire. The monastic diet for penitents is specified by Gildas which is bread and relish with butter on Sundays, as well as vegetables, eggs, cheese, milk and buttermilk – hardly penitential at all, since the only sacrifice is the beer and meat that are mentioned for others to eat. The stricter *Book of David* lists bread, salt and pease porridge, but later monastic diets at Llancarfan mention fish and milk. Cadog is reputed to have given a cask of beer and a fat sow as well as fifty wheaten loaves to the soldiers who came to demand food from him. There is further mention in the Colloquy[54] of breads, fats, milk of many kinds, chicken, cheese and broth for feasts, and ale, wine, cider and mead to drink.

Giraldus Cambrensis (1188) comments on the 'strange habit' of serving the main dish on bread rolled out large and thin and baked fresh each day. This sounds like Persian bread, rolled out as thin as a sheet, which is thrown against the hot walls of an oven, or like a large Indian Nan. Or could it be like the pikelet, which originally stems from Wales, for this is a thick batter mixture, the dough being thinned enough by the addition of milk to run across the stone. Whatever its nature it sounds good. The Welsh, like the Bretons, have always loved pancakes – *crempog*. Giraldus goes on to mention the plentiful supply of meat and poultry, evoking a varied and nourishing diet, perhaps only lacking in green vegetables, although the peasantry, as in Ireland, ate seaweeds, particularly rich in all the vitamins. They reared sheep, cattle, pigs and some goats. They also ate river and sea fish; there are mentions of monastic rights over rivers, lakes and estuaries which show us how concerned they were about fishing rights. Also, one gets the impression that cornfields were as common as pasture, that the arable land available was divided equally, that their food staples were bread and meat and there was plenty of dairy produce. This was a land of plenty, thinly populated and able to export some of its livestock and corn.

As in Ireland, there is in Wales a poem that turns everything into cheese. It has not as yet been translated, and the date is much later than *The Vision of MacConglinne*. It is by Deio ap Ieuan Ddu (fl.1460–80) a Cardigan man who sang eulogies. The story goes that someone told the poet that the abbot of Bardsey, Nadog ap Madog, was an extremely generous man, so the poet hired a boat and visited the island with a prepared eulogy for him. He discovered on his visit, however, that the abbot was an old skinflint, for he was only given bread, cheese and buttermilk, so instead of presenting him with the prepared ode, he went home and produced another: 'The Ode of the Cheese'.

Unlike *MacConglinne*, a work which the poet must have known (making this a case perhaps of early plagiarism or merely creating in a current mode), and in which everything is described in terms of fat, bacon, ham, cheese, buttermilk and cream, Deio ap Ieuan Ddu only uses cheese. Perhaps it was particularly bad, dry and sour cheese he had been given, for the term 'bitter cheese' is used. Thus, every corner of the abbot's dwelling is full of goat's milk and cheese; his cloak and alb like his milking pail are all cheese. Morning, midday and evening meals, his Christmas fare, are all cheese; his only occupation is cheese-making as he is too miserly to employ staff, whilst the only bards that sing to him are his cows, his goats and his chickens. When the poet talks of Christmas fare, we get a glimpse of the food the abbot would have eaten; he has no relish or sauce, no pie, roast or boiled food, no brawn, no poultry or spit to cook it on, there is no butler to serve him, no staff to cook for him and for New Year's Day – also celebrated with a feast – the poet wishes him eighteen kinds of cheese, with two large pails full of buttermilk and a profusion of curdled milk.[55]

It is impossible to say without reading the whole text whether like *MacConglinne* it is an attack upon the Church as a whole, or just the abbot personally; nevertheless what one does have is a vivid impression of the wealth of good food available. Certainly this picture does not conflict with the accounts that have come down to us[56] where up to the sixteenth century even the Welsh peasantry enjoyed a diet which was certainly more abundant than many peasants in England, and possibly Ireland. The peasantry of Scotland too in this period, certainly on the mainland, enjoyed an adequate diet. There was plenty of milk, cheese and eggs, barley bread and bacon broth in abundance, including meats of all kinds.

As in England the Welsh diet was based upon bread, but Welsh bread was made out of barley which had added beer barm to the dough, so that it fermented and made a lighter mixture. Thrust back into the uplands, they could only grow barley, rye and oats, so their pottage made with meat (being more fortunate than their English cousins) and wild greens was thickened with barley or oats. Rye bread was made but not liked; it was only eaten for medicinal reasons.[57] They also made porridge out of either oats or barley, mixed with water and boiled with added salt; it was eaten with buttermilk. *Llymru* was also made from oatmeal where it was steeped in water for a length of time, then strained and the water boiled until it became almost solid. As noted earlier, this dish travelled east to England where it was eaten with enthusiasm under the name of flummery. Gervase Markham praised the dish for its extreme goodness and explained that some ate it with honey, others with wine or strong beer. A coarser version of this dish called sucan was made from the soaked husks and leavings from the oats that had been ground; in north Pembrokeshire and south Cardiganshire it was called *uwd* or *uwd sucan*. For centures, it became the noonday meal for farmworkers, who had huge tin milk dishes carried to them filled with a quivering brown jelly. It was eaten with spoons with added beer or milk and stacks of bread spread with salted butter.

After Henry VIII's Act of Union with Wales in 1536 most of the arable land was enclosed, yet it was not necessarily cultivated. Even in Anglesey, a fertile area, only one-eleventh of the cultivated land was under cereals. Very little wheat was grown and only such oats and barley as were needed for home consumption. However, the open field with its multiple owners was still functioning in 1620. In the south-east and north-eastern parts below the 600 ft level where the Norman manorial system had made itself felt, a few open arable fields persisted for nearly 200 years longer and were not enclosed until the eighteenth century. In Wales there was no right to common pasturage on the autumn stubbles, for there was no need; there was enough common and waste land to graze the peasants' few livestock. When the great wave of enclosures occurred in the eighteenth century it was these lands that were taken, and their loss was deeply resented by the peasantry.

Wales was a difficult land to farm as so much is mountainous and farms straddle mountain and plain, upland and valley which gives great environmental diversity. Hence, it is impossible to generalise about the size and structure of the landed estates or of their constituent farms. However, the selective building up of large estates was already clear by 1640, and throughout the late seventeenth century caused the virtual extinction of the lesser gentry. Big properties at Crosswood and Gogerddan in Cardiganshire spread over a variety of farming environments. The 28,000 acres of Gogerddan extended from saltmarsh to the mountainous sheepwalks on Pumlumon.

Opportunities and means of marketing the produce were all-important, which is why the farms in easy reach of the port at Liverpool or Bristol were profitable. Inland the seasonal fairs, some held at market towns, others in wide-open spaces, did brisk business. To these went the droves of cattle on their long walk to distant buyers (see below).

By 1700 Wales had become a competitive supplier of agricultural produce, beyond its traditional strength in cattle and wool. John Aubrey thought that Pembrokeshire corn came in after the Civil War and cites evidence that the Monmouthshire dealers began to take corn to Bristol around 1660. The bakers found that Welsh wheat yielded more flour than English grain bought at Warminster and was no dearer, thanks to water transport. North Wales too was producing more. John Lloyd described the Vale of Endyrnion in the 1690s on the upper Dee, near Corwen: 'I am sure we live plentifully in it, God make us thankful,' and goes on to list the good husbandry that had been employed. Henry Rowlands speaks of the improvements in Anglesey of marl, lime and sand added to the soil.

From the seventeenth century onwards the Welsh peasantry were not freeholders but tenants. In Wales the system of land-holding was influenced by the proximity to England and by intermarriage of Welsh and English families: the landlords tended to be remote estate owners operating through agents or poverty-stricken squires interested only in their rents and exercise of their sporting rights. It was not until the end of the eighteenth century that landlords started to invest in buildings and other improvements, though always with interest charges added to the rents. So there was always great estrangement between the people and the landlords, leading to an increasingly wide economic and cultural barrier, a legacy that was to foster the spread of rebellious Nonconformity.

Snowdonia in the 1690s was bleak and taxing. A visitor to Llanberis found, 'the best bread being black, tough and thick oat-bread, they have neither miller, fuller, and any other tradesman but one taylor; there's not a cock, hen or goose, nay ne're an oven in ye parish.' Cattle had to be stall-fed through the winter, and sheep still grazed on grass, where brutally cold winters could decimate the flocks. Wild animals, such as polecat, pine marten and wild cat were numerous in the terrain, finding good cover in the woodlands. On level tracts of tillage field crops grew: wheat, barley, oats, rye, peas, vetches and even clover.

Market business was affected by adverse weather; cold spells were acute in the Welsh uplands, where the growing season was short at the best of times. There was a disastrous winter in 1739-40; the diarist Owen Thomas noted 'the great frost' as beginning on 23 December 1739 and lasting until 10 February 1740; it was still freezing at night throughout April and there was snow on the mountains into May. The peasants now suffered, their diet reduced to oat bread, wild foods and if they were near the coast, the gathering of seaweeds, especially laver. This was boiled until it was a purée, then mixed with oats and fried. Of course, the landed gentry lived as well as they did across the border, aping fashionable manners in eating.

The typical cottages of Wales and the north of England were of mud-and-stud or wattle-and-daub construction, though here and there more substantial ones of brick and stone were built, especially where industrial development and labour shortages encouraged such building.

Migration from the rural areas of England and Wales to the towns and overseas has shown that there was a considerable increase in the numbers moving in the 1850s, followed by a check in the 1860s, and then an even higher outflow in the 1870s and 1880s. Between 1851 and 1871 the number of agricultural workers fell by twenty-two per cent. The Welsh migration came to a head in the 1880s. The worker might be paid in sacks of corn and potatoes at rates above the market price, in cider unfit for sale, in carcasses of stock that had died of disease, and his cottage would be wretchedly small, of mud walls and a thatched roof consisting of one room with a floor of clay or broken stone. In an exceptionally bad village there would be either no allotments or gardens, or the rents charged for them would be exorbitant. (By 1866 there were as many as 646,000 allotments and gardens of an eighth of an acre or more, 93,000 potato patches and over 9,000 cow gates or rights to graze a cow on lane verges and spare ground.)

The Gentry

Elizabeth Morgan paid 2s 0d for 800 oysters, and a lobster cost 3d. There were plenty of oysters at Penmon and the poor of Anglesey found employment in dredging and then pickled them in barrels for export. In 1739 Sir William Bulkeley sent thirteen live lobsters and a bag of samphire to his daughter in Liverpool by sea, giving the mate 1s 0d to take care of them. This was rock samphire, which grew in the rocks and on Anglesey's cliffs, which was pickled; it has fleshy aromatic leaves and should not be confused with marsh samphire. Much salmon was caught and what was not eaten fresh was potted under a thick layer of clarified butter. On Anglesey, surrounded on three sides by the Irish Sea, where these reports come from, much sea fish was eaten: flatfish, coalfish (coley), prawns, crabs, cockles and mussels.[58]

A church ceremony at the beach on Holyhead began the herring season in September. The Reverend Thomas Ellis wrote: 'They are preparing for the herring harvest and so I must very soon again kneel on the sea shore.' Fish, especially shellfish, was thought to be very good for complaints of the chest. 'Conway herring good against cough, raw oysters with much liquor in them are excellent, mussels and cockles in their own liquor boiled are excellent, in short all sea fish which have plenty of sea in them.'[59] William Bulkeley noted that in 1735 herring were being sold for seven or eight for a penny. When a season brought in a great catch it was noted that it contributed to the support of the poor inhabitants being then their principal food.

Chicken and ducks were 3d each; guinea fowl was also eaten, but the main staples were meat, beef, mutton and pork. Pork was surprisingly cheap; a roasting pig cost 1s 0d in 1738, but it must have been a suckling pig, for William Bulkeley bought a side of pork weighing 46 lb at 1³/₄d per pound and a little later complained of rising inflation: 'paid 16s 6d for a Small Pig which might have been bought ten years ago for 9 shilling.' Venison was cheaper: a haunch cost 5s, bought from the gamekeeper of one of the deer parks, while a side of young venison was bought from Llabfechell market for 1s 3d. At Christmas they ate beef and mutton and on Christmas Eve William Bulkeley killed a sheep 'for my own use and to distribute to the poor'. He writes a description of a turtle found which had been driven on shore by a great storm.

> . . . none ever seen upon the Coasts of England before, as I could learn, but they are very common in the West Indies . . . I had the guts taken out which were near as large as those of a Cow – had a prodigious quantity of blood and when washed clean I had a great quantity of the flesh cut out of it and dressed like Beef Steaks and some of it I had stewed and it eat very like Beef, it had a Bladder as large as a sheep's, what flesh remained within the Shell I had it salted and hung in the air and sun to dry . . . . We dined today upon the Turtle, part of it was broiled at the fire and part was stewed. All of it eat well enough not much unlike the beef steaks, but I think the broiled pieces were best.

In 1753 they were unable to feed their livestock throughout the winter, at a time when in England livestock were being fed with turnips, swedes and rape cake, and so the livestock was slaughtered, butchered and salted. Lady Bridget bought 1,200 lb salt which cost her £3 8s. The hunting was good, however, and Sir William shot pheasant, partridges, teal, widgeons, plovers, woodcock, snipe and wild ducks. Then there were the puffins on Priestholm Island and South Stack, the headland beyond Holyhead: 'Puffins resort thither in great abundance leaving it sometime in August or at furthest the beginning of September, great many barrels of which are yearly sent up to London where they are sold at no small price.' Parties of gentry with their servants would sail to Priestholm in the summer to see the menfolk have sport, for as well as puffins there were also rabbits and other sea fowls. The puffins were pickled in vinegar and spices, which must have cut through the oiliness of the flesh. Five dozen pickled puffins cost 4s 0d and the gentry kept a couple of barrels as part of their kitchen stores. They must have been much favoured for Elizabeth Morgan had a recipe on how to make pickled pigeon look like puffin; on their estates they all had large stone dovecotes and ate pigeon regularly throughout the winter.

One of the Morris brothers, William, described a typical dinner enjoyed at his home, helpfully listing where all the ingredients had come from: 'April codlings, lobsters and crabs from the ocean, radishes from my garden, pepper from India, ketchup from Llechychled, wine from Portugal and France, small beer from Holyhead and Liverpool beer, cheese from Chester and butter from Llanfigel, French cress and radish from Paradwys.' What an excellent dinner this sounds. William was fond of gardening; he grew both carrots and potatoes and had soft fruit in a walled garden.

Icehouses were built upon the island; in fact for the elite they had become part of the necessary architecture, for one was built in 1755 at Plas Gwyn at the same time as the house was built. Another essential building was the brewhouse so that home-brewed ale, drunk by everyone, could be made. William Morris, however, thought that toddy was the drink of the island, which was made from brandy, hot water and sugar. Coffee, tea and chocolate were to oust ale within this century. As early as 1711, Lady Bridget was the first to introduce Anglesey to the new beverages; she bought 6 lb 'chocolat' for 13s 6d, 1 lb coffee for 6s 6d and 1/4 lb tea, by far the most expensive, for 9s 6d. Within twenty years tea had become essential to the upper classes; in 1736 Elizabeth Morgan bought twelve cups and saucers of porcelain, two 'slope' bowls, a china milkpot and seven teapots. Tea drinking seems to have been resented by the men as a women's activity; Lewis Morris was glad that the Customs men had seized 'a bag of pernicious tea without which women's prattling tongues are as dry as chips'. His brother William wrote sadly when William Bulkeley died in 1760: 'Farewell now to the harp, there will only be there now a gang of women drinking tea.'

They were aware, for how could they not be, that the poor suffered and ate coarse food: Lewis Morris talked of the gruel which the poor ate and that barley bread was the common household bread of the island, while his brother William boasted of how he and other parishioners in Holyhead had enjoyed the best wheaten loaf from Dublin. The poor ate *potes blawd*, a flour and water broth with salt boiled to the consistency of porridge.

Cattle Droves

As we have seen, a large proportion of the cattle eaten in England was brought in for fattening from Wales, Scotland, and later Ireland. The great trade in Welsh cattle goes back to the Middle Ages. Anglesey cattle, which were the hardy black longhorns found down the length of coastal Wales, swam the Menai Strait as their start to the long journey to Barnet Fair. The scene was described by an eighteenth-century writer:

> They are urged in a body by loud shoutings and blows into the water and as they swim well and fast, usually make their way to the opposite shore. The whole herd proceeds pretty regularly until it arrives within about 150 yards of the landing place, when, meeting with a very rapid current formed by the tide eddying and rushing with great violence between the rocks that encroach far into the Channel, the herd is thrown in the utmost confusion. Some of the boldest and strongest push directly across and presently reach the land; the more timorous immediately turn around and endeavour to reach the place from which they set off; but the

greatest part, borne down by the force of the stream, are carried towards Beaumaris Bay and frequently float to a great distance before they are able to reach the Caernarvonshire shore.[60]

Other cattle went by boat; from Pembrokeshire, Carmarthen and Brecknock, across the Severn or from Tenby they sailed to the Somerset ports. The chief route from south and central Wales was by land through Herefordshire, Ross, Ledbury and Tewkesbury where they pastured on the South Midland fields, or went on to Essex and Kent then to the London butchers. By the eighteenth century the black cattle included dun-coloured and parti-coloured beasts, useful both for beef and milk. Farmers in the Welsh hills kept sheep and reared young stock also destined for the fattening farms of the Midlands and the south-east of England; while they reared these animals they also had the benefit of their wool, milk, butter and cheese which they sold in the local Welsh markets.

In Scotland the cattle were driven from the Hebrides and swam Kyle Rhea, the narrowest channel between Skye and the mainland, which was notorious for its strong currents and inshore eddies. But few beasts were ever lost, for the drovers had a method that they swore saved their cattle: they placed a rope around the lower jaws to keep the mouth open to keep the tongues free.

> The reason given for leaving the tongue loose is that the animal may be able to keep the salt water from going down its throat in such a quantity as to fill all the cavities in the body which would prevent the action of the lungs; for every beast is found dead and said to be drowned at the landing place to which this mark of attention has not been paid. Whenever the noose is put under the jaw all the beasts destined to be ferried together are led by the ferryman into the water until they are afloat, which puts an end to their resistance. Then every cow is tied to the tail of the cow before until 6 or 8 be joined. A man in the stern of the boat holds the rope of the foremost cow. The rowers then ply the oars immediately.[61]

In the long journey southwards sometimes the cattle were bled to make the drovers' black puddings which with oatmeal and a ram's horn of whisky provided their staple fare.

Both the Welsh and the Scottish drovers had their own particular routes, but both attempted to keep to the higher ground and the moorlands, so as to avoid the hard roads which injured the cattle's feet and the lanes that traversed the enclosed land and which were too narrow.

Welsh Food

In Wales there is also a legend, as in Ireland, that the potato arrived on its shores with a shipwreck of a barque from Ireland. It had certainly arrived early in the seventeenth century; two writers in 1664 speak of the growing popularity of the potato in Wales, how they prosper and increase exceedingly, and there is another reference in 1667: 'Potatoes with white and ash coloured flowers are planted in many fields in Wales.' In 1688 potatoes were seen growing in fields adjoining the highways.[62]

Recipes that are inherently Welsh tend to be breads, which include the famous speckled fruit bread *bara brith* made with buttermilk. Other recipes are enriched with the butter and dairy products which were plentiful from the earliest days. One of the most basic of all north European dishes, the meat and vegetable stew cooked in a cauldron or now in a large saucepan is called *cawl*. This seems to be especially loved, perhaps because of the mixture of bacon joint and beef with leeks which forms the essence of the dish; it is mentioned by writers like Richard Llewellyn and recalled by the old with great nostalgia. The meal was a movable feast; any vegetable could be included and it was eaten over a series of days, some swore that the older it got the better it tasted. Some versions had parsley sauce added, made from the floury potato water; others had cabbage and root vegetables such as parsnips. On some days only the vegetables were eaten, while at other times just the meat, which was a way of making the dish last. A nineteenth-century recipe cooks the meat first, which is taken from the cauldron, then vegetables, herbs and oatmeal are added to the stock and that is stewed for half an hour. This was dinner on the first day and became breakfast for the next three days. There were *cawls* made with broad beans; others made with wood pigeons.

Potatoes were mashed and eaten with added buttermilk stirred in, or roasted beneath the meat or cooked with the bacon. Another distinctive dish was onion cake (*teisen nionod*), made from layers of onions, then potatoes dotted with butter, and moistened with beef stock. There are, oddly enough, not so many recipes for leeks, which grow well in Wales and hence became the national emblem, mainly because they tended simply to take the place of onions in recipes of onions; there are, however: *pastai cennin*, a pasty of chopped leeks and bacon enfolded in a short pastry crust; cooked leeks mixed with mashed potato, rather like a leek colcannon, to form a nest around hard-boiled eggs covered in cheese sauce; and there is a famous leek soup, *cawl cennin*, in which leeks and potatoes are cooked with stock, butter and milk; this is, of course, the same as vichyssoise which stemmed from the French country soup potage *à la bonne femme*. It was inevitably the French version that became known in England (chilled it was an easy and economical banquet dish), though the recipe could just as well have been borrowed from the Welsh, except they never served it chilled.

Salmon was poached in milk with a bay leaf, then served with parsley sauce using the milk in which the fish was cooked. Herrings were salted, potted and soused; oysters were made into a soup, plunged into batter and fried, or, in an early eighteenth-century recipe for oyster loaves, poached in wine with sweetbreads and herbs and stuffed into loaves which are warmed in the oven. (This, of course, is much the same as the Anglo-Saxon recipe and Lady Craven's, see pages 31 and 231). From the same book come oyster sausages, for which oysters are parboiled, then chopped with sage, herbs, anchovies mixed with egg yolks, breadcrumbs, suet, pepper and nutmeg; spoonfuls of the mixture are then fried.[63] A shoulder of mutton could be stuffed with oysters, capers and samphire, while oysters with anchovies, butter and lemon make a pie. There are several recipes for cockles to be made into a pie, as well as their being mixed with eggs and bacon fat, as were limpets and winkles.

Welsh mutton and lamb are still famous and there were many eighteenth-century recipes given for roasting, boiling and stuffing both, even for making hams out of mutton; curing mutton legs by rubbing them with black treacle started the process off. Mutton pies were a traditional dish at Gower wedding feasts. The meat was eaten with rowan jelly, red currant jelly and mint sauce, though mutton with laver sauce was popular near the coast. Laver, when it is cooked for hours and turned into a purée, becomes laverbread and is particularly delicious.

Historians have varying explanations as to how Welsh Rabbit got its name or whether it came from Wales at all. Hannah Glasse gives a recipe of plain toasted cheese under its name, but then gives a recipe for Scotch Rabbit which has no mustard, but further complicates matters by adding a third recipe called English Rabbit where the bread is soaked in red wine. By 1885 it was referred to as Welsh Rarebit and amazingly luxurious versions were given by chefs like Brillat-Savarin. Ale was always drunk with the dish and by the end of the nineteenth century it began to be made with ale, with the cheese melted into it.

The Twentieth Century

What is clear is that the cooking of Ireland, Scotland and Wales is based on oats, barley and dairy products and it emphasises these in the many breads, both sweet and savoury, which all these countries excel in. As in rural England, their cuisines by the middle of the nineteenth century were altered by the advent of technology, commercial instant foods and the corner shop. This process accelerated in the twentieth century, as the corner shop itself became more and more generalised, stocking everything that their customers had need of. At the beginning of the nineteenth century a chandler's, for example, might stock knitted stockings, wines and spirits, by the middle of the century they would have added tea and sugar and by the end of the century half the shop would have tins and dried packets of food. The advent of blended tea (Horniman and Cassell had been making up small packets of tea in foil-lined paper since the 1850s) allowed shopkeepers to store one or two types of brands of tea without having to be a specialist in tea-blending, as the old-type grocers were. The multiple grocers concentrated on low-priced, readily available, well-displayed general groceries and provisions of an even quality. Apart from tea and sugar, salt and pepper they stocked pickles and relishes, flour, rice and some dried fruits; and dairy products, which included the cheaper, imported Cheddar cheeses from Canada and Dutch Edam.

As towns grew and urbanisation spread a greater variety of grocer's shops opened servicing their locality and competing with each other. The traditional high class grocer continued to flourish, carrying a very wide range of commodities, many of them imported, which was aimed at the richer customer. These luxury foods and delicacies enabled them to continue to combine the specialist trades of both the grocer and the provision dealer. Fixed purpose-built shops, as opposed to market stalls, dominated the trading centre of the growing towns, augmented by the weekly market and by the dispersed shops in the spreading outlying districts.

Each region reacted differently to these new influences, as regional surveys in the 1950s show. The Scots, Welsh and Irish all have a tradition of not eating a wide range of vegetables, and of only growing one or two. A history of self-sufficiency in farming must presumably explain their high consumption of eggs, but what explains the high consumption of salt in the Highlands and Wales but not in Ireland? Is it that for centuries the Highlands and the Welsh lived off salted mutton throughout the winter? (Highland butter is traditionally much saltier than Lowland.) The Welsh relied for centuries on their own supplies of meat and distrusted butcher's meat; in fact, they used the term as abuse. They took to canning and freezing, as being reliable methods of preservation, while the Scots did not, being exceptionally resistant to the sale of chilled and frozen meat in the inter-war period. Yet the Scots consume a large amount of processed meat pies, cakes and ice cream. They are also unaccountably choosy when it comes to buying tins, liking tinned soups, baked beans, spaghetti, sweet puddings, fruit juices while only buying in small amounts tinned fish, peas, fruit, milk and cream.

By the middle of the nineteenth century in England an urban diet had evolved which was dependent upon the new commercial foods; in Ireland, Wales and Scotland the diet took longer to spread and, in some distant rural areas, dependent on one small shop, the urban diet possibly did not reach it until the 1930s or 1950s. However, it was inevitable that this diet now reflected what was eaten in the whole of the British Isles, and that regional differences, discussed in this chapter, had now had commercialisation superimposed upon them. What is exciting is that by the end of the century these differences were being rediscovered and regional foods were being revalued. They were seen as rich testaments to living communities; a struggle began to unearth more from archive material and people's memories of their childhood and to save these dishes for new generations.

CHAPTER 8

Glories of the Country Estate

The eighteenth century saw the continuation of land enclosures; the process of agricultural improvement demanded it. Between two and three million acres of open fields, commons and wastelands were enclosed in the last half of the century. So huge and radical were these that, coupled with fast industrial growth in the new Midland towns, they were to change rural populations forever. Severe rural poverty and deprivation were caused, as we shall see, but these massive enclosures in themselves truncated the heritage of rural cooking, a loss that at the time no one noticed or thought worth commenting on.

Many observers then and later discussed the merits and disadvantages of the agricultural revolution, but none pointed out what it meant to the culture of English cooking. Every cuisine has its roots within the peasant traditions, which are constantly being replenished by ideas and practices that are forced to be creative within economic limitations. In such cooking there is a reliance on cereals, wild plants and game; many of these ideas are then filched by more affluent parts of society (see Beistyn, page 82) and this flow constantly replenishes a national cuisine. It is this profound enrichment from below that our national cuisine was now to lose.

It had already lost its head, both figuratively and literally: the court style and conspicuous consumption of France which it fleetingly looked as if we might possess under the early Stuarts, was lost when we executed a king. The Hanoverians, who were pawns in a Whig aristocracy, were unable to lead a developing cuisine, as they were simple honest trenchermen, eating like a country squire. However, the glories of the country estate were then worth hymning.

Enclosures

Land values almost doubled between 1700 and 1790 as vast expanses were brought under cultivation; the merits of the new, improved farming, using new technology like Jethro Tull's famous seed drill had increased yield by almost half. Arthur Young spoke for many when he said that, 'No small farm could effect such great things as have been done in Norfolk. Great farms are the soul of Norfolk culture; split them into tenures of a hundred pounds a year and you will find nothing but beggars and weeds in the whole country.'[1] There were over 4,000 Acts of Enclosure in Britain between 1750 and 1850. As the fields were enclosed, woodlands and wastes disappeared and a new pattern of hedges, walls, fences and roads took shape. In the 1760s Smollett described it as 'smiling with cultivation . . . parcelled out into beautiful enclosures'. Many a fortune was made out of the process: rent rolls rose and farm profits were boosted. Attacks were made upon the new farmers as 'oppressors of the indignant many' and Young himself came to feel that it led to human suffering; there is no doubt he thought that the poor were injured 'and in some cases grossly injured'. Nevertheless he felt it was inevitable; the economy was expanding, the population rising, but, 'In a great Kingdom there must always be hands that are idle, backward in the age of work, unmarried for fear of having families, or industrious only to a certain degree.'

At the end of the seventeenth century, Gregory King, author of *National and Political Observations and Conclussions upon the State and Condition of England in 1696*, had estimated that there were around 330,000 farmers. About half of them were tenants who farmed the land belonging to the great landlords and gentry. The rest were owner-occupiers, farming their own land and sometimes renting additional land from a landlord; these farmers probably had no more than twenty acres. Below these small owners were the cottagers and labourers. Because most farms were small they could be worked with the help of the farmer's family and one extra labourer. The cottagers had the right to use the common for grazing a few beasts and for getting fuel; they also had a small plot of land where they grew vegetables and corn for making their own flour and bread. Once the common land and his own plots were enclosed and belonged to the local landlord the cottager had no fuel to light a fire; nor did he have land to grow vegetables and herbs or on which to graze his few animals. Many cottagers and farm labourers sold what they had and emigrated to America, others attempted to find work in the growing towns and cities in the new factories being built. There, under the slavery of long hours and pittance wages, their diet declined to bread, jam, tea and sugar.

The ruling classes, the nobility and the new rich had now absorbed most of the fertile land of England; the bulk of these large farms were still run by tenants and by the end of the century these constituted three-quarters of all farms in England. Arthur Young is vicious in his criticisms of these tenant farmers who make themselves ridiculous by aping the style of their landlords, buying pianofortes for their parlours and post-chaises for driving their wives to assembly rooms, placing their servants in livery, sending their daughters to boarding schools and their sons to university to be made parsons. By 1790 the landowners themselves had incomes of £10,000 a year (possibly £1,000,000 in today's money), some a great deal more. As early as 1715 the Duke of Newcastle's estates were bringing in £32,000, and by 1800 almost a quarter of England's landed wealth was owned by peers of the realm. By the end of the century England's population had risen to nine million, eighty per cent of whom still lived in the country. An anonymous rhyme summed up the horror of the enclosures for the rural labourer:

> They hang the man and flog the woman
> That steals a goose from off the common

But leave the greater criminal loose
That steals the common from the goose.

Enclosure turned land into absolute private property and quickened suspicion of both
the law that enshrined that process and the justices of the peace who administered it;
it was one more demonstration of Oliver Goldsmith's dictim that 'Laws grind the
poor and rich men grind the law.'[2]

What happened to our heritage of rural cooking? The cottagers and farm labourers
who moved to the industrial towns had no means to buy food or even cook it, so those
habitual daily recipes which had been a central part of their life must have been lost
within a few years. These people for the most part were illiterate, so the recipes that
had once been passed on from generation to generation now vanished. No other
European country suffered this experience, for the industrial revolution occurred
later and in countries where the land mass was great, as in France, the rural traditions
continued undisturbed. The dispossessed farmworkers who emigrated to the
American colonies took their recipes with them; once there they must have used
familiar techniques and skills on new and unfamiliar ingredients, creating new
dishes.[3] We can see in *A Booke of Cookery* and *A Booke of Sweetmeats*, which once
belonged to Martha Washington, recipes that are wholly English and representative of
the sixteenth century. Unfortunately these recipes are more characteristic of the
landed gentry than they are of a labouring class.[4] Some recipes in regions of Britain
survived because they were from distant rural parts untouched by change and these
recipes are discussed later. (See page 352 – Appendix II.)

Change and Display

English society was hierarchical and highly status conscious, but the status was not
necessarily determined by birth; it was a society based upon achievement when
status, honours, money and titles followed. It was charged throughout by the spirit
of emulation, as are all successsful consuming societies. Not only did vast numbers
of people achieve a station in life that was superior to that in which they were born,
but also those people that stayed within the same stratum nevertheless emulated the
life-style immediately above them. So in England the fashions of the aristocracy and
gentry were copied by merchants, farmers and their families, even by their servants
and labourers. The moralists were shocked that shopkeepers carried swords, servants
wore velvet and a mere maid would powder her hair, while the labouring classes now
insisted on eating wheaten bread. There was a flood of religious tracts complaining
of the spread of luxury, indulgence and Godless existence where life and soul
depended on what colour ribbon you wore and how many dishes at dinner you
served. Nor did such tracts care for the new pursuit, the reading of novels, for their
plots tended to revolve also on the spur of social emulation, so that after many
vicissitudes the heroine must end happily married to a country gentleman, lord of
many acres. Newspapers also fostered such ambitions: the first daily started
publication in 1702 and by 1760 there were four daily London papers and six which

appeared thrice weekly, as well as thirty-five provincial papers.

With so much money flowing in, the nobility spent lavishly on improving great estates, building palatial houses, landscaping parks, moving villages, buying elegant furniture, pictures and silver and buying wine for its cellars. Food was, of course, central to its wealth and enjoyment; meals occupied a good part of the day and night and the dining room became a significant room in the house with its own especially designed furniture. Before, tables and chairs had tended not to be permanent fixtures, but were set up or carried in from other rooms. Such an arrangement was no doubt left over from the days when medieval monarchs were always on the move and dined from trestle tables and benches covered in tapestries and cushions which could all be dismantled.

The food was now brought to the table by servants course by course, and the wine glasses were refilled by the butler at the sideboard. There were still two courses, while dessert was considered separate from the dinner proper as was the banqueting course of the previous century; the sweetmeats were now called confectionery. A soup tureen was laid at one end of the table as part of the first course for those people who liked to begin the meal with a bowl of soup. On the table would be a set of silver casters for sugar, pepper and mustard; later in the century cruet sets grouped together in a holder were made in silver, pewter and china. An epergne, which was an intricate piece of pottery with branches for dishes or candles and places for cut flowers, stood at the centre of the table; these were developed during the 1720s and they often held casters and cruets, sauceboats and spice boxes. This florid but often highly impressive centrepiece with its glass dishes could be changed throughout the meal.

An etiquette book of 1730 stated: 'Coughing, yawning or sneezing over the Dishes should be carefully avoided; I have been oftentimes in pain to see People, not altogether unaquainted with the Rules of Good Manners, guilty of this Indecorum.'[5] Forks had only two tines widely spaced; it is a sign of the growing refinement in food and table manners that as the cooked dishes contained smaller morsels covered in a sauce, a two-tined fork could not cope in spearing them. The knife, having a rounded end, served as a shovel, especially in the difficult art of eating peas, and such an act was then thought to be the height of good manners.

If we wish to see how the gentry aspired to eat, we can turn to *The Complete Practical Cook* (1730), in which Charles Carter, former cook to the Duke of Argyll, gives sample menus for dinners throughout the year, so that a nobleman might choose what he thinks fit. There are dinners for visiting royalty and even a banquet for a coronation. Obviously Mr Carter was ambitious, for though he had worked with English ambassadors abroad and the Duke of Argyll, he had not been cook to a king. His dinner for March has two courses and begins with a choice of crayfish soup with carp dumplings or a chicken soup; once these have been taken, the two dishes put in their place are a platter of stuffed pike, flounders and eels and a leg of mutton. On the sideboard there are a baron of beef and a venison pasty. Upon the table there are lobster patties, a fricassée of lamb, a roast turkey, a calf's foot pudding and a Westphalia ham pie (we must not forget that the Hanoverian dynasty was reigning and a taste for German foods was fashionable), as well as assorted spring salads. This is but the first course and when these have been tasted, they are taken away and a second course appears. We have green (young) geese and ducklings, asparagus, chicken peepers and squabs, buttered crabs and shrimps in their shell, a chine of salmon and smelts, gollard eels and a ragout of sweetbreads.

There is no dessert course given, but one menu later in the year suggests a centrepiece of a grand pyramid of sweetmeats and fruit, surrounded by pistachio cream, raspberry cream, iced chocolate cream, iced lemon cream, syllabubs coloured and syllabubs plain. Porcelain figures adorned the dessert course, half naked musicians plucking at their lutes, shepherdesses and lovelorn shepherds, cupids in fancy dress and strutting birds, all added to a remarkable display where how the food looked took priority over how it tasted. 'How ravishing those eighteenth-century tables must have looked when the crystallised fruit, the oranges and raisins, the spun sugar confections, the trays of syllabubs, the pyramids of jellies, the dishes of little almond cakes shaped into knots and rings and bows, the marchpanes spiked with candied fruit, the curd tarts and all the sweetbreads were spread.'[6]

Breakfast was served at half past nine or ten with tea or chocolate and hot buttered bread, perhaps with cheese or toast. Toast was an English invention said to be necessary because the houses were so cold and the butter so hard that it was only on toast that it was spreadable. Carl Philip Moritz, a German pastor, was highly pleased at the invention; he wrote: 'One slice after another is taken and held to the fire with a fork till the butter soaks through the whole pile of slices.'[7] Dinner was served at about four or five and supper at ten; after the dessert had been served at dinner, the ladies retired to the drawing-room for tea or coffee, while the men remained to smoke and drink port, while also passing around the chamber pot which, when not in use, was housed in specially made cupboards.

Tables were spread with white damask or plain linen cloth and set with pieces of silver, or fine pewter in the more modest homes. Pewter was fairly cheap and once polished emulated silver in a satisfactory manner. The poor used wooden platters. The dinner tables of the aristocracy laid out with many silver dishes was a sight aimed to impress the diner and fill him and her with awe and respect for the magnificence of their hosts. 'Often the table had a theme of gardens and landscapes; cottages thatched with vermicelli stood beside islands fashioned from meringues, sugar constructions of the Temple of Solomon overlooked ponds that reflected the moon and stars. These displays were either specially made or else hired for the evening'; later Wedgwood made many of the sugar paste figures into porcelain.[8]

The Technology of Cooking

One of the results of the industrial revolution, of iron smelting and the use of coal, was the emergence of technological innovations in the kitchen but they were slow to happen. It took time for anyone to consider whether the difficulties of cooking in front of an open fire could be modified.

The age-old method of suspending a cooking pot over a fire limited the meal to that one pot, though experience taught ingenuity. This recollection is from an

Oxfordshire farm as late as the 1920s:

> Somehow on a great black grate our mother concocted wonderful meals
> – tasty and filling. In a great oval pot that was suspended over a good fire
> she cooked hunks of fat bacon along with potatoes and cabbage. The
> vegetables were put in string nets to keep them separate. When they were
> cooked she would fish them out with the aid of a fork. Then into the same
> water and along with the bacon she would drop a suet pudding, perhaps
> a roly-poly or a currant 'spotted dick', and sometimes just a plain suet to
> be eaten with golden syrup on it as a special treat.[9]

The Ladies' Dictionary of 1694 warned the gentry against entering the kitchen because
the heat of the fire made servants hot and fretful. The open fire allowed boiling and
roasting, but bread and pastries had to be baked. The beehive-shaped stone or brick
oven built into the wall had been the answer for hundreds of years. (See below.) In the
north of England, however, baking stones were used in the embers of a fire where a
flat dough was cooked; these were generally unleavened coarse breads made from
barley and rye; another method for making bread, which was thousands of years old
and only disappeared in the nineteenth century, was to use baking pots – the iron pot
was turned upside down over a heated stone placed in the embers of a fire. This was
a particularly Celtic method, used in Wales, Ireland, Devon and Cornwall.

Ovens were of masonry, built into the wall in the shape of a beehive (most of the
surviving ones in houses and cottages are now made into deep cupboards). Early in the
morning on baking day a large fire was lit inside the oven (using whatever cheap
material there was, gorse or broom bushes, dried turf) and allowed to rage away; then
the ashes were swept away and the raised dough pushed inside. It was important for
the oven to be completely sealed and the oven door had to fit exactly, and the difficulty
was how to tell that the oven was hot enough. One method was to observe the colour
of the bricks and how they changed; some threw a handful of flour against the side of
the oven and if it burned in sparks the oven was hot enough. When built efficiently
these ovens retained heat for twenty-four hours. The bread was baked first, when the
oven was hottest, then the large meat pies and fruit flans, then the rolls, buns, cakes
and biscuits; then when all the baking was done, pillows were dried and fluffed, and
rose leaves and herbs dried for pot-pourri. Without thermometers cooks had to rely
on habit and instinct (we have seen how Mrs Pepys with her new oven burnt the pies)
and old recipes sometimes give rough guides, as in 'not so hot as for manchetts'.[10]

Early in the century the iron-smelting industry had begun seriously in Wales; in
1720 John Hanbury was making tinplate at Pontypool. Tinplate rolling machines
replaced the previous method of beating tin sheets with hammers, and methods of
tinned iron improved. So did all the articles needed for pies, tarts and flans; there
were nests of baking hoops, patty pans and paste cutters, rowel wheeled pastry jiggers,
pastry moulds stamped with a design and tin baking sheets to place them all on.
Biscots, biscakes, puffs, macrooms, whiggs, plumb cakes, seed cakes, queen's cakes and

all manner of meat, chicken, game and fruit pies, as well as a variety of breads were baked in the brick built ovens on baking day.

By the eighteenth century all the boiling and roasting was still done over an open fire. It must have been obvious to anyone walking through the kitchens that most of the heat from the fire was dispersed into the kitchen, or went up into the chimney and almost by-passed the piece of meat hanging there. Yet for over 150 years no one considered it. This was because women servants were in charge of the cooking and no gentlemen troubled to consider the issues within their working lives.

Spits in front of the fire held the roasting meats, but these had to be turned, either by a turnspit, a small boy who made sure the meat 'was done to a turn', or by dogs encased in a wheel who ran on the spot. This was not efficient either, because the dogs would hide or run away at any indication that roasting meat was on the menu. In large country houses there were a few experiments in turning the spit by a water mill method, but this could only be done if the kitchen was near or above a stream. Later in the century turning was done by a smoke jack which made the hot air from the fire do the work, or a wind-up jack which was operated by winding up a weight. The smoke jack needed a steady supply of ascending smoke to rotate a fan which caused the spit to turn. These could not have worked well because they were rare. John Evelyn came across one and wrote: 'It makes very little noise, needs no winding up, and, for that, preferable to the more noisy inventions.' The roasting time needed for the meat could be speeded up by a wooden screen lined with shiny tin in front of the spit to reflect the heat back to the meat. A roaster, a small tin machine that just fitted over the bars of the grate, was described as 'convenient and effectual . . . has within itself a dripping pan . . . also a door at the back to open for basting and salting the meat.'[11]

The fat from the meat dripped down into a long, narrow, iron trough, and was called 'dripping'; it was collected and stored in a greasepan and later used for making rushlights and candles. When coal began to supersede wood as fuel, a fire basket had to hold the coals. These were handy to perch trivets on for holding kettles and saucepans, which warmed on one side but not on the other, so had to be continually turned. Later in the century the various types of spit were superseded by a clockwork mechanism wound up by a key. With iron foundries eager to sell to the new rich, all sorts of appliances were invented, likely to appeal to the mistress who had rarely cooked in her life, but who would think it 'just the thing for young Mary': there was a hanging griller looking rather like a paper rack; a down hearth toaster for slices of meat or bread on a long handle which could be turned once one side was done; a griller with an adaptable support for a basin or plate; as well as pieces like salamanders which had been part of a kitchen since medieval times. An inventory of a farmer's kitchen gives a surprising amount of cooking equipment considering his status: it included three different spits and two dripping pans, nine dishes of pewter, a large iron skillet and a smaller iron skillet, an old iron kettle and three iron porridge pots, as well as much else.

In the middle of the century an iron oven with a grate underneath called a perpetual oven was made. (One was installed in Shipton Hall, Halifax, in 1750 for the

Reverend John Lister, which cost him 4 guineas.) It nearly always had to be placed near the main fire as it shared the flue and chimney, so it appeared to be combined; hence the kitchen range was born. Soon after the kitchen range began to acquire side boilers for heating water and ovens for baking; these innovations came from the north of England, the centre of the iron industry. By then new smelting techniques made it possible to make iron thinner which gave lighter hollow ware, tinned on the inside, blacked and stoved outside. In 1763 a copper mine was found in Anglesea, and saucepans and frying pans began to be made of this much lighter and prettier material which was immediately popular. Earlier copper had been scarce and expensive and most of it went to make brass.

For the next fifty years various changes were made to the oven in an attempt to get it to trap and then regulate the heat, but no one understood the science of convection, so these experiments failed. In 1776, however, a British-born American, Benjamin Thompson, who had spied for the British in the War of Independence, returned to England and observed the extraordinary waste of heat involved. He was elected a fellow of the Royal Society and then, given permission by the Government, left for Munich and entered the service of the Elector of Bavaria where he stayed for fifteen years, finally being created Count Rumford, a count of the Holy Roman Empire. Having already contributed to science seminal theories on heat, he returned to England again in 1798 and founded the Royal Institution of Great Britain. He was again amazed and baffled at the inefficient systems of cooking. Writing on the imperfections of kitchen fireplaces 'now in common use', Count Rumford commented:

> The great fault in the construction of kitchens in private families, particularly in Great Britain, is . . .. that the fireplaces are not closed. The fuel is burned in a long open grate called a kitchen range over which the pots and kettles are freely suspended or placed on stands . . . The loss of heat and waste of fuel in these kitchens is altogether incredible.

He summarised the inadequacies by remarking that 'more fuel is consumed in it to boil a tea-kettle than, with proper management, would be sufficient to cook a dinner for fifty men.' His remedy was that:

> Each boiler, kettle, stewpan should have its separate closed fireplace. Each fireplace should have its grate for fuel and its separate ashpit closed by a well fitting door and furnished with a register for regulating the air intake.

The Count then invented a closed oven, a hollow sheet iron cylinder 18 inches in diameter and 24 inches long with a door at one end. This was set horizontally in brickwork and heated underneath by a small fire; it had a steam tube attached to the top of the oven to carry off steam which escaped in roasting. Count Rumford arranged a blind tasting of two roasts of mutton from the same carcass, one from his oven, the other roasted on a spit in front of a fire. His oven carcass was unanimously preferred. He went on to popularise James Watt's steam engine, to invent the double boiler and the drip coffee pot, which was on much the same principle as our present cafetière except that there was a space beneath where it dripped through. The first patent for a closed kitchen range was taken out in 1802.

Poorer houses made do without this equipment, or even a spit; they hung the meat on a hook and chain which was twisted and it slowly revolved in front of the fire, but the cauldron, hung from another chain, remained the most common cooking utensil. Next to the fire in the farmhouse kitchen was the salt box; it was handy to dip into, and its position ensured that the contents were always dry. A knife box hung on a nail, the knife handles of bullock horn or buckhorn. Cooking implements hung above, skimmers, ladles, and a large fork for extracting a bulky piece of meat from the cauldron. On the mantelpiece were stoneware mugs, tobacco jars and beer jugs, brass candlesticks and possibly a pewter pepper pot and one or two horn mugs.

Tea Time

At the beginning of the eighteenth century tea-drinking belonged to the upper classes; it was a sign of their position and affluence for the clothes, china and furniture that accompanied the drink were elegant and highly fashionable. Queen Anne liked to take her Bohea[12] cold with a little Bols[13] added. From the beginning tea had been highly taxed: liquid tea sold in the coffee houses was taxed at 8d a gallon, but in 1689 this was replaced by a customs duty of 5s per pound on the leaf itself. By the end of the century tea had become a staple drink of the masses. It was a dramatic change, so how had it happened?

The process had occurred fairly rapidly in the first few decades of the century: from London tea-drinking moved to the fashionable centres of Britain, to Bath and other spas, to York and Edinburgh, then to towns and lastly to the countryside. To avoid customs duty smuggling was rife and respectable people happily colluded with it. Sir Robert Walpole, the King's principal minister, used an Admiralty barge to bring his smuggled wine up the Thames and was applauded. At his parsonage in Norfolk Parson Woodforde (see page 237) knew that a tap on the window at night meant the local smuggler had arrived. On 29 March 1777 he wrote:

> Andrews the smuggler brought me this night about 11 o'clock a bagg of Hysons Tea 6 Pd weight. He frightened us a little by whistling under the Parlour Window just as we were going to bed. I gave him some Geneva and paid him for the tea at 10/6 per Pd.[14]

So much tea was smuggled into the country that in 1736 the tea dealers had petitioned Parliament, claiming that half the tea in the country had entered it illegally.

As the effect of the enclosures tightened upon society, those home-made effusions from wild currants and berries that were the source of so much home-made wine-making, dried up. In Manchester around 1720 society dispensed home-made wine at an afternoon call, but by the middle of the century they were offering tea. In June 1776 Parson Woodforde took on a new maid and as part of her wages (5 guineas a year) agreed that she was to have tea twice a day. His annual tea bill was £3 8s, but this did not include what he paid Andrews, the smuggler. In 1783 he notes that three of his neighbour's maids took tea with their own maids that afternoon – a perfect example of the servants aping their betters which so many moralists complained was the ruin of the century. Parson Woodforde does not even think it worthy of comment, as it had become such common practice. In 1767 the reformer Jonas Hanway, who was an acute observer of the diet of working people, but a purist who hated spirits and thought butter a luxury, was horrified when he found that labourers mending the roads were clubbing together to buy tea-making equipment. He also noticed that a vendor sold tea to harvest workers.

From 1723 the Government's response to the smuggling scandal was to lower the tax; it continued to go down gradually until the middle of the century, which allowed tea to become generally far more popular than hitherto. However, when coffee was becoming the staple drink among families in other European countries, why should tea appear to be taking the same role here? There were several reasons. France and Holland had direct access to their coffee supplies through their colonies in Java and the Antilles, while our trade interests were monopolised by the East India Company with its strong China connection. Here in Britain, the image of the coffee drinker had from the very beginning been a highly masculine one, bound up with politics and commerce, and was not easily assimilated into the domestic scene; similarly from the very beginning tea drinking had been a feminine pursuit associated with the decorative arts. Medical opinion approved of it too, as boiling the water destroyed the bacteria in a very dubious water supply. Tea could also be drunk without milk and the leaves dried and re-used; it had also by 1760 become widely available, and almost a quarter of all shops now stocked it. At Twining's shop in London, customers could buy from a selection of blends that were mixed in their presence and offered to them for tasting. Tea, in being so acceptable to the growing bourgeoisie, gave respectability, sobriety and an air of authoritative security to the drink. The aura tea possessed was its most powerful attraction to the lower classes.[15]

At some time in the first half of the century it became usual to add sugar to hot tea, perhaps because the black Bohea and Congou teas were very strong and bitter. Certainly our sugar imports grew. Sugar consumption rose from 4 lb per person per year in 1700-10 to 8 lb in 1720-30 and to 11 lb in 1770-80.[16] There is a direct correspondence between the tonnage of tea and the amount of sugar imported throughout. By the end of the eighteenth century we were the biggest importers of both in the world; the level of British consumption of tea was one quarter of the world's supply. Milk was added to tea in the nineteenth century but it was not unknown before. Thomas Garway refers to it in his handbill of 1660, and Rachel, Lady Russell wrote to her daughter in 1698: 'Yesterday I met with a little bottle to pour milk out for tea, they call them milk bottles, I was much delighted with them and so put them up for presents to you.' The East India Company's sales of oriental porcelain included milk pots, with or without covers, in 1706 but not earlier.[17]

It is not surprising that labourers now felt that sweetened tea gave them energy, so that it became very quickly a daily and addictive beverage, entrenched as a staple with their meals. By the end of the century when prices rose because of disastrous harvests, hot sweet tea was a necessity, drunk three times a day with the tea kettle kept simmering on the hob. Labourers were spending ten per cent of their budgets on tea and sugar and only 2.5 on beer. Jonas Hanway, of course, still thought that it was 'pernicious to Health, obstructing Industry and impoverishing the Nation'.

The French and Hannah Glasse

By the eighteenth century there was a clear distinction in people's minds between French and English cooking, though whether the gulf was as wide as people thought is debatable. Certainly in some respects the two styles were very different. The subject is further complicated by the fact that France itself was a highly emotive subject: the century had begun with the Duke of Marlborough winning a series of astonishing military victories against Louis XIV. Though Marlborough was ousted in 1710, the British army backed by Protestant allies was by 1712 massed on the borders of France ready to march on Paris. It was then that without our allies' knowledge we secretly signed a peace treaty and deservedly gained the pejorative title of 'perfidious Albion'. It was Jacobite (Roman Catholic) sympathisers within the British Government who had ousted Marlborough from his command and reneged on our allies; this same faction with the help of Louis had planned to place the Stuart Pretender upon the throne and to reject the Hanoverian succession. To the general populace anything French was traitorous, Catholic, and an insidious threat. The Catholics, it seemed to them rightly, were eager to regain control of England; even the recent Act of Union with Scotland was suspect for everyone knew how Papist the Highlands were. However, French chefs and the food they produced were popular with the aristocracy who thought that French recipes were superior to the English; therefore, to prefer English food was a sign of patriotism and Protestantism, and these feelings went deep. Nevertheless French food was also fashionable and the pull of fashion was incredibly powerful in this century, as we have seen. Besides, food has a will of its own, born from a combination of planned accidents; it absorbs influences from wherever it attracts. English food had already borrowed from every country that Englishmen had visited and enjoyed, and it would hardly retrench now.

Mrs Glasse's fulminations against French cooking have amused historians and food writers, for she represents the ambivalence I have described above. Let us examine her more closely. *The Art of Cookery made plain and easy by a Lady* (Hannah Glasse 1747) went through many editions, was amazingly popular and went on selling through into the next century. She poaches from other cookery books published in the first half of the century, so the book is highly representative.[18] Ann Cook, who in 1755 devoted sixty-six pages of her *Professed Cookery* to criticising Mrs Glasse's recipes, puts her finger on various flaws where she obviously did not cook the recipe first, or had made mistakes in amounts of the ratio of meat or butter to rice, or been far too generous with the amount of salts when she pots venison and beef. This comes, one surmises, in Mrs Glasse having been too hasty in her borrowings.

Mrs Glasse writes to enlighten the servants, ' that every servant who can but read will be capable of making a tolerable good cook'. She wishes to instruct the 'lower sort', and uses expressions they will understand, for she says great cooks 'have such a high way of expressing themselves that the poor girls are at a loss to know what they mean'. So Mrs Glasse is a teacher, an aspect all the women writers were very conscious of. Their instructions were part of the civilising process; if it did not teach young girls how to possess the attributes of being a lady, at least they could minister to them with skill and elegance, thus ensuring employment for their lifetimes.

This down to earth approach must have been appealing, but surely Mrs Glasse's success was also due to a practical appreciation of the art of economy and an obvious irritation with French extravagance and deceit, which is at once apparent in her introduction. 'If Gentlemen will have French cooks, they must pay for French tricks,' she announces tartly, then continues:

> A Frenchman in his own country would dress a fine dinner of twenty dishes and all genteel and pretty, for the expense he will put an English lord to one dressing dish. I have heard of a cook that used six pounds of butter to fry twelve eggs, when, everybody knows that understands cooking, that half a pound is full enough. But then it would not be French. So much is the blind Folly of this Age, that they would rather be imposed on by a French booby, than give encouragement to a good English cook.

Her strictures against the French continue throughout the text. After giving a detailed recipe on the French way of dressing partridges, Mrs Glasse adds: 'This dish I do not recommend; for I think it an odd jumble of trash, by that time the cullis, the esssence of ham, and all the other ingredients are re-reckoned, the partridges will come to a fine penny; but such receipts as this, is what you have in most books of cookery yet printed.' She then gives seven sauces which use a cullis and concludes: 'It would be needless to name any more; though they have much more expensive sauce than this. However, I think here is enough to show the folly of these fine French cooks.' Then, Cassandra-like, she prophesies bankruptcy for these large French estates. She is writing just thirty years before the Revolution.

The time of writing is very important, for Mrs Glasse was compiling and writing the book when the 1745 rebellion had thrown England into a great panic; the Jacobite army had marched south into England as far as Derby and was only a few days' march from London itself. It seemed then that George II and the Hanoverian lineage would be short-lived, that Charles Edward Stuart, the Young Pretender, would be back upon the English throne and the British Isles would return to Catholicism. No wonder Mrs Glasse was vindictive in her writing of France and its cooking, for if the Stuarts were back in power that would be the style of cooking celebrated everywhere. It would have been like a British cook in 1940 saying how great and marvellous was German cuisine and looking forward to the time when we should all be eating it.

It follows that in Glasse we should find an English cuisine, holding at bay most of the French and other national ideas. This is not so, however. She welcomes a 'Pellow' or a 'Currey' in the Indian way, for example. Like other cookery writers, Mrs Glasse reflected the current interest and enjoyment of Indian spices and ketchups. These had been brought back to Britain by retired East India Company officials, who often had their favourite recipes made up in their own kitchens.[19] Some of her recipes are termed 'in the French way', although they would have been familiar to an English medieval cook. She stuffs a hind saddle of mutton beneath the skin with truffles, onions, lemon peel, parsley, thyme, mace and cloves. She cannot resist saying of another French dish, Cutlets *à la Maintenon*, that it is a 'very good dish'; the cutlets are stuffed, then baked *en papillote* (as we would describe it, for this term was not used then). Her stuffing is minced veal, beef suet, spice, sweet herbs and yolks of eggs (*à la Maintenon* now means a soubise [onion] purée with sliced mushrooms, truffles and pickled tongue). She spreads French terms around in her recipes without a shred of embarrassment (*à royale, à la dauphine*) and gives many recipes for 'fricaseys'; the latter were interpreted as fry-ups and thus as much an English medieval dish as a contemporary French one.

It was one of the misunderstandings of the sixteenth and seventeenth centuries that recipes 'in the French manner' were so often cooking methods used here before the Reformation, which were then re-imported back into England in the mistaken impression that they were new and French. It must have been galling for Mrs Glasse to know that Frenchmen were being employed by the British aristocracy and being paid ten times as much as she was, while also being given the freedom to spend ten times as much on the food and its preparation. She must have looked at the methods used and found them on so many occasions not worth the extra work, ingredients and expense.

Where did this English awe of French culinary arts, which is obviously flourishing in Hannah's lifetime, begin? It has to go back to Robert May, inculcated in French skills and techniques, and his work for the English Catholic nobility, who looked to France as an example of all things wise and good. To sit down to a meal in the French fashion must have been to celebrate a rite common to international Catholicism centred on Rome, and the more the dishes reflected such a style the deeper the reverence felt. This was the cooking England would have had, if the Reformation had never happened; this was the cooking to which England could return if it came back to the rule of Rome. The Hanoverian Kings were solidly in power in Mrs Glasse's lifetime; there was no chance of a return to Rome in the immediate future (except for the panic felt in 1745). British Catholics kept a low profile, for the legislation against them was fierce and of great bigotry. Of course, the character of the food eaten then was given no significance by anyone of whatever belief, but the difference in the style of food and the groups that ate it is clearly apparent now. Hannah Glasse may enthuse over plain and economical cooking (and Mrs Bradley after her), expressing disgust and horror for the French style, but the sub-text speaks powerfully to us. The

Englishness of the former represented values of freedom, an elected Parliament, an English Church free of foreign domination, food without taint, fresh from the English soil, while food in the French manner was something quite insidious, almost, she makes us feel, a contamination, a creeping infection, to be much feared and halted if at all possible. She admits, with a cross sigh, that such recipes are to be expected, but makes her readers feel guilty for wanting them.

Sea Travel

Mrs Glasse's Chapter Eleven is specifically for captains of ships and deals with recipes intended to last, which can be taken on voyages. It begins with a ketchup to keep twenty years which is made from strong stale beer, a pound of anchovies, shallots, ginger, mushrooms, mace, cloves and pepper. She gives a fish sauce which is also made from anchovies, spices, lemon and horseradish. Two spoonfuls will be sufficient with a pound of butter, she says, as a sauce for boiled fowl or veal. (Mrs Raffald also makes these sauces up and then keeps them to add to gravies for meats and fish.) These magnificently, intensely flavoured sauces, are so powerful in their heat and spices one feels Mrs Glasse's pleasure at the thought that they could never appear in the French cuisine. Nor would the almost forty recipes for pickles from walnuts, oysters, red currants to elder shoots in imitation of bamboo. (Varenne pickles only a very few vegetables in vinegar and salt with perhaps a bay leaf.) There are over twenty recipes for potting meats and fish from venison to mackerel.

Are these recipes really going to be incorporated into a ship's stores for a long voyage of exploration? Did James Cook's expeditions around the world from 1768 to 1780 carry Hannah Glasse recipes? In his journals for July 1772 Cook gives an account of the provisions placed aboard the *Resolution* and *Adventure* to feed 201 men. On the *Resolution*, the greatest quantity is almost 60,000 lb of ship's biscuit; 17,000 lb of flour is listed with 14,000 lb of pork and only half that of salt beef. There are 19 tons of beer, 642 gallons of wine, 1397 gallons of spirit; there are quantities of dried peas, wheat, oatmeal, butter, cheese, sugar, olive oil, vinegar, suet, raisins, salt and malt. What makes Cook's provisions strikingly different from others, however, is the quantities of various types of 'anti-scorbuticks'; he had 19,000 lb of 'sour krout' as well as salted cabbage, portable broth, saloupe, mustard and something entitled 'mermalade of carrots'. Cook explains that only 'portable broth' was ever used before in the stores. This was beef broth reduced so that it jellied; a cube of it was then mixed with boiling water and given to the sick at the discretion of the surgeon. The rest of the men had it boiled with the peas on Mondays, Wednesdays and Fridays because they were meatless days. Saloupe was lemons and oranges kept for the sick and scorbutic only. Mustard was given to everyone in the belief that it was an anti-scorbutic. The mermalade of carrots was the juice of yellow carrots 'inspissated till it is the thickness of flued honey', which was recommended by Baron Storsch of Berlin. Cook quotes him as saying, 'a spoonful of this Marmadlade, mix'd with Water, taken now and then will prevent the Scurvey, it will even cure it if constantly taken.' Cook adds, 'It is much used by the poor in Germany.' The provisions were to last two years.

They also had fishing lines, nets and hooks and some empty barrels in order to take on 400 gallons of Madeira wine. There is, of course, no mention of any of Mrs Glasse's recipes, but some of her preserves might well have been on board, or ketchups and pickles very similar to hers, as the officers brought their own personal supplies, having been given jars of various preserves by their mothers, wives and sweethearts. On deck there was also a menagerie of horses, cows, sheep, pigs, chickens and even a goat who eventually circled the globe twice. The livestock was there to produce milk and eggs but also to leave on desert islands so as to populate them with useful food animals. John Thompson was Cook's cook on the first voyage and he had to slaughter, prepare and cook cormorant, penguin, dog, walrus and quantities of unidentified plants, as well as the salt beef, pork and dried peas. He used a stove that burnt wood (the best fuel was coniferous logs and coconut shells), and could only accommodate two copper vessels with a capacity of 5 to 10 gallons each to feed 100 men daily. The ship's company was divided into messes of four persons sitting together and eating out of the one dish. The officers and gentlemen ate separately from the crew in the Great Cabin with windows out at the stern. The men were not always happy at what they had to eat: 'It was No Uncommon thing when Swallowing Over these Messes to Curse him heartily and wish for gods sake that he Might be Obledged to Eat such Damned Stuff Mixed with his Broth as Long as he Lived . . .'[20]

In September 1769, Joseph Banks, the naturalist on board, wrote in his journal:

> Our bread indeed is but indifferent, occasioned by the quantity of Vermin that are in it, I have often seen hundreds, nay thousands shaken out of a single bisket. We in the Cabbin have however an easy remedy for this by baking it in an oven, not too hot, which makes them all walk off, but this cannot be allowed to the private people who must find the taste of these animals very disagreeable, as they have everyone a taste as strong as mustard or rather spirits of hartshorn.

Later the same day he notes that Dr Solander has been unwell, so he opened Dr Hulme's Essence of Lemon Juice which 'proved perfectly good, little if at all inferior in taste to fresh lemon juice'. Then he comments that a pie was made from the North American apples that Dr Fothergill had given him, which proved to be very good; he goes on to note that 'our ships beef and Pork are excellent as are the peas; the flour and oatmeal which have at some times failed us are at present and have in general been very good.'

In April 1769 Banks tells us that he ate constantly of the 'Sower crout', until the salted cabbage was opened, which he found he preferred. He noticed that his gums swelled and he had a few pimples on the inside of his mouth, so:

> I then flew to the Lemon Juice which had been put up for me according to Dr Holmes method described in his book . . . Every kind of liquor which I used was made sour with the Lemon Juice, so that I took near 6

ounces a day of it. The effect of this was surprising, in less than a week
my gums became as firm as ever . . .

Cook at first found that the sailors would not eat the sauerkraut, so he used a ploy he
had found never failed; he ordered that every day a dish should be placed on the
officers' table and all should partake of some without fail. Within a week he found that
all the sailors insisted on eating it and he had to place an allowance on the amount
everyone now ate. Cook comments: 'the moment they see their Superiors set a Value
upon it, it becomes the finest Stuff in the World . . .' Seven years later Captain Cook
addressed the Royal Society of London and was awarded the Copley Gold Medal for
his paper as the best experimental research of that year for the method that preserved
the health of the crew. Cook had allowed each man to have 4 lb sauerkraut per week
which gave every man 40 mg vitamin C daily. (10 mg vitamin C daily will prevent
scurvy.) Cook also insisted that the men ate fresh greens boiled in their broth every
day, but this could only happen when they were close to land when crew members
could row ashore and pick wild leaves.

They used the produce of the islands whenever they landed, but they also planted
cereals and vegetables: turnips, carrots, parsnips, peas, beans, melons and
strawberries. In New Zealand the Maoris were already cultivating large acreages, and
they found sweet potatoes, yams and pumpkins. As well as the breadfruit tree which
fascinated them, Cook relates how in 1773 they salted their own pork in New Zealand:
'In the cool of the evening the hogs were killed and dressed, then cut up, the bones
taken out and the Meat salted while it was yet hot, the next Morning we gave it a
second salting, packed it into a cask and put to it a sufficient quantity of Strong Pickle,
great care is to be taken that the meat be well covered with pickle other wise it will
soon spoile.'

In July 1769 when anchored at Tahiti Cook lists the fruit and vegetables upon the
island which they are eating: Bread fruit, cocoa-nuts, bananas, plantains, a fruit like an
apple (*Spondias dulcis*), sweet potatoes (*Ipomoea Batatas*), yams (*dioscorea alata*), a fruit
known by the name of Eag melloa (*Eugenia malaccensis*) and reckoned most delicious,
sugar cane, which the inhabitants ate raw, a root of the salop kind called by the
inhabitants pea (*Tacca leontopetaloides*), the root also of a plant called Ethee (*Cordyline
terminalis*), and a fruit in a pod like a kidney bean which when roasted can be eaten like
a chestnut and is called Ahee (*Inocarpus edulis*), the fruit of a tree called wharrra
(*Pandanus tectorius*) something like a pineapple, the fruit of a tree called by them Nano
(*Morinda cirifolia*), the roots of a fern (*Angiopteris evecta*), and the roots of a plant
called Theve (*Amorphophallus campanulatus*).

Their tame animals numbered hogs, fowls and dogs; the latter, the sailors had
discovered, were as delicious as English lamb. Cook is amazed at the variety of the sea
food. He remarks how astonishing it is that the wealth of food upon the island allows
the natives the freedom not to have to cultivate, though he notices that their main food
is vegetables and these they either bake or boil. What makes Cook so remarkable a man
and so valuable to history is not only his observation and tenacity in noting everything,

but the fact that he and his men try every possible food they stumble across. Such a willingness made the men vulnerable to the odd toxins; there was an occasion when they ate water hemlock, another time when they consumed mussels infected with red tide; and they also suffered agonies from eating a poisonous reef fish. Other than the occasional belly ache, however, they survived remarkably well after such long voyages, without anyone becoming mortally ill from scurvy.[21]

Cook constantly amazes one with how enterprising he was. In May 1779 at Unalaska, finding the ground beginning to be clear of snow, he led a party ashore and found nettle tops and onions which they collected. Then he tapped the birch trees which gave a 'good quantity of clear, sweet juice'. Back on board the company were given an allowance of brandy to drink with the juice every day for as long as it lasted. It was far too early in the year for any other vegetables. Cook noted that the ones they found were too advanced in decay, but what he found instead were berries; he ordered one-third of his crew by turns to go ashore and pick them, and a good quantity were procured from the natives. They caught salmon trout and once a magnificent halibut weighing 254 lb. They received from the natives a rye loaf which encased spiced salmon and surmised that this present must have been from some Russians in the area, so they sent back bottles of rum, wine and porter. In South Georgia Cook was so heartily sick of salt beef that he noted he much preferred penguin. The flesh was 'reminiscent of bullock's liver'; they were 'tolerably palatable and very nutritive'. Cook's voyages lasted only nine years, before he was killed by the natives in the Sandwich islands in 1779.[22]

Cook's dietetics are all the more impressive because he disregarded Admiralty orthodoxy; their ineptitude had led to a long catalogue of disasters. Two Elizabethans, Sir Richard Hawkins and Sir John Lancaster, had both recognized the value of lemons in the treatment of scurvy and had written journals detailing the fact. The Admiralty had ignored them. Between 1740 and 1744 George Anson took five ships and two store ships to circumnavigate the globe. The ships were overrun with rats and the men with lice; when crossing the Atlantic there was a devastating epidemic of fever and dysentery which killed ninety men; off the coast of Brazil mosquitos attacked the convalescents; a captain died of cerebral malaria while men fell sick with scurvy, as well as asthma, idiocy, lunacy and convulsions, which imply multiple vitamin deficiencies. One of the captains, Cheap, had lost all self-respect, and was covered with filth, alive with vermin, and a human anthill, whose legs were as big as millposts, though his body appeared to be nothing but skin and bone. His memory gone and failing even to recall his own name, he lapsed into a stumbling passive state. From that ship of 243 men only thirty-seven finally survived. On other ships men continued to die, until off the coast of Chile they ate turnips, radishes, scurvy grass and goats' flesh. A few men from another ship had survived by finding at Tierra del Fuego wild celery and other greens. When Anson finally returned he had lost nearly 1,500 men and only 150 returned home. Anson was interviewed by the influential physician Richard Mead, who thought that the anti-scorbutic properties of fresh vegetables and fruits were due to their astringency and hence recommended vinegar and bitters as a substitute for further sea voyages. He also thought ships should be better ventilated and suggested extraction tubes. The Admiralty at once implemented both suggestions.[23]

White Bread and Potatoes

The eighteenth century saw the rise in consumption of both the wheaten loaf and the potato so that both eventually became a staple of the working class diet. At the end of the century in 1798 Arthur Young notes: 'The usual diet of labourers in Hull and its neighbourhood is wheaten bread, with the cheapest sort of butcher's meat, potatoes and fish.' In the early part of the century workers had been content with a loaf of mixed rye and wheat; the changeover to a completely wheat loaf had occurred by the 1770s. Young notes the change as early as 1767: 'Rye and barley bread, at present, are looked on with a sort of horror even by poor cottagers, and with some excuse, for wheat now is as cheap as rye and barley were in former times.'[24] At that time it had been estimated that in England about 4$\frac{1}{2}$ million people lived on wheat and rye and about 1$\frac{1}{2}$ million on barley and oats. By the end of the century the number of people who would eat only wheat bread rose steadily, not only as the price of wheat went down, but as the idea that to eat white bread was a mark of privilege available to all gained more and more credence.

Of course, white bread from the earliest times was always a symbol of nobility and affluence, but in the Middle Ages the peasants had hardly any opportunity to eat it, except for the remnants in waste food thrown out of the castle kitchens. Through the ages white bread gained greater symbolic value, reflecting white damask tablecloths, cleanliness and purity, but also social status. To be able to eat it occasionally must have meant that one was climbing the social ladder, and to eat it every day, must surely be somehow significant that success and prosperity had almost arrived. The adoption of white bread was not only a sign of the hunger for status, but also evidence of an egalitarian spirit pervading the English class structure. It marks the end of the downtrodden peasant content with his lot, and clearly states that I am as good as the next man and the slogan of the French Revolution is applicable this side of the Channel too.

By 1795 the supremacy of wheaten bread was for all practical purposes complete, apart from in the north. Its success was all the more dramatic for after 1770, as produce rose in price and meat vanished from their tables, the workers had still insisted on eating white bread, and not the cheaper, coarser barley loaf; it was white bread and cheese that had become the staple food. They would rather turn to the two despised foods, potato and rice, despised because they were associated with the Irish and the coolie (the Chinese East End labourers) whom people regarded socially as little better than slaves, than return to eating the coarse, brown rye and barley loaves. Middle-class commentators saw little virtue in this new fad; it was merely another sign of the inferiority of the working class. 'The flour must be divested of its bran and in a fit state for the most luxurious palate, or it is rejected not only by the affluent but by the extremely indigent,' said Lewis Magendi in 1795, and Squire Bevan of Riddlesworth Hall, Norfolk, commented: 'Our Labourers reject anything but wheaten bread.' Lord Sheffield, the same year, wrote: 'The poor are too fine mouthed to eat inferior bread till imperious necessity compels them.' In the end it was 'imperious necessity' and Government policy that led not back to the rye and barley loaf, but onwards to the potato.

The acceptance of the potato was slow. When Young toured the country in the 1760s, he noted it was Lancashire, the nearest area to Ireland, where the potato was first fully established. The moist warm climate and the deep moss soil were particularly suitable for the tubers and Formby claimed to be the first site of their cultivation in the 1670s. Tolls had to be paid on every potato load going into the Michaelmas market in Wigan in 1680, but their immediate neighbours were not far behind. They were being grown in north-east Cheshire as early as the 1680s and by 1700 there is a reference to a potato bed at Garstang. There they are cooking a dish called lobscouse, a highly flavoured dish of meat, potatoes and onions, which became particularly associated with the seamen of the Lancashire ports.[25] (In time Lobscouser became a nickname for a sailor.) The first field crop was grown in this county and by the middle of the century it had built up an export trade, the first of its kind in England, and was sending consignments of potatoes out to Gibraltar as well as sending twenty shiploads annually to Dublin.

A pamphlet on potatoes published in 1799 by one Hezekiah Kirkpatrick, who lived on the High Road between Warrington and Wigan, gives intelligent advice on their cultivation and cooking. The author admits he is not a Lancastrian, but aware of the superior attention given to this useful vegetable by the county wishes to render a service by introducing the potato to other counties. He deals with various methods of cultivation, storage and subsequent use of the land, includes four pages of recipes and details the uses of potato starch in textiles and the potatoes themselves for also feeding livestock.

He gives some space and detail to boiling potatoes in the Lancastrian way. The potatoes were peeled, placed in barely simmering water and cooked slowly (no cooking time is given); constant testing was needed to see the moment they were done; then they were drained, salted and placed back in the dry saucepan by the fire where they were left, after shaking the pan a little until they become fluffy. Eliza Acton also gives the recipe in *Modern Cookery* (1845). Kirkpatrick recommends potatoes sliced, seasoned and placed over minced beef or mutton and onion. He mentions that the dish may be made from cold meat, but considers it not so palatable. He also gives a recipe for mashing the potatoes and placing them in scallop shells or small cups to be made brown and crisp before the fire or with a salamander. He recommends them as being palatable and frugal dishes.

In 1772 early potatoes were selling at 2s 6d a pound, a high price which suggests that people so relished eating the very first crop that they would pay more than a labourer's weekly wage. The potatoes had to be brought into market still attached to the roots otherwise no one would buy them. In 1795 John Holt writes that there is 'general strife betwixt the Kirkdale and Wallasey gardeners, who can produce the first early potato at Liverpool market'.[26] The rich were paying their gardeners to cultivate the potatoes over hot beds so that they could eat them at Christmas. Mr Butler, gardener to the Earl of Derby, practised this every year at his seat at Knowsley.

Other parts of England were slow to follow the Lancastrian lead, however. Possibly this was because the official view was distinctly unenthusiastic. 'Potatoes are generally thought to be an insipid root: but when they are cultivated in a good mixed soil, they are not without their admirers: the smaller roots and knots are commonly preserved for a succeeding crop.'[27] In the district around Doncaster potatoes were grown as a field crop but only to be fed to the horses. In the neighbourhood of the larger towns in the North and West Ridings of Yorkshire potato crops began to be important by the 1760s. In fact the crop followed these burgeoning industrial towns, as well as appearing far more often as a field crop in the enclosed system of agriculture and not in the open fields. The reasons are obvious: firstly, it had not taken long for farmers to discover how economical the crop was to grow, since the yield of tubers was great and it was easily sold in the market with a new and growing population, who had to provide cheap meals that were also filling. Secondly, it was the large farms that were more economically attuned to the needs of the market and could put large acreages to the crop. Agricultural writers were not encouraging. They were convinced the potato was not a crop for the small garden, but should be assiduously cultivated in the fields. In 1756 Thomas Hale was very specific: 'It should be put in the hands of the farmer, especially near big towns.'[28] By 1770, when Mrs Austen (see page 255) advised a tenant's wife at Steventon near Basingstoke to plant potatoes in her garden, the answer she received was: 'No, no, they are all very well for you gentry, but they must be terribly costly to rear.'[29]

At the beginning of the eighteenth century the smallholder was consuming a varied diet: milk, butter, cheese, whey and buttermilk, cabbage, turnips, parsnips, carrots, onions and potatoes, apple pie, pease-pies, puddings and pancakes; gruel, flummery and frumenty. Meat and fish did not appear: the first was too expensive and the second, because of poor roads and communications, never found its way inland.[30] For a time the landless labourer could not have enjoyed so wide a range, nor so ample a supply of food. This was reflected in the institutions; in 1714 the Bristol Workhouse fed its inmates three times a day on meat, green vegetables, turnips and potatoes; in the Bedfordshire Workhouse there was meat six times a week, wheaten bread and cheese for supper, milk and bacon. They were fortunate that they were not attempting to drink milk in the midst of any of the big cities.

In *The Expedition of Humphry Clinker* (1771), Tobias Smollett sums up the trade in fresh milk in the following passage:

> . . . carried through the streets in open pails, exposed to foul rinsings discharged from doors and windows, spittle, snot, and tobacco quids, from foot passengers; overflowings from mud carts, spatterings from coach wheels, dirt and trash chucked into it by rogueish boys for the joke's sake; the spewing of infants, who have slabbered in the tin measure, which is thrown back in that condition among the milk, for the benefit of

the next customer; and, finally, the vermin that drops from the rags of the nasty drab that vends this precious mixture, under the respectable denomination of milkmaid.

By the last quarter of the century dark clouds had begun to gather on the horizon. The American War of Independence meant that the Nottingham hosiery workers were thrown out of work, and the invention of the spinning jenny began to withdraw work from the cotton spinners. Unemployment began to rise. Adam Smith was convinced that the potato could replace wheat as the mainstay of the poor, and estimated that an acre of land under potatoes would yield an equivalent in food to three acres of wheat and could therefore maintain a larger population. The harvests of the 1790s were disastrous, especially in 1794 and 1795, causing widespread distress. The Government published a series of well informed articles on the 'Cultivation and Uses of the Potato' which advocated its adoption by workers as a cheap substitute for wheat. They championed varieties of potato to grow and eat, while there was another variety to be grown for feeding livestock. They also encouraged people to use potatoes in bread, assuring the public that 12 lb potatoes added to 20 lb wheaten flour would make 42 lb of excellent bread.

Commentators were not enthusiastic, however: 'The poor will not eat potatoes if they can get anything else,' said Thomas Ruggles. 'I believe the daintiness of the poor to be the chief obstacle,' thought Thomas Butts in 1794. Other landowners, however, agreed with the labourers in the value and nutrition of white bread. 'The poor allege that as they live almost entirely on bread, they cannot perform their tasks without good bread,' said John Wickens from Dorset in 1795. 'They have nothing but bread and they want the best,' Charles Onley pointed out very reasonably in the same year, and Bernard James agreed: 'The principal food of the Poor is the whitest bread of which they eat but little else, and they must have it of the most nourishing kind.'[31]

The poor were distrustful of this new food that was being thrust upon them with such enthusiasm, but the price of white bread continued to rise; meat and cheese had doubled in price and milk, as a result of the enclosures, was unobtainable in many parts of the country. They had to eat. The Board of Agriculture had said: 'Potatoes and water alone, with common salt can nourish men completely . . . they are perhaps as strong an instance of the extension of human enjoyment as can be mentioned . . .' The clergy up and down the country were urged to tell their flocks of the incomparable advantage of potato bread. The Prime Minister, Pitt, suggested a loaf made from maize and potato was very pleasant and nutritious. But to little avail – out of ninety-eight different districts only seven reported that any of the 'poor' had used potatoes in their bread. However, with hunger being the dominant factor, the poor now began to grow and use potatoes as a vegetable, though they resolutely refused to substitute them for wheat in their bread. The distress caused by the second bad harvest of 1795 induced many cottagers who still had a tiny plot of land to grow the root. *The Times* of 10 September 1795: 'From the apprehension of a second year of scarcity, potatoes have been everywhere planted and their produce has been generally great.' Industrial workers had already been buying potatoes from the market, now the rural workers were growing them and from thence on potatoes appear as an item in the family budget.

Whether white bread or the potato was the mainstay of the meal was subject to circumstances for the next thirty years: in times of good harvests when the price of bread fell, the white loaf reigned almost supreme; but when economic conditions were harsh the potato returned to occupy the centre of the table.

Women Cooks

Elizabeth Raffald (née Whitaker) was born in 1733, one of four sisters. It is thought her father did some teaching. As a very young girl she went into service and almost certainly learnt there how to make confectionery. There was a shortage of good servants in the eighteenth century; because of social mobility, there was a scramble to better oneself, so servants were always leaving. Though the great houses had a pool of young people in the children of their estate workers, no sooner were they trained than they left to find better positions or to get married. Servants attempted to save money from the 'perks' offered: the master and mistress's clothes could be sold on, they had a right to sell candle ends and they were given tips by visitors.

In 1760 Elizabeth got a new position as housekeeper at Arley Hall in Cheshire, where her duties included looking after the servants, buying fish, tripe, oysters, lemons and lobsters from the vendors who visited the house, keeping an account which the steward vetted every month, as well as preserving, pickling, making wines and table decorations, cakes and confectionery to be offered at that now established ritual the mistress's tea. The steward settled meat bills and those for the London goods, which was where the spices were ordered: cinnamon, cloves, mace and nutmeg. (The list is basically no longer than the Earl of Bedford's a century before.) The new housekeeper also had game from the estate and all the garden produce, as well as ice from the icehouse to make her ice cream.

The gardener at Arley Hall was one John Raffald, and he and Elizabeth were married early in 1763; however, they now had to leave the Hall as great houses insisted that servants should be unmarried. They travelled to Manchester and opened a shop where Elizabeth advertised Yorkshire Hams, Tongues, Newcastle Salmon, potted meats, portable soups (on which Captain Cook was to rely), sweetmeats, lemon preserve and mushroom ketchup, cakes and table decorations. She also began a register office so that employers could find servants, while also compiling and writing her book *The Experienced English Housekeeper*. Unfortunately, the registry could also be mistaken for something rather dubious, so Elizabeth Raffald had to place another advertisement to make that clear: 'As several of Mrs Raffald's friends in the country have mistook her Terms and Designs of her Register Office she begs leave to inform them that she supplies Families with Servants, for any place, at ONE shilling each.'

In 1766 they moved to a more central shop in Market Place near to the principal inn, The Bull's Head, and next to the markets. Her many advertisements detail the wide range she offers to the public: 'creams, possets, jellies, flummery, lemon cheese cake, best boiled tripe, pickled walnuts, coffee, tea and chocolate of the finest sorts'.

Amidst all of that, it is thought that she gave birth to sixteen daughters, but only six were baptised and only three survived their mother. As so many cookery books were pirated, Mrs Raffald chose to publish hers by subscription in 1769 and sample pages were placed in shops for inspection. This was a huge success; the public responded to her experience and authority and the book went on into thirteen editions well into the next century as well as selling twenty editions in America.

Elizabeth Raffald states that the book contains 'near 800 original recipes most of which never appeared in print', a claim heard often but which is possibly true in her case, for her recipes are practical, there is a marvellous no nonsense approach and her writing is clear and concise. Many of the recipes could be used today without making any changes. She frequently uses alegar, which was a vinegar made from ale or beer; she used it to rub fish with before poaching or as a flavouring. She is writing twenty-five years after Mrs Glasse and she does not mention the French or their influence, nor does she bother with a 'cullis' or coulis. Her sauces seem eminently sensible and trouble-free, such as one for salmon which is simply chopped fennel and parsley added to melted butter. Perhaps the most complicated is the alternative sauce for salmon which she also suggests is good for all kinds of boiled fish. She begins with a strong stock of meat and vegetables, which she calls gravy, adds to it an anchovy, a teaspoon of lemon pickle, a meat spoonful of the liquor from walnut pickle, some of liquor that the fish was boiled in, a stick of horseradish, a little browning and salt. This is boiled together, thickened with a *beurre manié*, then strained and sent to table.

I don't know whether 'browning' is the first mention of this ingredient, which was familiar enough in my childhood as a commercial bottle with its thick, black gummy liquid, a spoonful of which was always added to the gravy for the Sunday joint. Mrs Raffald gives a recipe for it, which begins with butter and sugar cooked together until it caramelises, then red wine, jamaica pepper, six cloves, four shallots, two or three blades of mace, three spoonfuls of mushroom ketchup, salt and rind of a lemon are added; it is boiled together, and bottled when cool. This sounds delicious and so does the gravy sauce for the fish to which it is added. It also strikes me as equal to any reduced sauce, or coulis by a French chef. She writes: 'I have given no directions for cullis, as I have found by experience, that lemon pickle and browning answer both for beauty and taste (at a trifling expense) better than cullis, which is extravagant.' So in her sauces, which one might suppose were more vulnerable to French influences than any other dish, we can only discern a wholly British character. Mrs Raffald does not bother, like Mrs Glasse, to argue truculently with the fussiness and expense of French cooking; she almost ignores it completely. She says: 'And though I have given some of my dishes French names, as they are only known by those names, yet they will not be found very expensive, nor add compositions, but as plain as the nature of the dish will admit of.' Her book is the second work (see Mrs Bradley below) to celebrate the quintessence of British cuisine: country produce cooked simply with sauces of intense flavour. Let us look briefly at other cookery books written before Mrs Raffald's.

There were the private recipe collections in the homes of the gentry. 'The Lady Cravens Receipt-Booke (privately owned), 1697-1704, is perhaps representative of these. Elizabeth Craven died in childbirth aged twenty-five, and not surprisingly, considering her early death, the receipt book has many blank pages. What makes her collection interesting, however, is firstly a recipe for oyster loaves which must have its roots in the Anglo-Saxon version. (See page 31.) Here the loaves are small rolls with the interior crumb removed, the oysters are poached in white wine and chopped onion with pepper, salt, mace, nutmeg and cloves, then much butter is added and they are poured into the bread rolls which are baked in a hot oven. Secondly, food preparation, storage and cooking have not changed since Elinor Fettiplace's time, a hundred years earlier. Lady Craven dries peas and beans for keeping throughout the winter, she pickles purslane, French beans and artichokes. She makes a ragout of pigeons, where they are trussed as for baking, then beaten so that the bones are broken, then seasoned with pepper, salt, mace and cloves. They are larded, then floured, then poached in a strong broth, stewed until tender until no more broth is left, then chopped sweetbreads, mushrooms, artichoke bottoms are added with wine, herbs and lots of butter. This is cooked for a while and the pigeons are served in the sauce. There are recipes for cheeses, including Angelot; Lady Fettiplace gave a recipe for this, and it is little changed. The cheese once set is rubbed with salt and butter. Lady Craven also gives recipes for cream cheese, winter cheese and little straw cheeses. She has four recipes for mushrooms, including one on how to pickle them. They are peeled, boiled, then placed in white wine vinegar with cloves, mace and pepper. She says the same pickle will do for 'cowcumbers'. The first recipe is for almonds to make into comfits, they are boiled in syrup, left to cool, then more sugar is added and they are boiled again; the process continues for days until the syrup is hard.

Mrs Anne Hawtrey's Receipt Book for 1689 (privately owned) has a collection of recipes that seem quite familiar: a peas pottage for example for which the dried peas are soaked, then boiled with a ham bone; a fricassée of chicken, where the chopped pieces are fried in butter until brown, then poached in broth and wine; the sauce for it is thickened with egg yolks. As you read on you realise that so many of the recipes are quite lost to us, such as roasted rabbit with oyster stuffing, or a stewed breast of veal, or minced pies from beef with nutmeg, cinnamon, lemon, sack and sugar. Her recipes include how to make thick cheese, almond cheesecakes, lemon custards, quince cream, cabbage and clotted cream, how to candy angelica, how to pickle anchovies, green French beans, walnuts, cowcumbers and cockles, how to preserve barberries, plums and morello cherries, and how to make apricot cakes, raspberry cakes and apple pudding. As in the sixteenth century, the household receipt book is also the repository of all medicinal cures and wisdom; here one can read how to prevent miscarrying, how to make Mrs Buster's powder for convulsions, to purge gently, to make vapour water, to cure deafness and the bite of a mad dog. And how to make 'Mr Whissellers pultice' which is good for any sore or swelling. These two books, at the cusp of the new century, reflect the last few hundred years, and in no way anticipate Mrs Raffald's sixty years later.

The first wildly successful cookery book of the eighteenth century was Eliza Smith's *The Compleat Housewife* (1727); it went through almost 100 editions and was published up until 1773. It included 500 receipts, and in 1742 it became the first cookery book to be published in America. She says of herself that she had been constantly employed in fashionable and noble families. If the soup she made for them on fast days is anything to go by they sacrificed nothing. This, in fact is the nub, as her recipes still reflect medieval concepts of luxurious fast day dishes, mixing meat and fruit, of almonds and verjuice. Her noble families are surely of the old faith and of great piety. Eliza herself quotes the Bible with relish:

> That Esau was the first Cook I shall not presume to assert; for Abraham gave Order to dress a fatted Calf; but Esau is the first person mentioned that made any Advances beyond plain Dressing, as Boiling, Roasting etc. For tho' we find indeed that Rebeckah his Mother was accomplished with the Skill of making savoury Meat as well as he, yet whether he learned it from her, or she from him, is a Question, too knotty for me to determine.

Quite Eliza, so why mention it? Yet the mixture of Biblical quotation and kitchen lore was obviously loved by her eighteenth-century public.

A fasting day 'soop' is made from spinach, chervil, sorrel and lettuce with herbs sautéed in butter, then simmered in water with pepper and salt and an onion stuck with cloves, a stale French roll cut into slices and pistachio nuts. It continues to simmer, then is thickened with eight egg yolks mixed with a little white wine and the juice of a lemon; a toasted French roll is then placed in the bowl, the soup is poured over and it is garnished with ten or twelve poached eggs.

Both a lamb pie and a chicken pie are made with the addition of fruit, damsons, gooseberries, citron and lemon chips, all mixed with butter. A sauce or caudle is added afterwards made from sack, white wine, verjuice and sugar. A white leach is made with milk, almonds and rosewater, set with isinglass and flavoured with grains of musk and oil of mace or cinnamon. These are medieval recipes still alive and well in the 1720s.

To mumble rabbits and chickens, she suggests stuffing them with parsley, onion and liver, and boiling them. When they are half done, the flesh should be torn from the bones in flakes, and with the stuffing boiled with white wine, butter, nutmeg; it is then thickened with a little flour and served on sippets. This is another medieval recipe unchanged from the twelfth century. To collar salmon, Hannah Glasse gives a recipe almost word for word the same as Eliza Smith's. Recipes on how to collar beef, veal, or venison, were all popular, because it is a way of keeping a dish for some days. A strip of meat or fish is beaten thin, a stuffing made and spread over it, then it is rolled up and tied, and poached in a pickling liquor where it is left to remain until cold. It is kept in the liquor and served sliced with some of the liquor. A goose, turkey or leg of mutton *à la daube* is a recognisable recipe that we might use still today. On the other hand, we have quite forgotten the popularity of cucumbers cooked in butter and served with meat. Eliza Smith gives a method of potting swans, which will also do for goose, duck, beef or hare. She colours milk with marigolds when making cheese.

She gives a direction when pickling samphire 'to pick your samphire from dead or withered branches'; this, of course, is rock samphire which is no longer picked and eaten. Today we eat marsh samphire.

One of the most impressive cookery writers of the century was Martha Bradley. *The British Housewife, or the Cook, Housewife or Gardener's companion*, by Mrs Martha Bradley, late of Bath was published in 1760, in two volumes, with 725 pages in all. Unlike earlier cookery writers, Mrs Bradley explains everything in great detail beginning with the produce itself: for example, caviare is the roe of the sturgeon, prepared and dried. Then she tells you how it is caught, prepared and sent all over Russia. Capers and 'cayan' pepper are dealt with as efficiently. She is highly informative and is the first real educator in food for the literate classes. Her book is well indexed and could be used today as a food encyclopaedia of general interest. (She does, however, make occasional mistakes, such as believing that soy sauce was made from a purplish mushroom with a wrinkled surface resembling that of morel.)

The importance of Mrs Bradley's work is that it is the first and only book before Mrs Raffald's which is written for the British housewife as opposed to an English gentlewoman. One can imagine it being the kitchen standby of an Irish housekeeper of a great estate in County Wicklow, or being read with avidity by the wife of a sea captain in Swansea, or a doctor's wife in Edinburgh. This is food for the literate masses and classless, written in an easy style, succinct and pragmatic. Mrs Bradley is interested in communicating information and does so brilliantly. She is incredibly comprehensive as she writes: 'directing what is to be done in the providing for, conducting and managing a family throughout the year'. She goes on to tell you what the book contains:

> . . . a general account of fresh provisions of all kinds. Of the several foreign articles for the Table, pickled or otherwise preserved; and the different kinds of spices, salts, sugars and other ingredients used in pickling and preserving at home: showing what each is, whence it is brought, and what are its qualities and uses. Together with the nature of all kinds of foods and the method of suiting them to different constitutions. A bill of fare for each month, the art of marketing . . .

And so she goes on. Was there anything that the British housewife needed to know that wasn't in this book? What of the recipes, however? If this book is a great social leveller the recipes should be as practical as the advice, and here surely are recipes that dispense with the frivolities.

Her recipe for boiling any fowl, even a turkey, is simple enough: put in enough water, she directs; too little water makes the bird look brown and dirty. A chicken needs only 15 to 20 minutes but a turkey will take about an hour. (All birds then were far smaller than intensively farmed poultry now.) A fowl to be roasted is basted with butter and dredged with a little flour, and that is all. (Flour had now been fully accepted as a thickening medium.) To roast a fowl pheasant fashion is to truss it like a pheasant (keeping the head on), lard it with bacon and serve it with a sauce associated with pheasant. People are fooled by this dish, she tells us, and when they have both real and fake pheasant on the table, often prefer the fowl. Here, we suddenly see, is a writer on the side of the kitchen staff, ready and eager to deceive her employers, the wealthy or the gentry. She does also give a recipe for roasting a good, fine fowl, which should be stuffed with oysters mixed with a glass of white wine; then the fowl is buttered and larded with bacon before it is roasted. She tells us how to boil a goose which will need an hour and the water merely has the addition of salt and parsley. It is served with cabbage – 'let them be well boiled' – and she finishes the recipe by telling us that a boiled salted goose served with pickled red cabbage is an excellent dish. She gives a recipe for a stuffed shoulder of mutton in which the stuffing is composed of oysters, anchovies, hard-boiled eggs, onion, nutmeg, thyme and winter savory; it is served with a sauce of red wine and oyster liquor, which one knows would be marvellous. And there are many other recipes that strike one as delicious. In her brisk manner she has a way of cutting through what she considers to be unnecessary; she gives a recipe for a goose *à la daube* which is not what we would recognise as such, but is merely a goose served cold seasoned with lemons, bay and chives, having been boiled and wrapped in a napkin.

She finished that recipe with this observation: 'The French dress partridges, pheasants and other Game this way but the tame fowls do better.' Now we know, Mrs Bradley has spoken. Her suspicion of French influences is also seen in her explanation of the 'cullis'. 'These are a particular article of the French Cookery, which we have not named in the preceding months, because victuals made to be dressed in a plain way do very well without them; but they are essential to made dishes, and will be found very useful on many other occasions.' She then gives various recipes that are similar to the ones Patrick Lamb gave fifty years earlier. So the French get a rather grudging acknowledgement that the cullis is not really essential to good food but at times can be useful in ragouts and rich soups. It is the expense, of course, that alarms the English cooks, she writes of a ragout of cabbage: 'The French are so extravagant at their great tables that they use such a ragoo as this as a sauce.'

Is Mrs Bradley guilty of over-cooking the vegetables, however? Her advice on savoys, cabbages and cauliflowers is to boil until the stalks are tender. Her further advice on cabbage is after this to chop it up, mix it with butter and boil for another five minutes, then to send it to the table mashed. Little doubt there that the cabbage would stink of sulphur while it cooked, or come to the table soggy. Historically throughout northern Europe all brassicas were cooked slowly in the cauldron for great lengths of time; the tradition was that cabbages should be well and thoroughly cooked. However, Mrs Bradley observes in her recipe for cauliflower that the boiling time must be watched carefully, for over-cooking was a common fault. Also, her recipe for cooking spinach is perfect: she observes it needs no water added, just a little salt and it would be cooked in a few minutes; then it should be drained and sent to table with a little butter.

Mrs Bradley and Mrs Raffald are celebrating both the birth and instant flowering of the British cuisine; they are solidly bourgeois, pragmatic, sensible; they eschew time-wasting in the kitchen, dislike fussiness, and yet value clear, distinct flavours and the quality of their produce. They are not much influenced by any French notions of gastronomy; in fact both ignore it, yet they are open to ideas from British travellers and colonialists. Mrs Raffald gives a recipe for Indian Pickle or Piccalillo and one in imitation of Indian Bamboo. Mrs Bradley lists and describes many imported foods, including dried mushrooms and truffles; the latter which she regards as so tasteless they are a waste of time. These women writers were Protestant and churchgoers; in fact it is very likely that Mrs Raffald was in the Collegiate church at Manchester when Ann Lee created a rumpus, for which she was fined and jailed before she left for America to found the American Shakers.[32]

The Country Estate

The recipes and style of cooking on country estates were based on a supply of fresh country produce which was unequalled in its richness, variety and flavour. Indeed, with this kind of produce there was little need of culinary adornment, for it was cooked plainly and briefly. In *Humphry Clinker* Tobias Smollett's country gentleman character, Matthew Bramble, makes an oft-quoted boast that sums up the richness of country produce:

> At Brambleton Hall . . . my table is furnished from my own ground; my five year old mutton, fed on the fragrant herbage of the mountains that might vie with venison in juice and flavour; my delicious veal, fattened with nothing but the mother's milk, that fills the dish with gravy; my poultry from the barn door, that never knew confinement, but when they were at roost; my rabbits panting from the warren; my game fresh from the moors; my trout and salmon struggling from the stream; oysters from their native banks . . . My salads, roots, and pot herbs, my own garden yields in plenty and perfection; the produce of the natural soil prepared by moderate cultivation. The same soil affords all the different fruits which England may call her own, so that my dessert is every day gathered from the tree; my dairy flows with the nectarious tides of milk and cream, from whence we derive abundance of excellent butter, curds and cheese; and the refuse fattens my pigs, that are destined for hams and bacon.

Bramble then goes on to make a point by point comparison with what is available in London, unfavourable in all respects to the city.

Gilbert White began work on his garden at Selborne in 1749 and the following year was planting forty different varieties of vegetables, including artichokes, endives, mustard and cress, white broccoli, skirret and scorzonera, marrowfat peas, leeks, squashes, cucumbers, all manner of lettuces and a crop of onions to pickle. He became obsessed with growing melons and by the mid-1750s had dug out a hot bed, referred to as a melon ground; it was 45 ft long and used thirty cart loads of dung annually.[33]

When living in Oxford he would purchase salad leaves from the Botanical Gardens to complement lobsters, crabs and oysters, olives, almonds, Seville oranges and strawberries, for all of which he had a great liking. Back home he was energetic in planting out asparagus beds, sowing his first potatoes and tending to the cucumbers on the hot bed. He wrote of potatoes: 'They have prevailed by means of premiums within these twenty years only, and are much esteemed here now by the poor, who would scarcely have ventured to taste them in the last reign.' In 1761 he planted a large number of fruit trees and made a fruit wall for his espaliers.

In Stuart times it had become the custom to build a kitchen garden with stillrooms in each corner, handy for processing the large number of medicinal herbs that were grown. Sometimes these plots, still planned on the four field system of medieval pattern, had earth walls planted with wallflowers; this was common in the north, though in the south it was more customary to build the walls out of brick or stone. Nevertheless, Gilbert White builds earth and straw walls and remarks how attractive they are.

We cannot but be impressed at the great range of vegetables and fruit grown on the eighteenth-century country estate. There were cabbages, in numerous varieties to obtain a succession from April to October, such as red cabbages, the Aberdeen red, the dwarf and the large, five varieties of savoy, fourteen of borecole (these are more brassicas, but cavolo nero is now sometimes referred to as borecole); Russian kale which was sometimes blanched like seakale, cauliflowers, broccoli, eighteen varieties of peas including sugar snap, ten varieties of broad bean, several varieties of kidney bean and scarlet runners, turnips, sometimes grown as seedlings and used in salads (it was Charles I's favourite salad, so John Evelyn tells us), a new sort of violet carrot, parsnips, beetroots, skirrets, scorzonera and salsify (sometimes eaten like asparagus in the spring), radish seed pods used in salads and pickles, spinach, white and red chard, orach, New Zealand spinach brought back by Joseph Banks, Good King Henry (a relation of spinach, the tops of which were blanched in the spring), and sorrel, used in soups, sauces and salads. Then there were onions, leeks, garlic and shallots. It was thought that more asparagus was grown in London than anywhere else in the world; some growers had over 100 acres in cultivation in Deptford and Mortlake. Globe artichokes were grown in three varieties: the French conical, the globe and the dwarf globe. There were cardoons and rampion (the roots were eaten raw like radish and its leaves used in winter salads); alexander was going out of favour but celery was grown instead; celeriac was used for soups. For salads and flavourings they grew and used chicory, mustard and cress, lamb's lettuce, water cress, burnet, wood sorrel, purslane, parsley, tarragon, fennel, chervil, dill, horse radish, nasturtiums, marigolds, borage, balm, thyme, sage, clary, rock samphire, wormwood, liquorice, mint, marjoram, savory, basil, rosemary, angelica, anise, coriander, rue, caraway, hyssop, camomile, elecampane, tansy and costmary.

As for fruit, quinces were used for marmalade, for making tarts and for flavouring apple puddings; medlars were bletted before being eaten or used for jelly. They grew 140 varieties of peaches and nectarines, seven of apricots, 100 of plums, forty of cherry. Mulberries were grown under glass, gooseberries grew wonderfully well in Lancashire. Currants were grown in fifteen different varieties and raspberries in nine; they grew the hautbois strawberry (*fragaria elatior*), as well as alpine and wood strawberries. Joseph Banks had introduced the cranberry. Five varieties of walnuts were grown, as well as the sweet chestnuts and filberts. Pineapples were being cultivated under glass, as well as grapes, peaches, melons, figs and cucumbers, while oranges and lemons had their own elegant buildings. At a garden in Salcombe, Devonshire, there were orange trees all over 100 years old and producing fruit as large and fine as any in Portugal.

Of course all this cultivation relied on a large number of gardening servants who worked hard for a small wage. The raised beds, the hot bed, the large number of glass houses, the paths, borders and hedges all required constant attention and a head gardener who was skilled in a job that required scientific precision at propagation, pruning, fumigation, forcing, delaying ripening, storage and packing, companion planting, espaliers and fan-training.

Every country house had a kitchen garden on which they relied for their produce. Even the most modest of households like Jane Austen's home had its hens, pigs, sheep or cow and a wealth of game birds, hares and rabbits that could be shot or snared almost on their doorstep and if not the sea coast, at least a lake or river nearby. This was the century when all these foods met on the table and were free of the commercial instant mixes that would so infect the cooking of the following centuries; the table was also free of the imported foods, which would in due course arrive across oceans to dilute the harvest of local foods on which all then lived. If the squire was fortunate enough to possess a skilled and experienced cook who had read her Mrs Raffald, Glasse or Bradley then the food served must have been notable. There was a pride in the Englishness of this cuisine, which crops up in novels and plays of the period: there was distaste for 'made-up' dishes, and the liking for plain roasted food with a sharp sauce seemed honest and true, reflecting values which were being communicated to the rest of the world. Nevertheless I believe this idea of 'plain' was more an abstract concept than a reality: the food in the cookery books is highly and imaginatively seasoned, and the British male's palate was well attuned to these additions, as will be seen from the recipe below.

Another hindrance to our perceiving the true glories of the eighteenth-century diet is that when we read an account of it, all the colourful gustatory details are missing and the food strikes one as banal, because of the personality of the diarist. I don't believe it to be so: for example, if pork sausages are mentioned, we are not told that they were flavoured with spinach, rosemary, sage, oysters, mace, shallots, onions, cloves and mace. This, however, is a recipe of Henry Howard's from *The British Cook's Companion* of 1729 and very good it sounds.

Parson Woodforde

James Woodforde was born in 1740, and was five years old when Bonnie Prince Charlie's army reached Derby; his father, rector of Ansford and vicar of Castle Cary, would have been greatly alarmed and that concern and outrage must have spread through the house. Certainly the adult James in his reactions to events like the French Revolution takes a solidly conservative view utterly representative of his class and cloth. James went to New College, Oxford, in 1759, was ordained a deacon in 1763 and became a curate in Somerset in the same year. In the following year he was ordained a priest at Wells Cathedral. From 1776 to 1803, the year he died aged 63, he lived at Weston Longeville Parsonage in Norfolk, looked after by his niece, Nancy, for he never married. He began his diary the year before he left for Oxford and continued it until a few months before his death; its value to us is that often he recorded what he ate and drank at home, and more particularly when he went out to dine with grander neighbours or enjoyed festive dinners with the bishop, or at his Oxford college. It allows us to see in this one instance what the middle classes, comfortably off but not in the least affluent (he kept two maidservants, two menservants and a boy) ate everyday.

How far had Mrs Bradley and Mrs Raffald influenced the cooking in the kitchen of a country parsonage? What cookery books were in the kitchen to be referred to? Did his niece use one to make her cakes, tarts and puddings? We do not know for certain the answer to these enquiries, but if we look at the food eaten it tells us something.

At Oxford in August 1763 Woodforde dines at High Table 'upon a neck of venison and a Breast made into a Pasty, a Ham and Fowls and two Pies. It is a venison Feast which we have once a year about this time.' In Somerset he plants in his garden in February, peas, beans, radishes and Spanish onions. In 1766, while out to dinner, he tastes a pineapple for the first time, but unlike Evelyn he does not comment on how he found it. There is, in fact, a dearth of evaluation on the food he eats, no analysis of taste or criticism of a sauce, for example. His main criticisms are kept for his servants and almost his most adverse comment upon them is to find them 'saucy'.

In March the following year he starts to take a decoction of alder stick in water: 'I do really think that I have gained great benefit from it, half a pint each morning; it must be near the colour of Claret.' Alas, he does not say why he takes it, but then he is reticent and, sadly for us, discreet. Red alder (*Alnus serrulata*) was taken for diarrhoea, indigestion and dyspepsia. A week later he is bled, just two ounces of blood for which he paid 2s and 6d but comments: 'My blood was verey rich and, therefore proper to be bled.' On 5 April 1768 his tenants paid him their rents and he gives them dinner: a loin of veal roasted and a good plum pudding. He goes to a dance two weeks later and is up until two in the morning; he had a dinner of roasted shoulder of mutton and a plum pudding as well as veal cutlets, frill'd potatoes, cold tongue, ham and cold roast beef and eggs in their shells. In September a friend from Oxford stays, to whom he gives hashed mutton and a roasted neck of pork. In October 1770 he gives a dinner for five friends, who have:

> fine tench caught from my brother's pond, Ham and 3 Fowls boiled, a plumb pudding; a couple of Ducks roasted, a roasted neck of pork, a plumb tart, an apple tart, Pears, Apples and Nutts after dinner; White wine and Red, Beer and Cyder. Coffee and Tea in the evening at six

o'clock. Hashed fowl and Duck and Eggs and Potatoes etc for Supper. We did not dine until four o'clock – nor supped till ten.

In 1775 he took the Oath of Abjuration to which every employee of Church and State had to swear; this ritual oath ensured that no descendants of James II would ascend the throne. If Hannah Glasse cooked for churchmen or civil servants she would have been aware of the state fear of being overrun by Jacobites and surrendering the country back to Roman Catholicism. Woodforde, of course, was happy reading the 39 Articles in Weston Church before a crowded congregation and declaring 'my assent and consent to the Liturgy'. In 1776 he moved to Weston Longeville where he took on the new maids and, as we have seen, agreed that part of their pay would be tea twice a day. In December his tenants visited to pay him their tithe (one-tenth of their income); he gave them a good dinner, they sat down at two to drink punch and ale, six bottles of wine and a gallon and a half of rum; they have roasted beef, a boiled leg of mutton and 'plumb puddings in plenty'. One hopes they thought their tithe dinner was worth the loss of a tenth of their produce, but like their parson, one doubts that they questioned the status quo, though such questions were being asked elsewhere in America and across the Channel.

In 1777 Woodforde goes to friends for a Rotation Club meeting where he dines on another boiled leg of mutton, a batter pudding and a couple of ducks. In March he goes fishing and catches two brace of pike, one fine perch, some gudgeons and a few flat fish. In September some friends dine with him and he gives them fine tench taken from his pond, a boiled rump of beef, a roasted goose and a pudding. One of the ladies, a Mrs Howes, 'found great fault with many things especially about stewing the fish – she could not eat a bit of them with such sauce etc.' In May 1778 he catches 'the largest pike, it weighed 7 pounds', and at Lenswade Bridge a few days later he catches another: 'a prodigious fine pike which weighed 8 pound and a half and it had in his belly another pike of about a pound'. With friends he drinks 'a dish of tea'.

His dinners generally seem still to be structured in two courses, though as we have seen, the courses seem similar. In September he spends the day with his grand neighbours, the Custances, and he eats there for dinner 'some common fish, a leg of mutton roasted and a baked pudding', all in the first course, while a roast duck, 'a Meat Pye, Eggs and Tart' were in the second. For supper 'We had a brace of Partridges roasted, some cold tongue, Potatoes in Shells and Tarts.' In May 1779 the Howes and others return to dine and he gives them a dish of 'maccarel', three young chickens boiled and some bacon, roasted neck of pork and a hot gooseberry pie. They laugh so much because they have sent Mrs Howes to Coventry that the Parson gets the 'Hickupps'. Obviously Mrs Howes was complaining of the fish again. One wishes he had been more forthcoming. In October he dines with friends and has for dinner a boiled leg of pork, a roasted turkey and a couple of ducks; for supper a couple of boiled fowls, a roasted pheasant and some cold things. 'Dinner and Supper served up in China Dishes and Plates. Melons, Apples and Pears, Walnuts and small nuts for a desert'.

After church in January 1780 he dines with Sir Edward Bacon and company at the Calf's Head and has boiled fowl and tongue, a saddle of mutton roasted on the side table and a fine swan roasted with currant jelly sauce for the first course. He has for the second course a couple of wild fowls called dunfowls (small wading birds – dunlins), larks, blancmange, tarts and a good dessert of fruit which included a damson cheese. He comments: 'I never eat a bit of Swan before and I think it good eating with sweet sauce. The swan was killed 3 weeks before it was eat and yet not the lest bad taste in it.' The next year he visits a friend in Dereham who lodges over a barber's and has dinner with him; a fine lobster and mutton steaks were sent over from the King's Arms. In May he entertains the Howes again and others to dinner; he gives them his great pike which they roasted with a 'Pudding in its Belly', with some 'boiled Trout, Perch, Tench, Eel and Gudgeon fryed, a Neck of Mutton boiled and a plain Pudding for Mrs Howes'. The company were all very impressed by the largeness of the pike and how moist it was. He gave another pike to Mr Howes when they left. One hopes that Mrs Howes coped with all the fish at dinner and was grateful for the gift. The next month in June he entertains the Custances with a couple of boiled chickens, a tongue, a boiled leg of mutton with capers and batter pudding for first course; for the second he gives them a couple of roasted ducks with green peas, some artichokes, tarts and blancmange. After dinner he offers them almonds, raisins, oranges and strawberries. He comments that the peas and strawberries were the first gathered by him that year – it is 8 June. Two months later they dine at New Hall with the Custances and have a ham and two fowls boiled, some young beans, veal collops and hash mutton for the first course; for the second, a roast duck, baked puddings and apple tart. In January of the next year his niece, Nancy, is very busy all morning making cakes, tarts, custards and jellies for an entertainment. At the tithe audit in 1882 he serves a dinner of salt fish, a leg of mutton boiled with capers, a knuckle of veal, a pig's face, a fine sirloin of beef roasted and plenty of plum puddings. These, which are an obvious favourite at the Parsonage, are boiled suet puddings with dried fruit and spices; Mrs Glasse flavours hers with ginger and nutmeg, makes it with milk and eggs and boils it for five hours.

In April 1783 the Parson dines with friends, including the Howes, and has a leg of lamb boiled, a piece of roasted beef, a baked plum pudding, some crabs, tarts, raspberry creams and hung beef, grated. In June he dined with the Custances and had beans and bacon, a chine of roasted mutton, a giblet pie, hashed goose, a rabbit roasted with young peas, tarts, pudding and jellies. In August he enjoys a rather grander dinner of perch and trout, a saddle of mutton roasted, beans and bacon, a couple of fowls boiled, patties and some white soup in the first course; on the second course he has roasted pigeons and duck, 'piggs pettytoes', sweetbreads, raspberry cream, tarts and puddings and pippins. Mrs Raffald gives a recipe on how to dress a 'Pig's Pettitoes', which are boiled suckling pigs trotters: she makes a gravy with the heart, liver and lights, then shreds them small into the liquor; she adds white wine and lemon, butter and flour, flavours with nutmeg and thickens with egg yolk and cream. She lays bread (sippets) upon a platter, splits the boiled trotters in two, lays them on top of the bread skin side up and pours the sauce over them.

When the Parson gets up especially early, he breakfasts on mutton broth. He always eats especially well when he's with the Custances, even if they are all travelling; on one occasion they all dined with a mutual friend, Mr Micklethwaite, where they have 'a very genteel dinner. Soals and Lobster sauce. Spring Chicken boiled and a tongue, a Piece of rost Beef, Soup, a fillet of Veal rosted with Morells and Truffles, and Pigeon Pye for the first course – sweetbreads, a green Goose and Peas, Apricot Pye, Cheesecakes, Stewed Mushrooms and Trifle.' He was impressed by Mr Micklethwaite's silver buckles which cost between '7 and 8 pounds'. In August 1790 he sends a dozen very fine apricots from his best tree, an Anson, to the Custances and they send back some fine black grapes from Mackay's Hot House; Mackay was a gardener in Norwich. That Christmas he eats roast beef and plum puddings. At the tithe dinner the following year they get a sirloin of roasted beef, a boiled marrow bone of beef, a boiled leg of mutton with caper sauce, a couple of rabbits with onion sauce, some salt fish boiled with parsnips and egg sauce and plenty of plum puddings.

In August 1794 he has 'a very genteel dinner' with friends and neighbours at Hungate Lodge:

> First Course at the upper end, stewed Tench, Veal Soup, best part of a Rump Beef boiled, 2 roast Chicken and a Ham, Harrico Mutton, Custard Puddings, backed Mutton Pies, Mashed Potatoes in 3 Scollop Shells brown'd over. Roots. 2 Dishes. Second Course. At the upper end, Rabbits fricasseed, at the Lower End Couple of Ducks rosted, Trifle in the Middle, blamange, Cheesecakes, Maccaroni, and small Raspberry Tartlets. Desert of Fruit mostly that sent by me to them, Peaches, Nectarines and three kinds of Plumbs.

Both Mrs Glasse and Mrs Raffald give recipes on how to 'harrico' mutton; they use the neck and cut it into chops which are fried, then the meat is stewed with root vegetables, celery and asparagus are added, the sauce reduced, and then it is served. Mrs Glasse adds chestnuts and herbs to hers. Mrs Glasse's custard pudding is made in a wooden bowl with a pint of cream, a little flour, five yolks and two whites of egg, salt, nutmeg, three spoonfuls of sack, sugar to taste, a cloth is tied over the bowl and it is boiled for half an hour. The pudding is turned out onto a dish and melted butter is poured over it. For her rabbit fricassée, the rabbit is cut into small pieces, then egg and breadcrumbed, flavoured with mace and nutmeg, then fried in butter; once done a rich red wine gravy is made as a sauce. How interesting to see that blancmange, that relic from an early tenth-century Arab recipe that was to become such a medieval favourite, is eaten quite often. Mrs Raffald gives a recipe for a clear blancmange, which is calf's foot jelly mixed with cream, almonds and rosewater (a kind of distillation of the source recipe though not suitable for a fast day) and two others made with isinglass, one dyed green with spinach juice.

On one level there is something uninspiring about Parson Woodforde and his companions' diet; there is far too much of it and surely the repetition of a variety of roasted and boiled meats day in and day out would become tedious. There can be no doubt, however, that it is representative of the age. The middle classes lived well and here is the proof of it. Fish came from the ponds, rivers and estuaries of East Anglia. Perch and trout are thought rather grand but eels are simply fried. Tench is eaten frequently, but it is a fish we never see now; it is a member of the carp family and weighs 4 lb or more. Pike is also served whenever the Parson caught one; these fish are either boiled or stewed, and served plain, for once when the tench came with a sauce Mrs Howes complained and would not eat it. They often eat sea fish like sole and mackerel, and salt fish is served quite often, especially for the tithe dinners – perhaps to remind the tenants of their status.

They also eat venison and game birds, although mostly the Parson serves beef, mutton and veal plainly cooked and with a separate sauce, referred to as a gravy. If the recipes in the cookery books were followed, of course, this sauce would be intensely flavoured, made from red wine, lemons, herbs and spices. They also eat young chicken and geese boiled, ducks, hens, capons and older geese roasted. There are very few made dishes like the fricassée of rabbit, which are made for special occasions. Plum puddings are served so often they must have been making these daily; egg custards of various kinds are the next choice. Root vegetables appear frequently, but the summer vegetables are a source of some excitement; the first garden peas are always recorded and so are the cucumbers and lettuces, so salads must have been enjoyed, as was the fresh fruit, the plums, nectarines and strawberries.

This food because of its freshness and its simplicity of preparation and cooking would not have been dull to the diners themselves (or indeed to us now if we were eating it); it is possibly that Parson Woodforde fails to bring it to life. We do not know how well the food was cooked, of course. I cannot help but think of William Verrall's condemnation of some aspects of English ham: 'We serve it up generally not half soaked, salt as brine, and almost as hard as a flint, and our sauce most times nothing more than a little greasy cabbage and melted butter, and sometimes for garnish an ugly fowl or two, or half a dozen pigeons badly trussed.'[34] When Woodforde ate dinner alone there was of course less food; later in his life, when he recorded his food daily, it is just 'boiled beef and a suet pudding' or 'Veal soup, Veal Collops, and Bacon and a brace of Partridges roasted and Apple Dumplins',[35] but there's no doubt that his diet tended towards stodge. Overeating, obesity and gout were afflictions of the age, being a well-known target of the caricaturist.

There is comfort and security in these meals; the security funds the indignation Woodforde feels when the King is mobbed by an angry crowd as he travels in his coach from St James's Palace; it fuels the horror he expressed when Marie Antoinette is guillotined, 'all anarchy and confusion', and he is content to pay heavy taxes in order to fight the rebels in the American colonies. James Woodforde never questions such matters as the Rotten Boroughs returning members, that a theft of over 40s is punishable by death, that the slave trade is nothing but a respectable institution, that men can be press-ganged into the navy, that the Catholics are hated and feared by honest God-fearing people. He is confined within his limitations, just as his diet is; he never ventures to eat anything alien to him – there is no whisper of garlic for example, for that belongs to France, to people who are the enemy and have been for hundreds of years. Once dining out he had a dish with morels and truffles in it (dried and imported) but they bring forth no comment. The cookery books of the time are not without imagination and enterprise; indeed, they are full of it. Though the Parson goes hare-coursing, however, does he ever eat it jugged or 'florendined' (boned, stuffed and rolled), does he take his partridges paned (minced, flavoured and baked in moulds) or have his beef in olives or his lamb fricasséed? No, he does not, yet these dishes appear in the cookery books of the time. It is not that his kitchen skills are limited, for servants and his niece Nancy wish to please him and would contrive to cook any amount of delicious dishes for him; it is simply that he is content with the plain fare he eats, or does not much notice it if it isn't plain so cannot record it. Basically Parson Woodforde is a plain man, but we fall into an error if we think the food he eats is as plain and uninteresting as it sounds.

CHAPTER 9

Industry and Empire

When did the quality of British food begin to decline, for by the early twentieth century the reputation of our food was depressingly low? How early in the nineteenth century did the seeds of that decline germinate? Abraham Hayward in his *Art of Dining* (1852) thought that gastronomy had emigrated to England in the years following Waterloo. The chef Louis Eustache Ude, writing in 1813, thought that 'Cookery in England, when well done, is superior to that of any country in the world.' So it would appear that the first quarter of the nineteenth century won international gastronomic approval, but perhaps the salient phrase in Ude's remark is the qualification 'when well done'. This chapter and those following will attempt to pursue what went wrong with British cooking, the reasons for its decline and exactly when this began to happen.

A Leap Forward
The nineteenth century was one of great expansion and change, which succeeded in making the rich richer (often beyond the dreams of avarice) and the poor poorer, sinking to depths of neglect, exploitation and the inevitable malnutrition, which earlier had only been experienced in medieval famines. This was pinpointed by a writer in 1840: 'Society has been startled by the discovery of a fearful fact, that as wealth increases, poverty increases in a faster ratio and that in almost exact proportion to the advance of one portion of society in opulence, intelligence and civilisation, has been the retrogression of another and more numerous class towards misery, degradation and barbarism.'[1]

Britain was the home of the industrial revolution and of a triumphant bourgeoisie; both Carlyle and Marx agreed that the successful industrialist was the new aristocrat. From the great period of canal building which had reached its peak in the 1790s, there was a sense among the affluent of an immense leap forward, which seemingly had no end, and where human and animal strength was to be replaced by machines. At the same time there was this astonishing feeling that the country was shrinking: distance was no longer a formidable problem; food could travel now from one end of the country to the other within a short space of time; and new methods of travelling, by water, road and rail, succeeded each other within decades. Firstly there was the canal system, which looked forward to linking great rivers like the Severn, Mersey, Thames and Trent; the Leeds and Liverpool canals were joined; and the coal from the Duke of Bridgewater's coal mines at Worsley in Lancashire could be brought to Manchester by barge. Secondly, there were improved roads and coaches: in 1754 there were six firms operating coaches from Manchester to London, a journey that took four days; thirty years later the time had been cut by half and by 1816 there were 200 land carriers transporting goods to and from Manchester in wagons and carts; by 1830 there were fifty-four passenger coaches travelling every day. Thirdly, the railway network began between Liverpool and Manchester in 1830. Between 1825 and 1835, Railway Acts were passed permitting railway buildings, and by 1838 there were already 500 miles of track. But this was nothing. In the next four years there was a railway boom, when fifty-four companies concerned with nearly 1,500 miles of track were approved; and so the network grew. The most notorious of the railway contractors, Thomas Brassey, left over £3,000,000 on his death in 1870.[2] There were plenty of critics of this new method of travelling who thought it far too democratic, and that it would lead heaven knows where. 'A dangerous tendency to equality,' was Disraeli's phrase in his novel *Sybil* (1845), and the headmaster of Rugby School, Dr Arnold, thought it was 'destroying feudalism forever'.

Industry had already changed the British Isles irrevocably. A German visitor in 1844, J.G. Kohl, wrote of 'black roads winding through verdant fields, the long trains of waggons heavily laden with black treasures . . . burning mounds of coal scattered over plain, black pit mouths, and here and there an unadorned Methodist chapel', and he was speaking of the countryside. The new towns were another deep scar upon what was once farming land. A visitor to Manchester in 1814 wrote:

> The cloud of coal vapour may be observed from afar. The houses are blackened by it. The river which flows through Manchester, is so filled with waste dye-stuffs that it resembles a dyer's vat.

Government policy was determined by manufacturing interests; a strong belief in free trade was ignored when the British home market might be damaged by imports.

In 1750 there had only been two cities in Britain with more than 50,000 inhabitants – London and Edinburgh. By 1801 there were eight and in 1851 there were twenty-nine. There was a sudden population increase of eighteen per cent between 1811 and 1831 spread all over the country, but mostly in the manufacturing towns; many migrants flooded into the towns from the country so that by 1851 many villages were smaller than they had been thirty years before. Between 1700 and 1801 the population rose from 6^1/$_4$ million to 10^1/$_2$ million – at least a tenth of whom were paupers.

London, by the middle of the century, had fifteen per cent of the population and an insatiable demand for food and fuel, which transformed the south and east of England into one huge larder; London drew regular supplies into its maw not only from them but also from remoter parts of Wales and England. The productivity of the coal mines of Newcastle was thus stimulated. We were the first industrial society, far in advance of our neighbours across the Channel. As in the example of the

Reformation and the Civil War, such factors changed us irrevocably from other European countries even again to the extent of what we ate.

The Disappearance of Peasant Cooking

What was perhaps one of the most startling differences between Britain and the continent was the decline of the peasantry in Britain.[3] The growth of a market economy had already undermined local self-sufficiency and enmeshed the village in a network of cash sales, for it was not immune to the popularity of the imported foods, such as tea, coffee and sugar. The smallholder who cultivated his own plot had become a rarity, except in the Celtic fringe and in other out of the way areas in the north and west. By 1750 the land had been swallowed up through the enclosures acts into the hands of a few thousand landowners. They leased their land to tens of thousands of tenant farmers, who operated it with the labour of some hundreds of thousands of farm labourers who were nearly always hired. Also much of the work of the small industries, such as cloth, hosiery, and metal goods, was sent out to rural workers, turning the peasant into a cash earner. Villages now became full of knitters and weavers working in their single cottage room. Deprived of the ability to grow vegetables or keep hens, and in fact having no time for either, the cottage artisan worked long hours and lived on a diet that was little better than his cousin in the industrial town.

What the change had wrought was to erase the English rural cuisine; there were now no ingredients for the soup or pottage flavoured with wild greens, thickened with dried peas or beans and if they were lucky a bacon hock bone to give added lustre and flavour. Eliza Acton, who was born in 1799, must have been aware of this, for she notices that the making of soup seems to have entirely disappeared: 'The art of preparing good, wholesome, palatable soups, without great expense, which is so well understood in France, and in other countries where they form part of the daily food of all classes of the people, has hitherto been very much neglected in England.' And she further adds a note: 'The inability of servants to prepare delicately and well even a little broth suited to an invalid, is often painfully evident in cases of illness, not only in common English life, but where the cookery is supposed to be of a superior order.' The servants, of course, came from that very class that had no ingredients or heating to boil such a soup; they had gone into service in order to survive. A hundred years before Eliza Acton, Mrs Glasse had given over twenty recipes for soups, and Mrs Raffald had started her book with a chapter upon them. In *The Cook's Oracle* (1817) Dr Kitchiner includes a chapter on broths and soups, but complains that the English soup has an excess of spice and not enough roots. For the affluent at least soup was surely still one of the dishes amongst the first course at dinner, but if we are to believe Eliza Acton (and no one is a more honest observer than she) soup was hardly eaten in the first half of the century, although it is listed in all the cookery books. Although it appeared on menus soup as a separate course altogether at formal dinner parties did not appear until the 1850s. We shall return to these cookery books later.

What the farm labourers' hard-earned wages (and in the first three decades of the

1800s they were paid between 3s and 4s a week, when a 4 lb loaf cost 1s 2d and a pound of butter cost 9d) bought was tea, sugar, white bread and potatoes. Sir Frederick Eden comments in 1797: 'No vegetable is, or ever was, applied to such a variety of uses in the North of England as the potatoe; it is a constant standing dish, at every meal, breakfast excepted.'[4] But often they did not even have the means to cook the potatoes. Arthur Young, who wrote a series of forty-eight *Annals of Agriculture* between 1784 and 1809, commented in 1795, that: 'Our cottagers are without bedding, without fuel, unless stolen, and in many places inhabiting buildings, or rather ruins, which keep out neither wind nor rain . . . the whole is a disgrace to Christianity.' He goes on further: 'The common lands should be served out to them and they would save themselves with potatoes and a cow . . . a man with 10 children should have 4 and a half acres.'[5]

In his journeys on horseback in the 1820s around the counties near to London, Cobbett grows passionately indignant as to the plight of the rural labourer:

> I saw in one single farmyard here more food than enough for four times the inhabitants of the parish; and this yard did not contain a tenth, perhaps, of the produce of the parish; but, while the poor creatures that raise the wheat and the barley and cheese and the mutton and the beef are living upon potatoes, an accursed Canal comes kindly through the parish to convey away the wheat and all the good food to the tax eaters and their attendants in the Wen.[6]

He comments later that the more he sees good corn country, the more miserable and poverty-stricken are the labourers.

> The cause is this, the great, the big bull frog grasps all. In this beautiful island, every inch of land is appropriated by the rich.

Near Leicester he is horrified at the miserable sheds of the labourers beside the beautiful churches and impressive vicarages.

> Look at these hovels, made of mud and straw; bits of glass, or of old cast off windows, without frames or hinges frequently, but merely stuck in the mud wall. Enter them and look at the bits of chairs and stools; the wretched boards tacked together to serve for a table; the floor of pebble, broken brick, or of the bare ground . . .

As late as the 1830s over ninety per cent of the food consumed in Britain was grown in these islands. British farmers had to feed a rapidly expanding population. Before the Agricultural Revolution farmworkers were hired annually at the great hiring fairs; they lived in and ate at the farmer's table, so most of their income was in kind. Now the men were hired weekly, daily or by the job required and paid a miserable cash wage. The growing wealth of the tenant farmers themselves gave them socially mobile aspirations, which made them into remote and unfeeling masters; old familial bonds between employer and workman had been broken. Productivity rose, however, because more and more land was under the plough. In 1844 a Suffolk clergyman wrote of his villagers:

> They have no village green or common for active sports. Some thirty years ago, I am told, they had a right to a playground in a particular field, at certain seasons of the year, and were then celebrated for their football; but somehow or other this right has been lost and the field is now under the plough . . .[7]

The landed interests were paramount; the workforce could be exploited with the connivance of Parliament, until the Corn Laws were abolished in 1846. The game laws had now become of horrific severity; desperately hungry villagers were driven to poach, but landlords, parsons and farmers continued to erect barriers against trespass of private property. Gamekeepers patrolled the woods with firearms and the poachers, once caught, were either hanged or transported.

Success in business and sudden wealth were an open sesame to the ranks of the gentry, and a gentleman had a country house with a large estate and hundreds of acres of farmland; eventually he also had a seat in Parliament, perhaps a knighthood or peerage, while his wife became a lady instructed by dozens of etiquette books on how to behave in polite society, how to manage servants, and how to choose a menu for every occasion. Manners ruled this aggressively upwardly mobile society and manners began to exert rigid limitations upon the food eaten.

A New Town

As early as the 1770s Thomas Percival, a doctor and founder of the Manchester Literary and Philosophical Society, had estimated the population of Manchester to be over 29,000, making it one of the more crowded of urban settlements. The food needs of such a sudden congregation of this number required new supplies and distribution dependent on the resources of its near neighbours, the counties of Lancashire and Cheshire. A traveller in Lancashire in 1800 thought the agriculture was much neglected, while another observer of Cheshire thought that agricultural improvements had made but slow progress. It was thought by them that though farmers and their families worked hard in both counties they received scant return for their labours.

Early in the century, very little of the meat was produced locally, except for veal and pork; all the cattle were driven from a distance. Meat was a by-product of dairy farming, farmers sold their calves to butchers either soon after birth or after a few months' fattening and when the milk yield of cows fell they were slaughtered. Pigs were kept in the towns, sometimes in the houses themselves. Irish immigrants were blamed for this, but there is plenty of evidence from court records of pigs running wild in the streets so the practice was common before the major wave of Irish immigration.

Butchers sometimes kept herds of pigs next to their premises, but as more and more sanitary regulations crept in it became more difficult. In 1866 the Salford authorities complained of 'a passion or infatuation amongst many of the working classes for pig breeding and pig fattening', but ten years later they were managing to clear away the pigs without too much resistance. Sheep from the Welsh borders were brought into Cheshire and were fattened for sale to Manchester, and local farmers, seeing the profit, began also to graze flocks of sheep and to keep more pigs. The sheep that grazed on the high eastern Lancashire hills, and were considered half starved were now brought down into the valleys to be fattened. Farmers much further afield in Northumberland, Durham and Westmorland now felt it worthwhile to fatten their livestock for sale in the Midlands, though Manchester turned towards the Yorkshire grazing area of the Craven which had bred longhorn cattle.

With the advent of steam traffic across the Irish sea livestock could be sent from Dublin to Liverpool; a voyage of seven days was reduced to fourteen hours. These cattle and sheep had been fattened up in Ireland and were now ready to be slaughtered by the Liverpool butchers. By the late 1820s it was expected that the new railways would carry livestock; cattle and sheep wagons were built and a cattle station developed at Broad Green, Liverpool. However, railways met competition from the canals which had all been built in the previous century, and by the mid 1830s the number of pigs that travelled to Manchester from Liverpool was evenly divided between rail and water. Even by the 1850s about half of the cattle still travelled by road. The railways were more successful on long journeys from Scotland and the north, and by the 1860s more cattle were being eaten in Manchester from these regions than Ireland. Cumber-land and Westmorland also supplied bacon and ham. The lower paid workers, if they ate meat at all, bought the cheaper cuts of bacon or salted and pickled pork.

As we have seen, Lancashire had cultivated potatoes from the middle of the seventeenth century. Now they had a hungry market in Manchester and supplies of early potatoes, as well as main crop, were sent from the Wirral and Ormskirk to Liverpool and Manchester. They were producing a prodigious amount, something like 6,000-8,500 tons per year; some were exported to Ireland, however, and surplus was fed to livestock. Market gardens around Warrington and Altrincham had sprung up from the 1780s, producing cabbages, peas, beans, carrots, turnips and onions with a very small amount of cucumbers and asparagus. From the 1820s the wholesale price of potatoes, carrots, onions and turnips was reported in the local newspapers and until 1846 the price was low and unchanged; the potato blight which struck then made prices rocket, but from 1850 the price fell again. From the 1850s onwards, the railways brought in supplies of peas from Evesham, Yorkshire and Nottinghamshire, and apples from Worcestershire and Kent; the affluent in Manchester, a growing number with industry booming, now also bought supplies of delicacies from America.

In the latter part of the 1700s experiments had taken place on how to get supplies of fish inland: live cod in seawater tanks came by barge down the canals, carriages with ventilated boxes suspended to reduce jolting were also tried, but both methods proved too expensive. In the nineteenth century, weekly supplies began to arrive from Scarborough; cod, haddock and lobsters took two days to travel. As early as 1831 there is a record of oysters sent by rail from Liverpool, but rail transport for fish failed to catch on to any great extent until the 1840s when fish prices were stabilised on the east coast and the price of cod fell from 6d to 2d per pound. The amount of fish carried by rail then rose from $3^{1}/_{2}$ tons to 80 tons a week. By the 1850s Hull and Grimsby were supplying fish to Manchester, and later both Yarmouth and Lowestoft. Nevertheless the difficulties of keeping fish fresh loomed large: ten fishmongers were fined in October 1844 for selling 'diseased' herrings and another two were charged the next year in respect of fifty unwholesome salmon. That the authorities were watchful and prosecuted the fishmongers goes some way to explain the fact that the cases declined after the 1870s.

In Liverpool there were 500–600 cows in town dairies, but none at all in Manchester. The activities of various sanitary inspectors in the period 1780–1880 show the overall unimportance of town milk. Among countless reports of insanitary slaughterhouses and piggeries, dairies were hardly ever mentioned.[8] Manchester, like many of the new towns, was supplied by the surrounding countryside; a ten-mile radius was thought the safe limit, for more than this and the milk was bound to arrive sour.

By 1825 these growing industrial towns were being supplied by canal, a smoother journey than by road which shook the milk about, and it arrived in the centre of Manchester twice a day. The Manchester, Bolton and Bury Canal had a special milk boat and now many dairies outside the towns switched from cheese and butter production to the supply of raw milk. The Bridgewater canal also had a special milk boat, which travelled along the Cheshire branch. Hundreds of milk cans were commonly to be seen stacked on the wharves in Manchester.

In 1844 the Manchester and Birmingham Railway started bringing milk to Manchester from farmers close to the Manchester-Crewe part of the line. By 1846 the traffic amounted to 100–150 milk cans a day. As the capacity of the cans varied from 9–18 gallons it is impossible to estimate how much milk was produced and drunk, but it was thought no more than a weekly consumption of 1.4 pints. By 1869 most of Manchester's milk supply was coming by rail.

By 1855, the early milk trains had also made their appearance in London. Adulteration was a great problem. In the 1850s milk was bought wholesale at 3d a quart and retailed at 4d, but the addition of only ten per cent of water increased the profit by forty per cent. It was estimated that seventy-four per cent of milk was adulterated with water, in a ratio of anything from ten to fifty per cent water to milk. The 1863 report claimed milk had been diluted by the addition of four to six times its volume.[9] It was pointed out that the food value was thereby much reduced.

By 1855 both dried milk powder and condensed sweetened milk had come on to the market; the first was too expensive for the working classes, but condensed milk quickly became a big success. With all the fat skimmed off, it was, however, nutritionally deficient in both vitamins A and D, so rickets became common among working class children. As flies were attracted to the open tins containing this sticky liquid, it also played a part in the gastritis and enteritis which killed one-third of infants before 1914.[10] Raw milk was a perfect carrier of infection, especially bovine tubercle bacillus. Between the years 1896 and 1907, a tenth of Manchester and Salford's milk supply was found to be contaminated with the bacillus.[11] Milk can also carry scarlet fever, and incidence of this infection was as high in the rural districts of Manchester as in the central poorer regions.

In 1845 Engels inveighed against the deceit practised 'in the sale of all articles offered to workers', instancing potatoes which were shrivelled and bad, stale cheese, rancid bacon and meat which was old, tough and partially tainted. He criticised small shopkeepers of generally using false weights and measures. Adulteration of food reached its height after 1850 when public concern began to mount leading to the acts of 1872 and 1875, which are thought to have been conducive to some improvement; certainly they form the basis of the present laws relating to food safety.

At times of poverty, as in the cotton famines of the 1860s, overall consumption of food fell, mostly in meat and potatoes, though bread consumption also fell; the sugar intake decreased least of all, suggesting that people were surviving on sweetened tea, bread and treacle. More oats were eaten as porridge, the only ingredient that was cooked, possibly overnight in the embers of a fire.

A Manchester clergyman wrote: 'There is not a town in the world where the distance between the rich and the poor is so great or the barrier between them so difficult to be crossed.' An American, Colman, was far more depressing in 1845 when he wrote of the Manchester poor: 'wretched, defrauded, oppressed, crushed human nature lying in bleeding fragments all over the face of society. Every day that I live I thank Heaven that I am not a poor man with a family in England.'[12]

Servants and Cooks

As the new booming industries produced more affluence in the middle classes so domestic servants grew in number, for the safest way of distinguishing oneself from the working class was to employ them. Their number increased substantially in the second half of the century, growing from 900,000 in 1851 to 1,400,000 in 1871; there were then 90,000 cooks, slightly more than this number of housemaids, and 16,000 private coachmen. From 1870 among the upper and middle classes, the birthrate began to fall when birth control methods were discovered; given a choice between a higher living standard or more children the married couple chose the lifestyle, so with smaller households servant numbers began to decline.

From the first quarter of the nineteenth century the fate of British cooking was essentially in the hands of a burgeoning bourgeoisie and its kitchen staff. How intelligent, skilled and knowledgeable the cook was, and how trained and experienced, was of course, checked out by the mistress who would judge her suitability. But mistresses like putative cooks come in all shades of accomplishment and all too often the cooking of many a middle-class household must have been a hit and miss affair. That great bond of familial loving care between a mother and her brood which was at the centre of cooked meals was now broken; the intimacy that lies at the heart of so many created dishes was shattered. Where it might still have existed in working-class families, the mother would be only too thankful to have scraps to feed her young, and these far too often were uncooked.

Cooks, however, were now almost certainly to be literate and there were plenty of publications to give her advice of the most detailed kind. Dr Kitchiner, whose 1817 book *The Cook's Oracle* went through many editions until 1840, gives over a chapter to advice for the cook and other servants. He begins by suggesting that immediately the cook arrives she should get into 'good graces' of the other servants, especially those that waited on table; she should not listen to gossip, requesting an early interview with the master and mistress and trusting in her own judgement. If she was a good cook she would soon become a favourite domestic, which would excite envy, hatred and malice in her fellow servants. He advises her to be an agreeable companion in the kitchen without compromising her duty to her patrons in the parlour. She should ask her employers these questions:

> Do they like their roasts of a gold colour, or well browned and if they like them frothed?[13] Do they like Soups and Sauces thick or thin, or white or brown, clean or full in the mouth? What Accompaniments are they partial to? What flavours they fancy, especially of Spice and Herbs? . . . Be extremely cautious of Seasoning High – leave it to the Eaters to add the piquante condiments, according to their own palate and fancy . . . Enter into all their plans of Economy . . . many things may be readdressed in a different form from that in which they were first served.

He then gives examples of cold leftovers reheated which are less than stimulating, but I will return later to the Victorian preoccupation with using up food remains.

Two factors in the advice above would generate a decline in cooking; a willingness to connive and abet the master's economy drives in the kitchen could easily succeed in too many mediocre dishes and in addition it would encourage a tendency towards blandness through a fear of pungent herbs, especially garlic, upon the breath; this was a cardinal social sin which would have been sufficient cause to be ousted from society forever. There was a third reason against which Kitchiner also warns. The structure of a middle-class home did not help the serving of meals. Kitchiner writes: 'Long before dinner is announced all becomes lukewarm; and to complete the mortification of the grand Gourmand, his meat is put on a sheet of ice in the shape of a Plate, which instantly converts the gravy into jelly and the fat into something which puzzles his teeth and the roof of his mouth as much as if he had Birdlime to masticate.'[14] He advises a complete meat screen with a hot closet and plate-warmer; this was like a Dutch oven but on wheels, about 3½ ft wide by 1 ft deep.

But that was only one problem. Kitchiner complains of 'modern-built town houses' which have no proper place to preserve provisions, except a hanging safe; if you feared meat would not keep, then it should be par-roasted or par-boiled. As to the cooking range, he warns against 'deleterious vapours and pestilential exhalations of the charcoal . . . the glare of a scorching fire and the smoke so baneful to the eyes and complexion'. He ends by summing up: 'Besides understanding the management of the Spit, the Stewpan, and the Rolling Pin, a Complete Cook must know how to go to Market, write legibly, and keep Accounts accurately.'

When Mrs Beeton (see page 270) was writing (1859-61), the cook was paid £20-£40 a year, which included an extra allowance for tea, sugar and beer; if no extra allowance was made, she was paid £14-£30. Mrs Beeton thought it essential that the cook rise very early in the morning 'for an hour lost in the morning will keep her toiling, absolutely toiling, all day'. Her first duty was to set her dough for the breakfast rolls if that had not been done the previous night. She lit the fire and boiled the kettle, went to the breakfast room and made things ready, she cleaned the kitchen, pantry, passages and kitchen stairs all before breakfast. Though Mrs Beeton lists all this under the duties of the cook it is her charges, the scullerymaids, who do the work. After breakfast the cook gave directions and made preparations for the different dinners of the household and family. The cook answers the back door in the morning, as it is the tradesmen who call.

Her main duty of the day is in the preparation and cooking of the dinner; she must take upon herself all the dressing and preparation of the principal dishes; while these are cooking, she must be busy with her pastry, soups, gravies, ragouts etc. Stock must be at hand with sweet herbs and spices for seasoning. Vegetables and sauces must be ready, while dishes must stand for some time covered on the hot plate or in the hot closet until the order to serve is given from the drawing room. 'Then comes haste, but there must be no hurry.' The cook takes charge of the fish, soups and poultry, the kitchenmaid of the vegetables, sauces and gravies. These are now all put into the appropriate serving dishes. Everything has to be timed to prevent it getting cold. Great care has to be taken that between the first course and the second no more time is allowed to elapse than is necessary. When the dinner is over the cook has to look to her larder to preserve the leftovers 'to keep everything sweet and clean'.

Mrs Beeton considers that 'Modern cookery stands so greatly indebted to the gastronomic propensities of our French neighbours, that many of the terms are adopted and applied by English artists to the same as well as similar preparations of their own.'[15] There is no rage, as in Mrs Glasse, at French culinary fashions, in fact we gather that according to Mrs Beeton British cooking has absorbed what it wants and adapted it in a seamless marriage. The Napoleonic Wars finished almost fifty years earlier, and even though Cobbett, writing in the 1820s about defending the country against French Jacobins, elsewhere showed an active hatred of Catholics, time has moved on and there is not an iota of such feelings in Mrs Beeton. She goes on to explain fifty-five different French terms from aspic to vol-au-vent. (Miss Acton explains thirty-five French terms in her book, while Dr Kitchiner uses a few but explains nothing.) On garlic Mrs Beeton comments:

The smell of this plant is generally considered offensive, and it is the most acrimonious in its taste of the whole of the alliaceous tribe. . . . On the continent, especially in Italy, it is much used, and the French consider it an essential in many made dishes.

Kitchiner makes a garlic vinegar from 2 oz of chopped garlic with a quart of vinegar, but observes: 'The Cook must be careful not to use too much of this; a few drops of it will give a pint of Gravy a sufficient smack of the Garlic, the flavour of which, when slight and well blended, is one of the finest we have – when used in excess it is the most offensive.' Then to be on the safe side he adds: 'The best way to use Garlic is to send up some of this Vinegar in a Cruet, and let the Company flavour their own Sauce as they like.' Miss Acton gives a recipe for a Mild Ragout of Garlic or *L'ail à la Bordelaise* where the garlic is boiled in water, but the water is changed three times in the 15 to 25 minutes of cooking. She says: 'By changing the water in which it is boiled, the root will be deprived of its naturally pungent flavour and smell and rendered extremely mild.' We know that such a change of water is unnecessary, that garlic becomes mild in flavour when cooked. This fragment of cooking lore was not known to Miss Acton, who is nearly always as thorough and pernickety as her great admirer Elizabeth David. I would suggest that this was because Miss Acton showed a nervousness about the use of garlic, which is shared by the other cookery writers mentioned above, and that therefore she had not cooked it often enough. This recipe and one for garlic vinegar are the only ones in the book.

Servants slept in the attics and ate and lived almost exclusively in the basements; they moved around the house silently and if possible invisibly, using tradesmen's entrances and back stairs. From the 1810s cooking was done on the closed range which had an oven, boiler, hot plate and hot closets which could bake, boil, roast, steam, stew and heat flat irons, and provided ten gallons of boiling water. It was made of cast iron; Count Rumford had already pointed out that this absorbed the heat and radiated it out into the room and that ovens were better made out of brick. Cast iron was the material of the age. It used up a great amount of coal and had to be cleaned every morning early before being lit; this labour depended on a willing workforce, so only the comfortably off in their large suburban villas installed them. The closed range had its ashes and cinders raked, its flue cleaned, its grease removed, the steels polished with bathbrick and paraffin, the iron parts blackleaded and polished and finally its hearth washed and polished.[16] How this monster must have been cursed by succeeding teenage girls on their hands and knees early in the morning.

In the rows of substantial new villas being built throughout the century around the new towns and cities, consuming the green fields which the sheep and cattle had so recently grazed on, kitchens were located in the basements above the cellars next to coal holes with pantries and washrooms grouped around the tradesmen's entrance. Stairs led up to the ground floor with a corridor towards the dining room; trays laden with dishes were heavy, and serving a meal was laborious work; keeping it hot was always a knotty problem. Corridors were not well lit, gaslights gave only a dim glow and gas mantles needed constant attention if they were to remain bright. Later in the century a hatch worked with weights and pulleys was built into the kitchen and the dining room located above it, which simplified the ritual of serving. In larger houses the kitchens might be located in another wing of the house and dishes would have to travel longer distances, only to be placed in another warming oven nearer the dining room, waiting to be served. At Chatsworth it took the butler six minutes to walk from the kitchen to the dining room. Such systems could never produce good food.

Jane Austen and the Brontes

We may obtain a glimpse of the food that people ate in the first half of the century if we examine Martha Lloyd's *Household Recipe Book*.[17] She was a friend of Jane Austen's who came to live and cook for them, and eventually, eleven years after Jane's death, married her brother, Admiral Sir Frances Austen. A couple of decades later the novels of the Bronte sisters give us details of the type of food they ate. Both homes were parsonages, so they are variations on a theme that we have already examined in the Norfolk home of Parson Woodforde. The Reverend George Austen's stipend was £600 a year to care for his two small livings, Steventon and Deane, a mile apart, in Hampshire. On this he supported a wife and eight children. Mrs Austen was industrious, however, and was often seen even when quite elderly hoeing her vegetable patch; she also kept a poultry yard where she reared chickens, turkeys, geese, ducks, guinea fowl and bantams. She taught her maids how to make butter and cheese, bake bread, brew beer, cure bacon and hams and make all kinds of preserves, pickles and home-made wines. There was nothing unusual in this; on their limited income the Austens were counted as lesser gentry, most of whom would have attempted self-sufficiency. What was bought in, of course, was the ubiquitous tea, sugar and some citrus fruit. In the garden they planted (for George Austen worked in the garden too) fruit trees and a strawberry walk.

At Chawton Cottage near Alton where they lived from 1809 until Jane died in 1817 they had an enclosed garden and some fields where they kept five Alderney cows, pigs and some sheep as well as being able to grow wheat. Jane took an interest in food from a child, after a nursery meal with two nieces she wrote: 'Caroline, Anna and I have just been devouring cold souse and it would be difficult to say who enjoyed it most.' Souse was a medieval dish which became Elizabethan Christmas fare: 'brawn, pudding and souse and good mustard withal'. It was pickled pork made in the winter; the hind parts, ears, cheek, snout and trotters were soaked in brine with ale or verjuice or wine added, and they were then made into a brawn. It was a way of using every scrap of the pig left over from the butchering of the carcass.

As George Austen kept a coach they travelled and visited grand relations; after stopping once in Devizes Jane wrote to her sister, Cassandra, that the dinner was good: 'Amongst other things we had asparagus and a lobster, which made me wish for you.' On visits to her rich relations Jane gathered recipe ideas and took them back home to try. 'I am very fond of experimental housekeeping,' she wrote in 1798, 'such as having an ox cheek now and then . . . I mean to have some little dumplings put into it . . .' Jane's favourite brother, Henry, kept a French cook, and she was fond of M. Halavant's cooking. After sending her brother one of their turkeys, she wrote to Cassandra: 'Pray note down how many full courses of exquisite dishes M. Halavant converts it into.' At the height of the Napoleonic Wars M. Halavant's post might seem surprising, but the Prince Regent led the way, as his own cook was Carême.

At Chawton Jane ordered China tea from Twinings, but warned Cassandra that her brother liked coffee with his breakfast, which was taken late, about 10 a.m. Staying at Stoneleigh Abbey in 1806, Mrs Austen wrote: 'At nine we meet to say prayers in the Chapel. Then follows breakfast, consisting of Chocolate, Coffee, and Tea, Plumb Cake, Pound Cake, Hot Rolls, Cold Rolls, Bread and Butter and dry Toast for me.' The hour they dined grew later over the years: in 1798 they sit down to dinner at half past three; in 1805 they dine at four, occasionally at five; by 1808 'we never dine now before five'; in fashionable households dinner was now at 6.30. As the gap between breakfast and dinner widened people began to feel pangs of hunger and cold meats, pickles, cakes and jellies were laid out on the sideboard; there was also a growing fondness for picnics, which later in the century would become an enthusiastic passion. Sir John Middleton in *Sense and Sensibility* was 'a blessing to all the juvenile part of the neighbourhood, for in summer he was for ever forming parties to eat cold ham and chicken out of doors'.

When Jane's rich uncle, James Leigh Perrot, was in London on one occasion for consultation with Dr Budd, he dined at Hachetts. 'Our dinner was Mackerel at top, chicken on one side and beans and bacon the other; Peach and Cherry tart succeeded.' No doubt he made an excellent breakfast the next morning, but hunger struck him and he took giblet soup, giving this snack a name; he refers to it as 'luncheon'. The words 'nuncheon' and 'nunch' occur as early as the fourteenth century. Johnson's *Dictionary* (1755) gives 'nunchin' as 'a piece of victuals eaten between meals', but defines lunch and luncheon 'as much food as one's hand can hold'.[18] In a French-English dictionary of 1580, the French *lopin* is translated as 'a lumpe, a gobbet, a luncheon'.[19] From then on food in a great lump was referred to as luncheon. Jane uses the word earlier in a letter (1808) where she spells it 'noonshine'. Perhaps far more apt than the correct spelling. Her word is a mixture of two in use at the time, 'noonings' and 'nuncheon'. Mrs Rundell's *A New System of Domestic Cookery* (1806) stated: 'When noonings or suppers are served (and in every house some preparation is necessary for accidental visitors) care should be taken to have such things in readiness as are proper for either.' In 1811 Jane uses 'luncheon' in *Sense and Sensibility* and later, in 1813 when *Pride and Prejudice* was published, Lydia and Kitty Bennet buy salad and cucumber and add 'such cold meat as an inn larder usually affords' so as to make 'the nicest cold luncheon in the world'. The word is now in full use.

As we have seen with Parson Woodforde, a dinner invitation from friends or neighbours was extended to include supper with the interval in between filled with card playing or musical entertainments. Jane described a 'delightful evening' spent with her young niece Anna with neighbours in Chawton: 'Syllabub, Tea, Coffee, Singing, Dancing and a Hot Supper at eleven o'clock'. Tea was also beginning to be

Street Food and Markets

STREET BREAKFAST.

From the earliest times street food was an essential part of the urban scene. It was cheap, hot, nutritious and tasty and often was the mainstay of the working man's diet, as well as providing a hot item for the family's evening meal. Produce markets were the cornerstone supporting the distribution of food to the urban population. They existed in all cities and towns of any size.

Top left: Street breakfast, 1825. (8)

Top right: London food stall, 1877. (8)

Middle right: Covent Garden market, London, 1897. (8)

Bottom left: The People's Market, Bradford, Yorkshire, circa 1880. (8)

Bottom right: Selling hot, roasted chestnuts in the street, 1930s. (8)

Food for the Working Classes in the Mid-Nineteenth Century

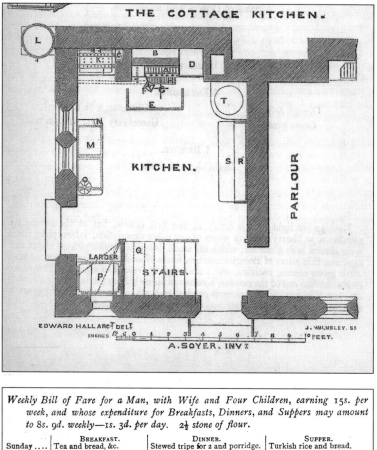

THE COTTAGE KITCHEN.

KITCHEN.

PARLOUR

LARDER

STAIRS.

EDWARD HALL ARCT DELT
INCHES · FEET.
A. SOYER, INVT
J. WALMSLEY, SC

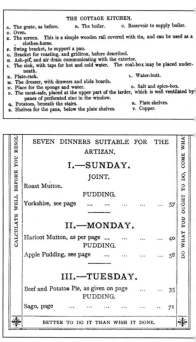

THE COTTAGE KITCHEN.

A. The grate, as before.　B. The boiler.　C. Reservoir to supply boiler.
D. Oven.
E. The screen. This is a simple wooden rail covered with tin, and can be used as a clothes-horse.
F. Swing bracket, to support a pan.
G. Bracket for roasting, and gridiron, before described.
H. Ash-pit, and air drain communicating with the exterior.
I. The sink, with taps for hot and cold water. The coal-box may be placed underneath.
K. Plate-rack.　　　　　　　　　　　　　L. Water-butt.
M. The dresser, with drawers and slide boards.
N. Place for the sponge and water.　　　o. Salt and spice-box.
P. The meat-safe, placed at the upper part of the larder, which is well ventilated by panes of perforated zinc in the window.
Q. Potatoes, beneath the stairs.　　　　R. Plate shelves.
S. Shelves for the pans, below the plate shelves.　T. Copper.

SEVEN DINNERS SUITABLE FOR THE ARTIZAN.

CALCULATE WELL BEFORE YOU RESOLVE

DO WHAT YOU OUGHT TO DO, COME WHAT

I.—SUNDAY.

JOINT.

Roast Mutton.

PUDDING.

Yorkshire, see page 57

II.—MONDAY.

Haricot Mutton, as per page 40
PUDDING.
Apple Pudding, see page 58

III.—TUESDAY.

Beef and Potatoe Pie, as given on page ... 35
PUDDING.
Sago, page 71

BETTER TO DO IT THAN WISH IT DONE.

MANNER OFTEN MAKETH FORTUNE.

HONESTY IS THE HANDMAID OF VIRTUE.

WHO WILL NOT BE COUNSELLED CANNOT BE HELPED.

IV.—WEDNESDAY.

Hashed Mutton, page 28
PUDDING.
Oatmeal, page 62

V.—THURSDAY.

Tinned Meats, cold, see page 34
Pancakes, page 65

VI.—FRIDAY.

Mutton Broth, recipe for which see page ... 6
PUDDING.
Suet Pudding, page 57

VII.—SATURDAY.

Pot-au-Feu, see page 11
Rhubarb Pie, see page 59

AN EVIL LESSON IS SOON LEARNED.

Weekly Bill of Fare for a Man, with Wife and Four Children, earning 15s. per week, and whose expenditure for Breakfasts, Dinners, and Suppers may amount to 8s. 9d. weekly—1s. 3d. per day. 2½ stone of flour.

	BREAKFAST.	DINNER.	SUPPER.
Sunday	Tea and bread, &c.	Stewed tripe for 2 and porridge.	Turkish rice and bread.
Monday....	Coffee and bread, &c.	Stew, soup No. 2, potatoes.	Cabbage and dumplings.
Tuesday ..	Oatmeal porridge, &c.	Sheep's head and dumplings.	Potato rice.
Wednesday	Tea and bread, &c.	Sheep's head and rice.	Crowdie and bread.
Thursday ..	Coffee and bread, &c.	Sheep's head and dumplings.	Remains of crowdie & bread.
Friday	Oatmeal porridge.	Carrot soup and dumpling.	Rice porridge.
Saturday ..	Coffee and bread, &c.	Bacon and potatoes, broken-bread pudding.	Suet dumplings.

Top left and *top right:* The beginnings of social reform redirected interest into the eating habits of the working classes. Soyer, who had applied himself to the feeding problems of the military, also began to consider the needs of the working man. He designed the ideal kitchen for the country cottage. A simple but functional arrangement. (4)

Middle left: In *Beeton's Penny Cookery* of 1880, a daily menu was proposed for the working man using the cheapest cuts of meat and offal. The sheep's head does for three suppers, and they still observe Friday as a meatless day. Note too the complete absence of green vegetables. (9)

Middle right and *bottom right:* A skilled artisan would be eating simple fare like these dishes described in a publication of 1888. This is basic food which would remain much the same for working people until the 1950s. (10)

Women Cooks and Writers who have been particularly significant in the History of British Food.

Top left: Elizabeth, Countess of Kent, author of the first recorded printed cookery work by a lady, published in 1653. (11)

Top right: Elizabeth Raffald, 1769, a practical cook of enormous ingenuity who was not impressed by French influences. (12)

Bottom right: Mrs Agnes B. Marshall (1855-1905). She invented and sold a unique design of ice-cream machine and early refrigerator called Ice Caves, as well as writing books on ices which popularised ice cream and sorbets. She also invented the cone or cornet, and was an influential teacher who ran her own cookery school. (13)

Top left: Mrs C. F. Leyel (1880-1957). She wrote cookery books of great taste and style filled with ingredients from the Mediterranean and the Middle East. She founded the Society of Herbalists and the Culpeper shops. (14)

Top right: Elizabeth David, who reintroduced the love of Mediterranean food to the British palate. (15)

Bottom left: Mrs Beeton's influence was so profound because Ward Lock, the publishers, bought the rights and implemented constant re-editing of the work over the years. There was little original Mrs Beeton left by the twentieth century. (8)

Bottom centre: Jane Grigson (1928-90) was a fine prose stylist who wrote perceptively of food in the British tradition. Her influence on deepening the awareness of good quality food in the British public was immeasurable. (16)

Bottom right: Delia Smith, the Mrs Beeton of television, a practical teacher, who succeeded in taking the mystique out of cooking. (17)

Some Male Innovators of Food Throughout the Centuries

Top left: Sir Kenelm Digby, 1669. (18)

Top right: John Evelyn, 1699. (19)

Middle left: William Kitchiner, 1817. (20)

Middle centre: Alexis Soyer, 1846. (21)

Middle right: Charles Elme Francatelli, 1846. (22)

Bottom right: George Auguste Escoffier (1846-1935), whose best known saying was 'Above all, make it simple.' Advice which neither he nor his disciples kept to. He was chef at the Savoy from 1889-98 controlling eighty cooks, then at the Carlton Hotel until he retired in 1920. He exerted a huge influence on haute cuisine in Britain; the worst excesses of it are expressed in his recipe for veal Orloff, where the veal is braised, sliced, reassembled with truffles and onion sauce between the slices then glazed with a cheese-laden Mornay sauce. However, his influence on British cookery was very pervasive. (23)

Kitchens Through the Ages

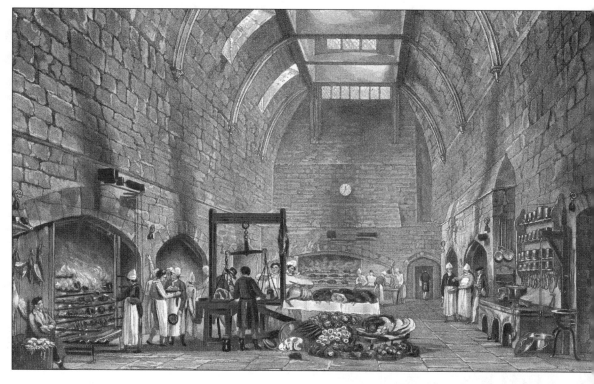

Above: A representation of the kitchens of Windsor Castle done in the 1840s which purports to be a depiction of it in the sixteenth century. However, the dress of the waiting staff appears to be eighteenth century. All the light comes from above and there are no wall sconces to be lit for the evening. Haunches of beef are being weighed and scores of joints and large fowls are being spit roasted; all the vegetables are heaped upon the floor. (3)

Right: A picture of a Still Room showing the lady of the house making *eau de vie,* with her cook in the background about to bake sugared cakes, ratafias or comfits. On the shelves and the table there are cone sugar and spices with a hanging sieve. This is the frontispiece of the second edition of Hannah Woolley's book published in 1662 at the start of the Restoration. (24)

Opposite page
Top left: One of the copper plates from Martha Bradley's *The British Housewife* published in 1770 which showed the manner of trussing all kinds of game, wild and tame fowls. Here a goose is about to be spit-roasted by the cook, while a maid pulls the mechanism to turn the spit with a suckling pig on it already in front of the fire. A hare and a duck and two small birds hang in the game room, there is a teapot and a sugar sifter on the mantlepiece, while another maid finishes two pies for baking. (25)

Top right: The frontispiece from Elizabeth Hammond's *Modern Domestic Cookery* published in about 1820 which shows a capacious plate warmer in front of a mechanical spit which is wound with a key and rings a bell when it is completed. The cook is placing a funnel into a pie ready to pour hot gravy into it from the small saucepans in the *bain marie;* a piece of beef and a capon roast in front of the fire. (26)

Bottom: A drawing to show the efficiency and cleanliness of a gas kitchen in 1824. The large gas jets set upon tiles are made to hold gallon saucepans. One is astonished that such an advance in technology took another twenty years before anyone showed enthusiasm for it. This was largely because there was a fear of explosions. (27)

The Development of the Modern Domestic Kitchen

All the kitchens are light and airy and show a reaction against clutter and a new awareness of hygiene with austere lines and surfaces that are easy to clean. Note that in all four there is no food exposed, all is hidden away in cupboards.

Top left: A kitchen in 1919. (8)

Top right: In 1936 there is a new Aga and an emphasis on chrome and steel. (8)

Bottom left: In the 1950s hot water comes via a geyser and there is a preponderance of plastic. (8)

Bottom right: A highly expensive Smallbone kitchen in the new millennium. The extractor hood and the built-in furniture in the centre of the room are new developments. Not only the food has disappeared, but now even the smell of the cooking must be quickly erased. (28)

served now in the interval between dinner and supper.

Martha Lloyd does not bother to write down in her book instructions for the roasting and boiling of joints and birds; these pages are reminders of favourite methods and recipes which she and the Austen family enjoyed. She begins with a collection of soups. Jane wrote that she was not ashamed to ask their doctor, a Mr Lyford, to sit down to dinner when he called unexpectedly, as they were just about to eat pease-soup, a spare rib and a pudding. Here, when the family were alone, one sees how modest the table was. Soup gets mentioned often in Jane's novels, for it was always served at balls and dances; a large tureen of hot soup fortified with wine, spice and lemon, warmed the guests as they arrived from a journey in an unheated coach. This, of course, contradicts Miss Acton, though not her statement that a soup was unable to be made by the very poor.

Martha's pease soup was flavoured with celery, onion, pepper, salt, mint, parsley and spinach. Just a small handful, she says; I suspect it was to give colour. The most interesting addition was two anchovies and half a spoonful of sugar. But there could be no doubt that the 'pease' would override the other flavours as she uses two quarts and does not specify the amount of water. This, I estimate, would make enough soup for about twelve people and still have some left over. Other soup recipes include a Veal Soup from a Mrs Hartly, which is made from a knuckle of veal and a ham bone with a head of celery and sweet herbs; it is stewed for four hours, skimmed then left to cool, the fat taken off, strained and finally thickened with cream, white breadcrumbs and a little flour. A white soup was made from a gravy from any kind of meat, thickened with pounded egg yolks, sweet almonds and 'as much cream as will make it a good colour'. A Swiss Soup Meagre is a *Soup Maigre*, meaning a vegetable soup without meat, which appears in all the recipe books, as it was eaten regularly in France as a dish for fast days. In Britain it seems to have been eaten because we liked it. Martha's recipe uses cabbage, lettuces, endive, sorrel, spinach, chervil, onions, parsley, beet leaves, cucumber, peas and asparagus which gives us a picture of what was growing in the garden outside the kitchen door. All these vegetables are cut up fine and stewed in a quarter of a pound of butter with a small teaspoonful of flour; then boiling water is poured over and the soup is stewed further; then the yolks of three eggs are added in a teacup of cream and the juice from some Seville oranges. This seems to me an excellent recipe. The flour, as in Martha's other recipes, is such a small amount, for she thickens with egg yolks and cream and the addition of the Seville oranges would lighten and be stimulating in the final flavour.

There are several sauces to have with fish, the simplest being two anchovies simmered in a little water with horseradish, elder vinegar, white wine, and a little mushroom ketchup thickened with a little butter and flour. Another begins with a pint of port, a quarter of a pint of vinegar, pepper, cloves, mace, nutmeg, onion, bay leaves, thyme, parsley, bits of radish and anchovies; it is boiled until the anchovies dissolve, then it is bottled, stored and used to flavour melted butter. A sauce to have with sea fish is made from pounded crawfish or lobster shells, mixed with gravy, cinnamon, and crusty bread all stewed together until it is strong; then it is strained and mixed with butter and anchovy. The most interesting sauce comes from Captain Austen who eventually was to marry the cook, and who is obviously not afraid of strong flavours: he uses two heads of garlic, cutting each clove in half with an ounce of cayenne, two spoonfuls of Indian soy, and two ounces of walnut ketchup or pickle, placed in a quart bottle and filled with vinegar. 'Cork it close and shake it well. It is fit for use in a month and will keep good for a year.'

There are recipes for hogs' puddings, scotch collops, how to hash a calf's head, to make pigeon pies, sausages, little patties and rissoles, a 'receipt to make curry after the India manner', vegetable recipes, and how to make macaroni and toasted cheese. There are recipes for rice pudding and 'Blanch Mange' which is ground almonds, cream, sugar and isinglass – so here is mawmenny again. There is a recipe for a trifle using sponge fingers or 'Naples biscuits', which is identical to the sixteenth-century one for 'foole' and one for 'Bread Pudding' which is bread, suet and dried fruit mixed with four eggs and boiled for four hours. There is a New College Pudding, Orange Pudding, a Baked Apple Pudding and Lemon Mince Pies, all of them excellent recipes that we would enjoy today.

What is interesting is how the remnants of medieval ideas and ingredients linger on, yet how contemporary Martha's recipes also are. The food the Austen family ate was squarely based on the freshest of produce; it was well flavoured with fresh herbs, and at times intensely flavoured with spices and home-made sauces. Here, in the first decade of the century, there was no fear or nervousness of pungency in the cooking; it was gutsy and relaxed. We are still within the age of the glories of the country estate and the meals the Austens enjoyed must have been the most delicious and certainly inherently British of any age. If we want to see what the best of British cooking is then I think much of it is contained in this slim book.

The food the Brontes ate was rather different, but they lived much farther north and had less money than the Austens. They started the day according to their servant, Sarah Garrs, with 'a plain but abundant breakfast of porridge, milk, bread and butter'. They dined at 2 p.m. on 'Plain roast or boiled meat and for dessert . . . bread and rice puddings, custards and other slightly sweetened preparations of eggs and milk'. The last meal of the day was tea which they ate in the kitchen.[20] Other details about their diet can be gleaned from the novels; every type of meal is mentioned in them as well as Christmas, wedding feasts and picnics. Different characters choose a different time of meal for dinner to show their class status. Mrs Reed, for example, the housekeeeeper in *Jane Eyre*, likes to eat dinner early at midday if there is no company, while Mr Lockwood in *Wuthering Heights* asks for dinner at 5 p.m., but Nelly, one of the most strongly individual women in fiction, insists on serving it at the latest at one o'clock. So much for social pretension. Mr Lockwood is the only one to drink coffee except for Charlotte's Belgian characters; all the others drink tea. Tea as a meal is popular among the farming families. They hardly ever drink milk, it is for the young and invalids, when it is boiled with sugar.

The aristocratic Isabella has to eat porridge once married to Heathcliff and attempts to take it upstairs away from the servants. The meat and poultry are either mutton or chicken; beef features little. Fish only gets one fleeting mention in the whole Bronte oeuvre: in Anne Bronte's *Agnes Grey* Mrs Bloomfield lists the major dishes for dinner as 'Turkey, grouse and fish'. It seems extraordinary, yet considering the lack of decent roads, it is not surprising that little fresh fish arrived in Haworth, which is what one surmises.

This is plain food, far plainer than the meals Jane Austen was delighting in; there is no mention of pigeon pie, a green herb sauce, asparagus, green peas, cheesecake and trifle, which were everyday dishes in Chawton. The dinner table in Haworth seems almost as bleak as the moors surrounding it: roast mutton (Was there ever caper or onion sauce? One somehow doubts it.), with boiled potatoes and cabbage, followed by a custard or boiled suet currant pudding. For breakfast there was porridge, for they are in the north, and bread and butter. Surely they made preserves and pickles? If so, there's no inkling of it; in the novels, characters who like sweet things appear almost weak in their craving.

Both parsonages are more representative of the eighteenth century in their food habits than the nineteenth. But what in food terms was characteristic of this age?

Breakfast

If the British are known for any culinary achievement it is the great British breakfast and it was in this century that it achieved its status. Even in the nineteenth century bacon for breakfast would become almost *de rigueur*, even for the lower classes, as long as they could afford it. In 1901 a railworker earning 44s per week, with two children and a lodger, ate for his breakfast bacon on every day except Sunday, when he had a sausage, and Thursday, when he ate ham; with this he had bread and butter and tea.

At the beginning of Victoria's reign the essence of the breakfast, eggs and bacon, with the eggs cooked in a variety of ways, had already become the expected way to start the day. The meal began with porridge or cream of oatmeal (exactly the same dish but with the Scottish connotation omitted), continued with the cooked part, and finished with toast and marmalade; coffee or tea was drunk with it. Both the porridge and the eggs and bacon could be cooked beforehand and left in heated dishes upon the sideboard for the master and mistress to help themselves.

As our immense resources of economic power exalted our position in the world our importance grew in international affairs. Apart from the Crimean War we kept aloof from the great wars of Europe in the years 1854-78 and only involved ourselves in colonial expansion and Far Eastern skirmishes. It was the policy of prestige, which Palmerston pursued, that we need not court the favour of any power in particular; his actions showed that a 'pax Britannica' had now replaced the old 'pax Romana' and in 1850 in Parliament he made that clear by saying that the strong arm of England would protect any British subject abroad if they suffered injustice and wrong. Our annual export and imports of goods trebled in value between 1850 and 1870. We were considered 'the workshop of the world': we produced two-thirds of the world's coal, perhaps half its iron and five-sevenths of its supply of steel. The British Empire, of which Canada, India and Australia formed the greater part, was booming and immigration from England to these new lands was rising.

As a family became richer the breakfast grew, almost as a reflection of the power and affluence of the British Empire itself. As the map of the world glowed pink, the sideboard in the morning room began to be laden with extra dishes. It already had a choice of cold cuts, comprised of sliced meats, and perhaps even a whole leg of ham or tongue (for the master was fond of cutting his own in chunks); it was a short step to dipping chicken or pheasant legs in mustard and heating them up in the oven. Left-over rice was a boon, for it could be turned into kedgeree (another dish stemming from India) with a few fillets of smoked haddock, a spoonful of curry powder and the Victorian standby which crept into so many dishes, a few hardboiled eggs; mixed and reheated it could be piled up onto a warm silver salver.

When Mrs Beeton's famous book was first published in 1861, breakfast had hardly got into its stride, but she devotes three small paragraphs to the subject:

> Suffice it to say, that any cold meat the larder may furnish, should be nicely garnished, and be placed on the buffet. Collared and potted meats, or fish, cold game or poultry, veal-and-ham pies, game-and-rump-steak pies are all suitable dishes for the breakfast table . . .

As to hot dishes, Mrs Beeton lists:

> broiled fish, such as mackerel, whiting, herrings, dried haddocks, etc; mutton chops and rump steaks, broiled sheep's kidneys, kidneys *à la maître d'hôtel* (with butter, parsley and lemon juice), sausages, plain rashers of bacon, bacon and poached eggs, ham and poached eggs, omelets, plain boiled eggs, *oeufs-au-plat*, poached eggs on toast, muffins, toast, marmalade, butter . . .

In the summer she advises a bowl of flowers and fresh fruit to be added to the table. The 1888 edition of the book added some vegetarian dishes.

A Breakfast Book of 1865, suggesting a huge number of other dishes which it claims are 'more or less in daily request for our ordinary breakfasts', makes Mrs Beeton's list appear modest. Here, as well as Mrs Beeton's choice, one may have brawn, pickled pork, curries and devilled bones, fried potatoes, pork chops, veal cutlets, bloaters and anchovies. As well as this, the cook could make up dishes like ham toast, croquettes, hashed game and rissoles (the last three being very useful for getting rid of the leftovers). Then there were savoury puddings, savoury pies, galantines and meat in jelly, but snobbism has set in, for black puddings 'are not bad in their way, but they are not among the things we would make to set before our friends'.[21]

Major L., who published *Breakfasts, Luncheons, and Ball Suppers* in 1887, divides breakfasts into four types: the family breakfast; the *déjeuner à la fourchette*, where the items were introduced in courses similar to dinner; a cold collation (which must produce an ornamental effect); and the *ambigu* which is 'an entertainment of a very heterogeneous character, having the resemblance to a dinner, only that everything is placed upon the table at once; relevés, soup, vegetables, and hot entremets are held to be ineligible. Our everyday breakfasts are in a small way served *en ambigu*, inasmuch as broiled fish, cold pasties, devilled bones, boiled eggs, cold ham etc. all appear together.'[22] Major L. sounds too, too much, but totally characteristic of his age. One is relieved that the term *ambigu* did not catch on, though it would be a useful term for so many functions today, as Major L. meant an ambiguous medley.

These are breakfasts designed for the weekend house party; Major L. suggests that they should contain a variety of items and he repeats much of what we have heard before: he thinks that sportsmen can eat whatever they like, but he is concerned that ladies should be more abstemious though he admits that 'they rarely eat meat for breakfast'. By meat he means roasts and cutlets because he then goes on to list what ladies may eat; this includes ham, bacon, chicken, kidneys, roast larks, broiled ducklings and devilled turkey.

Cookery books gave detailed menus for breakfasts for ten or twelve people, seasonal breakfasts throughout the year, breakfasts for every day throughout three months; new ideas spawned a medley of dishes from pickled oysters, shrimps, plovers' eggs and Russian caviar – tossed. (As the last comes under hot dishes, one fears that it might have been cooked.) Even dishes that involved much cooking, such as blanquette of lamb, a mayonnaise of turbot, a raised pie of pigeons and periwinkle patties, were all seriously suggested. Did people follow these ideas? I suppose ambitious society hostesses might have taken the books to their housekeeper and requested them to tell cook to make periwinkle patties for Sunday breakfast. One hopes the cook had enough sense to say that the periwinkles were unavailable.

Such opulence and conspicuous consumption of luxuries is reminiscent of Renaissance princes, medieval kings and Roman emperors. As their capital grew so did male headgear: top hats became taller, accentuating the height and impressiveness of the male, just as the skirts the women wore grew rounder, larger and more womblike accentuating the breeding fecundity beneath. By the later part of the century, the amount of capital in the hands of the rich appeared almost an embarrassment to them. They were constantly searching for ways to invest the money abroad; gambling money away in South America on shaky investments and being conned in the Far East seemed an integral part of extreme wealth. From 1881–4 Britain invested abroad at the average rate of £29,000,000 per year.

Street Food

The well-established tradition of street food continued into the Victorian era. The range of food offered to the public by itinerant traders in the London streets was a prolific medley, conjuring up the vigorous hybrid society it catered for. In one sense it can be compared with our own contemporary supermarkets where everything is immediately accessible to the hungry shopper. The Victorian, as he strolled the streets, could have eaten or taken back home hot eels, pickled whelks, oysters, sheep's trotters, pea soup, fried fish, ham sandwiches, hot green peas, kidney puddings, boiled meat puddings, beef, mutton, kidney and eel pies and baked potatoes. For dessert there were tarts of rhubarb, currant, gooseberry, cherry, apple, damson, cranberry and mince pies; plum dough and plum cake; lard currant, almond and many other varieties of cake as well as of tarts; gingerbread-nuts and heart-cakes; and Chelsea buns, muffins and crumpets, street ices and in Greenwich Park strawberry cream could be purchased at 1d a glass.[23]

To drink there was tea, coffee and cocoa, lemonade, Persian sherbet, elder cordial or wine, peppermint water, curds and whey, and rice milk. From the beginning of the century new articles had appeared, such as Brazil nuts, rhubarb, cucumbers, pineapples and ginger beer. The coffee stall superseded the saloop stall.[24]

In the midst of the century it was estimated that there were 500 traders in pea soup and hot eels, which were often sold together from the same stalls. Near the Bricklayers Arms at the junction of the Old and New Kent Roads a hot eel man sold what a customer described 'as spicy as any in London, as if there was gin in it'. The price of eels was a half penny for five or seven pieces and three parts of a cupful of liquor; the charge for a half pint of pea soup was a halfpenny. The most successful trader was one in Clare Market, who on one Saturday sold 100 lb of eels, but on an average Saturday he sold 80 lb.

Sheep's trotters were sold in London, Liverpool, Newcastle-on-Tyne, and some other major cities. It paid the fellman to dispose of his trotters by cooking them to be sold to the poor rather than selling them to the gluemaker, as the price of glue and size had fallen by mid-century. The trotters were scalded for half an hour; small boys then scooped out the hoofs which were sold for manure, or to manufacturers of Prussian blue used by painters. Women were then employed to scrape the hair off without injuring the skin, and the trotters were then boiled for a further four hours.

Baked potatoes were sold from about 1835 onwards throughout the winter months. The cleaned potatoes were taken to the bakers to be cooked in large tins for about an hour and a half. They were then taken from the bakehouse in a basket protected by green baize to keep them warm, and then placed in tins, some of which were highly decorative with brass ornaments; the tins stood on legs with an iron fire pot beneath, and there was also a compartment for butter and salt.

Whelks were brought to London live and boiled for ten minutes. 'They never kicks as they boils, like lobsters or crabs, they takes it quiet,' Mayhew reports a whelk dealer saying. They are sold from two to eight a penny depending on their size, and for sale in public houses they were carried around in a jar. 'People drinking there always want to eat. They buy whelks not to fill themselves, but for a relish.' They were seasoned with pepper and vinegar.

At the beginning of the century there existed a trotting butcher, who would carry raw meats into the suburbs with a horse and cart; his appearance might be hailed as saving a walk of a mile to a butcher's shop. As the suburbs merged together shops appeared among them and hawking butchers, unable to afford a horse and cart, made do with meat in a basket carried on their shoulders; the meat was mostly pork and veal, which did not weigh so heavily as beef and mutton; and they were also hawked around the pubs.

In the late 1830s a man who had been unsuccessful in keeping a coffee shop in Westminster hit upon the idea of vending ham sandwiches outside the theatre as the audience left. Ham, loaves and mustard were all that were required and he was immediately successful, making 10s a night, half of which was profit. He was soon joined by others, lads in service, errand boys, potboys, footboys or lads hawking around the inns. Around the theatres, concert rooms and music halls there were about seventy such hawkers of ham sandwiches.

The sellers of hot green peas go back, as we have seen, to the medieval era; the cry of 'hot peas-cod' meant that the peas were not shelled but boiled in the pod; they were eaten by being dipped in melted butter with a little pepper, salt and vinegar, and then drawn through the teeth to extract the peas, the pod being thrown away. Pea-sellers carried a round or oval tin pot with a swing handle with a ladle attached; the pan was wrapped around with a thick cloth to retain the heat. Mayhew observed only four of them: three were ladies who were shoemakers in the daytime and pea-sellers in the evening; the other was a man who had been in the trade for twenty-five years.

Another ancient streetseller was the pieman. The meat pies were made from beef or mutton, the fish pies from eels; the fruit from apples, currants, gooseberries, plums, damsons, cherries, raspberries or rhubarb, according to the season – and occasionally from mincemeat. By the 1850s the trade had almost been destroyed by the pieshop. The pieman visited the taverns and cried out, 'Here's all 'ot, toss or buy! Up and win 'em.' This is the only way the pieman could get rid of the pies; the customer tossed a coin and the pieman called head or tail; if he won, he received 1d and did not give a pie, if he lost the pie is free. Often the customers used the pie to throw at each other, or at the pieman. As one might surmise, the pies were not highly thought of as food.

Rice milk was made by boiling four quarts of skimmed milk with one pound of rice which had already been boiled in water for an hour; the addition of the rice increased the quantity to six quarts. Some sellers sweetened the milk, but others left it to the customer to sweeten it when they purchased. Mayhew noticed that the sellers of curds and whey were not doing very good business; the curds were sold in mugs with a spoon in each, 'but those that affect a modern style have glasses'.

The street pastries were of a strong flavour, attributable to the use of old or rancid butter, but this taste was enjoyed, especially by the young. Such food sold in the street included meat and fruit pies, boiled meat and kidney puddings, plum duff or pudding, and an almost infinite variety of tarts, cakes, buns and biscuits. Plum dough was a boiled currant pudding, either made in a ball or more frequently a 'roly-poly'. Duffs were boiled in cotton bags in coppers or large pans and were sold for half a penny each. Thirty years before Mayhew, Yorkshire pudding with raisins had been popular. About thirty Jewish pastry cooks who all lived in Whitechapel made all the pastries; the street vendors, who had other jobs in the daytime, bought from the pastry cooks. They sold coventrys (three-cornered puffs with jam inside), raspberry biscuits, cinnamon biscuits, chonkeys (a kind of mincemeat baked in a crust), Dutch butter cakes, Jews' butter cakes, bowlas (round tarts made of sugar, apple and bread), jumbles (thin crisp cakes made of treacle, butter and flour); and jams or open tarts with a little preserve in the centre.

Four thousand costers visited Billingsgate fish market on a Friday morning to buy oysters, soles, red-headed gurnets (gurnards) and cod, as well as eels placed on large cabbage leaves to keep them from writhing and falling off. Women held bunches of twigs for stringing herrings; there were blue, black piles of small live lobsters with their bound-up claws and long feelers; there were transparent smelts on ice whelks stood in sackfuls, yellow shells piled up at the top; and turbots were strung up so that their white bellies shone like mother-of-pearl.

The costermongers themselves ate in the streets. They breakfasted at a coffee stall; for 1d they procured a small cup of coffee and two thin slices of bread and butter, for dinner they bought 'block ornaments', their name for the small dark-coloured pieces of meat exposed on the cheap butchers' blocks or containers. Half a pound cost 2d, and they cooked them in a pub taproom. If they were in a hurry they bought a pie or saveloys with a pint of beer or a glass of neat gin called a 'short'. On Sunday they enjoyed a joint of roasted shoulder or half shoulder of mutton with 'lots of good taturs baked along with it'.

Fish and Chips

One of the earliest references to fried fish itself is made in *Oliver Twist*, first published in serial form between 1837 and 1838, where a fried fish warehouse is mentioned. This tallies with Mayhew who in the late 1840s spoke to a fried fishseller who mentioned he had been in the trade for seventeen years. The fried fish was sold with a slice of bread and it was hawked around the London pubs, the cry of the seller being 'fish and bread, a penny'. This fishseller had been a gentleman's servant, had married a servant maid, had a family and then neither of them could get a situation. He told Mayhew, 'I've lived in good families, where there was first-rate men-cooks, and I know what good cooking means.' He made 7s-10s each night (on a good night he sold 120 pieces), and half of that was profit. His wife opened a fried fish stall too, opposite wine vaults, and she made nearly half as much as he did on his rounds. Later in *Memoirs of Alexis Soyer* (1859) the editors[25] described Soyer buying fried fish and eating it as he walked through Soho. Frying fish was a good way of arresting its deterioration; Mayhew talks of fish-frying areas around Bishopsgate, the Inns of the Court and near London Bridge, where Jews often plied the trade.

Chip shops which only fried potatoes also existed; they were associated with slums and poverty, and were often run by widows in their front rooms, with an old boiler filled with rank lard set up on a block of bricks, with a small coal fire underneath. The tiny terraced houses would have stunk of fat, but people were content to buy chips wrapped in newspaper and ate them in the back room or took them home. In the latter part of the century, the greatest density of chip shops was in the industrial districts of Lancashire and Yorkshire between Oldham and Bradford, and it is thought it was in this area that the marriage of the chip with a piece of fried fish occurred. When exactly this was no one seems to know.

A method of preparing chip potatoes is detailed by Dr Kitchiner who suggests that after peeling the potato curls should be shaved off it, and then fried in lard or dripping. In her 1845 *Modern Cookery for Private Families* Eliza Acton copies the idea and improves it; she calls them potato ribbons, and pares them in long strips; she also cuts potatoes into chip-like lengths and described this as 'an admirable way of dressing potatoes, very common on the Continent, but less so in England than it deserves to be'. She was right, for the fried potato can be traced back to 1755 to Menon's *Les Soupers de la Cour*, while Audot in 1823 gives a recipe for *pommes frites* that must be *bien cassantes*, while Carême is very specific about the thickness of the raw potato which must be one twelfth of an inch.[26]

In 1861 Mrs Beeton gives a recipe for fried potatoes in the French fashion in which the potatoes are peeled and sliced, but it is obvious these are cut into rounds, then fried. Kitchiner's alternative method was to slice the potato a quarter of an inch thick, but neither method seemed to catch on until much later. Who was the first to have a chip stall is disputed. Some say it was Edward de Gurnier, who in 1865 had a stall with his wife in the Green Market, Dundee, where they sold fried chipped potatoes and boiled peas, a 'buster' for a halfpenny a saucerful.[27] Two years earlier John Lees had built a hut in Mossley and sold pea soup and pigs' trotters; on a visit to Oldham he found a man selling chipped potatoes in the 'French and American style' which was thought of as *à la mode*. Lees moved to a shop opposite and copied the style claiming it to be 'The Oldest Chip Restaurant in the World'.

In the US, the shaving method of chipped potatoes is now called Saratoga chips, in honour of George Crum, the chef at Moon's Lake House at New York's fashionable nineteenth-century spa, Saratoga Springs. It is said that in 1853 George Crum, impatient because a customer had sent back his French fries complaining that they were too thick, cut the potato as thinly as he could in a spirit of irony. As it caught on and spread throughout the country, a machine was invented to make these parings. At least this story points to the fact that chips were known and loved in America before 1853 and that they originally came from France. In fact, the story goes that French fries were brought back by Jefferson in the mid 1780s, and there is a note with corrections in his hand that points to it.[28] Further, the ribbon technique is given in a recipe in *The Virginia Housewife* (1824) by Mary Randolph which went through 19 editions throughout the century. Ude gives a recipe for fried potatoes in 1813, but there they were cut when raw in rounds as thick as two-penny pieces; this is the style that Mrs Beeton followed.

Frying ranges began to appear in Britain in the mid 1860s; there was even a version of a frier on a handcart which had a tall chimney. The earliest ranges were made of cast iron and heated by coal; tinsmiths fashioned the pans to hold the fat. Faulkner & Company of Oldham began manufacturing ranges between 1870 and 1875, by which time the fried fish shop was a booming business. At the same time deep-sea trawlers were coming into greater use, bringing abundant supplies of cheap Icelandic cod into the northern fishing ports. Yorkshire friers found that haddock was the most popular while Lancashire preferred hake though both were enthusiastic about cod. By 1914 fish and chip shops were selling 800,000 fish suppers every week.

They had become a central part of the working class diet. Cheap and convenient, and wrapped in newspaper, they were easy food to be eaten in a relaxed way outside on the street or taken back home and shared out, sometimes reheated in the oven for a few minutes. Salt and malt vinegar were available at the shop for seasoning, while back home in the latter part of the century the sauce bottle, either HP or tomato ketchup, became an inevitable addition. Some fish and chip shops had austere dining rooms where you could also get bread and marge and a hot cup of tea. The fragments of batter were given away free and the very poor could scrounge a cup of soup which was the dregs from the mushy pea saucepan.

The Food of the Poor

By the middle of the nineteenth century urbanisation had deprived millions of people of experiences that had been commonplace for humankind before. A London street-sweeper remarked to Mayhew that, 'I've never tasted honey, but I've heard it's like sugar and butter mixed.' Others had never seen a wheatfield or realised that it had any connection with bread. The sweeper earned 12s 6d a week; his food cost him 1s a day and beer 6d. On most days he ate boiled salt beef at any taproom; he didn't care for vegetables except for onions and cabbage, which he ate smoking hot with plenty of pepper. Mayhew observed that working scavengers or nightmen seemed fonder of strong flavoured and saltier food than other working men; they had 'a great relish for highly salted cold boiled beef, bacon or pork, with a saucer full of red pickled cabbage or dingy looking pickled onions, or one or two strong, raw onions, of which most of them seem as fond as Spaniards of garlic'. This sort of meat, 'sometimes profusely mustarded, is often eaten in the beer shops with thick shives of bread, cut into big mouthfuls with a clasp pocket knife'.

Another sweeper had bread, butter and coffee for breakfast, for dinner a saveloy with potatoes or cabbage, or a faggot with the same vegetables, or fried fish, or a pudding from a pudding shop or soup from an eating house; then his tea was the same as breakfast. The coster-boys lived off what they could scrounge and beg, but when in work they 'are fond of good living', as Mayhew puts it, and would choose a relish at breakfast, a couple of herrings or a bit of bacon. They never dined except on a Sunday when they would have a fourpenny plate of meat at a cookshop. They were very fond of pudding and should a plum duff at an eating house contain an unusual quantity of currants the news soon spread and the boys then endeavoured to work that way so as to obtain a slice.

The coster-girls started to sell when they were about seven, hawking oranges, apples, watercress or violets; they left home at four or five in the morning to go to the markets, they were on the streets until ten at night having nothing in all that time except one meal of bread and butter and coffee. They seldom got meat except on Sunday.

Industrial workers earned only a little more than costers; the London compositors, the highest paid of all artisans, earned £1 17s 6d in 1810. Their bread and flour cost 6s, 14lb of meat cost them 10s 6d for a week for one man, his wife and two children. Skilled workers and factory operatives earned about one pound a week, and after 1825, when potatoes had been accepted as part of the daily diet, they lived off those, and a little meat, bread, tea, sugar and milk.

A Manchester operative in 1832 rose at five in the morning, worked at the mill from six to eight, then returned home for half an hour for breakfast of tea, coffee and a little bread, returning to work until noon; dinner was potatoes with melted lard or butter poured over them and if they were lucky a few pieces of fat bacon. Work then began again at one o'clock, and continued until seven in the evening; before going to bed he ate his last meal of tea and bread.[29]

This was a subsistence diet which was barely adequate for survival and malnutrition was rife among the working class, which in 1867 over three-quarters of the 24,100,000 inhabitants of Great Britain. This comprised office workers, shop assistants, shopkeepers, foremen and supervisory workers, who were all slightly better paid than the unskilled.

In 1861 Charles Elmé Francatelli wrote and published *A Plain Cookery Book for the Working Classes*, which contained simple and nutritious recipes like boiled beef, pea soup, bacon and cabbage broth; but he, a pupil of Carême, former chef to Queen Victoria and chef de cuisine at the Reform Club, found it difficult to continue such a theme for a hundred pages. So we find baked suckling pig, baked goose, stewed steak, and baked skate creeping in. But as Francatelli knew, often the poor did not have a fire or stove to cook on and in his introduction he gives a list of necessary equipment and its cost, eleven items which cost £6 12s 4d. – six weeks' work for the highest paid artisan, almost a fortune.

Agricultural workers earned far less. Farmhands in the 1870s took home 7s 6d a week. The spread of labourers' allotments, which had been encouraged by national policy since early in the century, was what saved most of these low-paid farming families from starvation. Even so, this meant labouring for long hours in all weathers and on rations that were meagre, especially if there were young children. The mother might glean enough corn to keep the family in flour for much of the year; if the father had a few rows in an allotment for potatoes, he could grow peas and cabbages. Potatoes were eaten for breakfast, dinner and supper, and were often added to the bread dough. In the winter they might eat swedes and parsnips or buy two pennyworth of scrap meat from the butchers. The mother would make potato pies for the men to take with them for the day. If they kept a pig, they sold most of the carcass in return for boots, shoes, clothes and food, but kept back remnants to cure so as to flavour soups throughout the year. They made a 'mock tea' from burnt crusts and boiling water, and bread would be soaked in boiling water first before being added to milk for breakfast.[30]

In towns there was a greater range of cheap foods, so the reliance on the potato was not so pronounced. Forty per cent of the working class lived in abject poverty on a weekly wage of between 18s and 21s. It was calculated in 1899 that a couple and three children living off 21s 8d spent half of that on food which included no meat at all, their rent was 4s and the rest was clothing and fuel.[31] In Liverpool, a farthingsworth of milk could be bought, even delivered to the house. But by the end of the century food habits had altered radically, for those families that were not struggling on subsistence began to eat fruit in the form of jam and the imported banana, which supplemented or replaced apples as the only fresh fruit eaten by the urban poor. Also, the neighbourhood shop began to stock a greater variety of food, in competition with the new chain stores which suddenly flowered. In 1880 there were ten chains of butchers, by the end of the century there were 2,000, while from twenty-seven chains of grocers there grew to be 3,444. Shoe shops and menswear shops followed; women's wear came more slowly, and this sudden boom quietened to a more steady growth in the new century.

The rise of urban society, often clustered around an industrial nucleus, led to another important movement which would alleviate the worst rigours of poverty: the co-operative movement. Its origins are found in the eighteenth and early nineteenth centuries, in the Woolwich Co-operative Flour Mill (1760), the Hull Co-operative Corn Mill (1797), the Sheerness Baking Society and others, which were all dedicated to the reduction of flour prices and the supply of unadulterated, full weight produce, to people who had only latterly been stripped of the means to grow their own. In 1844 a group of twenty-eight poor weavers from Rochdale opened a small store in Toad Lane. They had been unsuccessful in a strike and sixteen of them were disciples of the philanthropist and socialist, Robert Owen, whose imaginative schemes had been dedicated to a more equitable life for the working man. They called themselves the Pioneers and stored goods, at first food and clothing, in the shop to sell for cash at local retail prices, while any profit they made would be shared out at the end of the year to their customers. They sold flour, oatmeal, butter and sugar, later tea and other groceries and later still, coal and furniture. Their purpose was to improve the moral character of trade rather than to make large profits, but the movement successfully cut out the middle man, reduced the price of necessities and was a form of saving. It became popular and after 1850 scores of societies sprang up in the north and the Midlands. In 1862 fifty co-operative stores in the Manchester region formed the English Co-operative Wholesale Society (CWS); by 1873 it boasted 250,000 members and an annual turnover of £2,000,000; by 1876 it possessed a fleet of ships and depots, and agencies and plantations in four continents. By 1890 the CWS had grown to 700,000 members and an annual turnover of about £7,700,000. Though some critics considered the CWS had now become a self-perpetuating bureaucratic machine, a great impersonal business enterprise, the CWS still fought for fairness in the marketplace in the interest of its customers, and more importantly it still gave its customers 'a divvy'. It was a key element in the struggle of working people and they went on flocking to the Co-op for food, clothing and housing. It was the best deal as consumers they had ever had.[32]

CHAPTER 10

Victorian Food

The Victorians redefined the female gender, a process that can be inferred from the title page of Mrs Beeton's book when she uses a quotation from Milton: 'Nothing lovelier can be found/In Woman, than to study household good.' Mrs Beeton does not give the reference, but these two lines are from *Paradise Lost*, Book IX, when Adam is speaking to Eve on their role in the 'work which here God hath assigned us'. The next line is also significant: 'And good works in her husband to promote'. Milton is full of advice on the roles in marriage: the husband 'shades thee and protects/The wife, where danger or dishonour lurks,/Safest and seemliest by her husband stays,' which the Victorians took to their hearts. This passage comes immediately before the Serpent tempts Eve. So Mrs Beeton's choice of quotation is that the housewife should strive to be like Eve before The Fall, her picture of the female is of an innocent but loving helpmate of man. The Victorian era split the female psyche into two: the idealistic and innocent woman who makes continual self-sacrifices becomes the mother of the ideal family and is therefore the ideal housekeeper; and the fallen woman, Eve the temptress, the whore and sexual betrayer. It was a terrible inheritance, because for several generations afterwards the British male was to see women either as a mother or a whore.

Household management, of course, is all about making the man of the house happy and comfortable. Mrs Beeton was not the first to say so, other female writers had constantly made such a point: the woman was there to serve the man, by inference she was nowhere near his equal. The redefinition of genders had begun in the seventeenth century when the capitalist entrepreneur had needed a wife to be a decorative symbol of his commercial success and not, as in previous centuries, a working partner. As this attractive piece of living art, she was expected to be witty, even feckless, an amusement to entertain her partner and his friends. Two hundred years after Milton, the Victorians had jettisoned this frivolity and taken the poet's earnest God-fearing words defining gender roles in marriage as a theological blueprint. The Victorian upper and middle class woman was expected to be passive, compliant, modest, fecund and maternal without a mind or a will of her own. She was not expected to cook. Others did that for her, as others changed the babies' nappies and bathed the children, so others wrung the chicken's neck and gutted the salmon. In this bewildering world young wives must have found Mrs Beeton's book a true godsend.

Isabella Beeton

The woman whose name evokes Victorian cooking was born in 1836 and died in 1865 aged twenty-eight from puerperal fever after giving birth to her second surviving son.[1] She was born in Milk Street off Cheapside in the City of London, the eldest child of Elizabeth and Benjamin Mayson. In 1841 her father died and left her mother with four children, but luckily she had another suitor in the wings, Henry Dorling, who married her two years later. He was Clerk of the Course at Epsom and the whole family went to live there while her mother bore her second husband thirteen children.

Isabella met Sam Beeton in 1855; she was a capable young woman who was well used to looking after the large family, which grew up first in Epsom and then in a large house built for them in Croydon. Isabella fell in love with the young publisher, who was inclined to be sickly and was thought a bit of a rake, but he was charming and deeply romantic. He was also extremely ambitious and soon after they met had started the *Boys' Own Journal* which was an immediate runaway success. In 1856 they married and went to live in Chandos Villas, Pinner. It must have been difficult for Isabella to appreciate how hard Sam worked; he rarely got back before midnight and was off again early in the morning after a cold bath. If he missed the last train back from Euston, then he walked from Fleet Street to Pinner, a distance of about sixteen miles. Isabella always left him a hot supper either in a warm oven or on two plates on two saucepans.

Sam was eager to publish a book of cookery and for Isabella to write it. A friend of theirs, Mrs English, wrote frankly to Isabella: 'I see difficulties . . . Cookery is a Science that is only learnt by Long Experience and years of study which of course you have not had.' She recommends that Isabella compile a book of recipes taken from a:

> . . . Variety of the Best Books Published on Cookery and Heaven knows there is a great variety for you to choose from. One of our best Woman Cooks who is now retired whom I know told me recently one of the Best and Most Useful Books is Simpson's Cookery, Revised and Modernised.

This letter appears not to have discouraged Sam and Isabella, and Mrs English was anxious that they meet the Duke of Rutland's cook, a Mr Orpwood who is 'a very clever little fellow in his Profession and a Great Economist and very minute and cleanly in his kitchen.' Mrs English went on to add:

> You will find the Stockpot is the great secret of the kitchen. Without it nothing can be done, with it everything can be done.

Sam, fortunately for us, ignored the advice of Mrs English and in his *Englishwoman's Domestic Magazine* wrote to housewives requesting recipes which would be tried and tested then published; 'We shall be exceedingly obliged to any lady who will spare us a few minutes to write out for us some of her choice recipes and thus make the EDM a means whereby her knowledge and skill may be communicated to the world for the benefit of all.'

The response was amazing, recipes arrived by every post and a terrifying process of sorting, classifying, testing and duplicating began. With the help of her younger sister, Lucy, Isabella whirled about the Pinner kitchen, beating eggs and mixing pastry, butchering, baking and boiling, conscientious in testing every recipe to examine whether it worked and whether it was good enough to be included. Jenny Lind, the famous singer, was represented by Soup *à la Cantatrice* which was beneficial to the chest and throat (it was made from sago and eggs) and Soup *à la Solferino* from a war correspondent present at the battle of Solferino in 1859; Isabella proudly writes that this is a Sardinian recipe which has been slightly Anglicised to improve it. One wonders what changes she made, for it is a recipe for flour, egg, cream and butter dumplings cooked in a bouillon. (I suspect she added the cream and butter.)

In the hard winter of 1858 she turned her house into a soup kitchen and was making 'Soup for Benevolent Purposes', giving out large helpings to the poor. The children of Pinner brought their bowls and took some soup home with them. The recipe is in the book and it was made from ox cheek, trimmings of beef and a few bones with lots of odds and ends of vegetables; it was thickened with rice or pearl barley, and its only seasoning was salt and pepper. She made 8 or 9 gallons of the soup every week and estimated the cost at 1½d per quart; she says: 'The soup was very much liked, and gave to the members of those families, a dish of warm, comforting food, in place of the cold meat and piece of bread which form, with too many cottagers, their usual meal, when, with a little more knowledge of the cooking art, they might have, for less expense, a warm dish every day.' How well meaning and warmhearted she is, yet sadly she shows her ignorance: the cottagers would have loved to have cooked soups themselves, but possibly did not have the means to make a fire.

A report by Dr Edward Smith in 1863 investigated indoor workers, needlewomen, kid-glove stitchers and shoemakers and discovered, 'They are exceedingly ill fed and show a feeble state of health.' Half the families never received any butcher's meat and those who did made their Sunday dinner from a pennyworth of sheep's brains or a pennyworth of black pudding; they survived on bread, potatoes, sugar, milk and tea.[2]

Beeton's Book

From 1859-61 the completed *Book of Household Management*, compiled and edited by Isabella, was published in monthly parts. Strangely enough, Sam, always an eager businessman, did not advertise the event, yet it caught on quickly. Women all over Britain eagerly awaited the parts, then began to collect them and stick them together. As the months rolled on, there could be no doubt of their popularity, so Sam made plans to publish them in volume form as soon as possible. Why did they make such an immediate impact? Considering the ambitious range of the book, which in its comprehension and scope no single woman could possibly hope to embody, one would be inclined to think that it might put off a housewife by the sheer size of the role she had to play. But this was a nation of Empire builders, challenges were stimulating and nothing was too vast for them not to conquer.

Isabella was at pains to structure the book so that it was easy to refer to; she had been made impatient by other such books and took great care that hers would not have the same fault. (This chapter is based on the first and best edition of the book.) The index at the front is over thirty pages long, from accidents to Yorkshire pudding. Secondly, she is comprehensive; the forty-four chapters range from a summary of the mistress's duties (which begins with a quotation from Proverbs, 'Her children arise up, and call her blessed') to legal memoranda. There is little doubt it really does include everything one needs to know about managing a household. Thirdly, she knew her audience; she knew what the middle classes needed to know, for from early adolescence she had looked after sixteen younger siblings and observed her mother manage their own busy household. No book before was so authoritarian in its advice ('Cleanliness is also indispensable to health . . . cold or tepid baths should be employed every morning') or so thorough in its detail ('As the visitors are announced by the servant, it is not necessary for the lady of the house to advance each time towards the door, but merely to rise from her seat.'). Fourthly, the recipes are representative of a very large readership: Isabella did not invent these recipes; they reflect what the middle classes were eating and cooking in the midst of the nineteenth century. No cookery book had succeeded in publishing such information before. Nor can there be any doubt that this burgeoning and affluent society wanted to continue to eat what it liked, and bought the book to ensure such an outcome.

The book therefore reflects a picture of a society in a very exact and detailed manner; part of the book's success must have been the clarity of this self-portrait. It served as a document to secure an image that was comforting; the women who perused its pages did not see smugness or arrogance but righteousness and leadership; they did not see domestic tyranny, but order and cleanliness, and were not irritated by constant moral harping and niggardly ethical strictures, but delighted by Mrs Beeton's piety and pragmatic moral sense. In reflecting a society, however, she also helped to propagate it; such a detailed memorandum was referred to by succeeding generations who took it all to heart, so that Mrs Beeton became the household bible of management. She writes in her preface that what had moved her in the beginning to write such a book was the 'discomfort and suffering brought upon men and women by household mismanagement'. Perhaps she was thinking of David Copperfield's wife, Dora, and her constant mistakes like buying a barrel of unopened oysters for a dinner party when they possessed no oyster knife to open them. 'I have always thought that there is no more fruitful source of family discontent than a housewife's badly cooked dinners and untidy ways,' Isabella wrote.

How good are the recipes? She divides the food up into seventeen chapters which follow the stages of a dinner party. She begins with soups, starting with a rich, strong stock, immediately followed by medium, economical stock (the liquor that the meat has boiled in with added trimmings and vegetables) and white stock (based on veal and poultry). She then gives a recipe for browning. Alas, this is nothing but burnt sugar and water; she says in France they add onion, but she does also add that the process of browning should be discouraged as it can impart a slightly unpleasant flavour to the stock. One hundred years earlier Mrs Raffald had given a recipe for browning which included pepper, cloves, shallots, mace, mushroom ketchup, salt, lemon, red wine and butter as well as sugar. This would have added a delicious note of complex piquancy to any gravy, but eighteenth-century culinary zest for flavouring had gone. Dutifully, even though she disapproved of the practice, Isabella gives directions on how to make burnt sugar and water and to bottle it. Within a few decades gravy browning would be commercially produced, unfortunately from such a recipe as hers.

Her soup chapter is alphabetical (as all the chapters are), continuing with almond soup, based on mutton broth (so this bears no relation to a medieval fast-day soup) and thickened not only with almonds but with egg yolks and cream. She gives soups for the poor and the rich: there is a bread and a potato soup as well as lobster and turtle soup, which she admits is founded on M. Ude's recipe; nevertheless when giving instructions on how to kill and butcher the turtle, she appears to know how to do it herself. This chapter includes eighty different soups, from all over Britain.

Her fish chapter begins with the biology of fish (yes, she tries to give the reader a comprehensive education) and continues with directions on how to dress the fish before cooking. She begins with anchovies: how to make anchovy butter or paste, how to pot them, and how to make anchovy toast with a warning about adulterations in the commercial pastes. She continues with barbel and brill; often she does not give exact cooking times, and that fish, for instance, should be simmered until it is done, for it depends upon the size; but when she does give a time it strikes me as far too long. She goes on to cod, carp, crabs and crayfish, and ends with several recipes on whiting. The turbot, as are other fish, are simmered in water and salt. There is never any addition of wine, herbs or spices. In *The French Cook*, M. Ude gives a recipe for a court bouillon for poaching fish with carrots, parsley roots and leaves, thyme, bay leaves, mace, cloves, and two bottles of white and two bottles of red wine plus salt, but he adds:

> This manner of boiling fish is too expensive in England, where wine is so dear; and very good court bouillon cannot be made with vinegar. Besides fish with court bouillon is always eaten with oil and vinegar, which is not customary in England.

So there we have it. The French authority M. Ude, who published his book in 1813 and who was working in England then, was as ignorant as Mrs Beeton of the English medieval tradition of poaching fish in wine, stock and herbs. Mrs Beeton did not set out to be innovative, or to bring back older English culinary traditions, nor is she that much interested in the final flavour or how it might be improved. What she does is to set in tablets of stone what is considered good cooking practice about 1860.

After fish, Isabella then gives a chapter on sauces, pickles, gravies and forcemeats, beginning with anchovy butter. The Victorian fear of pungent flavourings vanishes in this chapter; the menfolk would obviously insist on having powerful sauces and pickles, especially when out subjugating the natives in the colonies. She gives a recipe for camp vinegar that includes a head of garlic and cayenne and does not comment on using it cautiously. There is chilli vinegar made with fifty fresh chillies to one pint of vinegar; the chillis are cut in half and infused in the vinegar for two weeks. She says, 'This will be found an agreeable relish to fish, as many people cannot eat it without the addition of an acid and cayenne pepper.' One sympathises, for the fish would be overcooked and tend to the tasteless. She gives an Epicurean Sauce for steaks, chops, gravies or fish, which owes more to Mrs Raffald's Browning than anything else and is also bottled. There is also a 'very superior' recipe for Indian Pickle, with garlic, horseradish, ginger, cayenne and mustard seed. The Victorians were very keen on substitutes, so there is a recipe for caper sauce that is made from parsley boiled until 'it is a bad colour'.

There can be no doubt that meat lies at the centre of the British diet: her recipes for beef, lamb and mutton take up 200 pages, with a further 100 pages on poultry and game, while there are only fifty pages on vegetables. In the chapter on meat cookery there are many recipes that begin with cold roast beef, alerting the reader to the fact that left-over cooked meat was a continual challenge. Isabella calls this 'Cold Meat Cookery' and it marks a sharp decline in British cooking. At first glance the titles give the wrong impression: Baked Beef is sliced cold beef laid in a casserole interleaved with root vegetables, herbs and gravy reheated in the oven for half an hour. Beef cake is cold roast beef minced, mixed with bacon and egg, shaped into rissoles and fried. Slices of cold beef can be covered in mushrooms and gravy and reheated; or slices of cold roast beef can be fried in butter, then covered with chopped boiled cabbage which is also fried in butter. She calls this Bubble and Squeak. Cold roast beef can be curried with the addition of a dessertspoon of curry powder and a wineglass of beer. Other recipes included hashed beef, minced beef, beef rissoles, cubes of cold beef in a batter like toad-in-the-hole, for which she also gives a recipe, using steak and kidney; then there is cold meat cookery with mutton, where it is endlessly minced in a variety of recipes. Cold mutton cutlets can also be rejuvenated by being rolled in egg and breadcrumbs and fried in dripping; diced cold mutton could be mixed with cooked rice, suet and seasoning, shaped into sausages, rolled in egg and breadcrumbs (another Victorian favourite) and fried – these were called Dormers. Cold mutton is made into pies, hashed, of course; she adds a note that 'Many persons express a decided aversion to hashed mutton . . .' and goes on to defend the dish if properly done. Cold mutton can be turned into collops with the addition of spices, and again can be placed cold in a batter and called 'toad-in-the-hole'.

Her section on pork reveals a somewhat equivocal attitude to the pig; she is repulsed by its feeding habits, 'his gluttonous way of eating', and thinks they must be prone to disease; she then condemns the Jews for their 'usual perversity and violation of the divine commands' by keeping herds of swine. There is an unhappy anti-semitic flavour in the whole passage, but in this she is only representative of Victorian society.

It is obvious, however, that her love for ham and bacon is too strong to banish the pig from the kitchen and she gives directions for curing bacon. She gives few recipes for pork compared to the ones for beef and mutton and only one in cold meat cookery for both pork and veal. Her recipes for game are, as one would expect, comprehensive, beginning with blackcock where she mentions that some cooks roast the birds covered in a vine leaf; recipes follow for wild duck, hare, grouse, corncrake, leveret, partridge, pheasant (five recipes), plovers, ptarmigan, quail, snipes, teal, venison (two recipes), widgeon, woodcock and even the capercailzie, which she believed to be extinct in Britain. She then devotes a few pages to the carving of each bird.

Mrs Beeton appears to come into her own on the subject of puddings and pastry. Perhaps it is here that her readers waxed enthusiastic and sent in the most imaginative recipes. She starts off with general remarks, full of sensible advice on flour, butter, suet and lard, then continues with types of patty-pans and moulds; then comes a lengthy section on how to make puff pastry before we are into the puddings proper. There are over 100 different puddings and over sixty further creams, fritters, jellies and blancmanges. It is no wonder when one reads the emphasis upon dessert that Britain, with more than twice the per capita consumption, used almost half of all the sugar beet consumed in Europe, as well as by far the greater part of the overseas cane-sugar imported into Europe. Apples are made into various puddings, fifteen in all: there is a Bakewell Pudding, which is very rich and made with puff paste; an orange batter pudding; six different bread and butter puddings; five different suet and fruit boiled puddings; there are some suitable for picnics, gooseberry puddings, ginger puddings, iced puddings, rolled treacle puddings and even a Quickly Made Pudding. Then there are milk puddings, made from rice (four recipes), sago, tapioca and semolina, on which she adds a note:

> After vermicelli, semolina is the most useful ingredient that can be used for thickening soups, meat or vegetable, of rich or simple quality. Semolina is softening, light, wholesome, easy of digestion, and adapted to the infant, the aged and the invalid.

The milk pudding came into prominence within this century. Mrs Raffald gives recipes for only three made with rice, as does Eliza Acton. Kitchiner gives two. But they all ignore the other starches which Mrs Beeton and her readers love so much. Milk puddings were thought excellent for invalids and the young, a notion that the twentieth century, still so influenced by Mrs Beeton, took on board. It stemmed from her fervent belief in the efficacy of milk for all ailments: 'This bland and soothing article of diet is excellent for the majority of thin, nervous people, especially for those who have suffered much from emotional disturbances . . .' Was she thinking of her husband by any chance, a highly active man with tendencies towards manic-depression and who possibly had a secret sado-masochistic life?[3] She goes on, 'Milk is in fact a nutrient and a sedative at once . . . from no other substance, solid or fluid, can so great a number of distinct kinds of aliment, be prepared as from milk.'

Mrs Beeton's book shows us in vivid detail all that is good and bad in British cooking, but because she was an honest reporter she did not try to change any errors she saw (as in the use of browning) but included them, so that she supports the status quo; in supporting it she fosters and entrenches it. Her cold meat cookery would become the standby of lodging houses and institutions, of provincial cafes and myriad homes from every class which could not or would not buy it fresh. It should never have been enshrined within the pages of a cookery book for she gave it respectability. It was a method of disguising old food as fresh, for few of the masters and mistresses would have recognised the roast beef of a few days before resurrected as Baked Beef or Beef Cake and would have been under the impression that cook had made the dish from freshly slaughtered butcher's meat. Such cooking came about because of the urge to economise; if the master's table did not finish the dish it became food for the servants who were not fussy. But in such an affluent society why should economy be a presiding motive in the kitchen? Because social climbing necessitated a great show of wealth when entertaining, and to pay for the cost at other times the family ate more modestly. *Punch* was full of such cartoons depicting social pretension and the hypocrisy and facades it involved.

She was not, by far, the first to give respectability to the re-use of cooked meat; the French cooks had done so before her. In 1813 Ude, in his best-selling book *The French Cook*, gives a recipe for beef hash, but specifies it is for the servants and also says it must not be reheated for long otherwise it will be tough. Alexis Soyer in his *Modern Housewife* of 1849 writes for the middle-class housewife of differing means and imagines one, a Mrs B., whose husband's fortunes change from being a small shopkeeper to a prosperous merchant and the way her cooking changed over the years. In version one she has roast beef on Sunday, hashes it on Monday and makes a stew of it with vegetables on Tuesday; on the Wednesday she has fish if it is cheap, on Thursday pork, but on Friday they eat the remains of the pork. Two years later her husband's business is doing so well that Mrs B. is feeding three clerks who live with them; her meals have become more intricate, but on Monday two of Sunday's dishes are rejuvenated and so it continues until the end of the week. Later, becoming still more affluent, Mrs B. says that the remains of their extensive dinners are required for breakfast, lunch, nursery and servants' dinners.

Hodge-Podge, one of the most favoured recipes, was simply a mixture of leftover meats cut up into pieces combined with any old vegetables in leftover gravy. Alexis Soyer simply calls his recipe for the same dish 'Remains'. Nothing is wasted was a proud cry of the Victorian housekeeper. Whereas in the past and on the continent the scraps were fed to the pigs and chickens outside the kitchen door, now they were thrust beneath a floury sauce, reheated and sent up to the nursery. This is a product of urbanisation, the result of being cut off from the country roots, but it also springs from an obsession with how pennies can be saved, for the Victorian entrepreneur knew that riches and success would follow if the pennies were hoarded. No cookery books before or since, except in the war years, have been quite so full of remonstrations to make food that is economical; this is all the more astonishing when one knows that Britain was riding upon a tidal wave of profit. Or was it?

The growth of urbanisation marked Britain out as quite different from any other country. In 1851 about a quarter of British males were employed in agriculture; this figure dropped to seventeen per cent in 1881 and twelve in 1900. In France, Germany, Denmark, Sweden and the United States throughout that time over half of the labour force worked on the land. The acreage devoted to wheat in Britain had halved by the end of the century; we supplied less than a quarter of our own needs in butter, cheese and pork and even less in beef, mutton and lamb. We could no longer be considered a farming nation; factories, slum terraces with open cesspits running between them and shops, shops, shops had been built upon the green fields.

We all know that leftovers used with dexterous flair can make an excellent dish. There is an account by a French *bon vivant* in the Second Empire that celebrates the art when he speaks of *croquettes Périgord*:

> These croquettes are truly delicious, the day after such luxurious feasts as those served on meat eating days, with subtle and patient skill the finely chopped meat of the preceding day blends, mingles, harmonizes, somehow comes together in a single dish. Garlic scented roast beef and leg of lamb, a subtle hint of roast veal rump, the delectable aroma of chicken, quail and partridge with their exquisite bouquet – each makes its own contribution and adds its own touch to the admirable whole . . . It perfumes the entire house. Then they arrange it on a platter, a masterpiece, a golden pyramid browned in fat, topped with a bonnet of green parsley. . . . Sometimes these croquettes made from a variety of meats are hidden by an artistically browned batter, similar to the way some cooks prepare salsify or artichoke hearts. But when served in this way it is a venial sin if the chopped meats are not ornamented with lovely slices of black truffles, cooked in champagne.[4]

One can imagine any number of French cooks working in England making such croquettes: the women would be delighted, for the croquettes were perfect to nibble on and toy with, while the men would be longing for a large piece of underdone beef. Yet how often were the leftovers turned into gastronomic art?

To the society she wrote for, Mrs Beeton's strength was that her book covered all social occasions, from the grandest to the most modest, but it also gave recognition and seemingly also approval to domestic practices that had become ingrained. It was an extraordinarily good-mannered book; for example, when talking of the origin of sugar beet she avoids pointing out that its discovery was prompted by the English naval blockade of France in the Napoleonic Wars. Instead she says, 'circumstances having, in France, made sugar scarce'. On family relations she taught moral virtues gently; she instilled into the pages a sense of politeness, restraint and caution, she gave credibility and distinction to the middle classes who had had no champion before. She knew exactly who her readers were as when she advised against dinners *à la Russe* in households without sufficient resources. They were scarcely suitable for small establishments, she thought, as they required a large number of servants.

A la Russe

At the time that Mrs Beeton's book was first published there was a change in the way that dinner was served for the most fashionable segment of society. The previous dining style had been called *à la Française* and involved, as we have seen, a number of different dishes being placed on the table all at once as a first course, with the diners helping themselves and others. When these were eaten and removed, the second course involved more dishes being placed in the same position. If there was a haunch of meat to be carved then the host carved at the head of the table. This sometimes caused accidents: a large goose might fly into a lady's lap, or fat spurt into someone's eye. It also meant that at a large dinner party the host carved for some length of time before being able to sit down himself to eat. For festive meals at home, most of us still go in for this method of dining; several dishes are placed on the table, we help ourselves, while the host or head of the family carves the joint or bird. Such an arrangement often helped or hindered romantic matters, as Jane Austen wrote to her sister:

> I could see nothing very promising between Mr P. and Miss P.T. She placed herself on one side of him at first, but Miss Benn obliged her to move up higher; and she had an empty plate and even asked him to give her some mutton without being attended to for some time. There might be some design in this . . . (Jan. 1814)

Carving became an accomplishment of gentlemen, one of the minor arts of polite life; 'to dance in hall and carve at board' were classed together, according to Meg Dods. Not only did everyone have to have a good portion of the meat, but the carver must leave the joint looking as presentable as possible, 'sometimes by rearranging the garnishing over it or, as in the case of fish, by folding it beneath part of the napkin on which it was served,' wrote William Kitchiner. When the first course was finished the host gave a signal to the servant to remove the dishes; the signal was as discreet as possible, so that servants would silently enter to do the work. (I recall in a private home in the 1950s a bell upon the floor near the host's feet which could only be heard in the kitchen.) After the second course all the plates and cutlery were removed. The richer the host the more dishes at each course and the more servants to bring and take them away.

So why change the manner of service at all, for surely *à la Française* allowed for conspicuous consumption in the grand manner? The change allowed the host much greater control over the event; it was a method of structuring the dinner with rules for the time of dining, the pace of the meal, rules for how to serve it, how to eat it and to whom to speak.[5] It allowed for the dining table to be laid with epergnes, posies, folded napkins and decorative flower displays, the finest glass and all the silver with printed menus. Table decor was highly significant, showing at once the expense the host had gone to and his position in society. The new service relied on butlers, footmen and parlourmaids to serve all the dishes individually offering to each diner from the left the dish on a silver salver, while the butler carved the meat at the sideboard. At the grandest dinners there was almost a footmen to each guest; to have servants swarming around guests gave considerable prestige to the host. It was not so much the visible splendour that held a guest in awe and respect, however, but the unseen rules of etiquette, the secret code that imposed the strictest and most pernickety dos and don'ts on the social outsider, rules that had to be learnt in order to become part of such a society, and which, if broken, meant ostracism.

It could be a minefield, particularly for a young woman entering society. She would be paired off with a gentleman in the library some minutes before dinner began. Name cards would be placed upon the table with a folded table napkin hiding a bread roll at the place setting. After sitting down she would first take off her gloves which were laid in her lap, and then covered with her table napkin; she would place the roll to her left. At each setting there were two large knives, three large forks, a silver knife and fork for fish and a tablespoon for taking the soup; on the right there would be a wide-rimmed glass for champagne, a small one for sherry and a coloured glass for hock. The dessert spoon and fork were not placed upon the table, but would appear for the sweet course; the salad would be served on a small crescent-shaped plate placed on her left. Both plates were used at once, meat taken from the main plate and salad from the other.

Part of the fashion was to serve an hors-d'oeuvres as a beginning to these grand dinners; this would be served from a large platter with several partitions containing, for instance, anchovies, olives, prawns, oysters; you were intended to take a small morsel of one or two to be eaten with a knife and fork on a small plate. This cutlery would be removed before the soup which would be a choice of two. Mrs Beeton gives a menu for twelve people in November and offers Hare Soup or Julienne Soup, followed by Baked Cod or Soles *à la Normandie*, then the entrées,[6] then meat, fowl, game and sweets. 'All entrées, such as patties, or mince, must be eaten with a fork only; but when sweetbreads, cutlets or game enter into the composition of the dish, a knife is of course requisite.'[7]

For her November dinner party Mrs Beeton recommends lobster patties, croustades of marrow with *fines herbes*, a *riz de veau aux tomates* and mutton cutlets with *soubise* sauce, all of them entrées. These might be followed by a sirloin of beef, braised goose, boiled fowls with celery sauce and a bacon cheek with sprouts. Everything would be cleared away before the dessert course and a silver slice used to remove all the crumbs; the wine glasses would go only to be replaced with three fresh ones, for claret, port and sherry. The fruit already on the table would be handed around by a servant after the dessert plate with a finger glass, doily, and dessert knife and fork had been placed before each person. Etiquette demanded you should remove the finger bowl from your plate, placing it on the doily on the left; you might then dip your fingertips into the water. The hostess, after the ladies have finished, should bow to the lady on her husband's right and rise from her seat; this was the signal for the ladies to retire, led by the lady of the highest rank with the hostess the last to leave. For the inexperienced all this rigmarole must have been a nervous nightmare, but it was meant to be; such detailed rules were a secret code to keep *hoi polloi* at bay, firmly outside the castle walls.

Why should this new form of service be named 'in the Russian manner'? The change had been a long time happening; Dr Kitchiner had said, 'It would save a great deal of time etc if poultry, especially large turkeys and Geese were sent to the table ready cut up.' A little later Meg Dods hoped 'to see the day when all large troublesome dishes will be taken to the side-table and carved by a *maître d'hôtel* or whoever waits on the company, as is now the general practice of France, Germany and Russia.' The two forms of service almost merged into each other; to call the new one *Russe* was one way of differentiating it from what had gone before. It was said that the manner derived from the Czar's mode of dining and was introduced into France at the peace of 1814 in honour of the Russian Emperor, but this is uncertain. What is clear is that it ushered in not only a more rigid way of entertaining hemmed around with formality, but also a more lavish use of French terms and dishes. What now grew up in the last half of the century was pseudo-French cooking, an anglicised version of Gallic dishes adapted to banquets and grand dining but which omitted much of the essential qualities of the originals.

French and British Cooking

French cooking had been fashionable ever since the Restoration, when it had been associated with Papism and the Jacobite cause. In the nineteenth century these associations had faded away. In the seventeenth century, if we look at William Verrall, Charles Carter and others, there had been French chefs working for Roman Catholic families and the cooking they created was very nearly authentic. By the late eighteenth and early nineteenth centuries French chefs were more common and not only allied with great aristocratic families. Jane Austen's brother, the banker, had one who wrought 'exquisite dishes' from the turkey sent from Chawton.

The first French cook who came to prominence in Britain was, as we have seen, Louis Eustache Ude. His father had been cook to Louis XVI and he briefly followed him in that position until the Revolution. He was *maître d'hôtel* to Princess Letizia Bonaparte, but found that unsatisfactory, so he came to England, where he became chef to Lord Sefton, and was happy. On Lord Sefton's death he went to the Duke of York and finally became director of St James's Club; after he retired on an annuity bequeathed by Lord Sefton, he published *The French Cook* in 1813; so successful was it that it was republished many times up to 1833. He was sensitive to Roman Catholic fast-day requirements because he mentions adapting recipes on those times. When an English m'lord appointed a French chef he knew he was also possessing a fragment of French history, an additional aura that boosted such chefs' renown. Ude begins his book with the statement 'Broth is the foundation of Cookery,' (so this is where Mrs Beeton's friend got the idea from) and goes on to describe the various types. Ude has obviously adapted his own cooking to British tastes – see his method with fish below. Besides, every chef had to adapt to the tastes of his employer and Ude gives a recipe of a *ramequin* Lord Sefton's way: it is puff paste with layers of Parmesan folded over several times and baked. This is one of the dishes that Mrs Beeton uses without acknowledging the source.[8] Her book shows Ude's influence, for there is no difference in the making of soups and sauces except that Mrs Beeton has many more of them.

(There are almost fifty years between the two books.) British cooking had by then absorbed a bastardised French influence.

Ude boils salmon, John Dory, turbot and even a sturgeon in salt and water. In 1759 Verrall had written of his chef, M. Clouet: 'He never boiled any fish of any sort in the plain way,' and continued by giving several recipes of fish poached in wine, herbs and sauces. Ude's section on pastries is quintessentially French, and Mrs Beeton, as if knowing there was no real competition here, again uses his recipe, calling it French Puff Paste; she also gives Soyer's recipe for puff paste and throughout her book borrows from Soyer frequently, again not always acknowledging her source. (This, of course, in many cases may simply be as a result of her readers sending in unacknowledged borrowed recipes.)

Because of this idolisation of French chefs, there was no chance of an English chef learning how to practise British cooking. In fact British cooking was disdained by the rising middle classes as something inferior. That a whole nation could embrace the cooking of a nation that had been historically its fiercest rival and enemy might seem astonishing. But Britain in this century felt itself to be far superior to any other nation in the world, and that like Ancient Rome before it, it could steal with impunity any idea or culture it thought desirable. Hence, French titles for a bastardised French cooking were utterly reasonable. With the disdain for British cooking came a disdain for the female cook, and most domestic cooks were women for the very good reason that they cost less. Marcham, the Duke of Rutland's French chef at Belvoir Castle, was paid £147 in 1810, rising to £161 14s in 1814 while a woman cook would have received something like £14.⁹ The average female cook in a middle–class home need not even have been literate, only to have picked up a vague knowledge of cooking from being a parlourmaid at her previous place of work; untrained and unskilled she learned as she went along. The middle classes, however, if they were honest and not in pretentious mood, really loved British cooking; the very heart of their meals was meats, boiled and roasted, great haunches (if they were rich enough) of beef, mutton and pork, with a gravy made from their juices and drippings; these they enjoyed almost daily. They were aware that roast beef and Yorkshire pudding were thought by their superiors to be inferior food, yet beef with lashings of mustard and horseradish sauce remained an integral part of the food of chop houses, inns and taverns all over Britain.

What the British thought was French cooking was a radical adaptation towards their own tastes; as much as an Indian restaurant gives a British interpretation of curry today. Secondly, many of these so-called French influences were medieval, and had been enjoyed here for hundreds of years; after the Reformation we had forgotten about them. The tragedy for our own cuisine was that this snobbish idolisation of the French cuisine, which reached its peak in the latter half of the nineteenth century, made us feel that British cooking was far inferior. Without skills expended upon it and without credence, it very often did become inferior; it was thus despised even more and became a butt for jokes. Other factors in the same century conspired to help its fall. (See end of chapter.)

Cheap Imports

Food imports up to the nineteenth century had always been limited to foods such as dried fruits and spices, which could travel distances without spoilage; the problem with other foods was how to keep them free of harmful bacteria. The answer to the problem, which would radically change world economy and trade, began quietly with some experiments by a Frenchman. Nicolas Appert, a Parisian confectioner, discovered that he could preserve food by putting fresh food in glass jars, standing the jars in hot water to expel air and then hermetically sealing them with alternate layers of cork and wax. In 1804 Appert was awarded a prize by Napoleon who saw the discovery as of military strategic importance. An Englishman, Peter Durand, conceived the idea that tin might be more suitable as a medium as it was lighter, cheaper and more amenable to being shaped, while it could conduct heat more efficiently than glass and would not be vulnerable to breakages in transport. He took out a patent for the use of tin canisters in 1810. In the early 1820s the firm Donkin & Hall, having bought the patent from Durand, was supplying the Admiralty with canned meats for use in ships' stores, and by 1839 tin-coated steel containers were widely used all over the world. It was there the can stayed for the next two decades until the American Civil War in the 1860s, where as Napoleon had foreseen, tin cans of meat that could be quickly opened were a convenient way of getting a quick nutritious meal inside a fighting soldier.

The meat-canning industry as well as armaments quickly began to flourish and by the 1870s tinned meat was being exported to Britain from the States, Australia and Argentina, where a canning industry with the name of Fray Bentos had started by the River Plate in 1871. The meat was not of good quality; it was mostly boiled mutton from Australia, and canned with sinews and fat, so it looked highly unattractive. A number of food poisoning scares had made the British public nervous and they were suspicious of the new product. Its only charm was its cheapness: it cost from 5d-7d per lb, half that of fresh meat. Fray Bentos Corned Beef first appeared in 1876 and soon became popular with the working classes as it could be sliced and placed between bread as a packed lunch.

The canning technique was now being applied to milk, fish, vegetables and fruit. The commercial manufacture of tinned condensed milk had begun in the 1850s in America and Switzerland, and was a success despite its drawback of contributing to the increase of rickets and other diseases. Fruit canning began in California in the late 1860s and by the 1880s tinned peaches, apricots, pears, cherries and pineapples were part of the store cupboard in middle-class kitchens and became integral to quick desserts. By the 1870s canned salmon from Columbia and Alaska was exported all over the world. (In Britain Crosse & Blackwell began canning salmon as early as 1849, opening a factory in Cork.)

A small tin cost around 9d and was far too expensive for the working classes, but it became yet another standby of the middle-class kitchen. In 1880 a firm in Maine first produced cans of pork'n'beans; fifteen years later H.J. Heinz of Pittsburgh, Pennsylvania came up with the recipe for baked beans in tomato sauce, but it was another ten years before the first tins were on sale in the north of England, only to receive a lukewarm response.

It took thirty years of experiments with freezing in order to achieve the refrigerated hold packed with mutton and beef in the SS *Strathleven* when she sailed from Melbourne to London in 1880. Meat that sold in Australia for only 1½d could sell in London for 5½d; the voyage opened the flood gates to cheap meat imports from USA which sent pork, from the Argentine with its beef and from New Zealand with its lamb. By 1902 more than 56 lb per head per year was being eaten in Britain; the farmer at home only contributed less than half of our requirements.

By the end of the nineteenth century such meat was now affordable at least once a week for the working classes, whose wages had risen. A joint of beef, pork or lamb could be eaten on Sundays and the remains used up on the weekdays. After all, such necessary economies had been authorised by the middle classes emboldened by eminent cookery writers, hence rehashed food for the weekday diet became the normal routine for the average working family.

Convenience Food

In the second half of the century, industry and technology began to be an integral part of Britain's food supply; it was another factor that crept into Britain's kitchens and did them fatal injury, a harm they are still reeling from – convenience food.

It began innocently enough. In the late 1860s roller mills came into use. Millers liked to use 'hard' American wheat; it was cheaper and also had a high gluten content, which was good for rising, but it did not grind well beneath the milling stones and gave a brown flour. Bakers used additives to whiten the loaves, using anything from chalk, alum and ammonium carbonate to ground-up pipe clay, powdered bones, gypsum and ground stone. (Adulteration of food had reached such alarming proportions that in 1875 the Government at last passed the Sale of Food and Drugs Act that formed the basis of food law until 1955.)

Porcelain rollers were the answer, giving the miller more control over the refinement of the flour by passing it through a series of rollers, so that the bran and wheatgerm that gave the flour its colour could be sifted out. A roller mill in Glasgow in 1872 began producing white refined flour and the invention spread rapidly; by the end of the century everyone wanted pure white flour without wheatgerm. It was a necessary prelude to the sliced loaf, which arrived in the 1930s. It was also a significant change in status, for that centuries-old symbol that white bread had always stood for could now be eaten by the whole of society, even the very poor, as part of its daily diet. Brown bread was slowly to become the status of elitism where it still is today. There was one exception to this universal trend: the firm of Hovis (from the Latin construction *hominus vis* – strength of man) which began marketing its loaf in the 1890s; it was formed by millers who manufactured a flour that retained a high amount of wheatgerm; the formula was patented in 1885 by Richard Smith, a miller from Stone in Staffordshire. In 1898 the Hovis Bread Company was founded.

On the heels of the roller mills there came new processed, packeted, bottled and canned food, which made the life of the cook beneath stairs easier. It erased some time-wasting chores of beating and sieving, which helped to streamline her cooking by reducing the time she spent at the stove, but affected the original flavour of many dishes by rendering them even blander. It gave them an artificial flavour and texture which some would find addictive and others repellent.

These commercial packages included quick-acting compressed yeast, self-raising flour and baking powder, which made bread and cake making simpler; there was shredded suet, custard powder without eggs, blancmange made of flavoured gelatine mixed with dried milk and concentrated egg powder, and jellies in various flavours. As well as farmhouse cheeses, there were now great blocks of cheese matured very quickly, and tins of sweetened, condensed milk. Margarine was made from beef fat and milk; there were bulk dried vegetables and dried packets of soup mix; commercially bottled pickles and sauces; and cans of vegetables and fruit.[10] There were mixes for gravy, beef tea from a jar for invalids and tins of tripe, peas and beans; meals were now augmented by these first convenience foods.

The 1870s were years where the food industry began to boom: biscuit, jam and chocolate manufacturing were among the first to lead the way, with confectionery manufacturers such as Fry, Rowntree and Cadbury. Another great change in the national diet was the emergence of breakfast cereals which were imported from the States. They were a product of the policies of various vegetarian groups and dietary reformists,[11] but the concept originally came from Dr John Harvey Kellogg, director of the 'medical boarding house' which later became a sanatorium at Battle Creek, where he developed his concept of 'natural foods'. In the 1860s he formulated Granola, the first ready-cooked breakfast cereal, made from a mixture of wheat, oatmeal and maize baked in a slow oven. In 1896 he produced Granose, the first flaked cereal food made of wheat, and three years later the cornflake, which was to invade and take over Britain. By the 1890s all the manufacturing processes to treat cereals had been invented and a rash of flaking, toasting, puffing and extrusion dominated this new breakfast industry. Shredded Wheat was invented in 1892 by Henry D. Perky of Denver, Grape Nuts in 1898 by Charles W. Post, Puffed Wheat in 1902 by Alexander Anderson and Toasted Oat Flakes in the 1890s by the Beck Cereal Company of Detroit. (My mother, as a small child, remembered a free sample of Shredded Wheat arriving through the letter box – this would be around 1907-09. It arrived without instructions or they were not read, and her family sampled it straight, decided it was most unpleasant and never tried it again for years.)

Whether it was quick breakfasts that needed no cooking or a custard made from a powder, British cooks now relied on a host of manufactured goods, which required no skill, erased any singularity and further deprived it of its rural roots.

The Rise of the Fancy Biscuit

Biscuits originally were not fun or destined to give pleasure at all; they did you medicinal good, or they were ship's biscuits. At Deptford, Portsmouth and Plymouth the victualling authorities in the King's dockyards set up their own baking establishments for the navy where these biscuits were produced. They were a kind of hard, dry bread made to be carried to sea and consisting only of flour and water. The process was mechanised in 1833. The medicinal biscuit was made by Dr William Oliver (1695-1764) of Bath, to be chewed with the medicinal waters, and by Dr John Abernethy (1764-1831). It was Lemann's of Threadneedle Street, London (founded in 1747), which brought out the first recorded non-medicinal biscuit to commemorate the marriage of the Duke of York in 1791. This was copied by small London pastrycooks or confectioners, who made sweet biscuits as a sideline during the daytime, using the ovens that baked bread throughout the night.

It was Quakers who were the pioneers in fancy biscuit-making, concerned in the manufacture of goods that could do no harm to anyone, free from adulteration and fairly priced. In the late 1830s Jonathan Dodgson Carr, a miller and baker of Carlisle, began to design machinery for cutting and stamping biscuits. By 1846 Carr's of Carlisle, which believed it was the first to mechanise the process, was producing 400 tons of biscuits in a year. Another Quaker, miller and confectioner George Palmer, joined up with his cousin, Thomas Huntley, who made biscuits entirely by hand in his Reading shop; they built a small factory behind the shop and were producing biscuits early in the 1840s. Ten years later they were making biscuits containing butter, eggs, milk and flavourings, caraway, cinnamon, essence of lemon and orange flower. By 1870 they were the largest biscuit company in the world, making 120 varieties and claiming that their names Ginger Cob and the Osborne had been borrowed by others, including Carr's.

Peek Frean & Co. was established in Bermondsey by 1860 making fancy biscuits; among them were the Garibaldi and the Marie, but half its output was ship's biscuit. All the biscuit manufacturers had used agents to recruit family grocers all over the country to stock their biscuits. By the 1860s Huntley and Palmer had 700 retailers in nearly 400 different towns throughout the British Isles. In the next decade the chain grocers like Liptons and Home & Colonial Stores, seeing how profitable biscuits had become, made their own arrangements for manufacturing them. Towards the end of the century Scottish and Irish firms like McVitie & Price, Macfarlane Lang and Jacob's of Dublin began to impinge upon the English market.

The rise of the fancy biscuit was due to the changes in meals and the time they were eaten, to the affluence of the middle classes and the spread of tea drinking. They were also amazingly convenient, sold in charming tins that could be re-used. Between 1840 and 1860, when large breakfasts were being eaten and people dined at five, lunch or luncheon was a snack of a beverage and bread and cold meats; biscuits easily fitted into this meal or as the other snack eaten before retiring to bed. During his large hunting breakfasts, R.S. Surtees' Mr Jorrocks consumed a few ship's biscuits, which were probably a generic name for plain biscuits, while the ladies of Mrs Gaskell's *Cranford* nibbled a lady's biscuit with their mid-morning wine. Long before mechanisation, in Jane Austen's *Emma*, Savoy and Sponge biscuits were served at evening parties, so the biscuit had long been there.

In the beginning the new sweet biscuits were priced high, and so could only be eaten by the upper classes or the well-heeled. By far the most expensive were Huntley and Palmer's Rout biscuit for formal parties, which cost 2s a pound; Ratafias, Lemon and Orange Dessert and Raspberry biscuits cost 1s, while Ginger Nut and Osborne cost 6d, a quarter of what labourers earned in a day. In 1859 Huntley and Palmers sold six million pounds and Peek Frean's one million pounds. Biscuits became fashionable for the affluent clergy and institutions such as Oxford and Cambridge colleges, public schools and gentlemen's clubs.

By the 1860s, as the solid Victorian villas began to spread in the suburbs around the centre of London, mealtimes were changing again. Breakfasts were served earlier for the Victorian businessman had to travel to work, while dinner time was now around seven to give the paterfamilias time to return home. Luncheon and afternoon tea now became common; at both these meals biscuits were served, biscuits for cheese for the gentleman at his club, and sweet biscuits for tea at home for the mistress and her guests. By the late 1870s Huntley and Palmer were selling 37 million pounds of biscuits a year and Peek Frean another 17 million.[12]

As did tobacco barons and big brewers, food producers sometimes came to national prominence as well as local eminence: the Colmans of Norwich, the Frys of Bristol, the Cadburys of Birmingham were all seen as leaders of British industry. Some of them reinforced their market power by the shrewd use of advertising: Hovis was perhaps the most brilliant, giving away baking tins which had its name imprinted upon the side so that it appeared on the bread itself; but Oxo, Rowntree and Bovril all used early poster design to great effect. The mustard and starch manufacturer, Colmans, established an advertising department to create new marketing ideas as early as 1870.

Drinking Milk

As London grew in size its food demands covered the whole country, which inevitably changed the nature of farming, so that farmers turned to artificial fertilisers for their land and concentrated winter feeds for their livestock. Railways helped to bring in fresh produce from the country, but in such quantity that mono-culture crept on to the acres, which brought the problem of disease and deterioration of quality. In 1847 the *Lancet* had condemned the unhygienic character of London's milk supply, which was hardly surprising when you read a description of the cowsheds in Golden Square behind Piccadilly Circus:

> Forty cows are kept in them, two in each seven foot space. There is no ventilation, save by the unceiled tile roof, through which the ammoniacal vapours escape . . . Besides the animals, there is at one end a large tank for grains, a storeplace for turnips and hay, and between them a receptable into which the liquid manure drains, and the solid is heaped . . . the stench thence arising is insufferable.[13]

By 1855, the early milk trains had made their appearance in London, bringing the milk in churns. As the capacity of the churns varied from 9-18 gallons it is impossible to estimate how much milk was produced and drunk, but it was thought no more than a weekly consumption of 1.4 pints, a little more than Dr Edward Smith's figure (see below). In country districts, small towns and the suburbs of cities milk was sold from handcarts or horse-floats by retailers who were either part of the farm that had produced the milk or buyers who had bought directly from them. If farmers did not actually deliver the milk, then they drove the milk to the nearest railway station and from there it would travel into the nearest town or city. The urban areas were already divorced from links with the producers in the country; the London market drew its supplies of milk from Essex and Suffolk, fifty miles or more distant, and then as it grew ever larger, from even further afield, from Wiltshire, East Dorset and Somerset, and from the Midlands as far north as Derbyshire.

The demands of London converted farmers who were making butter and artisan cheeses from summer grass milk into selling the milk (this was milk of the highest quality for cheese-making) and influenced them to change their methods so that they could produce winter milk too. This meant autumn calving cows, fodder crops and the purchase of concentrates, which produced milk of less quality but perfectly suitable for drinking.

In the 1860s Dr Edward Smith's report to the Privy Council on the food of the labouring classes found that the average person drank less than one pint of milk per week. As the milk supplies came from further and further away, it brought the twin problems of souring and adulteration. As people could not rely on milk not going off through the night, deliveries of milk arrived very early in the morning in time for breakfast, having travelled by train in the night. The further away from London the milk came from, the more special milk depots and creameries had to be built beside the railway depot to ensure the milk was cooled before the journey. London firms advertised that they delivered three times daily, inflicting upon the roundsman a working day of 13-14 hours. The cooling rooms at the depots helped, but in the hot summers of 1893 and 1911 people ran short of milk because of sourness. All the hot summers of the 1890s through to the First World War produced a rise in infant mortality which was ascribed to summer diarrhoea. In hot years when there was an epidemic infected milk was considered to be a factor.

By the 1890s pasteurised milk had made its appearance and the first milk bottle arrived by 1900; both took some time to be accepted. By then the diet of rural labourers had much improved; a survey in 1902 showed that their consumption of raw milk was between 3 and 7 pints of milk per week. It was not until 1910 that a few firms had adopted pasteurisation or sterilisation. People had complained rightly that both changed the flavour and the latter tinged the milk grey; also some doctors rejected it as lacking in any nutritive qualities. Despite the introduction of the bottle, as late as the 1920s pasteurised milk was still being delivered in the usual manner dipped from a churn into jugs provided by the housewife. Bottling milk helped to prevent adulteration by the roundsmen, but the supply of bottles, their cleaning, sterilisation and capping were expensive extras for the dairy. The most serious problem, however, was tuberculosis in the dairy herd: of 750 samples of milk taken by health inspectors at London railway stations in 1913, a tenth were found to contain active tubercle bacilli and it was discovered that the infection was rampant in those dairy herds that provided winter milk. This did not cause panic, however, as it was believed that bovine tuberculosis could not be transmitted to human beings.[14]

Reasons for the Decline of British Cooking

Britain in the nineteenth century was an aggressively, socially mobile society, and people in fierce competition to gain a place on the next rung of the ladder formed rigid rules and regulations as a method of selection. These rules were comprehensive, covering the whole lifestyle, and any infringement in the codes of dress, deportment, language, family and the rituals of entertaining and offering food, ensured an obstacle to social improvement possibly for a lifetime. To court social disapproval was to become a pariah which few were brave enough to contemplate. There was a real fear of difference and a strong need within every class for sameness amongst its members, all, of course, aping the class above. Hence there was a mass movement towards the bland and the nondescript which food reflected. The appearance of the food was more important than the flavour and to achieve the right look, flavour was either secondary or entirely ignored.

A part of this was a delight in mock recipes: the most famous was Mock Turtle Soup made from a calf's head, which bore no relation to the flavour of real turtle soup which had a greenish hue and was, as Mrs Beeton puts it, the most expensive soup to be brought to the table. She advises that a tin of turtle flesh which contains the green fat would be more economical than buying a live turtle. Mock turtle cost 3s 6d a quart while the real thing cost a guinea. There were many other recipes which were a kitsch version of something else: mock crab was made from coarsely grated Leicester or Cheshire cheese mixed with chicken, tossed in mustard and salad oil and piled up in a crab shell.[15] A boiled salad, made from potato, celery, brussel sprouts and beetroot, with a superhuman effort of the imagination pretended to be a lobster salad.[16] None of these three dishes added any fishy essence so that it might taste like produce from the sea; taste was of no concern for the dishes were aping their superiors as were the diners themselves.

It is the unsophisticated, untroubled by the anxieties of social climbing, who can often see through the facades of their age, like this streetseller who told Henry Mayhew: 'I don't know nothing of the difference between the real thing and the mock, but I once had some cheap mock in an eating house, and it tasted like stewed tripe with a little glue.'

There was a belief that raw or undercooked food was bad for you, since it harboured germs, and so everything had to be thoroughly cooked and boiled. Medical opinion was divided on this, but whatever the experts said on the subject the public were suspicious of raw vegetables. Mrs Beeton fostered this opinion: 'As vegetables eaten in a raw state are apt to ferment on the stomach, and as they have very little stimulative power upon that organ, they are usually dressed with some condiments, such as pepper, vinegar, salt, mustard, and oil. Respecting the use of these, medical men disagree, especially in reference to oil, which is condemned by some and recommended by others.' She gives two pages to salads out of 1,112 and begs the cook to ask her employer on the use of such vegetables as the spring onion and the radish. The Victorians loved both because they were decorative, but the fear of them upon the breath, or what they might do to the digestion would have induced women to have avoided them. Imagine those platters and bowls of uneaten salad going back downstairs to the kitchens where the footmen could then chew on onions and radish to their hearts' delight spending the rest of the night and day burping with pleasure.

The Victorian middle class was nervous of pleasure, not in feeling it, but in showing it: any outward exhibition of pleasure should be controlled, so a sensual appreciation of food, any rolling around the mouth of an oyster for example, would be deeply shocking; it would in fact be vulgar and reminiscent of the working class. So anything that gave any possible potential pleasure was viewed with suspicion, as being an instigator towards the road to ruin and social downfall. Food must be eaten with a show of decorum; if hungry, one should never show it; meats should be sliced small and thinly; one should eat slowly, masticating thoroughly. A mouth bulging with food was disgusting and to speak while the mouth was full, well, again only the working class male behaved so. A social dinner party was viewed as a minefield where the civilised veneer could crack to show the Darwinian beast beneath. There was nervousness as to what food could do to one. (Though the subject of this book does not cover drink, it is perhaps worth pointing out that the Temperance movement grew in power in this century.) Food should be tamed to make it powerless, and the only effective way of doing that was to make it uninteresting and unattractive.

The Victorian era used food as a moral weapon to condition the young. Various writers throughout the century wrote books on child-rearing, which were eagerly bought by a middle class anxious over matters of moral guidance. Dr Pye Henry Chavasse was one of the most authoritative and best-selling of these authors: 'His tone appears to owe more to a vengeful deity'[17] than anything else. His view on desserts and cakes was extreme:

> I consider them so much slow poison. Such things cloy and weaken the
> stomach and thereby take away the appetite and thus debilitate the frame.
> If the child is never allowed to eat such things, he will consider dry bread
> a luxury.[18]

Notice the child is 'he'. New emphasis was given to the doctrine of original sin by the revival of Protestantism and the growth of non-conformist religions, hence children were viewed in a new and darker light. These tots were bundles of original sin which had to be disciplined and purged from it. It was considered that food was a strong persuader. This attitude continued until well into the next century. For example in W.B. Drummond's *The Child: his Nature and Nurture* (1901), the author thought tasty titbits should not be allowed in a child's diet, 'if for no other reason than they are apt to make the children discontented with the plain and wholesome food with which they are perfectly satisfied so long as they have never had anything else'.

The modern Irish novelist Molly Keane, writing about her first four years, came to the realisation that 'nursery food was so disgusting that greed, even hunger, must be allayed elsewhere'.[19] Ruth Lowinsky in 1931, looking back on her childhood, wrote: 'When we were children it was considered good for our souls as well as our bodies to be continually fed on any food we disliked.' The Victorians felt certain that they were highly civilised; anything untouched by civilisation made them nervous and not a little frightened. Darwin's theory of evolution with its suggestion that the primate was a distant cousin seemed at first horrific and blasphemous. Children too could be untamed and unruly, not unlike that primate at times, and so they were punished severely, beaten and starved, to crush the devil within.

'Aunt Marjorie was always alert for greed in the young,' Molly Keane continued, 'a vice that was a depravity to be commented on and corrected whenever evident . . . for years I had a sensation of shame as well as guilt about second helpings; a deep rooted sense that the enjoyment of food was unattractive, something to conceal.' Nursery food was plain and monotonous. The day began with bread and milk or porridge for breakfast; mutton and vegetables were considered suitable for dinner.' Lady Sybil Lubbock, in her book *From Kitchen to Garret* about her childhood in the 1880s, was still eating a nursery luncheon of boiled or roast mutton, mashed potatoes, greens and rice pudding; there was also steaming potato water for chilblains.[20] These meals were often made unpalatable by careless cooking or by resentful and angry relationships between the nurse and the cook. Nursery quarters behind baize doors and at the top of the house cut children off from the rest of the family and were unpopular with staff, for bowls of hot water had to be carried upstairs as well as trays of food, which tended to be furnished with left-overs from downstairs with concessions to juvenile taste or stature. The formidable lines of Dr Watts against lying might also serve as a warning against food:

> Then let me always watch my lips,
> Lest I be struck to death and Hell,
> Since God a book of reck'ning keeps,
> For every lie that children tell.

Ursula Wyndham in *Astride the Wall* recalls:

> greasy mutton, overcooked vegetables wallowing in the water they had been cooked in, burnt rice puddings . . . This prison fare was the unsupervised production of the kitchen maid, whose more important task was to assist the cook in preparing many courses for the dining room twice a day.[21]

Mrs Leyel comments in 1925: 'The repugnance of many English children for green vegetables is explained by the dishes of stringy, watery, tasteless, tough green leaves that are sent up for nursery dinner, a relic of the Victorian days when grown-up people ate far too much meat, and when butter was regarded as a superfluous luxury for children brought up almost exclusively on starch.'[22]

Gwen Raverat, writing in the 1950s about her late Victorian childhood, asks: 'Surely our feeding was unnecessarily austere?' They began the day with porridge without sugar or salt, with toast and butter; if they had jam there was no butter, for they could not have both. For tea there was only bread and butter again, no cakes, unless they had visitors when there would be sponge cake, which the children nibbled the ends off.[23]

Nor did children's food improve when they went away to board at public school, if anything it got worse. Harold Acton recalls the food at Lawnwood Crammar as blotched oily margarine, hairy brawn and knobbly porridge smuggled into his handkerchief and thrown down the lavatory.[24]

Gwen Raverat was puzzled that her loving parents were so severe; it was difficult if not impossible to understand how those who love you could plunge vulnerable growing lives into such regimented days erased of all pleasures. Yet those parents in their defence would have said it was all done with love, though such regimes allowed those with a sadistic cast of nature to give full reign to it. The *zeitgeist* of the age demanded such severity, but why should it? Why should it have inflicted upon children such a regimen of disgustingly unpalatable food, bequeathing them with a diffidence for food throughout their lives which in turn affected their children; it was only after the Second World War that as a nation we managed to emerge from this baleful inheritance.

At the heart of Victorian society there was guilt. The wave of affluence, which brought the middle classes into prominence with an excess of capital to be spent on opulent household furnishings and on palatial municipal constructions, also intensified the guilt they felt about being surrounded by poverty and pauperism. Victorian religion was a sadistic one: it encouraged men to flay their souls and spirits with arduous tasks and penances; eating plain food was but one of them and inflicting it upon your children became a religious duty.

The reasons for the decline of British cooking were, firstly, the Enclosures Acts which removed the constant stimulus that peasant cooking gives to any nation's cuisine; our roots were cut away. Secondly, Victorian society praised French cooking and belittled the traditional British cuisine, so that no distinguished cook was encouraged to develop it and lead the way. Thirdly, as the first industrial society we became to a great extent urbanised, which created new and acceptable practices not conducive to good food. Fourthly, the architecture of the suburban villa and the hierarchy of servant labour drove a wedge between kitchen and dining room, turning cooking into a mercenary duty. In addition to which there was a dearth of experienced cooks. With the huge expansion of the middle classes needing more and more kitchen staff; illiterate and untrained women were employed as cooks who could only muddle through, presenting their employers with overcooked, tasteless meals, which they learnt to accept rather than lose their staff. Fifthly. the advent of technology in canning, packaging, freezing and retailing was enthusiastically and uncritically embraced in the kitchen, bringing standardised tastes and textures. Sixth, a fear of the untamed, the raw, the hearty and the vulgar caused dishes to be bland and over-refined with their emphasis upon appearance rather than flavour. Seventh, religious zeal made bad cooking acceptable and insensitivity over food praiseworthy. Eighth, and this factor was to continue with even greater disaster into the twentieth century – war. Wars caused naval blockades and the halt of food supplies from distant countries, severely limiting the diversity of ingredients on which British cooking had traditionally relied. The Crimean War (1853-1856) and then the Boer War (1899-1902), though both only of three years' duration, halted supplies. Lastly, in the seventeenth century, we had lost a royal court that thought of food as a developing aesthetic form. Our monarchy thereafter followed bourgeois practice; it was the bourgeoisie that took over the role of food guardians and in the eighteenth century fulfilled the role admirably. It was totally unaware of the role it played, however, so tragically threw it away; instead, it pursued a French culinary chimera, which they often felt inadequate to create.

By the end of the nineteenth century, all these factors had combined to wreak their havoc upon the British kitchen, without the British people being quite aware of what had happened. They remained smug, defensive and not a little arrogant on the British food they offered to guests from other nations, they found criticism of their food hard to accept. For the process of its decline had occurred at their finest hour, so how could the sustenance of Empire builders be in any way inadequate?

CHAPTER 11

Food for All

Edwardian society was distinguished by an orgy of conspicuous waste; a society that senses its impending end tends to throw itself into mad excess. Headed by that symbol of indulgent luxury, King Edward VII, it was to be seen at Biarritz, Cannes, Monte Carlo and even Marienbad consuming a sequence of similar meals characterised by an abundance of cream, butter, sugar and animal protein. These meals continued on steam yachts and private trains and at opulent country houses where a weekend visit might stretch into weeks complete with horse racing, the massacre of game birds and adulterous liaisons within its own set.

The idea of the British Empire still irradiated this class, bequeathing it with notions of racial superiority; a vague Darwinism had been allowed in suggesting that certain races were better fitted to survive than others. The imperialist spirit was all about civilising the native, giving it the Christian values that the Anglo-Saxon race fostered. These values had been created by clergymen, boys' fiction writers, poets, journalists and schoolmasters, and popularised a cult of Anglo-Saxon manhood, a compound abstraction of ideas comprising self-discipline and self-sacrifice, heroism, patriotism, skill at games and a sense of fair play. Square-jawed, blond, muscular and blue-eyed, this paragon disdained creature comforts and was entirely ignorant of gastronomy; in fact he took a distant and diffident attitude to all food.

The social structures behind such a creation were the public schools, which in the second half of the nineteenth century (set more or less free from all government control) had actively encouraged an anti-intellectual, anti-scientific, games-dominated Tory imperialism, which had fuelled all these ideas. It also gave a daily, practical illustration of the unimportance of food in the inedibility of their meals. The end product of such an education tended to be a conservative, cautious Christian gentleman with a stunted imagination who could read Latin and Greek, but who could barely taste the difference between an overdone Brussel sprout and a turnip.

Food for Heroes
In the winter of 1899-1900 many thousands of young men came to enlist for the British infantry, like their blond strong heroes in a G.A. Henty novel, only to find they were unfit for service; malnutrition throughout infancy had stunted growth and given them heart afflictions, poor eyesight, hearing and bad teeth. Thirty-eight per cent were turned away.

The Victorian diet continued much the same until the First World War; for the upper and middle classes the diet depended wholly upon staff:

> There is such a multitude of servants that elaborate hierarchies have to be created below stairs. Housekeepers, butlers, valets and personal maids are even more relentlessly snobbish than their masters and mistresses.[1]

In all those households it had become habitual to fortify the occupants of the best bedrooms with a cup of tea before rising. Staff had to be up and working very early, preparing the breakfast rolls and the breakfast trays for the ladies who would be served in bed. Cook was expected to be down by 6.45 and to find all the housemaids busy cleaning the house and laying the fires; she began to prepare breakfast which was eaten by 8 a.m. or 8.30 a.m. Prayers often preceded this meal with the staff in serried ranks all kneeling.

In the great country houses breakfast could continue until 10.30:

> There were pots of coffee and of China and Indian tea, and various cold drinks. One large sideboard would offer a row of silver dishes, kept hot by spirit lamps, and here there would be poached or scrambled eggs, bacon, ham, sausages, devilled kidneys, haddock and other fish. On an even larger sideboard there would be a choice of cold meats – pressed beef, ham, tongue, galantines – and cold roast pheasant, grouse, partridge, ptarmigan. . . . A side table would be heaped with fruit – melons, peaches and nectarines, raspberries . . . there were always scones and toast and marmalade and honey and specially imported jams.[2]

In lesser households breakfast meant porridge with cream and sugar, buttered eggs and bacon, perhaps a kedgeree, coffee, tea, toast and marmalade.

Working Class Food

In 1886 almost a quarter of adult males earned less than 20 shillings a week, and this remained relatively unchanged until 1914. Charles Booth thought that the urban poor were all more or less 'in want, ill nourished and poorly clad'. Food expenditure was the largest item in the family budget: nearly sixty per cent of income went on food, most money being spent on meat, which amounted to roughly one quarter of the income. Because of the cost both meat and dairy produce were eaten in small amounts, the staple food being bread and potatoes. The meat was often just a flavouring. 'The tiny amounts of tea, dripping, butter, jam, sugar, and greens, may be regarded rather in the light of condiments than of food.'[3]

Charles Booth noticed that if the father was in regular employment family meals became more regular:

> For dinner, meat and vegetables are demanded every day. Bacon, eggs

and fish find their place at other times. Puddings and tarts are not uncommon, and bread ceases to be the staff of life.

But other observers saw what a struggle achieving the regular meal could be:

> Potatoes are an invariable item. Greens may go, butter may go, meat may diminish almost to vanishing point, before potatoes are affected. When potatoes do not appear for dinner, their place will be taken by suet pudding, which will mean that there is no gravy or dripping to eat with them. Treacle, or – as the shop round the corner calls it – 'golden syrup' will probably be eaten with the pudding, and the two together will form a midday meal for the mother and children in a working man's family.[4]

When there was no animal protein sugar took its place which determined the type of starch eaten.

Children's meals followed a less regular pattern:

> Bread is their chief food. It is cheap; they like it; it comes into the house ready cooked; it is always at hand, and needs no plate or spoon. Spread with a scraping of butter, jam or margarine, according to the length of the purse of the mother, they never tire of it as long as they are in an ordinary state of health. They receive it into their hands and can please themselves as to where and how they eat it. It makes the sole article in the menu for two meals a day. Dinner may consist of anything from the joint on Sunday to boiled rice on Friday. Potatoes will play a great part as a rule, at dinner, but breakfast and tea will be bread.[5]

Food was very carefully distributed among the members of the family. The father, the breadwinner, took the lion's share, especially in animal food. If the family was thrifty the husband would have a morsel of meat or bacon daily throughout the week, but his wife and children would only eat it once a week. The meat is bought for the men; the chief expenditure upon food was on the Sunday joint and the following day it was eaten cold but only by the father. What cooking the mother did tended only to be for her husband as the children made do on 'pieces'. Most working-class homes had no gas installed, hence no gas ovens; solid fuel was too expensive, so ovens were rare. In the towns in houses with multi-occupancy one oven might do for several families. The eating of food was never a social occasion, except for a funeral which was termed, 'a slow walk and a cup of tea'.

> To boil a neck of mutton with pot herbs on Sunday and make a stew of pieces on Wednesday, often finishes all that has to be done with meat. The intermediate dinners will ring the changes on cold neck, suet pudding, perhaps fried fish or cheap sausages, and rice or potatoes.

Breakfast and tea, with the exception of the husband's rashers, consist of tea, and bread spread with butter, jam or margarine.'[6]

Nutritionists and social observers were horrified at the paucity of food on which the working classes were obliged to live, and constantly drew the attention of government to their plight:

We see that many a labourer, who has a wife and three or four children, is healthy and a good worker, although he earns only a pound a week. What we do not see is that in order to give him enough food, mother and children habitually go short, for the mother knows that all depends upon the wages of her husband.[7]

Growing children suffered particularly from the shortage of fats, dairy produce, fresh vegetables and fruit in the diet. Rickets became exceedingly common in children before 1914. Symptoms that were noticed were dry scaly skin, thin wispy hair and nutritional deficiencies were thought to be factors contributing to the incidence of disease in infancy and early childhood; over 140,000 deaths of children under five formed almost twenty-eight per cent of all deaths in England and Wales in 1913.[8]

Milk Crisis

By 1900 the diet of the rural labourers had much improved. A survey in 1902 showed that their consumption of raw milk was between 3 and 7 pints of milk per week. Much of this milk would have been used in cooking, for the milk pudding was still a staple part of diet and a large amount of it would have been added to tea, as 8 oz of tea was consumed per person each week. It is interesting to compare that intake with a later survey from 1924-34 of the average middle-class home, which shows that the raw milk consumption was only 2.8 pints; in these homes, however, the consumption of other foods and the range of foods eaten are much greater.

When just before the First World War hospitals began to test the milk they were alarmed to find massive infection with 'B. Coli' and other impurities. In 1916-17 twenty out of thirty samples of milk delivered to Manchester hospitals carried more than 1,000,000 bacteria per centilitre. Milk supplied through infant welfare centres in London to mothers and babies in the same year was also generally contaminated.[9] The introduction of tuberculin tests showed how far herds were infected. Measures to improve the quality and hygiene of the milk supply were started by the wholesalers and the larger retailers who were concerned at public alarm and decline in sales. They installed pasteurisation and bottling plants with regular testing of milk.

Within a few months of the outbreak of the First World War there were shortages of foodstuffs for the dairy herds, and many roundsmen had enlisted; the supplies of milk began to fall and the price rose making it too expensive for the poorer families. In 1915 United Dairies was formed from two separate companies; it began by controlling half of the wholesale trade in London, and throughout the war continued to buy up wholesalers and retailers in the milk trade. It claimed its objective was to rationalise the industry and to make economies in horses, dairies, equipment and roundsmen. Though this 'milk combine' was attacked in the House of Commons as a dangerous monopoly the Astor Committee appointed to look into the affair was impressed by its efficiency. Nevertheless, it advised the Government to take immediate control of milk supplies, and after the war to buy out the firms that controlled it. In May 1918 the Government accepted this report and authorised the Ministry of Food to take over the premises and plants of milk distributors; the head of United Dairies was brought on to the new Milk Control Board to show the Government how this new nationalised industry should be run. The farmers hated the idea, however, and the Ministry of Food found it impossible to rationalise the milk prices – they had estimates ranging from 2s 9d to 4s 9d per gallon. The Armistice and a change of government swept the whole issue off the map and the Milk Control Board withered away.

In 1918 when the price of milk rose to 10d a quart, local authorities were allowed to provide free milk to the poor from Welfare Centres. Alarmed at the malnutrition in working-class children, the Government also provided free milk and school meals. Various nutritional studies from the beginning of the century had discovered that it was only the young, invalids and the old who drank milk by itself, for other adults drank most of their milk in hot drinks and consumed the rest in milk puddings. Milk consumption changed little in the first thirty years of the century. By 1925 nearly all of the milk sold in London was pasteurised.[10]

At all times between 1921 and 1938 at least one out of every ten citizens of working age was unemployed. In seven out of those eighteen years at least three out of every twenty were unemployed; in the worst years one out of five. It was in this era that the Milk Marketing Board was born to stabilise milk prices and to ensure that free milk would be available to all schoolchildren.

Due to pasteurisation there was now a firm belief in the health-giving properties of cows' milk (which to a certain extent continues today). The League of Nations had summed it up: 'Milk is the nearest approach we possess to a complete food . . . it contains all the materials essential for the growth and maintenance of life in a form readily assimilable by the body . . . milk should represent a large proportion of the diet of every age.' But compared to other European countries we lagged behind in milk consumption, coming sixth in the league at only drinking 3.5 pints per week while Switzerland drank 8.9 pints. Throughout the 1930s milk drinking took on almost a glamorous appeal; certainly the new milk bars that were springing up in the High Street, copied from America with their chromium-plated interiors, high bar-counter stools and flavoured fruit shakes, were popular with the young throughout the era.

Not unexpectedly the highest consumption of milk was by the rich at 5.30 pints per week, while the poor only drank 1.57 pints. This difference is shown even more dramatically in the case of cream: the wealthy consumed seventy times the amount that the poor did; in fact cream was about as rare in the working-class home as caviare or oysters. Milk was, of course, used in puddings, custards and cereals as well as being added to tea, coffee and cocoa. All classes used milk in puddings, custards and cereals, though the poor used less. It was only in coffee that there was a noticeable class difference as the poor hardly ever drank it.

The Milk in Schools scheme which began in 1934 supplied a third of a pint of milk daily to half of elementary schoolchildren, increasing their consumption to 22 million gallons a year. By 1939 it was discovered that twelve-year-old boys were three inches taller and eleven pounds heavier than their fathers had been twenty years earlier. The Milk Nutrition Committee in 1938-9 found that schoolchildren on free milk showed quicker aptitude and intelligence.

The highest raw milk intake belongs to the 1950s where we drank 4.78 pints per person per week, compared to 1985 where our consumption was only 3.82.[11] This, I would suggest, was due to the end of rationing in 1953 where the range of foods available was limited and the milk pudding was still a fixture on the dining table. But after this peak milk consumption fell, possibly due to public awareness of milk being a source of saturated fat. From then on skimmed milk began to go on sale, and though whole fat milk fell by eight per cent skimmed milk sales more than trebled.

J. Lyons & Co. Ltd

In the midst of the century almost every town and city in the British Isles had a catering establishment with J. Lyons' name upon it, while nearly every kitchen in the land had his tea or cakes. How did part of our diet become so standardised? J. Lyons & Co. Ltd. was born from the Temperance movement of the late Victorian period.

Because in towns the provision of catering facilities for the growing tribe of office workers and shop girls was so rudimentary and largely based upon the public house, Dining Rooms began to spring up serving cheap, simple food. The Temperance movement then began to open public coffee houses, where people could sit in comfortable surroundings, which were almost exact replicas of their alcoholic cousins. After the initial success these places began to lose custom; people could happily drink ten pints of beer but failed to drink more than two cups of coffee. To save themselves, coffee tavern proprietors began to serve food; sandwiches, sausages, Melton Mowbray pies, pastries and bread. The motto of one such chain, Pearce & Plenty, was 'Quality, Economy, Despatch'. There, a lunchtime menu was: steak pudding and potatoes 5d, two sausages and potatoes 4d with tea at 1d or 1½d. Around the same time the Express Dairy opened 'milk and bun' shops.

The Lyons business was run by two families, the Salmons and the Glucksteins, who were so bonded by intermarriage that they almost formed one family group. They were well known for a thriving tobacco business called Salmon & Gluckstein and when Montague Gluckstein (who had noticed how inadequate the food was at exhibitions) wanted to go into catering they felt a new name should be chosen. Montague's brother Isadore was engaged to a girl who had a distant relation running a stall at the Liverpool Exhibition; as he had some experience they approached him and offered him a job. This included giving the new scheme his name, although the entrepreneurs behind it remained Salmon & Gluckstein. His name was Joseph Lyons (later chairman of the public company), who was then credited with the idea of the Joe Lyons teashops. He began with a tea pavilion at a Newcastle exhibition in the 1890s; when the exhibition closed, Lyons continued to keep the tea pavilion open and hired a Hungarian orchestra at a cost of £150 per week to provide the entertainment. The tea pavilion flourished, leading to a chain of teashops uniform in price and decoration. The menu was lighter and more sophisticated than those of Pearce & Plenty, appealing to lady shoppers and the growing army of girl typists. Their cheapness, speed and cleanliness became the Lyons watchwords. In the 1920s the profit on a full-scale meal in a teashop was reckoned to be less than a farthing.

They had triumphed in exhibition catering, leading to a chain of teashops and exploiting the Temperance market; they then assailed that temple of gastronomy – the high-class restaurant. The Trocadero opened in 1896 on a site that the caterers described as 'the centre of pleasure-seeking London'. It was slowly being accepted that it could be respectable to take women out to dine and even to entertain guests in restaurants. 'Men don't dine at their clubs nowadays; they go with their wives or the wives of others to partake of the restaurant dinner . . . they have become the greatest feature of the Night Side of London high life.'[12] At the Trocadero you could have the *table d'hôte* inclusive of wine for as little as 5s with a regimental band as entertainment. The menu was in French: an *Escalope de Veau Charbonnière* was priced at 4s; this was an egg- and bread-crumbed piece of veal with mushrooms, aubergines and truffles fried in butter mixed with a few capers. Coffee was sold as Cafe Moka and cost 9d. By 1900 they had also opened the Throgmorton Restaurant directly opposite the Stock Exchange; this had both a high-class restaurant and another dispensing cheap refreshments for city clerks. The first Lyons Corner House opened in 1909.

Lyons also bought the Regent Palace Hotel at Piccadilly Circus. On the ground floor there was the Rotunda Cafe where in the 1920s the in-drink was 'Gin and It'. The restaurant had a *table d'hôte* for 2s 3d, where you could start with hors d'oeuvre or a grapefruit *en coupe* or *Crème Santé*; the next course was a *Filet de Bar Frit Orly* or *Curry d'Oeuf Madras*, followed by the meat course. On offer also might be *Pied de Veau Portugaise* or Steak and Kidney Pie or Roast Pork Sauce *Reinette*; the vegetables to accompany them might be *Panais à la Crème* or *Pommes Mousseline*. To follow there might be either a Baked Apple or *Glace à l'Orange* or *Fruits Frais*. I can just remember food like this and it was dreadful. The food was basically British, cooked without care, given a French title simply because it was thought the diner would be conned into thinking it better. The disdain for British food was just as great. Although Steak and Kidney Pie was popular (a pity that they did not cook the dish as a pudding, i.e. wrapped in suet, using absolutely vital ox kidney needed for the dish – both would have been even more popular), the general attitude coloured the kitchen's attitude, providing a choice of products not at their best cooked in an offhand way. By this time the British public knew no better, so they flocked to these huge and gaudy eateries and ate happily.

Lyons became the country's largest caterer in the inter-war period; it had 250 teashops, three Corner Houses, each capable of seating up to 3,000 people and both the Trocadero and Throgmorton's. Lyons' waitresses, or the 'nippys' as they were called, were accepted as a symbol of public service. The cups of tea sold in the shops were produced from the finest blends. The most popular meal in the teashops, roast beef and two vegetables, cost only 10d and a *table d'hôte* lunch at a Corner House cost as little as 1s 6d. The most expensive item was a lobster mayonnaise at 2s 6d, but hors d'oeuvres ranged from 4d-9d. The price was dependent on what you chose: there were tinned sardines, anchovies and celery, hard boiled egg in mayonnaise, diced beetroot and sliced cucumber in malt vinegar, soused herring, potato salad, tomato salad, Russian salad, cole-slaw, sweet corn with diced red pepper (from a tin), cocktail onions, marinaded mushrooms (also from a tin), slices of honeydew melon with dyed scarlet maraschino cherries, diced ham and gherkins. All of these were immensely popular; their strong and variegated colours had aesthetic appeal which was so sadly missing then from most British food. Soups cost 5d, whitebait 9d, mutton cutlet 8d, roast beef 11d, ices from 3d upwards and meringue Chantilly 5d.

The Corner Houses had many different departments, and there were three orchestras on different floors. Both in their menus and in their restaurants, they used French words and titles cleverly, words that were not too obscure but still gave that element of style and mystery, to make their lower middle class customers feel that they were visiting something classy and special, and yet still affordable. There was Cafe de Petit Repas open day and late into the night, and a cocktail lounge called L'Apéritif. On the menu there was Clear *Jardinière* and Jugged Hare *Bourguignonne*. There was also a Sun Vita Cafe selling Soda Fountain specialities; hairdressing shops; wine and spirit counters; flowers, chocolates, cakes, candy, cigarettes and grocery counters – and a theatre ticket office.

Because of the popularity of the food, products began to be sold from a counter near the entrance of the shop as early as 1904. First, it was packages of tea, then cakes, ice cream and bread. Special recipes were devised by Lyons' laboratories to reflect public taste, while factory buildings were specially designed by Lyons' engineers to cope with production on a scale hitherto unknown. Visitors to their site were astonished to learn that the daily production of Swiss rolls could be measured in miles.[13]

Lyons owed its success to brilliant planning and a sensitivity to seeing public needs and trends, combined with a belief in a tiny profit margin on individual products, but huge sales of them. To a large degree it standardised food tastes to a very limited range of flavours and ingredients (banned from its food, for example were all herbs except parsley and mint, as well as garlic, black pepper, cayenne, paprika and, of course, chilli). Even though it introduced foreign dishes like kebabs and moussaka in the Corner Houses they were reduced to a blandness suitable for the British palate. It also took over much of the traditional roles of home baking: bread, pies and tarts could now easily be bought, even delivered and the term 'baking day' became an anachronism. Yet making cakes, especially sponges or fruit cakes, still remained a central part of home cooking and perhaps the most popular.

First World War

Though wages remained the same in 1914 as they had been in 1895 the cost of living rose sharply from 1910-13 bringing a rash of strikes not seen since the early 1890s. The Edwardian bubble had burst, more or less with the death of the King in 1910. In the next few years the real world would obtrude in a far more bleak manner than the rituals of Black Ascot, when the Royal Enclosure went into deepest mourning but still did not forgo its champagne and strawberries. In 1912 forty million days were lost through strikes, and emigration rose in those years preceding the war.

It was that Government-manipulated sense of fair play, of fighting against the bullies that brought us into the conflict; though Serbia was seen as a small nation struggling to be independent, no one really cared, but when Germany invaded 'little Belgium', trampling on its neutrality, there was a moral cause to unite the public. No one imagined, nor has it yet been fully appreciated, that victory in this terrible war would hinge upon food.

Food policy had been a subject of a Royal Commission since 1905, when the Government realised that with a high amount of imported foods the British Isles would be especially vulnerable at times of war. Four-fifths of Britain's wheat supplies were imported from Canada making that dangerous journey across the Atlantic; from August 1914 the price of wheat rose from 36s a quarter to 70s in May the following year. The public were asked to make voluntary sacrifices on bread, meat and sugar. Asquith, the Prime Minister, had created five ad hoc committees concerned with food supply by January 1915. With a shortage of imported foods, the British diet changed; a Ministry of Food was established to control and direct supplies, while agriculture was hugely expanded.

David Lloyd George, appointed minister for munitions in 1915, was deeply concerned that munition workers should have adequate nutrition; in 1916 a Health of the Munition Workers' Committee was set up under the chairmanship of Sir George Newman, who encouraged factories to establish canteens. Already it had been realised that the physical fitness of the worker had an important bearing on the output of the factory. All the new factories had restaurants decorated in pleasant colours which provided breakfast, dinner and tea. A three-course dinner cost 4d, Scotch Broth cost one halfpenny, stew 2d, mince and potatoes 3d, meat pies 3d. *The Times* of 30 September 1916 stated: 'The provision of proper meals for the workers is indeed an indispensable condition for the maintenance of output on which our fighting forces depend, not only for victory but for their very lives.'

Today, we would find the food offered in factory canteens uninspiring, but considering that the workers all came from families which had been struggling for decades to alleviate hunger pangs this food would be luxury: chop and mashed potatoes, roast beef, mashed potatoes and vegetables, steak pie and potatoes, liver, onions and potatoes, tripe and onions, fish, parsley sauce and potatoes, fish pie, Shepherd's pie and puddings all for a few pennies each. Soups were not popular, possibly it was thought because many of them went back to a bowl in the evening which with bread and cheese was supper. They were offered Haricot Bean soup,

Spring Soup, Kidney, Tomato, Lentil, Vermicelli, Scotch Broth, Green Pea and Potato – but Scotch Broth was by far the most popular.

At the time of the Armistice in November 1918, one million meals were being served daily in industrial canteens. It was said that if you gave workers a canteen they could be proud of, the canteen would soon be proud of its workers. It was soon learnt that the most efficient method of serving food was to have portions already upon hot plates and to have soup, meat and sweets at separate counters. 'A factory canteen, apart from its primary object of supplying wholesome food under favourable conditions, has in it great possibilities as a social institution, where workers meet, make friends, and learn to be part of, and take part in, the life of what should be a valuable humanising influence.'[14]

Within these war years the whole basis of the factory canteen was explored with astonishing success. Once the war ended and all the food restrictions were lifted, however, industry fell back into apathy. For ten years or so there was comparative stagnation, because of lack of understanding and suspicion of the science of industrial welfare.

For the first two years of the war the food problem in Britain was not acute; in that time plans were made to build up a secret reserve of wheat supplies and sugar rationing was considered. But by June 1916 German U-boats had become a threat to merchant shipping, and when Lloyd George became prime minister in late 1916 he created the role of a Food Controller. According to Sir William Beveridge, by the summer of 1917 'complete control over nearly everything eaten and drunk by forty million people' had been established. Sugar was rationed by January 1916, but there were queues for meat, bread and other products. Two weeks before Christmas 1917, *The Times* reported long rows of women queuing for margarine outside multiple shops in London, some with infants in their arms and many with children at their skirts. Bread and potatoes were never rationed, but staple prices had to be subsidised in 1917 and potatoes were often in short supply. General rationing was only brought in by February 1918, and this abolished the queuing which had been looked upon with horror. (It was to return with a vengeance in 1940 and became a facet of the British character forever lampooned.)

> On the whole the people have been fed and fed, in the circumstances remarkably well. If there has been any class discrimination, it has been the working classes who have benefited by it, as it should be, not those with money or special privileges.[15]

Indeed, working-class British women and children were better fed than they had been before 1914, owing to improved employment, canteen meals and easier access to the weekly pay packet. Rationing continued until 1920, but for the first time in the history of this land, there was food for all distributed fairly. Tragically, it was not to last for with peace declared the imperative soon waned; it was to return, but it took another war to provoke it.

The story in Germany was strikingly different; even though in the spring and summer of 1918 German forces had made advances into the Allied lines, there was a crisis within Germany itself. By early summer 1917 military food reserves were being drawn upon to feed civilians; munitions workers were getting only two-thirds of their pre-war calories, the fat ration was down to 4 oz a week and industrial output fell. Civilians severely malnourished so that their immune systems were enfeebled were dying. According to one observer who visited Germany at the end of the war, 'The people were physically and mentally enfeebled . . . in a condition of dull depression and lassitude; they had no feeling of national honour; they had completely lost the will to victory.'[16] Lack of food, caused by the Allied naval blockade and lack of foresight in planning and rationing what food they had from the beginning of the war, led them in November to negotiate an Armistice.

The Ministry of Food, sadly, was short-lived. It was described by the President of the Food Manufacturers' Federation as 'a continual source of irritation to traders and no little yearly expense'. Editorials in *The Grocer* attacked the idea of a permanent Ministry of Food as being unreasonable and unnecessary, a view that agreed with the general mood throughout the food industry of ending controls and returning to free markets.

In the inter-war years the Co-Operative movement went from strength to strength. By 1929 membership had increased to six million and by the outbreak of war in 1939 to over eight and a half million, taking twenty per cent of the total trade in groceries and provisions and over a quarter of the milk trade. Its shops reflected closely all the current food fads and trends, and during this period moved into the south and west of England, appealing now to the middle classes as well.

Social Upheaval

A new age had begun; the evidence of social injustice was too blatant for the authorities to dismiss any more. In the summer of 1917 the Minister of Education justified the raising of the school-leaving age to fourteen on the grounds that 'industrial pressure on the child' should cease. He had already abolished all school fees in elementary schools; he was concerned that talent should not be wasted. He appealed to the increased feeling of solidarity generated by the war and argued that conscription, which had caused so much liberal concern, implied that 'The boundaries of citizenship are not determined by wealth'. Two years later the Government passed a Housing Act which laid on local authorities the duty of surveying the housing needs of their areas and submitting plans for new estates to be subsidised from state funds. Suddenly, the working classes were to be housed and their children freely educated.

One of the effects of war was early marriage; contraceptives were increasingly taken for granted, and every village chemist was now selling them. Not unexpectedly there was a rise in adultery, illegitimacy and divorce. Nonconformist strictures began to look old-fashioned and its canons of behaviour absurd. The moralists picked on women drinking in pubs, their boyish figures and short skirts for denunciation. The war had shattered the sense of security that had cocooned the Victorian age. When husbands, sons and lovers could be blown to bits in the next second people began to live for the present.

The great landowners, feeling the economic chill which nibbled at their assets, sold off some of their land, and one quarter of England and Wales passed from being tenanted land into the possession of farmers in the thirteen years after 1914. Some sold their huge London houses. Devonshire House, built in Piccadilly opposite the Ritz by William Kent in the eighteenth century, was sold for £1,000,000 in 1919 and pulled down in 1924.

In both 1919 and 1920 there was a dramatic wave of strikes; when the General Strike was called in May 1926 it was effectively crushed by voluntary workers from the middle and upper classes who took over the main services, driving buses and trains, and emptying rubbish. The class war was never so fierce and brutal; the top class irradiated by that sense of fair play felt it was being blackmailed by cunning working men with the shadow of Bolshevik Russia behind them.

In a society so disrupted with no beliefs or ideals to unite it, falling into fragmentation like the empire it was about to lose, the food everyone ate was bound to change as radically. Staff had left domestic service in droves for work in the new industries; after the war they failed to return preferring to work in offices and shops. No longer could meals be made by indifferent and resentful servants whose cooking skills (with honourable exceptions) were limited. For the most part, the middle classes were now reduced to one maidservant, who was a glorified char and au pair, and only some households also had a cook.

Of course, for the rich there were still servants, but the food eaten was a very pale shadow of the pre-war diet; both the number of courses and the amount eaten had shrunk. Edwardian pretension had been stripped away, and the need to impress was less urgent. The lessons of the war with its horrible stalemate, armies glued down in mud and blood, where no aristocratic field marshal or monarch made a ha'porth of difference, where the values of sportsmanship and fair play were risible, had been felt by the Establishment, if not absorbed. It was aware that its role in the world had altered dramatically.

Accordingly, the rituals of the meal became more modest as its assessment of itself became more cautious, as apprehensiveness grew over Stalinist Russia. In 1932 on the eve of Hitler's rise to power in Germany, and at the height of the Depression, 2,750,000 British people were unemployed, standing in long queues waiting for work outside Labour Exchanges. For these people their diet fell to a level that was barely above subsistence. In this world Hitler was seen by some of the upper classes as a saviour, a bulwark against Communism to be appeased and palliated. This was the world of the society hostesses, where the King who was shortly to abdicate took cocktails and nibbled canapés with his American mistress, a world where the food was influenced by that huge country, its silver screen and its packets of cereals.

British Canned Food

In the early part of the twentieth century canned food was still viewed by certain quarters in society with suspicion; food poisoning scares in the past had scared off the affluent and except for condensed milk and bully beef, most canned foods were too expensive for the working classes. The war helped to change people's views; soldiers recently returned from the horrors of trench warfare had fond memories of tinned food. Increased production, once free from wartime restrictions, brought fierce competition among canned producers, which reduced the price dramatically and imports of canned foods soared.

In 1922 there were only three firms in Britain producing canned foods, compared with over 2,000 in the United States. The British share in this market was absurdly low: canned meat was only fifteen per cent, canned fish 1.8, canned vegetables 5.1, canned fruit in syrup 2.7 and condensed milk 23.9. In 1926 Smedleys was the first to introduce a fully automatic, high-speed pea-canning plant, after their chairman, S.W. Smedley, had visited the United States. Peas remained the most important British product to be canned. Within a short time other British canners were turning out British fruits and vegetables to compete with the imported varieties: strawberries, raspberries, loganberries, cherries, damsons and apples.

By the early 1930s all sorts of vegetables could be bought in cans: asparagus, beetroot, baked beans with pork, carrots, celery, mushrooms and spinach. Over eighty factories were now in production in the UK and with prices falling steadily because of the Depression, the consumption of canned foods became commonplace. Between 1920 and 1938 the consumption of canned vegetables, fish, meat and fruits rose dramatically. However, this did not halt the popularity of the imported cans, except for canned peas. To keep the factory working throughout the year, British canners used the dried pea and rehydrated it; they marketed them as 'Readi-Peas' and found they were an immediate success.[17]

In 1939 Ambrose Heath compiled a book of recipes to be made from canned foods, which includes a list of the cans available. There are nearly sixty soups, including five types of consommé, over ninety fish, including five types of anchovies, one with pistachios, and twelve types of herring, including one smoked, as well as tinned ormers, oysters and pike quenelles. He lists 218 types of meat, including sixteen beef; chicken comes in eleven different versions, including tamales; there are fourteen different types of galantine, seven types of lamb and eighteen of meat roll. There are 100 kinds of vegetables, including okra, sea kale, samphire and truffles; ninety-seven varieties of fruit, thirteen sauces and forty miscellaneous, which includes four different types of spaghetti.[18] Heath himself thought the scope of his list was 'portentous if not horrific', but it was not even comprehensive. He revised and republished the book for wartime in 1943 under the new title *Good Dishes from Tinned*, but as these goods were by then all on the point system most of them would have been unlikely to have endured. (The point system was a form of rationing whereby goods carried their own ratings and were available according to supply. Each consumer had a set number of weekly points.)

Diet in the Thirties

In a poll taken in the late 1930s Mrs Beeton's book was used by nearly half of the housewives, though many more read it from the upper social grades (determined mainly by income) than the poorer. The next most popular cookery books were books from MacDougall's Flour, or the gas or electric companies. Gas cookers were used by three-quarters of the population and very few used electric. Solid fuel cooking was even lower, but as the survey was only in urban areas that would have been expected. The most popular food cooked at home was cakes followed by soups, then jams and preserves. Home-made soups were particularly popular in London, Glasgow and Newcastle while jam-making appealed particularly to housewives in Cardiff and Liverpool.

With milk now delivered twice a day and meat, fish and greengroceries delivered every day or every other day, the housewife needed only to buy enough perishable food for a day, but following the American example, domestic refrigerators were being installed and the newest flats and houses had kitchens with spaces made for them. Forty per cent of the top social grade had a refrigerator but only sixteen per cent of the next grade down and the lower grades had none; three-quarters of those refrigerators were electric. (In the thirties my grandparents had a small gas refrigerator table height, while we had a tall electric one.) As was to be expected, London was the area that had the highest proportion of refrigerators installed.

The percentage of family income spent on food declines steadily as the social scale rose. The poor spent just over half (those with less than 10s per head per week) while the wealthiest group spent a little under one-eighth. A male over fourteen spent 5s 11d a week. This is at prices prevailing in 1933. The highest number of people across the classes stored enough food in the home to last a week; in fact the middle income groups stored more food than either the poorest or the wealthiest. One-fifth of people kept only sufficient food in reserve to cover a single day.

The highest proportion of people ate breakfast between eight and nine; all classes had bread, rolls or toast with butter, only the poor also ate margarine while only the rich had marmalade. Rather more of the rich tended to have a cooked breakfast than the poor; over seventy per cent of the rich ate eggs, bacon or ham while only thirty per cent of the poor did so. Taking fruit juice also declined steadily from rich to poor as did eating tomatoes. A working-class breakfast without a very strong cup of tea was unthinkable. Coffee was only drunk by the rich and was a sign of social standing. In all social scales except the wealthiest 'dinner' was a much more popular designation for the midday meal than 'lunch'. (Seventy years later this designation is not so cut and dried: 'dinner' remains the name only in the labouring classes while 'lunch' is used by almost everyone else.)

The food eaten at this meal also changed with each class, except for meat which appears classless, though lower income groups ate more offal. While the rich ate fish the poor were choosy; all classes ate potatoes but the rich ate more green vegetables, fruit and salad, which the poor entirely ignored. Half the population, of whatever class, ate this meal at home. Forty per cent of the rich ate at a restaurant while only four per cent of the poor did so; the lower income groups tended to take packed food while the rich had never heard of such a practice. There were two types of tea eaten, afternoon tea and high tea, but at both the same beverage is drunk. The time the meal is eaten designated the type. Afternoon tea in well-to-do homes was taken from 4 p.m. to 4.30 p.m., but as one descends the social scale the tea-time hour became later and later; yet as the working man's day became shorter, high tea was eaten when he returned home. The average time in 1933 was around 5 p.m. instead of 6 p.m. or even 6.30 p.m., as was the case before 1914. At afternoon tea bread and butter and cakes were served, but at high tea there were potted meats, pies, sausages and ham and even fish and chips. At weekends crumpets, muffins and a choice of cakes were offered at afternoon tea. Hot cooked meats were not the only difference in high tea: margarine and sometimes dripping were on the table instead of butter; potatoes and other vegetables were sometimes eaten as well as puddings. What was similar was that jams and preserves were on the table with cakes, buns and pastries. (Seventy years later both these meals have almost vanished entirely, except as part of a day's trip out.)

The names for the evening meal also divided the classes sharply: dinner was only used by the highest social class; supper gained ground as one moved down the social scale. Even the middle classes preferred to use the word supper. In the poorest working class group only seven per cent ate anything after high tea. The wealthy ate dinner between 7.30 p.m. and 8 p.m., while the poor ate supper after 9 p.m. Forty per cent of the rich began their dinner with soup or fish; they tended to eat more poultry and game than meats and green vegetables and salads, while they also ate more fruit and cheese than at earlier meals. The working classes ate fish and potatoes, cheese and bread, and drank tea or cocoa.

Less than half of the meat eaten in the UK then was homebred; half the supplies of lamb and mutton came from New Zealand; and three-quarters of the bacon and ham came from Denmark. One-third of the meat supply, beef and veal, pork, bacon, poultry and game, was British and meat consumption as a whole was rising; though we were in fourth place, the three leading Commonwealth countries, New Zealand, Australia and Canada, ate more meat than we did.[19] According to the 1930s poll, beef consumption had fallen slightly in recent years, while that of mutton and lamb had risen; it was thought that smaller families demanded smaller joints. Bacon was the one meat that appeared to be classless; the weekly consumption hardly changed from rich to poor, though with beef, mutton and pork less than half was eaten by the poor than the rich. The amount of meat eaten falls steadily as one descends the social scale; the only brake on the British avidity for meat was an economic one. The joint reigned supreme in the British home; prepared meat dishes which were not based on leftover scraps of roasted joint hardly existed. So much for the French influence on our cooking.

The consumption of eggs declined with the social scale; the rich ate around six eggs per head per week, the poor only two. In the 1930s we ate more fish, 12.3 oz than Europe and the United States.[20] The rich ate over double the amount of fresh fish than the poor, and surprisingly four times the amount of tinned fish, salmon and sardines being the most popular varieties.

The richest class in this survey[21] had at least two live-in servants and one gardener, a house with at least ten rooms, a high priced car or more than one car, a luxury flat in town, and children at public or private schools. These were the factory owners, stockbrokers, bankers, business executives and landowners. The poorest lived in a council house or tenements, and were lower grade office or warehouse clerical staff, semi-skilled and unskilled employees.

Other surveys throughout the 1930s had shown that the agricultural worker was among the worst fed of English workers, that thirty-three per cent of children were of sub-normal nutrition, and that the average consumption of fresh milk was 0.3 pints. *The Times* in 1936 concluded that 'one half of the population is living on a diet insufficient or ill-designed to maintain health'. Poor families first satisfied their hunger with cheap carbohydrate foods accompanied by innumerable cups of sweetened tea, and only after that might they turn to protein food or fresh vegetables high in vitamins if they could afford it.

Rebirth of a Cuisine

The social upheavals that occurred throughout the war and afterwards caused not only radical changes in what everyone ate, but also made gastronomes rethink some of the basic tenets of good eating. Foremost among them was was Mrs Leyel (1880-1957), a herbalist who opened Culpeper House in Baker Street in 1927. The year before she had published *The Magic of Herbs* and founded the Society of Herbalists. Just as importantly, in 1925 she published with a friend, Olga Hartley, *The Gentle Art of Cookery*. This is a remarkable book, and a key book for Elizabeth David who wrote a preface for the 1974 edition. Mrs David believed it to be a 'small classic of English culinary literature', and was fascinated and stimulated by Mrs Leyel's use of the ingredients of Eastern cooking, such as almonds and pistachio nuts, apricots and quinces, saffron and honey, rosewater, mint, dates and sweet spices. Mrs David wondered whether she ever would have learnt to cook at all, 'had I been given a routine Mrs Beeton to learn from instead of the romantic Mrs Leyel, with her rather wild and imagination-catching recipes'.

Mrs Leyel was intelligent, civilised and rebellious; she fought the Establishment in two big court cases in the 1920s and won. After the war, deeply shocked at the plight of ex-servicemen, which the Government was ignoring, she raised £350,000 for them by means of a ballot. She was prosecuted immediately under the Lottery Act, won her case, and then faced second charges under the Betting Act; after she had won that case she succeeded in legalising ballots for charity. Unlike Mrs Beeton with her quotation of Miltonic gender definition, Mrs Leyel chose a much more apt quotation from John Ruskin which attempted to define cookery:

> It means the knowledge of all herbs and fruits and balms and spices, and all that is healing and sweet in the fields and groves, and savoury in meats. It means carefulness and inventiveness and willingness and readiness of appliances. It means the economy of your grandmothers and the science of the modern chemist . . .

The fundamental point in this astonishing cookery book, which Elizabeth David could not have known as the earliest recipes had not then come to light, is that Mrs Leyel was simply reviving ingredients and recipes which had been loved in Anglo-Norman cookery. There is a chapter on flower recipes with a chrysanthemum salad, a nasturtium salad, eggs cooked with marigold, all of which the English medieval court would have loved, for their beauty as much as their flavour. (As we saw earlier, the French court never used flowers in cooking.) She has a chapter on almonds, giving recipes for soups, pastes and creams, all of which would have been very familiar in medieval cooking; she has another chapter on chestnuts with soups, salads and the most delicious of puddings. Further chapters on soups, fish, eggs and meat with their intelligent comments are all highly individual and owe their attractiveness to the way they have reinterpreted traditional Anglo-Norman culinary inventiveness for a new age.

Mrs Leyel was not alone.

> By 1928 I had struck a rich line of research. We had the finest cookery in the world, but it had been nearly lost by neglect; a whole lifetime would not be sufficient for one person to rediscover it.

The words belong to Florence White who founded the English Folk Cookery Association, but there were very few subscribing members, as English cookery was disdained with such snobbish fervour that most people would have paid a subscription to keep away. Florence White gave a series of six weekly broadcasts and the public responded by sending her recipes. The result was *Good Things in England* published in 1932, which contains 853 recipes and celebrates our culinary heritage. Both these books broke away from Mrs Beeton and the unending new editions of her book, which was constantly being revised by the publishers to meet, what they felt, were the fresh demands of a new age; they were in fact only dissipating the original.

Another cookery writer who recorded the change that occurred after the war was Alice Martineau, who wrote: 'Food fashions have greatly changed. Large parties where the principal entertainment was the dinner, have given way to brief but well selected menus . . .'[22] Mrs Leyel, Florence White, Alice Martineau and others were part of a brief flowering of English gastronomy, which Arabella Boxer explored recently.[23] She found it regrettable, as must we all, that this trend was cut short by the outbreak of the Second World War in 1939. 'Such things take time to reach all levels of society, and this one had hardly had time to spread beyond the sophisticated world in London and the south before war was declared, and the country was plunged into austerity.' A cuisine, if it is to be accepted by all classes in society, is reinterpreted by them and ideas from the working classes, being generally more robust and tasty, are often taken up by the classes above them – mustard and crème brûlée being but two.

English cooking, as practised by rich people of taste (it is a rare combination), was influenced by the United States; a number of American women had married Englishmen of influence, such as Nancy Astor and her niece, Nancy Lancaster, Emerald Cunard and Wallis Simpson. Again, past English culinary triumphs which had been taken to the new colonies in the seventeenth century, were now returning in more sophisticated versions: roast squab served with a grape salad, cheesecakes, new flavours, grapefruit and avocado became fashionable.

The new style of cooking was understated; it eschewed peasant earthiness as one would expect, for we had lost our peasant roots. Fresh produce was now cooked simply, presented elegantly and was eaten with a sharp contrasting sauce. The ingredients were cooked separately, not mixed together as in the French tradition. There was an emphasis on clear soups, and a liking for jellied consommé and aspic-covered chicken; but in an age that was the first to be conscious of dieting and the need to be fashionably thin, one might expect the food to be lighter, for the fish to be briefly poached and the chicken breasts to be grilled. Both would be served with an attractive sauce, of course, such as Sauce Duglère with the fish and that still starring favourite of the Victorians, Devil Sauce made with English mustard, curry powder, cayenne and tabasco mixed with butter, flour and cream. Devilled chicken or game was also a favourite lunch or supper dish, served either hot or cold.

There was a new emphasis on vegetables, cooked briefly and on mixed salads, another American influence. But, oddly enough, here our own royal family led the way. King George V liked to have his vegetables served after the main course as a separate dish. Many households followed this example, serving a vegetable dish alone, and some more enterprising cooks liked to turn them into soufflés. Alice Martineau described the vegetable soufflés made by Lady Wilton's chef at Melton: 'a soufflé of small Brussels sprouts, boiled very soft with well-beaten eggs and cream one night, the next, a soufflé of white Jerusalem artichokes or asparagus, and the third night one of spinach which, boiled with cream and whipped up with eggs was a delicate green colour with a brown top'.[24]

In the 1920s a mixed salad, now a rather tired cliché, was considered a new dish from America. Before salad here had usually only been leaves,[25] now it had tomato, cucumber and spring onion mixed in with the leaves. In a little book published in 1925, *Green Salads and Fruit Salads*, Mrs Leyel, so much our contemporary in her culinary taste, advises 'purslain, rampion, skirret, scalions and sampier' with shoots of 'nettles, tarragon, sorrel and corn salad' to be added to cos lettuce leaves, and begins her book with John Evelyn's list of English salad herbs. However, a characteristic recipe for a composite salad at the height of fashion then might be Mrs Martineau's Hollywood Salad, which had two heads of lettuce, one head of broccoli briefly cooked, four devilled eggs, three small tomatoes, a small tin of sweetcorn, a cup of celery strips with a plain French dressing or the 'new buttermilk' dressing to be served at a ladies' lunch party with baby lobsters cut in halves, very thin wafers of ham and brown bread and butter sandwiches with a powdering of cheese inside. The buttermilk dressing was mayonnaise, onion juice (a particular craze), lemon juice, mustard, paprika, white pepper and thick buttermilk or sour cream.[26]

Mrs Martineau's book, published in 1938 at the close of this interwar era, is both pragmatic and advanced in its style and advice. Take her chapters on meat and poultry: a tournedos steak is carefully cut, oiled, seasoned then cooked briefly under a hot grill and served with an anchovy sauce; the lamb cutlets have olive oil rubbed in them; she uses an oatmeal stuffing in a loin of lamb and in pheasant; she advises soy sauce with veal cutlets and even gives a recipe for raw beef sandwiches. Her chicken is spatchcocked and sprinkled with thyme, parsley, onion and mushroom, a young chicken is stuffed with cream crackers, oysters, cooked chestnuts and cream; while her jugged hare has added chocolate, squabs (first eaten in America) are steamed, casseroled and roasted.

It is the lighter dishes that personify this new cooking, however: soups of green peas or asparagus, baked eggs and soufflés, scrambled eggs in black butter with artichokes, soufflés of smoked haddock and savoury custards, crab mousse and fish chowder, steamed scallops and devilled soft roes. Arabella Boxer describes the cuisine: 'Meals became shorter and more informal, and the dishes themselves more light hearted. Meals were rarely more than three courses, except for a formal dinner, and a more relaxed attitude became the norm.'

Then wartime austerity arrived as complete and daunting as the blackout. Rationing began the whole structure recalled from the First World War: the books were already printed; the hostesses closed their London houses, retired to the country and informed their gardeners that they must dig for victory. Mrs Boxer claims the cuisine then vanished, and when after the war Elizabeth David's books on Mediterranean food were published they exerted another influence altogether. But did the interwar cuisine really disappear? I very much doubt it; in fact the proof that it had an almost immediate effect upon the middle and lower middle classes resides on my bookshelves.

New Technology and Middle-Class Cooking

The *Radiation Cookery Book*, which went through eighteen editions from 1927, came with the New World gas oven. These practical guides to cooking given away with the new technology had a more potent influence on the cooking of the nation than any other cookery books. I have the one published in 1935, which belonged to my mother; it has a small section on hors d'oeuvres, another on food for invalids and one on preparation of sweetmeats, such as how to make almond fondant and peppermint creams. There is also a short chapter on vegetarian dishes.

The same social forces that brought the hostesses' stylish cooking into being, operated also upon the creation and sale of this cookery book. New technology and loss of domestic staff are the two most potent, which propelled the hostess into the kitchen to learn from her one resident cook, and which also made the cookery book give a long section on dinners that could be cooked in the oven without any attention being given to the food inside. Other influences, which I explored briefly earlier, were grouped around the concept of the new woman, no longer chained to a sink or hot stove, but needing and succeeding in being an individual in her own right; cooking and recipes could fade into the background.

The gas oven was an incredible step forward for the cook, because the heat could be controlled from a very low simmer to a blazing boil. By 1939 it was estimated that there were between eight and nine million gas cookers in Britain and that three-quarters of all families had one. The remaining quarter without one were because they lived in areas with no mains gas supply, for by now even the very poor cooked on a gas ring as well as keeping an open fire, which was used for warmth in addition to cooking food. Penny-in-the-slot meters were available from the 1880s, whereby you paid for the gas daily; these were commonplace in all homes except for the rich. Electric cookers made much slower process in being accepted by the public, though they were available from the early 1900s, but the electric heating elements were at first inefficient, in 1914 for example it took 15-20 minutes to boil two pints of water and 35 minutes to preheat an oven. Cookers were much improved throughout the 1920s and by the 1930s the design of saucepans had changed to make them fit more completely on the heating rings which cut the time of cooking by half. Even by 1936 only six per cent of British families cooked by electricity. After the war this rose rapidly to thirty per cent in 1961 and by 1980 electricity had almost half of the market.[27]

From the early years of the century women had seen electricity as a 'new servant', capable of liberating them from household drudgery. The General Electric Company advertised their product by saying as much, the electric home was where cooking was 'hygienic, uniform and economical, where cleaning is an easy and pleasant job . . . where ample heating, clean, smokeless, fumeless is always available'. There was an Electrical Association of Women to help promote and sell the product. Their President, a Mrs Ashley, said she wanted electricity to be the best friend of the middle class woman, and of the poor woman. 'I want the people who have only one servant, or none, to have cheap power in their homes.'[28] There was also a range of different electrical appliances which would cut down housework to a few hours a week rather than the twenty-six hours estimated: electric irons, whistling kettles, toasters, portable fires, water heaters and wash-boilers.

Cooking by solid fuel which in some form or other had been done for countless centuries depended upon gruelling labour (hauling coal or logs around) and tiresome chores (cleaning, raking and stoking); all of these vanished. The new machines were easy to clean, simple to use and in addition the cookery books handed out with the ovens explained step by step how to cook a great range of foods. No wonder they were popular.

Naturally, the recipes changed, because the heat could be regulated down to the smallest degree. Sauces were more easily made, for there was little chance now of their burning or sticking; other dishes could be left unattended, with no need for constant basting. What the combination of new technology, few staff and a much more active lifestyle brought about was quick dishes, food that only needed brief cooking and the simplest presentation. (The effect of fresh food being kept in the refrigerator was not yet an influence, as by 1948 only two per cent of the population had one; there were also daily deliveries of every perishable food.)

The women who compiled the *Radiation Cookery Book* were obviously aware of the cooking of Mrs Leyel, Mrs Martineau, Lady Sysonby and others, and had absorbed much of it, for some of their recipes, such as celery creams, anchovy biscuits, scalloped artichokes and seakale might well have been served at the smartest party. So the book is far from being without sophistication. They give, for example, a recipe for frying parsley, but unlike Mrs Beeton they tell you it should turn to a dark green. The fact that such recipes, with many others typical of the new style of cooking, reached three-quarters of the population has not been properly registered before, because these stylish recipes – Salmi of Game, Roast Teal, Chaudfroid of Chicken – were lost among other more banal ones. The book had also been well grounded in Mrs Beeton and her disciples, representing a sturdier more earthbound cuisine, fuel for the working man such as Tripe and Onions, Toad-in-the-Hole, Sausage Pudding, and Baked Stuffed Heart. There are different cooking times given for a sheep's, bullock's or calf's heart. This was a common dish in our home, and the blood made a dark rich gravy.

Yet, what a relief, there are no recipes for leftovers. In a recipe for curried mutton, the neck of mutton is uncooked, cut from the bone and chopped into cubes; the same for the soup Hodge-Podge, which is now basically shin of beef or scrag end of mutton with vegetables, pulses, potatoes and dumplings added in the last twenty minutes, casseroled in the oven for over two hours at a very low temperature. The book is full of culinary skill which had been thoroughly adjusted to the new age that the gas oven ushered in. It also obviously had a Scot upon the team, for there are over twenty Scottish recipes, from Cock-a-Leekie and Kail Broth to Free Kirk Pudding and Haggis, but alas, there are only two Welsh recipes and one Irish.

It also makes mistakes, seen from our view. At the end of the book it lists fifty whole dinner menus, which include, enterprisingly, four vegetarian ones; these menus are for a main course with vegetables and a cooked pudding (another section of the book gives cold sweets); in its urgent desire to make the role of the cook in the home an easier one every menu is cooked in the oven and needs no attention through the specified time given – often an hour. Unfortunately, it sometimes suggests vegetables which should not have to endure an hour in the oven beneath the main dish. Both Brussel sprouts and peas are given this treatment, though the root vegetables in other menus benefit from it. Menu 33 suggests a brace of roast pheasants with potatoes, bread sauce and the braised Brussel sprouts cooked with a few bacon rinds, but with these go a Cranberry and Apple tart; elsewhere there is a recipe for making real custard with cream, sugar and egg yolks.

Mistakes are made by everyone: Mrs Martineau in giving a recipe for stuffed aubergines adds a last note: 'On the stuffing depends the flavour of the dish as the aubergines have none!' Mrs Leyel tells of an English cook she knew who was asked to fry a vegetable marrow. She flatly refused and explained that it was 'against nature' for a vegetable marrow to be fried, it must always be boiled. I was delighted to find in this *Radiation Cookery Book* instructions for cubing and then frying the marrow in butter.

Second World War

In 1939 Britain was only thirty per cent self-sufficient in food compared with eighty-six for Germany; it was urgent that huge changes be made in our agricultural policy. They had, in fact, already begun, for as Nazi Germany had grown powerful, the

British Government had started to make some provision for a possible war. In 1936 a Food Defence Plans Department had been set up. British agricultural output had been greatly expanded throughout the 1930s, with the help of subsidies and various marketing schemes; it helped too that the old landed aristocracy was selling out to its tenant farmers who were concerned to work hard at wresting a living from the land. Throughout the war with the help of the Dig for Victory campaign arable acreage rose by half from twelve to eighteen million acres to provide food for the domestic market, so that valuable tonnage could be saved in supplies coming by sea. Unskilled land girls were drafted into the country for a considerable amount of this work; the number of sheep, pigs and poultry fell substantially, though the number of cattle (felt to be essential because of milk) rose by about ten per cent.

One of the most significant advances, however, was the new understanding of the science of nutrition led by such men as John Boyd Orr of the Rowett Institute in Aberdeen, which had been founded to study the subject. Orr's previous work in the 1930s on the relationship between poverty, inadequate diet and poor health had been invaluable in discovering the diet for optimum requirements for health and energy. At the outbreak of war Orr calculated that only a third of the population were living above that optimum requirement. 'The health line of the Home Front may become as important as the Maginot Line,' warned Orr in 1940.[29] The Government was now clear that adequate nutrition was part of the war effort, and that it would be hugely strengthened with an energetic workforce in the factories, the homes and services. It was convinced from the beginning that food must be rationed and that everyone must have a fair share. Orr was an idealist; he believed that the war would destroy a great many nineteenth-century ideas of the supreme importance of trade and money-making. He believed that:

> The post-war Government in dealing with food will have as its objective the welfare of the whole population. Supply will be regulated, not by trade interests, but according to the needs of the people, and in price fixing, the price of essential foods will be fixed in accordance with the purchasing power of the poorest.

Orr told the Government that with sufficient bread, fat (butter or margarine), potatoes and oatmeal, there would be no starvation. What worried them was that it was obvious from pre-war surveys that there were deficiencies in calcium, vitamin A and vitamin B1 (caused by a preference for white flour). Margarine was therefore fortified with vitamins A and D and white flour was not used for bread-making. Lord Woolton took over the Ministry of Food in April 1940 and Jack Drummond was appointed to head a food-advice division. From then on the Ministry poured out a steady stream of sensible advice, information, recipes, suggestions and encouragement with brilliant use of radio pulling in known and popular comics like Gert and Daisy (Elsie and Doris Waters) to get over to the public important nutritional facts. Not only was the radio used, there were advertisements everywhere, news flashes in cinema, leaflets and booklets. From them all, the British learnt that eating wisely for health was part of defeating Hitler. If hungry, starch would fill you up. 'Rations go twice as far this way,' said the soup advertisements. 'Start with platefuls of piping hot, thick, appetizing soup, and plenty of bread. It's filling and satisfying and you can make do with smaller servings of the rationed foods . . .'

Irene Veal, who wrote a book of recipes for wartime, dedicated it to Lord Woolton, 'who taught British women to cook wisely'. She continued in her preface:

> Never before have the British people been so wisely fed or British women so sensibly interested in cooking. We are acquiring an almost French attitude of mind regarding our food and its careful preparation, and the demand for good and practical recipes is continually increasing.

The public began to understand that vegetables must be cooked briefly, otherwise valuable vitamins would be lost, that the cooking liquid must be saved for soup, that it was good to eat raw vegetables everyday, that carrots were essential for seeing in the dark. They were taught that potatoes contained vitamin C as well as oranges, which with other citrus fruits and bananas were unobtainable. After two years the public were slimmer and livelier and this was not lost on the women. In 1943 one of their most popular magazines, *Woman*, commented:

> Food discoveries that ought to stay long after there's no stringent need for them are our new habits of eating raw vegetables in salads, raw cabbage and raw carrot; our new wisdom in cooking vegetables so that all the goodness and health-giving qualities stay in; our wartime substitute for a glass of fruit juice which is a glass of the water that the vegetables were cooked in . . .[30]

One of Jack Drummond's innovations was the process of dehydration, which reduced eggs, milk and bananas to a powder; again this saved on shipping space, as did importing boneless meat like 'spam' and corned beef. Every home in the land ate both gratefully, though while dried foods were used in cooking (their added nutritional value was well known) the thought of making scrambled eggs from dried egg never stimulated the salivary glands. What food rationing did do was to force everyone to grow their own vegetables; however small a patch people owned, lawns and flower beds were dug up, soil was dug, fertilised and planted with a year round supply of potatoes, vegetables and salads; it also forced people to pick from the wild, blackberries and rosehips, sloes and bullaces for making jams; though sugar was severely rationed, other sweeteners were tried, honey was precious, maple syrup unobtainable, and the herb Sweet Cicely was found to be not all that sweet. Damsons were used for cheese, rowans for jelly, beechnuts made into a butter, pine kernels could be gathered and roasted, the cones used for fuel, chestnuts made into a soup and walnuts pickled.

Books by the French Vicomte de Maudit, the first with a preface by Lloyd George (who really did know his father), was amazingly informative on how to live completely from the wild. He gave recipes for roasted and grilled squirrel and for making squirrel tail soup, for wood pigeon pie and stewed starlings; recipes for making marmalade from just the peel and a sugarless pudding – made from dried fruits; as well as how to cook with flower pots and scallop shells and how to make a water bottle from a brick. There were a host of self-help books published throughout the war years on every possible topic.

But how severe was the rationing? Rationing began in January 1940 for bacon or ham at 4 oz per week; 12 oz of sugar were allowed and 2 oz of tea – so old leaves were re-used. (Coffee was not important enough to be rationed.) Four ounces of fat were allowed, 2 oz each of margarine and butter, and cheese was rationed in May 1941 at 1 oz per week, which was barely a mouthful. Jam, honey and golden syrup, mincemeat, marmalade and lemon curd all went on ration coupons, though the amount varied from 8 oz to 2 lb a month. Extra sugar was allowed in the jam-making season.[31] A points system allowed for luxuries such as canned salmon, sardines or baked beans, American sausagemeat in a tin, condensed milk or cream crackers; their points value changed, becoming higher as the stores ran low, and so in this way the housewife had the illusion that she enjoyed some freedom of choice. Spam was ubiquitous; it turned up sliced cold with pickled onions for a funeral breakfast, and was chopped up small in vol au vents for a wedding, it was fried in lard or covered in breadcrumbs or batter.

Under such severe limitations could gastronomy survive? Mario Gallati, who was the manager of the Ivy, admitted that sometimes all they had on the menu was tripe and onions and spam, but they had to invent variations on what ingredients they had.

> For instance, I used to make a kind of mayonnaise with flour and water put into the mixing machine with vinegar, mustard and a bit of powdered egg. It made me shudder to serve it, but every one took this kind of 'ersatz' food very much in their stride.[32]

As restaurants could not charge more than 5s for a meal, if they managed to get game birds or salmon, even crayfish and had a supply of vegetables and herbs, they made up their costs by charging far more for the wine. Shooting game depended upon spare cartridges, which were precious so older methods of trapping and snaring were brought back into use.

Most people muddled on and attempted their best to rustle up a meal that would at least be edible, but they failed miserably if they struggled to keep to conventions. Spam was not beefsteak and it was little good pretending otherwise. The natural cooks with a flair for making anything edible into something stylish were unfazed and accepted the challenge, using a large amount of wild foods. Half the battle, they discovered, was not to let on what was the real nature of the food people were eating. Nettle soup, for example, was eaten with far more enthusiasm when people were told it was sage and onion. Theodora Fitzgibbon queued for hours to buy horsemeat and made enormous pâtés and jellied tongues which everyone enjoyed, thinking it was beef; another time she made a pie out of rooks and let them believe it was grouse. When she complained to the butcher that all the offal had disappeared and that:

> All the animals seemed to be born without tongues, tails, hearts, kidneys, livers or balls, he winked at me, a great arm went under the counter, and he flung up a half-frozen oxtail. I had never cooked one before, but even today I can taste the thick gravy and see our grease spattered lips as we chewed on the bones. Unrationed rabbit was the salvation for many people in a low income group. Frying was quite difficult, as lard was rationed and olive oil only obtainable at a chemist on a doctor's prescription, so sometimes we were reduced to liquid paraffin. At least we didn't suffer from constipation.[33]

It was impossible to defend the quality of the wartime sausage. Sausages were unrationed and became a butt for jokes. The manager of my father's building works referred to them as 'them breads'. Their ingredients were best not enquired into, as offal was rarely on sale; it was suspected that unmentionable parts of the carcass were minced up and used, but certainly sausages contained a high proportion of cereals and their flavour was feeble. The Ministry of Food had stipulated that the minimum meat content of luncheon sausage, breakfast sausage, meat galantine and polony might not be less than thirty per cent. Before 1939 it had been eighty. They overlooked the fact that when the meat content of sausages is depressed lower than twenty per cent, the flavour of meat falls below the threshhold of taste altogether and the manufacturer might just as well make his sausages with no meat at all.[34]

People were reduced to strange behaviour:

> One Northampton woman who saw a dog dashing out of a butcher's shop with a large piece of suet in his mouth, followed him on her bicycle and watched him bury the suet. 'When the dog was safely away I went to the spot and confiscated the hidden treasure . . . I took home that suet, cut out the mauled part and then made suet pudding.'[35]

By the third year of the war the nation had adjusted to the new diet; by the end of the war they were not a little surprised to know that they had never been healthier. Child mortality rates had never been so low, fewer mothers had died in childbirth, fewer babies had been stillborn, children were taller and sturdier; this was a reflection of their daily regulation milk, orange juice and halibut liver oil, and added to that trio I recall a most delicious bottle of rose hip juice. There was a much lower rate of tooth decay, deaths from TB were down, there were fewer anaemic women and children. All of this had been achieved when there were fewer doctors, dentists, nurses and health visitors because the majority were all with the armed services. Overall, the rich had eaten a great deal less and the poor had eaten adequately and well. The message was simple: Government food control was able to give society a good mixed diet which benefited their health. Why could they not do it in the future? The answer was that people hated to be under that amount of control, if it was not in wartime conditions. However, rationing would continue for longer than anyone dreamt possible.

The Age of Austerity

When the war finished Britain expected, if not the lap of luxury, at least a few bananas, a haunch of beef, pork with real crackling, a dozen eggs and perhaps, with any luck, half a pint of cream and a bottle of whisky. But it was not to be. The population was alienated as much by the petty regulations as the lack of luxuries that had been common enough in the 1930s. When the public read that a costermonger with a licence for vegetables had been hauled up for selling rhubarb because it was a fruit, or that a restaurant was in trouble for serving asparagus, not lawfully on the same plate with the meat balls but as a separate course, or that a farmer's wife was fined for serving the Ministry snooper with Devonshire cream for his tea, or a shopkeeper for selling home-made sweets that contained his own ration of sugar, then it lost its temper and heaped most of the blame on the new Labour Government.

The British had to endure food rationing for fourteen years (1939-53) and after the war put up with even more scarcity. Bread was rationed for the first time from 1946 to 1948; the meat ration was cut and even potatoes were rationed for a year. In restaurants bread was also placed on a points system, so it counted as a single dish in a meal which comprised the maximum three dishes. If, however, it was served as bread and cheese or as sardines or baked beans on toast or even Welsh rarebit, it didn't count as an extra course, unless the customer had soup beforehand and wanted bread with it; they then forfeited a right to have the pudding. There was then the matter of the vanishing dried egg. We had at last, it seemed, grown to love this protein powder and when in the negotiations with the United States over post-war loan schemes, it disappeared, there were questions asked in the House of Commons.

The bakers were furious that bread was rationed and faced with the quantities of form-filling they complained that Britain had become like Nazi Germany. Sadly, the main reason for bread rationing was so that we could send flour to occupied Germany, as the civilians there were having to survive on 1,000 calories a day. Another baker observed bitterly that the quality of British bread – greyish coloured, with a low fat and high chalk content – was so bad it hardly needed rationing at all.

> It will ration itself. We have never used worse flour. It is thirty-five per cent cattle food.[36]

There was a housing shortage and if you did have a house, there was not even enough coal to warm one room in it. Bombed cities were trying to clear ruined buildings and rubble, clothes were still rationed, there was no soft fruit in the shops because the Ministry had taken it all to make jam, beer was weak and whisky had vanished entirely.

In 1947 there was a freak winter when the snow fell blocking roads and railways with fourteen foot-high snowdrifts and the country was paralysed for weeks. Ice floes were seen off the Norfolk coast, on the hills thousands of sheep lay dead in the snow. Then instead of the spring arriving the floods came; forty miles of the River Severn spilled over, the Thames swelled to the width of three miles below Chertsey and a million people in London were without a water supply. It was the worst winter since 1880. The Government poured money into distress funds, housing drives, farming subsidies, but the food and fuel prospects were worse than ever. The floods had destroyed 80,000 tons of potatoes and a further 70,000 acres of wheat; thirty-two per cent of the hill sheep had died and 30,000 cattle.

What is astonishing is how very conservative the British were in what they refused to eat; they found tuna fish disgusting. I suspect no one knew how to cook it properly, for its dark bloody flesh[37] must be placed under a running cold tap until the flesh is bloodless and pale, the colour of tinned tuna. The depths of their revulsion was unleashed when given whalemeat; it was cooked like stewing steak but it tasted fishy, which was the main critical condemnation. Shock and deep horror were felt by all. Again it should have had the cold water treatment before being cooked, or been marinaded in vinegar and spices. This simply illustrates how very reclusive our island race had grown; we had no idea at all of what others ate, no idea at all that whalemeat was a staple in the diet of the Inuit or our recent enemy, the Japanese. (If the last fact had been known, no one would have touched it, such was the depths of feeling.) But how did the Inuit process it and cook it? Did anyone bother to ask? No, we still had immense pride in our own idiosyncrasies which we felt strongly were healthy and normal. Yet there were people in Britain who could cook whalemeat and make it delicious. At one Lyons Corner House they were selling 600 whale steaks a day by 1947 simply by not labelling it. Raymond Postgate wrote that he knew a City restaurant 'where for months city gents consumed the steaks in great gollops, happily convinced they were eating on the black market and spiting Mr Strachey . . . If they had known they were not breaking the law they would have left in a huff.'[38]

The depth of British revulsion was kept for snoek, however. One would think at a time when the butter and meat ration had been cut, the bacon ration halved and after a winter and spring of catastrophe, a new tinned fish which was cheap and unrationed, for it was only on points, would be greeted with delight. Snoek is its South African name; in Australia it is called barracouta (not to be confused with barracuda, a different fish). Snoek (*thyrsites atun*) lives in the seas of the southern hemisphere, grows to a length of 135 cm (54 inches) and is often smoked. It was planned that ten million tins of this fish would replace Portuguese sardines, whose import was restricted by exchange problems. Wholesalers had already tried it and pronounced it tasteless and unpalatable. But the Minister had already spent £857,000 on the fish and, what is more, eaten it in sandwiches. He had pronounced it 'good, palatable, but rather dull'. The Government published eight recipes when the first consignment arrived in May 1948: *snoek piquante* was mashed, mixed with chopped spring onions, vinegar, syrup, pepper and salt, to be eaten cold with salad. It cost 1s 4½d for a half pound tin and took only one point, thirteen points less than red salmon.

Nevertheless the British housewife was unimpressed; by the summer of 1949 more than a third of the snoek imported since 1947 was still unsold. The Ministry hopefully put out more recipes: snoek sandwich spread, snoek pasties, snoek with salad. In September 1947 the price was reduced, but it still remained unsold; three weeks later with tinned tomatoes and various tinned meats it came off the points system, and then people forgot about it. Eighteen months later among the celebrations of the Festival of Britain a large amount of new tins labelled: 'selected fish food for cats and kittens', went on sale in the shops.[39] The public was biased against the food because it was now suspicious of all Ministry announcements; it disliked the imposition laid upon it of having to eat some new food; besides, the fish was unexciting and it had a ridiculous name, so how could anyone treat a food called snoek seriously? Also, the Ministry recipes were hardly adventurous or imaginative; they were far too cautious. Their *piquante* was not *piquante* enough; some curry powder and cayenne might have cheered the fish up. A southern hemisphere fish needed southern hemisphere recipes, but if not that, a few ideas borrowed from the new Jamaican immigrants would have made a huge difference.

Until 1948 there had been very few black and coloured immigrants arriving in England, but in that year 547 immigrants arrived from Jamaica alone. By 1951 the Caribbean population was 15,300 and ten years later it had risen to 171,800; now there were women and children too. The Indian, Pakistani, African and Asian numbers were barely half of this number, but continually rising. There were also Cypriot, Maltese, Hong Kong and Malaysian peoples, all of whom would enrich our cuisine. The new immigrants worked in hospitals and on the railways where there were grave labour shortages, but they met with persistent discrimination and there were serious disturbances with Teddy Boys going 'niggerhunting'. As always, neighbours complained of cooking smells from curries and spice mixes, which the English thought were offensive.

The dour and depressing kitchen scene across the land was set against the beginnings of mighty changes in our agriculture, which began with the 1947 Agricultural Act passed by the new Labour Government and designed to save the farmer in its structure of subsidies, from the insecurities of pre-war farming. There was an eightfold increase in the use of nitrogen fertilisers between 1953 and 1976. In 1950 there were still 300,000 horses working on farms, by 1979 there were only 3,575; in 1945 there were 563,000 regular full time farm workers, in 1980 there were 133,000.

By 1950 food controls gradually began to lessen. In January milk rationing was suspended; in May hotels and restaurants were freed of the 5s limit and the number of courses eaten. In autumn 1953, flour, eggs and soap were unrationed and it all finally ended in 1954 when fats, including cheese and meat came off ration. Now, if you had the money you could begin to buy more or less anything you wanted to eat. There were still restrictions on the amount of money you took abroad, so doing an eating tour of France was impossible. But what had happened to British cooking in these fourteen years?

Cordon Bleu

The Constance Spry Cookery Book was published in 1956; Spry and her colleague and friend, Rosemary Hume, had been working on it for almost ten years throughout the worst years of austerity. In the foreword Constance Spry tells of a conversation with a student on the eve of war who had suggested that after the war she should add cookery lessons to her flower programme. The student added, 'I think we shall need it.' Spry adds the statement, 'showing in this constructive suggestion a prophetic vision'.

Did her students lack all culinary skill and knowledge? The answer is, unfortunately, yes. This particular student saw the future stretching bleakly in front of her with not one servant to do her bidding. From the onset of war all the servants had gone, and these were the people who for good or ill had coped mostly with all the cooking for the middle and upper classes. Constance Spry's students and those who learnt cooking at Rosemary Hume's Cordon Bleu Cookery School all came from this class (in fact the first section in their book is on food for a cocktail party). They well knew that after the war the servants would not return, and that if they did not learn to cook, no one else would do the job.

'Remembering as I do the days of immensely long, boring, wasteful dinners, remembering too the starvation which was all too often at our very doors, I cannot forbear to remind you how much respect ought to be paid to food, how carefully it should be treated, how shameful waste is.' Mrs Spry was grateful for the rationing system at which they grumbled so incessantly as it had meant 'the immensely better and fairer distribution of food among all grades of society'. She thought that the contemporary cook-hostess had the best of it, for she saw her efforts appreciated and heard the food discussed, 'which is a pleasant innovation, for talk about food used to be taboo'. This gives us a clue to that Victorian/Edwardian past into which Mrs Spry was born in 1886, when the food was allowed to decline; food was not discussed, it was bad manners to comment on the food eaten, whether to praise or criticise it. Obviously, when that happens the subject becomes moribund.

In 1953 food was discussed, however, and no wonder for throughout the war people could think of little else but how to make what little food there was appetising. Once food reappeared again in all its variety, yes, it was discussed endlessly – the corpse had stirred and was returning to life. Spry's book with Hume is an excellent illustration of where British food was at the time, but it is restricted to the class from which their devoted students came, who were 'in effect an English variant on the French style'.[40] For that reason the Cordon Bleu style of cooking never permeated much further into society; it became rather a joke and was also instantly recognisable in being a little over fussy in presentation and tending towards the bland in flavour.

Earlier, in 1952, another book had been published which had far more influence over the way the majority cooked, *The Penguin Cookery Book* by a New Zealander, Bee Nilson. Taking both books together, we can see where British cuisine was in the midst of the century before other influences arrived, which had been waiting in the wings.

Firstly, on that old controversy of French influences, Mrs Spry in her Introduction apologises:

> The incidence of French words is no snobbery, or I hope not. It is sometimes difficult to find a suitable English equivalent for them; if you try you will find that often the English words lack nicety of description. Sometimes a translation sounds downright unappetising. Do you like the sound of 'paste of fat liver'?

The point that Mrs Spry overlooks is that 'a paste of fat liver' strikes us as odd, because we have no tradition of making it. If we had had overstuffed geese or ducks ever since medieval times in some town in Devon we would almost certainly know the dish by the name of that town. However, her note above is misleading: she does not just use French expressions for French dishes, which would have been acceptable; in her section on chicken most of the following recipes are variations on *poulet*, which could easily have been English recipes. This becomes ridiculous when in the fish chapter in three recipes for *colin* (hake), she specifies cod without an explanation. In fact she expresses nervousness about buying fish and admits to only recently daring to cook skate; one supposes that the fishmonger stocked hake and she failed to recognise it. The fish chapter with its unending list of French recipes makes me impatient with Mrs Spry. Surely she knew of the work of Mrs Leyel and Florence White, surely she was aware that there were excellent English recipes for fish which she could have used? That at this vital moment in our culinary history she took the easy route of agreeing with her colleague that there was no question that French cuisine was superlative seems to me a sell-out. However much she protests above, the impression is that French terms are used throughout for snobbish reasons and snobbish reasons only. But then we are in the land of Cordon Bleu.

In the style of Mrs Beeton, Spry and Hume include a chapter titled '*Rechauffés*', which is for dishes based on leftover meat, another called '*Pièces Froides*' which is full of galantines, terrines and pâtés, another deals with *petits gâteaux*, *petits fours* and *gros gâteaux*, and of course under egg dishes we have *oeufs* this, that and the other. The book, over 1,200 pages long, is astonishingly comprehensive; over fifty years later it still remains an excellent work of reference and can still be used with perfect results as a cookery book. But it attempted to fix the British cuisine in an aspic that had already melted; it taught the leisured classes how to cook in the manner of the nineteenth century, a useless requirement in 1955.

The fish chapter in the Penguin book is quite practical: without necessarily naming a fish it goes into detail about different methods of cooking, boiling, poaching, steaming, stewing, grilling and of course, frying. It gives recipes for a fish pie, for soused herrings and fish baked in stock or wine. It has ten suggestions for using various canned fish in recipes and a section on shellfish and how to make 'Hot Buttered Crab', though throughout whenever butter is mentioned it adds 'or margarine', though it does say earlier that 'butter is by far the ideal fat'.

This cookery book, which sold many millions of copies in the early 1950s, lacks all enthusiasm for its subject; it treats food like domestic science (the author taught it at North London Polytechnic); it is severely pragmatic, and totally without any imagination. It is a rule book, which if followed carefully will give plain and edible results, but, I imagine, little enjoyment. Certainly this book is not about gastronomy or about the traditions of a rich English cuisine; it delivers to you the bald facts and does not attempt to make them appetising. Moreover, so much of the information one would rather not have at all: 'Hors-d'oeuvres are meant to be appetizers at the beginning of the meal to stimulate the flow of digestive juices and help digest the food which will follow.' But Bee Nilson is excellent on the cooking of vegetables and on the dangers of eating too much sugar. This was a perfect book for people who were never going to love food or express much interest in it, but who felt that they should learn to cook as a duty. This, I fear, was a general feeling for many people in the 1950s: they were unexcited by the food they ate, but knew that they had get on and eat the wretched stuff.

Both books together did nothing to destroy the conviction among the British that their cooking was the worst in the world, nor did we know why we had reached such a nadir of genuine awfulness.

Fifties' Food

The state of our food was partly a hangover from the war; so many dreary short cuts still existed in the use of food substitutes. (Dried egg, for example, did not curdle like egg yolks when used to thicken sauces.) Hotels and restaurants that boasted of their gourmet cooking tended to overcook food and serve it sodden with water, or they failed to season it, or else it was oversalted and excessively peppered; they served ill-butchered meat, stale fish smothered with a floury sauce, mixed butter and marge together, used bottled mayonnaise, mock cream (another leftover from the war); used false pie crusts which had had no previous contact with the food beneath it, packet soups, gravy cubes and gravy browning, and had the nerve to present a cheeseboard full of dried and sweaty scraps of hard cheese, mostly Danish Blue and factory-made Cheddar. One of the most common crimes was to bone and roast meat, then allow it to go cold, then cut slices paper thin on a meat slicer to be warmed and served up with ersatz gravy. Had no one before realised, as did Raymond Postgate, that Britain was packed full of wild food which was edible and delicious, and at times of rationing or austerity such a larder could be raided to the full? In his seminal article which launched *The Good Food Guide* Postgate wrote:

> There is, and there has been for a long time, plenty of chickens, poultry, rabbits, geese, game, salmon, sole, cod, herring and all kinds of fish: and of vegetables when they are in season . . . Food is ill-cooked in hotels and restaurants, or it is insufficient, or it is badly and rudely served up – or all three. The pretence that this is due to Ministry of Food regulations will not do any more.[41]

By 1951 the first edition of *The Good Food Guide* was in print and sold 5,000 copies. It only had just over 500 entries from Aberdeen to Wembley, all based on the recommendations of readers of the *Leader Magazine*. The beginnings of a gastronomic revolt against bad food, ill-informed cooking and sloppy service had begun.

Now, as well as newly designed gas cookers, we also had a refrigerator, television and cookery programmes with Marguerite Patten, Philip Harben and later in the 1950s, Fanny Cradock with her stooge husband. She, in a ridiculous ball gown and white fox fur stoles, gave an ersatz glamour to her cooking which was heavily biased towards French dishes. After the years of rationing, meat returned to become a central ingredient; the Sunday joint reigned supreme with its leftovers eaten cold or rehashed as shepherd's pie or curry.

Frozen peas arrived and were an instant big hit; peas were now being eaten throughout the year. Other frozen foods followed, and fish fingers became a children's favourite meal. Instant coffee took over from Camp coffee essence which had been flavoured with chicory, a Continental addiction that never caught on here. Steak and chips became a favourite choice when eating out, though the appearance of fried scampi was a close runner-up; *quiche lorraine* was a popular snack or lunch in pubs and delicatessens, while pasta began to be eaten more. The new steak houses that began to spring up found that prawn cocktail was a favourite starter, and when the prawns were available frozen, which began in the 1960s, it could also be made at home. The middle classes socialized now by giving dinner parties, beginning inevitably with pork or chicken liver pâtés followed by *coq au vin*.

The invention of the espresso coffee machine by Achille Gaggia resulted in the coffee bar with its false coloured ceilings and rubber plants. By 1960 there were 2,000 of them, where young people could meet, discuss, read and write, eking out a cup of espresso or cappuccino for several hours. They vanished almost as suddenly as they arrived, as Italian caterers realised that there was more money to be made if they served food and obtained a drinks' licence. The Italian *trattoria* began to spread in the 1960s; every provincial town had one with its check tablecloths and plastic grapes, and on the menu its long list of different pastas and veal dishes – how very welcome they were. In London there were also the superior *trattorie*, owned by Mario and Franco and designed by Apicella in white and black tiles, which served sophisticated Italian food with style. But the Italians were not, by far, the most invasive foreign influence on our high streets. This era also saw the rise of Indian and Chinese restaurants, whose spicy meals were a more than welcome change.

Looking back on those years when I was growing up, I ask myself what did I know of good or bad food in that time? All children know is what they enjoy or dislike, and each of us seem to be born with idiosyncratic likes and dislikes which could have their roots in genetic or environmental causes. Mine were a negative response to pasteurised dairy products, especially milk, and to all kinds of liver, though oddly enough not pâtés. My mother was a good, natural cook, eager to try new ingredients and recipes when they came her way. Looking back now on my childhood, I enjoyed two separate dishes made perfectly and learnt to cook both in my late teens. Now, I consider they are two of the greatest British dishes and I've never had either cooked better than in those early years. The first I ate at my grandmother's home and it was roast beef with Yorkshire pudding cooked beneath the joint; she had learnt that method from her grandmother so it goes back to the eighteenth century. The beef is cooked on a rack and its juices drop down into the batter; the centre of the pudding never puffs up, and is rather sloppy and very meaty. The charm of it is that one has a slice of the centre batter and a slice of the crispy outside piece too. There's no gravy, the bloody juices of the meat suffice. However, my most favourite dish as a child and an adult (until I gave up eating meat in middle age) was steamed steak and kidney pudding with its suet top but not its sides, which my mother made. It was essential that ox kidney was used and no other, the amount of kidney to steak had to be equal and the pudding had to steam slowly for all of three hours. These are two simple meat dishes, but great ones individual to our cuisine.

As a very young man in the middle 1950s I cooked other dishes than these, such as *piperade*, for at John Lehmann's literary parties, I had met an extremely shy Mrs David, nestling close to writers like Elizabeth Bowen, William Plomer and even Dame Edith Sitwell, on one occasion resplendent upon a sofa wearing her Tudor toque with her skirts spread out like any monarch. Like me, Mrs David did not appear to belong anywhere, and I had already been bewitched by her writing.

Elizabeth David

It was John Lehmann who published in 1950 Elizabeth David's *A Book of Mediterranean Food*, followed by *French Country Cooking* in 1951, both books illustrated by John Minton. After his publishing business collapsed, her third book, *Italian Food*, was brought out by Macdonald's in 1954. The influence her books had was immediate. Their power was due to the strength of her prose which in the most economical style evoked countries of taste, texture and colour that we all longed to experience too.

Arabella Boxer makes the point in her introduction[42] that in our embrace of the Mediterranean world we forgot our own English food. That is so up to a point, but what we were embracing in reality, though we did not know it, were the past influences that had once created our own medieval food. Mrs Leyel, thirty years earlier, had done the same. It was as if our national atavism had been pricked alert and awoke to a world that had once been ours and that we now needed to regain. The shallots, garlic and saffron, the almonds and pistachios, the mixture of sweet and savoury, of dried fruits and lemon zest, of lentils and chick peas were all somehow faintly familiar. We seemed to have no tradition of them because we could only go back as far as Victorian bourgeois cooking; before that through the diaries of Parson Woodforde and Pepys we learnt only of roast meats and steamed puddings; nothing to be proud of, we thought naively. Earlier historians of medieval food had been disapproving of the flavourings:

> A large proportion of the receipts in all the cookery books prescribe spices, even for food which, according to modern taste, would be far better without them . . . the practice of smothering ordinary meats with

spices . . . quinces are not merely boiled but flavoured with rose water
. . . the highly spiced dishes that one encounters in India, in northern
Africa, and in out-of-the-way districts of Italy and Spain today
differ in no essential particulars from those that chiefly characterize
medieval cookery.[43]

And there was the nub of it, said by a food historian whose opinion was that medieval food sounded thoroughly disgusting, akin to the foreign muck on the continent.

Pre-Reformation cooking had continued to grow and develop in France without interruption, but the Reformation in our own national psyche seemed to have built a barrier between us and the past. Perhaps Henry VIII's instigation and enforcement of it was so brutal and bloody it inhibited our awareness, was too painful to consider. Each time thereafter that we took an influence from across the Channel we believed it to be a completely new one; in the seventeenth century we absorbed some of the ideas of La Varenne, but most of those were also medieval.

Reading Mrs David was like rediscovering a part of oneself that had been so utterly lost we were unaware of its existence. As Mediterranean longings permeated society in the late 1950s so the first package tours made it possible for people with slim incomes to go abroad and to sample the food first hand. Pre-war only the rich and the upper classes travelled abroad (my mother never went further south than the Isle of Wight). Strange vegetables began to appear in the grocers – peppers, courgettes, avocadoes and aubergines. London's Soho had streets where the smells were a heady mixture of garlic, coffee and Parmesan, where you could buy home-made pasta, olive oil and Parma ham. At home one could cook the dishes eaten abroad little knowing that one was returning to smells and flavours once loved by our ancestors.

Going Ethnic

Our taste for the curry ever since the eighteenth century had been a strong one. Led by Mrs Raffald and Mrs Glasse, almost immediately after the part colonisation of the sub-continent, recipes for pickles, ketchups, kedgeree and curried mutton appeared in all the English cookery books. We absorbed this spicy food as our own. Now in the 1960s Indian restaurants began to open in towns, large and small, all over the British Isles; these were a boon to vegetarians for it was the only world cuisine in which a meal lacking animal protein was regarded as commonplace.

Almost at the same time immigrants from Hong Kong and the New Territories fleeing from the fear of Maoist China arrived in Britain and began working in the service industries. From there it was a short step to opening a restaurant; by 1970 there were around 4,000 Chinese catering businesses in the UK, many of these being take-away shops. Their success was certainly due to a combination of the cheapness of the dishes and the spicy flavours which in a harmless manner easily become addictive.[44] But sweet and sour meat dishes (the number one Chinese favourite), for example, were also a favourite medieval dish, so again here was a spectrum of flavours that not so long before had been part of our own cuisine.

By 1965, thirty-one per cent of people who ate out regularly visited Chinese restaurants, eight per cent went to Indian, five to Italian and another five to French. In the 1963 edition of *The Good Food Guide* eight Chinese and six Indian restaurants were felt to be good enough to be listed in London, while there were eight more Chinese and four Indian in the rest of the UK. It was only in the late 1960s that regional Chinese differences began to appear, and there were noticeable differences between Canton, Hong Kong and Shanghai, between the wheat-based menus of north China and the rice-based food of the coastal south; dim sum, snacks steamed in baskets, became popular, as did crisp fried duck rolled in pancakes with hoi-sin sauce. Later still, other differences appeared, as in the more specialised Szechuan, hot with its own aromatic pepper. The discerning British gastronome learnt to search out the Chinese restaurant that attracted the largest Chinese clientele, and to appreciate the Chinese cuisine that they ate so enthusiastically.

Throughout the 1970s and 1980s, various Indian regional differences in restaurants also began to attract English customers. The British bureaucrats and the military had always centred on the meat-eating Muslim north, Pakistan and Bangladesh. But now wider audiences grew to appreciate the mild pilaus, sweet dhansaks and cream kormas of north India, and clay ovens, tandoors, for dry roasting of yoghurt-marinated chicken were imported. Nepal, Goa and the vegetarian Gujerat, the Tamil cooking of the south, were all regions to find appreciative British audiences. Yet the most favourite dish still remained sweet and sour pork, or sweet and sour anything. We cannot escape our past.

Observers of our eating patterns considered that we embraced every new world cuisine because of the paucity of our own. On the contrary what we were embracing was the return of flavours that once had been part of our own tradition.

CHAPTER 12

The Global Village

In the post-war years there was great concern among nutritionists and food scientists that with a burgeoning world population we would not have enough to eat, and, most particularly, that there would not be enough protein foods for all. At that time there was a belief that we should eat more protein in our diet (even though the evidence from the war years showed how healthier a society was with very little). Obesity statistics today suggest we now eat too much. This post-war anxiety fuelled desperation to boost agricultural production and allowed the pharmaceutical industries on to the farm with chemicals, prophylactics and hormones to stimulate production into ever-greater output. The average yield of wheat rose by 10 cwt per acre to reach 32 cwt in the twenty years from 1949 to 1969. Factory farming became widespread in egg, chicken, pork and bacon production. These new farming methods placed an increasing premium upon capital, access to capital, and the terms on which it was available became crucial for a farm's survival; this was encouraged both by the NFU and the Agricultural Act of 1967. As technology, mechanized drills, tractors and combine harvesters, and use of pesticides for weeding instead of hoeing came in, so human labour was lost and now only two per cent of people work on the land. The old-style farms disappeared, hedges and spinneys were eradicated in deference to the machine, streams were diverted and ponds filled in; any water that was left was soon polluted by animal slurry and the run-off of chemicals from the fields stretching bleakly to the horizon growing their single crop. More and more food production tasks were done in factories and processing units and fewer were carried out in farms. As industrial farming took over so the quality of our food declined; there might be more of it but all the flavour had drained away. It was cheap, however, and though at first the public noticed the disadvantages, it did not seem unduly worried.

This dramatic change in farming now allows a farmer to produce far more food than ever before. In fact, we have a surplus of food, which increases every year, and which costs us, the taxpayer, a phenomenal sum in dumping it; as it rots away it is cast back into the land. Though working conditions are now easier there is greater expense in the input of fossil fuels, pesticides and nitrates. The farmer has been forced away from an intimate understanding of the natural environment and the creatures in it, to an ever-increasing attempt to control and manipulate nature by artificial means. We see this vividly in the claustrophobic conditions in which thousands of animals are reared, conditions that decimate them to such an extent that if it were not for a regular, daily supply of prophylactic drugs they would collapse and die long before their brief term of life – as seven per cent of them do. Chickens have been genetically improved for rapid growth on a very high protein diet; they live for six weeks (a chicken's natural life span is about six years) in these unhygienic conditions reaching their 3 lb weight. These creatures are slaughtered and processed in factories, thirty per cent of them with broken bones due to handling. A chicken takes roughly an hour from arriving upside down squawking to have its throat cut, to when it is polythene wrapped and ready for the lorry to deliver to the supermarket. The few facts above have been widely promulgated in our society, yet chicken remains the most popular meat eaten, possibly because the carcass meat is now the cheapest flesh-protein available, far cheaper than in the 1950s. What is still not widely known is that the soiled chicken litter with parts of dead and rotten birds in it filled with chicken faeces and urine is processed and fed to cattle. Since the BSE scare feeding of cattle with mammalian protein had been halted, but not avian protein. Never in the past, in all its unhygienic practices, was a nation's food supply so badly contaminated as ours is at present and given official blessing.

Health Foods

Disgust with factory farming was a strong factor in stimulating organic agriculture and the health food movement, which took off in the 1960s, giving rise to the Cranks restaurant in Soho and a chain of nationwide health shops. By the 1980s these shops numbered 1,200 with a turnover of £80 million a year. The journalist Nicholas Tomalin, writing at the time, thought sceptically that its customers were buying 'hope and innocence in a sullied, dangerous technological world'.[1] Health foods went hand in hand with a resurgence in the vegetarian movement; fuelled by reports of the cruelty, lack of welfare and added chemicals in their feed that livestock had to endure, many people stopped eating meat altogether.[2] Food poisoning outbreaks tripled in the 1980s; 9.5 million people are affected by it each year, a sixth of the population. Salmonella from chickens and eggs, listeria from a number of sources and the BSE scare (bovine spongiform encephalopathy or 'mad cow disease') all served to turn people away from animal protein; the last scare saw a decline in sales of beef. When Max the cat died of FSE (the feline version of 'mad cow') meat sales collapsed by a third overnight.

In the 1980s there was a series of reports on diet, the first in 1983 by NACNE (National Advisory Committee on Nutrition Education) which the Government tried to suppress. Its main findings were that a healthy diet should be very low in saturated fats (found mainly in animals), high in fibre (meat has no fibre), low in refined foods, salt and sugar, and high in fruit and vegetables. The consumption of animal protein should fall and vegetable protein rise. These reports also gave added incentive to a vegetarian diet or one very low in animal proteins – game birds, for example, have no saturated fat at all. All this information fuelled an active and at times almost militant response away from industrialised food towards a meatless diet, a fostering of farm and organic shops or turning towards growing your own vegetables and fruits. The majority of people on low incomes, however, many of them trapped in meaningless jobs, living on bleak housing estates, found that it was easier to buy highly processed food that was easily available and not to question its quality.

Fast Food

The frozen food market grew from 100,000 packets of frozen fruit and vegetables in 1954 to 360 million in 1960. The freezer cabinet, which could even take an entire butchered carcass, began to be purchased in affluent homes, especially in country houses. Convenience foods, often comprising a whole meal on a plastic tray, were also becoming a big seller; many people now tended to eat their evening meal while watching television.

After the end of rationing food retailing went through a dramatic transformation, when the principle of self-service was introduced from the United States. At first many thought it to be a passing fad. It was the co-operative movement that pioneered the idea. By 1950 there were already 600 of their self-service stores in operation. Once food rationing ended there was a rush to open many more, and within three years there were 3,000. These numbered many larger stores with over 2,000 square feet of selling space, which were dubbed supermarkets; by 1962 there were 12,000 of them.

This proved to be a problem for the old multiple traders, such as Home and Colonial who often only had narrow shops about 12 ft wide, and were ill-suited to sell the huge range of goods that the modern shopper now demanded. They were slow to reorganise themselves and though by 1965 they had 400 supermarkets they had been overtaken by a number of giant national supermarket chains like Tesco and Fine Fare, where the competition was fierce, emphasising low prices with the aid of high-powered advertising, and special offers. Centralized buying of produce by supermarket chains led to monoculture and large industrial farms, while smaller farmers were squeezed out of the market, unable to produce the quantities required.

Self-service meant a different type of food; everything, which before had been cut from larger blocks to the customer's requirements, was now pre-weighed and wrapped before sale. In the early 1990s around one-third of the products were the supermarket's own label; this is twice the amount in the rest of Europe. Supermarkets claim that they respond to the customers' requirements but they stock foods in abundance that may have little nutritional value but certainly have a generous profit margin; these are the most glossily packaged and are given the most advertising – breakfast cereals being the prime example. No small grocer's shop could begin to stock the wide range of cereals eaten now. Junk food is another example of poor nutritional value, a big profit margin and glossy packaging, which is stocked to excess by supermarkets, many of them making their own brand versions. Junk food is food that is highly processed, that is likely to be composed only of refined flour and milk solids, sugar, salt and chemical flavourings, or made up from odds and ends of animal carcasses which have been processed, surfaced, sequestrated, humected, emulsified and anti-oxided and turned into blocks of pap.

It is the supermarket that dictates the bulk of the national diet, linked to effective television advertising; it has become more like the Orwellian concept of Big Brother, ever watchful to the slightest yearning, ready to satiate or to harness it to some mercenary end. We are in its thrall; for many harassed mothers with small children, a visit to the supermarket is almost a form of entertainment, as well as a necessary trip for essential goods. Another American import that crept into our high streets in the 1950s was the fast food shops, which were then independently-owned eating rooms giving a standardised meal which could be eaten in house or taken away: the foods offered were roast chicken, pizza, steaks or hamburgers. A few variations of this main component were offered; also on the menu were non-alcoholic drinks and tinned fruit, cream or ice cream desserts. These fast food outlets were immediately successful; younger people flocked there, using them as meeting places. At first they were deplored by older people as 'cheap American food', but well within two decades they became established as a regular part of the British diet. Families took their young children there for meals, especially on day trips. By 1992 the sales in burger bars were by far the most successful, though closely followed by our own traditional fish and chips, then pizza and roast chicken which were almost level with ethnic take-aways.

Fast food has entered the home in tandem with refrigerators, freezers and microwaves, to complete the chain which extends the reach of the food factory into the home by providing the technology to store and prepare its products easily, and with minimal ability.[3] Most people now lack the basic skills needed to transform a relatively few, inexpensive ingredients into meals. The BBC's *Food Programme* instanced two young women, who had no idea how to cook dried pasta, so bought it tinned though it was three times the price. This is an obvious result of the fact that cooking was removed from the curriculum of schools in the early 1980s under a regime of educational cuts under the Thatcher government.

Diet towards the Millennium

By the 1990s Britain had become a society where in order to eat people were not obliged to cook at all; there were enough convenience foods stored in the refrigerator or freezer for people merely to heat them up. This tendency has grown. In fact, convenience foods do not have to be stored in the home; in poorer families they are often bought daily. Many new apartments built in London's West End now have no kitchens or cooking facilities, other than a microwave and a power point for boiling a kettle.

A Mass Observation survey, as reported by David Pocock,[4] tells a disparate story of how we ate in the early 1980s. Breakfast times differ, dependent on what time work began. A shop assistant's husband with no children in Southport got his own breakfast at 5.30, with cereal, toast and tea, while she would eat muesli, toast, cheese and tea at around 7.30. An all-night lorry driver ate his breakfast at 2 p.m. The average time was between 7 a.m. and 8 a.m., with family members sitting down whenever they were ready; the wife and mother often ate no breakfast at all, but drank a few cups of tea while she ensured that everyone else ate. If there was a cooked breakfast, even just a boiled egg, it was always the man who ate it, unless it was a Sunday when everyone might have bacon and egg. For all, there was a preponderance of branded cereal types, which are eaten with skimmed milk and sugar.

Tea and coffee were drunk by both sexes at elevenses, often with a sweet biscuit, while the midday meal could be for many young women just a snack, sometimes only a Yorkie, Kitkat or a Mars bar. Working men and women took a packed lunch, which they sometimes called dinner; if they bought food to eat at midday they referred to it as a snack. A working-class family stuck stubbornly to the term 'dinner' even if it was just sandwiches. But the word 'lunch' seemed to be winning, as the majority used it for their snack food eaten at midday, reverting back to the original meaning given by Dr Johnson, 'as much food as one's hand can hold'. However, there was also the 'business lunch', which was in a restaurant and included alcohol, wine instead of beer.

Lunch at home was mostly for the retired and was generally the most substantial meal of the day, with two courses of meat and two veg and a pudding, with custard made out of a packet, followed by a cup of tea. In the evening this couple might have had 'something on toast' – cheese or baked beans. A retired secretary in Berkshire living on her own always had a joint on Sundays, which lasted her through the week for three other main meals. She was following a Victorian tradition. As she was not working she only had toast and marmalade for breakfast but would have a light tea of grilled cheese or an egg, though no supper.

The great majority of women who lived alone or who were looking after one small child ate very little at lunchtime, only tea and bread and butter in the afternoon and later a snack of egg or cheese. Unemployed people seemed to fare no better, living off bought sandwiches, rolls, biscuits and instant coffee, always with milk and sugar. Afternoon tea as a main meal and a social event seemed to have altogether vanished, except in hotels or tea shops visited on holiday or a trip out. The coffee morning had replaced it, which had its heyday in the 1970s and 1980s; it is now rarer unless held to raise money for some charitable event. The food eaten was wholly ersatz; the coffee was instant granules and the food bought biscuits, though sponges and homemade cakes could be made.

Was the evening meal called dinner or supper? Some people claimed that they got invited out to supper more often than dinner, that supper meant at least one course less and it was expected that a bottle of wine should be taken. If the evening meal is the most substantial of the day then it is called dinner; a couple from Southport wrote that they would sit down to eat around 6.30 or 7 p.m., and have grapefruit or soup, then chicken, liver, or other meat, potatoes or rice, vegetables then stewed fruit, ice cream or a pudding or melon. A childless working couple in Bristol took turns to cook, whoever had had an easier day, and they ate omelettes, chops, frozen vegetables, Chinese takeaways, kebabs and curries. There does not seem to me much cooking here, merely thawing and heating up.

In families with children of different ages few of them ever sat down altogether to any meal, whether breakfast or supper, on a weekday. Sunday lunch, however, still seemed to be a ritual where they all expected to eat together.

In a family in Kent one son, having had a cafeteria lunch at school, returns at 5 p.m. to cereals, sandwiches and cake; a little later a working son returns for a cooked two-course meal which is his tea; and our correspondent, together with her husband and youngest son who have had a substantial lunch, sit down to their tea or salad or 'something on toast' and cake at about 6.15.[5]

The joint was still the most common feature of Sunday lunch and beef the most favoured meat with Yorkshire pudding; in fact, such was the pudding favoured that it could appear with other meats – roast lamb or pork. It was a two-course meal which was generally eaten between 1 and 2 p.m. though some families preferred to eat it at 7 or 7.30 p.m. The second course was described as pudding, dessert or sweet and was generally stewed or tinned fruit with custard, cream or ice cream. Wine was nearly always drunk with this meal. Guests tended to be invited on a Saturday evening, when extra care would be taken and the meal would begin with a starter.

Though convenience foods were easily obtainable, it is interesting to note that people still took pride in their own cooking and would do it for special occasions. The convenience foods were used on weekday evenings when people were tired after a long day's work. When they had time they cooked and when they cooked they favoured traditional foods – roast meats and Yorkshire pudding. Though the scope of the Victorian meal had shrunk with the families that were eating, the main course in essence had not much changed since the time when domestic cooking was created for a small group of friends, the time of Pepys.

Did much change in the 1990s? The Mass Observation documents cover a great range of topics, but the subject of food is one that is returned to frequently. The decade began with the eggs and salmonella scare: one ninety-one-year-old woman was not put off in the least, and thought it right that the minister should have spoken out, though wrong that she was made to resign. She said wisely that she always bothered about getting her eggs from a good source and made sure they were free range. Another retired woman did stop making her own homemade advocaat, which was brandy mixed with egg yolks and lemonade, but because of listeria threw her Camembert away and returned to eating Cheddar, which she preferred anyway.

Most correspondents were shocked and angry at the food scares; shopping, they felt, had become a minefield, they had become far more sympathetic to a vegetarian diet and were gradually adopting one.

In the spring of 1995 Mass Observation suggested in one of its directives that correspondents should write a day diary and picked a date in March. This was to ensure that people did not pick a particular day which flattered them, but an arbitrary day, whether typical or not. Two seventy-year-olds had a day trip out to their nearest town; she had fish and chips for lunch and he ate shepherd's pie with a fruit dessert and a pot of tea. All a widow aged sixty-one ate all day was tea, cider, toast, marmalade, cheese and salad sandwiches, plasticised strawberries, summer fruit pudding, bread and semi-skimmed milk; she had added up the total calories, which were 800; she said she was trying to lose weight. A sixty-eight-year-old retired secretary gave her husband tinned tomato soup heated in the microwave for lunch; she and her daughter had a chicken burger and a pot of tea. She went out shopping at KwikSave for buns, bread rolls, milk, sauce and yoghurts. They had another cup of tea at five and a cup of cocoa and a cheese roll for supper at 10 p.m. Another retired woman had a breakfast of orange juice, bran sticks, wholemeal bread with marmalade and two cups of tea; for lunch she had minced beef with a Bulgarian red wine which had been opened the day before to go with venison, followed by a rice pudding; tea at 5.30 p.m. consisted of wholemeal scones and chocolate cake, and at 10 p.m. there was instant coffee and a digestive biscuit before going to bed. A thirty-eight-year-old female author had breakfast in bed at 8.30, brought by her husband and consisting of marmite on toast and Earl Grey tea (she suffered from severe rheumatoid arthritis). Her lunch was a chicken burger with sprouts, mushrooms, potatoes and afterwards steamed jam pudding. At 6 p.m. she had V8 vegetable juice and at 7.20 p.m. soya cottage cheese and marmite on bread, chocolate sponge cake and Earl Grey tea; she was allergic to dairy products.

A student nurse had a takeaway about once a month, which was usually Chinese or Indian but occasionally fish and chips. A head teacher aged fifty-two breakfasted on two cups of tea, plus a bowl of organic porridge oats with sultanas cooked with water in the microwave. At a 10 a.m. meeting in a hotel she ate a chicken sandwich and a cup of tea, at 1 p.m. another cup of tea and a salad sandwich; at 8.40 p.m. she had a supper of fresh French bread and turkey with another cup of tea. A woman aged thirty-three breakfasted on Kellogg's branflakes with skimmed milk early in the morning; she got to work by 8 a.m., and had her first cup of tea at 9 a.m.; she had a packed lunch of sandwiches, cheese spread, homemade tuna pâté or homemade hummus and a banana; for supper she ate homemade aloo samosas with chick peas and green chilli and two pitta breads. She described herself as having 'a passion for food, particularly ethnic', and found English food 'dull and uninspiring'. A thirty-one-year-old unemployed woman had breakfast with her boyfriend in bed, consisting of orange juice, cornflakes and a cup of tea; she made him a packed lunch of four slices of wholemeal bread made into one Cheshire cheese sandwich and one corned beef with Branston pickle (she thought the last was 'yucky stuff'), plus a pear. She had lunch with a friend in a cafe at 1 p.m., drinking a pot of tea and eating a huge slice of chocolate cake. When her boyfriend returned she made him pancakes with diet Coke; later they went out to see a film and eat chips and popcorn. She commented that they usually ate much better than this:

> I'm a veggie who'd ideally like to have an organic garden plot to grow my own veggies in. We eat a lot of veg and fruit usually and I certainly don't have choccy cake, pancakes and Maltesers all in one day.

A sixty-year-old JP with five daughters drank coffee (made by her husband) and ate half a slice of wholewheat toast; at 9 a.m., still hungry, she made herself a cup of peppermint tea; at 11 a.m. she had coffee and biscuits; at 12.30 p.m., meeting a friend for lunch, she had a salmon and salad sandwich (she was on a diet); at 4 p.m. she had a cup of peppermint tea; at 4.30 p.m. her husband had an omelette and chips and she had two vegetarian sausages and two whole onions cooked in the microwave. She spent the evening in court and went to bed at 11 p.m. still hungry.

A male teacher aged thirty-five ate breakfast around 7.45 a.m. and had fresh orange juice, a bowl of All-Bran topped up with some bran flakes and a cup of tea, made up his packed lunch of a round and a half of granary bread with smoked turkey, a low fat fruit yoghurt, a carrot and a Granny Smith apple; after a day at school he returned home at 4.30 and had a Sainsbury's frozen tagliatelle cooked in the microwave, a banana, chocolate biscuits and a cup of tea. A student aged twenty-four who was unemployed ate a big bowl of muesli with extra dried fruit when he got up; at 10.30 he had black coffee and a small cherry bakewell tart in a cafe with a friend; for lunch at another cafe he had a hot sausage sandwich on brown bread and a mug of tea. Back home at 4.30 he put the remains of last night's dinner back in the oven; it was pasta with cheese sauce with Welsh sausages and onion mixed in. While it was heating he ate some more mixed dried fruit in natural yoghurt, then fell asleep for three-quarters of an hour. Not long after he wakes up one of his housemates offered some food; she was making a fish balti of cheap filleted coley, pasta sauce, curry powders and frozen fresh leaf coriander which they ate with rice. He spent the evening with friends where they drank coffee and got stoned. At 10.30 p.m. on his way home he stopped at a new convenience store and bought some chocolate raisins and a three-pack Belgian Frangipanes labelled Cakes for the Connoisseur. He commented it was 'clearly very average seven-eleven-type munchy food. It amazes me the extent to which late night stores seem to almost consciously cater for stoned people'.

In the summer of 1997, correspondents gave their views on being overweight. Few people commented negatively, they looked upon obesity as all part of the variety of life, and in fact were distressed if they heard rudeness towards fat people: 'I think society can be very cruel to overweight people.' 'The whole idea of being a certain shape and weight is largely due to the magazines.'

For celebrations a Scottish woman arranged her children's birthdays by providing crisps, sausage rolls and cakes; the oldest child preferred friends to stay overnight with what she called proper grown-up food (pizzas or burgers) with a cake made in the shape of a car or a teddy bear covered in butter icing. The children arrange a surprise forty-second birthday party for her with 'a mountain of food buffet style'. At Christmas one woman's family always ate beef with horseradish sauce and mustard and Yorkshire pudding, roast potatoes, sprouts, sweetcorn, carrots and home-grown runner beans from the freezer. The runner beans were a family tradition for she recalled as a child the beans were salted in stone jars. They followed this with Christmas pudding, fresh fruit salad, mince pies and a special trifle; this was followed by cheese and biscuits. They drank Asti Spumante throughout and fresh fruit juices. For her birthday they had lunch at a local Beefeater restaurant, where she remembered that the children thanked the waitress for serving them.

On the subject of genetically modified foods a seventy-two-year-old retired teacher commented: 'I'm disturbed, but more by the behaviour of the media than any danger to health from the food.' A seventy-seven-year-old retired man thought GM foods were okay as long as they were properly tested, but he strongly objected to having to eat them because they were forced on to the market. Another retired man, born in 1926, regarded it as 'an insidious move towards total control of what we eat', seeing it as a step towards the destruction of the whole eco system. A man aged fifty-two did not trust the Government: 'We are becoming too arrogant at tinkering with and ignoring nature.' A single forty-seven-year-old civil servant commented: 'Once again the unacceptable face of American capitalism raises its head' and looks forward to the time they are banned. Another seventy-six-year-old thought that in his opinion Montsanto's assurances flew in the face of history.

On the question of BSE a retired secretary aged sixty-nine thought the whole thing had been blown out of proportion; a young woman aged thirty-nine stopped eating beef altogether; another, forty-seven years old, thought it very worrying, but food and health scares had become commonplace; she added that she couldn't do without eating beef, and she felt she had to have red meat three times a week, but she hated the fact that the Government had made cows into cannibals. She reflected that organic farming was the only way to safeguard our food. A family which ate a lot of beef, a roast always on Sundays, mince to make burgers, beef stews in the winter, steak for supper, was worried and considered giving it up, but then decided they enjoyed it too much. One repeated a joke, swearing that she heard a person saying: 'I've got a lot of beef in my freezer, I shall wait until this BSE scare has died down before I eat it.' There was a general revulsion over animals that are given their own kind to eat. It would seem that the people who already ate beef and enjoyed it, went on doing so, but that the ones who ate very little gave it up without any sacrifice, just to be on the safe side.

How representative of our food consumption is the above? Firstly the reader should remember that the people that write to Mass Observation are self-selected; they wish to record these experiences for future social historians. As honestly as they can they set their own personal records down, so this cannot be an average cross-section of society. From a wealth of documentation my own selection of reading was arbitrary, and my choice inevitably subjective, so the above cannot claim to be representative.

Nevertheless, the overall impression from this limited perusal is that society now relies almost completely on convenience foods. When working people start the day with a bowl of cereals with milk and sugar, and drink tea; throughout the day they eat biscuits and sandwiches and drink more tea; once at home, few of them seem to cook a proper meal themselves from raw ingredients. If the meal is hot, it is something to be placed in the microwave to be heated through. Mealtimes for the younger people appear to have been jettisoned completely; they eat when they are hungry, which is possibly how they were fed as babies. They also eat a mixture of foods that might strike older people as not compatible. Though everyone, young and old, is aware of what comprises a healthy diet, there appears to be from the above records only a very rough simulation of it now and again.

This, if I am honest, is exactly what I and my friends do as well. The correspondents are individuals with strong beliefs and decided opinions, otherwise they would not have elected to join the scheme, but for the most part their food habits tend to be conformist, showing an overriding conservatism in their food choices. This shows up the limitation of the foods on offer and the way advertising guides the consumer into ever narrower choices, rather than the lack of intelligence and freedom in the individual.

Farming Crisis

The two last decades of the twentieth century were fraught with a crisis from zoonosis, the ability of the human population to catch diseases from animals. A continuing theme in history. We had had the scientists working for a Tory government informing the public that Bovine Spongiform Encephalopathy (BSE) could not be caught by humans, which it then was. This was soon followed by anxiety over genetic engineering which was hyped by multinationals and a newly elected Labour government, as the solution to many ills in the food system. This was followed by an outbreak of Foot and Mouth Disease which led to an over-zealous culling of livestock with a refusal to countenance vaccination. It was obvious soon after the millennium that the methods involved within intense farming methods pursued for maximum profit were giving us sick animals and a polluted environment. Some radical changes had to take place.

On the issue of genetic modification of crops there was public concern that Government trials being grown in the UK would contaminate traditional crops grown in the same area. Critics argued that organisms in the soil, bees, birds, insects, tractor wheels and the wind itself would be able to take pollen from GM crops, enabling them to grow many miles away. They were proved to be right; research from Canada has shown that GM rape has combined with various weeds to produce a superweed resistant to pesticides. Public anxiety has modified to a small degree through current Government policies, while making the multinationals themselves retrench to rethink their methods of selling the concept to the public.

What is the point of GM food except to make profits for the multinationals? Ideas that are being worked on are fungus resistant lettuce, virus resistant melon with longer shelf life, peas with a higher sugar content, and disease resistant tomatoes with high levels of the nutrients beta-carotene and lycopene. Another result of anti-GM research shows that the new combination of DNA is far from stable; once outside the laboratory it can continue to modify in unexpected ways. This meddling with natural evolution could bring unforeseen and disastrous results.

But does GM food taste better? No. This is because no scientist yet has discovered the secret of the combination of thousands of trace minerals, which the right soil and the right climate gives to a certain plant, bequeathing it with its magical and mysterious secret flavours. As to feeding the hungry of the world, a claim many multinationals make, their golden rice with added vitamin A, for example, would have to be eaten in such great quantities every day for it to have any effect that it would be impossible. If current trends continue, however, in twenty years GM crops could account for the vast majority of foods available, as well as functional foods, designed for specific health or other dietary purposes.[6]

We live in a global village. We presently import seventy per cent of our organic food. The ecological effect of this air freight concerns a minority mindful of the ethics, as do the issues of mono-culture and the production of fruits and vegetables for rich countries by the developing world, instead of depending on their own indigenous crops. This minority wants to see the localised organic farming movement rejuvenated, so that there is always an alternative to the supermarkets in easily accessible farmers' markets. It wishes Government farm and food policies to be less concerned with global competitiveness and more with sustainable agriculture.

At the beginning of the twenty-first century the sad conclusion we are forced to reach is that farmers no longer control our food supply; it is corporate power with submissive governments in tow that control land use, the distribution of water, the growing fields; it is they who own the seeds, the pesticides and nitrates that are used on the land, it is corporate power that owns the factories which process the produce, which own the patents to those processes and the businesses that will advertise them. Corporate power manipulates world trade and government food policies, its ethos influences management at all levels so that food production, retailing technology and marketing tools are all developed in specialised ways to influence the consumer to eat in a particular way, to continue in a lifestyle which profits the producer. The result in our food supply is a diet which is unhealthy, banal, tasteless and devoid of national characteristics.

World Trade

Is there an answer to the tyranny over our food supply that corporate power exerts? One exists, and it necessitates strengthening and improving our democratic institutions to compete with the new economic relations of the global market place. It means broadening the democratic base of ownership to include some control of economic resources so as to counterbalance the concentration of power in corporate hands. The co-operative model is a perfect one to employ for here the power rests with the individual and it is a decentralised system; it allows individuals to influence through a democratic process their economic behaviour in the workplace or at the point of consumption. A co-operative movement which is truly competitive in the world market, in which the consumers have a say in the actual produce bought and sold and where the profits are shared equitably among the grower, the buyer and the consumer would be a remarkable step forward. It would give back to the consumer the control that was lost when industry took over from cottage produce 200 years ago. 'Until democracy is extended to our economic behaviour, democracy is incomplete.'[7]

Britain is part of the affluent and industrialised West and within the last fifty years the diets of its countries have gradually become similar. The American fast food franchises with the burger leading the way has in fact infiltrated Eastern countries too, mainly because of the attractiveness the United States way of life has in the developing world. Britain led the way in the post-war years in being the first disciple of this culture. The diet of all the Western countries has been now permeated by

American-style junk food and convenience refined industrialised food, eaten to a great extent by the young, but used by all classes and all ages; has this affected the national cuisine of each country? The odd thing is that the traditional cuisine appears to co-exist quite happily and be quite uncontaminated by the newcomer. But can this be true of Britain where the public are not aware of possessing any vigorous endemic cuisine?

British consumers can buy goods from almost any country in the world. They can eat in almost any style: Indian, Thai, Turkish, Italian, Spanish, Japanese, Greek and many more. These cuisines, like the French in the nineteenth century, are adapted to British tastes, so they are in no way authentic, but a bastardised version of the genuine cooking. The British freedom of choice, with both supermarkets and small ethnic stores stocking all the necessary ingredients, is astonishing and reflects a booming world trade in even the most obscure of foods. We live in a global village and the freedom it gives to roam from one country to another in the space of an evening is awesome. Because of the rich diversity of foods brought into the UK and sold to the public, one might conclude that our traditional cuisine is in danger of being lost. There is obvious confusion over this very question because the British people are uncertain – apart from roast beef – as to what their traditional cuisine is or whether they have one at all. Sybil Kapoor, in her introduction to *Simply British*, sums it all up:

> Friends took me aside to question how I could possibly include curry or pizza in a book on British cooking; surely, they argued, these are Indian or Italian dishes. In their minds Lancashire hot pot or roast beef were typically British, and other more obviously foreign dishes had no part in our national cuisine, modern or not. Yet even they could not give a clear definition as to what makes British food British. Others questioned the value of writing about British food at all, since in their opinion, our indigenous food is so intrinsically bad as to be unworthy of special attention.[8]

The Essential British Cuisine

The OED defines the word cuisine as a manner or style of cooking, kitchen, or culinary department, and its use in Britain dates from 1786; the eve of the French Revolution and the flight of so many French chefs who had been employed by the aristocracy to England. The British still feel deep inferiority about their food and many of our gourmets are quick to disparage British cooking while praising French. However, I believe we have a great cuisine and one that goes back to the tenth century, a thousand years of history, a time span which this book has attempted to cover.

I admit that we have some trouble in recognising the value of our own cooking, because it is so diffuse. But the last fifty years, in our embrace of ethnic food, the more esoteric, aromatic and spicy the better, are a clue to our own traditions; for this kind of cooking remained for almost 500 years the feasts of kings and princes in our own land; even though only two per cent of the population sat down to these feasts, the thousands of cooking staff, tasted and nibbled, while the pungent aromas, tidbits and scraps permeated downwards, and finally out to the beggars tearing at wheaten crusts soaked in a fiery ginger sauce. Surely it is significant that the favourite sauce of the poorest people in early medieval London, bought from the fast food cook shops, was garlic and ginger and that the favourite ethnic sauce in the last fifty years is sweet and sour?

Because of the Reformation this imaginative and ingenious cuisine was lost; its incredible fast day recipes with almonds used as dairy substitutes had far too intense and intimate associations with Papism for it to survive in the court of King Henry VIII. But I am convinced this kind of cooking entered our national psyche and has made us ever since eager to taste it again.

Twinned with this are the roasted and boiled carcass meats, the exterior burnt and caramelised crusts of great haunches and legs of cattle and boar, always eaten with hot and pungent sauces, mustard, horseradish and garlic. After the Reformation the emphasis changed to this type of simpler, plainer cooking and this was used, almost as propaganda, to signify our Protestant Englishness. Mind you, there was something to boast about; our carcass meat had been famous throughout history, especially the beef cattle (though not the breeds we are familiar with now) which grew fat on rich pasture. Equal to our love of beef was our passion for bacon. At least the British breakfast is famous; bacon and ham have been an essential aspect of our love affair with food since Anglo-Saxon times and we have been faithful to this love ever since.

Running a close third as a favoured meat was our mutton, either roasted or boiled, or in the Elizabethan period 'carbonadoes', for which thin fillets were cut, salted then grilled briefly over a very hot fire, so that the meat was scorched, then served with onions, garlic and vinegar. We never see mutton now; the public have grown indifferent to the meat and the sheep tend to be slaughtered too young.

Meat stewed in red wine sauces, with plenty of added herbs and covered in pastry, sounds essentially French, yet both our countries loved this dish in many different forms throughout medieval times and for centuries afterwards, even if the British at various times used cider or beer as the cooking medium. The British excelled in meat pies of all shapes and sizes too, and cookshops from the earliest period sold them in their thousands. Perhaps the most essentially British meat dish is the steak and kidney pudding, steamed for many hours over a low fire – but surely so is crisp pork crackling and boiled salt beef. This is a dish hardly ever eaten now except by the Jewish community, yet it was the most common meat dish we ate throughout the winter, boiled with carrots and herb dumplings. A love of game birds is also part of our British character a huge range was hunted, snared and trapped in the medieval period, then simply roasted or else used in a variety of pies.

Like the rest of the northern European countries we smoke, salt and pickle fish, although the colder countries further north excel at a much greater variety of fish. Yet our smoked salmon is justly famous and has been for many years; for centuries a humble dish like soused herrings dominated the people's cooking on the East Coast; boned rolled with onions, spiced and cooked in vinegar in a warm oven they almost melted in the mouth. Now we have now lost our shoals of herrings through over-fishing and if a few fresh herrings appear the contemporary cook is not interested. Most of them go to be cold-smoked for kippers in Scotland and the Isle of Man. Kippers are still inherently British, although their history only goes back to the nineteenth century. The theory of medieval humours also gave us fried fish in egg and breadcrumbs, a quintessential British dish.

Shrimps abound in the shallow waters around our coasts and have provided cheap, tasty and nutritious food for coastal people for many centuries. Whenever there was a glut they could be preserved by being potted in clarified butter and stored. Great quantities of eels were eaten throughout our history, but the habit has now faded, leaving only a few eel and pie shops in East London and some stalls still selling their jellied eels with parsley. Eels were always eaten with green sauce, a sauce made from crushed green herbs, onion tops, chives, mint, parsley pounded with oil and verjuice added.

Of all the vegetables we grew and loved, peas are the most durable, from the chick pea of the Middle Ages, the staple pulse in the people's stews to pease pudding (made from yellow or green split peas, the very smell of which no British person I know can resist), or to the mushy peas of the north; we find the dried pea in all its forms irresistible. This is akin to our liking of the broad bean, forms of which we grew for many hundreds of years, dried to preserve them through the winter and eaten in our soup/stews almost daily. We also delight in watercress, grown since the Roman times, and sacred to the Anglo-Saxons with its fresh, tangy, peppery leaves characteristic of the tastes we love.

We excel in producing hard mature cheeses, Cheddar is at least 600 years old, but again what a great pity none is produced now without being pasteurised; butter, the cooking medium of these islands when unpasteurised, is one of our greatest products. It is still being produced in small artisan farms and sold locally.

This strikes me as a rich variety of magnificent foods which are inescapably British and which have their roots in a thousand years of cooking. What is more, we are still surrounded by almost all of them. They continue to be eaten and enjoyed, yet we still deny their greatness – with some astonishing exceptions; we still want to decry their worth, still want to face the rest of the world and join it in making fun of our supposedly culinary desert. Is it possible that we can at last learn to be proud of our cuisine, can we cast off the terrible Victorian heritage that made us feel so inferior and so unworthy? I pray that these pages may help us do just that.

Rebirth of the British Cuisine

With all these rich materials, a rise in the demand for organic produce, and the popularity in farmers' markets which sell local, organic ingredients, there is also an undeniable resurgence in great British cooking. This lies at the other end of the spectrum from the situation evident in Mass Observation, for human beings are complicated creatures full of paradox, so the same people that eat convenience foods will also enjoy a quality meal in a restaurant which has been made from local organic produce and cooked with imaginative skill by a chef aware of British food traditions.

What are the causes behind this new interest and respect for good food, which are constantly fuelled by the media? No doubt one reason is the steady influx of new foods and products on sale in supermarkets, ethnic stores, delicatessens and quality greengrocers. Our medieval liking for new flavours, oriental spices and Mediterranean ingredients has been fully satiated with ethnic shops which generally have a fresher supply of products than can be found elsewhere. When in former years we would have passed these foods by feeling both suspicious and ignorant of their nature or how to cook them, now we benefit from television gurus like Delia Smith who use them and patiently explain their value. Delia Smith's popularity has placed her in the position of a Mrs Beeton of our age, for she reflects the trends that already exist and then turns them into a runaway success; for example she used both balsamic vinegar and Maldon Sea Salt on her television programmes, some several decades after gastronomes had been habitually using them. But the great worth of Delia Smith is her ability to teach and simplify, taking the mystique out of the craft and turning a skill into something approachable which all can do. Besides, she works within the British tradition, keeping alive recipes of the farmhouse kitchen, while easily absorbing new ingredients.

The success of television cookery programmes and the influence of television cooks on our food and lifestyle has not yet been fully absorbed, but, for example, Jamie Oliver and Gary Rhodes before him, have no doubt made it trendy for young men to be creative in the kitchen. Long may that influence continue, for its social impact upon male and female relationships could be considerable. The media play a huge part in this new interest in food, which can be dated as starting in the late 1970s, for by the 1980s most national newspapers had a weekly food page.

Good pub food is also a contemporary phenomenon; beginning in the 1980s it was not uncommon to have a chef on the premises cooking hot food that had a British Mediterranean style to it. A boom in restaurants of all types and grades has continued throughout this time; within the huge choice of dishes on offer it might be difficult to discern that a new form of British cooking has been established. Yet it is undoubtedly flourishing in a wide range and infinite variety, but with its roots firmly within the heritage of our cuisine. Perhaps the most vigorous exponent of the farmhouse tradition which goes back many hundreds of years – in fact, many of his dishes would have been proudly displayed and consumed hungrily at medieval banquets – is Fergus Henderson of St John restaurant in London. Here is served roast bone-marrow with parsley salad, lamb's trotters with faggots, pot-roast brisket and a stew of lamb's tongues. Another is Paul Heathcote in Lancashire, in whose restaurant trotters and ham shanks are a speciality, the former served in a puddle of rich sauce, boned and filled with diced meat in a contrasting sauce, intensely flavoured and caramelised. Fish is not neglected in either restaurant; it is briefly seared and served with strong sauces and shredded vegetables. There are also plenty of other chefs who are working securely within British traditions, such as Gary Rhodes, who at his restaurant The Greenhouse was serving smoked eel salad with piccalilli, crisply fried black pudding, and calf's liver and bacon with mashed potato and onion gravy. The Castle Hotel at Taunton serves potted pigeon or duck, shredded cabbage, and steamed fillets of plaice with spring onions. There is Shaun Hill at the Merchant House in Ludlow with its Michelin star; two other restaurants in the same area also have stars and all use high quality local ingredients imaginatively. And Richard Corrigan at the Lindsay House in London who also specialises in modern Irish cooking and delights in the use of offal. Gifted chefs in this new British tradition are in fact too numerous to mention and are spread across Britain. It is a culinary phenomenon, which has been noticed by foreign visitors who are now beginning to understand that the old horror stories about British food are no longer true.

The state of our food at the beginning of the new millennium is complex and contradictory. On the one hand we have world corporate power with its heavy investment controlling a food supply which is uniform and bland, on the other we have sprinkled across the land individuals with the passion and spirit to retain traditional methods of rearing and cultivation and the skill to cook the product perfectly. We are the guardians of our traditions; the more we know and respect them, the better we are equipped to protect them from the financial predators of the modern world.

APPENDIX I

Wild Food Plants of the British Isles

Many of these plants would have been eaten by peoples living on these islands since the last Ice Age, when the land became habitable again. As the Romans introduced so many of their favourite plants, foods and flavourings, which were left uncultivated after they relinquished control of England, the list reflects the edible plants growing wild here from roughly AD 450. There are around a hundred plants listed here. There are also edible mammals, birds and their eggs, fresh water fish and sea fish that can be caught from the shore, all of which are indicated in Chapter 1, and all of these would have been eaten by the peasants.

This list cannot be comprehensive; many plants have become extinct in the last 1,000 years, most of them in the last 150. Many more are threatened with extinction. The plants listed are not likely to have been growing in every area of the British Isles, but if there were only a few of each category growing in the neighbourhood, there would have been enough to augment the diet of the very poor. The information on where plants grew, at what time of year they appeared, and what part of them could be harvested and when, would be passed down from mother to daughter. Girls when still small infants would have been taken out to the fields, hills, shore, cliffs and woods to learn the art of gathering. The names, preparation and cooking of plants would have been essential learning from the moment they could walk and run by themselves. Various regions have different names for the same plant; many of the names indicate how they were prepared and cooked.

The following categories are not watertight, as often the whole of a plant would be used, seeds, leaves, flowers, stem and root (as in Fat Hen). In such cases, I have listed the plant only once.

Leaves

Sea Cabbage *(Brassica oleracea)*: Grows on cliffs, and is an ancestor of garden cabbage, though this was domesticated from Mediterranean stock. A strong-tasting brassica, needing long slow cooking; its flavour would have permeated the whole dish and the breaking down of its sulphur compounds would have made the dish smell strongly. I am sure such a smell would then have counted as appetising, but we can

344

only surmise that Anglo-Saxons had a quite different register of aromas that were attractive or repulsive than we do. (See page 12.)

Buckrams, Ramsons or **Bear's Garlic** *(Allium ursinum)*: The common wild garlic that grows in woodlands, it was eaten raw with cheese and with boiled bacon. One of the first green vegetables in spring. The oil was also distilled and used medicinally.

Calamint, wild basil *(Calamintha officinalis)*: Has an aromatic scent, looks like a small pink flowered dead nettle. Brewed as tea or made into a syrup.

Caraway *(Carum carvi)*: Very common and popular in medieval times, used in cakes and breads, pungent leaves sometimes used in salads, the seeds also made into comfits.

Coltsfoot *(Tussilago farfara)*: Plant used for centuries as a cough syrup and a candy. Leaves made into herbal tobacco.

Comfrey *(Symphytum officinale)*: Used to set broken bones, its Scottish name is 'boneset'. Also named Saracen root, which suggests it was brought over by Crusaders. Highly mucinlaginous, the juice was used to wash wounds, then the pulp was wrapped in a linen cloth and packed around the fracture exactly as we now use plaster. Comfrey still grows around the sites of old monasteries. Used also as fodder for cattle and horses, new leaves can be eaten like spinach.

Coriander *(Coriandrum sativum)*: Extensively grown in Essex; the wild plant is common there. Used in spice powders and pickles and in curing meat.

Docks *(Rumex)*: Used to wrap up cheese and butter for the market, and with sorrel cooked into a sauce.

Germander *(Teucrium scorodonia)*: Used in brewing ale before hops took over; it clears the beer and gives it a dark colour and bitter flavour.

House Leek *(Sempervivium tectorum)*: Juice used as an eye lotion.

Lamb's Lettuce *(Valerianella locusta)*: Appeared at lambing time in March and it was picked and eaten as a salad.

Leeks *(Allium porum)*: Eaten like spring onions.

Lettuce *(Lactuca: verosa and serriola)*: Juice dried into brown cakes and used as a form of opium. A medieval housebook of the early fifteenth century mentions the dried juice being given to produce sleep for surgery.

Lovage *(Ligusticum scoticum)*: East coast fishing trade brought the herb south, but in earlier times it was associated with Scotland, where it was eaten as a salad, but also boiled, and where it was called 'Sirenas'.

Orach *(Atriplex angostepolia)*: Boiled as greens, young leaves used in salads.

Common Orach *(Atriplex patula)*: Leaves are eaten. Useful to add to a mixed salad, there are two kinds, red orach and golden orach.

Charlock *(Sinapis arvensis)*: Leaves boiled; called Corn-cail in Dublin, Colonsay in Hebrides. Turner in 1548 called it Oarlock or Wyld Cale. This is a poor cousin of kale and would have been used where kale failed to grow, boiled in the pottage.

Scurvy Grass *(Cochlearia officinalis)*: Abundant in Scotland, found on sea cliffs and shore, rich in vitamin C. The whole plant would have been used, leaves, stalks, flowers and berries, crushed and the juice was either added to ale or made into a medicinal potion. But as it tasted unpleasant, spices and sugar were added; it was used as a remedy for various ills until in the sixteenth century it became well known as a cure for scurvy and taken on long sea voyages. Then it became almost fashionable, as in London there existed scurvy grass streetsellers.

Here is a recipe of Dr Parry's: 'Of the juyce of scoury-grasse one pint; of the juyce of water-cresses as much; of the juyce of succory, half a pint; of the juyce of fumitory, half a pint; proportion to one gallon of ale; they must be all tunned up together.'[1]

In the 1650s a fashionable woman began the day with a glass of this tonic, much as we might drink freshly squeezed orange juice. Later, early in the nineteenth, sandwiches of scurvy grass were eaten and a 'spring juice' was created, which was a mixture of watercress, scurvy grass and Seville oranges. But it fell out of fashion when the much nicer drink of watercress and lime was discovered. In the sixteenth century when it was realised that it cured scurvy, apothecaries wondered whether it might be the *Britannica herba* of Dioscorides. In Germanicus Caesar's campaign of AD 14 across the Rhine, his legionaries fell ill with a scurvy-like affliction; the Frisians seeing this taught the soldiers to take this herb and they were miraculously cured. Gerard described the disease accurately: 'The gums are loosed, swolne and exulcerate; the mouth grevously stinking; the thighes and legs are withall verie often full of blewe spots, not unlike those that come of bruses: the face and the rest of the bodie is oftentimes of a pale colour; and the feet are swolne, as in the dropsie.'

Watercress *(Nasturtium officinale)*: It was boiled or eaten raw. Anglo-Saxons believed it to be sacred, and it remained popular throughout the centuries; rich in vitamin C it was also a cure against scurvy.

Winter Cress *(Barbarea vulgaris)*: I grow this plant myself as a winter salad, and it thrives in very cold weather; it is very peppery, and called by Turner Wound Rocket, as the leaves were pounded and used as a poultice on wounds.

Chickweed *(Stellaria media)*: Used in salads or sandwiches. Has a slight cucumbery taste. Grows rampant on manure and around animals.

Spring Beauty (US term) *(Claytonia perfoliata)*: Eaten raw in salads or boiled. This is delicious, the leaves are quite crunchy and it looks appealing. It was brought from US early in the nineteenth century, for it was not observed in Britain until 1852.

Good King Henry *(Chenopodium bonus-henricus)*: Young shoots and flowery tops boiled and eaten. A poor man's spinach. The name stems from the early sixteenth century, of course, but the plant itself is indigenous to northern Europe. It's good to eat if picked young.

Fat Hen *(Chenopodium album)*: Seeds, containing fat and albumen, are eaten. Ancient food plant found in stomach of peat bog men and other early remains. Leaves, boiled and eaten, also makes red or golden dye. In Ireland and Western Highlands called 'wild pottage', so it must have been used daily. It is a useful plant in that it grows very quickly on animal dung and general livestock detritus. In Normandy they call it *grasse-poulette* because it flourishes inevitably around wherever the chickens are. When I kept doves it grew beneath the dovecote. Seeds are also ground to make flour, which tastes like buckwheat. Leaves can also be cooked, ground and mixed with butter.

Beet *(Beta vulgaris)*, called wild spinach: Leaves eaten with pork or bacon. Roots are also boiled and eaten. These leaves are very good indeed, excellent stir-fried in a little oil and eaten cold as a salad.

Glasswort *(Salicornia stricta)*: The poor pickled it, though its main use was for glassmaking as it is rich in soda. It grows in estuaries and salt marshes all around the European coastline, appearing in June. To make glass, the plant was dried, burnt and the ash, then called barilla, was gathered and exported to the Mediterranean. Sir Thomas More (1478) names it in a list of plants that would improve 'many a poor knave's pottage . . . glasswort might afford him a pickle for his mouthful of salt meat'. We now know this as marsh samphire, and confuse it with the rock samphire which grows from cliffs.

Wood Sorrel *(Oxalis aceto sella)*: One of the most ancient wild leaves to be used as a seasoning, as its common names often refer to food. It has a sharp lemony flavour. In Somerset it is called 'bread-and-cheese and cider' or 'butter and eggs'. It was commonly eaten with bread and cheese, but also obviously in omelettes. Its other common name is 'allelujah', as it first appears in spring around the time of Easter and was associated with Christian celebration. The name allelujah for wood sorrel is also used in France, Spain and Italy, so its name and usage are certainly medieval. It was also chopped and made into a green sauce or added to soups. There is a connection between the use of wood sorrel in cooking and the term 'julienne', which is a corruption of allelujah. When wood sorrel was chopped and used in soups, the leaves would disappear and the tiny stalks were left. When wood sorrel was no longer used, chefs chopped vegetables into matchsticks to simulate the sorrel stalks.

Fool's Watercress *(Apium nodiflorum)*: Herb used in cooking of meat pies and pasties.

Ground Elder *(Aegopodium poda graria)*: These are highly delicious, they have a strong aniseed flavour, and when young the leaves are good for salads. Also the leaves can be lightly boiled and eaten.

Rock Samphire *(Crithium maritimum)*: Pickled, also minced with butter. It grows on cliffs and tastes strongly of the essence of herbs, very savoury and meaty. It was a huge favourite throughout the Middle Ages and on until over picking and its contamination with lesser samphire, both golden and marsh, put people off the product. Rock Samphire was gathered in the Isle of Wight and the Isle of Man, packed into barrels and pickled in brine, then sent to London markets. You can still find the plant, best picked in the summer months before it seeds itself. It grows all over the beaches in the South of France, but the French are ignorant of its gastronomic quality.

Lovage *(Ligusticum scoticum)*: Leaves eaten, cooked or raw.

Bistort *(Polygonum bistorta)*: Leaves boiled. Easter Ledger pudding eaten in the Lake District at Easter. Ledger, logia, Astrologia from French *Aristolochia clematis*, plant of best birth. Bistort in *The Grete Herball* of 1526 'hath virtue . . . to cause to retayne and conceyve'.

Sorrel *(Rumex Acetosa)*: Green sauce for fish, leaves boiled with pork or goose.

Nettle *(Urtica Dioica)*: Young leaves eaten as soup. Nettles also made cloth.

Water Mint *(Mentha aquatica)*: Leaves for flavouring.

Wild Marjoram *(Origanum vulgare)*: Leaves used for tea.

Wild Thyme *(Thymus serpyllum)*: Used for tea.

Wood Sage *(Teucrium scorodonia)*: Used for tea.

Chamomile *(Anthemis nobilis)*: Used for tea.

Milk Thistle *(Silybum marianeum)*: Remove prickles, young leaves can be eaten, blanched as salad, and stalks eaten after peeling and soaking to remove bitterness.

Chicory Succory *(Cichorium intybus)*: Brought here by Romans. Leaves blanched for salad. In France, it is known as *Barbe de Capuchin*.

Chives *(Allium schoenoprasum)*: Leaves eaten.

Cowslip *(Primula veris)*: Leaves eaten in salad, mixed with other herbs for stuffing meat. Cowslip salad made from petals dipped in white sugar. Flowers make a delicate wine.

Elder *(Sambucus nigra)*: Elder flowers make wine or vinegar, berries make juice and wine, jam, chutneys, ketchup and are also used in cooking in cakes and muffins (like blueberries).

Dandelion *(Taraxacum officinale)*: Blanched leaves in salads, or used for wine and beer.

Salad Burnet *(Poterium sanguisorba)*: Leaves used in salads. Named to distinguish it from Great Burnet (both used as a salve for wounds).

Roots, Bulbs, Shoots, Seeds and Tubers

White Water Lily *(Nymphaea alba)* and **Yellow Water Lily** *(Nuphar lutea)*: Both roots were dried, ground and used medicinally, but also to make flour from.

Dittander *(Lepidium Latifolium)*: Grows in salt marshes. The roots were used like horse radish, but extremely hot, burning and bitter.

Horse Radish *(Armoracia rusticana)*: Introduced from Friesland (probably first of all indigenous to eastern Europe) where it was made into a sauce for boiled meat. German name is *Meerettich* – sea radish.

Jack-by-the-Hedge *(Alliaria petiolata)*: Hedge garlic, used to make a spring sauce, eaten with salt fish. Or used in salad or bulbs boiled and eaten with boiled mutton.

Sea Kale *(Crambe maritima)*: Shoots boiled and eaten in early spring. French called it *chou mann d'Angleterre*.

Fireweed, Rosebay Willow *(Chamaenerion augustifolium)*: Young shoots boiled and eaten like asparagus.

Bitter Vetch *(Lathyrus montanus):* Tubers eaten fresh and raw, or tied in bundles to dry, used also to flavour whisky. Gerard likened taste to chestnuts.

Rampion *(Campanula rapuncullus)*: Its white root was boiled and eaten, or finely sliced and used in a salad.

Rhubarb *(Rumex alpinus)*: Monk's rhubarb used as a standard aperient in place of the expensive imported rhubarb root. Another plant that appears around the site of old monasteries.

Sea Holly *(Eryngium maritimum)*: The blue sea holly which has a huge root which was dug up and candied with sugar and rosewater; its flavouring was used as a chewing gum against plague infection.

Wild Arum *(Arum maculatum):* Used as a base for salop, but the extreme acidity has to be washed out of the root before the starch can be used. Used as a starch before the import of West Indian arrowroot.

Sweet Cicely *(Myrrhis odorata)*: Anise flavour, roots boiled and eaten with oil and vinegar. Leaves also used to flavour puddings.

Fennel *(Foeniculurn vulgare)*: Roots eaten raw and cooked. Leaves also used as flavouring. Of the cultivated variety William Coles in *Nature's Paradise* (1650) said, 'Both the seeds, leaves and root of our garden fennel are much used in our drinks and broths for those that are grown fat, to abate their unwieldiness and cause them to grow more gaunt and lank.'

Wild Parsnip *(Pastinaca sativa)*: Roots boiled and eaten, also used as pig food and mixed with bran for horses. Cooked and pounded parsnip used to eke out flour in bread. Parsnips improved after frost. Lenten food, eaten with salt fish, mixed with hard-boiled eggs and butter. Parsnips eaten with mustard. Made into wine, beer and spirits in Ireland. Brewed with malt instead of hops.

Cow Parsnip *(Heracleum spondylium)*: Roots possibly eaten but mostly gathered for pig food.

Wild Carrot *(Daucus carota)*: In the Hebrides roots eaten raw. Flowers used by herbalists.

Hops *(Hurnulus lupulus)*: Shoots cooked and eaten. Flowers used to flavour and preserve beer.

Alkanet *(Anchusa officinalis)*: Used to colour cheeses a golden red. Now a rare plant, but sometimes found in clumps at the site of old cheese farms.

Asparagus *(Asparagus officinalis prostratus)* (Also called **Sperage** or **Sparrow Grass**): Used in salads and sauces.

Wild Angelica *(Angelica sylvestris)*: Pink and purple stems and seeds eaten.

Black Bindweed *(Polygonurn convolvulus)*: The seeds have starch content. Boiled and eaten.

Pale Persicaria *(Polygonurn lapathifolium)*: They grow with the corn and are inevitably eaten.

Buckwheat *(Fagopyrum esculentum)*: Brought from Asia by the returning Crusaders; its French name is Saracen Corn. It was cultivated here as food for pheasants; now increasingly used to make flour from.

Lady's Bedstraw, Cheese Rennet *(Galium verum)*: Used for stuffing mattresses and for curdling milk, for flavouring sheep's and goats' cheese. Used in Cheshire, Gloucestershire and the Highlands.

Wild Celery (Smallage) *(Apium graveolens)*: Eaten raw or cooked. Brought here by the Romans. Commonly eaten right up to the nineteenth century, has a strong and lovely flavour, excellent for cooking as celery soup.

White Mustard *(Brassica Alba)* and **Black Mustard** *(Brassica Nigra)*: Romans brought both to England. The Anglo-Saxons loved it. The seeds were pounded and steeped in wine. The name derives from *Mustum*, the must of grape juice, and *ardens*, meaning burning. In 1623 Gerard wrote: 'The seed of mustard pounded with vinegar is an excellent sauce, good to be eaten with any grosse meates, either fish or flesh, because it doth help digestion, warmeth the stomache and provoketh appetite.' Mustard was made up into balls with honey and vinegar and a little cinnamon and this is how it was sold; when needed, it was mixed with more vinegar. It was particularly collected around Tewkesbury in Gloucestershire.

Fruits

Barberry *(Berberis vulgaris)*: Red fruits make a jam or jelly; candied, eaten as sweets; used as a fever drink or made into a punch. Fruit can be pickled. Rouen was the centre for *confitures d'épine vinette*. Roots boiled in lye to dye wool yellow; bark used with alum to dye linen yellow. *Berberis* is Arabic name for fruit. Naturalised in medieval gardens.
Blackberry, Bramble *(Rubus fructicosus)*: Berries eaten, raw or cooked.
Raspberry *(Rubus idaeus)*
Bungleberry, Bunchberry, Stoneberry *(Rubus saxatilis)*
Dewberry, Blue Bramble *(Rubus caesius)*
Strawberry *(Fragaria vesca)*
Blackthorn *(Prunus spinosa)*: Sloes, ancestor of plums. Makes wine, flavours spirits.
Bullace *(Prunus domnestica)*: Made wine, if kept for long enough resembled port.
Medlar *(Mespilus germanica)*: Welsh brewed an ale from fruits, also cider, jellies and jams. Eaten with game.
Crab Apple *(Malus sylvestris)*: Jelly and wine, mixed with apples in a tart.
Red Currant *(Ribes sylvestris)*
Black Currant *(Ribes nigrum)*
Gooseberry *(Ribes urva-crispa)*
Cowberry *(Vaccinium vitis-idaea)*: Berries eaten, also makes jelly.
Bilberry, Whortleberry *(Vaccinium mytillus)*: Berries used in tarts, jelly, jam or raw. In the Hebrides the leaves are dried and used as tea.
Cranberry *(Oxycoccus palustris)*
Crowberry *(Empetrum nigrum)*
Broom *(Sarathamnus scoparius)*: Wine was made from the flowers. The twigs, tied into bundles and chopped neatly at the end, were used, as its name suggests, for sweeping the hearth or the bread oven. Birch besom was used for the cobbled yard. All parts extensively used medicinally.
Roses *(Rosaceae)*: Hips made into a drink or jam.

Nuts

Sweet Almond *(Amygdalus communis var. dulcis)* and **Bitter Almond** *(var. amara)*: Brought to Britain by the Romans, became wild, cultivated after 1562, admired then chiefly for its blossom. The nuts are free of starch. In the Middle Ages almonds were an important article of commerce in Central Europe, for consumption in cookery was enormous. Jeanne d'Evreux, Queen of France, listed in an inventory 20 lb sugar and 500 lb almonds. Nuts give oil; when nuts are ground and mixed with water they make a most delicious milk. A butter can be made from ground almonds (the milk can be churned like cow's milk), sugar and rose water.

Beechnut *(Fagus sylvatica)*: The nuts of beech called mast have always been used for food to feed animals and humans; pigs let loose in the woods will consume all the mast that has fallen and grow fat on it. The mast will yield oil (similar to hazel in flavour) used for cooking and burning.

Hazel *(Corylus avellana)*: These nuts have been eaten from the earliest times. Much admired in the ancient world.

Sweet Chestnut *(Castanea sativa)*: Romans introduced it to England. The nuts were thrown onto a fire and scorched in the embers, as they are still eaten; they can also be ground into flour and used in cooking, made into soups, fritters and stuffings, or preserved in sugar or syrup as *marron glacé*.

Walnut *(Juglans regia)*: There is some evidence that walnuts existed before the Romans, but their enthusiasm for them must have made the tree popular. The nuts produce an oil used for cooking and for salads. The shells were used for a black hair dye.

Fungi

These were a movable feast, for they arise out of the earth always in new and unexpected places. The fact that a few are poisonous and/or hallucinatory would have been learnt and remembered. They were treated with awe. Here are a few which are the most common: parasol *(Lepiota procera)*, milk mushroom *(Lactarius deliciosus)*, chanterelle *(Catharellus cibarius)*, common mushroom *(Agaricus campestris)*, horse mushroom *(Agaricus arvensis)*, edible bolet *(Boletus edulis)*, giant puff ball *(Lycoperdon bovista)*.

Seaweeds

Laver *(Porphyra lacinata)*, lettuce ulva *(Ulva lactuca)*, carrageheen moss *(Chrondus crispus)* also known as Irish Moss and Iceland Moss; when boiled it forms a jelly. Dulse *(Rhodyrnenia palmata)* boiled and eaten with butter; there are two other dulse *(Dilsea edulis)* and the pepper dulse *(Lawrencia pinnatifida)*; this last is found all around the coast of Britain and is hot to the taste, hence makes an excellent pickle. Its leaves are not unlike those of the oak tree enlarged. Bladderwrack *(Fucis vesiculosis)*: Used as manure all round the coast. Gives 20–40 lb potash to the ton. Also burnt to produce smoke for flavouring and drying bacon and fish. Cattle are fed with it.

APPENDIX II

Traditional British Cooking

This list is far from being comprehensive and some of the inclusions will make no sense unless the book and its conclusions have been read. I have tended to choose the dishes that have had longevity, but then there are also distinctly national dishes like fish and chips or tomatoes which have merely had 120 years. Pasta, of course, has been with us since 1100 and curry mixtures for flavouring for more than 300 years. For various reasons, some of these dishes are no longer cooked, and have therefore become obscure; but all are worth making, seeking out and certainly eating. See the Bibliography for recipe books which deal only with traditional British food. Lastly, the greatness or not of dishes in the following collection is wholly determined on the culinary skill employed in their making. British cooking, in its inherent simplicity, can be destroyed very easily, another aspect of its vulnerability to abuse.

England

Soups: Pea Soup, made from dried peas, or beans or lentils flavoured with wild herbs and a ham or bacon bone. White Soup, made from almonds, onion and flavoured with lemon. Hare Soup, the carcass and vegetables, butter, wine and peppercorns. Oxtail Soup, oxtail, vegetables, herbs and spices, (mace, cloves, peppercorns) and sherry. Clear Pheasant Soup.
Fish: Poached Cod with Parsley Sauce. Jellied Eels with Green Sauce. Fried Plaice in egg and breadcrumbs. Fried Whitebait. Fish Pie. Dressed Crab. Poached Salmon with Cucumber. Grilled Mackerel with Gooseberry Sauce. Grilled Dover Sole. Buttered Lobster. Potted Shrimps. Bloater Paste. Fish and Chips. Bass in white wine herb sauce. Baked Pike with Ginger Sauce. Soused Herrings.
Meat: Roast Beef and Yorkshire Pudding with horseradish and mustard. Steak and Kidney Pudding. Boiled silverside of salt beef with carrots. Roast Saddle of Mutton with Rowan Jelly. Boiled Mutton and Onion Sauce. Shepherd's Pie. Roast Pork with Crackling and Apple Sauce. Calves' liver and bacon. Tripe and onions. Mixed Grill. Pork Pie. Ham. Bath chaps. Beef or Mutton Curry. Sweet and Sour Pork. Pasta.
Poultry and Game: Roast Duck with green peas. Roast Goose with sage and onion stuffing and apple sauce. Roast Pheasant with bread sauce and watercress. Roast Partridge. Game Pie. Jugged Hare. Rabbit Pie.
Vegetables: Asparagus, globe artichokes (these were popular and grown in England),

cabbage, savoy and red cabbage, celery, broad beans, peas, lentils, runner beans, tomatoes, kale, spinach, broccoli, sea kale, leeks, beetroots, parsnips, potatoes.

Puddings: Roly-Poly. Spotted Dick. Sussex Pond. Bread and Butter Pudding. Cabinet Pudding. Plum Pudding. College Pudding. Caramel Pudding. Ginger Pudding. Treacle Pudding.

Other Desserts: Apple Pie. Bakewell Tart. Treacle Tart. Trifle. Mince Pies. Blancmange. Stewed Fruit. Gooseberry Fool. Summer Pudding. Lemon Curd. Strawberry Shortcake.

Savouries: Angels on Horseback, Scotch Woodcock. Smoked cod's roe on toast. Ham Croutes. Soft Roes on Toast. Anchovy Toasts. Devilled Sardines. Kippers on Toast. Macaroni Cheese. Buck Rabbit. Cheese Soufflé. Smoked Haddock Soufflé.

Tea: Plum Cake, Pound Cake. Jam Roll. Gingerbread. Parkin. Banbury Cakes. Bath Buns. Muffins. Crumpets. Sally Lunn.

Regional Specialities: Cornish Pasties, Squab Pie, Leek and Pilchard Pie from Cornwall. Cumberland Rum Butter and Currant Cake. Devonshire Potato Cake and Boiled Apple Dumplings. Lancashire Eccles Cakes, their Hot Pot and Oldham Parkin. Melton Mowbray Pork Pies and Whetstone Cakes from Leicestershire. Norfolk Dumplings and Yarmouth Bloaters. Pickled Salmon from Northumberland. Banbury Apple Pie from Oxfordshire and Oxford Pudding. Buckwheat Cakes from Shropshire. Oliver Biscuits and Somerset Frumety from Bath. Lemon Syllabubs from Staffordshire. Almond Pudding and Aldeburgh Sprats from Suffolk. Richmond's Maids of Honour from Surrey. Lardy Johns from Sussex. Derwentwater Cakes from Westmorland and Devizes Pie from Wiltshire.

Scotland

Soups: Scotch Broth. Cock-a-leekie. Powsowdie. Nettle Soup. Fat Brose. Kail Brose. Feather Fowlie. Friar's Chicken. Lorraine Soup. Hotch Potch. Poacher's Soup. Grouse Soup. Cullen Skink. Partan Bree. Mussel Soup.

Fish: Cabbie Claw. Crappit Heids. Partan Pie. Herring in Oatmeal. Pickled Herring. Poached Salmon with Anchovy Sauce. Pickled Salmon. Arbroath Smokies. Smoked Haddock. Cropadeu. Stewed Oysters. Limpet Stovies. Fried Trout. Grilled Lobster.

Meat: Haggis. Minced Collops. Scots Kidney Collops. Highland Beef Balls. Forfar Bridies. Veal Flory. Boiled Gigot with Turnip Purry. Small Mutton Pies. Spiced Bacon.

Poultry and Game: Roast Red Deer. Venison Collops. Venison Pasty. Roast Grouse. Kingdom of Fife Pie. Chicken Stovies. A Stoved Howtowdie with Drappit Eggs. Scots Rabbit Curry.

Vegetables: Buttered Peas. Colcannon. Kailkenny. Rumbledethumps. Neep Purry. Clapshot. Stovies. Scots Potato Pies. Scots Potato Fritters.

Puddings: Holyrood Pudding. Scots Marmalade Pudding. Cloutie Dumpling. Almond Flory. Greengage Frushie.

Desserts: Scots Trifle. Cranachan. Atholl Brosie. Caledonian Cream. Whim-Wham.

Scots Flummery. Whipt Sillabubs.

Savouries: A Scots Rabbit. Scots Woodcock. Scots Eggs. Nuns Beads. Green Dumplings. Kipper Creams.

Cakes and Shortbreads: Dundee Cake. Montrose Cake. Oatcakes. Scots Shortbread. Ayrshire Shortbread. Petticoat Tails. Black Bun. Edinburgh Gingerbread. Broonie. Parlies Abernethy Biscuits. Edinburgh Gingerbread.[2]

Wales

Soups: Broths and Cawl (Welsh for soup) based on mutton, beef or wood pigeon, with added root vegetables, leeks and broad beans, the recipes vary and so do the names. But they are distinctively Welsh and provide one pot meals. There is also a buttermilk soup, for buttermilk is a major ingredient in bread, cakes, pikelets, flummery and also added to potatoes. Oyster Soup. Pig's Liver Soup (Cawl haslet).

Fish: Poached Salmon with Laver Sauce. Salmon Steaks with onions and Butter Sauce. Teifi Salmon Sauce. Pickled Mackerel. Grilled Herrings with Mustard Sauce. Fried Oysters. Oyster Loaves. Cockles Penclawdd. Welsh Cockle Pie. Cockles and Eggs.

Meat: Mutton stuffed with Oysters. Welsh Mutton Hams. Spiced Mutton. Welsh Venison. Mutton Pies. Thick Bacon Slices and Potatoes (Cig moch). Haslet. Granny Morgan's Brawn. Scruggins Cake. Black Pudding. Pembrokeshire Faggots. Liver, Bacon and Onions. Savoury Pies. Goose-Blood Pudding. Chicken and Leek Pie. Welsh Salt Duck. Lobsgows. Bidding Pie. Welsh Lamb Pie.

Vegetables: Leeks. Potatoes. Anglesey Eggs. Laver. Cabbage. Marrow. Pease Pudding.

Puddings: Apple Cakes. Cranberry Tarts. Spiced Rhubarb Crumble. Rhubarb Shortcake. Gooseberry Pudding. Quince Fool. Apple and Ginger Fool. Violet Pudding. Welsh Cheesecake. Welsh Curd Cakes. Monmouth Pudding. Snowdon Pudding. Welsh Pudding. Blackberry Bread Pudding. Dowset. Whitepot. Pancakes.

Cakes and Breads: Pembrokeshire Buns. Souly Cakes. Welsh Cakes. Moist Cake. Welsh Cinnamon Cake. Ginger Bread. Anglesey Cake. Threshing Cake. Bara Brith. Pikelets. Bakestone Bread. Barley Bread. Sour Oatmeal Bread.[3]

Northern Ireland

Soups: Irish Farm Broth. Brotcham Roy. Clam and Cockle Soup. Mutton Broth. Nettle Soup. Watercress Soup. Pea Soup. Bairneach (Limpets) Soup. Wild Mushroom Soup.

Fish: Soused Herring or Mackerel. Lobster with Butter Sauce. Potted Smoked Mackerel. Poached Salmon. Pickled Salmon. Salt Cod with White Sauce. Cockles with Melted Butter. Scallops with Cream. Potted Shrimps. Fish Cakes with Garlic Butter.

Meat: Ulster Irish Stew. Boiled Mutton. Beef and Guinness Stew. Corned Beef with Cabbage. Spiced Beef. Spiced Ox Tongue. Pig's Head with Cabbage. Pig's Tails with Swede. Brawn Crubeens. Black Puddings. Goose Pudding. Stuffed Heart. Drisheen from Cork.

Poultry and Game: Pigeon Pie. Woodcock Potted Pie. Rabbit and Hare Pie. Roast

Venison. Venison Stew. Poached Chicken with Parsley Sauce.

Vegetables: Champ. Colcannon. Boxty. Stampy. Potato Oaten Cakes. Buttered Cabbage. Carrot and Parsnip Mash. Leeks. Celery. Curly Kale. Seakale. Beetroot. Sorrel Pie.

Puddings: Apple Dumplings. Apple Fritters. Irish Apple Cake. Burnt Cream. Jam Pudding. Irish Sherry Trifle. Bread and Butter Pudding. Pancakes. Carragheen Moss Blancmange.

Breads and Grains: Soda Bread, white and brown. Bocaire. Rye Bread Oatcakes. Potato pancakes. Dulse Soda Scones. Porridge. Barmbrack. Simnel Cake. Potato Apple Cake.[4]

Notes

Publication dates are those of editions consulted.

INTRODUCTION

1   Hieatt, Constance B., Jones, Robin F., *Two Anglo-Norman Culinary Collections*, edited from British Library Manuscripts. Additional 32085 & Royal 12. C. X11.

2   Hill, Christopher, *The World Turned Upside Down* (Penguin 1972).

3   Mead, William Edward, *The English Medieval Feast* (Allen & Unwin 1931).

4   Feild, Rachel, *Irons in the Fire* (Crowood 1984).

CHAPTER 1: Prologue: The Land

1   A measure of capacity containing 4 pecks or 8 gallons.

2   Anglo-Saxon herbals of great range, foresight and wisdom.

3   Quoted in Magennis, Hugh, *Anglo-Saxon Appetites* (Four Court Press 1999).

4   Ibid.

5   Ibid, 'Seasons of Fasting'.

6   Cumin (*cuminum cyminum*), native of the eastern Mediterranean and the Near East, an important spice in ancient Egypt and in the Mycenaean palaces of the fourteenth century. It came to England via the Rhineland and Lotharingia, which were granted a licence to sell pepper, wax and cumin.

7   Rick Stein was shown hedge fishing by some Dorset fishermen off Chesil Beach. They went out in a small rowing boat and dragged a net in a semi-circle, with one end staked to the beach; then they drew in the catch of mackerel.

8   Aelfric: *Colloquy*, ed. G.N. Garmonsway (Methuen's Old English Library 1939). Bishop Aelfric (fl. c.955–c.1010), considered the greatest prose writer and grammarian of his time, wrote books to instruct monks and a Colloquy to teach Latin, which gives portraits of contemporary life.

9   These same tracks are now, of course, our roads, country lanes and footpaths.

10   An amber equals 4 bushels.

11   Aelfric: *Colloquy, op.cit.*

12   Quoted in Fell, Christine, *Women in Anglo-Saxon England* (Colonnade Books 1984).

13   Ibid.

CHAPTER 2: Anglo-Saxon Gastronomy

1   Tacitus, *Germania*, ch.23; trans Mattingly (Penguin Classics 1951).

2   Aelfric: *Colloquy, op.cit.*

3   Knowles, David, *The Monastic Order in England: a History of its Development from the Times of St Dunstan to the Fourth Lateran Council, 943-1216* (CUP 1949).

4   *Anglo-Saxon Conversations. The Colloquies of Aelfric Bata*, ed. Scott Gwara; trans. and introduction, David W. Porter. Colloquy 21 (Boydell Press 1997).

5   Ibid. Colloquy 25.

6   Ibid. Colloquia Difficiliora, 1.

7   Hagen, Ann, *A Handbook of Anglo-Saxon Food and Drink: Production and Distribution* (Anglo-Saxon Books 1992).

8   Aelfric: *Colloquy, op.cit.*

9   As the kidneys' function in mammals is to remove waste and excess substances from the blood and change them into urine, I have often thought it odd that such an excretory organ should be eaten at all. Perhaps this was an early taboo now faded which might in our days of factory farming be resurrected.

10   Of the *dolichos* family, which is both pole and dwarf in growth.

11   Anthimus, *On the Observance of Foods*, translated and edited by Mark Grant (Prospect Books 1996).

12   An oatmeal dish from the Welsh *llymru* which spread into Cheshire and Lancashire, and which was made from oatmeal steeped in water, then strained and boiled, until it became solid like a blancmange.

13   See Hagen, Ann, *op.cit.*

14   This was a fermented fruit drink, as beer from hops was not made until the sixteenth century.

15   All infectious diseases of cattle were referred to as murrain, these could have been any of the diseases we are familiar with now that cause such havoc in contemporary farming.

16   Quoted in Hagen, *op.cit.*, from which this analysis of Anglo-Saxon infestation derives.

CHAPTER 3: Norman Gourmets 1100-1300

1   Froissart, *Chronicles*, ed. Brereton, Geoffrey (Penguin 1968).

2   His obesity at the end of his life is thought to have had a genetic cause.

3   Quoted in Bartlett, Robert, *England under the Norman and Angevin Kings 1075-1225* (Clarendon Press 2000).

4   *Ecclesiastical History of Orderic Vitalis*, edited and translated with introduction and notes by Chibnall, Marjorie (Clarendon Press, Oxford, 1969-1980).

5   Martin, *Description of the Western Isles of Scotland*, quoted in Seebohm, M.E., *The Evolution of the English Farm* (Allen & Unwin 1952).

6   Neckam, A., *De Naturis Rerum*, quoted in Hieatt, Constance; Butler, Sharon, *Curye on Inglysch* (OUP 1985).

7   We have noted the Anglo-Saxons' love for this spice.

8   Dyer, Christopher, *Everyday Life in Medieval England* (Hambledon Press 1994).

9   *Rumex Sanguineus* (Bloodwort) a red-veined dock, grown as a pot herb in gardens and eaten as a vegetable, not unlike spinach.

10   Wright, Clifford, A., 'Cucina Arabo-Sicula and Maccharruni', Vol 9, (Al-Masaq 1996-97).

11   Charles Perry has pointed out that there are many Arabic recipes for mawmenny that do not have almonds or chicken in them and are also in different colours.
See *PPC 31*, 'Isfidhabaj, Blancmanger and No Almonds' (1989).

12   France then was only a small region around Paris while the Counties of Champagne, of Bourbon, of Auvergne and others were vassals of the French monarch.

13   Wright, Clifford, A., *A Mediterranean Feast* (William Morrow & Co. 1999)

14   Shaida, Margaret, *The Legendary Cuisine of Persia* (Grub Street 2000).

15   Hieatt, Constance; Butler, Sharon, *Curye on Inglysch* (OUP 1985).

16   *English Historical Documents, c.500-1042,* trans. Whitelock, Dorothy (OUP 1979).

17   Some of the monks who arrived with the Norman kings had trained at the medical school of Salerno where the *Antidotarium Nicolai* originated, a collection of prescriptions deriving from Greek and Arabic sources which remained in use for several centuries.

18   London paid sixteen-point-eight per cent of the total taxation, Boston fifteen-point-seven per cent, Southampton 14.3%, Lincoln 13.3%, and Lynn 13.1%.

19   The word apothecary derives from *apotheca* meaning the place where wine, spices and herbs were stored.

20   Nightingale, Pamela, *A Medieval Mercantile Community: The Grocer's Company and the Politics and Trade of London 1000-1485* (Yale University Press 1995).

21   Norman, Jill, *The Complete Book of Spices* (Dorling Kindersley 1990). In this comprehensive manual the author lists 49 spices.

22   There is a contemporary account from Peter of Blois (quoted in *Eleanor of Aquitaine* by Alison Weir, Pimlico 2000) of eating at Henry II's court, where the bread was unbaked and the meat and fish rotten. It is so exaggerated that one cannot take it literally. Peter was a man of acerbic wit and fine sensibility and, one infers, loyal to Queen Eleanor whose aesthetic temperament must have been more in tune with his own life than the raucous and wild company he had found himself among.

23   Scully, Terence, *The Art of Cookery in the Middle Ages* (Boydell Press 1995).

24   Henna itself comes from the tree *Lawsonia inermis*.

25   Oil came from a variety of wild plants, also rape oil was imported from Flanders and rape was also grown in medieval gardens. Linseed oil from cultivating flax was also used.

26   The Anglo-Saxons would boil a mixture of fish in an iron cauldron – possibly the source of the term 'kettle of fish'.

27   Cobb, H.S., *Overseas Trade of London: Exchequer Custom Accounts 1480-81* (London, London Record Society 1990).

28   Woolgar, C.M., *The Great Household in Late Medieval England* (Yale University Press 1999).

29   Dyer, Christopher, *Everyday Life in Medieval England* (Hambledon Press 1994).

30   Carp were only introduced in the late fourteenth century and took some time to be accepted.

31   Harvey, Barbara, *Living and Dying in England 1100-1540* (Clarendon Press 1993).

32   Austin, T., (ed), *Two Fifteenth Century Cookery Books: Harleian MS 279,4016* (Early English Text Society 1888).

33   Dyer, *op.cit.*

34   Wilson, C. Anne, *Food and Drink in Britain* (Constable 1973).

35   Carlin, Martha, 'Fast Food and Urban Living Standards in Medieval England' from *Food and Eating in Medieval Europe*, ed. Martha Carlin; Joel T. Rosenthal (Hambledon Press 1998).

36   FitzStephen, William, *A Description of London*, trans. H.E. Butler (Historical Association Leaflet 1934).

37   The Victorians decimated the population by their organised shoots and the drainage of the marshes. The bird is still very rare.

38   In Colchester in 1301 only 3% of the taxpaying households had a kitchen.

39   The fire was the centre of the house, the source of heat and light for all classes. Among the poor a gift of fire was carried to neighbours inside a hollowed out giant puff-ball.

40   Dyer, *op.cit.*

41   Adamson, Melitta Weiss, 'The Games Cooks Play: Non-Sense Recipes & Practical Jokes in Medieval Literature' from *Food in the Middle Ages: A Book of Essays* Garland Medieval Casebooks 12 (London and New York 1995).

CHAPTER 4: Anarchy and Haute Cuisine 1300-1500

1   Mintz, Sidney, *Tasting Food, Tasting Freedom* (Beacon Press 1996).

2   Quoted in C. Anne Wilson, *op.cit.*

3   This was public land used by the peasant to graze livestock, grow food and gather wood for his cooking, enclosed by hedges or fences by the local landowner for his sole use, later such acts were legalised by Parliament.

4   The Plantagenet character was an obsessive one; one idea would take hold and everything else would be sacrificed towards it.

5   Hunt, Alan, *Governance of the Consuming Passions. A History of Sumptuary Law* (Macmillan 1996).

6   Saaler, Mary, *Edward II* (The Rubicon Press 1997).

7   Ziegler, Philip, *The Black Death* (Penguin, 1969).

8   Saaler, Mary, *op.cit.*

9   Quoted in Ziegler, *op.cit.*

10   Ibid.

11   Constance Hieatt in the Introduction to her *An Ordinance of Pottage* (Prospect Books 1988) deals with the intricacies of the various manuscripts and the differing interpretations of the recipes by historians throughout the centuries.

12   Landsberg, Sylvia, *The Medieval Garden* (British Museum Press 1995).

13   Quoted in Stead, Jennifer, 'Bowers of Bliss: The Banquet Setting' in *Banquetting Stuffe*, ed. C. Anne Wilson (Edinburgh University Press 1986).

14   A version of this recipe with others was found in a collection in Samuel Pepys' library.

15   The amount spent upon food in the royal households was carefully graded dependent on the importance of each person. For example, a duke related to King Edward III with a company of 300 horse was allowed £15 13s 4d per day, every man and horse was allowed 12s per day. A duke who was not of the blood royal was allowed £10 13s 4d, a viscount 55s, while a knight having in his company ten men was only allowed 12s. These amounts rose with inflation throughout the years, but the system remained unchanged for hundreds of years.

16   This is a recipe that I have cooked and the figs, prunes and sultanas poached with the partridge make a delicious sauce.

17   Swabey, ffiona, 'The Household of Alice de Bryene, 1412-13', in *Food and Eating in Medieval Europe*, ed. Carlin, Martha; Rosenthal, Joel T. (Hambledon Press 1998).

18   See Norman, Jill, *The Complete Book of Spices* (Dorling Kindersley 1990).

19   Wilson, C. Anne, *Food and Drink in Britain* (Constable 1973).

20   Variously spelt 'bestys' or 'beastlyns' or also called 'firstings'.

21   Hartley, Dorothy, *Food in England* (Macdonald 1954).

22   Marcel Boulestin thought it originated at Trinity College, Sir Harry Luke believed it was Corpus Christi.

23   Dyer, Christopher, *Standards of Living in the Later Middle Ages* (CUP 1989).

24   *The Paston Letters 1422-1509*, ed. J. Gairdner (London 1872).

25   Harvey, Barbara, *Living and Dying in England 1100-1540. The Monastic Experience* (Clarendon Press, Oxford 1993).

26   Ibid.

27   Wilson, C. Anne, *Food and Drink in Britain, op.cit.*

28   Hallam. H.E., ed. 'The Worker's Diet', *The Agrarian History of England and Wales*, Vol. 2, 1042-1350. General ed. Joan Thirsk (CUP 1988).

29   Ibid.

30   Trow-Smith, R. A., *History of British Livestock Husbandry to 1700* (London 1957).

31   Hallam, H.E., ed. 'England before the Norman Conquest.' *The Agrarian History of England and Wales*, Vol 2. General ed. Joan Thirsk (CUP 1988).

32   Quoted in Wilson, C. Anne, *op.cit.*

33   Boorde, Andrewe, *A Dyetary of Helth* (Kegan Paul, London 1870).

34   Plat, Sir Hugh, *Sundrie new and Artificial remedies against Famine* (1596). Quoted in Drummond, J.C., *The Englishman's Food* (Jonathan Cape 1958).

35   Wilson, C. Anne, *op.cit.*

36   Webb, Diana, *Pilgrimage in Medieval England* (Hambledon & London 2000).

37   Dyer, Christopher, *op.cit.*

38   Lampreys are still eaten in Spain, Portugal and Bordeaux, while they are smoked in Finland. They fell out of favour in the nineteenth century, while pollution in our rivers has now greatly diminished their numbers.

39   Wilson C. Anne, *op.cit.*

40   The name dates from the eighteenth century and came from France, where the sauce was flavoured with vinegar and bitter herbs and appeared to have an asp-like bite.

41   Dyer, Christopher, *op.cit.*

42   Wilson C. Anne, 'The Evolution of the Banquet Course: Some Medicinal, Culinary and Social Aspects' from *Banquetting Stuffe* (Edinburgh University Press 1986).

43   Wilson C. Anne, *Food and Drink in Britain, op.cit.*

44   Dyer, Christopher, *op.cit.*

45   Ibid.

46   Jane Austen mentions eating it with enjoyment later. See page 255.

47   This account depends on Harvey, Barbara, *Living and Dying in England 1100–1540. The Monastic Experience, op.cit.*

48   Barbara Santich believes the word to derive from Persian/Arabic *sikbaj* meaning vinegar stew. See Alan Davidson, *The Oxford Companion to Food* (OUP 2000).

49   Woolgar, C.M., *The Great Household in Late Medieval England* (Yale University Press 1999).

50   The name was used pejoratively; it came from Middle Dutch *lollaert*, meaning mumbler, and applied to heretical sects. Here it was used to mean followers of Wycliffe.

51   A term coined by Sir Walter Scott.

52   Briggs, Asa, *A Social History of England* (Weidenfeld & Nicolson 1983).

53   See Briggs, Asa, *op.cit.*

54   Ibid.

55   Ibid.

56   Quoted in Strong, Roy, *The Story of Britain* (Pimlico 1998).

57   Quoted in Curtis-Bennett, Sir Noel, *The Food of the People* (Faber & Faber 1949).

58   Ibid.

CHAPTER 5: Tudor Wealth and Domesticity

1   Giving an erroneous impression that we were being influenced by French dishes.

2   Briggs, Asa, *A Social History of England, op.cit.*

3   McGrath, Patrick, *Papists and Puritans Under Elizabeth I* (Blandford Press 1967).

4   Crawford, Patricia, *Women and Religion in England 1500–1720* (Routledge 1993).

5   Ibid.

6   Whiting, Robert, *The Blind Devotion of the People* (CUP 1989).

7   Ibid.

8   Heinze R.W., *The Proclamations of the Tudor Kings* (CUP 1976).

9   Youngs, Frederick, A., *The Proclamations of the Tudor Queens* (CUP 1967).

10   Heal, Felicity; Holmes, Clive, *The Gentry in England and Wales, 1500–1700* (Macmillan 1994).

11   *The Agrarian History of England & Wales*, Vol IV 1500–1640, ed. Joan Thirsk (CUP 1967).

12   Beys were the so-called 'new draperies' like 'shaloons' and 'perpetuonos' which were cheap, light, less durable but highly amenable to changes in fashion. These profitable draperies were made by immigrant labour.

13   Elinor Fettiplace (see page 124) mentions them roasted, or sliced with butter, rosewater, sugar, salt and the juice of Seville oranges. This is a method still used by Americans at Thanksgiving.

14   'Feaberrie' in Cheshire, 'feabes' in Norfolk, and 'grozer' or 'grozet' in Scotland, probably from the corruption of the French *groseille*.

15   Gooseberries in France are called *groseilles à maquereau* because of their association with the cooking of mackerel.

16   Dodd, A.H., *Life in Elizabethan England* (Batsford 1961).

17   *The Star Chamber Dinner Accounts*, Commentary by Andre L. Simon (The Wine and Food Society 1959).

18   Markham, Gervase, *The English Hus-wife*, 1615.

19   Quoted in Hibbert, Christopher, *The English, a social history, 1066-1945* (Grafton Books 1987).

20   *A Proper Newe Booke of Cokerye* (Cambridge MS c1560), ed. C.F. Frere (Cambridge 1913). Also *A Booke of Cookry Very Necessary for All Such as Delight Therein*, Gathered by A.W. (1584).

21   Quoted in Barber, Richard, *Cooking and Recipes from Rome to the Renaissance* (Allen Lane 1973).

22   *The Lisle Letters*, ed. Muriel St Clare Byrne (Penguin 1981).

23   Burton, Elizabeth, *The Elizabethans at Home* (Secker & Warburg 1958).

24   Plat, Sir Hugh, *Delightes for Ladies*, 1602 (London 1948).

25   A gibe at France and its barbarous tastes in food.

26   Sim, Alison, *Food and Feast in Tudor England* (Sutton Publishing 1997).

27   The tongue of an ox, cow, bullock or heifer.

28   Meads, D.M., ed. *The Diary of Lady Margaret Hoby, 1559-1605* (George Routledge 1930).

29   *The Elizabethan Home. Discovered in Two Dialogues* by Claudius Hollyband and Peter Erondell and Edited by M. St. Clare Byrne (Cobden-Sanderson 1930).

30   This was a name since the twelfth century applied to round cheeses from Brie and Camembert country.

31   A cheese greatly admired at this time, 'by age waxing mellower and softer and more pleasant of taste, digesting whatsoever went before it, yet itself not heavy of digestion.' Quoted in C. Anne Wilson, *op.cit.*

32   Thomas Cogan thought Banbury cheese to be better than Cheshire: 'for therein you shall neither taste the rennet nor salt, which be two special properties of good cheese.'

33   *The Elizabethan Home, op.cit.*

34   St Clare Byrne, M., *Elizabethan Life in Town and Country* (Methuen 1925).

35   Isinglass is made from the air bladders of freshwater fish – notably the sturgeon. Hartshorn jelly is made from the shavings of hart's horns. Both are transparent and gelatinous.

36   Edited by Hilary Spurling (Viking Salamander 1986).

37   C. Anne Wilson in 'A Cookery Book and Its Context: Elizabethan Cookery and

Lady Fettiplace', *PPC 25* (1987) is critical of Spurling, believing that this is only a fragment of an original family receipt book.

38   I recall a vogue for this same dessert in the 1950s.

39   Quoted in Stead, Jennifer, 'Navy Blues: the Sailor's Diet, 1530-1830' from *Food in the Community,* ed. C. Anne Wilson (Edinburgh University Press 1991).

40   Hartley, Dorothy, *Food in England* (Macdonald 1954).

41   Laslett, Peter, *The World We Have Lost* (Methuen 1965).

42   Later reissued as *Five Hundreth Pointes of Husbandrie* in 1573.

43   See Braudel, Fernand, *The Wheels of Commerce* (Collins 1982).

44   Borrowed from France with its roots in both Latin and Greek.

45   Hentzer, Paul, *A Journey into England in the Year 1598. Printed in Fugitive Pieces on Various Subjects*, vol II (London 1765), quoted in Beeverell, James, *The Pleasures of London*, translated and annotated by W.H. Quarrell (Witherly & Co. London 1940).

46   Quoted without source in Claire, Colin, *Kitchen Table* (Abelard & Schumann 1964).

47   Wilson, C. Anne, ed., *Banquetting Stuffe* (Edinburgh University Press 1986).

48   In 1513 the King of Portugal offered the Pope a lifesize effigy of himself surrounded by 12 cardinals and 300 candles all made out of sugar.

49   Quoted in Baldwin Smith, Lacey, *Elizabethan World* (Hamlyn 1967).

50   Barclay, John, *Icon Animorum* (1614). Quoted in Hill, Christopher, *The World Turned Upside Down* (Penguin 1972).

CHAPTER 6: A Divided Century

1   Mennell, Stephen, *All Manners of Food* (Blackwell 1985).

2   Hill, Christopher, *The Century of Revolution 1603-1714* (Nelson 1961).

3   In 1612 the Earl of Salisbury was receiving £7,000 a year from the silk monopoly, the Earl of Suffolk £5,000 from currants, the Earl of Northampton £4,500 from starch.

4   Quoted in Hill, *op.cit.*

5   Ladurie, E. Leroy, 'Peasants' in *New Cambridge Modern History*, XIII., ed. P. Burke (CUP 1979).

6   Hill, Christopher, 'A Bourgeois Revolution?' in *Collected Essays*, Vol. 3 (Harvester Press 1986).

7   Davenant, Charles, *Discourses on the Publick Revenues and on the Trade of England, by the Author of Ways and Means* (1698).

8   Quoted in Hill, Christopher, 'The Poor and the People' in *Collected Essays, op.cit.*

9   See Pullar, Philippa, *Consuming Passions* (Hamish Hamilton 1970). Stephen Mennell (*op.cit.*) has argued convincingly against such a trite and populist theory.

10   Hill, Christopher, *The World Turned Upside Down* (Penguin 1972).

11   Cohn, Norman, *The Pursuit of the Millennium* (Paladin 1970).

12   His life and work are dealt with in detail in my book *Vegetarianism – A History* (Grub Street 2001).

13   Named after Leonard Mascall who published *The Booke of Arte and Maner, howe to plant and graffe all sortes of trees*, published in 1572.

14   Bacon, Francis, 'On Gardens', an essay 1625, quoted in Roach, F.A., *Cultivated Fruits of Britain* (Blackwell 1985).

15   Thick, Malcolm, *The Neat House Gardens: Early Market Gardening around London* (Prospect Books 1998).

16   Ibid.

17   *The Agrarian History of England and Wales*, Vol. IV, ed. Thirsk, J. (CUP 1967).

18   May, Robert, *The Accomplisht Cook* (Prospect Books 1994).

19   Ibid.

20   Hamlyn, Matthew, *The Recipes of Hannah Woolley* (Heinemann 1988).

21   Burnett, John, *Liquid Pleasures* (Routledge 1999).

22   Ibid.

23   Lehmann, Gilly, 'Food and Drink at the Restoration, as seen through the diary, 1660-1669, of Samuel Pepys'. (This essay was based on a computer analysis of the food eaten.) (*PPC* 1998).

24   Quoted in Driver, Christopher; Berriedale-Johnson, Michelle, *Pepys at Table* (Bell & Hyman 1984).

25   Defoe, Daniel, *A Tour Through England and Wales* (Everyman ed. 1928).

26   Ibid.

27   Pepys, Samuel, *The Diary of Samuel Pepys*, Vol IV 1663, ed. Latham, R.C.; Matthews, W. (Harper Collins 1995).

28   The salted, pressed dried female roe of the striped grey mullet or tunny. It is an old eastern Mediterranean delicacy, known in ancient Egypt. Rare to find now, though I have eaten it in the past.

29   Preserved or pickled from the Latin *condire* to season or pickle.

30   Quoted in Driver, Christopher, ed., *John Evelyn, Cook* (Prospect Books 1997).

31   McKendrick, Neil; Plumb, J.H.; Brewer, John, *The Birth of the Consumer Society* (Europa, London 1982).

32   Mennell, Stephen, *All Manners of Food* (Blackwell 1985).

33   *The Agrarian History of England and Wales*, Vol V ii, ed. Thirsk, Joan (1985).

34   General works on husbandry stood alongside specialist treatises by authors such as Sir Hugh Plat, Thomas Hill, Edward Maxey and Leonard Mascall.

35   Samuel Hartlib was granted a pension for publicising various utilitarian plants, and army garrisons as far afield as Kirkwall taught the locals how to grow cabbages.

36   Marshall, W., *The Rural Economy of the West of England* (1796) quoted in Chambers, J.D.; Mingay, G.E., *The Agricultural Revolution 1750-1880* (Batsford 1966).

37   *The Diary of Samuel Pepys*, Vol VIII 1967 (Harper Collins 1995).

38   Folio, *In the Savoy* (printed by Thomas Newcomb 1687), privately owned.

39   Succory (*chicorium intybus*), a root needing to be blanched, was thought to have medicinal qualities, and to be good for the stomach and liver.

40   Marcoux, Paula, 'The Thickening Plot: Notable Liaisons between French and English Cookbooks, 1600-1660' (*PPC 60*, 1998).

41   See Mennell, *op.cit.*

CHAPTER 7: Other Island Appetites

1   Introduction by Professor Wollner to *The Vision of MacConglinne*, ed. Kuno Meyer (Nutt, London 1892). We are now familiar with the *goliardi* from Carl Orff's *Carmina Burana*.

2   Ibid.

3   *The Vision of MacConglinne, op.cit.*

4   Ibid.

5   Kelly, Fergus, *Early Irish Farming* (Dublin Institute for Advanced Studies 1997).

6   Ibid.

7   Proc.R.I.A., LV, C, pp8 ff, Professor Dillon.

8   Quoted in Lucas, A.T., 'Irish Food Before the Potato', *Gwerin 3*, no 2, Dec. 1960.

9   Ibid.

10   Hunt, H., *De contemptu mundi I*, quoted in Bartlett, Robert, *England under the Norman and Angevin Kings, 1075-1225* (OUP 2000).

11   Sexton, Regina, *A Little History of Irish Food* (Kyle Cathie 1998).

12   Donaldson, J., *Husbandry Anatomized* (1697).

13   Bellhaven, Lord, *The Countrey-Man's Rudiments* (1699).

14   Quoted in Sexton, *op.cit.*

15   Lysaght, Patricia, 'Continuity and Change in Irish Diet' in *Food in Change*, ed. Fenton, Alexander; Kisbán, Eszter (John Donald Publishers 1986).

16   Woodham-Smith, Cecil, *The Great Hunger* (Harper 1962).

17   Allen, Darina, *Irish Traditional Cooking* (Kyle Cathie 1998).

18   Aneirin, 'The Gododdin' (sixth-century) in *The Oxford Book of Welsh Verse in English*, ed. Jones, Gwynn (OUP 1977).

19   Johnson, Samuel, *A Journey to the Western Islands of Scotland*, 1775.

20   Fenton, Alexander, 'Food and the Coastal Environment' in *Food in Change, op.cit.*

21   Cheape, Hugh, 'Pottery and Food Preparation, Storage and Transport in the Scottish Hebrides' in *Food in Change, op.cit.*

22   Handley, J.E., *Scottish Farming in the 18th Century* (Faber & Faber 1953).

23   Brown, P.H., *Scotland before 1700* (1893).

24   *Scottish Society 1500-1800*, ed. Houston, R.A.; Whyte, I.D. (CUP 1989).

25   Quoted in ibid.

26   See Houston and Whyte, *op.cit.*

27   *General View of the Northern Counties*, quoted in ibid.

28   *The Cottagers of Glenburnie* (9th edition 1832).

29   Taillevent, *Le Viandier* (1312-1395). (Paris 1892).

30   Sue Lawrence in *Scots Cooking* (Headline 2000) gives two alternative derivations: from Shetland where the dialect word for codling is kabbilow, and because of the trade between Scotland and Holland she suggests it is likely that the Dutch for cod, *kabeljauw*, was responsible.

31   Bingham, Madeleine, *Scotland under Mary Stuart* (Allen & Unwin 1971).

32   Ibid.

33   Ibid.

34   Bristed, J., *A Pedestrian Tour through part of the Highlands of Scotland in 1801*, quoted in Handley, *op.cit.*

35   Cave, Sir Thomas, *A Diary of a Journey from Stanford Hall to the North of Scotland and back in the Year 1763*, quoted in ibid.

36   McNeill, F. Marian, *The Scots Kitchen* (Blackie 1929).

37   Quoted in Fenton, *op.cit.*

38   Quoted in McNeill, *op.cit.*

39   Ibid.

40   Quoted in Handley, J.E., *op.cit.*

41   Robertson, G., *Rural Recollections* (1829).

42   Macdonald, J., *An Economical History of the Hebrides and Highlands of Scotland* (1808).

43   Ibid.

44   Johnson, Samuel, *A Journey to the Western Islands of Scotland* (1775).

45   *Ordinance Gazetteer of Scotland.*

46   Robertson, G., *General View of Midlothian* (1793).

47   Robertson, G., *General View of Agriculture in the Southern Districts of the County of Perth* (1794).

48   Lettice, J., *Letters on a Tour through various parts of Scotland in the year 1792.*

49   *Memoirs of a Highland Lady*, quoted in McNeill, F. Marian, *op.cit.*

50   Smiles, *Lives of the Engineers, Metcalfe-Telford* (1904).

51   Firth, C.H., *Scotland and the Protectorate* (1899).

52   McNeill, *op.cit.*

53   Davies, Wendy, *Wales in the Early Middle Ages* (Leicester University Press 1982).

54   Evans, J.G., *The White Book of Mabinogion* (Pwllheli 1907).

55   I'm indebted to Canon T.J. Prichard for this explanation and the translation of excerpts of this early Welsh poem.

56   Owen, George (1552-1613), quoted by Davies, D.J. (1933), *The Economic History of South Wales* (Cardiff 1933).

57   Freeman, Bobby, *First Catch Your Peacock* (Image Imprint 1978).

58   Lady Bridget Bulkeley's accounts of food and drink (1709-11) and the accounts of Elizabeth Morgan of Henblas, Llangristiolus (1734-73) are quoted in Ramage, Helen, *Portraits of an Island* (Anglesey Antiquarian Society 1987).

59   *The Letters of Lewis, Richard, William and John Morris*, ed. Davies, J. H., quoted in Ramage, *op.cit.*

60   Aikin, Arthur, *Journal of a Tour through North Wales* (London 1787).

61   Haldane, A.R.B., *The Drove Roads of Scotland* (Thomas Nelson & Sons 1952).

62   See Salaman, Redcliffe, N., *The History and Social Influence of the Potato* (CUP 1949).

63   Williams, Meryell, *Ystumcolwyn* (Peniarth collection, NLW).

CHAPTER 8: Glories of the Country Estate

1   Young, Arthur, *Six Weeks Tour Through the Southern Counties of England* (1768).

2   Briggs, Asa, *A Social History of England* (Weidenfeld & Nicolson 1983).

3   American cookery books began to be published in the eighteenth century and have recipes for baked beans, chowders, soft gingerbreads, pumpkin pie and turkey with cranberry sauce.

4   See Karen Hess and her brilliant introduction and footnotes in *Martha Washington's Booke of Cookery* (Columbia University Press 1981).

5   Emmerson, Robin, *Table Settings* (Shire Publications 1991).

6   David, Elizabeth, 'Banketting Stuffe' (*PPC 3* 1979).

7   Girouard, Mark, *Life in the English Country House* (Yale 1978).

8   Shipperbottom, Roy, Introduction to *The Experienced English Housekeeper* by Elizabeth Raffald (Southover Press 1997).

9   Cookson, Caroline, 'The Technology of Cooking in the British Isles, Part 1: Before the Use of Gas' (*PPC 1* 1979).

10   Feild, Rachael, *Irons in the Fire* (Crowood Press 1984).

11   Ibid.

12   The finest black tea from the Wu-i Hills north of Fuhkien, which after 1704 became the name for all tea, even the poorest, and the infusion itself.

13   Named after Lucas Bols who began manufacturing gin at Schiedam in 1575, known in French as *eau de genièvre*.

14   Woodforde, James, *The Diary of a Country Parson 1758-1802*, ed. Beresford, John (OUP 1978).

15   Burnett, John, *Liquid Pleasures* (Routledge 1999).

16   Ibid.

17   *PPC 52* (May 1996).

18   See Jennifer Stead in *PPC 13 & 14*, and Priscilla Bain in *PPC 23*. Between them they have detected over 360 recipes copied from other books out of a total of 972. No doubt there are more.

19   The origins of Worcester Sauce began in a similar manner.

20   Burkhardt, B.; McLean, B.A.; Kochanek, D., *Sailors and Sauerkraut* (Gray's 1978).

21   Ibid.

22   *Cook's Voyages of Discovery*, ed. Barrow, John (Everyman 1906).

23   Watt, Sir James, 'Some Consequences of Nutritional Disorders in Eighteenth Century British Circumnavigations' from *Starving Sailors*, ed. Watt, J.; Freeman, E.J.; Bynum, W.F. (National Maritime Museum 1981).

24   Young, A., *Farmers' Letters* Vol 1. (1771).

25   Countess Morphy in *British Recipes* (Herbert Joseph 1936) gives Lobsgows under Welsh recipes as a mutton stew with onions, root vegetables and potatoes boiled for over two hours. Bobby Freeman also considers it a north Welsh dish (see *First Catch Your Peacock, op.cit.*).

26   Shipperbottom, Roy, 'Cooking Potatoes in the North of England: A Rare Document of 1796' (*PPC 45* 1993).

27   Laurence, John, *A New System of Agriculture* (1726).

28   Hale, Thomas, *A Compleat Body of Husbandry* (1756).

29   Austen-Leigh, E., *A Memoir of Jane Austen* (1870).

30   Baxter, Richard, *The Poor Husbandman's Advocate* (John Ryland 1926).

31   Salaman, Redcliffe N., *The History and Social Influence of the Potato* (CUP 1949).

32   See Shipperbottom, Roy, Introduction to *The Experienced English Housekeeper* by Elizabeth Raffald, *op.cit.*

33   Mabey, Richard, *Gilbert White* (Century 1986).

34   Verrall, William, *Cookery Book*, 1759 (Southover Press 1988).

35   Woodforde, James, *The Diary of a Country Parson 1758-1802*, ed. John Beresford (OUP 1935).

CHAPTER 9: Industry and Empire

1   Laing, Samuel, *National Distress: Its Causes and Remedies*, quoted in Burnett, John, *Plenty and Want* (Routledge 1966).

2   Briggs, Asa, *A Social History of England* (Weidenfeld & Nicolson 1983).

3   Hobsbawm, E.J., *Industry and Empire* (Penguin 1968).

4   Eden, Sir Frederick, *The State of the Poor*, quoted in Drummond, J.C., *op.cit.*

5   Quoted in Salaman, Redcliffe N., *op.cit.*

6   Cobbett, William, *Rural Rides* (Penguin 1967).

7   Quoted in Hobsbawm, E.J., *op.cit.*

8   Scola, Roger, *Feeding the Victorian City: The Food Supply of Manchester 1770-1870* (Manchester University Press 1992).

9   Ibid.

10   Burnett, John, *Plenty and Want, op.cit.*

11   Scola, Roger, *op.cit.*

12   Briggs, Asa, ed. *Chartist Studies* (Macmillan 1959).

13   This is a method of adding flour to the meat fat to make a paste as in a roux, then rolling the joint in it and finishing the roasting so that the outside gets a crust.

14   *The Cook's Oracle*.

15   *Beeton's Book of Household Management*, ed. Beeton, Isabella (facsimile edition, Southover Press 1998).

16   Davidson, Caroline, *A Woman's Work is Never Done: A History of Housework in the British Isles 1650-1950* (Chatto & Windus 1982).

17   Hickman, Peggy, *A Jane Austen Household Book with Martha Lloyd's Recipes* (David & Charles 1977).

18   Palmer, Arnold, *Movable Feasts* (OUP 1984).

19   Wilson, C. Anne, ed. *Luncheon, Nuncheon and Related Meals* (Sutton 1994).

20   Lucraft, Fiona, 'Food and Eating in the Bronte Novels', *PPC 62* (1999). This is a fascinating essay, especially for all Bronte enthusiasts; my very brief summary does it no justice.

21   Quoted in White, Eileen, 'First Things First: The Great British Breakfast' in *Luncheon, Nuncheon and Related Meals*, ed. Wilson, C. Anne, *op.cit.*

22   Quoted in ibid.

23   Henry Mayhew, *Mayhew's London*, ed. Quennell, Peter (Spring Books 1972).

24   The word dates from 1712 meaning a drink of powdered salep, but it was later made from sassafras with added milk and sugar. Salep was an orchid root imported

through the East India Company. It was powdered, then added to water until it thickened, then flavoured.

25   Volant, F. & Warren, J.R.

26   Hess, Karen, 'The Origin of French Fries', *PPC 68* (2001).

27   Shipperbottom, Roy, 'Fish and Chips', *Proceedings of the Oxford Symposium* 1997. I'm indebted for this paper to the late Mr Shipperbottom.

28   See Hess, Karen, *op.cit.*

29   Burnett, John, *Plenty and Want, op.cit.*

30   Salaman, *op.cit.*

31   Rowntree, B. Seebohm, *Poverty, a Study of Town Life* (1901).

32   Lewis, Gary, *The Middle Way* (Brolga Press 1992).

CHAPTER 10: Victorian Food

1   He became Sir Mayson Beeton who survived until 1947.

2   Burnett, John, *Plenty and Want, op.cit.*

3   Spain, Nancy, *The Beeton Story* (Ward Lock 1956).

4   Quoted in Aron, Jean-Paul, 'The Art of Using Left-overs: Paris, 1856-1900', from *Food and Drink in History*, Vol. 5, ed. Forster, Robert; Ranum, Orest (Johns Hopkins University Press 1979).

5   Mars, Valerie, 'A la Russe: The New Way of Dining' in *Luncheon, Nuncheon and Related Meals, op.cit.*

6   Today we think of entrée as a main course, but then the entrée followed the fish and preceded the main; they were hot dishes in a sauce – croustades, timbales, or cold dishes like pâtés.

7   Quoted in ibid.

8   See 'Pastry Ramakins to serve with the cheese course', *Beeton's Book of Household Management* (facsimile edition, Southover Press 1998).

9   Mennell, Stephen, *All Manners of Food, op.cit.*

10   Black, Maggie, *A Taste of History* (British Museum Press 1993).

11   See Spencer, Colin, *Vegetarianism – a History* (Grub Street 2001).

12   Corley T.A.B., 'Nutrition,Technology and the Growth of the British Biscuit Industry 1820-1900', in Oddy, Derek J.; Miller, Derek S., ed. *The Making of the Modern British Diet* (Croom Helm 1976).

13   'An Address to the Inhabitants of St James's Westminster, by a retired Churchwarden', Hon. F. Byng, 1847, quoted in Drummond, J.C., *The Englishman's Food, op.cit.*

14   The same belief about BSE was strongly held in the 1980s.

15   Black, Mrs, *Superior Cookery* (Collins 1898).

16   *Janey Ellice's Recipes 1846-1859* ed. Wentworth, Josie A. (MacDonald and Janes 1975).

17   Mars, Valerie, 'Parsimony amid Plenty', Food Culture & History (London Food Seminar 1993).

18   Quoted in ibid.

19   Keane Molly, *Nursery Cooking* (MacDonald 1985).

20   King-Hall, Magdalen, *The Story of the Nursery* (Routledge 1958).

21   Quoted in Boxer, Arabella, *Book of English Food* (Hodder & Stoughton 1991).

22   Leyel, Mrs C.F.; Hartley, Miss Olga, *The Gentle Art of Cookery* (Chatto & Windus 1925).

23   Raverat, Gwen, *Period Piece* (Faber and Faber 1954).

24   Acton, Harold, *Memoirs of an Aesthete* (Artellus 1948).

CHAPTER 11: Food for All

1   Priestley, J.B., *The Edwardians* (Sphere 1970).

2   Ibid.

3   Reeves S.P., Magdalen, *Round About a Pound a Week* (1913).

4   Ibid.

5   Ibid.

6   Ibid.

7   Rowntree, B. Seebohm, *How the Labourer Lives: A Study of the Rural Labour Problem* (1913).

8   Oddy, D.J., 'A Nutritional Analysis of Historical Evidence: The Working Class Diet 1880-1914' in *The Making of the Modern British Diet*, Oddy, Derek J.; Miller, Derek S. ed. (Croom Helm 1976).

9   'Astor Committee on the Production and Distribution of Milk' (1918).

10   Whetham, Edith, 'The London Milk Trade, 1900-1930' in *The Making of the Modern British Diet*, Oddy, Derek J.; Miller, Derek S. ed., *op.cit.*

11   Burnett, John, *op.cit.*

12   Machray, R., *The Night Side of London* (1902).

13   Richardson D.J., 'J. Lyons & Co. Ltd: Caterers & Food Manufacturers, 1894 to 1939' (Oddy and Miller o*p.cit.*).

14   Curtis-Bennett, Sir Noel, *The Food of the People* (Faber 1959).

15   Ibid.

16   Griggs, Barbara, *The Food Factor* (Viking 1986), quoted in Boyd Orr, Sir John; Lubbock, David, *Feeding the People in Wartime* (Macmillan 1940).

17   Johnson, James, *A Hundred Years' Eating* (Gill & Macmillan 1977).

18   Heath, Ambrose, *Open Sesame: two hundred recipes for canned goods* (Nicolson & Watson 1939).

19   New Zealand ate 236 lb per head per annum, Australia 202 lb, Canada 144 lb and the UK 140 lb; these figures were for the years 1930-4.

20   In order following us were Denmark at 7.7 oz, Germany 6.4 oz, France 5.6 oz, USA 4.6 oz, Italy 3.4 oz and Switzerland 1.9 oz.

21   Crawford, Sir William; Broadley H., *The People's Food* (Heinemann 1938).

22   Martineau, Alice, *More Caviare and More Candy* (Cobden-Sanderson 1938).

23   Boxer, Arabella, *Book of English Food* (Hodder & Stoughton 1991).

24   Quoted in ibid.

25   *Cassell's Cookery Book* (1884) does, however, suggest a salad of leaves, tomato, potato and celery.

26   Martineau, *op.cit.*

27   Davidson, Caroline, *op.cit.*

28   Ibid.

29   Boyd Orr, Sir John; Lubbock, David, *Feeding the People in Wartime, op.cit.*

30   Quoted in Griggs, Barbara, *The Food Factor, op.cit.*

31   By the end of the war weekly rations for an adult were: meat by price 1s 2d (roughly 1 lb), bacon or ham 4 oz, sugar 8 oz, butter and margarine 6 oz, cheese 2 oz, chocolate and sweets 3 oz, cooking fat 1 oz, tea 2½ oz, preserves 4 oz.

32   Driver, Christopher, *The British at Table 1940-1980* (Chatto & Windus 1983).

33   Fitzgibbon, Theodora, *With Love* (Century 1982).

34   Pyke, Magnus, *Townsman's Food* (Turnstile Books 1952).

35   Longmate, Norman, *How We Lived Then* (Hutchinson 1971).

36   Cooper, Susan, *Snoek Piquante. The Age of Austerity* (Penguin 1963).

37   Tuna on sale now at the fishmonger has already been drained.

38   Postgate, Raymond, *Leader Magazine*, 23 June 1949.

39   Cooper, Susan, ibid.

40   Driver, Christopher, ibid.

41   *Leader Magazine*, 20 May 1950.

42   Boxer, Arabella, *Book of English Food* (Hodder & Stoughton 1991).

43   Mead, William, Edward, *The English Medieval Feast* (Allen & Unwin 1931).

44   The food we habitually take is always an addiction; I am not referring necessarily to monosodium glutamate, or strong Indian tea or coffee which we know are very addictive, for toast and marmalade or baked beans on toast can also be.

CHAPTER 12: The Global Village

1   Quoted in Driver, Christopher, *op.cit.*

2   For a detailed account see Spencer, Colin, *Vegetarianism – a history, op.cit.*

3   Tansey, Geoff; Worsley, Tony, *The Food System* (Earthscan 1995).

4   Introduction to Palmer, Arnold, *Movable Feasts: Changes in English Eating Habits, op.cit.*

5   Ibid.

6   'After FMD: Aiming for a Values-Driven Agriculture' (Food Ethics Council 2001).

7   Gary Lewis, whose thoughts on the co-operative movement I've summarised.

8   Kapoor, Sybil, *Simply British* (Michael Joseph 1998).

APPENDIX I

1   Diary of John Manningham, 1602-03 (Camden Society Publication No 99, 1868).

APPENDIX II

2   See McNeill, Marian, *The Scots Kitchen, op.cit.*, and Bibliographies in other Scots cookery books.

3   Freeman, Bobby, *First Catch Your Peacock, op.cit.*

4   Allen, Darina, *Irish Traditional Cooking* (Kyle Cathie 1998); Sexton, Regina, *A Little History of Irish Food* (Kyle Cathie 1998).

Glossary

Albae michiae: white bread eaten by the abbot and gentry in the monastery.

Albus panis: another type of white bread as above.

Almond milk/butter: the nuts are blanched, peeled then ground to a fine powder; water is added to make milk, but only a little water to make a thick, spreadable paste referred to as butter.

Angelot: by the eleventh century the Augelot or Angelon cheeses, products of the ancient Pays d'Auge, existed, probably created in a monastery or with monastic guidance. By the thirteenth century they were called Angelot, the name of a coin which pictured a young angel defeating a dragon. The cheese is mentioned in the first part of *Roman de la Rose* by Guillaume de Lorris published around 1236. The Normans brought the cheese to England where it remained immensely popular.

Arancina: saffron-coloured rice moulded into a ball with meat or cheese at its centre, made purposely to look like oranges. The Italian rice croquette *Suppli* is obviously derived from it.

Aundulyes: an Anglo-Norman sausage made from the large guts and stuffed with chopped entrails highly seasoned, then smoked.

Bain-marie: literally 'Maria's bath' is a method of baking delicate dishes like moulded egg custards, heating them slowly in a pan filled with hot water inside the oven. The method was invented by an alchemist of the first century AD who lived in Alexandria, Maria the Jewess, who wrote under the name of Miriam the Prophetess, sister of Moses. She is considered the most practical of all the early alchemists. Maria invented other laboratory equipment including a still called a *tribikos*, but it is her water bath that forever carries her name. Mrs Beeton never uses the *bain-marie* for cooking, but only as a receptacle for keeping food hot. Patrick Lamb gives this title to a beef consommé recipe.

Banquet: in the Tudor and Stuart age the word had two meanings, one which we are now familiar with, to mean a great and important feast; the second meaning was to denote the special final course of such a meal, made up of a wide variety of sweetmeats washed down with sweet herbal fermented drinks; recipes for the last appear in *The Closet of Sir Kenelm Digby.*

Barbel *(Barbus barbus):* a large river fish can weigh up to 10 lb, not now considered edible as its eggs are thought to be poisonous.

Baulks: Anglo-Saxon term for narrow strips of raised turf that divided individual acres. They are still visible as ridges where fields have become pasture for the last few hundred years.

Beistyn: The first milking of the cow after calving. Dorothy Hartley in *Food in England* writes: 'Bestys', or 'Beastlyns' or 'Firstings' is golden yellow, and thick as double cream; it should be thinned down with four times its quantity of plain milk, sweetened, and set in a cool oven with some simple flavouring – a vanilla pod, or cinnamon stick. It will set exactly like the richest egg custard. A good finish is to cover the top with damp sugar, and crisp it under the grill or before the fire; the sweet caramel crust, in contrast to the smooth custard, is pleasant.'

Bisae michiae: brown or black bread eaten by monks in the monastery.

Blanch Powder: a flavouring condiment made from refined sugar, powdered ginger and other spices like cinnamon.

Blaunche de sorre: white dish of Syria.

Blaunche doucet: medieval term for a sweet white dish.

Blaw maungere: dish of white meat or fish and rice.

Botargo: salted, pressed roe of the grey mullet which was served sliced thinly with lemon juice.

Bragot: a seventeenth-century drink made with ale, honey, spices and herbs.

Brant *(Branta bernicla):* Brent goose, winter visitors to Britain from the Arctic tundra, all but died out in the 1930s. Rich, lean, dark flesh, much favoured for eating.

Bruet: meat or game cooked in a broth, the liquid always well spiced often thickened with breadcrumbs and egg yolks as well as coloured with parsley juice or red sanders.

Chardequynce: similar to the Spanish quince paste available today and the forerunner of marmalade. Quinces and warden pears were cooked with honey, wine, ginger and cinnamon to a dark rich pulp. A preserve which lasted.

Chewettes: small pastries with a filling of pork, onion, chicken and spices or for fish days, a filling of haddock, cod, cream and herbs. The pasties were sometimes fried instead of baked. By the latter part of the fifteenth century these pasties, filled with minced pork or veal, spices and herbs, were given the name of 'hats'.

Cobbi: another word for a small brown loaf eaten by the working monks, likely to be small and round, baked at the bottom of the oven where they developed a good crust. The word Cob is still used to describe such a loaf.

Cock-ale: a seventeenth-century recipe whereby a cock is boiled in 8 gallons of ale with 4 lb raisins, three nutmegs, mace, dates and 2 quarts of sack. It is then bottled and can be drunk after a month.

Cockatrice: a conceit of the banquet table where a cock and a suckling pig are cut in half, stuffed with forcemeat, then sewn together, boiled, roasted and gilded.

Collup/collop: a slice of meat.

Comfit: a sweetmeat made from a fruit or root preserved in sugar.

Coney: rabbit, the Normans reintroduced them into England and very soon in the game parks there were huge warrens.

Conversi: a better class of corrodian.

Corrodian: a rich gentleman who chooses to spend his declining years in a monastery.

Costmary or alecost *(Tanacetum balsamina):* a herb from the Mediterranean used to flavour food and in Gerard's time ale. It got its name because the aroma reminded the English of the very expensive putchuk or costus which grew in the highlands of Kashmir.

Coulis/cullis: a term for a sauce of any kind, the name stemmed from the funnel used for straining the sauce, called a couloir.

Cubeb *(Piper cubeba):* a berry belonging to the pepper family in common use until the end of the seventeenth century.

Curfew: a large brass or copper cover which covered the embers at night. The word came from the French *couvre-feu.* At a fixed hour in the evening a bell was rung as a signal that all fires were to be extinguished. The word came to mean the hour of ringing, as well as the actual bell.

Darioles: small tarts, one recipe was for eggs and cream with chopped dates, figs, prunes and sugar. Another recipe specifies a quart of cream and forty egg yolks to make twenty custard tarts.

Dillegrout: a white soup made from almond milk and dill leaves, it was served traditionally at Coronations because it was thought that William the Conqueror gave to his cook, Tezelin, the lordship of the manor of Addington, as a reward for creating the soup. The lord of the manor always brought the soup to the newly crowned king.

Dominicus panis canonicorum: white bread that is blessed eaten in the monastery.

Drage: another term for dredge-corn, which is generally a mixture of barley and oats, but can be any mixture for sowing and used in the making of ale.

Electuaries: a herbal remedy mixed with sugar or honey made up like a sweet or pastille.

Endored: gilded, painted with egg yolk then roasted for a moment or covered in gold leaf.

Entremets: means literally between dishes, can be applied to all the dishes that come after the roast, but is generally applied to the vegetable dishes which accompany the main course.

Eringo *(Eryngium maritimum):* grows on the seashore and has massively long phallic-shaped roots which bequeathed a mythical aphrodisiac quality; the roots were candied and eaten. Also the young tender shoots when blanched can be eaten like asparagus. A candied eringo industry grew up around Colchester but declined in the nineteenth century.

Fleur frite: a term used by La Varenne for what was to become the 'roux' where the flour soaks up the fat and makes a paste which is cooked slightly before adding stock as a basis for a sauce.

Floated water meadows: an agricultural technique used in the seventeenth century.

Flummery: a flavoured cream set with calves' foot, isinglass or hartshorn, made with almonds for Lent. The earlier traditional flummery came from Wales and was set with thoroughly boiled oatmeal.

Frumenty: boiled wheat grains mixed with almond milk or cows' milk, thickened with well beaten egg yolks, flavoured then coloured.

Galingale: now galingal *(Kaempferia galinga)* but also in medieval England the roots of the plant (*Cyperus Longus*), a member of the ginger family, were a popular flavouring in foods and sauces.

Garfish *(Belone belone):* a long thin sea fish with a brilliantly coloured green back.

Gastel: the Norman French word for cake which became 'wastel' meaning fine white bread.

Gaufres: the Norman version of waffles made from a flavoured batter which would have been very similar to our own.

Gauncil: garlic sauce made with garlic, saffron, milk and wheat flour always eaten with roast goose.

Gitte: Anglo-Saxon word for black cumin made into a relish.

Grains of Paradise *(Amomum melegueta):* a spice related to cardamom, with a hot peppery taste.

Haburdens: summer-cured dried cod, also called 'Poor John'. In Shakespeare's *The Tempest*, Trinculo says of Caliban: 'He smells like a fish – a very ancient and fish-like smell – a kind of, not of the newest, poor john.'

Hauseleamye: chicken in a green sauce coloured by parsley.

Hausgeme: minced veal in a sauce coloured red.

Hippocras: red wine with spices added, generally ginger, cinnamon and grains of paradise, sweetened with honey. It took its name from the bag through which it was strained, said to resemble Hippocrates' sleeve.

Hydromel: another fermented honey drink popular in the seventeenth century. (See Mead and Metheglin.)

Jelly of Flesh: a speciality of Norman cookery. In the fourteenth century it comprised 'swine's feet, and snouts, and the ears, capons, coneys, calves feet' boiled in wine, vinegar and water. The liquor was then strained, spiced and coloured and when set it was decorated. There are intricate directions for colouring the dish in several shades.

Kickshaws: derived from *quelques choses* which meant in the sixteenth century an elegant and dainty dish, but came to be derogatory in the following two centuries to mean all that was pretentious in French cooking.

Lac de matutino: the milk from that morning given to harvest workers. In the summer it would not have kept any longer than a few hours after milking.

Lampern *(Lampetra fluviatilis):* the river lamprey, after five years in the river the lamprey migrates to the sea becoming the sea lamprey (*Petromyzon marinus*) for two years; it then attaches itself to a migrating trout or salmon (they are parasites sucking blood) and hitches a free ride back to rivers where it will spawn.

Lechemeat: cold set dishes that need to be sliced. The slices were called leaches and were eaten with a wine sauce. They were often made from almond milk as a Lenten dish.

Leechdoms: Anglo-Saxon books of herbal remedies.

Ling: used to describe dried cod in general, specifying a better quality of fish than stockfish itself.

Lozenges: this was a dough made from flour, water, sugar and spices, cut in a lozenge pattern and fried in oil; these were served in a wine syrup with added dried fruit and spices. Polenta, of course, can be made in exactly the same way now, as can other flour pastes, made for example from chick pea flour.

Lucanian sausage: a smoked and heavily spiced sausage made with minced pork and pine kernels, popular in the ancient world and still surviving in many forms today.

Macerouns: early form of macaroni where the pasta is in flat ribbons and not tubes.

Macrows: another form of pasta – a flat noodle.

Manchet: white bread of the finest quality made from flour which had been two or three times sieved. Manchets were small loaves weighing no more than 6 ounces.

Marmalada: see chardequince above, the Tudor name for the preserve made from quinces and then other fruits – pears, apples, damsons and medlars.

Maslin: mixed grain, rye, barley and wheat, applicable to the flour and the bread made from it.

Mawmenny: a favourite medieval dish which changed over the 500 years it was prepared. Inspired by an Arabic recipe it began as spiced minced chicken in almond milk mixed with breadcrumbs, egg yolks and a setting agent. The forerunner of the dessert we know as blancmange.

Meath: a fermented honey, rosemary and ginger drink. Sir Kenelm Digby gives several recipes of various types.

Methegelin: a spiced honey fermented drink which Sir Kenelm Digby gives recipes for.

Milfoil *(Achillea Millefolium):* the common yarrow, the leaves are many and finely divided (literally thousand leaved).

Mortrews: a boiled dish of finely ground food in a broth. Other spellings are 'morterel' or 'mortrellus'.

Mullein *(Verbascum thapsus):* commonly called Aaron's Rod, can grow to 2 metres or more, has grey woolly leaves and yellow flowers, seeds itself in most country gardens and allotments; some love its effect in the herbaceous border. The Anglo-Saxons believed that Mercury had given Mullein to Ulysses when he came to Circe to ward off her evil. It was used medicinally to cure coughs, gripes and piles.

Murrain: cattle plague from *mori*, to die. Chroniclers were not specific in noting characteristics of diseases in livestock. All pestilence was termed a murrain.

Neat's tongue: the tongue of an ox, bullock, cow or heifer.

Noonings/nuncheon/noonshine: various names for lunch or luncheon as the concept of such a meal appeared at the beginning of the nineteenth century.

Oleo/olio/oglia: a fashionable dish in the seventeenth century which could include almost anything, but essentially had meat, fowl, game, a variety of vegetables, herbs and spices simmered for some hours in wine and stock. All the cooks gave different recipes, including Robert May, Patrick Lamb and La Varenne. Its origin was the peasant fare of the Basque country where anything brought back by the hunter was cooked in the pot; it survived in Spain, not only as a dish but as a phrase – *olla podrida*, a mish-mash.

Orach *(Atriplex hortensis):* a tall plant comes in red or gold with small heart-shaped leaves, used for salads.

Pandemain: a high class white bread, very similar to wastel (see below) the name derives from *panis domini*, the sacramental bread.

Peasecods: pea pods cooked whole and sold as street food, dipped in butter the peas are sucked out and the cods thrown away.

Pellitory *(Parietaria diffusa):* Grows out of walls and used for kidney stones, troubles of the bladder, coughs, burns and inflammation.

Penidia: twisted sticks of sugar like barley-sugar sticks, thought to cure the common cold.

Periwinkle *(Littorina littorea):* a tiny shellfish sold already boiled and eaten with vinegar and pepper with the aid of a pin.

Pottage: this term covers a range of dishes from the thick cereal and vegetable soup, the mainstay of the peasants' diet, to soup/stews of meat, game and fish, subtly spiced, in a royal banquet.

Powder Fort: a flavouring spice mixture which was hot, so pepper and ginger predominated.

Principal Pudding: a boiled suet pudding stuffed inside a sheep's stomach, flavoured with mace, nutmeg, cinnamon, ginger, every kind of dried fruit and ground almonds with sometimes rose water, orangeflower water, musk and ambergris to intensify the perfume. Eaten on Festival days at the monastery.

Puddingis: an Anglo-Norman sausage made from minced pork and pig's blood highly seasoned.

Pyonada: a medieval sweetmeat, made from sugar and pine nuts. See electuaries above.

Ramsons *(Allium ursinum):* wild garlic, place names like Ramsbottom derive from where they grew. John Gerard (1545-1612) wrote in his Herbal that in the Low Country fish sauce was made from the leaves which 'maye very well be eaten in April and Maie with butter, of such was are a strong constitution, and labouring men'.

Raysons of Corinth: currants because they came to be referred to simply as 'corinth'.

Rennet: anything used to curdle milk in the making of cheese. The active substance is a single enzyme rennin which disables casein. Traditionally made from the stomach of a young animal and surrounded by rituals and folklore. There are many recipes which are all variations on much the same process. The lamb, kid or calf must be a suckling, after slaughter the stomach with its contents must be hung to dry for several weeks, then it is sealed in a jar where it can keep dry for a year. One litre of water is then needed to soak a half-vell (the lining of the stomach) of lamb or goat, 4 litres are needed for a calf's vell. One soup spoon of rennet serves for 10 litres of milk. Vegetable rennet is found in thistle, fig and Ladies' Bedstraw *(Galium verum)*.

Rockling *(Ciliata mustela):* a small fish; the adult reaches 25 cm (10 in), found in the North Sea inshore in early summer, a bottom feeder can sometimes be seen in tidal pools.

Rubia *(Rubia peregrina):* Wild Madder, used for colouring. The roots do not give the same brilliant red as the true madder *(Rubia Tinctorum)* but a rosy pink.

Salmagundy: an intricate seventeenth-century salad of herbs, eggs, roast capon, anchovies and other cold meats and fish. The name was derived from the old French *salmigondis* but was subsequently corrupted into Solomon Gundy which has still survived in North America.

Salpicon: a stuffing for veal, beef or mutton. Patrick Lamb gives a recipe with over ten main ingredients and herbs.

Sanap: an embroidered and decorated overcloth which covered the plain white cloth upon the top table; upon it would be placed other decorative pieces, like an ornate salt cellar made out of silver or gold and often jewel encrusted.

Saucistres: an Anglo-Norman sausage made from lean pork, spices and herbs.

Sawsedges: Tudor spelling of sausages.

Skirret *(sisum sisarum):* a species of water parsnip, a popular root vegetable grown all over Europe until the end of the eighteenth century.

Snoek *(Thyrsites atun):* a fish of the southern hemisphere canned, then imported to Britain in great quantities after the Second World War to help feed the nation in the worst years of rationing. But the British nation was suspicious, hated the name and disliked the taste. It is thought that the unused stock was relabelled as cat food.

Souse: parts of the slaughtered pig not used for anything else; the ears, cheeks, snout and trotters were boiled with water, wine and spices, often ginger, mace, cloves, pepper and coriander seed, until tender, left to cool then the fat skimmed off. More salt,wine and spices were added, and it was barrelled in its jelly. One of the Christmas foods, Jane Austen writes of eating it with relish.

Spikenard: used as an oil and a perfume and occasionally in cooking; the leaves, root and the 'spike', an ear that grows from the rhizome, were used.

Squails: short weighted sticks used for bringing down small prey, squirrels, small game and even apples.

Stepponi: a seventeenth-century drink made from raisins, sugar, lemons and water.

Stockfish: dried fish of the cod family like pollack and whiting, which has to be soaked before cooking. Sir Kenelm Digby gives two recipes for preparing stockfish; it is a long process which begins with the dried fish being thoroughly beaten, then soaked in water for 14 hours, then boiled in the water for 6 or 7 hours at least. Then the water is pressed out; it is seasoned with pepper and mustard, and boiled again for an hour in milk, then placed in a dish with melted butter, seasoned and stewed again before it is ready.

Subtleties/sotelties: elaborate sugar sculptures which ended each course at a medieval banquet. Allegorical figures, castles, trees and animals were all vividly depicted and brightly coloured. After being admired they were eaten. There is a description of the feast given by Cardinal Wolsey to the French ambassadors in 1527 in which there is a realistic depiction of St Paul's Church with its tall steeple. 'There were beasts, birds, fowls of divers kinds and personages, most lively made counterfeit in dishes, some fighting, as it were with swords, some with guns and crossbows, some vaulting and leaping, some dancing with ladies, some in complete harness, jousting with spears.'

Succory *(Cichorium intybus):* chicory, the root was used medicinally as well as the leaves and flowers in salads. For a salad it was earthed up like endive to blanch it and became fashionable in the sixteenth and seventeenth centuries.

Sucket/Succade: fruit conserves eaten in the banquet course. These were citrus fruits, bitter oranges, lemons and pomegranates conserved in a sugar syrup.

Sumac: powdered berries from the sumac shrub used extensively for flavouring food in the Middle East, tastes both sour and fruity rather like tamarind.

Surae michiae: a different type of black or brown bread eaten by monks in the monastery.

Swinecress *(Apium nodiflorum):* more commonly called Fool's Watercress as it grows with the watercress, which is cooked in pies and pastries. But in some parts of the country *Coronopus squamatus* or Wart's Cress is also called swinecress, and the seeds are used for flavouring.

Talbotays: dishes where the blood is used in the cooking broth as in many of the hare recipes.

Tragopogon porrifolius *(Salsify):* an edible root sometimes called 'oyster plant' for, with a leap of the imagination, the flavour vaguely resembles the oyster.

Wastel: the best, white, wheaten bread, the flour was sieved several times, from the Norman French *gastel* or cake.

Wether: a castrated ram.

Wormwood *(Artemisia Absinthium):* an aromatic plant of bitter flavour.

Verjuice: unripe grapes which in northern Europe were otherwise wasted were fermented to form a fruit vinegar used in cookery and pickling. Later crab apples were used. They were substituted for the lemons unobtainable in any quantity in England and which the Crusaders had enjoyed.

Zedoary *(Curcuma zedoaria):* an aromatic root related to turmeric, native to India and Indonesia.

Glossary of Conversions

acre: area of 40 poles long by 4 broad (4,840 square yards). The size used to vary. Before the time of Edward I, it was reckoned to be as much as a yoke of oxen could plough in a day.

amber: dry measure equalling 4 bushels.

bushel: measure equalling 4 pecks or 8 gallons (36.4 litres). The imperial bushel (from 1826) equals 2218.192 cubic inches. The Winchester bushel, established by Henry VIII, was slightly smaller. Before that, it varied from place to place or according to the commodity.

cwt: see hundredweight.

d. abbreviation for pre-decimalisation pence.

farthing: one-quarter of a pre-decimal penny.

furlong: originally the length of a furrow in a common field, then theoretically a square of 10 acres. The furlong varied but was usually 40 poles; now 220 yards, one-eighth of a mile.

gallon/imperial gallon: equals 8 pints (4.55 litres).

hide: 120 acres, the size of which could vary.

hundredweight (abbrev. cwt): 112 pounds, or 8 stones, or 50.74kg.

kilderkin: cask for ale or fish equivalent to half a barrel. In the sixteenth century it was defined as 18 gallons of beer, 16 of ale.

lb: abbreviation for pound (weight).

ore: (originally ora, a unit of currency brought to Britain by the Danish invasion. In the Domesday Book it was reckoned as 20d. It was also a measure of weight; in the Domesday Book it was used for ounce, or a 12th part of a Saxon pound.

ounce (abbrev. oz): one-sixteenth of a pound.

peck: dry measure equal to one quarter of a bushel, or 2 imperial gallons.

penny/pence (abbrev. d): there were 240 pre-decimalisation pennies to £1.

pint: equals 568 millilitres. 8 pints equal 1 imperial gallon.

pole: equals 5½ yards.

pound: in currency, £1 equalled 240 pre-decimalisation pence, and 20 shillings. In weight: 1 lb equals 453 grams.

quart: equals 2 pints.

quarter: dry weight measure equal to 8 bushels.

sester: now obsolete liquid measure for beer or wine. A sester-penny was a charge made on every sester of beer brewed.

shilling (abbrev: s): in pre-decimalisation currency there were 20 shillings to the pound. A shilling was worth 12d.

stone: equals 14 lb.

tun: a cask for wine or beer of definite measure: its capacity was 4 hogsheads, or 210 imperial gallons for wine/216 of beer.

Picture Credits

(1) Wright, Thomas, *The Homes of Other Days*, 1871. Collection Latham.

(2) Sandford, Francis, *The History of the Coronation of James II*, 1687. Collection Latham.

(3) Collection Latham.

(4) Soyer, Alexis, *The Gastronomic Regenerator*, 1846. Collection Latham.

(5) *Murray's Modern Domestic Cookery*, 1851. Collection Latham.

(6) Henderson, William Augustus, *The Housekeeper's Instructor*, c. 1790. Collection Latham.

(7) Briggs, Richard, *The English Art of Cookery*, 1788. Collection Latham.

(8) Mary Evans Picture Library.

(9) *Beeton's Penny Cookery Book*, c. 1880. Collection Latham.

(10) *Good Things Made Said and Done for Every Home and Household*, 1888. Collection Latham.

(11) Countess of Kent, Elizabeth Grey, *A Choice Manual*, 1653. Collection Latham.

(12) Raffald, Elizabeth, *The Experienced English Housekeeper*, 1769. Collection Latham.

(13) Marshall, Mrs A.B., *Larger Cookery Book*, 1891. Collection Latham.

(14) Courtesy of Culpeper Ltd.

(15) David, Elizabeth, *Summer Cooking* (Museum Press 1955). Collection Latham.

(16) Grigson, Jane, *Good Things*, 1971. Collection Latham.

(17) Smith, Delia, *The Food Aid Cookery Book* (BBC 1986).

(18) Digby, Sir Kenelm, *The Closet of Sir Kenelm Digby, KT., Opened*, 1910 edition. Collection Latham.

(19) Evelyn, John, *Silva*, 1706 edition. Collection Latham.

(20) Kitchiner, William, *The Housekeeper's Oracle*, 1829. Collection Latham.

(21) Soyer, Alexis, *The Modern Housewife*, 1850. Collection Latham.

(22) Francatelli, Charles Elme, *The Cook's Guide*, 1861. Collection Latham.

(23) Escoffier, A., *A Guide to Modern Cookery*, 1907. Collection Latham.

(24) Wooley, Hannah, *The Ladies Delight*, 1662. Collection Latham.

(25) Bradley, Martha, *The British Housewife*, c.1770. Collection Latham.

(26) Hammond, Elizabeth, *Modern Domestic Cookery*, c.1820. Collection Latham.

(27) Cooke, Conrade, *Cookery and Confectionery*, 1824. Collection Latham.

(28) Courtesy of Smallbone & Co. (Devizes) Limited.

Select Bibliography

This list does not include particular issues of Petits Propos Culinaires, *which I have found useful, though they are cited in the footnotes. But this volume owes a debt of gratitude to the publication as a whole, and to the Oxford Food Symposium itself, which I have always found stimulating and enriching.*

The citation dates given are to the editions consulted.

Acton, Harold, *Memoirs of an Aesthete* (Artellus 1948)

Adamson, Melitta Weiss, ed., *Food in the Middle Ages: A Book of Essays*, Garland Medieval Casebooks 12 (New York and London 1995)

Aelfric, *Colloquy*, ed. G.N. Garmonsway (Methuen's Old English Library 1939)

Allen, Darina. *Irish Traditional Cooking* (Kyle Cathie 1998)

Anthimus. On the Observance of Foods, trans and edited by Mark Grant (Prospect Books 1996)

Austin, T., ed. *Two Fifteenth Century Cookery Books*: Harleian MS 279, 4016, Early English Text Society 1888

Baldwin Smith, Lacey, *Elizabethan World* (Hamlyn 1967)

Barber, Richard, *Cooking and Recipes from Rome to the Renaissance* (Allen Lane 1973)

Bartlett, Robert, *England under the Norman and Angevin Kings* 1075-1225 (OUP 2000)

Barrow, John, ed., *Cook's Voyages of Discovery* (Everyman 1906)

Beeton, Isabella, ed. *Beeton's Book of Household Management* (Southover Press 1998)

Bingham, Madeleine, *Scotland under Mary Stuart* (Allen & Unwin 1971)

Black, Maggie, *A Taste of History* (British Museum Press 1993)

Bober, Phyllis Pray, *Art, Culture & Cuisine* (University of Chicago Press 1999)

Boxer, Arabella, *Book of English Food* (Hodder & Stoughton 1991)

Boyd Orr, Sir John; Lubbock, David, *Feeding the People in Wartime* (Macmillan 1940)

Braudel, Fernand, *The Wheels of Commerce* (Collins 1982)

Brears, P.C.D., *The Gentlewoman's Kitchen* (Wakefield Historical Publications 1984)

Briggs, Asa, *A Social History of England* (Weidenfeld & Nicolson 1983)

Burkhardt, B.; McLean, B.A.; Kochanek, D., *Sailors and Sauerkraut* (Gray's 1978)

Burnett, John, *Liquid Pleasures* (Routledge 1999)

Burnett, John, *Plenty and Want* (Routledge 1966)

Burton, Elizabeth, *The Elizabethans at Home* (Secker & Warburg 1958)

Byrne, M. St.Clare, *Elizabethan Life in Town and Country* (Methuen 1925)

Byrne, M. St.Clare, ed. *The Lisle Letters* (Penguin 1981)

Byrne, M. St. Clare, ed. *The Elizabethan Home. Discovered in Two Dialogues by Claudius Hollyband and Peter Erondell* (Cobden-Sanderson 1930)

Carlin, Martha; Rosenthal, Joel T. ed., *Food and Eating in Medieval Europe* (Hambledon Press 1998)

Chambers, J.D.; Mingay, G.E., *The Agricultural Revolution 1750-1880* (Batsford 1966)

Chibnall, Marjorie, ed. and trans., *Ecclesiastical History of Orderic Vitalis* (Clarendon Press, Oxford, 1969-80)

Claire, Colin, *Kitchen Table* (Abelard & Schumann 1964)

Cobb, H.S., *Overseas Trade of London: Exchequer Custom Accounts 1480-81* (London Record Society 1990)

Cobbett, William, *Rural Rides* (Penguin 1967)

Cohn, Norman, *The Pursuit of the Millennium* (Paladin 1970)

Cooper, Susan, *Snoek Piquante: The Age of Austerity 1945-1951*, ed. Michael Sissons and Philip French (Penguin 1964)

Crawford, Patricia, *Women and Religion in England 1500-1720* (Routledge 1993)

Crawford, Sir William; Broadley, H., *The People's Food* (Heinemann 1938)

Curtis-Bennett, Sir Noel, *The Food of the People* (Faber & Faber 1949)

Davidson, Alan, ed., *The Oxford Companion to Food* (OUP 2000)

Davidson, Caroline, *A Woman's Work is Never Done. A History of Housework in the British Isles, 1650-1950* (Chatto & Windus 1982)

Davies, D.J., *The Economic History of South Wales prior to 1800* (Cardiff 1933)

Davies, Wendy, *Wales in the Early Middle Ages* (Leicester University Press 1982)

Defoe, Daniel, *A Tour Through England and Wales* (Everyman ed. 1928)

Dodd, A.H., *Life in Elizabethan England* (Batsford 1961)

Driver, Christopher; Berriedale-Johnson, Michelle, *Pepys at Table* (Bell & Hyman 1984)

Driver, Christopher, ed., *John Evelyn, Cook* (Prospect Books 1997)

Driver, Christopher, *The British Table 1940-1980* (Chatto & Windus 1983)

Drummond. J.C., *The Englishman's Food* (Jonathan Cape 1958)

Dyer, Christopher, *Everyday Life in Medieval England* (Hambledon Press 1994)

Dyer, Christopher, *Standards of Living in the Later Middle Ages* (CUP 1989)

Elias, Norbert, *The Civilizing Process: The History of Manners and State Formation and Civilization*, trans. Edmund Jephcott (Blackwell 1994)

Emmerson, Robin, *Table Settings* (Shire Publications 1991)

Feild, Rachel, *Irons in the Fire* (Crowood 1984)

Fell, Christine, *Women in Anglo-Saxon England* (Colonnade Books 1984)

Fenton, Alexander; Kisbán, Eszter, ed., *Food in Change* (John Donald, Edinburgh, 1986)

Fitzgibbon, Theodora, *With Love* (Century 1982)

FitzStephen, William, 'A Description of London', trans. H.E. Butler (Historical Association Leaflet 1934)

Freeman, Bobby, *First Catch Your Peacock* (Image Imprint) 1978

Girouard, Mark, *Life in the English Country House* (Yale 1978)

Griggs, Barbara, *The Food Factor* (Viking 1986)

Hagen, Ann, *A Handbook in Anglo-Saxon Food and Drink: Production and Distribution* (Pinner, Middlesex: Anglo-Saxon Books 1992); *A Second Handbook of Anglo-Saxon Food and Drink: Production and Distribution* (Hockwood cum Wilton, Norfolk: Anglo-Saxon Books 1995)

Hale, John, *The Civilization of Europe in the Renaissance* (Fontana 1994)

Hallam, H.E., ed., *The Agrarian History of England and Wales*, Vol. 2, 1042-1350, Gen. ed. Joan Thirsk (CUP 1988)

Hamlyn, Matthew, *The Recipes of Hannah Woolley* (Heinemann 1988)

Handley J.E., *Scottish Farming in the 18th Century* (Faber & Faber 1953)

Harrison, Molly, *The Kitchen in History* (Osprey 1972)

Hartley, Dorothy, *Food in England* (Macdonald 1954)

Harvey, Barbara, *Living and Dying in England 1100-1540* (Clarenden Press Oxford 1993)

Heal, Felicity; Holmes, Clive, *The Gentry in England and Wales, 1500-1700* (Macmillan 1994)

Heath, Ambrose, *Open Sesame: two hundred recipes for canned goods* (Nicolson & Watson, 1939)

Heinze R.W., *The Proclamations of the Tudor Kings* (CUP 1976)

Hess, Karen, ed. *Martha Washington's Booke of Cookery* (Columbia University Press 1981)

Hibbert, Christopher, *The English, a social history, 1066-1945* (Grafton Books 1987)

Hickman, Peggy, *A Jane Austen Household Book with Martha Lloyd's Recipes* (David & Charles 1977)

Hieatt, Constance, *An Ordinance of Pottage* (Prospect Books 1988)

Hieatt, Constance; Butler, Sharon, *Curye on Inglysch* (OUP 1985)

Hill, Christopher, *The World Turned Upside Down* (Penguin 1972)

Hill, Christopher, *The Century of Revolution 1603-1714* (Nelson 1961)

Hobsbawm, E.J., *Industry and Empire* (Penguin 1968)

Houston, R.A.; Whyte, I.D., *Scottish Society 1500-1800* (CUP 1989)

Hunt, Alan, *Governance of the Consuming Passions. A History of Sumptuary Law* (Macmillan 1996)

Johnson, James, *A Hundred Years' Eating* (Gill & Macmillan 1977)

Kapoor, Sybil, *Simply British* (Michael Joseph 1998)

Keane, Molly, *Nursery Cooking* (MacDonald 1985)

Kelly, Fergus, *Early Irish Farming* (Dublin Institute for Advanced Studies 1997)

King-Hall, Magdalen, *The Story of the Nursery* (Routledge 1958)

Knowles, David, *The Monastic Order in England: a History of its Development from the Times of St. Dunstan to the Fourth Lateran Council, 943-1216* (CUP 1949)

Landsberg, Sylvia, *The Medieval Garden* (British Museum Press 1995)

Laslett, Peter, *The World We Have Lost* (Methuen 1965)

Lawrence, Sue, *Scots Cooking* (Headline 2000)

Lewis, Gary, *The Middle Way* (Brolga Press 1992)

Leyel, Mrs C.F.; Hartley, Miss Olga, *The Gentle Art of Cookery* (Chatto 1925)

Longmate, Norman, *How We Lived Then* (Hutchinson 1971)

Mabey, Richard, *Gilbert White* (Century 1986)

Magennis, Hugh, *Anglo-Saxon Appetites* (Four Court Press 1999)

Mars, Valerie, 'Parsimony amid Plenty. Food Culture & History' (London Food Seminar 1993)

Martineau, Alice, *More Caviare and More Candy* (Cobden-Sanderson 1938)

May, Robert, *The Accomplisht Cook* (Prospect Books 1994)

Mayhew, Henry, *Mayhew's London*, ed. Peter Quennell (Spring Books 1972)

McGrath, Patrick, *Papists and Puritans Under Elizabeth I* (Blandford Press 1967)

McKendrick, Neil; Brewer, John; Plumb, J.H., *The Birth of the Consumer Society* (Europa, London 1982)

McNeill, F. Marian, *The Scots Kitchen* (Blackie 1929)

Mead, William Edward, *The English Medieval Feast* (Allen & Unwin 1931)

Meads, D.M., *The Diary of Lady Margaret Hoby, 1559-1605* (George Routledge 1930)

Mennell, Stephen, *All Manners of Food* (Blackwell 1985)

Mintz, Sidney W., *Tasting Food, Tasting Freedom* (Beacon Press 1996)

Nightingale, Pamela, *Medieval Mercantile Community. The Grocer's Company and the Politics and Trade of London. 1000-1485* (Yale University Press 1995)

Norman, Jill, *The Complete Book of Spices* (Dorling Kindersley 1990)

Oddy, Derek J.; Miller, Derek S., ed. *The Making of the Modern British Diet* (Croom Helm 1976)

Palmer, Arnold, *Movable Feasts* (OUP 1984)

Pepys, Samuel, *The Diary of Samuel Pepys*, ed. R.C. Latham and W. Matthews, Vol. IV 1663 (Harper Collins 1995)

Plat, Sir Hugh, *Delightes for Ladies* (Crosby Lockwood & Son, London 1948)

Priestley, J.B., *The Edwardians* (Sphere 1970)

Pullar, Philippa, *Consuming Passions* (Hamish Hamilton 1970)

Pyke, Magnus, *Townsman's Food* (Turnstile Press 1952)

Raffald, Elizabeth, *The Experienced English Housekeeper*, Introduction by Roy Shipperbottom (Southover Press 1997)

Ramage, Helen, *Portraits of an Island* (Anglesey Antiquarian Society 1987)

Raverat, Gwen, *Period Piece* (Faber and Faber 1954)

Saaler, Mary, *Edward II* (The Rubicon Press 1997)

Salaman, Redcliffe. N., *The History and Social Influence of the Potato* (CUP 1949)

Scola, Roger, *Feeding the Victorian City. The Food Supply of Manchester 1770-1870* (Manchester University Press 1992)

Scully, Terence, *The Art of Cookery in the Middle Ages* (Boydell Press 1995)

Seebohm, M.E., *The Evolution of the English Farm* (Allen & Unwin 1952)

Sexton, Regina, *A Little History of Irish Food* (Kyle Cathie 1998)

Shaida, Margaret, *The Legendary Cuisine of Persia* (Grub Street 2000)

Sim, Alison, *Food and Feast in Tudor England* (Sutton Publishing 1997)

Spain, Nancy, *The Beeton Story* (Ward Lock 1956)

Spencer, Colin, *Vegetarianism – a History* (Grub Street 2001)

Spurling, Hilary, ed., *Elinor Fettiplace's Receipt Book* (Viking Salamander 1986)

Star Chamber Dinner Accounts, The, Commentary by Andre L. Simon (The Wine and Food Society 1959)

Strong, Roy, *The Story of Britain* (Pimlico 1998)

Tansey, Geoff; Worsley, Tony, *The Food System* (Earthscan 1995)

Thick, Malcolm, *The Neat House Gardens, early market gardening around London* (Prospect Books 1998)

Thirsk, Joan, ed., *The Agrarian History of England and Wales*, Vol. IV, 1500-1640 (CUP 1967); Vol. VII Agrarian Change (CUP 1984). General ed. Finberg, H.P.R.; Thirsk, Joan

Trow-Smith, R. A., *History of British Livestock Husbandry to 1700* (Routledge Kegan Paul 1959)

Tuchman, Barbara W., *A Distant Mirror* (Penguin Books 1979)

Verrall, William, *Cookery Book 1759* (Southover Press 1988)

Webb, Diana, *Pilgrimage in Medieval England* (Hambledon & London 2000)

Wentworth, Josie A., *Janey Ellice's Recipes 1846-1859* (MacDonald and Jane's 1974)

Whitelock, Dorothy ed., *English Historical Documents c500-1042* (OUP 1979)

Whiting, Robert, *The Blind Devotion of the People* (CUP 1989)

Wilson, C. Anne, *Food and Drink in Britain* (Constable 1973)

Wilson, C. Anne, ed., *Food in the Community* (Edinburgh University Press 1991)

Wilson, C. Anne, ed., *Banquetting Stuffe* (Edinburgh University Press 1986)

Wilson, C. Anne, ed., *Luncheon, Nuncheon and Related Meals* (Sutton 1994)

Woodforde, James, *The Diary of a Country Parson 1758-1802*, ed. John Beresford (OUP 1978)

Woodham-Smith, Cecil, *The Great Hunger* (Harper 1962)

Woolgar C. M., *Household Accounts from Medieval England*, 2 vols (Oxford 1992-93)

Woolgar, C. M., *The Great Household in Late Medieval England* (Yale University Press 1999)

Wright, Clifford, *A Mediterranean Feast* (William Morrow & Co. 1999)

Youngs, Frederick A., *The Proclamations of the Tudor Queens* (CUP 1967)

Ziegler, Philip, *The Black Death* (Penguin 1969)

Index